Kaplan Publishing are constantly finding new ways to make a difference to your studies and our exciting ~~online~~ offer something different to students looki

KU-475-852

This book comes with free MyKaplan online resources so that you can study anytime, anywhere. **This free online resource is not sold separately and is included in the price of the book.**

Having purchased this book, you have access to the following online study materials:

CONTENT	ACCA (including FBT, FMA, FFA)		FIA (excluding FBT, FMA, FFA)	
	Text	Kit	Text	Kit
Electronic version of the book	✓	✓	✓	✓
Check Your Understanding Test with instant answers	✓			
Material updates	✓	✓	✓	✓
Latest official ACCA exam questions*		✓		
Extra question assistance using the signpost icon**		✓		
Timed questions with an online tutor debrief using clock icon***		✓		
Interim assessment including questions and answers	✓		✓	
Technical answers	✓	✓	✓	✓

* Excludes BT, MA, FA, FBT, FMA, FFA; for all other papers includes a selection of questions, as released by ACCA
** For ACCA SBL, SBR, AFM, APM, ATX, AAA only
*** Excludes BT, MA, FA, LW, FBT, FMA and FFA

How to access your online resources

Kaplan Financial students will already have a MyKaplan account and these extra resources will be available to you online. You do not need to register again, as this process was completed when you enrolled. If you are having problems accessing online materials, please ask your course administrator.

If you are not studying with Kaplan and did not purchase your book via a Kaplan website, to unlock your extra online resources please go to www.mykaplan.co.uk/addabook (even if you have set up an account and registered books previously). You will then need to enter the ISBN number (on the title page and back cover) and the unique pass key number contained in the scratch panel below to gain access. You will also be required to enter additional information during this process to set up or confirm your account details.

If you purchased through the Kaplan Publishing website you will automatically receive an e-mail invitation to MyKaplan. Please register your details using this email to gain access to your content. If you do not receive the e-mail or book content, please contact Kaplan Publishing.

Your Code and Information

This code can only be used once for the registration of one book online. This registration and your online content will expire when the final sittings for the examinations covered by this book have taken place. Please allow one hour from the time you submit your book details for us to process your request.

Please scratch the film to access your unique code.

Please be aware that this code is case-sensitive and you will need to include the dashes within the passcode, but not when entering the ISBN.

KAPLAN

PUBLISHING

ACCA

Strategic Professional – Options

Advanced Audit and Assurance (AAA)

Study Text

British library cataloguing-in-publication data

A catalogue record for this book is available from the British Library.

Published by:
Kaplan Publishing UK
Unit 2 The Business Centre
Molly Millars Lane
Wokingham
Berkshire
RG41 2QZ

ISBN 978-1-78740-600-1

Acknowledgements

These materials are reviewed by the ACCA examining team. The objective of the review is to ensure that the material properly covers the syllabus and study guide outcomes, used by the examining team in setting the exams, in the appropriate breadth and depth. The review does not ensure that every eventuality, combination or application of examinable topics is addressed by the ACCA Approved Content. Nor does the review comprise a detailed technical check of the content as the Approved Content Provider has its own quality assurance processes in place in this respect.

The IFRS Foundation logo, the IASB logo, the IFRS for SMEs logo, the "Hexagon Device", "IFRS Foundation", "eIFRS", "IAS", "IASB", "IFRS for SMEs", "IFRS", "IASs", "IFRSs", "International Accounting Standards" and "International Financial Reporting Standards", "IFRIC" and "IFRS Taxonomy" are Trade Marks of the IFRS Foundation.

Trade Marks

The IFRS Foundation logo, the IASB logo, the IFRS for SMEs logo, the "Hexagon Device", "IFRS Foundation", "eIFRS", "IAS", "IASB", "IFRS for SMEs", "NIIF" IASs" "IFRS", "IFRSs", "International Accounting Standards", "International Financial Reporting Standards", "IFRIC", "SIC" and "IFRS Taxonomy".

Further details of the Trade Marks including details of countries where the Trade Marks are registered or applied for are available from the Foundation on request.

This product contains material that is ©Financial Reporting Council Ltd (FRC). Adapted and reproduced with the kind permission of the Financial Reporting Council. All rights reserved. For further information, please visit www.frc.org.uk or call +44 (0)20 7492 2300.

Contents

Introduction

This document references IFRS® Standards and IAS® Standards, which are authored by the International Accounting Standards Board (the Board), and published in the 2019 IFRS Standards Red Book.

How to use the materials

These Kaplan Publishing learning materials have been carefully designed to make your learning experience as easy as possible and to give you the best chances of success in your examinations.

The product range contains a number of features to help you in the study process. They include:

(1)   Detailed study guide and syllabus objectives

(2)   Description of the examination

(3)   Study skills and revision guidance

(4)   Study text

(5)   Question practice

The sections on the study guide, the syllabus objectives, the examination and study skills should all be read before you commence your studies. They are designed to familiarise you with the nature and content of the examination and give you tips on how best to approach your learning.

The **Study Text** comprises the main learning materials and gives guidance as to the importance of topics and where other related resources can be found. Each chapter includes:

- The **learning objectives** contained in each chapter, which have been carefully mapped to the examining body's own syllabus learning objectives or outcomes. You should use these to check you have a clear understanding of all the topics on which you might be assessed in the examination.

- The **chapter diagram** provides a visual reference for the content in the chapter, giving an overview of the topics and how they link together.

- The **content** for each topic area commences with a brief explanation or definition to put the topic into context before covering the topic in detail. You should follow your studying of the content with a review of the illustration/s. These are worked examples which will help you to understand better how to apply the content for the topic.

- **Test your understanding** sections provide an opportunity to assess your understanding of the key topics by applying what you have learned to short questions. Answers can be found at the back of each chapter.

- **Summary diagrams** complete each chapter to show the important links between topics and the overall content of the syllabus. These diagrams should be used to check that you have covered and understood the core topics before moving on.

- **Question practice** is provided at the back of each text.

Quality and accuracy are of the utmost importance to us so if you spot an error in any of our products, please send an email to mykaplanreporting@kaplan.com with full details, or follow the link to the feedback form in MyKaplan.

Our Quality Coordinator will work with our technical team to verify the error and take action to ensure it is corrected in future editions.

Icon Explanations

 Supplementary reading – These sections will help to provide a deeper understanding of core areas. The supplementary reading is **NOT** optional reading. It is vital to provide you with the breadth of knowledge you will need to address the wide range of topics within your syllabus that could feature in an exam question. **Reference to this text is vital when self-studying.**

 Definition – Key definitions that you will need to learn from the core content.

 Key point – Identifies topics that are key to success and are often examined.

 Test your understanding – Exercises for you to complete to ensure that you have understood the topics just learned.

 Illustration – Worked examples help you understand the core content better.

 Tricky topic – When reviewing these areas care should be taken and all illustrations and test your understanding exercises should be completed to ensure that the topic is understood.

 Tutorial note – Included to explain some of the technical points in more detail.

 Footsteps – Helpful tutor tips.

 Links to other syllabus areas – This symbol refers to areas of interaction with other parts of your syllabus, either in terms of other ACCA papers that you have studied, or may go on to study, or even further professional qualifications that you may decide to pursue on completion of ACCA.

Reference to ISA paragraph numbers are for copyright purposes only. Students are not required to learn this level of detail.

Online subscribers

Our online resources are designed to increase the flexibility of your learning materials and provide you with immediate feedback on how your studies are progressing. Ask your local customer services staff if you are not already a subscriber and wish to join.

If you are subscribed to our online resources you will find:

(1) Online reference ware: reproduces your Study Text online, giving you anytime, anywhere access.

(2) Online testing: provides you with additional online objective testing so you can practice what you have learned further.

(3) Online performance management: immediate access to your online testing results. Review your performance by key topics and chart your achievement through the course relative to your peer group.

Syllabus for September 2020 to June 2021

Syllabus background

The aim of ACCA Advanced Audit and Assurance (INT & UK) is to analyse, evaluate and conclude on the assurance engagement and other audit and assurance issues in the context of best practice and current developments.

Objectives of the syllabus

- Recognise the legal and regulatory environment and its impact on audit and assurance practice.

- Demonstrate the ability to work effectively on an assurance or other service engagement within a professional and ethical framework.

- Assess and recommend appropriate quality control policies and procedures in practice management and recognise the auditor's position in relation to the acceptance and retention of professional appointments.

- Identify and formulate the work required to meet the objectives of audit assignments and apply the International Standards on Auditing.

- Evaluate findings and the results of work performed and draft suitable reports on assignments.

- Identify and formulate the work required to meet the objectives of non-audit assignments.

- Understand the current issues and developments relating to the provision of audit-related and assurance services.

Core areas of the syllabus

- Regulatory environment

- Professional and ethical considerations

- Quality control and practice management

- Planning and conducting an audit of historical financial information

- Completion, review and reporting

- Other assignments

- Current issues and developments.

Approach to INT and UK syllabus elements

Due to the alignment of the INT and UK syllabus elements, one text has been produced to address both variants. Both streams apply the principles of International Standards on Auditing (ISAs) and International Financial Reporting Standards (IFRS® Standards).

The International variant has been used as the basis of the text. Any variances relevant only to the UK syllabus (such as compliance with the Companies Act 2006) are identifiable by reference to sections preceded with "UK syllabus". All test your understandings have also been appended to reflect any UK specific variations.

ACCA Performance Objectives

In order to become a member of the ACCA, as a trainee accountant you will need to demonstrate that you have achieved nine performance objectives. Performance objectives are indicators of effective performance and set the minimum standard of work that trainees are expected to achieve and demonstrate in the workplace. They are divided into key areas of knowledge which are closely linked to the exam syllabus.

There are five Essential performance objectives and a choice of fifteen Technical performance objectives which are divided into five areas.

The performance objectives which link to this exam are:

1   Ethics and professionalism (Essential)

2   Governance risk and control (Essential)

3   Prepare for an plan the audit process (Technical)

4   Collect and evaluate evidence for an audit (Technical)

5   Review and report on the findings of an audit (Technical)

The following link provides an in depth insight into all of the performance objectives:

https://www.accaglobal.com/content/dam/ACCA_Global/Students/per/PER-Performance-objectives-achieve.pdf

Progression

There are two elements of progression that we can measure: first how quickly students move through individual topics within a subject; and second how quickly they move from one course to the next. We know that there is an optimum for both, but it can vary from subject to subject and from student to student. However, using data and our experience of student performance over many years, we can make some generalisations.

A fixed period of study set out at the start of a course with key milestones is important. This can be within a subject, for example 'I will finish this topic by 30 June', or for overall achievement, such as 'I want to be qualified by the end of next year'.

Your qualification is cumulative, as earlier papers provide a foundation for your subsequent studies, so do not allow there to be too big a gap between one subject and another. We know that exams encourage techniques that lead to some degree of short term retention, the result being that you will simply forget much of what you have already learned unless it is refreshed (look up Ebbinghaus Forgetting Curve for more details on this). This makes it more difficult as you move from one subject to another: not only will you have to learn the new subject, you will also have to relearn all the underpinning knowledge as well. This is very inefficient and slows down your overall progression which makes it more likely you may not succeed at all.

In addition, delaying your studies slows your path to qualification which can have negative impacts on your career, postponing the opportunity to apply for higher level positions and therefore higher pay.

You can use the following diagram showing the whole structure of your qualification to help you keep track of your progress.

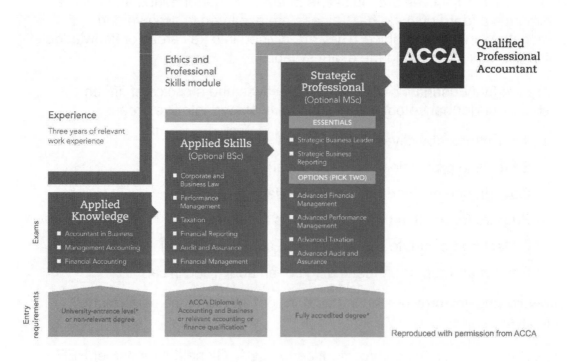

Reproduced with permission from ACCA

Syllabus objectives

We have reproduced the ACCA's syllabus below, showing where the objectives are explored within this book. Within the chapters, we have broken down the extensive information found in the syllabus into easily digestible and relevant sections, called Content Objectives. These correspond to the objectives at the beginning of each chapter.

Syllabus learning objective	Chapter reference
A REGULATORY ENVIRONMENT	
1 International regulatory frameworks for audit and assurance services	
(a) Explain the need for laws, regulations, standards and other guidance relating to audit, assurance and related services.[2]	1
(b) Outline and explain the need for the legal and professional framework including:[2]	1
(i) public oversight of audit and assurance practice	
(ii) the impact of corporate governance principles on audit and assurance practice (UK: the impact of the UK Corporate Governance Code on audit and assurance practice)	
(iii) the role of audit committees and impact on audit and assurance practice.	
2 Money laundering	
(a) Define 'money laundering' and discuss international methods for combatting money laundering.[2]	2
(b) Explain the scope of criminal offences of money laundering and how professional accountants may be protected from criminal and civil liability.[2]	2
(c) Explain the need for ethical guidance in this area.[2]	2
(d) Describe how accountants meet their obligations to help prevent and detect money laundering including record keeping and reporting of suspicion to the appropriate regulatory body.[2]	2
(e) Explain the importance of customer due diligence (CDD) also referred to as Know Your Customer (KYC) and recommend the information which should be gathered as part of CDD/KYC.[2]	2

<table>
<tr><td>(f)</td><td>Recognise potentially suspicious transactions and assess their impact on reporting duties.[2]</td><td>2</td></tr>
<tr><td>(g)</td><td>Describe, with reasons, the basic elements of an anti-money laundering program.[2]</td><td>2</td></tr>
</table>

3   Laws and regulations

<table>
<tr><td>(a)</td><td>Compare and contrast the respective responsibilities of management and auditors concerning compliance with laws and regulations in an audit of financial statements.[2]</td><td>4</td></tr>
<tr><td>(b)</td><td>Describe the auditors' considerations of compliance with laws and regulations and plan audit procedures when possible non-compliance is discovered.[2]</td><td>4</td></tr>
<tr><td>(c)</td><td>Discuss how and to whom non-compliance should be reported.[2]</td><td>4</td></tr>
<tr><td>(d)</td><td>Recognise and recommend when withdrawal from an engagement is necessary.[2]</td><td>4</td></tr>
</table>

B   PROFESSIONAL AND ETHICAL CONSIDERATIONS

1   INT: Code of Ethics for Professional Accountants

UK: Code of ethics and conduct

<table>
<tr><td>(a)</td><td>Explain the fundamental principles and the conceptual framework approach.[1]</td><td>3</td></tr>
<tr><td>(b)</td><td>Identify, evaluate and respond to threats to compliance with the fundamental principles.[3]</td><td>3</td></tr>
<tr><td>(c)</td><td>Discuss and evaluate the effectiveness of available safeguards.[3]</td><td>3</td></tr>
<tr><td>(d)</td><td>Recognise and advise on conflicts in the application of fundamental principles.[3]</td><td>3</td></tr>
<tr><td>(e)</td><td>Discuss the importance of professional scepticism in planning and performing an audit.[2]</td><td>7</td></tr>
<tr><td>(f)</td><td>Consider the ethical implications of the external auditor providing non-audit services to a client including an internal audit service.[2]</td><td>3</td></tr>
<tr><td>(g)</td><td>Assess whether an engagement has been planned and performed with an attitude of professional scepticism, and evaluate the implications.[3]</td><td>7</td></tr>
</table>

2   Fraud and error

(a)   Identify and develop an appropriate response to   4
circumstances which indicate a high risk of error,
irregularity, fraud or misstatement in the financial
statements or a given situation.[2]

(b)   Compare and contrast the respective responsibilities of   4
management and auditors for fraud and error.[2]

(c)   Describe the matters to be considered and recommend   4
procedures to be carried out to investigate actual and/or
potential misstatements in a given situation.[2]

(d)   Explain how, why, when and to whom fraud and error   4
should be reported and the circumstances in which an
auditor should withdraw from an engagement.[2]

(e)   Consider the current and possible future role of auditors   4
in preventing, detecting and reporting error and fraud.[2]

3   Professional liability

(a)   Recognise circumstances in which professional   4
accountants may have legal liability and the criteria that
need to be satisfied for legal liability to be recognised.[2]

(b)   Describe the factors to determine whether or not an   4
auditor is negligent and discuss the auditor's potential
liability in given situations.[2]

(c)   Compare and contrast liability owed to client with liability   4
owed to third parties (i.e. contract vs establishing a duty
of care).[3]

(d)   Evaluate the practicability and effectiveness of ways in   4
which liability may be restricted including the use of
liability limitation agreements.[3]

(e)   Discuss and appraise the principal causes of audit   4
failure and other factors that contribute to the
'expectation gap' (e.g. responsibilities for fraud and
error) and recommend ways in which that gap may be
bridged.[3]

C   QUALITY CONTROL AND PRACTICE MANAGEMENT

1   Quality control (firm-wide)

(a)   Explain the principles and purpose of quality control of   5
audit and other assurance engagements.[1]

(b)   Describe the elements of a system of quality control   5
relevant to a given firm.[2]

(c)   Evaluate the quality control procedures that are in place   5
for a given firm and assess if they have been
appropriately applied in a given engagement.[3]

2   Advertising, tendering and obtaining professional work and fees

    (a)   Evaluate the appropriateness of publicity material including the use of the ACCA logo and reference to fees.[2]   6

    (b)   Outline the determinants of fee-setting and justify the bases on which fees and commissions may and may not be charged for services.[3]   6

    (c)   Discuss the ethical and other professional problems, for example, lowballing, involved in establishing and negotiating fees for a specified assignment.[3]   6

    (d)   Recognise and explain the matters to be considered prior to tendering for an audit or other professional engagement and explain the information to be included in the proposal.[2]   6

3   Professional appointments

    (a)   Explain the matters to be considered and the procedures that an audit firm/professional accountant should carry out before accepting a specified new client/engagement or continuing with an existing engagement, including:[3]   6

        (i)   client acceptance

        (ii)   engagement acceptance (new and existing engagements)

        (iii) establish whether the preconditions for an audit are present

        (iv) agreeing the terms of engagement.

    (b)   Recognise the key issues that underlie the agreement of the scope and terms of an engagement with a client.[2]   6

D   PLANNING AND CONDUCTING AN AUDIT OF HISTORICAL FINANCIAL INFORMATION

1   Planning, materiality and assessing the risk of material misstatement

    (a)   Define materiality and performance materiality and demonstrate how it should be applied in financial reporting and auditing.[2]   7

    (b)   Evaluate business risks, audit risks and risks of material misstatement for a given assignment.[3]   7

    (c)   Discuss and demonstrate the use of analytical procedures in the planning of an assignment.[3]   7

(d)	Explain how the result of planning procedures determines the relevant audit strategy.[2]	7
(e)	Explain the planning procedures specific to an initial audit engagement.[2]	7
(f)	Recommend additional information which may be required to assist the auditor in obtaining an understanding of the entity.[2]	7
(g)	Discuss how transnational audits may differ from other audits of historical financial information (e.g. in terms of applicable financial reporting and auditing standards, listing requirements and corporate governance requirements).[2]	8
(h)	Recognise matters that are not relevant to the planning of an assignment.[2]	7

2   Evidence and testing considerations

(a)	Identify and describe audit procedures (including substantive and tests of control) to obtain sufficient, appropriate audit evidence from identified sources to support the financial statement assertions and disclosures.[2]	9
(b)	Assess and describe how IT can be used to assist the auditor and recommend the use of automated tools and techniques such as audit software, test data and other data analytics where appropriate.[2]	9
(c)	Recommend additional information which may be required to effectively carry out a planned engagement or a specific aspect of an engagement.[2]	9
(d)	Apply the further considerations and audit procedures relevant to initial engagements.[2]	9
(e)	Apply analytical procedures to financial and non-financial data.[2]	7 & 9
(f)	Explain the specific audit problems and procedures concerning related parties and related party transactions.[2]	9
(g)	Recognise circumstances that may indicate the existence of unidentified related parties and recommend appropriate audit procedures.[2]	9

3   Audit procedures and obtaining evidence

(a) Design appropriate audit procedures relating to:[3]   9 & 20

    (i)   inventory (including standard costing systems)

    (ii)   non-current assets

    (iii)   intangible assets

    (iv)   biological assets

    (v)   investment properties

    (vi)   assets held for sale and discontinued operations

    (vii)   financial instruments

    (viii) fair values

    (ix)   government grants

    (x)   leases

    (xi)   impairment

    (xii)   provisions, contingent liabilities and contingent assets

    (xiii) borrowing costs

    (xiv) employee benefits

    (xv)   share-based payment transactions

    (xvi) taxation (including deferred tax)

    (xvii) related parties

    (xviii) revenue from contracts with customers

    (xix) statement of cash flows

    (xx)   business combinations

    (xxi) events after the end of the reporting period

    (xxii) the effects of foreign exchange rates

    (xxiii) segmental reporting

    (xxiv) earnings per share

    (xxv) changes in accounting policy

    (xxvi) payroll and other expenses

(b) Explain how the auditor's responsibilities for   9, 11
corresponding figures, comparative financial
statements, and 'other information' are discharged.[3]

(c)	Explain the auditor's main considerations in respect of social and environmental matters and how they impact on entities and their financial statements (e.g. impairment of assets, provisions and contingent liabilities).[2]	17

4 Using the work of others

(a)	Recognise when it is justifiable to place reliance on the work of an expert (e.g. a surveyor employed by the audit client).[2]	9
(b)	Evaluate the potential impact of an internal audit department on the planning and performance of the external audit.[2]	9
(c)	Assess the appropriateness and sufficiency of the work of internal auditors and the extent to which reliance can be placed on it.[2]	9
(d)	Recognise and evaluate the impact of outsourced functions on the conduct of an audit.[3]	9

5 Group audits

(a)	Recognise the specific matters to be considered before accepting appointment as group auditor to a group in a given situation.[3]	8
(b)	Identify and describe the matters to be considered and the procedures to be performed at the planning stage, when a group auditor considers the use of the work of component auditors.[3]	8
(c)	Identify and explain the matters specific to planning an audit of group financial statements including:	8

- assessment of group and component materiality

- the impact of non-coterminous year ends within a group

- changes in group structure or a complex group structure.[2]

(d)	Recommend and discuss the communications and content therein to be provided by the group auditor to the component auditor in a given situation.[3]	8
(e)	Recognise the audit problems and describe audit procedures specific to:	8

- a business combination including the classification of investments

- the determination of goodwill and its impairment

- group accounting policies

- intra-company trading

- equity accounting for associates and joint ventures
- changes in group structure including acquisitions and disposals
- accounting for a foreign subsidiary.[3]

(f)	In respect of the consolidation process identify and explain the relevant audit risks and audit procedures necessary to obtain sufficient appropriate evidence.[3]	8
(g)	Consider how the group auditor should evaluate the audit work performed by a component auditor.[2]	8
(h)	Explain the responsibilities of the component auditor before accepting appointment, and the procedures to be performed in a group situation.[2]	8
(i)	Justify the situations where a joint audit would be appropriate.[2]	8

E COMPLETION, REVIEW AND REPORTING

1 Subsequent events and going concern

(a)	Design audit procedures to identify subsequent events which may require adjustment to, or disclosure in, the financial statements of a given entity.[2]	10
(b)	Evaluate indicators that the going concern basis may be in doubt and recognise mitigating factors.[2]	10
(c)	Recommend audit procedures, or evaluate the evidence that might be expected to be available and assess the appropriateness of the going concern basis in given situations.[3]	10
(d)	Assess the adequacy of disclosures in financial statements relating to going concern and explain the implications for the auditor's report with regard to the going concern basis.[3]	10 & 11

2 Completion and final review

(a)	Explain the use of analytical procedures in evaluation and review.[3]	10
(b)	Assess whether an engagement has been planned and performed in accordance with professional standards.[3]	5 & 10
(c)	Evaluate whether reports issued are appropriate in the circumstances.[3]	5 & 10
(d)	Evaluate as part of the final review the matters (e.g. materiality, risk, relevant accounting standards) and audit evidence to confirm if sufficient and appropriate evidence has been obtained.[3]	10

(e)	Justify the review procedures which should be performed in a given assignment, including the need for an engagement quality control review and recommend additional procedures or actions needed in the circumstances.[2]	5 & 10
(f)	Evaluate the use of written representations from management to support other audit evidence.[2]	10

3 Auditor's reports

(a)	Determine the form and content of an unmodified auditor's report and assess the appropriateness of the contents of an unmodified auditor's report.[3]	11
(b)	Recognise and evaluate the factors to be taken into account when forming an audit opinion in a given situation and justify audit opinions that are consistent with the results of audit procedures.[3]	11
(c)	Critically appraise the form and content of an auditor's report in a given situation.[3]	11
(d)	Assess whether or not a proposed audit opinion is appropriate.[3]	11
(e)	Advise on the actions which may be taken by the auditor in the event that a modified auditor's opinion is issued.[3]	11
(f)	Explain the implications for the auditor's report on the financial statements of an entity where the opinion on a component is modified in a given situation.[2]	8
(g)	Recognise when the use of an emphasis of matter paragraph, other matter paragraph and KAM disclosure would be appropriate.[3]	11
(h)	Discuss the courses of action available to an auditor if a material inconsistency or material misstatement exists in relation to other information such as contained in the integrated report.[2]	11

4 Reports to those charged with governance and management

(a)	Critically assess the quality of a report to those charged with governance and management.[3]	11
(b)	Advise on the content of reports to those charged with governance and management in a given situation.[3]	11

F OTHER ASSIGNMENTS

1 Audit-related and assurance services

(a) Describe the nature of audit-related services, the circumstances in which they might be required and the comparative levels of assurance provided by professional accountants and distinguish between:[2]

    (i) audit-related services and an audit of historical financial statements

    (ii) an attestation engagement and a direct engagement.

12

(b) Describe the main categories of assurance services that audit firms can provide and assess the benefits of providing these services to management and external users.[3]

12

(c) Describe the level of assurance (reasonable, high, moderate, limited, negative) for an engagement depending on the subject matter evaluated, the criteria used, the procedures applied and the quality and quantity of evidence obtained.[3]

12

2 Specific assignments

- **Due diligence**   15
- **Review of interim financial information**   13
- **Prospective financial information**   14
- **Forensic audits**   16

For each of the other assignments listed above:

(a) Define and describe the purpose of each type of assignment and analyse the appropriate level of assurance that may be offered by a professional firm in relation to these assignments:[3]

(b) Evaluate the matters to be considered before accepting the engagement, including any ethical and professional considerations.[3]

(c) Plan the assignment to gather suitable evidence and provide an appropriate level of assurance in line with the objectives of the assignment.[2]

(d) Discuss the level of assurance that the auditor may provide and explain the other factors to be considered in determining the nature, timing and extent of examination procedures.[1]

(e) Describe and recommend appropriate substantive, examination or investigative procedures which can be used to gather sufficient appropriate evidence in the circumstances.[2]

(d)	Examine the financial position of a company and determine whether it is insolvent.[2]	19
(e)	Identify the circumstances where administration could be adopted as an alternative to liquidation, and explain the benefits of administration compared to liquidation.[2]	19
(f)	Explain and apply the priority for the allocation of company assets.[2]	19

5 Reporting on other assignments

(a)	Analyse the form and content of the professional accountant's report for an assurance engagement as compared with an auditor's report.[2]	12
(b)	Discuss the content of a report for an examination of prospective financial information.[2]	14
(c)	Discuss the effectiveness of the 'negative assurance' form of reporting and evaluate situations in which it may be appropriate to modify a conclusion.[3]	12

G CURRENT ISSUES AND DEVELOPMENTS

Discuss the relative merits and the consequences of different standpoints taken in current debates and express opinions supported by reasoned arguments.

1 Professional and ethical developments

(a)	Discuss emerging ethical issues and evaluate the potential impact on the profession, firms and auditors.[3]	3
(b)	Discuss the content and impact of exposure drafts, consultations and other pronouncements issued by FRC (UK only) and IFAC and its supporting bodies (including IAASB, IESBA and TAC).[3]	1 & 3

2 Other current issues

(a)	Discuss current developments in auditing standards including the need for new and revised standards and evaluate their impact on the conduct of audits.[3]	1
(b)	Discuss current developments in business practices, practice management and audit methodology and evaluate the potential impact on the conduct of an audit and audit quality.[3]	1, 7, 9
(c)	Discuss current developments in emerging technologies, including big data and the use of automated tools and technologies such as data analytics and the potential impact on the conduct of an audit and audit quality.[3]	1 & 7

The superscript numbers in square brackets indicate the intellectual depth at which the subject area could be assessed within the examination. Level 1 (knowledge and comprehension) broadly equates with the Knowledge module, Level 2 (application and analysis) with the Skills module and Level 3 (synthesis and evaluation) to the Professional level. However, lower level skills can continue to be assessed as you progress through each module and level.

For a list of examinable documents, see the ACCA website.

The examination

Examination format

Section A will comprise a Case Study, worth 50 marks, set at the planning stage of the audit, for a single company, a group of companies or potentially several audit clients. Candidates will be provided with detailed information, which will vary between examinations, but is likely to include extracts of financial information, strategic, operational and other relevant financial information for a client business, as well as extracts from audit working papers, including results of analytical procedures.

Candidates will be required to address a range of requirements, from syllabus sections A, B, C and D, thereby tackling a real world situation where candidates may have to address a range of issues simultaneously in relation to planning, risk assessment, evidence gathering and ethical and professional considerations.

Four professional marks will be available in Section A and will be awarded based on the level of professionalism with which a candidate's answer is presented, including the structure and clarity of the answer provided.

Section B will contain two compulsory 25 mark questions, with each being predominately based around a short scenario.

One question will always predominantly come from syllabus section E, and consequently candidates should be prepared to answer a question relating to completion, review and reporting.

There are a number of formats this question could adopt, including, but not limited to, requiring candidates to assess going concern, the impact of subsequent events, evaluating identified misstatements and the corresponding effect on the auditor's report. Candidates may also be asked to critique an auditor's report or report which is to be provided to management or those charged with governance.

The other Section B question can be drawn from any other syllabus section, including A, B, C, D and F.

Quality control and ethics

The auditor's assessment of effective quality control procedures and consideration of ethical issues are fundamental to all stages of the audit and therefore these concepts could be examined in any section of the exam.

Current issues

Syllabus section G on current issues may be examined in Section A or B as appropriate. Current issues is unlikely to form the basis of any question on its own but instead will be incorporated into the Case Study or either of the Section B questions dependent on question content and the topical issues affecting the profession at the time of writing.

	Number of marks
Section A	
Planning, risk assessment, gathering evidence, ethical and professional considerations, quality control, current issues	46
Professional marks	4
	───
	50
Section B	
Completion, review and reporting	25
Any area of the syllabus from:	25
• Regulatory environment	
• Ethical and professional considerations	
• Quality control and practice management	
• Planning and conducting an audit of historical information	
• Other assignments	
• Current issues	
	───
	100

Total time allowed: 3 hours 15 minutes

Examination tips

We recommend that 15 minutes should be spent reviewing the format and content of the requirements so that you understand what you need to do.

Read each question carefully.

If 15 minutes are spent reading the examination requirements, this leaves three hours to attempt the questions:

- Divide the time you spend on questions in proportion to the marks on offer.

- One suggestion for this examination is to allocate 1.8 minutes to each mark available (180 minutes/100 marks), so a 25 mark question should be completed in approximately 45 minutes. If you plan to spend more or less than 15 minutes on reading, your time allocation per mark will be different.

Unless you know exactly how to answer the question, spend some time **planning** your answer. Stick to the question and **tailor your answer** to what you are asked. Pay particular attention to the verbs in the question.

Practise plenty of questions to improve your ability to apply the techniques.

Spend the last few minutes reading through your answers and making any additions or corrections.

If you get completely stuck with a question leave it and return to it later.

If you do not understand what a question is asking, state your assumptions. Even if you do not answer in precisely the way the examiner hoped, you may be given some credit, if your assumptions are reasonable.

You should do everything you can to make things easy for the marker. The marker will find it easier to identify the points you have made if your answers are legible and well spaced out.

Be concise but make sure you explain your points in sufficient depth.

Make sure that each point is clearly identifiable by leaving a line space between each of your points. DO NOT write an essay.

Question 1 will ask you to present your answer in the form of briefing notes or other document. So use the correct format, there will be professional marks to gain here.

Don't panic if you realise you've answered a question incorrectly. Try to remain calm, continue to apply examination technique and answer all questions required within the time available.

Strategic Professional CBE

From March 2020, ACCA introduced Strategic Professional computer based examinations (CBE) in selected locations. Strategic Professional CBE will be extended to other locations over time, across subsequent examination sessions. Once CBE are offered in a location, the paper-based exam will no longer be available. For more information regarding when Strategic Professional CBE will be introduced in your market, please refer to the ACCA Global website.

This Study Text is appropriate for both CBE and paper-based exams. It is essential that students who will be sitting the CBE become familiar with the CBE environment as part of their exam preparation. For additional support please refer to the ACCA Global website.

Study skills and revision guidance

This section aims to give guidance on how to study for your ACCA exams and to give ideas on how to improve your existing study techniques.

Preparing to study

Set your objectives

Before starting to study decide what you want to achieve i.e. the type of pass you wish to obtain. This will decide the level of commitment and time you need to dedicate to your studies.

Devise a study plan

Determine which times of the week you will study. Split these times into sessions of at least one hour for study of new material. Any shorter periods could be used for revision or practice. Put the times you plan to study onto a study plan for the weeks from now until the exam and set yourself targets for each period of study – in your sessions make sure you cover the course, course assignments and revision.

If you are studying for more than one exam at a time, try to vary your subjects as this can help you to keep interested and see subjects as part of wider knowledge.

When working through your course, compare your progress with your plan and, if necessary, re-plan your work (perhaps including extra sessions) or, if you are ahead, do some extra revision/practice questions.

Effective studying

Active reading

You are not expected to learn the text by rote, rather, you must understand what you are reading and be able to use it to pass the exam and develop good practice. A good technique to use is SQ3Rs – Survey, Question, Read, Recall, Review:

(1) **Survey the chapter** – look at the headings and read the introduction, summary and objectives, so as to get an overview of what the chapter deals with.

(2) **Question** – whilst undertaking the survey, ask yourself the questions that you hope the chapter will answer for you.

(3) **Read** through the chapter thoroughly, answering the questions and making sure you can meet the objectives. Attempt the exercises and activities in the text, and work through all the examples.

(4) **Recall** – at the end of each section and at the end of the chapter, try to recall the main ideas of the section/chapter without referring to the text. This is best done after a short break of a couple of minutes after the reading stage.

(5) **Review** – check that your recall notes are correct.

KAPLAN PUBLISHING

You may also find it helpful to re-read the chapter to try to see the topic(s) it deals with as a whole.

Note-taking

Taking notes is a useful way of learning, but do not simply copy out the text. The notes must:

- be in your own words
- be concise
- cover the key points
- be well-organised
- be modified as you study further chapters in this text or in related ones.

Trying to summarise a chapter without referring to the text can be a useful way of determining which areas you know and which you don't.

Summarise the key points of a chapter.

Three ways of taking notes:

(1) **Make linear notes** – a list of headings, divided up with subheadings listing the key points. If you use linear notes, you can use different colours to highlight key points and keep topic areas together. Use plenty of space to make your notes easy to use.

(2) **Try a diagrammatic form** – the most common of which is a mind-map. To make a mind-map, put the main heading in the centre of the paper and put a circle around it. Then draw short lines radiating from this to the main subheadings, which again have circles around them. Then continue the process from the sub-headings to sub-sub-headings, advantages, disadvantages, etc.

(3) **Highlighting and underlining** – you may find it useful to underline or highlight key points in your study text – but do be selective. You may also wish to make notes in the margins.

Revision

The best approach to revision is to revise the course as you work through it. Also try to leave four to six weeks before the exam for final revision. Make sure you cover the whole syllabus and pay special attention to those areas where your knowledge is weak. Here are some recommendations:

Read through the text and your notes again and condense your notes into key phrases. It may help to put key revision points onto index cards to look at when you have a few minutes to spare.

Review any assignments you have completed and look at where you lost marks – put more work into those areas where you were weak.

Practise exam standard questions under timed conditions. If you are short of time, list the points that you would cover in your answer and then read the model answer, but do try to complete at least a few questions under exam conditions.

Also practise producing answer plans and comparing them to the model answer.

If you are stuck on a topic find somebody (a tutor) to explain it to you.

Read good newspapers and professional journals, especially ACCA's **Student Accountant**, this can give you an advantage in the exam.

Ensure you **know the structure of the exam** – how many questions and of what type you will be expected to answer.

During your revision attempt all the different styles of questions you may be asked.

Further reading

You can find further reading and technical articles under the student section of ACCA's website.

Technical update

This text has been updated to reflect Examinable Documents September 2020 to June 2021 issued by ACCA.

Regulatory environment

Chapter learning objectives

This chapter covers syllabus areas:

- A1 – International regulatory frameworks for audit and assurance services

- G – Current issues and developments.

Detailed syllabus objectives are provided in the introduction section of the text book.

PER

One of the PER performance objectives (PO4) is governance risk and control. You contribute to effective governance in your area. You evaluate, monitor and implement risk management procedures, complying with the spirit and the letter of policies, laws and regulations. Working through this chapter should help you understand how to demonstrate that objective.

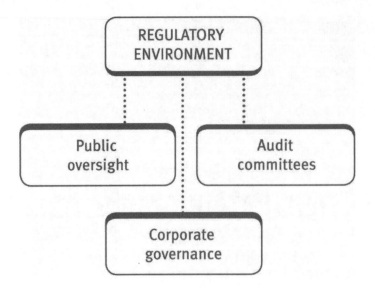

 Exam focus

This chapter considers the reasons behind the mechanisms for regulating assurance services and how standards of corporate governance are maintained. You need to have an awareness of recent developments in the profession, which will require you to read around the topic to develop your understanding and develop an ability to form your own opinion and reach your own conclusions.

1 The need for assurance services

 Assurance professionals provide reports that give an independent opinion as to whether the subject matter complies with pre-determined criteria. This enables the end user of that information to place more or less reliance on that information when making decisions.

Decision makers within financial markets need to have the confidence to make **informed decisions**. In order to make these decisions they need information they can trust. The main investment decisions that take place concern the buying and selling of shares. Without credible, reliable information at their disposal, investors cannot make those decisions.

It is not just shareholders who rely on this information, there are a range of other stakeholders who also rely on assurance services. For example, it is common for banks to seek audited financial statements and independently examined forecasts before making lending decisions. Many companies request audited financial statements before buying from, or supplying a company.

As well as investments in businesses, other stakeholders must make decisions about how to deploy resources: suppliers, customers, employees and prospective lenders all need information before making significant decisions that could have damaging financial repercussions.

2 Regulation of the profession

 Regulation of the accountancy profession was covered briefly in Audit and Assurance at the Applied Skills level. The Advanced Audit and Assurance syllabus looks at regulation from a broader perspective.

As a result of financial scandals, and the public concern that followed, many changes were implemented in the global auditing and accountancy profession.

Examples of developments include:

- The IAASB's International Standards on Auditing (ISAs) have been adopted or are being used as a basis for national standards in over 100 countries worldwide. The World Federation of Exchanges endorsed the IAASB's standard setting process and ISAs.

- The Code of Ethics for Professional Accountants has been adopted by many member institutions.

- Legislative changes have been established to introduce new corporate governance requirements. The most famous of these, The Sarbanes Oxley Act (SOX) in the US, led to the creation of the Public Company Accounting Oversight Board, who create standards for listed entities and conduct inspections of audit firms' work.

- The Public Interest Oversight Board was set up in 2005 to oversee the International Federation of Accountants' auditing and assurance, ethics, and education standard setting activities and its membership compliance programme.

Global regulation

The main problem is that harmonisation requires national regimes to adopt ISAs. Many countries have adopted ISAs but they have been adapted to suit local customs/laws and, as a result, many differences still exist in the quality of audits worldwide.

The need for regulation

Business failures, particularly large, high-profile businesses, cause loss of confidence within global financial markets. Confidence in the reliability of financial information is essential to the functioning of these markets. Whilst it is not the only factor in helping to achieve confidence, good quality, independent audit and assurance has a key role to play. A series of recent and high profile corporate failures has eroded trust in the assurance market and, as a result, mechanisms for increased regulation of the auditing profession have been introduced.

Self-regulation

The accountancy profession introduced standards to regulate financial reporting and shortly afterwards auditing standards were introduced. Standards were set **by** the accounting profession **for** the accounting profession to follow.

Self-regulation seemed to make sense because the accountancy organisations usually had a 'public interest' remit written into their constitutions and they understood financial reporting and auditing better than anyone.

However, high profile corporate failures, such as Enron have led to the questioning of self-regulation as a satisfactory mechanism.

Global Regulation

The globalisation of business, professions and investment markets has been rapid. Once businesses started to cross national borders it soon became clear that the variation of laws and regulations in different countries made life difficult, both for the multinationals and the professions trying to provide services to them. This realisation led to the foundation of the International Federation of Accountants (IFAC).

IFAC is structured to operate through a network of boards and committees.

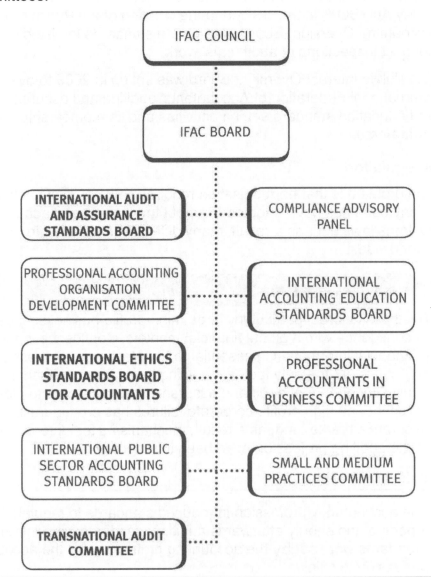

Detailed explanation of IFAC structure

The International Federation of Accountants (IFAC) is the global organisation for the accountancy profession. It was formed in 1977 and is based in New York. As at 1 January 2020, IFAC has more than 175 member bodies of accountants (including the ACCA), representing 3 million accountants from 130 separate countries.

IFAC's overall mission is to serve the public interest, strengthen the worldwide accountancy profession, and contribute to the development of strong international economies by establishing and promoting adherence to high quality professional standards.

The structure of IFAC is as follows:

The **IFAC Council** comprises one representative from each member body. It meets once a year and elects the board.

The **IFAC Board** is responsible for setting policy and overseeing the work of the various committees.

The **IFAC Nominating Committee** makes recommendations regarding the composition of IFAC boards, committees and task forces.

The main bodies to be aware of are:

- The **International Auditing and Assurance Standards Board:** develops and promotes ISAs and other assurance standards to improve the uniformity of auditing practices and related services throughout the world.

- The **International Ethics Standards Board for Accountants:** promotes the Code of Ethics. Significantly, the committee continually monitors and stimulates debate on a wide range of ethical issues to ensure that its guidance is responsive to the expectations and challenges of individuals, businesses, financial institutions and others relying on the work of accountants.

- The **Transnational Auditors Committee:** deals with issues arising from cross-border auditing. It is the executive committee of the Forum of Firms (FoF), open to all firms performing or wishing to perform transnational audits. The TAC is discussed in chapter 8.

Other constituent bodies include:

- The **Compliance Advisory Panel**

- The **Professional Accountancy Organisation Development Committee**

- The **International Accounting Education Standards Board**

- The **Professional Accountants in Business Committee**

- The **International Public Sector Accounting Standards Board**

- The **Small and Medium Practices Committee.**

IFAC has encountered a number of difficulties in carrying out its role:

- It was set up by, and continues to be financed by, the accountancy profession worldwide. It therefore represents a self-regulatory body. It is suggested that this is an inappropriate mechanism for regulating the audit profession.

- National interests still apply leading to the implementation of international standards being bogged down in arguments between different national approaches.

- Its members are the professional accountancy bodies, whose authority has been eclipsed to some extent by the power of the largest accountancy firms.

The need for Global Accounting Networks

Although companies have had their securities listed in both the European and US markets for a number of years, the ability to be based virtually anywhere in the world, and to manufacture, sell and manage businesses on a truly global basis is a more recent phenomenon. Global businesses need global professional firms to support, advise and audit them. The emergence of the 'Big 4' global practices has been an accelerating process that has its origins in the 1970s. Similar globalisation has happened in the banking and assurance industries and the introduction of external shareholders into the securities markets has led to, e.g. Nasdaq from the US investing in the London Stock Exchange.

3 Corporate governance

 The principles of corporate governance were covered in detail in Audit & Assurance at the Applied Skills level. The main provisions are covered again here.

 Corporate governance is the system of rules, practices and processes by which a company is directed and controlled.

It is about ensuring public companies are managed effectively for the benefit of the company and its shareholders.

Corporate governance pronouncements tend to respond to corporate scandals that arise because unscrupulous management has:

- manipulated the share price for personal gain

- disguised poor results/mismanagement

- extracted funds from the company

- raised finance fraudulently.

High profile corporate failure: Carillion

In 2018, construction company Carillion collapsed after building up debts of £1.5 billion. The company was a major contractor for the UK government with contracts to build hospitals and schools as well as facilities management and ongoing maintenance. It was the second largest construction company in the UK and employed more than 43,000 people worldwide. The company took on too many projects and failed to realistically price the contracts resulting in huge cost overruns and losses being made. In December 2017 the major banks refused to lend more money to Carillion and in 2018 the company went into compulsory liquidation. This caused significant problems, not just for the shareholders who will receive nothing, but also for the significant number of employees who lost their jobs, the government contracts that were in progress that would not be completed, and for the suppliers who would not be paid.

One of the issues highlighted by Carillion was that of executive pay. Executive directors were earning significant amounts of money despite running the company into the ground. In 2016, the former chief executive director earned more than £2 million. The head of corporate governance at the Institute of Directors said that the collapse of Carillion suggests a lack of effective governance. Directors' remuneration allowed them to benefit despite the collapse of the company as there were no clawback conditions. The company could only request clawback from directors if there was gross misconduct or misstatement of financial results. The directors also received payoffs despite being responsible for the collapse.

The collapse of Carillion has also returned focus to the big accounting firms and their part in allowing companies to fail by not having raised the alarm much earlier.

The UK Corporate Governance Code

The Organisation for Economic Co-operation and Development (OECD) has produced a set of six principles of corporate governance to guide policy makers when setting regulations for their own country.

The six OECD Principles are:

- Ensuring the basis of an effective corporate governance framework

- The rights and equitable treatment of shareholders and key ownership functions

- Institutional investors, stock markets, and other intermediaries

- The role of stakeholders in corporate governance

- Disclosure and transparency

- The responsibilities of the board.

The UK Corporate Governance Code reflects the OECD principles.

The UK Corporate Governance Code is particularly important for publicly traded companies because large amounts of money are invested in them, either by 'small' shareholders, or from pension schemes and other financial institutions. The wealth of these companies significantly affects the health of the economies where their shares are traded.

The Code is split into five parts:

- Board leadership and company purpose

- Division of responsibilities

- Composition, succession and evaluation

- Audit, risk and internal control

- Remuneration.

The Code does not set out a rigid set of rules, instead it offers flexibility through the application of Principles and 'comply or explain' provisions and supporting guidance.

The main requirements of the Code are given below.

Board leadership and company purpose

Principles

- A successful company is led by an effective board whose role is to promote long-term sustainable success thereby generating value for shareholders.

- The board should establish the company's purpose, values and strategy. The directors should lead by example and promote the desired culture.

- The board should ensure that the necessary resources are in place for the company to meet its objectives. The board should establish a framework of effective controls to enable risk to be assessed and managed.

- The board should ensure effective engagement with, and encourage participation from shareholders and stakeholders.

- The board should ensure that workforce policies and practices are consistent with the company's values. The workforce should be able to raise matters of concern.

Main provisions

- The board should describe in the annual report how opportunities and risks to the future success of the business have been considered and addressed.

- The board should assess and monitor culture. Where behaviour throughout the business is not consistent with the company's purpose, values or strategy, the board should ensure management have taken corrective action.

- In addition to formal general meetings, the chair should seek regular engagement with major shareholders. The board as a whole should understand the views of the shareholders.

- When 20% or more of votes have been cast against the board recommendation for a resolution, the company should explain what actions it intends to take to understand the reasons behind the result.

- The board should understand the views of the company's other key stakeholders and describe how their interests have been considered in board discussions. For engagement with the workforce, the company should use a director appointed from the workforce, a workforce advisory panel or a designated non-executive director (NED).

- The workforce should be able to raise concerns in confidence and anonymously ('whistleblowing').

- The board should take action to manage conflicts of interest.

- Directors' concerns about the operation of the board or management of the company that cannot be resolved should be minuted. On resignation, a non-executive director should provide a written statement to the chair for circulation to the board if they have any concerns.

Division of responsibilities

Principles

- The chair leads the board and is responsible for its overall effectiveness.

- The chair should facilitate effective contribution of all board members.

- The chair should ensure that directors receive clear, accurate and timely information.

- The board should be balanced so that no individual or small group of individuals can dominate board decisions.

- NEDs should have sufficient time to meet their board responsibilities and should hold management to account.

- The board should ensure it has the policies, processes, information, time and resources it needs to function effectively and efficiently.

Main provisions

- The chair should be independent on appointment (see below for independence criteria).

- The chair and chief executive roles should not be taken by the same individual and the chief executive should not become the chair of the same company.

- At least half the board, excluding the chair should be independent NEDs.

- The board should identify the independent NEDs in the annual report. Independence would be deemed to be affected if a director:

  - is, or has been, an employee of the company or group within the last five years

  - has, or has had within the last three years, a material business relationship with the company either directly or indirectly

  - has received or receives remuneration in addition to a director's fee, participates in the company's share option or a performance-related pay scheme, or is a member of the company's pension scheme

  - has close family ties with any of the company's advisers, directors or senior employees

  - holds cross-directorships or has significant links with other directors through involvement in other companies or bodies

  - represents a significant shareholder

  - has served on the board for more than nine years from the date of their first appointment.

- One of the independent NEDs should be appointed as a senior independent director to provide a sounding board for the chair.

- The NEDs and the senior independent director should meet without the chair present at least annually to appraise the chair's performance.

- NEDs appoint and remove executive directors and scrutinise performance against agreed performance objectives.

- The responsibilities of the chair, chief executive, senior independent director, board and committees should be set out in writing and publicly available.

- The annual report should set out the number of meetings of the board and its committees and the attendance of each director.

- New appointments to the board should take into account other demands on the director's time. Full-time executive directors should not take on more than one NED role in a FTSE 100 company or other significant appointment. Appointments should not be made without prior approval of the board.

- Appointment and removal of the company secretary should be a matter for the whole board.

Composition, succession and evaluation

Principles

- Appointments to the board should be subject to a formal, rigorous and transparent procedure.

- An effective succession plan should be maintained for board and senior management.

- Appointments and succession should be based on merit and objective criteria and should promote diversity.

- The board and its committees should have a combination of skills, experience and knowledge.

- Annual evaluation of the board should consider its composition, diversity and how effectively members work together to achieve objectives.

Main provisions

- A nomination committee should be established to appoint board members.

- A majority of the committee members should be independent NEDs.

- The chair should not be a member of the committee when the committee is dealing with the appointment of their successor.

- All directors should be subject to annual re-election.

- The chair should not remain in post for more than nine years from the date of their first appointment. This period can be extended for a limited time to facilitate effective succession planning.

- Open advertising and/or an external search consultancy should be used for the appointment of the chair and NEDs.

- There should be a formal and rigorous annual evaluation of the performance of the board, its committees, the chair and the individual directors.

- The chair should consider having a regular external board evaluation at least every three years for FTSE 350 companies, and the external evaluator should be identified in the annual report.

- The annual report should describe the work of the nomination committee including the process used in making appointments, how the board evaluation has been conducted, the policy on diversity and inclusion and the gender balance of those in senior management.

Audit, risk and internal control including audit committees

Principles

- The board should establish formal and transparent policies and procedures to ensure the independence and effectiveness of internal and external audit functions and satisfy itself on the integrity of financial and narrative statements.

- The board should present a fair, balanced and understandable assessment of the company's position and prospects.

- The board should establish procedures to manage risk, oversee the internal control framework, and determine the nature and extent of the principal risks the company is willing to take in order to achieve its long-term strategic objectives.

Main provisions

- The board should establish an audit committee of independent NEDs, with a minimum membership of three, or in the case of smaller companies, two.

- The chair of the board should not be a member of the audit committee.

- At least one member must have recent and relevant financial experience.

- The committee as a whole must have competence relevant to the sector in which the company operates.

- The main roles and responsibilities of the audit committee include:

  - Monitoring the integrity of the financial statements.

  - Providing advice on whether the annual report and accounts are fair, balanced and understandable.

  - Reviewing the company's internal financial controls and risk management systems.

  - Monitoring and reviewing the effectiveness of the internal audit function.

  - If there is no internal audit function in place, they should consider annually whether there is a need for one and make a recommendation to the board.

  - Making recommendations in relation to the appointment and removal of the external auditor and their remuneration.

  - Reviewing and monitoring the external auditor's independence and objectivity and the effectiveness of the audit process.

  - Developing and implementing policy on the engagement of the external auditor to supply non-audit services.

- The annual report should describe the work of the audit committee including:

  - Significant issues considered relating to the financial statements.

  - How it has assessed the independence and effectiveness of the external audit process.

  - Where there is no internal audit function, an explanation for the absence and how internal assurance is achieved.

  - An explanation of how auditor independence and objectivity are safeguarded, if the external auditor provides non-audit services.

- The directors should explain in the annual report their responsibility for preparing the annual report and accounts.

- The board should carry out a robust assessment of the company's emerging and principal risks.

KAPLAN PUBLISHING

- The board should confirm in the annual report that it has completed this assessment, including a description of its principal risks, what procedures are in place to identify emerging risks, and an explanation of how these are being managed or mitigated.

- The board should monitor the company's risk management and internal control systems and, at least annually, carry out a review of their effectiveness and report on that review in the annual report. The monitoring and review should cover all material controls, including financial, operational and compliance controls.

- The board should state whether it considers it appropriate to adopt the going concern basis of accounting in preparing financial statements, and identify any material uncertainties to the company's ability to continue to do so over a period of at least 12 months from the date of approval of the financial statements.

- The board should explain in the annual report how it has assessed the prospects of the company, over what period it has done so and why it considers that period to be appropriate.

- The board should state whether it has a reasonable expectation that the company will be able to continue in operation and meet its liabilities as they fall due over the period of their assessment.

Remuneration

Principles

- Remuneration should be designed to promote the long-term sustainable success of the company. Executive remuneration should be aligned to the company purpose, values and long-term strategy.

- The board should establish formal and transparent procedures for developing the policy for executive directors' remuneration.

- No director should be involved in setting his own pay.

- Directors should exercise independent judgment and discretion when authorising remuneration, taking account of company and individual performance, and wider circumstances.

Main provisions

- A remuneration committee comprising a minimum of three independent NEDs should be established.

- The chair cannot chair the committee and can only be a member if they were independent on appointment.

- The remuneration committee should determine the policy for executive director remuneration and set remuneration for the chair, executive directors and senior management.

- The committee should review workforce remuneration and related policies taking these into account when setting the policy for executive director remuneration.

- NED remuneration should be determined by the board. It should reflect time commitment and responsibilities of the role and should not include share options or other performance related elements.

- Remuneration schemes should promote long-term shareholdings by executive directors. Shares awards should be released for sale on a phased basis and be subject to a total vesting and holding period of five years or more.

- Remuneration schemes should include provisions that enable a company to recover or withhold sums or share awards and specify the circumstances in which it would be appropriate to do so.

- Only basic salary should be pensionable and pension contribution rates should be aligned with those available to the workforce.

- Notice or contract periods should be one year or less. If it is necessary to offer longer periods to new directors the period should reduce to one year or less after the initial period.

- When determining the executive director remuneration policy and practices the committee should ensure remuneration arrangements are transparent, easy to understand, predictable, proportionate, and aligned to culture. The risks from excessive rewards should be identified and mitigated and the range of possible values of rewards should be identified and explained at the time of approving the policy.

- The work of the remuneration committee should be described in the annual report.

Relevance of corporate governance to external auditors

If a company complies with corporate governance best practice, the control environment of the company is likely to be stronger. There will be a greater focus on financial reporting and internal controls which should reduce control risk and inherent risk which together reduce the risk of material misstatements in the financial statements.

In addition, external auditors may be required to report on whether companies are compliant with the Code. For example, in the UK, external auditors of listed entities are required to report on whether the company is compliant with the UK Corporate Governance Code.

The audit committee of a company must also assess the effectiveness and quality of the external audit and monitor compliance with ethical standards.

4 Audit committees

Audit committees form part of the governance structure of an organisation.

The broad objectives of an audit committee are threefold:

- To increase public confidence in the credibility and objectivity of published financial information.

- To assist directors in meeting their financial reporting responsibilities.

- To strengthen the independent position of a company's external auditor.

The following requirements are taken from the Guidance on Audit Committees published by the Financial Reporting Council (FRC). The guidance is designed to assist company boards when implementing the Corporate Governance Code.

- Companies with a premium listing are required to comply with the Code or explain why they have not done so.

- Audit committee arrangements should be proportionate to the task and will vary according to size and complexity of the company.

- All directors have a duty to act in the interests of the company. However, the audit committee must act independently from the executive to ensure that the interests of the shareholders are properly protected in respect of financial reporting and internal control.

- There should be a frank, open working relationship and a high level of mutual respect between audit committee chair and board chair, the chief executive and the finance director.

- Management is under an obligation to ensure the audit committee is kept properly informed. All directors must cooperate with the audit committee.

- The core functions of audit committees are oversight, assessment and review. It is not the duty of the audit committee to carry out functions that belong to others. For example, they should make sure there is a proper system in place for monitoring of internal controls but should not do the monitoring themselves.

- The board should review the audit committee's effectiveness annually.

Membership, appointment and skills

- The committee should comprise independent NEDs.

- The committee should have at least 3 members (2 for smaller companies).

- The committee as a whole should have competence relevant to the sector in which the company operates.

- At least one member should have recent and relevant financial experience with an appropriate professional accountancy qualification.

- Committee members should be independent of operational management.

- Appointments to the audit committee should be made by the board on the recommendation of the nomination committee taking into consideration the skills, experience and qualifications to meet corporate governance requirements.

- Appointments should be for a period of up to 3 years, extendable by no more than two additional 3-year periods.

- New members should receive induction and training should be provided to all members on a continuing basis as required.

Meetings

- The audit committee should hold as many meetings as the roles and responsibilities require and it is recommended that no fewer than three meetings are held.

- No one other than the audit committee chair and members is entitled to be present at a meeting of the audit committee. The audit committee will decide if non-members, such as the finance director, head of internal audit or external audit partner should attend a particular meeting.

- The audit committee should meet the external and internal auditors without management at least annually to discuss any issues arising from the audit.

- In addition to the formal committee meetings, the audit committee should keep in touch on a continuing basis with the key people involved in the company's governance.

Resources

- The audit committee should be provided with sufficient resources to undertake its duties.

- The company secretary should ensure information is provided to the audit committee on a timely basis.

- Funds should be provided to enable it to take independent legal, accounting or other advice when required.

Remuneration

- The remuneration should take into account the level of fees paid to the other members of the board.

- The chair will be paid more than the other members to reflect the additional responsibilities and demands on their time.

Relationship with the board

- The audit committee should report to the board on how it has discharged its responsibilities.

- Where there is disagreement between the audit committee and the board, adequate time should be allowed to resolve the disagreement and the audit committee should have the right to report the issue to the shareholders.

- The audit committee should not just rely on the external auditor to raise issues but should consider matters using their own initiative.

Annual reports

The audit committee should:

- Review and report to the board on the significant financial reporting issues and judgments made in connection with the preparation of the financial statements.

- Consider the appropriateness of significant accounting policies, significant estimates and judgments.

- Review the annual report and accounts and advise the board on whether they are fair, balanced and understandable.

Internal control and risk management

The board has ultimate responsibility for risk management and internal control but may delegate some functions to the audit committee such as:

- Reviewing the systems established by management to identify, assess, manage and monitor financial risks.

- Receiving reports from management on the effectiveness of systems and the conclusions of any testing carried out by internal and external auditors.

- Reviewing and recommending disclosures to be included in the annual report in relation to internal control and risk management.

Internal audit process

- The audit committee should regularly review the need for establishing an internal audit function.

- Where there is an internal audit function the audit committee should review and approve the internal audit plan. The plan should be aligned with the key risks of the business.

- The audit committee should ensure the function has unrestricted scope, the necessary resources and access to information to be able to perform its work in accordance with professional standards for internal auditors.

- The audit committee will approve the appointment or termination of the head of internal audit.

- The internal audit function should have a reporting line independent of the executive so it can exercise independent judgment.

- The audit committee should monitor and review the effectiveness of the internal audit function's work. This includes:

  - Confirming that the quality, experience and expertise of the function are appropriate for the business.

  - Meeting with the head of internal audit without the presence of management to discuss effectiveness.

  - Receive a report on the results of the internal auditors' work.

- The audit committee may consider an independent, third party review of the internal audit function's effectiveness.

External audit process

- FTSE 350 companies should put the audit out to tender at least once every ten years to enable the audit committee to compare the quality and effectiveness of the services provided by the incumbent auditor with those of other firms.

- The audit committee has primary responsibility for the appointment of the auditor including the tendering process and selection procedures.

- An annual assessment should be made of the qualifications, expertise, resources and independence of the external auditor.

- If the external auditor resigns, the audit committee should investigate the issues giving rise to the resignation.

- The audit committee should approve the remuneration and terms of engagement.

- The audit committee should monitor compliance with the Ethical Standards including the level of fees, former employees of the audit firm who now work for the company, partner rotation and non-audit services.

- The audit committee should set and apply a formal policy specifying the types of non-audit services which are approved.

- At the start of the audit, the audit committee should ensure that appropriate plans are in place for the audit including whether the planned materiality level and the resources are consistent with the scope of the work to be performed.

- The audit committee should discuss with the external auditor any matters which could affect audit quality.

- The audit committee should review and monitor management's responsiveness to the external auditor's findings and recommendations and should also review the written representation letter before it is signed.

- The audit committee should assess the effectiveness of the external audit process including:
  - asking the auditor to explain the risks to audit quality
  - whether the auditor has met the agreed audit plan
  - obtaining feedback from key people involved such as the finance director about the conduct of the audit
  - reviewing the content of the management letter and whether recommendations have been acted upon.

Communication with shareholders

The audit committee chair should be present at the AGM to answer questions.

A separate section of the annual report should describe the work of the committee. Specifically:

- A summary of the role of the audit committee.
- The names and qualifications of all members of the audit committee during the period.
- The number of audit committee meetings.
- The significant issues that the committee considered in relation to the financial statements and how these issues were addressed.
- An explanation of how it has assessed the effectiveness of the external audit process and the approach taken to the appointment or reappointment of the external auditor.

Benefits and drawbacks of audit committees

Benefits

- Improved credibility of the financial statements, through an impartial review of the financial statements, monitoring of the independence of the external auditors, and discussion of significant issues with the external auditors.
- The quality of management accounting will be improved as the audit committee is better placed to criticise internal functions.
- The control environment may be strengthened as the internal audit function will report to the audit committee increasing their independence and adding weight to their recommendations.
- Communication between the directors, external auditors and management may be improved.
- Conflicts between management and auditors may be reduced/avoided.
- The skills, knowledge and experience, and independence of the audit committee members can be an invaluable resource for a business.

- It may be easier and cheaper to arrange finance as the presence of an audit committee can give a perception of good corporate governance.

- It would be less burdensome to meet listing requirements if an audit committee (which is usually a listing requirement) is already established.

Drawbacks:

- Difficulties recruiting the right NEDs who have relevant skills, experience and sufficient time to become effective members of the committee.

- A fear that their purpose is to police executive management.

- NEDs may be overburdened with detail.

- NEDs are normally remunerated, and their fees can be quite expensive thereby increasing costs for the company.

 FRC Audit Quality – Practice aid for audit committees

The Corporate Governance Code requires audit committees to assess the quality and effectiveness of the external auditor. To help fulfil this requirement, the FRC has issued guidance to audit committees. Assessment of the external auditor should cover three main areas:

(1) **Inputs**

The audit committee should obtain evidence from a variety of sources including:

- Management

- Internal auditors

- Other company personnel

- External auditors

- Regulators.

(2) **Evaluation**

4 key elements of audit quality should be evaluated:

- Mindset and culture – adherence to high professional and ethical principles.

- Skills, character and knowledge – strong auditing skills developed through effective training and relevant experience.

- Quality control – identifying the risks to audit quality and establishing adequate controls to address these.

- Judgment – professional judgment is applied at all stages of the audit.

(3) Concluding and reporting

The audit committee should consider if they have sufficient evidence before concluding and reporting on the quality of the audit and the effectiveness of external audit. This includes whether:

- The auditor has communicated key accounting and audit judgments to the audit committee.

- The management letter demonstrates a good understanding of the business.

- Any changes made to materiality have been reported to the audit committee.

Board structures

There are two models of board structure adopted around the world:

- Unitary board structure – as used in the UK and Ireland and jurisdictions whose company law systems have a similar basis.

- Two tier/supervisory board structure – as used in the US and similar jurisdictions.

Unitary board characteristics

- Collective board responsibility

- No distinction in law between the responsibilities of executive and non-executive directors

- The need to distinguish between the function of executive and non-executive directors

- The need to establish board committees to monitor and act on different functions – nomination committee, remuneration committee, audit committee, etc.

Two tier system characteristics

- Lower level management (operating) board

    - Comprises executive management – CEO, CFO, Vice president, etc.

    - Operational responsibility for running the business

    - Coordinated by the CEO.

- Upper level supervisory board

    - Comprises non-executives, employee representatives, environmental groups and other stakeholders

    - Appoints, supervises and advises the management board

- Strategic oversight of the organisation
- Members elected by shareholders at the AGM
- Receives information and reports from the management board
- Coordinated by the chair.

Enron and Sarbanes Oxley

Enron

Before its bankruptcy, Enron employed approximately 22,000 people and was one of the world's leading electricity, natural gas, and communications companies. In 2001 its revenue peaked at nearly $101 billion. Much of the reported profit and position was sustained by institutionalised and systematic accounting fraud.

The story can be briefly summarised as follows:

- A significant portion of Enron's profits were the result of deals with special purpose entities (SPEs), which it controlled.

- Many of the entities were offshore, which allowed Enron to avoid taxes, move currency and hide overall company losses.

- Enron used an accounting technique known as marking to market, which effectively meant that Enron could recognise revenue and earnings on deals a long time before the actual revenue was realised.

- The huge profits Enron reported drove up its share price. This allowed executives (who knew about the offshore accounts and hidden losses!) to trade millions of dollars' worth of Enron stock to their own benefit.

- Share prices began to fall and Enron's massive liabilities started to exert pressure on its liquidity. This eventual led to problems with its debt agreements and credit downgrades.

- The lower credit rating increased the cost of Enron's borrowing to unsustainable limits.

- Wall Street analysts exposed a number of inconsistencies and problems with Enron's accounts and the extent of earnings management was exposed.

The fraudulent financial reporting at the heart of the Enron collapse has had major repercussions for the accountancy profession worldwide. It was one of the largest and most complex bankruptcy cases the world has ever witnessed. Consequent investigations identified numerous creative accounting techniques designed to improve reported profits and hide significant debts from investors.

The scandal that followed in the wake Enron's bankruptcy led to the collapse of one of the 'Big 5' accountancy firms, Arthur Andersen.

The role of Arthur Andersen in the financial fraud came under close public scrutiny and much of the trust in the auditing profession was lost. The firm was found guilty of obstruction of justice for destroying documents related to the Enron audit and was forced to stop auditing public companies (although the conviction was later thrown out by the US Supreme Court).

Sarbanes Oxley Act

The Sarbanes Oxley Act came into force as a result of the Enron corporate failure.

As well as dealing with the oversight of auditors, the act enforces certain governance responsibilities, such as:

- Implementation of sound systems of controls.

- Clear documentation of financial processes, procedures, risks, and controls.

- Evidence that management has evaluated the adequacy of the design and the effectiveness of operation of procedures and controls.

- Evidence that the auditor has adequately evaluated the design and operation of financial controls.

- Evidence that the audit committee has taken a keen interest in the effectiveness of controls.

- Explicit sign off procedures by the chief executive and chief financial officer.

Overview of the Act

'The primary benefit is to provide the company, its management, its board and audit committee, and its owners and other stakeholders with a reasonable basis to rely on the company's financial reporting. The integrity of financial reporting represents the foundation upon which this country's public markets are built.'

The key characteristics of Section 302

CEO and CFO need to certify that:

- The SEC report being filed has been reviewed

- The report does not contain any untrue statements or omit any material facts

- The financial statements fairly present the financial position, results of operations and cash flows of the company

- They are responsible for, and have designed, established, and maintained disclosure controls and procedures as well as evaluated and reported on the effectiveness of those controls and procedures within 90 days of the report filing date

- Deficiencies and material weaknesses in controls and procedures have been disclosed to the registrant's audit committee and external auditors

- Significant changes in internal control affecting transactions in the period have been reported.

The key characteristics of Section 404

When the accounts are filed, companies are required to include an annual internal control report of management over financial reporting which includes:

- Responsibilities for establishing and maintaining adequate internal controls and procedures.

- Conclusions about the effectiveness of the company's internal controls and procedures.

- An attestation by the company's registered public accounting firm on management's evaluation.

 UK syllabus: Audit and assurance regulations

Scope and authority of Audit and Assurance Pronouncements March 2013

Audit and Assurance regulations include:

- Quality control standards

- The Auditor's Code

- Ethical and engagement standards

- Guidance for auditors, reporting accountants and auditors involved with other assurance engagements.

Practice notes and bulletins are further forms of guidance but are less prescriptive than ISAs.

These regulations are applicable to:

- Statutory audits of companies in accordance with the Companies Acts

- Audits of entities in accordance with other legislation e.g. banks, charities, pension funds

- Public sector audits

- Other audits that are required to comply with UK standards.

Failure to apply the regulations will result in regulatory action which may include the withdrawal of registration and therefore eligibility to perform company audits.

Audit exemption

In accordance with the Companies Act 2006 those companies falling below the small company threshold are not required, in law, to have an annual audit. Companies may still choose to have one voluntarily.

The main criteria for audit exemption which apply from 1 January 2016 are:

- Turnover not exceeding £10.2 million
- Gross assets not exceeding £5.1 million
- The number of employees must not exceed 50.

In order to qualify, the company must meet two out of the three criteria.

 UK syllabus: Financial Reporting Council

The FRC is the UK Competent Authority for audit regulation.

Structure

The FRC board is supported by two committees:

- **Conduct Committee**

  Responsible for overseeing the FRC's work in promoting high quality corporate reporting. This encompasses monitoring of Recognised Supervisory and Recognised Qualifying Bodies (RSBs, RQBs), audit quality reviews (AQRs), corporate reporting reviews, professional discipline and oversight of the regulation of accountants and actuaries.

- **Codes and Standards Committee**

  Responsible for maintaining an effective framework of UK codes and standards for Corporate Governance, Stewardship, Accounting, Auditing and Assurance, and Actuarial technical standards.

  The Codes and Standards Committee has three councils:

  - Audit and Assurance Council
  - Corporate Reporting Council
  - Actuarial Council.

Role of the FRC

- Promote high quality corporate governance and reporting and high standards of corporate governance through the UK Corporate Governance Code.

- Encourage engagement between investors and Boards through the Stewardship Code.

- Set standards for corporate reporting, audit and actuarial practice, including ethical guidance for auditors and reporting accountants in the UK. The FRC issues International Standards on Auditing for use within the United Kingdom. The standards are supplemented and revised before issuing them, mainly in order to ensure they remain compliant with national laws, such as the Companies Act 2006.

- Monitor and enforce accounting and auditing standards. The Audit Quality Review team monitors the quality of the audits of listed and other major public interest entities. Part of this role involves performing audit inspections of large firms annually and smaller firms once every three years.

- Oversee the regulatory activities of the actuarial profession and the professional accountancy bodies and operate independent enforcement arrangements for public interest cases involving accountants and actuaries.

- Promote the principles, professional behaviour and culture which are collectively fundamental to quality audit outcomes, and which serve the public interest. The Conduct Committee ensures that appropriate standards are maintained by members and member firms, by operating an independent professional disciplinary scheme for accountants.

FRC's 7 key objectives for audit

- Auditors are trustworthy, act with integrity and professional scepticism, serve the public interest and consistently demonstrate that the objectives of audit and auditing standards are met.

- Audit is subject to appropriate oversight within a clear regulatory regime.

- Roles and responsibilities of auditors and Audit Committees are clear, and aligned with the interests and needs of investors.

- Audit is a sustainable business with adequate capacity, and sufficient levels of investment, competition and choice.

- Audit innovates to meet changing business and economic circumstances to improve audit quality.

- Global audits are effectively managed and overseen, and quality is consistent across international work.

- There is a mechanism for standard setting to be more responsive to the needs of users, and to respond to emerging issues on a more timely basis.

At the time of writing, the FRC is currently in transition to a new regulatory authority, The Audit, Reporting and Governance Authority (ARGA). This action is being taken in response to a number of high profile accounting irregularities over recent years, such as Carillion and Patisserie Valerie. The UK government ordered a review of the regulatory system which recommended the introduction of a new regulator. The FRC was criticised for being too close to those that it is supposed to regulate creating a conflict of interest resulting in an ineffective regulatory system. It is expected that ARGA will be more proactive in taking action against firms who fail to uphold the reputation of the profession.

Test your understanding 1

Becher Co is an independent construction company, dealing with large-scale contracts throughout the UK and with some international interest in Europe. Becher Co has recently established an audit committee, the members of which are very concerned about complying with corporate governance best practice, particularly since they are currently looking at the possibility of obtaining a stock exchange listing.

You are an internal auditor with the company and have been asked to conduct a review of how well the company is meeting relevant corporate governance requirements.

You are required to prepare a report that addresses the following.

(a) Explain the term 'corporate governance' and why it is important for companies to comply with relevant corporate governance requirements. **(5 marks)**

(b) Explain the key issues Becher Co needs to address to achieve effective corporate governance. **(5 marks)**

(c) Explain the role of the audit committee in relation to corporate governance. **(5 marks)**

(Total: 15 marks)

5 Chapter summary

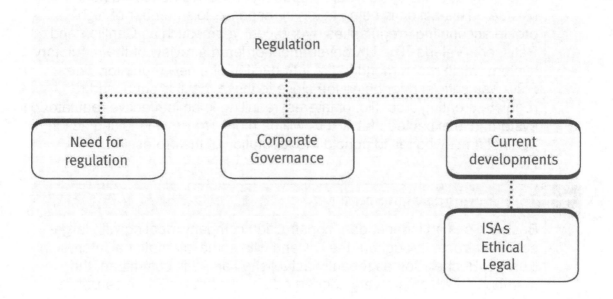

Test your understanding answers

 Test your understanding 1

(a) **Corporate governance**

Corporate governance concerns the way that a company is directed and controlled. It encompasses the following key aspects:

- The role of the board and audit committee.

- Overall control and risk management framework.

Corporate governance has become increasingly important in the wake of high profile accounting frauds. These frauds have had a damaging impact on the effective operation of world stock markets due to reductions in investor (and public) confidence in the roles of directors and company auditors.

Management and control is often more difficult to achieve in larger, more complex organisations. In addition, shareholders tend to be more remote from the directors who manage the company on their behalf. Having an agreed set of corporate governance standards therefore facilitates the adoption of good corporate governance practices and improves accountability to investor groups.

Failure to comply with these agreed standards of corporate governance could lead to significant penalties, namely:

- Fines and penalties, where corporate governance is enforced through law, the US for example. This could, in the most extreme cases, lead to imprisonment of directors.

- Penalties imposed by stock market regulators, such as removal from the listing.

- Replacement of board members.

(b) **Requirements of corporate governance**

The nature of issues to be addressed depends on the legal or listing requirements in place in the country of operation. However the following basic principles may be universally applied:

- The board should be responsible for the assessment of and response to risk.

- The board should be responsible for monitoring the effectiveness of the system of internal control.

- An independent system (including the use of committees) should be established to enable the effective recruitment and retention of directors.

- Communication with, and independence of auditors, should be overseen by the audit committee.

- There should be explicit and transparent reporting of compliance with corporate governance requirements/ principles.

UK Syllabus Focus: In the UK, listed companies must report on how, and whether, they have complied with the UK Corporate Governance Code.

(c) **Role of the audit committee**

The role and importance of the audit committee has increased as corporate governance requirements have been strengthened.

The audit committee should have at least three NEDs. One of the members should have recent and relevant financial experience to ensure the committee can be effective in its oversight of the financial reporting processes of the company.

All members should be independent of the company, i.e. have no direct involvement in the day to day running of its affairs.

The board chair cannot be a member of the audit committee.

The objectives of the audit committee are:

- To increase public confidence in the credibility and objectivity of published financial information.

- To assist directors in meeting their financial reporting responsibilities.

- To strengthen the independent position of a company's external auditor.

The audit committee should:

- Oversee the internal audit function.

- Assess the effectiveness of the external audit process and monitor audit quality.

- Ensure appropriate financial reporting processes are in place and ensure the annual report is fair, balanced and understandable.

- Ensure there is appropriate communication with shareholders on audit matters.

Money laundering

Chapter learning objectives

This chapter covers syllabus areas:

* A2 – Money laundering.

Detailed syllabus objectives are provided in the introduction section of the text book.

PER

One of the PER performance objectives (PO4) is governance risk and control. You contribute to effective governance in your area. You evaluate, monitor and implement risk management procedures, complying with the spirit and the letter of policies, laws and regulations. Working through this chapter should help you understand how to demonstrate that objective.

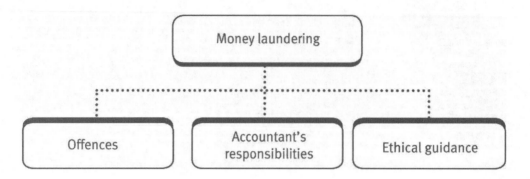

 Exam focus

Money laundering requirements may be knowledge based, in which you may be required to explain the basic elements of an anti-money laundering program or define and give examples of money laundering offences. You may also need to identify a potentially suspicious transaction and explain the accountant's responsibilities in such situations.

1 Definition of money laundering

 Money laundering is the process by which criminals attempt to conceal the true origin and ownership of the proceeds generated by illegal means, allowing them to maintain control over the proceeds and, ultimately, providing a legitimate cover for their sources of income.

Money laundering involves 3 main stages:

(1) Placement – where cash obtained through criminal activity is first placed into the financial system.

(2) Layering – where the illegal cash is disguised by passing it through complex transactions making it difficult to trace.

(3) Integration – where the illegally obtained funds are moved back into the legitimate economy and is now 'clean'.

Money laundering offences

- Acquiring, possession or use of criminal property.

- Concealing or disguising or transferring criminal property, or removing it from the country.

- Entering into, or becoming involved in, an arrangement which is known or is suspected to facilitate the acquisition, retention, use or control of criminal property by or on behalf of another person.

- Failure to report knowledge or suspicion of money laundering.

- Tipping off.

'Tipping off' means to carry out any action that may make suspected money launderers aware that they are under investigation, or prejudicing the outcome of an investigation.

No tipping off offence is committed when enquiries are made of a client regarding something that properly falls within the normal scope of the engagement or business relationship, or if an employee attempts to dissuade their client from conduct amounting to an offence.

Failure to disclose knowledge or suspicion of money laundering may include:

- Failure by an individual in the regulated sector to inform the Financial Intelligence Unit (FIU) or the firm's Money Laundering Reporting Officer (MLRO), as soon as practicable, of knowledge or suspicion that another person is engaged in money laundering, or

- Failure by MLROs in the regulated sector to make the required report to the FIU as soon as practicable if an internal report leads them to know or suspect that a person is engaged in money laundering.

If a business fails to meet its obligations under the Regulations, civil penalties or criminal sanctions can be imposed on the business and any individuals deemed responsible. This could include anyone in a senior position who neglected their own responsibilities or agreed to something that resulted in the compliance failure.

Criminal property and criminal conduct

Criminal property is property that has arisen from criminal conduct. Examples include:

- Property acquired by theft

- The proceeds of tax evasion

- Bribery or corruption

- Saved costs arising from a criminal failure to comply with a regulatory requirement.

Examples

Consider the following scenarios.

- Whilst preparing or auditing accounts you realise that a client has incorrectly reclaimed value added tax (or other national recoverable taxes) on the purchase of a motor car. You point this out to the client and propose an adjustment to the financial statements to provide for the additional tax that is due. You also advise the client that they must rectify this with the tax authorities. However, the client tells you that they have just had an inspection by the tax authorities that did not reveal the error and they do not wish to do anything further.

> - An auditor knowingly receives payment for one invoice twice (i.e. payment has been duplicated). The sole director has told the accounts department to ignore negative balances when they issue statements of account to customers hoping that they fail to notice.
>
> Errors and mistakes of the type illustrated above may not constitute criminal conduct, provided they are corrected. However, in both cases there appears to be an intention to gain a permanent benefit from another's mistake or to avoid a legal liability. As such, each of these cases would result in the accountant knowing or suspecting that a client is involved in money laundering.

2 Anti-money laundering program: basic elements

The main legislation and requirements below relate to the money laundering regulatory regime in the UK. The principles, however, are appropriate on an international basis.

Money Laundering Regulations impose certain obligations on financial services businesses, which are designed to assist in detecting money laundering and preventing the financial services organisations being used for money laundering purposes.

At a minimum, an anti-money laundering program should incorporate:

- Money laundering and terrorist financing risk assessment.

- Implementation of systems, policies, controls and procedures that effectively manage the risk that the firm is exposed to in relation to money laundering activities and ensure compliance with the legislation.

- Compliance with customer due diligence, enhanced due diligence and simplified due diligence requirements.

- Enhanced record keeping and data protection systems, policies and procedures.

In the UK, for example, these measures are covered by the Money Laundering Regulations 2017 (MLR 2017) with reporting to the National Crime Agency (NCA).

Money laundering and terrorist financing (MLTF) risk assessment

A written risk assessment must be carried out to identify and assess the risk of money laundering. The risk assessment must take into account information provided by the Supervisory Authority on risk factors in the sector. The following risk factors must also be taken into account:

- The firm's customers

- The countries or geographic areas where the firm operates

- The firm's products or services

- The firm's transactions, and

- The firm's delivery channels.

The risk assessment should be used to:

- Develop policies, procedures and controls to mitigate the risk of money laundering.

- Apply a risk based approach to detecting and preventing money laundering.

  The risk based approach recognises that the risks posed by MLTF activity will not be the same in every case and so it allows the business to tailor its response in proportion to its perceptions of risk. The risk based approach requires evidence-based decision-making to better target risks.

Internal controls

The firm must establish and maintain written policies, controls and procedures to effectively manage and mitigate the money laundering and terrorist financing risks identified in the risk assessment. These must be proportionate to the size and nature of the business, approved by senior management, regularly reviewed and updated and communicated internally within the firm.

Officer responsible for compliance

Firms must appoint a Money Laundering Compliance Principal (MLCP) and this person must be on the board of directors or a member of senior management. Sole practitioners with no employees are exempt from this requirement.

Firms must also appoint a nominated officer, Money Laundering Reporting Officer (MLRO), to receive internal suspicious activity reports and assess whether a suspicious activity report should be made to the appropriate regulatory body. The MLRO and MLCP may be the same person if the MLRO is sufficiently senior.

Employees

Firms must assess the skills, knowledge, conduct and integrity of employees involved in the identification, prevention or detection of money laundering, both before and during the course of their appointment.

Staff training must be provided on an ongoing basis in how to recognise and handle transactions and activities which may be related to money laundering.

Independent audit function

Firms must establish an independent audit function to assess the adequacy and effectiveness of the firm's anti-money laundering controls and procedures. Sole practitioners with no employees are exempt from this requirement.

Customer due diligence

Accountants are required to establish that new clients are who they claim to be by obtaining satisfactory evidence of identity from the client. This is often referred to as 'customer due diligence' or 'know your customer' procedures.

Businesses must apply these procedures at the start of a new business relationship, at appropriate points during the lifetime of the relationship and when an occasional transaction is to be undertaken. An occasional transaction is one which occurs outside of a business relationship and has a value of more than 10,000 Euros.

Customer due diligence must be performed as soon as is reasonably practicable after contact is first made between the two parties. Where satisfactory evidence of identity is not obtained by the accountant, the business relationship or occasional transaction must not proceed any further.

Customer due diligence involves:

- Identifying the client (i.e. knowing who the client is) and then verifying their identity (i.e. demonstrating that they are who they claim to be) by obtaining documents or other information from independent and reliable sources.

- Identifying beneficial owner(s) so that the ownership and control structure can be understood and the identities of any individuals who are the owners or controllers can be known. Reasonable measures should be taken to verify their identity on a risk sensitive basis.

- Gathering information on the intended purpose and nature of the business relationship.

 Information gathering

The business must be able to answer the following questions:

- Who is the client?
- Who owns/controls them?
- What do they do?
- What is their source of funds?
- Can you describe their activities?
- What will you be doing for them?
- What is its legal structure?

It may be helpful for the auditor to explain to the client the reason for requiring evidence of identity and this can be achieved by including this matter in the engagement letter.

Example engagement letter money laundering clauses

'In accordance with the *Proceeds of Crime Act 2002* and *Money Laundering Regulations 2017* you agree to waive your right to confidentiality to the extent of any report made, document provided or information disclosed to the *National Crime Agency* (NCA).

You also acknowledge that we are required to report directly to the NCA without prior reference to you or your representatives if during the course of undertaking any assignment the person undertaking the role of Money Laundering Reporting Officer becomes suspicious of money laundering.

As a specific requirement of the Money Laundering Regulations we may require you to produce evidence of identity of the company and its owners and managers. This will include for the business, proof of registration and address, and for the individuals, proof of identity and address. Copies of such records will be maintained by us for a period of at least five years after we cease to act for the business.'

Note: The above clauses include references to the relevant legislation and regulatory bodies in the United Kingdom. The references would be amended for the specific jurisdiction(s).

Basic identification procedures include:

- **For individuals (including key management personnel where the client is an entity):** inspection of evidence to establish the full name and permanent address of the client, e.g.
    - Driving licence
    - Passport
    - Recent utility bill to confirm the address.
- **For businesses:** inspection of evidence to verify company name, company number, address of registered office, e.g.
    - Certificate of incorporation
    - Lists of registered members and directors
    - Certificate of registered address.
- **For trusts:** inspection of evidence to establish and confirm:
    - Nature and purpose of the trust
    - Original source of funding
    - Identities of the trustees, controllers and beneficiaries.

Enhanced due diligence

For higher risk clients, enhanced due diligence must be carried out. Enhanced due diligence procedures include examining the background and purpose of the transaction and increased monitoring of the business relationship.

Simplified due diligence

For clients presenting a lower risk of money laundering, simplified due diligence may be carried out.

Enhanced record keeping

It is very important that accountants keep comprehensive records to show that they have complied with money laundering regulations, and protect themselves if there is an investigation into one of their clients.

Records must be kept of:

- All customer due diligence completed, including copies of the evidence inspected.

- Transactions with each client.

- Internal and external money laundering/suspicious activity reports.

Records must be held for five years after a relationship with a client has ended or the date a transaction is completed.

Reporting procedures

It is a criminal offence not to report knowledge or suspicion of money laundering. Money laundering regulations require that:

- A person in the organisation is nominated to receive disclosures (usually an MLRO).

- Anyone in the organisation, to whom information comes in the course of the relevant business as a result of which he suspects that a person is engaged in money laundering, must disclose it to the MLRO.

- Where a disclosure is made to the MLRO, they must consider it in the light of any relevant information which is available to the organisation and determine whether it gives rise to suspicion.

- Where the MLRO does so determine, the information must be disclosed to a regulatory body authorised for the purposes of these regulations (the FIU), such as the NCA in the UK.

- The MLRO completes a standard form that identifies:

  - Suspect's name, address, date of birth and nationality

  - Any identification or references seen

  - Nature of the activities giving rise to suspicion

  - Any other information that may be relevant.

Note that in the UK the obligation to report does not depend on the amount involved or the seriousness of the offence. There are no de minimis concessions.

Monitoring of policies and procedures

- The MLRO and appropriate senior management should together monitor the effectiveness of policies, procedures and processes so that improvements can be made when inefficiencies are found.

- Senior management should encourage relevant employees to provide feedback on the policies and procedures in place.

- When changes are made to policies, procedures or processes, these should be properly communicated to relevant employees and supported by appropriate training where necessary.

- The effectiveness of the MLTF systems must be independently reviewed. Independent does not necessarily mean external, but could be performed by internal audit, a compliance department or an internal quality function.

- Senior management responsible for compliance and the MLRO should monitor publicly-available information on best practice in dealing with MLTF risks, for example, by reading thematic reviews by regulators to improve understanding of good and poor practice.

Potentially suspicious transactions

There is no formal definition of suspicious. A suspicious transaction will often be inconsistent with the client's known or usual legitimate activities. Examples include:

- Unusually large cash deposits.

- Frequent exchanges of cash into other currencies.

- Overseas business arrangements with no clear business purpose.

3 The need for ethical guidance on money laundering

ACCA provides guidance in its Code of Ethics and Conduct in the area of money laundering.

This is needed because there is a clear conflict between:

(1) the accountant's professional duty of confidentiality in relation to his client's business, and

(2) the duty to report suspicions of money laundering to the appropriate authorities is required by law.

Professional accountants are not in breach of their professional duty of confidentiality if they report in good faith their knowledge or suspicions of money laundering to the appropriate authority.

Disclosure in bad faith or without reasonable grounds would possibly lead to the accountant being sued.

Financial Action Task Force

International efforts to combat money laundering

The Financial Action Task Force (FATF) is an international body that promotes policies globally to combat money laundering and terrorist financing. FATF issued recommendations to combat money laundering.

The recommendations included:

- International cooperation including extradition of suspects.

- Implement relevant international conventions on money laundering.

- Criminalise money laundering and enable authorities to confiscate the proceeds of money laundering.

- Implement customer due diligence, record keeping and suspicious transaction reporting requirements for financial institutions and designated non-financial businesses and professions.

- Establish a financial intelligence unit (FIU) to receive suspicious transaction reports.

  As an example, the UK FIU is run by the National Crime Agency (NCA).The NCA became operational in October 2013 and replaced the Serious Organised Crime Agency (SOCA).

FATF focuses on three principal areas:

- Setting standards aimed at combating money laundering and terrorist financing.

- Evaluating the degree to which countries have implemented measures that meet those standards.

- Identifying and studying money laundering and terrorist financing techniques.

ACCA guidance

The ACCA has issued Anti-money Laundering Guidance for the Accountancy Profession which is available from the ACCA website.

Test your understanding 1

You are the manager responsible for the audit of Sapporo Co, a chain of health and leisure clubs owned and managed by entrepreneur Izumi Smith. The audit for the year ended 31 March 20X5 is nearing completion and the draft financial statements recognise total assets of $27 million and profit before tax of $2.2 million. The audit senior has left the following file note for your consideration during your review of the audit working papers:

Cash transfers

During a review of the cash book, a receipt of $350,000 was identified which was accompanied by the description 'SJ'. Bank statements showed that the following day a nearly identical amount was transferred into a bank account held in a foreign country. When I asked the financial controller about this, I was told to speak to Izumi, as she has sole responsibility for cash management. According to Izumi, an old friend of hers, Seiko Jones, has loaned the money to the company to fund further expansion and the money has been invested until it is needed. Documentary evidence concerning the transaction has been requested from Izumi but has not yet been received.

Required:

Evaluate the implications for the completion of the audit, recommending any further actions which should be taken by your audit firm.

(5 marks)

4   Chapter summary

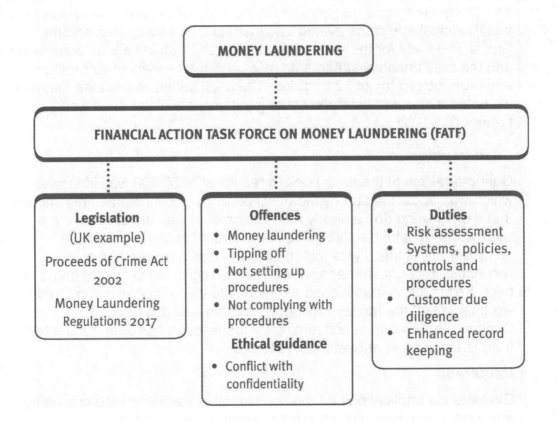

Test your understanding answers

Test your understanding 1

Cash transfers

This unusual, unexplained cash transfer into a foreign bank account may indicate that Izumi is using Sapporo Co to carry out money laundering. Money laundering is defined as the process by which criminals attempt to conceal the origin and ownership of the proceeds of their criminal activity, allowing them to maintain control over the proceeds and, ultimately, providing a legitimate cover for the sources of their income.

It is possible that the proceeds of criminal activity have been placed into Sapporo Co's bank account to enable them to transfer the funds into a foreign account, thus providing them with the appearance of legitimacy and creating a trail which is difficult to trace to the original source. This process is known as 'layering'. According to ACCA's Anti-money laundering guidance for the accountancy profession, money laundering can result from a single transaction such as the cash placed into Sapporo Co's bank account.

The fact that Izumi retains sole control over cash management and that the financial controller has no oversight or involvement in this indicates weak controls over cash, for example, there appears to be no segregation of duty which may be the intention of Izumi to facilitate illegal activity.

The failure to provide any documentary evidence, despite the request to do so by the audit team, arouses further suspicion. It is also possible that the company is being used as a vehicle for money laundering without Izumi's knowledge. It is possible that the money has been accepted in good faith without the source of the funding being adequately verified.

The amount which has been transferred represents 1.3% of total assets, which is material to the financial statements. The engagement, and particularly matters relating to cash transactions, should now be considered as high risk and approached with a high degree of professional scepticism. The audit files should now be subject to an independent second partner review. The firm may also wish to seek legal advice given the potential legal implications of dealing with a client involved in money laundering.

To properly assess the impact of the transaction on the financial statements, the audit firm needs to understand the accounting entries which have been made. The debit side of the entry would be to cash, and the audit team should enquire as to where the credit side of the entry has been recognised. Possibly the credit has been recognised as revenue or possibly it has been contra'd against the cash payment which was made the next day.

The situation should be reported as soon as possible to the firm's Money Laundering Reporting Officer (MLRO). The MLRO is responsible for receiving and evaluating reports of suspected money laundering from colleagues within the firm. They will make a decision as to whether further enquiries are required and, if necessary, will make reports to the appropriate authorities.

Finally, care must now be taken during the remaining audit that no-one 'tips off' the client that their activity is being treated as suspicious and that a report will be made to the MLRO. 'Tipping off' the client could prejudice any consequent investigation and may itself be considered a criminal offence, depending on relevant legislation. A tipping off disclosure may be made in writing or verbally, and either directly or indirectly so the audit team must ensure that when discussing the matter with Izumi, he is not alerted to the suspicions of money laundering.

KAPLAN PUBLISHING

Code of ethics and conduct

Chapter learning objectives

This chapter covers syllabus areas:

- B1 – Code of Ethics for Professional Accountants

- G1 – Professional and ethical developments.

Detailed syllabus objectives are provided in the introduction section of the text book.

PER

One of the PER performance objectives (PO1) is ethics and professionalism. The fundamental principles of ethical behaviour mean you should always act in the wider public interest. You need to take into account all relevant information and use professional judgement, your personal values and scepticism to evaluate data and make decisions. You should identify right from wrong and escalate anything of concern. You also need to make sure that your skills, knowledge and behaviour are up-to-date and allow you to be effective in your role. Working through this chapter should help you understand how to demonstrate that objective.

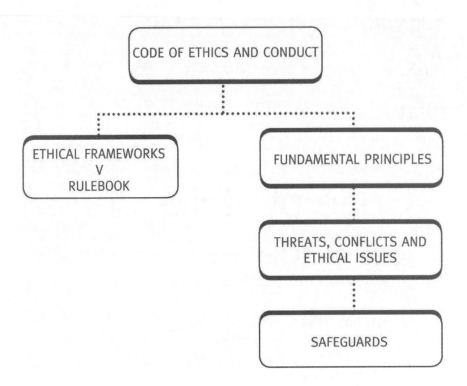

 Exam focus

- Professional and ethical considerations are a key element of the syllabus and will feature in every exam.

- A typical requirement will ask you to evaluate the ethical and professional issues in a scenario. Note that this incorporates all of the fundamental principles, not just objectivity, as well as professional issues discussed in subsequent chapters.

- Evaluation requires more than just identification and explanation of the threats. You will also need to consider the **significance** of the threat.

- You should consider any safeguards available to reduce the threat to an acceptable level as part of your evaluation.

- A question on ethics will require you to state the rules and principles and apply them to a scenario.

 Ethical issues were covered in detail in Audit and Assurance (AA) at the Applied Skills level. The knowledge from AA is examinable for AAA.

1 Conceptual framework

Ethical guidance can take either a principles-based approach or rules-based approach.

A conceptual framework relies on a principles-based approach. Both IFAC and the ACCA adopt a principles-based approach.

Principles-based approach	Rules-based approach
• Requires compliance with the spirit of the guidance. • Requires the accountant to use professional judgment. • Flexible, so can be applied to new, unusual or rapidly changing situations. • Principles may be applied across national boundaries where laws may not. • Can still incorporate specific rules for ethical situations likely to affect many firms.	• May be easier to follow because rules are clearly defined. • Needs frequent updating to ensure the guidance applies to new situations. • May encourage accountants to interpret requirements narrowly in order to get round the spirit of the requirements. • Virtually impossible to be able to deal with every situation that may arise, particularly across various national boundaries and in a dynamic industry.

The fundamental principles

The International Ethics Standards Board for Accountants (IESBA) has developed an International Code of Ethics for Professional Accountants, which applies to all professional accountants, whether in public practice or in business. This serves as the foundation for codes of ethics developed and enforced by member bodies of IFAC.

The ACCA Code of Ethics and Conduct ('the Code') is set out in Section 3 of ACCA's Rulebook. It applies to all ACCA members, affiliates and registered students.

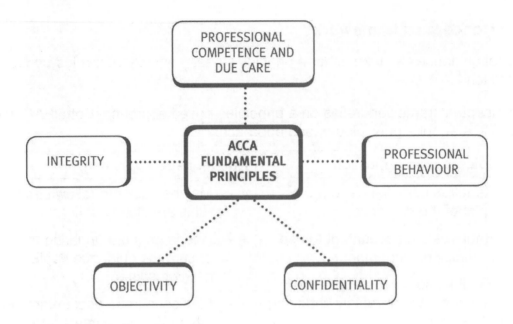

Fundamental principles definitions

- **Integrity:** Members should be straightforward and honest in all professional and business relationships.

- **Objectivity:** Members should not allow bias, conflicts of interest or undue influence of others to compromise professional or business judgments.

- **Professional competence and due care**: Members should attain and maintain professional knowledge and skill at the level required to ensure that a client or employer receives competent professional service based on current developments in practice, legislation and techniques. Members should act diligently and in accordance with applicable technical and professional standards when providing professional services.

- **Confidentiality:** Members should respect the confidentiality of information acquired as a result of professional and business relationships.
  Information should not be disclosed to third parties without proper and specific authority, unless there is a legal or professional right or duty to disclose. Such confidential information should not be used for the personal advantage of members or third parties.

- **Professional behaviour:** Members should comply with relevant laws and regulations and should avoid any conduct that discredits the profession.

[ACCA Code of Ethics and Conduct, Section 110.1 A1]

Current issue: Exposure Draft on Role and Mindset of Accountants

Proposed Revisions to the Code to Promote the Role and Mindset Expected of Professional Accountants

A consultation paper was issued in May 2018 called Professional Scepticism – Meeting Public Expectations. The paper sought views on the mindset and behavioural characteristics of professional accountants and whether the Code should be developed to promote such mindset and behaviours.

Responses to the consultation paper found clear support for the work of the IESBA and a project was initiated which will aim to:

- Revise the Code to describe the mindset and behavioural characteristics expected of all professional accountants.

- Explain the linkage between the role, mindset and behavioural characteristics expected of professional accountants and the fundamental principles.

- Address threats to compliance with the fundamental principles arising from bias, pressure and other impediments.

- Develop material to explain the linkage between the mindset and behavioural characteristics set out in the Code and expected of all professional accountants and the concept of professional scepticism as defined in the ISAs. Although the term 'professional scepticism' had been loosely used by some stakeholders to encapsulate that mindset and behavioural characteristics, there was a strong view that that term should be reserved for use only in an audit and assurance context and as defined in the auditing and assurance standards issued by the IAASB.

The exposure draft produced as a result of the consultation paper suggests the following key changes to the definitions of the some of the fundamental principles:

Objectivity

A proposed new definition of objectivity:

'to exercise professional or business judgements without being compromised by bias, conflict of interest or undue influence of, or undue reliance on, individuals, organisations, technology or other factors.'

Professional behaviour

The definition of professional behaviour to be enhanced to include a requirement to behave in a manner that is consistent with the profession's responsibility to act in the public interest.

Integrity

The definition of integrity to be amended to:

'...having the determination to act appropriately when confronting dilemmas or difficult situations.'

This includes standing one's ground when facing pressure to do otherwise and challenging others as and when appropriate, even when doing so creates potential adverse personal or organisational consequences.

Impact on the conceptual framework

When applying the conceptual framework, in addition to exercising professional judgment, the professional accountant must have an inquiring mind which means being open and alert for situations and information that might require further investigation and considering whether there is a need to critically evaluate the information obtained.

When applying the conceptual framework, the professional accountant should be aware of the risk of different types of bias, including, but not limited to:

- Automation bias – the tendency to favour output generated from automated systems even when human reasoning or contradictory information raises questions as to its reliability.

- Confirmation bias – the tendency to place more reliance on information that corroborates an existing belief than information that contradicts or casts doubt on that belief.

- Groupthink – the tendency to think or make decisions as a group that discourages creativity or individual responsibility.

- Representation bias – the tendency to base an understanding on a pattern of experiences, events or beliefs that is considered to be representative.

Pressure to breach the fundamental principles

An auditor or accountant may be asked to breach the fundamental principles by an employer, customer, supplier or lender.

The professional accountant should always apply the conceptual framework, which requires assessment of the significance of the threat and the application of an appropriate safeguard. They must not:

- Allow pressure from others to result in a breach of the fundamental principles.

- Place pressure on others which would result in a breach of the fundamental principles.

Examples of pressures:

- Being asked to misrepresent the financial statements

- Being asked to lie to the auditor

- Being asked to sign-off work as completed that you have not performed

- Being asked to inappropriately reduce the extent of the work performed.

Appropriate safeguards include:

- Discussing the matter with the individual exerting the pressure to try and resolve the issue.

- Discussing the matter with a manager, if the manager is not the individual exerting the pressure.

- Seeking advice from within the employer (e.g. Human Resources department).

- Using the organisation's formal dispute resolution process or whistleblowing policies.

- Seeking advice from the ACCA or other independent professional advisor.

- Seeking legal advice.

2 Ethical threats

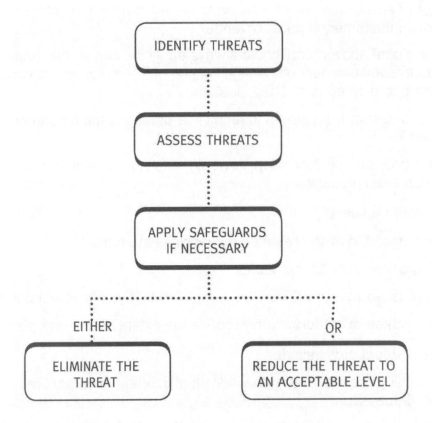

Ethical implications for non-audit services

When a practitioner provides non-audit services, ethical implications must still be considered before accepting the work.

A practitioner must always be competent to provide the service being requested.

In addition, if assurance is being provided, the practitioner must be objective, as a conclusion is being provided on a subject matter which will be relied upon by an intended user. For example, if a practitioner prepared a forecast for a client and then gave assurance on that forecast, a self-review threat would arise in the same way as a self-review threat would arise if the auditor prepared the financial statements they were auditing.

Therefore the threats listed above must still be assessed and safeguards implemented to reduce the threat to an acceptable level.

Identifying threats

Self Interest

- Own shares
- Fee dependency
- Gifts & hospitality
- Loans
- Business and personal relationships
- Employment with client
- Overdue fees
- Contingency fees
- Litigation with a client

Self Review

- Accounts preparation
- Internal audit
- Tax computations
- Valuation services
- Client staff joins the audit firm

Familiarity

- Long association
- Personal relationships
- Movement of staff between the firm and client
- Gifts & hospitality

Threats to objectivity

Intimidation

- Fee dependency
- Personal relationships
- Audit partner leaves to join client
- Litigation with a client

Advocacy

- Representing the client
- Promoting the client
- Negotiating on behalf of the client

Assuming management responsibilities

Assuming management responsibilities for an assurance client may also create threats to independence. In some jurisdictions, this is referred to as the **management threat**.

A firm must not assume management responsibilities as part of an assurance engagement or for an audit client. [R600.7]

Activities considered management responsibility:

- Setting policies and strategic direction.

- Hiring or dismissing employees.

- Directing and taking responsibility for employee's actions.

- Authorising transactions.

- Deciding which recommendations to implement.

- Reporting to those charged with governance on behalf of management.

- Taking responsibility for the preparation and fair presentation of the financial statements.

- Taking responsibility for designing, implementing and maintaining internal controls.

[600.7 A3]

The firm should take steps to ensure that client management makes all judgments and decisions. [R600.8]

Assessing the significance of threats

The assessment of, and response to, ethical threats is a key consideration for the audit firm. It is therefore critical that you can discuss the significance of a threat and recommend an appropriate safeguard.

Factors affecting the significance of the threat include:

- Value – e.g. when considering gifts and hospitality.

- Seniority of staff – e.g. when considering rotation of staff.

- Impact to the audit firm – e.g. when considering fee dependency.

- Materiality to the financial statements – e.g. when considering whether a non-audit service can be provided.

Safeguards

 A **safeguard** is an action or measure that eliminates a threat, or reduces it to an acceptable level.

The Code of Ethics provides guidance of safeguards for different types of threats to objectivity and independence.

Self-interest threats

Where the auditor has a financial or other interest that will inappropriately influence their judgment or behaviour.

Threat	Safeguards
Fee dependency Threats can be created if fees represent a large proportion of one partner or one office of the firm. [410.3 A4] Over-dependence could lead the auditor to ignore adjustments required in the financial statements for fear of losing the client. Factors relevant when evaluating the threat include: • Operating structure of the firm • Whether the firm is well established or new • The significance of the client to the firm. [410.3 A2]	*Non-listed clients* If fees from an audit client represent a large proportion of the firm's total fees, the firm should implement safeguards such as: • Increasing the client base to reduce dependency • Having an independent review of the work. [410.3 A6] *Listed clients* • A firm's independence is threatened, and should be reviewed, if total fees from a listed audit client exceed 15% of the firm's total fees for two consecutive years. • The firm should disclose the issue to those charged with governance at the client. • An independent engagement quality control review should be performed by a person not a member of the audit firm expressing the opinion, or by the professional regulatory body. This can be performed as either a pre-issuance review, before the 2nd year audit opinion is issued or a post-issuance review on the 2nd year audit before the 3rd year audit opinion is issued. [R410.4]

Threat	Safeguards
Gifts and hospitality Acceptance of goods, services or hospitality from an audit client can create self-interest, intimidation and familiarity threats as the auditor may feel indebted to the client.	Gifts and hospitality may not be accepted unless the value is trivial and inconsequential. [R420.3] Gifts and hospitality which are trivial and inconsequential but which are intended to improperly influence the behaviour of the recipient should not be accepted. [420.3 A2]
Owning shares/financial interests The auditor will want to maximise return from the investment and overlook audit adjustments which would affect the value of their investment.	A direct, or material indirect, financial interest in the audit client must not be held by: • the firm or a network firm • an audit team member or the immediate family of a team member • a partner working in the office connected with the audit engagement partner • any partner providing non-audit services to the audit client. [R510.4] An immediate family member may hold a financial interest such as pension or share options but must dispose of it as soon as practicable when the family member has the right to do so, e.g. when there is a right to exercise the option. [R510.5] Financial interests received indirectly e.g. by inheritance or gifted, must be disposed of immediately. [R510.9]

Threat	Safeguards
Overdue fees A self-interest threat may be created if a significant amount of fees is not paid before the auditor's report for the following year is issued. [410.7 A1]	• Obtain partial or full payment for the fees. • An independent reviewer should review the work performed to ensure objectivity has not been impaired. [410.7 A2] When fees remain overdue for a significant amount of time, the firm should consider whether the overdue fees constitute a loan, and whether it is appropriate to seek reappointment or continue with the engagement. [R410.8]
Loans and guarantees A loan or guarantee from (or deposit with) an assurance client that is a bank or similar institution will not create a threat to independence provided that: • it is on commercial terms, and • made in the normal course of business.	Loans and guarantees between an audit client and the firm, the audit team member, or their immediate family, that are not in the normal course of business or not on commercial terms are not permitted. [R511.5] Loans to audit clients are not permitted unless immaterial to the firm or individual, and the client. [R511.4]
Business relationships If audit firms (or members) enter into business relationships with clients (e.g. joint ventures, marketing arrangements), this leads to self-interest because the auditor would have an interest in the successful operation of the client. The purchase of goods and services from an assurance client would not normally give rise to a threat to independence, provided the transaction is in the normal course of business and on commercial terms. [520.6 A1]	A firm, network firm or audit team member should not have a close business relationship with an audit client unless any financial interest is immaterial and the business relationship is insignificant to the client, the firm or the audit team member. [R520.4] If the purchase of goods and services by an audit team member represents a material amount, that person should be removed from the audit team or they should reduce the magnitude of the transactions. [520.6 A2]

Threat	Safeguards
Potential employment with an audit client If a member of the engagement team has reason to believe they may become an employee of the client they will not wish to do anything to affect their potential future employment.	The firm must establish policies and procedures which require individuals to notify the firm of the possibility of employment with the client. [R524.5] Remove the individual from the assurance engagement. [524.5 A2] Perform an independent review of any significant judgments made by that individual. [524.5 A3]
Contingent fees The auditor would have incentive to ensure a particular outcome is achieved in order to maximise the audit fee. E.g. overlook audit adjustments that would reduce profit if the fee is calculated based on profit.	Fees based on a particular outcome, e.g. level of profits of the company, are not permitted for audit engagements. [R410.10] Contingent fees are not permitted for non-assurance services provided to an audit client if: • The fee is material to the firm. • The outcome of the non-assurance service is dependent on a future judgment related to the audit of a material amount of the financial statements. [R410.11]
Compensation and evaluation policies A self-interest threat is created when a member of the audit team is evaluated on, or compensated for, selling non-assurance services to that audit client. The significance of the threat will depend on: • The proportion of the individual's compensation or performance evaluation that is based on the sale of such services. • The role of the individual on the audit team. • Whether promotion decisions are influenced by the sale of such services. [411.3 A1]	**Key audit partners** A key audit partner shall not be evaluated on or compensated based on their success in selling non-assurance services to their audit client. [R411.4] **Audit team members** The firm shall: • Revise the compensation plan or evaluation process for that individual. • Remove that individual from the audit team. • Have a professional accountant review the work of the member of the audit team. [411.3 A2 – A3]

Threat	Safeguards
Actual or threatened litigation Litigation could represent a breakdown of trust in the relationship between auditor and client. This may affect the impartiality of the auditor, and lead to a reluctance of management to disclose relevant information to the auditor. [430.3 A1] The significance of the threat depends on the materiality of the litigation and whether the litigation relates to a prior assurance engagement. [430.3 A2]	It may be possible to continue other assurance engagements, depending on the significance of the threat by: • Discussing the matter with the client. [430.3 A1] • If the litigation involves an individual, removing that individual from the engagement team. [430.3 A3] • Having an appropriate review of the work done. [430.3 A4] If adequate safeguards cannot be implemented the firm must withdraw from or decline the engagement.

Familiarity threats

When the auditor becomes too sympathetic or too trusting of a client and loses professional scepticism, or where the relationship between the auditor and client goes beyond professional boundaries.

Threat	Safeguards
Long association of senior personnel Using the same senior personnel in an engagement team over a long period may cause the auditor to become too trusting/less sceptical of the client resulting in material misstatements going undetected. A self-interest threat may also be created as a result of the individual's concern about losing a longstanding client. [540.3. A2]	*Non-listed clients* • Rotate individuals off the audit team. • Change the role of the individual or the nature of the tasks they perform. • Perform an independent internal or external quality review. [540.3 A5 – A6] *Listed clients* • The engagement partner, EQCR or any other key audit partner must not act for a period of more than seven cumulative years ('time-on' period). • After the time-on period, the individual must serve a cooling-off period. [R540.5]

Threat	Safeguards
In relation to the individual the firm should consider: • The length and closeness of the individual's relationship with the client. • The length of time on the audit team. • The extent of direction, supervision and review of work of the individual. • The extent to which the individual has had the ability to influence the outcome of the audit. [540.3 A3 (a)] In relation to the audit client, the firm should consider: • Structural changes in the client's organisation. • Whether the client's management team has changed. • Whether the complexity of the subject matter has changed. [540.3 A3 (b)]	The cooling-off periods are as follows: • 5 years for an engagement partner. • 3 years for an EQCR. • 2 years for a key audit partner. [R540.11 – 13] In exceptional circumstances, a key audit partner may be permitted to serve a one year extension if continuity is important to maintain audit quality. [R540.7] If an audit client becomes a public interest entity, the length of time served as a key audit partner before the client became a public interest entity is taken into account. [R540.8] If a key audit partner was a key audit partner on that engagement at a different firm, the length of time served at the prior firm should be taken into account. [R540.18] An independent regulatory body may provide an audit firm with an exemption from partner rotation if the firm does not have sufficient people with the necessary knowledge and experience to enable partner rotation. [R540.9] During the cooling-off period, the individual shall not: • Be an engagement team member • Consult with the engagement team or client • Be responsible for, or provide, other professional services to the audit client. [R540.20]

Threat	Safeguards
Family and personal relationships A familiarity threat (and self-interest or intimidation threat) may occur when a member of the engagement team has a family or personal relationship with someone at the client who is able to exert significant influence over the financial statements (or subject matter of another assurance engagement). [521.4 A1]	*Audit team members* • Remove the individual from the engagement team. [521.4 A3] • Structure the engagement team so that the individual does not deal with matters that are the responsibility of the family member. [521.4 A4] *Other employees and partners of the firm* A firm should have policies and procedures in place to provide guidance when a partner (or employee) of the firm has a family or personal relationship with someone at the client who is able to exert significant influence over the subject matter, even when the individual is not a member of the engagement team. [R521.8] The firm should structure the individual's responsibilities to reduce any potential influence over the audit engagement and have an appropriate reviewer review the audit work performed. [521.8 A2]
Recruitment services Familiarity, self-interest or intimidation threats may arise if the firm is involved in recruiting senior personnel for the client. The firm may also be considered to be assuming management responsibilities. Reviewing qualifications and interviewing applicants to advise on financial competence is allowed. [609.3 A2]	Recruitment services may be provided to an audit client provided the client makes all management decisions including determining the suitability of the candidate, selecting a suitable candidate, determining employment terms and negotiating remuneration. [R609.4] The firm cannot provide recruitment services in respect of directors or senior management who would be in a position to exert significant influence over the financial statements. [R609.7]

Threat	Safeguards
Employment with an audit client A self-interest, familiarity or intimidation threat may arise where an employee or partner of the firm becomes a director or employee of an audit client (in a position to exert significant influence over the financial statements or other subject matter). [524.3 A1] The firm should ensure no significant connection remains between the individual and the firm, such as entitlement to benefits or payments from the firm, or participation in the firm's business and professional activities. [R524.4] The firm should consider: • The position taken at the client. • The involvement the person will have with the audit team. • The length of time since the individual was a member of the audit team. • The former position of the individual within the audit team. [524.4 A3]	• Modify the audit plan. • Assign individuals to the audit team who have sufficient experience in relation to the individual who has joined the client. • Have an appropriate reviewer review the work of the former audit team member. [524.4 A4] *Partners joining listed clients as a director or employee in a position to exert influence over the financial statements* Independence is compromised unless, subsequent to the partner ceasing to be a key audit partner or senior partner, the client had issued audited financial statements covering a period of not less than 12 months, and the partner was not a member of the audit team with respect to the audit of those financial statements. [R524.6] If a senior or managing partner of the firm joins a listed audit client, independence is compromised unless twelve months have passed since the individual was the senior or managing partner. [R524.7]

Self-review threats

Where non-audit work is provided to an audit client and is then subject to audit, the auditor will be unlikely to admit to errors in their own work, or may not identify the errors in their own work.

Threat	Safeguards
Accounting and bookkeeping services Preparing accounting records or financial statements for an audit client might create a self-review threat. [601.1] Accounting and bookkeeping services include: • Preparing accounting records and financial statements • Recording transactions • Payroll services. [601.3 A1] Discussing accounting treatments and proposing adjusting journal entries are a normal part of the audit process and do not create threats as long as the client is responsible for making decisions in the preparation of the financial statements. [601.3 A3]	*Non-listed clients* • A firm shall only provide a non-listed audit client with accounting and bookkeeping services which are routine or mechanical in nature. [R601.5] Services which are routine and mechanical in nature and therefore require little or no professional judgment include: • Preparing payroll calculations based on client-originated data. • Recording recurring transactions which are easily determinable. • Calculating depreciation when the client determines the accounting policy, useful life and residual value. • Posting transactions coded by the client to the ledger. • Posting client approved entries to the trial balance. • Preparing financial statements based on information in the client-approved trial balance. [601.4 A1] • Professionals who are not audit team members must be used to perform the service. • An appropriate reviewer who was not involved in providing the service should review the audit work or service performed. [601.5 A1]

Threat	Safeguards
	Listed clients A firm cannot provide a listed audit client with accounting and bookkeeping services. [R601.6] A firm can provide accounting services for divisions or related entities of a listed client if separate teams are used and divisions or related entities are collectively immaterial to the financial statements subject to audit. [R601.7]
Internal audit services In addition to the self-review threat, the auditor needs to be careful not to assume management responsibilities. The firm should consider: • The materiality of the related financial statement amounts. • The risk of misstatement of the assertions related to the financial statement amounts. • The degree of reliance that the audit team will place on the internal audit service. [605.4 A4]	The audit firm must be satisfied that management takes full responsibility for the internal audit activities and internal controls. [R605.4] Professionals who are not audit team members must be used to perform the service. [605.4 A5] A firm cannot provide internal audit services for a listed audit client, where the service relates to internal controls over financial reporting, financial accounting systems, or in relation to amounts or disclosures that are material to the financial statements. [R605.5]

Tax services

Providing tax services to an audit client might create a self-review and advocacy threat. [604.1]

Tax services include:

• Tax return preparation

• Tax calculations for preparing accounting entries

• Tax planning and advisory services

• Tax services involving valuations

• Assistance in the resolution of tax disputes.

[604.3 A1]

The firm should consider:

• The characteristics of the engagement.

• The level of tax expertise of the client's employees.

• The complexity of the tax regime.

[604.3 A2]

Threat	Safeguards
Tax return preparation Completion of tax returns does **not** usually create a threat. [604.4 A1]	No safeguards required.
Tax calculations	*Non-listed clients* – use professionals who are not audit team members to perform the service, and a reviewer who was not involved in providing the service to review the audit work or service performed. [604.5 A5] *Listed clients* – The firm must not prepare tax calculations of current or deferred tax where the figures are material to the financial statements. Where the figures are immaterial, the safeguards for non-listed clients should be applied. [R604.6]
Tax planning and advisory services In addition to the considerations in 604.3 A2, the firm should consider: • The degree of subjectivity involved. • Whether the tax treatment is supported by a private ruling and cleared by the tax authority. [604.7 A3]	A firm shall not provide tax planning and advisory services to an audit client when the effectiveness of the tax advice depends on a particular accounting treatment. [R604.8] When providing such services, the firm should use professionals who are not audit team members to perform the service, and a reviewer who was not involved in providing the service to review the audit work or service performed. [604.7 A4]
Tax services involving valuations If the valuation performed for tax purposes is not subject to external review and the effect is material to the financial statements, in addition to the considerations in 604.3 A2, the firm should consider: • The extent to which the valuation methodology is supported by tax law. • The degree of subjectivity. • The reliability of the underlying data. [604.9 A3]	When providing such services, the firm should: • Use professionals who are not audit team members to perform the service. • Have a reviewer who was not involved in providing the service to review the audit work or service performed. • Obtain pre-clearance from the tax authorities. [604.9 A4]

Threat	Safeguards
Assistance in the resolution of tax disputes In addition to the considerations in 604.3 A2, the firm should consider: • The extent to which the outcome of the dispute will have a material effect on the financial statements. • Whether the advice provided is the subject of the tax dispute. • The extent to which the matter is supported by tax law, regulation or established practice. • Whether the proceedings are conducted in public. [604.10 A3]	When providing such services, the firm should: • Use professionals who are not audit team members to perform the service. • Have a reviewer who was not involved in providing the service to review the audit work or service performed. [604.10 A4] A firm shall not act as an advocate for the audit client before a public tribunal or court in the resolution of a tax matter if the amounts are material to the financial statements. [R604.11] The firm is allowed to have a continuing advisory role e.g. • Responding to specific requests for information. • Providing factual accounts or testimony about the work performed. • Assisting the client in analysing the tax issues.
IT services IT services may create a self-review threat and also be considered to be assuming management responsibilities. The firm should consider: • The nature of the service. • The nature of IT systems and the extent to which they impact or interact with the client's accounting records or financial statements. • The degree of reliance that the audit team will place on the IT systems. [606.4 A1]	*All clients* When providing such services, the firm should use professionals who are not audit team members to perform the service. [606.4 A2] The audit firm must be satisfied that management takes full responsibility for the IT controls and systems. [R606.4] *Listed clients* A firm shall not provide IT systems services to a listed client that form a significant part of the internal controls over financial reporting or generate information that is significant to the financial statements. [R606.5]

Threat	Safeguards
The firm can provide IT services which involve: • Design or implementation of IT systems unrelated to internal controls or financial reporting. • Implementation of off-the-shelf accounting software that was not developed by the audit firm and does not require significant customisation. • Evaluating and making recommendations on a system designed or operated by another service provider or by the entity. [606.3 A2]	
Valuation services Providing valuation services to an audit client might create a self-review and advocacy threat. [603.1] The firm should consider: • The use and purpose of the valuation report, including whether the report will be made public. • The extent of the client's involvement in determining matters of judgment. • Whether the valuation will have a material effect on the financial statements. • The degree of dependence on future events that might create significant volatility in the amounts involved. • The degree of subjectivity. [603.3 A3] Some valuations will not involve significant subjectivity e.g. if the underlying assumptions are established by law or when techniques are widely accepted. [603.4 A1]	*All clients* • Use professionals who are not audit team members to perform the service. • Have an appropriate reviewer who was not involved in providing the service review the audit work or service performed. [603.3 A4] *Non-listed clients* Valuation services shall not be provided to audit clients if the valuation involves a significant degree of subjectivity and the valuation will have a material effect on the financial statements. [R603.4] *Listed clients* Valuation services that are material to the financial statements (regardless of subjectivity) should not be provided to listed audit clients. [R603.5]

Threat	Safeguards
Temporary personnel assignments The loan of personnel may create a self-review, advocacy and familiarity threat. [525.2] Staff may be loaned to the client provided: • The loan period is short. • The person does not assume management responsibilities. • The client is responsible for directing and supervising the person. [R525.4]	• Additional review of the work performed by the loaned personnel. • Not including the loaned personnel on the audit team. • Not giving the loaned personnel audit responsibility for any function that they performed during the loaned assignment. [525.3 A1]

Corporate finance services
 	
Self-review and advocacy threats may be created if a firm:
 	
• Assists an audit client in developing corporate strategies.
 	
• Identifies possible targets for the audit client to acquire.
 	
• Advises on disposal transactions.
 	
• Assists in raising finance.
 	
• Provides structuring advice.
 	
[610.3 A1]
 	
Factors affecting the existence and significance of any threat include:
 	
• The degree of subjectivity involved.
 	
• Whether the outcome will have a material impact on the financial statements.
 	
• Whether the effectiveness of the corporate finance advice depends on a particular accounting treatment.
 	
[610.3 A2]
	Where services can be provided:
	
	• Use professionals who are not audit team members to perform the service.
	
	• Have an appropriate reviewer who was not involved in providing the service review the audit work or service performed.
	
	[610.3 A3]
	
	Prohibited services
	
	• Corporate finance services that involve promoting, dealing in, or underwriting the audit client's shares. [R610.4]
	
	• Corporate finance services where
	
	  – the effectiveness of the advice depends on a particular accounting treatment or presentation in the financial statements
	
	  – the audit team has reasonable doubt as to the appropriateness of the accounting treatment, and
	
	  – the outcome will have a material effect of the financial statements.
	
	[R610.5]

Threat	Safeguards
Legal services Providing legal services to an audit client might create a self-review and advocacy threat. [608.1] Legal services can only be provided by legally trained, or authorised, personnel. [608.3 A3] The firm should consider: • The materiality of the matter in relation to the financial statements. • The complexity of the legal matter and the degree of judgment necessary. [608.4 A2]	Where services are provided, the firm should: • Use professionals who are not audit team members to perform the service. • Have an appropriate reviewer who was not involved in providing the service review the audit work or service performed. [608.4 A3] A partner or employee of the firm must not act as general counsel for an audit client. [R608.5] A firm shall not act in an advocacy role for an audit client when the amounts involved are material to the financial statements. [R608.6]
Client staff joins audit firm (recent service with an audit client) A self-interest, self-review, or familiarity threat may arise where an audit team member has recently served as a director or employee of the audit client. [522.2] When service with the audit client was prior to the period covered by the auditor's report, the significance of the threat will depend on: • The position the individual held with the client. • The length of time since the individual left the client. • The role of the audit team member. [522.4 A2]	The audit team should not include individuals who during the period covered by the auditor's report have served as a director or employee of the audit client. [R522.3] When service with the audit client was prior to the period covered by the auditor's report, an appropriate reviewer should review the work performed by the audit team member. [522.4 A3]

Threat	Safeguards
Serving as a director or officer of an audit client A self-review and self-interest threat will be created if an individual from the audit firm serves as a director or officer of an audit client. [523.2]	A partner or employee shall not serve as a director or officer of an audit client. [R523.3] A partner or employee shall not serve as company secretary for an audit client unless permitted by local legislation, management makes all relevant decisions, and the duties performed are routine and administrative in nature. [R523.4]

Advocacy threats

Promoting the position of a client or representing them in some way would mean the audit firm is seen to be 'taking sides' with the client.

Examples include:

- Representing the client in court or in any dispute where the matter is material to the financial statements.

- Negotiating on the client's behalf for finance.

- Loan of personnel from an audit firm to an audit client.

- Providing valuation services to an audit client.

- Providing tax services to an audit client.

Intimidation threats

Actual or perceived pressures from the client, or attempts to exercise undue influence over the assurance provider, create an intimidation threat.

Examples include:

- Fee dependency

- Gifts and hospitality

- Family and personal relationships

- Recruitment services

- Employment with an audit client

- Litigation between the audit firm and client.

Public interest entities (PIEs)

A public interest entity is one which is:

- Listed

- Defined by regulation or legislation as public interest

- Audited under the same independence requirements as a listed entity.

Audit firms are also encouraged to treat entities where there are a wide range, or significant number of stakeholders, as public interest entities e.g. banks, insurance companies and credit institutions.

UK syllabus – Safeguards from the FRC Ethical Standard

The FRC has issued a UK specific 'Revised Ethical Standard 2016' designed to ensure practitioners comply with ethical requirements. The standard refers to 'covered persons', 'persons closely associated' and 'other close family relationships'.

Covered persons include the partners and staff involved in the engagement, but could also be:

- Any other person placed at the disposal of the audit team e.g. an expert.

- Anyone in the audit firm with supervisory, management or other oversight responsibility for the partners involved in the engagement.

- Any other person in the firm who is in a position to influence the conduct or outcome of the audit.

Persons closely associated include immediate family members i.e. spouse and dependents.

Other close family relationships comprise parents, non-dependent children and siblings.

An individual can usually be presumed to be aware of matters concerning persons closely associated with them and to be able to influence their behaviour.

Many of the requirements extend to affiliated companies (i.e. subsidiaries).

Section 1 – General requirements and guidance

- The audit firm shall establish policies and procedures to ensure that the firm, and all those involved in the audit, act with integrity, objectivity and independence.

- The leadership of the audit firm shall take responsibility for establishing a control environment that places adherence to ethical principles above commercial considerations.

- The audit firm shall designate an ethics partner.

- The audit firm shall establish policies and procedures to prevent employees from taking decisions that are the responsibility of management of the audited entity.

- The audit firm shall establish policies and procedures to assess the significance of threats to the auditor's objectivity:

  (i) When considering whether to accept or retain an audit or non-audit service

  (ii) When planning the audit

  (iii) When forming an opinion on the financial statements

  (iv) When considering whether to provide non-audit services

  (v) When potential threats are reported.

- The audit engagement partner shall not accept or shall not continue an audit engagement if he or she concludes that any threats to the auditor's objectivity and independence cannot be reduced to an acceptable level.

- In the case of listed companies, an Engagement Quality Control Reviewer must be appointed who must:

  (i) Reach an overall conclusion on independence

  (ii) Communicate to those charged with governance at the client all significant matters that bear upon the auditor's objectivity.

Section 2 – Financial, business, employment and personal relationships

- The audit firm, partners, or persons closely associated with them shall not hold any financial interest in an audited entity.

- Audit firms, covered persons and persons closely associated with them shall not make loans to, or guarantee the borrowings of, an audited entity (and vice versa).

- Audit firms, covered persons and persons closely associated with them shall not enter into business relationships with an audited entity.

- An audit firm shall not second partners or employees to an audit client unless:
  - the secondment is for a short period of time, and
  - the audited entity agrees that the individual concerned will not hold a management position.

- Where a partner or employee returns to a firm on completion of a secondment to an audit client, that individual shall not be given any role on the audit involving any function or activity that they performed or supervised during that assignment.

- Where a partner joins an audited entity, the audit firm shall take action to ensure that no connections remain between the firm and the individual.

- Where a partner leaves a firm and is appointed as a director or to a key management position with an audited entity, having acted as audit engagement partner at any time in the two years prior to this appointment, the firm shall resign as auditor.

- A partner, or employee of the audit firm who undertakes audit work, shall not accept appointment:
  - to the board of directors of the audited entity, or
  - to any subcommittee of that board.

Section 3 – Long association with engagements and with entities relevant to engagements

- The audit firm shall establish policies and procedures to monitor the length of time that senior staff serve as members of the engagement team for each audit.

- Where senior staff have a long association with the audit, the audit firm shall assess the threats to the auditor's objectivity and independence and shall apply safeguards to reduce the threats to an acceptable level. Such safeguards include partner rotation or appointment of an engagement quality control reviewer. Where appropriate safeguards cannot be applied, the audit firm shall either resign as auditor or not stand for reappointment, as appropriate.

- Once an audit engagement partner on a non-listed client has held this role for ten years, careful consideration must be given as to whether their objectivity would be perceived to be impaired and rotation of the partner should be considered. If the partner is not rotated, other safeguards must be applied and the reason for not rotating must be communicated to those charged with governance.

- In the case of listed companies, the audit firm shall establish policies and procedures to ensure that no one shall act as audit engagement partner for more than five years, and should not return within five years. The audit committee may approve an extension of two years in certain circumstances.

- When the audit client becomes listed, if the audit engagement partner has already served four or more years they may continue for a maximum of two years.

- In the case of listed companies, the audit engagement partner shall review the safeguards put in place to address the threats arising where senior staff have been involved in the audit for a period longer than seven years.

Note: Listed companies are required to put the audit out to tender every ten years in accordance with EU regulations. This is an action that the company must take rather than the auditor.

Section 4 – Fees, remuneration and evaluation policies, gifts and hospitality, litigation

- Sufficient partners and staff with time and skill to complete the audit should be assigned, regardless of the audit fee charged.

- Audit fees should not be influenced by the provision of non-audit services to the clients.

- An audit shall not be undertaken on a contingent fee basis.

- The audit fee for the previous audit and the arrangements for its payment shall be agreed with the audited entity before the audit firm formally accepts appointment as auditor in respect of the following period.

- Listed client: fees for providing non-audit services shall be limited to 70% of the average audit fee for the last 3 years. Where the fees charged for non-audit services for a financial year exceed the audit fee for that year, disclose to the Ethics Partner and consider the need for safeguards.

- Where it is expected that the total fees receivable from a listed audited entity will regularly exceed 10% of the annual fee income (15% if non-listed) of the audit firm, the firm shall not act as the auditor of that entity.

- Where regular fee income is expected to exceed 5% (listed)/10% (non-listed) of the firm's fee income – disclose to the Ethics Partner and those charged with governance and consider whether safeguards need to be applied.

- New firms may find the economic dependence requirements difficult to comply with so should consider the use of an external quality control reviewer.

- The audit firm shall establish policies and procedures to ensure that the objectives and appraisal of members of the audit team do not include selling non-audit services.

- Where litigation with a client is already in progress, or where it is probable, the audit firm shall either not continue with or not accept the audit engagement.

- The audit firm, including employees, shall not accept gifts from the audited entity, unless the value is trivial.

- Audit firm employees shall not accept hospitality from the audited entity, unless it is reasonable in terms of its frequency, nature and cost.

Section 5 – Non-audit/additional services

- Anyone in the audit firm considering providing a non-audit service to one of the firm's audit clients must communicate the details to the audit engagement partner.

- Before accepting non-audit work, consider whether a reasonable and informed third party would regard the non-audit work as impairing the firm's objectivity and independence.

- Where safeguards are insufficient to mitigate the threats to independence, the non-audit work should not be accepted.

- General safeguards for non-audit services include separate teams for the audit and non-audit work and engagement quality control review of the work and conclusions of the audit team in relation to the non-audit service.

- Consider whether there is informed management i.e.

   - Objective and transparent information provided to the client.

   - The client has a genuine opportunity to decide between alternative courses of action.

   - A member of management has been designated to receive the result of non-audit services – this individual must have the capability to make judgments and decisions on the basis of the information provided.

   Without informed management it is unlikely that any safeguards could be effective against the management threat.

- Communicate matters that have a bearing on the auditor's objectivity and independence related to the provision of non-audit services to those charged with governance.

Prohibited non-audit services for listed clients:

- Tax services

- Taking part in management or decision-making

- Bookkeeping and preparing accounting records or financial statements

- Payroll services

- Design and implementation of internal controls, risk management procedures or information technology systems relating to financial information

- Valuation services (including actuarial valuation) where the valuation would have a material effect on the financial statements

- Legal services

- Internal audit

- Corporate finance services (including financing, investment strategy and promoting/dealing in or underwriting shares)

- Human resources services.

Section 6 – Provisions available for audits of small entities

When auditing the financial statements of a small entity **the audit firm is not required to**:

- comply with the requirement that an external independent quality control review is performed.

- comply with Section 5, relating to providing non-audit services. The firm is not required to apply safeguards to address the self-review threat provided there is informed management, more regular 'cold review' of audits where non-audit services have been provided and disclosure of the non-audit services in the auditor's report.

- comply with the requirement that where an audit partner joins the client the firm should resign and cannot accept appointment as auditor until 2 years have passed. The firm can continue as auditor provided there is no significant threat to the audit team's integrity, objectivity and independence and disclosure of the partner joining the client is made in the auditor's report.

- comply with the requirement for an external independent quality control review if fees from a client are expected to exceed 10% but not exceed 15%. There is no requirement for the independent quality control review, but the issue must be disclosed to the Ethics Partner and those charged with governance at the client.

UK Syllabus: Revised Ethical Standard Exposure Draft

FRC Revised Ethical Standard

In July 2019, the FRC proposed a set of more stringent ethical rules for auditors, in response to findings from recent audit enforcement cases and from audit inspections.

Key changes proposed include:

- A clearer and stronger 'objective, reasonable and informed third party test' which requires audit firms to consider whether a proposed action would affect their independence from the perspective of public interest stakeholders rather than another auditor. This is supported by additional material to encourage a wide-ranging assessment, which considers both the spirit and the letter of the standard.

- Enhancing the authority of the Ethics Partner function within audit firms, in order to ensure firm wide focus on ethical matters and the public interest, and to require reporting to those charged with governance where an audit firm does not follow the Ethics Partner's advice.

- The list of prohibited non-audit services that auditors of Public Interest Entities (PIEs) can provide to audited bodies has been replaced with a much shorter list of permitted services, all of which are 'closely related' to an audit or required by law and/or regulation. No other services can be provided.

The third party test

When considering whether the auditor has acted appropriately, in accordance with the ethical requirements, they should consider the perspective of an objective, reasonable and informed third party. Such a person is informed about the respective roles and responsibilities of an auditor, those charged with governance and management of an entity, and is not another practitioner. The perspective offered by an informed investor, shareholder or other public interest stakeholder best supports an effective evaluation required by the third-party test, with diversity of thought being an important consideration.

The Ethics Partner function

An ethics partner should be appointed by the senior management of the firm. The ethics partner has responsibility for ensuring the firm's compliance with supporting ethical provision. He or she must have the necessary seniority, relevant experience, authority and leadership levels.

In firms with three or fewer responsible individuals, it may not be practical to appoint an ethics partner. In these circumstances all partners will regularly discuss ethical issues amongst themselves.

If differences of opinion arise between the Ethics Partner and persons consulting them, the firm's policies and procedures for dealing with and resolving differences of opinion shall be followed. If in following those procedures, the firm concludes that the opinion of the Ethics Partner is not to be followed where it relates to an engagement on a public interest entity, the matter shall be reported to the firm's independent non-executives and to the Competent Authority. The engagement partner shall also report this matter to those charged with governance.

List of permitted services for public interest audit clients

Services required by UK law or regulation and exempt from the non-audit services cap:

- Reporting required by a competent authority or regulator under UK law or regulation for example;

    - Reporting to a regulator on client assets

    - In relation to entities regulated under the Financial Services and Markets Act 2000 (FSMA)

    - Reporting to a regulator on regulatory financial statements

    - Reporting on a Solvency and Financial Condition Report under Solvency II.

- In the case of a parent undertaking or controlled undertaking incorporated and based in a third country, reporting required by law or regulation in that jurisdiction where the auditor is required to undertake that engagement (such services can only be provided by network member firms in that jurisdiction and shall not be provided by the audit firm).

- Reporting on internal financial controls when required by law or regulation.

- Reports, required by or supplied to competent authorities/regulators supervising the audited entity, where the authority/regulator has either specified the auditor to provide the service or identified to the entity that the auditor would be an appropriate choice for service provider.

- Audit and other services provided as auditor of the entity, or as reporting accountant, in relation to information of the audited entity for which it is probable that an objective, reasonable and informed third party would conclude that the understanding of the entity obtained by the auditor for the audit of the financial statements is relevant to the service, and where the nature of the service would not compromise independence.

- Services which support the entity in fulfilling an obligation required by UK law or regulation, where: the provision of such services is time critical; the subject matter of the engagement is price sensitive; and an it is probably that an objective, reasonable and informed third party would conclude that the understanding of the entity obtained by the auditor for the audit of the financial statements is relevant to the service, and where the nature of the service would not compromise independence.

Services subject to the non-audit services cap:

- Reviews of interim financial information; and providing verification of interim profits.

- Extended audit or assurance work that is authorised by those charged with governance performed on financial or performance information and/or financial controls where this work is integrated with the audit work and is performed on the same principal terms and conditions.

- Additional assurance work authorised by those charged with governance performed on material included within the annual report of an entity relevant to an engagement.

- Reporting on government grants.

- Reporting on covenant or loan agreements, which require independent verification, including to third parties with whom the entity relevant to an engagement has a business relationship.

- Services which have been the subject of an application to the Competent Authority.

Where such services are provided, they shall not include any elements of those services subject to outright prohibition.

If a prohibited service is inadvertently provided, the audit firm may continue to carry out the statutory audit of the public interest entity only if it can justify, that such provision of services does not affect its professional judgment and the auditor's report. The audit firm shall report this in its auditor's report on the entity's accounts.

3 Confidentiality

Members acquiring information in the course of their professional work should not disclose such information to third parties without first obtaining proper and specific authority, unless there is a professional right or duty to disclose.

Confidential information may be obtained from:

- The firm or employing organisation

- Business relationships i.e. current clients

- Prospective clients and employers.

 Members of an assurance team should not disclose any information to anyone outside of the engagement team, whether or not they work for the same firm.

Circumstances in which disclosure is permitted or required

Disclosure of confidential information should only be made if:

- Disclosure is permitted by law and permission has been given.

- Disclosure is required by law e.g. to provide evidence in legal proceedings or disclosure is required to a regulatory authority. This would include money laundering reporting.

- There is a professional right or duty to disclose e.g.

    - To comply with a quality review of a professional body

    - To respond to an enquiry by a regulatory authority

    - To protect the member's interests in legal proceedings

    - To comply with technical and professional standards including ethical requirements.

Factors to be considered before disclosing confidential information include:

- Whether harm could be caused by the disclosure

- Whether all relevant information is known and substantiated

- Whether the information is to be communicated to appropriate recipients.

[ACCA Code of Ethics and Conduct 2018, Section 114]

Disclosure of confidential information: specific examples

Permitted or required by law

Where there is a statutory right or duty to disclose, the professional accountant will do so without obtaining permission of the client. The most common offences members are likely to encounter in their professional work are in relation to:

- Fraud or theft including fraudulent financial reporting, falsification or alteration of accounting records or other documents and misappropriation of assets

- Tax evasion

- Money laundering

- Drug trafficking or terrorism

- Insider dealing, market abuse, and bribery

- Offences under company law.

Public interest

An auditor may disclose information if they consider it to be in the public interest. There is no official definition of 'public interest'. The auditor must employ a combination of judgment and legal advice. A good rule of thumb is that if a member of the public could incur physical or financial damage that the auditor could knowingly have prevented, it is likely that the auditor has failed in their public duty.

In determining the need to disclose matters in the public interest the auditor should consider:

- The relative size of the amounts involved and the extent of the likely financial damage

- Whether members of the public are likely to be affected

- The likelihood of repetition

- The reasons for the client's unwillingness to make the disclosures

- The gravity of the matter

- Relevant legislation, accounting standards and auditing standards

- Legal advice obtained.

The auditor will be protected from the risk of liability provided that disclosure is made in the public interest, disclosure is made to an appropriate body or person, and there is no malice motivating the disclosure.

[ACCA Code of Ethics and Conduct, Section B1]

Conflicts of interest

A conflict of interest arises when the same audit firm is appointed for two companies that interact with each other, for example:

- Companies which compete in the same market

- Companies which trade with each other.

A conflict of interest may create a threat to the fundamental principles of objectivity and confidentiality.

It may be perceived that the auditor cannot provide objective services and advice to a company where it also audits a competitor.

Professional accountants should always act in the best interests of the client. However, where conflicts of interest exist, the firm's work should be arranged to **avoid the interests of one being adversely affected** by those of another and to prevent a breach of **confidentiality**.

In order to ensure this, the firm must **disclose** the nature of the conflict to the relevant parties and **obtain consent to act**.

The following additional safeguards should be implemented:

- Separate engagement teams (with different engagement partners and team members) who are provided with clear guidance on maintaining confidentiality.

- Review of the key judgments and conclusions by an independent person of appropriate seniority.

Measures which should be taken to reduce the threat of disclosure include:

- Procedures to limit access to client files

- Physical separation of confidential information including separate practice areas

- Signed confidentiality agreements by the engagement team members

- Specific training and communication.

If adequate safeguards cannot be implemented (i.e. where the acceptance/ continuance of an engagement would, despite safeguards, materially prejudice the interests of any clients), or if consent is refused, the firm must end or decline to perform professional services that would result in the conflict of interest.

[ACCA Code of Ethics and Conduct, Section 310]

Approach to exam questions: Ethical issues

Exam questions relating to ethical threats require you to evaluate the threats. Evaluation encompasses:

- Identification of the threat

- Explanation of the threat

- Evaluation of the significance of the threat

- Stating the actions the firm should take including the safeguards that should be implemented to manage the threat.

Example: the audit engagement partner owns shares in the audit client

Identify the threat

This is a self-interest threat as the partner has a financial interest in the audit client.

Explain the threat

The partner may overlook misstatements that if corrected would impact the value of the investment such as potential dividend payment or share value.

Evaluate the significance of the threat

The shares are owned by the audit engagement partner who has the greatest influence over the outcome of the audit as they are the person responsible for forming the opinion on the financial statements. Therefore the threat is significant.

Actions to be taken by the firm

The partner should sell the shares immediately and may need to be removed from the audit.

An engagement quality control review should be performed to assess the key judgments of the audit engagement partner to ensure objectivity has not been impaired.

It would be advisable for staff and partners of the firm to be reminded of the code of ethics in relation to financial interests, such as the need to disclose financial interests in clients and not to own shares in audit clients.

Test your understanding 1

You are an audit manager in Fox & Steeple, a firm of Chartered Certified Accountants, responsible for allocating staff to the following three audits of financial statements for the year ending 31 December 20X5.

Blythe Co is a new audit client. This private company is a local manufacturer and distributor of sportswear. The company's finance director, Peter, sees little value in the audit and put it out to tender last year as a cost-cutting exercise. In accordance with the requirements of the invitation to tender, your firm indicated that there would not be an interim audit.

Huggins Co, a long-standing client, operates a national supermarket chain. Your firm provided Huggins Co with corporate financial advice on obtaining a listing on a recognised stock exchange in 20X4. Senior management expects a thorough examination of the company's computerised systems, and are also seeking assurance that the annual report will not attract adverse criticism.

Gray Co has been an audit client for seven years after your firm advised management on a successful buyout. Gray Co provides communication services and software solutions. Your firm provides Gray Co with technical advice on financial reporting and tax services. Most recently you have been asked to conduct due diligence reviews on potential acquisitions.

Required:

Comment on the ethical and other professional issues raised, and recommend any actions that should be taken in respect of:

(a)   Blythe Co

(b)   Huggins Co

(c)   Gray Co.

(15 marks)

Test your understanding 2

Aventura International, a listed company, manufactures and wholesales a wide variety of products including fashion clothes and audio-video equipment. The company is audited by Voest & Co, a firm of Chartered Certified Accountants, and the audit manager is Darius Harken. The following matters have arisen during the audit of the group's financial statements for the year to 31 March 20X5 which is nearing completion:

(i)   During the annual physical count of fashion clothes at the company's principal warehouse, the audit staff attending the count were invited to purchase any items of clothing or equipment at 30% of their recommended retail prices.

(ii) The chief executive of Aventura International, Armando Thyolo, owns a private jet. Armando invoices the company, on a monthly basis, for that proportion of the operating costs which reflects business use. One of these invoices shows that Darius Harken was flown to Florida in September 20X4 and flown back two weeks later. Neither Aventura nor Voest & Co have any offices or associates in Florida.

(iii) Last week Armando announced his engagement to be married to his personal assistant, Kirsten Fennimore. Before joining Aventura in January 20X5, Kirsten had been Voest & Co's accountant in charge of the audit of Aventura.

Required:

Comment on the ethical and other professional issues raised, and recommend any actions that should be taken by the auditor in relation to these matters.

(15 marks)

Test your understanding 3

(a) Explain the importance of the role of confidentiality to the auditor-client relationship. **(5 marks)**

(b) Your firm acts as auditor and adviser to Blake Seven and to its four directors. The company is owned 50% by Brad Capella, 25% by his wife Minerva and 10% by Janus Trebbiano. Brad is the chief executive and Janus the finance director. Janus's sister, Rosella Trebbiano, has recently resigned from the executive board, following a disagreement with the Capellas. Rosella has now formed her own company, Blakes Heaven, in competition with Blake Seven.

Rosella is currently negotiating with her former co-executives the profit-related remuneration due to her and the sale of her 15% holding of shares in Blake Seven to one or all of them.

Rosella has contacted you to find out Brad's current remuneration package since he refuses to disclose this to her.

She has also requested that your firm continues to act as her personal adviser and becomes auditor and adviser to Blakes Heaven.

Required:

Comment on the matters that you should consider in deciding whether or not your audit firm can comply with Rosella's requests. **(10 marks)**

(Total: 15 marks)

Test your understanding 4 – UK syllabus only

Weller & Co is facing competition from other audit firms, and the partners have been considering how the firm's revenue could be increased. A proposal has been made that all audit managers should suggest to their audit clients that, as well as providing the external audit service, Weller & Co can provide the internal audit service as part of an 'extended audit' service.

Required:

Comment on the ethical and professional issues raised by the proposal to increase the firm's revenue. **(8 marks)**

4 Chapter summary

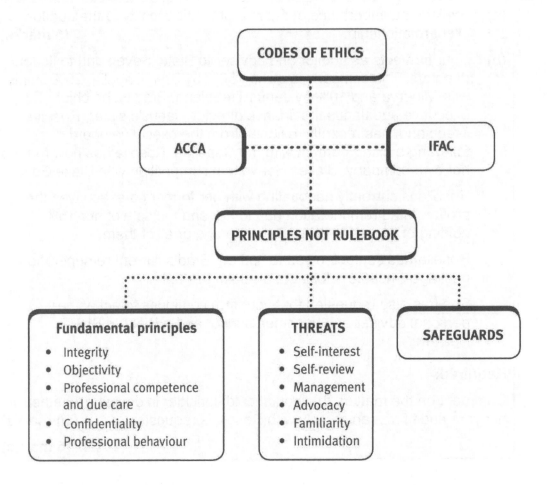

Test your understanding answers

Test your understanding 1

(a) **Blythe Co**

Intimidation and self-interest threats to objectivity may be created as the audit was put out to tender as a cost-cutting exercise. A threat to the fundamental principle of professional competence and due care also arises.

Peter may have applied pressure by stipulating that there should not be an interim audit in order to reduce fees.

This could mean the audit firm does not obtain sufficient appropriate evidence to form an appropriate opinion.

Senior staff assigned to Blythe Co should be alert to the need to exercise a high degree of professional scepticism in light of Peter's attitude towards the audit. The audit senior allocated to Blythe Co will need to be experienced in standing up to client management such as Peter.

As Blythe Co is a new client, detection risk will be higher and an engagement quality control review partner should be assigned.

(b) **Huggins Co**

Self-interest

The self-interest threat may be great for Huggins Co as the company is listed on a recognised stock exchange which may give prestige and credibility to Fox & Steeple.

Fox & Steeple could be pressured into overlooking material misstatements to avoid the loss of a listed client. This may result in the firm issuing an inappropriate opinion on the financial statements.

The engagement fee may be significant and Fox & Steeple may not wish to do anything to risk losing this client.

The fee level should be monitored to ensure that recurring fees from Huggins Co do not exceed the level set out by the profession for more than two consecutive years [INT: 15% of the firm's total fee income, UK: 10% of the firm's total fee income].

Familiarity

The familiarity threat of using the same lead engagement partner on an audit over a prolonged period is particularly relevant to Huggins Co, which is now a listed entity.

The audit firm may lack professional scepticism when performing the audit and fail to detect material misstatements.

The engagement partner should be rotated after a predefined period [INT: 7 years, UK: 5 years].

Self-review

A self-review threat is created when the audit firm provides non-audit services which affect the financial statements such as providing assurance over the computerised systems relevant to financial reporting.

The auditor may be unlikely to identify errors in their own work. If errors are found, they may be unlikely to admit to them.

The threat is significant as Huggins Co is a national chain and a listed client therefore significant reliance may be placed on the systems by the auditor.

As Huggins Co is listed, the examination of the computerised systems should not be undertaken if the systems relate to financial reporting or internal controls as the threat would be too significant.

If the systems do not relate to financial reporting or internal controls, separate teams should be used for each service. The team assigned to the systems examination should have appropriate skills.

Intimidation

As Huggins Co is seeking assurance the annual report will not attract adverse criticism, an intimidation threat may be created.

Management of Huggins Co may put pressure on the auditors to allow them to omit disclosures which would generate adverse criticism.

The team must be aware of this risk and apply sufficient professional scepticism when performing the audit.

(c) **Gray Co**

Familiarity

Gray Co has been a client for seven years therefore a familiarity threat may be created if the same partner has been assigned for that time. The partner may become complacent and lack professional scepticism, possibly failing to challenge the client to the extent they would if it was a new client.

The threat is not significant at this time. Partner rotation will only be required if Gray Co becomes listed but the firm may wish to consider appointing an engagement quality control review partner in the future to ensure the audit is being performed with sufficient professional scepticism.

Self-review

Fox & Steeple provide technical advice on financial reporting as well as tax services. A due diligence engagement has also been requested. These additional services create a self-review threat.

The auditor will be auditing financial statements that have been prepared based on the advice of the firm and may therefore be reluctant to criticise the accounting treatment of certain elements as it would be seen to be criticising their own firm.

The threat may be considered significant depending on the nature of the advice and tax services provided. However, as Gray Co is not listed, the firm can still provide these services with safeguards applied.

Separate teams must be used and each team must have the relevant skills and competence for the service provided. The audit team of Gray Co will require staff with experience in financial reporting matters specific to communications and software solutions e.g. in revenue recognition issues and accounting for internally generated intangible assets.

Assuming management responsibilities/Management threat

The provision of advice may be seen to be acting in the capacity of management if the advice provided is acted on without any consideration of Gray Co's management.

Activities such as authorising transactions, taking responsibility for the preparation and fair presentation of the financial statements, taking responsibility for designing, implementing and maintaining internal controls relevant to financial reporting or determining or changing journal entries, should not be performed without obtaining Gray Co's approval and acknowledgement that they are ultimately responsible.

Tutorial Note: General matters affecting Fox & Steeple

- All three assignments have the same financial year-end, therefore resourcing of each engagement will need to be carefully planned.

- As a listed company, Huggins Co is likely to have the tightest reporting deadline.

- Time budgets will need to be prepared for each assignment to determine manpower requirements and to schedule audit work.

Test your understanding 2

(i) **Goods**

The acceptance of gifts or hospitality, particularly during the inventory count, may be perceived to be a self-interest threat to objectivity. The count should be performed in a neutral way but staff may ignore this in order to ensure they get their 'perk' of the engagement.

From an external perspective, this may be considered to be a bribe for a more relaxed inventory count check.

Inventory counts should be performed with the least disruption possible. Movements in inventory during the count increase the risk of incorrect procedures being performed. If staff are purchasing items during the day this constitutes inventory movement.

The offer should not have been accepted during the physical count and all offers of goods should have been discussed with the audit manager.

The value of the goods in question should be considered. 30% of manufacturer's recommended price amounts to a 70% discount. This is unlikely to be material to the client but may be significant enough to the audit team to be considered more than a 'trivial' gift.

The auditor should also consider whether the offer was an inducement to influence the auditor's judgment.

In general it is advisable to avoid accepting gifts. If it later transpired that there was a problem with the count or the subsequent inventory valuation there would be increased risk of negligence claims (i.e. the audit team were not sufficiently diligent or that they had accepted bribes).

(ii) **Services/hospitality**

Darius Harken has received a substantial benefit from his association with the audit client creating a self-interest threat. Darius may feel indebted to the client because of the gift and therefore overlook issues identified during the audit.

In addition it could be argued that Darius Harken is over-familiar with the chief executive Armando Thyolo. Darius may lack professional scepticism when auditing Aventura.

The value of this gift is likely to be significant and could be perceived to be outside the boundaries of a normal, professional relationship.

Darius Harken should not have accepted the use of the jet without the express permission of the audit engagement partner. It is possible that Darius may have paid for the use of the jet. However, the question of over-familiarity would still be relevant, as he could have used a commercial airline.

The fact that this arrangement only came to light during the audit of certain invoices suggests that Darius was intentionally withholding information about this beneficial transaction. Whilst there is no evidence that he tried to conceal it, a manager should understand his ethical position and concerns should be raised about his conduct.

Darius Harken should be removed from the audit immediately and potentially disciplined.

The requirement to have all gifts approved by a senior member of the audit team should be communicated to all staff to ensure this does not happen again.

All Darius' previous work on the client should be reviewed again before the auditor's report is signed to ensure that appropriate procedures have been carried out and that he has remained objective. Particular attention should be paid to all matters of the audit manager's judgment.

Darius should be asked whether he has used the jet on other occasions and this should be confirmed with Armando.

(iii) **Ex-audit staff employed by client**

As Kirsten was the accountant in charge (AIC), not the audit manager or partner, it is unlikely that a significant lack of objectivity could have impaired the audit opinion for the year ended 31 March 20X4 or for any interim work done in 20X5.

However, her work may have been influenced given that she has developed a personal relationship with Armando Thyolo.

Upon beginning the relationship with Armando, Kirsten should have been immediately removed from the audit engagement. Either the senior management team are responsible for a lack of professional due care when assigning team members, or Kirsten has acted with a lack of professional behaviour by not informing the firm of the relationship.

Kirsten is now a member of staff at Aventura. There is likely to be a strong familiarity threat between her and the current audit team. The audit team may be less sceptical when auditing the client because they trust Kirsten having worked with her in the past.

The audit files for 20X4 and 20X5, in particular the work of Kirsten, should be reviewed again. This should be done by an independent engagement partner.

The members of the audit team assigned to Aventura may need to be rotated in order to reduce the familiarity threat. A team from a different office could be used.

Test your understanding 3

(a) **The importance of confidentiality to the auditor-client relationship**

Confidentiality and security of information is one of the fundamental ethical principles. It applies to all professional accountants.

In particular:

- Confidential information is only disclosed to those entitled to receive it.

- Information obtained in the course of professional work is not used for purposes other than the client's benefit.

- Any decision to override the duty of confidentiality (e.g. if required by a court order) is taken after due consideration and discussion with professional colleagues.

- The duty of confidentiality continues even after an auditor-client engagement ceases.

- An accountant who moves into new employment must distinguish previously gained experience from confidential information acquired from their former employment.

- Prospective accountants must treat any information given by existing accountants in the strictest confidence.

As well as being a fundamental principal of the Code of Ethics, confidentiality is an implied contractual term.

In order to fulfil their duties, auditors require full disclosure of all information they consider necessary. A duty of confidentiality is therefore essential to ensuring that the scope of the audit is not limited as a result of information being withheld.

(b) **Matters to consider**

Rosella has made three requests:

(1) Disclosure of a former co-executive's level of remuneration

(2) Continuing to act as personal adviser

(3) Appointment as auditor and adviser to Blakes Heaven.

(1) Disclosure of remuneration package

In an audit appointment, the auditor owes a duty of confidentiality to the client (i.e. the company not individual shareholders or executives). There is no legal or professional right or duty to disclose client information on an ad hoc basis merely because it is available to the auditor.

It would be a breach of the audit firm's duty of confidentiality to Blake Seven (in acting as auditor) and Brad (in acting as adviser) to disclose the information requested when clearly there is no process of law or public interest involved.

The audit firm could only disclose the information to Rosella with Brad's consent. This is highly unlikely since Brad has refused to provide Rosella with the information directly.

The latest audited financial statements (which are available to Rosella in her capacity as a shareholder) may disclose Brad's remuneration for the previous year (e.g. as chair and/or highest paid executive). Rosella will need to wait for this information to be publicly available.

As a member of the company (i.e. shareholder), Rosella would also be entitled to inspect any relevant documents required to be held at Blake Seven's registered office (e.g. if Brad has a service contract with the company).

In general, the audit firm's working papers are its own property and any request for them (e.g. if Rosella requested a schedule of emoluments, etc.) should be refused.

The request to disclose Brad's remuneration must be declined. However, Rosella may be directed to alternative sources of information, which may be of use.

(2) Continuing as personal adviser

A conflict between the interests of Blake Seven (and its continuing directors) and Rosella (in a personal capacity) is likely to arise (e.g. over the valuation of Rosella's shareholding).

It would be inappropriate for one adviser to act for both parties in certain matters, such as negotiating a share price, without appropriate safeguards.

Valuing Rosella's shareholding and negotiating her profit-related remuneration may appear to threaten the objectivity of the audit of Blake Seven. Rosella may try to exert influence to overstate profits (e.g. over Janus, as her brother and finance director, as well as the auditor).

In particular it may be possible to advise Rosella on personal tax matters.

The firm may continue to act as Rosella's personal adviser subject to appropriate conditions and safeguards being put in place in respect of matters which may materially prejudice either client. For example:

– The agreement of Blake Seven (and the remaining directors)

– Advising one or all clients to seek additional independent advice.

However, given the apparent acrimony between Rosella and her former associates, it seems unlikely that Blake Seven would agree to such an arrangement.

(3) **Appointment as auditor**

A conflict between the interests of Rosella's new company, Blakes Heaven, and Blake Seven is likely to arise as the former has been set up in competition with the latter.

There is nothing improper in having both companies as audit clients if there are appropriate safeguards (e.g. different reporting partners and teams of staff for each audit engagement).

However, even with safeguards, the directors of Blake Seven (the Capellas in particular) may perceive that the involvement of the company's auditor with a competitor (in the capacity of auditor and adviser) could materially prejudice their interests. Also, that the new company has been set up with so similar a name suggests that Rosella may be quite aggressive in targeting Blake Seven's business.

In view of the adversarial relationship between Rosella and Blake Seven it would be prudent to include in their respective engagement letters a clause reserving the right to act for other clients subject to confidential information being kept secure.

The provision of other services (as adviser) could threaten the objectivity of the audit assignment. In particular, it would be inappropriate for the personal adviser to be the reporting partner or otherwise involved in the audit.

The audit appointment could only be accepted with appropriate safeguards (e.g. reporting partner and audit staff not involved in the audit of Blake Seven or the provision of other services). However, even with safeguards, if Rosella's appointments are accepted, Blake Seven may decide not to re-appoint the firm in future.

Test your understanding 4 – UK syllabus only

Weller & Co must ensure that any efforts to increase the firm's revenue do not create any threats to objectivity and independence. Offering an 'extended audit' service to clients such as providing an internal audit service to an audit client creates a self-review threat if the firm uses the internal audit work in the course of a subsequent external audit.

The self-review threat arises because of the possibility that the audit team will use the results of the internal audit service, without appropriately evaluating those results or exercising the same level of professional scepticism as would be exercised when the internal audit work is performed by individuals who are not members of the firm.

Performing a significant part of the client's internal audit activities increases the possibility that firm personnel providing internal audit services will assume a management responsibility. This threat cannot be reduced to an acceptable level.

Audit personnel should not assume a management responsibility when providing internal audit services to an audit client. Management responsibility may include, for example, performing procedures that are part of the internal control and taking responsibility for designing, implementing and maintaining internal control.

Section 5 of the FRC Ethical Standard states that the greatest threats to objectivity created by performing an internal audit service to an audit client are those of self-review and the management threat. It also acknowledges that the range of internal audit services is wide, and may not always be termed as such by the audited entity.

Audit firms are prohibited from undertaking an engagement to provide internal audit services to an audited entity where it is reasonably foreseeable that:

- For the purpose of the audit of the financial statements, the auditor would place significant reliance on the internal audit work performed by the audit firm, or

- For the purposes of the internal audit services, the audit firm would undertake part of the role of management.

Safeguards may be used to reduce the threat to an acceptable level, for example, by ensuring that external audit work and internal audit work are performed by separate teams. In addition, the audit work should be reviewed by a partner who is not involved with the audit.

Where internal audit services are supplied to an audit client, they should be the subject of a separate engagement letter and billing arrangement, and should also be pre-approved by those charged with governance of the audited entity.

Professional responsibilities and liability

Chapter learning objectives

This chapter covers syllabus areas:

- A3 – Laws and regulations

- B2 – Fraud and error

- B3 – Professional liability

Detailed syllabus objectives are provided in the introduction section of the text book.

PER

One of the PER performance objectives (PO1) is ethics and professionalism. The fundamental principles of ethical behaviour mean you should always act in the wider public interest. You need to take into account all relevant information and use professional judgement, your personal values and scepticism to evaluate data and make decisions. You should identify right from wrong and escalate anything of concern. You also need to make sure that your skills, knowledge and behaviour are up-to-date and allow you to be effective in your role. Working through this chapter should help you understand how to demonstrate that objective.

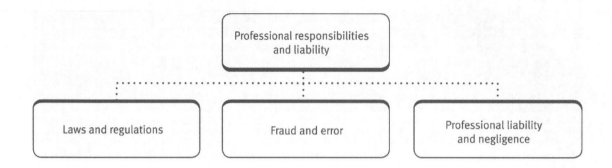

Professional responsibilities and liability

Laws and regulations

Fraud and error

Professional liability and negligence

 Responsibilities in relation to laws and regulations and fraud and error were covered in Audit and Assurance at the Applied Skills level. Negligence was covered in Corporate and Business Law at the Applied Skills level.

Exam focus

Professional issues are usually examined alongside ethical issues but can be examined in their own right. Typical exam questions may ask for respective responsibilities of management and auditors in respect of fraud & error or laws & regulations, or could ask whether an auditor is liable in a given situation.

1 Laws and regulations

Guidance relating to laws and regulations in an audit of financial statements is provided in ISA 250 (Revised) *Consideration of Laws and Regulations in an Audit of Financial Statements.*

Non-compliance with laws and regulations may lead to material misstatement if liabilities for non-compliance are not recorded, contingent liabilities are not disclosed, or if they lead to going concern issues which would require disclosure or affect the basis of preparation of the financial statements.

 Non-compliance – Acts of omission or commission, either intentional or unintentional, committed by the entity, which are contrary to the prevailing laws or regulations. Non-compliance does not include personal misconduct unrelated to the business activities of the entity.
[ISA 250, 12]

Responsibilities of management

It is the responsibility of management, with the oversight of those charged with governance, to ensure that the entity's operations are conducted in accordance with relevant laws and regulations, including those that determine the reported amounts and disclosures in the financial statements. [ISA 250, 3]

> ### Management responsibilities
>
> In order to help prevent and detect non-compliance, management can implement the following policies and procedures:
>
> - Monitoring legal requirements and ensuring that operating procedures are designed to meet these requirements.
>
> - Instituting and operating appropriate systems of internal control.
>
> - Developing, publicising and following a code of conduct.
>
> - Ensuring employees are properly trained and understand the code of conduct.
>
> - Monitoring compliance with the code of conduct and acting appropriately to discipline employees who fail to comply with it.
>
> - Engaging legal advisors to assist in monitoring legal requirements.
>
> - Maintaining a register of significant laws and regulations with which the entity has to comply.
>
> In larger entities, these policies and procedures may be supplemented by assigning appropriate responsibilities to:
>
> - An internal audit function
>
> - An audit committee
>
> - A compliance function.
>
> [ISA 250, A2]

Responsibilities of the auditor

The auditor is responsible for obtaining reasonable assurance that the financial statements taken as a whole, are free from material misstatement, whether due to fraud or error.
[ISA 200 *Overall Objectives of the Independent Auditor and the Conduct of an Audit in Accordance with International Standards on Auditing*, 11a].

Therefore, in conducting an audit of financial statements the auditor must perform audit procedures to help identify non-compliance with laws and regulations that may have a material impact on the financial statements.

The auditor must obtain sufficient, appropriate evidence regarding compliance with:

- Laws and regulations generally recognised to have a **direct effect** on the determination of material amounts and disclosures in the financial statements (e.g. company law, tax law, applicable financial reporting framework). [ISA 250, 6a]

- Other laws and regulations that may have a material impact on the financial statements (e.g. environmental legislation). [6b]

Further discussion of auditor responsibility

IFAC recognises that the auditors have a role in relation to non-compliance with laws and regulations. Auditors plan, perform and evaluate their audit work with the aim of providing reasonable, though not absolute, assurance of detecting any material misstatement in the financial statements which arises from non-compliance with laws or regulations. However, auditors cannot be expected to be experts in all the many different laws and regulations where non-compliance might have such an effect. There is also an unavoidable risk that some material misstatements may not be detected due to the inherent limitations in auditing.

Audit procedures to identify instances of non-compliance

- **Obtaining a general understanding** of the legal and regulatory framework applicable to the entity and the industry, and of how the entity is complying with that framework. [ISA 250, 13]

- **Enquiring of management and those charged with governance** as to whether the entity is in compliance with such laws and regulations. [15a]

- **Inspecting correspondence** with relevant licensing or regulatory authorities. [15b]

- **Remaining alert** to the possibility that other audit procedures applied may bring instances of non-compliance to the auditor's attention. [16]

- **Obtaining written representation** from the directors that they have disclosed to the auditors all those events of which they are aware which involve possible non-compliance, together with the actual or contingent consequences which may arise from such non-compliance. [17]

How to obtain a general understanding

- Use the auditor's existing understanding of the industry.

- Update the auditor's understanding of those laws and regulations that directly determine reported amounts and disclosures in the financial statements.

- Enquire of management as to other laws and regulations that may be expected to have a fundamental effect on the operations of the entity.

- Enquire of management concerning the entity's policies and procedures regarding compliance with laws and regulations.

- Enquire of management regarding the policies or procedures adopted for identifying, evaluating and accounting for litigation claims.

[ISA 250, A11]

Investigations of possible non-compliance

When the auditor becomes aware of information concerning a possible instance of **non-compliance** with laws or regulations, they should:

- Understand the **nature of the act and circumstances** in which it has occurred.

- Obtain further information to **evaluate** the possible effect on the financial statements.

[ISA 250, 19]

Audit procedures when non-compliance is identified

- Enquire of management of the penalties to be imposed.

- Inspect correspondence with the regulatory authority to identify the consequences.

- Inspect board minutes for management's discussion on actions to be taken regarding the non-compliance.

- Enquire of the company's legal department as to the possible impact of the non-compliance.

Communicating and reporting non-compliance

- The auditor should communicate non-compliance with management and those charged with governance, unless prohibited by law. [ISA 250, 23]

- If the auditor believes the non-compliance is intentional and material, the matter should be communicated with those charged with governance. [24]

- If the auditor suspects management or those charged with governance are involved in the non-compliance, the matter should be communicated to the audit committee or supervisory board. [25]

- If the non-compliance has a material effect on the financial statements, a qualified or adverse opinion should be issued. [26]

- The auditor should also consider whether they have any legal, regulatory or ethical responsibility to report non-compliance to third parties (e.g. to a regulatory authority). [29]

Engagement withdrawal

The auditor may consider the need to withdraw from the engagement (i.e. resign as auditor) if:

- management or those charged with governance do not take remedial action that the auditor considers appropriate, or

- the non-compliance raises doubts about the integrity of management or those charged with governance.

Withdrawing from the engagement cannot be a substitute for complying with other responsibilities in relation to reporting non-compliance. Therefore, if there is a responsibility to report the entity, the auditor must do so, they cannot resign to avoid having to make the report.

Ethical requirements may require a predecessor auditor to provide information on compliance with laws and regulations to an incoming auditor.

[ISA 250, A25]

Responding to Non-Compliance with Laws and Regulations

Ethical guidance on the professional accountant's responsibilities when non-compliance with laws and regulations (NOCLAR) is identified or suspected is set out in the Code of Ethics of both the IESBA and ACCA.

The accountancy profession is expected to act in the public interest. This means considering matters that could cause harm to investors, creditors, employees or the general public.

Examples of laws and regulations addressed in the requirements include:

- Fraud, corruption and bribery

- Money laundering, terrorist financing and proceeds of crime

- Securities markets and trading

- Financial services such as banking

- Data protection

- Tax and pension liabilities and payments

- Environmental protection

- Public health and safety.

Requirements do not apply to:

- Matters which are clearly inconsequential

- Personal misconduct unrelated to the business activities of the client.

Reason for the introduction of NOCLAR

NOCLAR was introduced because some of the major accounting scandals have been caused by professional accountants (PAs) being aware of serious issues but not reporting them due to concerns over breaching client confidentiality. This has caused damage to the reputation of the profession.

The new requirements have been brought in to enable PAs to decide how best to act in the public interest when they become aware of, or suspect, NOCLAR.

The PA must find the right balance between complying with the fundamental principle of confidentiality and acting in the public interest.

Objectives of NOCLAR requirements

- To enable PAs to comply with the fundamental ethical principles of integrity and professional behaviour.

- To enable companies to take prompt action to mitigate consequences of NOCLAR as the PA will have alerted them to the issue.

- To enable the PA to take further action as appropriate in the public interest.

Responsibilities of the professional accountant

Obtain an understanding of the matter

- Establish what legal or regulatory obligations are triggered, e.g. required to report, must not tip-off, must not disclose as confidential information.

- Apply knowledge, professional judgment and expertise. The accountant may consult on a confidential basis with others within the firm, a network firm or a professional body, or with legal counsel.

- Discuss the matter with management and those charged with governance. This may help to obtain an understanding of the matter and may prompt management to investigate the matter.

Address the matter

Discuss the matter with management and advise them to take appropriate action such as:

- Rectify, remediate or mitigate the consequences of the non-compliance.

- Deter the commission of non-compliance where it has not yet occurred.

- Disclose the matter to an appropriate authority where required by law or regulation or where considered necessary in the public interest.

- In a group audit, communicate NOCLAR to the group engagement partner or component auditor if not prohibited by law.

Determine what further action is needed

Assess the appropriateness of management's response including whether:

- The response is timely.

- The non-compliance has been adequately investigated.

- Appropriate action has been, or is being, taken to rectify, remediate or mitigate the consequences of non-compliance.

- Action has been or is being taken to deter non-compliance where it has not yet occurred.

- Appropriate steps have been taken to reduce the risk of re-occurrence.

- The non-compliance has been disclosed to an appropriate authority where appropriate.

- Determine whether to take further action in the public interest by applying the third party test – would a reasonable and informed third party conclude that the PA has acted appropriately in the public interest?

The PA should consider whether management integrity is in doubt, e.g. if management is suspected of involvement in the non-compliance, or is aware of the non-compliance but has not reported it to an appropriate authority within a reasonable period.

Further action may include:

- Disclosure of the matter to a regulatory authority even when there is no legal or regulatory requirement to do so. This will depend on the nature and extent of the actual or potential harm to the stakeholders.

  A PA may make disclosure to an appropriate authority without reporting to management in exceptional circumstances such as the risk of an imminent breach that would cause substantial harm.

- Withdrawal from the engagement and the professional relationship where permitted by law or regulation.

  A predecessor PA should provide, on request, the proposed PA with all relevant facts about the non-compliance as this may influence their acceptance decision.

Professional accountants performing non-audit services

If the PA is performing a non-audit service for an audit client of the firm, the matter should be communicated within the firm.

If the PA is performing a non-audit service to a client that is not an audit client, the matter should be communicated to the client's external auditor unless this would be contrary to law or regulation.

Senior Professional Accountants in Business (PAIB)

These are directors, officer and senior employees with the ability to make decisions about the control of the entity's resources.

These people should set the right tone at the top and establish a framework to prevent NOCLAR.

They should fulfil their professional responsibilities by:

- Obtaining an understanding of matters of actual or suspected non-compliance

- Discussing such matters with an immediate superior or next higher level of authority, as appropriate

- Communicating matters with those charged with governance

- Rectifying or mitigating consequences of NOCLAR

- Deterring NOCLAR

- Determining whether to notify the external auditor.

They must also apply the third party test to determine whether further action is required.

Further action may include informing the parent company if applicable, disclosing the NOCLAR to an appropriate authority and resigning from employment.

Other Professional Accountants in Business should:

- Escalate the matter to the next higher level of authority.

- Use internal whistleblowing procedures.

2 Fraud and error

Guidance regarding responsibility to consider fraud and error in an audit of financial statements is provided in ISA 240 *The Auditor's Responsibilities Relating to Fraud in an Audit of Financial Statements*.

 Definitions

Misstatement

A difference between the reported amount, classification, presentation, or disclosure of a financial statement item and the amount, classification, presentation, or disclosure that is required for the item to be in accordance with the applicable financial reporting framework. Misstatements can arise from fraud or error.
[ISA 450 *Evaluation of Misstatements Identified During the Audit*, 4a]

The distinguishing factor between fraud and error is whether the underlying action that results in the misstatement of the financial statements is intentional or unintentional.

Fraud

Fraud is an intentional act involving the use of deception to obtain an unjust or illegal advantage. It may be perpetrated by one or more individuals among management, employees or third parties.
[ISA 240, 12]

There are two categories of fraud that are of concern to auditors:

- Fraudulent financial reporting, and

- Misappropriation of assets.

[ISA 240, 3]

Misappropriation of assets means theft e.g. the creation of dummy suppliers or ghost employees to divert company funds into a personal bank account.

Fraudulent financial reporting in particular may be viewed as more prevalent nowadays for the following reasons:

- Increased pressure on companies to publish improved results to shareholders and the markets.

- Greater emphasis on performance related remuneration to comply with corporate governance best practice incentivises directors to inflate profits to achieve bigger bonuses.

- When trading conditions are difficult as has been seen over recent years, additional finance may be required. Finance providers are likely to want to rely on the financial statements when making lending decisions. Directors may make the financial statements look more attractive in order to secure the finance.

- If existing borrowings are in place with covenants attached, directors may manipulate the financial statements to ensure the covenants are met.

Error

An error can be defined as an unintentional misstatement in financial statements, including the omission of amounts or disclosures, such as the following:

- A mistake in gathering and processing data from which financial statements are prepared.

- An incorrect accounting estimate arising from oversight or a misinterpretation of facts.

- A mistake in the application of accounting principles relating to measurement, recognition, classification, presentation or disclosure.

[ISA 450, A1]

Errors are normally corrected by clients when they are identified. If a material error has been identified but has not been corrected, it will require the audit opinion to be modified.

Management responsibilities

The primary responsibility for the prevention and detection of fraud rests with both those charged with governance of an entity and with management.

Management should:

- Place a strong emphasis on fraud prevention and error reduction.

- Reduce opportunities for fraud to take place.

- Ensure the likelihood of detection and punishment for fraud is sufficient to act as a deterrent.

- Ensure controls are in place to provide reasonable assurance that errors will be identified.

- Foster, communicate and demonstrate a culture of honesty & ethical behaviour.

- Consider potential for override of controls or manipulation of financial reporting.

- Implement and operate adequate accounting and internal control systems.

[ISA 240, 4]

Auditor responsibilities

- Obtain reasonable assurance that the financial statements are free from material misstatement, whether caused by fraud or error. [ISA 240, 5]

- Apply professional scepticism and remain alert to the possibility that fraud could take place. [8]

- Consider the potential for management override of controls and recognise that audit procedures that are effective for detecting error may not be effective for detecting fraud. [8]

This can be achieved by performing the following procedures:

- Discuss the susceptibility of the client's financial statements to material misstatement due to fraud with the engagement team. [16]

- Enquire of management regarding their assessment of fraud risk, the procedures they conduct and whether they are aware of any actual or suspected instances of fraud. [19]

- Enquire of the internal audit function to establish if they are aware of any actual or suspected instances of fraud. [20]

- Enquire of those charged with governance with regard to how they exercise oversight of management processes for identifying and responding to the risks of fraud and the controls established by management to mitigate these risks. [22]

- Consideration of relationships identified during analytical procedures. [23]

Due to the inherent limitations of an audit, there is an unavoidable risk that some material misstatements may not be detected, even though the audit is properly planned and performed in accordance with ISAs. This risk is greater in relation to misstatement due to fraud, rather than error, because of the potentially sophisticated nature of organised criminal schemes. [5]

Responses to an assessed risk of fraud

- Assign responsibility to personnel with appropriate knowledge and skill. [ISA 240, 30a]

- Evaluate whether the accounting policies of the entity indicate fraudulent financial reporting. [30b]

- Use unpredictable procedures to obtain evidence. [30c]

Procedures

- Review journal entries made to identify manipulation of figures recorded or unauthorised journal adjustments:

  - Enquire of those involved in financial reporting about unusual activity relating to adjustments.

  - Select journal entries and adjustments made at the end of the reporting period.

  - Consider the need to test journal entries throughout the period. [33]

- Review management estimates for evidence of bias:

  - Evaluate the reasonableness of judgments and whether they indicate management bias.

  - Perform a retrospective review of management judgments reflected in the prior year.
    [33b]

- Review transactions outside the normal course of business, or transactions which appear unusual and assess whether they are indicative of fraudulent financial reporting. [33c]

- Obtain written representation from management and those charged with governance that they:

  - acknowledge their responsibility for internal controls to prevent and detect fraud.

  - have disclosed to the auditor the results of management's fraud risk assessment.

  - have disclosed to the auditor any known or suspected frauds.

  - have disclosed to the auditor any allegations of fraud affecting the entity's financial statements.
    [40]

Reporting of fraud and error

- If the auditor identifies a fraud they must communicate the matter on a timely basis to the appropriate level of management (i.e. those with the primary responsibility for prevention and detection of fraud). [ISA 240, 41]

- If the suspected fraud involves management the auditor must communicate the matter to those charged with governance. [42]

- If the auditor has doubts about the integrity of those charged with governance they should seek legal advice regarding an appropriate course of action. [A65]

- In addition to these responsibilities the auditor must also consider whether they have a responsibility to report the occurrence of a suspicion to a party outside the entity. Whilst the auditor does have an ethical duty to maintain confidentiality, it is likely that any legal responsibility will take precedence. In these circumstances it is advisable to seek legal advice. [44]

- If the fraud has a material impact on the financial statements the audit opinion will be modified. When the opinion is modified, the auditor will explain why it has been modified and this will make the shareholders aware of the fraud.

Engagement withdrawal

In exceptional circumstances the auditor may consider it necessary to withdraw from the engagement. This may be if fraud is being committed by management or those charged with governance and therefore casts doubt over the integrity of the client and reliability of representations from management.

The auditor should seek legal advice first as withdrawal may also require a report to be made to the shareholders, regulators or others. [ISA 240, A57]

Current issue: The future of fraud and the audit

Fraud is a controversial area for auditors, and the extent of auditor responsibility for the prevention and detection of fraud continues to be debated by the profession, governments and other stakeholders.

The Kingston Cotton Mill case (1896) emphasised that the reader of the auditor's report should have a realistic viewpoint of what the auditor's role should actually be.

The judge in the case set the benchmark for auditor responsibility when he said "An auditor is not bound to be a detective, or... to approach his work with suspicion, or with a foregone conclusion that there is something wrong. He is a watchdog, not a bloodhound."

Auditors are currently responsible for detecting material misstatements whether caused by fraud or error. However, misstatements due to fraud are, by their very nature, extremely difficult to detect. Auditors are not trained as, nor expected to be, forensic investigators and even the most experienced auditor may have failed to detect a material misstatement caused by fraud. Auditors do have a recognised responsibility for considering fraud when conducting an audit of financial statements, but the primary responsibility for fraud and error continues to rest with management, and those charged with governance.

However, the auditor's responsibility with respect to fraud could change. Many users would like to see auditors' responsibility for fraud extended. Auditors could be given responsibility for performing audit procedures specifically to detect fraud, possibly in those areas that are more susceptible to fraud. In order to achieve this, auditors would have to be given the training necessary to identify fraud. In addition, the extent of auditor's responsibilities would have to be defined. It would not be realistic to expect the auditor to detect all fraud. Some frauds (especially where collusion is involved) are almost impossible to identify.

The audit profession is dynamic and subject to much debate at the current time. It is not possible to know what the future holds, but perhaps auditors will be required to move towards the role of a bloodhound in the future.

Not absolute assurance

An auditor **cannot provide absolute assurance** over the accuracy of the financial statements because of such factors as:

- Nature of financial reporting:
  - The use of judgment by management.
  - Subjectivity of items in the financial statements.
- Nature of audit procedures:
  - Management may not provide complete information to the auditor.
  - Fraud may be sophisticated and well concealed.
  - The auditor does not have legal powers to conduct an official investigation into wrongdoing.
- The need to conduct the audit within a reasonable time and at a reasonable cost, therefore all items cannot be tested.

[IAS 200 *Overall Objectives of the Independent Auditor and the Conduct of an Audit in Accordance with International Standards on Auditing*, A47]

3 Legal liability

Liability to the client and liability to third parties

Liability to the client

- Liability to the client arises from contract law. The company has a contract with the auditor, the engagement letter, and hence can sue the auditor for breach of contract if the auditor delivers a negligently prepared report.

- When carrying out their duties the auditor must exercise due care and skill.

- Generally, if auditors can show that they have complied with professional standards including auditing standards and ethical requirements, they will not have been negligent.

Liability to third parties

A third party (i.e. a person who has no contractual relationship with the auditor) may be able to sue the auditor for damages, i.e. a financial award.

In the **tort of negligence**, the plaintiff (i.e. the third party) must prove that:

(1)   The defendant (i.e. the auditor) owes a duty of care, and

(2)   The defendant has breached the appropriate standard of care as discussed above, and

(3)   The plaintiff has suffered loss as a direct result of the defendant's breach.

The critical matter in most negligence scenarios is whether a duty of care is owed in the first place.

When is a duty of care owed?

A duty of care exists when there is a special relationship between the parties, i.e. where the auditors knew, or ought to have known, that the audited financial statements would be made available to, and would be relied upon by, a particular person (or class of person).

The injured party must therefore prove:

- The auditor knew, or should have known, that the injured party was likely to rely on the financial statements.

- The injured party has sufficient 'proximity', i.e. belongs to a class likely to rely on the financial statements.

- The injured party did in fact so rely.

- The injured party would have acted differently if the financial statements had shown a different picture.

Has the auditor exercised due professional care?

The auditor will have exercised due professional care if they have:

- Complied with the most up-to-date professional standards and ethical requirements.

- Complied with the terms and conditions of appointment as set out in the letter of engagement and as implied by law.

- Employed competent staff who are adequately trained and supervised in carrying out instructions.

Has the injured party suffered a loss?

This is normally a matter of fact. For example, if X relies on the audited financial statements of Company A and pays $5 million to buy the company, but it soon becomes clear that the company is worth only $1 million, then a loss of $4 million has been incurred.

Criminal vs. civil liability

Auditors' liability can be categorised under the following headings:

- Civil or criminal liability arising under legislation

- Liability arising from negligence.

Civil liability

Auditors may be liable in the following circumstances:

- To third parties suffering loss as a result of relying on a negligently prepared auditor's report.

- Under insolvency legislation to creditors – auditors must be careful not to be implicated in causing losses to creditors alongside directors.

- Under tax legislation – particularly where the auditor is aware of tax frauds perpetrated by the client.

- Under financial services legislation to investors.

- Under stock exchange legislation and/or rules.

The only possible penalty for a civil offence is payment of damages.

Criminal liability

Criminal liability can arise in the following circumstances:

- Acting as auditor when ineligible.

- Fraud, such as: theft, bribery and other forms of corruption, falsifying accounting records, and knowingly or recklessly including misleading matters in an auditor's report.

- Insider dealing.

- Knowingly or recklessly making false statements in connection with the issue of securities.

Penalties for criminal liability include fines and/or imprisonment.

In addition to the various civil and criminal liabilities the professional bodies that regulate accountants and auditors have various sanctions, such as warnings, fines, reprimands, severe reprimands and exclusion from membership for misconduct by members. Conviction of a criminal offence involving financial misconduct is normally sufficient to warrant exclusion from membership of a professional body.

Case Study: Bannerman

The Bannerman case (Royal Bank of Scotland (RBS) v Bannerman Johnstone Maclay (2002))

RBS provided overdraft facilities to APC Limited and Bannerman were APC's auditors. The relevant facility letters between RBS and APC contained a clause requiring APC to send RBS, each year, a copy of the annual audited financial statements. In 1998 APC was put into receivership owing money to RBS. RBS claimed that, due to a fraud, APC's financial statements for the previous years had misstated the financial position of APC and Bannerman had been negligent in not detecting the fraud. RBS contended that it had continued to provide the overdraft facilities in reliance on Bannerman's unmodified opinions.

Bannerman applied to the court for an order striking out the claim on the grounds that, even if all the facts alleged by RBS were true, the claim could not succeed in law because Bannerman owed no duty of care to RBS. The judge held that the facts pleaded by RBS were sufficient in law to give rise to a duty of care and so the case could proceed to trial. The judge held that, although there was no direct contact between Bannerman and RBS, knowledge gained by Bannerman in the course of their ordinary audit work was sufficient, in the absence of any disclaimer, to create a duty of care owed by Bannerman to RBS. In order to consider APC's ability to continue as a going concern, Bannerman would have reviewed the facilities letters and so would have become aware that the audited financial statements would be provided to RBS for the purpose of RBS making lending decisions. Having acquired this knowledge, Bannerman could have disclaimed liability to RBS but did not do so. The absence of such a disclaimer was an important circumstance supporting the finding of a duty of care.

Case Study: Caparo

The Caparo case (Caparo Industries v Dickman (1990))

Caparo Industries took over Fidelity plc in 1984 and alleged that it increased its shareholding on the basis of Fidelity's accounts, audited by Touche Ross. Caparo sued Touche Ross for alleged negligence in the audit, claiming that the stated £1.3 million profit for the year to 31 March 1984 should have been reported as a loss of £460,000. It was held in this case that the auditors owed no duty of care in carrying out the audit to individual shareholders or to members of the public who relied on the accounts in deciding to buy shares in the company. The House of Lords looked at the purpose of statutory accounts. They concluded that such accounts, on which the auditor must report, are published with the principal purpose of providing shareholders as a class with information relevant to exercising their proprietary interests in the company. They are not published to assist individuals (whether existing shareholders or not) to speculate with a view to profits.

Case Study: ADT Ltd v BDO Binder Hamlyn

ADT Ltd v BDO Binder Hamlyn (1995)

BDO BH were the joint auditors of the Britannia Security Systems Group. Before the 1989 audit was finished, ADT were considering bidding for Britannia, so an ADT representative met the BDO BH audit partner and asked him to confirm that the audited accounts gave a true and fair view and that he had learnt nothing subsequently which cast doubt on the accounts. The partner said that BDO BH stood by the accounts and there was nothing else that ADT should be told. ADT then bought Britannia for £105 million, but it was found to be worth only £40 million.

It was held that BDO BH owed ADT a duty of care when the partner made his statements, and the accounts had been negligently audited, so ADT were awarded £65 million plus interest. The shortfall in BH's insurance cover was £34 million. The partners were individually liable for that amount. BH appealed, and ADT agreed an out-of-court settlement.

Case Study: Lloyd Cheyham v Littlejohn de Paula

Lloyd Cheyham v Littlejohn de Paula (1985)

Littlejohn de Paula successfully defended themselves against a negligence claim in this case by showing:

- That they had followed the standard expected of the normal auditor, i.e. performed audit work in accordance with auditing standards.

- That their working papers were good enough to show consideration of the problems raised by the plaintiff and reasonable decisions made after consideration.

- That the plaintiff had not made all reasonable enquiries one could expect when purchasing a company. For example a review of the business was not undertaken upon investigating the purchase but only after purchase.

The judge, therefore, held that far too much reliance was placed on the accounts by the plaintiff and he awarded costs against the plaintiff to the defendant.

Restricting auditors' liability

Audit firms may take the following steps to minimise their exposure to negligence claims:

- **R**estrict the use of the auditor's report and assurance reports to their specific, intended purpose.

- **E**ngagement letter clause to limit liability to third parties.

- **S**creening potential audit clients to accept only clients where the risk can be managed.

- **T**ake specialist legal advice where appropriate.

- **R**espective responsibilities and duties of directors and auditors communicated in the engagement letter and auditor's report to minimise misunderstandings.

- **I**nsurance – professional indemnity insurance (PII).

- **C**arry out high quality audit work.

- **T**ake on LLP status.

- **S**et a liability cap with clients.

The impact of limiting audit liability

Some commentators have argued that limiting audit liability is contrary to the public interest, since auditors will be less motivated to do quality work if they know that they will not have to pay for their mistakes.

Other commentators say that this ignores the professional nature of the audit discipline. People choose to be audit partners because they want to do a high quality job for themselves and for society.

Methods of limiting audit liability

Liability caps

This could be a fixed amount (as in Germany), or a multiple of the audit fee. A possible adverse effect of the latter would be either to reduce the quality of work done, or to reduce the fee, as the lower the fee, the lower the liability.

In the UK such agreements were illegal until the Companies Act 2006, which now permits liability limitation agreements between auditors and companies, subject to shareholders' approval. The Act does not specify what sort of limit can be agreed, so a fixed cap, or a multiple of fees, or any other type, are all now possible.

Modification of the 'joint and several liability' principle.

Auditors are jointly and severally liable with directors where negligence claims are made, either under legislation, or under case law. This means that directors and auditors are held responsible together for the issue of negligently prepared and audited financial statements. If, say, the auditors and directors share the blame for falsifying records (i.e. the auditors did not detect it), the auditor may bear all of the costs if the directors have no resources to pay. The objective is to protect the plaintiff and maximise their chances of recovery of losses.

An associated problem is the fact that all partners and directors are responsible for the misconduct of other partners and directors in audit firms, regardless of whether they were directly involved in a particular audit. In the US, and now the UK, this problem is partly dealt with by limited liability partnerships.

Compulsory insurance for directors

If directors are partly to blame then they should be responsible for their share of the costs. If auditors must hold compulsory insurance in case of any claims it could be argued that directors should also hold insurance.

 Insurance for accountancy firms

One of the obligations of PAs in public practice is to ensure that, if their negligence has caused loss to a client, they have an insurance policy to pay any damages awarded.

- **Professional indemnity insurance (PII)** is insurance against claims made by clients and third parties arising from work that the PA has carried out.

- **Fidelity guarantee insurance (FGI)** is insurance against any liability arising through acts of fraud or dishonesty by any partner or employee in respect of money or goods held in trust by the accountancy firm.

The expectation gap

The **expectation gap** is the gap between what the public believe that auditors do (or ought to do) and what they actually do.

This expectation gap can be categorised into:

- **Standards and performance gap** – where users believe auditing standards to be more comprehensive than they actually are and therefore the auditor does not perform the level of work the user expects.

- **Liability gap** – where users do not understand to whom the auditor is legally responsible.

Bridging the expectation gap

Recent developments and proposals include:

- Educating users to reduce the standards gap e.g.

    - Auditor's reports now include greater detail of the auditor's responsibilities and key audit matters.

    - Written representation letters require management to sign to acknowledge their responsibilities in respect of the financial statements.

- Increasing communication between the auditor and those charged with governance regarding their respective responsibilities.

- Increasing the scope of the work of the auditor e.g. to require greater detection of fraud and error.

 Examples of the expectation gap

- Users believe that auditors are responsible for preventing and detecting fraud and error, while ISAs require auditors to have only a reasonable expectation of detecting material fraud and error.

- Users believe that they can sue the auditor if a company fails, while auditors maintain that it is the directors' responsibility to run their business as a going concern. It is not the auditor's function to protect individual shareholders if they make a poor investment decision.

- Users believe the audit firm will report externally all 'wrong doing' e.g. NOCLAR. The auditor will only report externally where there is a duty to do so.

- Users believe the audit firm will highlight poor performance by management. The objective of the auditor is to express an opinion on the truth and fairness of the financial statements. If poor decisions have been made, but the financial effects of these decisions have been properly reflected in the financial statements, there is nothing to mention in the auditor's report.

Disclaimer statements

Reaction to the Bannerman decision

In the Bannerman case the judge commented that, if the auditors had inserted a disclaimer statement in their report, then they would have had no legal liability to RBS who was suing them.

Following this case, the ICAEW recommended additional wording to be routinely included in all auditor's reports by ICAEW members:

> 'This report is made solely to the company's members as a body. Our audit work has been carried out so that we might state to the company's members those matters we are required to state to them in an auditor's report and for no other purpose. We do not accept responsibility to anyone other than the company and the company's members as a body, for our audit work or for the opinions we have formed.'

The ACCA's view is that standard disclaimer clauses should be discouraged since they could have the effect of devaluing the auditor's report. Disclaimers of responsibility should only be made in appropriate, defined circumstances (e.g. where the auditor knows that a bank may rely on a company's financial statements). The ACCA does not believe that, where an audit is properly carried out, such clauses are always necessary to protect auditors' interests.

In practice, the difference of opinion between the ICAEW and the ACCA may not be so great. If an ACCA auditor is not aware that a bank is going to place reliance on an auditor's report (so no disclaimer is given), then it seems likely under Caparo or Bannerman that no duty of care would be owed to the bank in any event.

Settlements out of court

Legal cases may be settled out of court due to negotiation between the plaintiff and the defendant.

Benefits

- Cost saving (i.e. lower fees).
- Time saving.
- Less risk of damage to reputation.

Drawbacks

- Does not address the importance of the practitioner's legal responsibilities.
- May be due to pressure from insurers, who are willing to risk a court settlement.
- Insurance premiums may still rise.

Test your understanding 1

You are an audit manager in Ebony & Co, a firm of Chartered Certified Accountants. Your specific responsibilities include planning the allocation of professional staff to audit assignments. The following matters have arisen in connection with the audits of three client companies:

(a) The finance director of Almond Co, a private limited company, has requested that only certain staff are to be included on the audit team to prevent unnecessary disruption to Almond Co's accounting department during the conduct of the audit. In particular, that Xavier be assigned as accountant in charge (AIC) of the audit and that no new trainees be included in the audit team. Xavier has been the AIC for this client for the last two years.   **(5 marks)**

(b) Alex was one of the audit trainees assigned to the audit of Phantom Co, a private limited company, for the year ended 31 March 20X4. Alex resigned from Ebony & Co with effect from 30 November 20X4 to pursue a career in medicine. Kurt, another AIC, has just told you that on the day Alex left he told Kurt that he had ticked schedules of audit work as having been performed when he had not actually carried out the tests.   **(5 marks)**

(c) During the recent interim audit of Magenta Co, a private limited company, the AIC, Jamie, has discovered a material error in the prior year financial statements for the year ended 31 December 20X4. These financial statements had disclosed an unquantifiable contingent liability for pending litigation. However, the matter was settled out of court for $4.5 million on 14 March 20X5. The auditor's report on the financial statements for the year ended 31 December 20X4 was signed on 19 March 20X5. Jamie believes that Magenta Co's management is not aware of the error and has not drawn it to their attention.   **(5 marks)**

Required:

Comment on the ethical, quality control and other professional issues raised by each of the above matters and their implications, if any, for Ebony & Co's staff planning.

Note: The mark allocation is shown against each of the three issues.

(Total: 15 marks)

Test your understanding 2

The audited financial statements of Lambley Trading were approved by the shareholders at the AGM on 3 June 20X5. On 7 June 20X5 the managing director of Lambley Trading discovered a petty cash fraud by the cashier. Investigation of this fraud has revealed that it has been carried out over a period of a year. It involved the cashier making out, signing and claiming petty cash expenses which were charged to motor expenses. No receipts were attached to the petty cash vouchers. The managing director signs all cheques for reimbursing the petty cash float. Lambley Trading has revenue of $2 million and the profit before tax is $150,000. The cashier prepared the draft financial statements for audit.

Your firm was responsible for the audit of Lambley Trading. No audit work was carried out on petty cash as the risk of material misstatement was considered low given the low level of petty cash expenditure.

Required:

(a) Briefly state the auditor's responsibilities for detecting fraud and error in financial statements.

(b) Consider whether your firm is negligent if the fraud amounted to $5,000.

(c) Consider whether your firm is negligent if the fraud amounted to $20,000. **(10 marks)**

Test your understanding 3

The audit of directors' remuneration at Colwick Enterprises, a limited company, has confirmed that the managing director's salary is $450,000, and that he is the highest paid director. However, a junior member of the audit team asked you to look at some purchase invoices paid by the company. Your investigations have revealed that the managing director has had work amounting to $200,000 carried out on his home, which has been paid by Colwick Enterprises. The managing director has authorised payment of these invoices and there is no record of authorisation of this work in the board minutes. The managing director has refused to include the $200,000 in his remuneration for the year, and to change the financial statements. The managing director says if you insist on modifying the audit opinion due to this matter, he will get a new audit firm to audit the current year's financial statements. The company's profit before tax for the year is $91 million.

Required:

Assuming the managing director owns 60% of the issued shares of Colwick Enterprises and refuses to amend the financial statements:

(a) Consider whether the undisclosed remuneration is a material item in the financial statements.

(b) Describe the matters you will consider and the action you will take:

- to avoid being replaced as auditor, and

- if you are replaced as auditor.

(c) Describe the matters you will consider and the action you will take to avoid being replaced as auditor, assuming Colwick Enterprises is a listed company with an audit committee, and the managing director owns less than 1% of the issued shares. **(10 marks)**

Test your understanding 4

You are the auditor of Promise Co. The finance director has asked for a meeting with you. She recently discovered that the purchase ledger manager has diverted $50,000 of company funds into his own bank account. The finance director has asked for an explanation as to why you did not highlight this issue during your recent audit. The profit for the year was $17.5 million.

Required:

Explain the matters you should discuss with the finance director at the meeting. **(6 marks)**

Test your understanding 5

You are the auditor of a chain of restaurants. You have read a newspaper report that guests at a wedding have fallen ill after eating at one of your client's restaurants.

Required:

In relation to this report, describe the audit procedures you should perform in respect of compliance with laws and regulations. **(5 marks)**

Test your understanding 6

The directors of Jubilee Co have asked your firm to provide a detailed report at the end of the audit listing all the deficiencies in the internal control system. They are unhappy that during the year discounts had been given to customers who did not qualify for them. They have expressed dissatisfaction with your audit firm as this control deficiency was not reported to them by your firm.

Required:

Draft points to include in your reply to Jubilee Co. **(5 marks)**

Test your understanding 7

Set out the arguments for and against allowing auditors to agree a contractual liability cap with clients. **(6 marks)**

4 Laws and regulations – summary

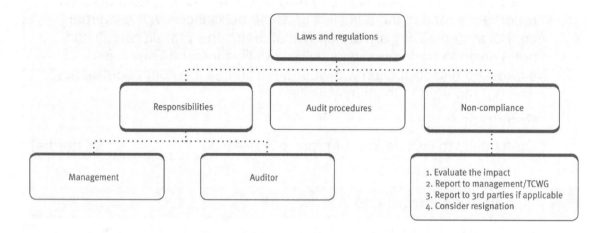

5   Fraud and error – summary

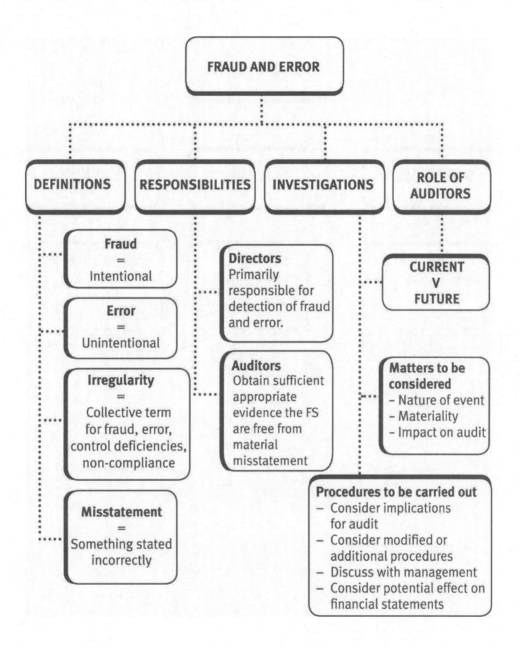

6 Legal liability – summary

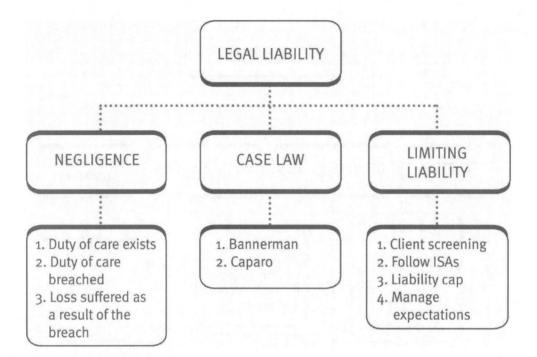

LEGAL LIABILITY

NEGLIGENCE

1. Duty of care exists
2. Duty of care breached
3. Loss suffered as a result of the breach

CASE LAW

1. Bannerman
2. Caparo

LIMITING LIABILITY

1. Client screening
2. Follow ISAs
3. Liability cap
4. Manage expectations

Test your understanding answers

 Test your understanding 1

The majority of marks will be awarded for application of knowledge to the scenario. Copying information from the scenario without analysis will not score well. Therefore, in your answer refer to the situations, companies and individuals described in the question.

(a) **Almond Co**

- There are many factors to be taken into account when allocating staff to an assignment, for example:
  - the number of staff and levels of technical expertise required.
  - logistics of time and place.
  - the needs of staff (e.g. for study leave, holiday).
  - what is in the client's best interest (e.g. an expeditious audit).

- A client should not dictate the audit team. If the finance director's requests are based solely on the premise that to have staff other than as requested would cause disruption then he should be assured that anyone assigned to the audit will be:
  - technically competent to perform the tasks delegated to them.
  - adequately briefed and supervised.
  - mindful of the need not to cause unnecessary disruption.

- Ebony & Co may have other (more complex) assignments on which Xavier (and other staff previously involved in the audit of Almond Co) could be better utilised.

- To reassign Xavier to the job may be to deny him other on-the-job training necessary for his personal development. For example, he may be ready to assume a more demanding supervisory role with another client, or he may wish to expand the client base on which he works.

- To keep Xavier with Almond Co for a third year may also increase the risk of familiarity with the client's staff. Xavier may be too trusting of the client and lack professional scepticism.

- If it is usual to assign new trainees to Almond Co then the finance director should be advised that to assign a higher grade of staff is likely to increase the audit fee as their charge out rates will be higher.

Conclusion

The finance director's requests should be granted only if:

(1)   they are in the interests of Almond Co's shareholders (primarily).

(2)   they meet the needs of Ebony & Co's staff.

(3)   Almond Co agrees to the appropriate audit fee.

(b)   **Phantom Co**

- Ebony & Co's quality control procedures should be such that:
    - the work delegated to Alex was within his capability.
    - Alex was supervised in its execution.
    - the work performed by Alex was reviewed by appropriate personnel (i.e. someone more senior than Alex).

- Alex's working papers for the audit of Phantom Co should be reviewed again to confirm that there is evidence of his work having been properly directed, supervised and reviewed. If there is nothing which appears untoward it should be discussed with Alex's supervisor on the engagement whether Alex's confession to Kurt could have been a joke.

- As Alex has already left not only the firm, but the profession, it may not seem worth the effort taking any disciplinary action against him (e.g. reporting the alleged misconduct to ACCA). However, ACCA's disciplinary committee would investigate such a matter and take appropriate action.

- It is likely that Ebony & Co will have given Alex's new employer a reference. This should be reviewed in the light of any evidence which may cast doubt on Alex's work ethics.

- As there are doubts about the integrity of Alex, his work should be reviewed again, to determine the risk that the conclusions drawn on his work may be unsubstantiated in terms of the relevance, reliability and sufficiency of audit evidence.

- The review process should have identified the problem. If the reviewer did not detect an evident problem this would indicate the review process was not effective and the reviewer should be (re)trained as necessary.

- The work undertaken by Alex for audit clients other than Phantom Co should also be subject to scrutiny.

Conclusion

As Kurt is already aware of the potential problem, it may be appropriate that he be assigned as AIC to audits on which Alex undertook audit work, as he will be alert to any ramifications. It is possible that Ebony & Co should not want to make the situation known to its staff generally.

(c) **Magenta Co**

- It appears that the subsequent events review was inadequate in that the impact of an adjusting event (the out-of-court settlement) was not considered.

- The financial statements for the year ended 31 December 20X4 contained a material error in that they disclosed a contingent liability (of unspecified amount) when a provision should have been made.

- The reasons for the error/oversight should be ascertained. For example:

  - Who was responsible for signing off the subsequent events review?

  - When was the review completed?

  - For what reason, if any, was it not extended to the date of signing the auditor's report?

  - On what date was the written representation letter signed?

  - Did the written representation letter cover the outcome of pending litigation?

- The error has implications for the firm's quality control procedures. For example:

  - Was the AIC adequately directed and supervised in the completion of the subsequent events review?

  - Was the work of the AIC adequately reviewed, to notice that it was not extended up until the date on which the auditor's report was signed?

- Ebony & Co may need to review and improve on its procedures for the audit of provisions, contingent liabilities and subsequent events.

- If the AIC (or other staff) involved in the prior year audit of Magenta Co was not as thorough as they should have been with respect to the subsequent events review, then other audit clients may be similarly affected.

- The auditor has a duty of care to draw the error/oversight to Magenta Co's attention. This would be an admission of fault for which Ebony & Co should be liable if Magenta Co decided to take action against the firm.

- If Ebony & Co remains silent and in the hope the error is unnoticed, there is the risk that Magenta Co will find out anyway.

- As the matter is material, it warrants a prior period adjustment (IAS® 8 *Accounting Policies, Changes in Accounting Estimates and Errors*). If this is not made, the financial statements will be materially misstated with respect to the current year and comparatives because the expense of the out-of-court settlement should be attributed to the prior period and not the current year's profit or loss.

- The most obvious implication for the current year audit of Magenta Co is that a more thorough subsequent event review will be required than the previous year. This may have a consequent effect on the time/fee/staff budgets of Magenta Co for the year ended 31 December 20X5.

- As the matter is material, it needs to be brought to the attention of Magenta Co's management, so that a prior year adjustment is made. If an adjustment is not made a modified opinion (qualified – 'except for') will be required.

Conclusion

The staffing of the final audit of Magenta Co should be reviewed and perhaps a more experienced person assigned to the subsequent event review than in the prior year. The assignments allocated to the staff responsible for the oversight in Magenta Co's prior period should be reviewed and their competence/capability re-assessed.

Test your understanding 2

There are two main aspects of auditing examined in this question:

- The role of, and potential liability of, the auditor in connection with the detection and prevention of fraud

- The concept of materiality.

Note: Misstatements of > 5% profit before tax and > ½ % revenue are considered material.

Lambley Trading

(a) Auditors should design their audit procedures to have a reasonable expectation of detecting material fraud and error in the financial statements.

An auditor would generally be considered to be at fault if he fails to detect material fraud and error. However, the auditor may not be liable if the fraud is difficult to detect because the fraud had been concealed.

A claim for negligence against the auditor for not detecting immaterial fraud or error would be unsuccessful, except in the circumstances described below.

An auditor may be negligent if he:

- Finds an immaterial fraud while carrying out his normal procedures and does not communicate it to the company's management. However, he may not be negligent if the evidence to support a suspected fraud is weak.

- Carries out audit procedures on immaterial items, of which the company's management is aware, and these procedures are not carried out satisfactorily, so failing to detect an immaterial fraud. For instance, there may be a teeming and lading fraud, and the auditor may check receipts from sales are correctly recorded in the cash book and sales ledger, but fail to check that the cash from these sales is banked promptly.

- Carries out audit procedures on immaterial items at the specific request of the company's management, and the auditor failed to detect an immaterial fraud due to negligent work. The management would have a good case to claim damages for negligence against the auditor.

(b) A fraud of $5,000 is 3.3% of the company's profit before tax, so it is immaterial.

As the auditor has carried out no work in this area, and is not responsible for detecting immaterial fraud, it is likely that he or she is not negligent.

It could be argued that the other audit procedures should have detected an apparent irregularity, such as analytical procedures. This might have indicated an increase in motor expenses compared with the previous year and budget, or the auditor could have looked at petty cash expenditure, which would show an increase compared with the previous year.

It could also be argued that the auditor should have looked at the absolute level of petty cash expenditure in order to decide whether to carry out work on the petty cash system. These arguments against the auditor are relatively weak, and it is unlikely that a claim for negligence would be successful. However, not detecting the fraud is likely to lead to a deterioration of the client's confidence in the auditor.

(c) A fraud of $20,000 is 13.3% of the company's profit before tax, which is material. It appears that the auditor may have been negligent in not carrying out any audit work on petty cash.

The auditor should design audit procedures so as to have a reasonable expectation of detecting material fraud or error. As no work was performed on petty cash there is no chance of detecting the fraud.

As a minimum, the auditor should have looked at the level of petty cash expenditure, comparing it with the previous year and the budget. This should have highlighted the increase in expenditure and led to the auditor carrying out further investigations.

As this is a petty cash fraud, it could be difficult to detect, but the cashier writing out and signing the petty cash vouchers, with no receipt attached, should have led the auditor to suspect the fraud.

It could be argued that the company has some responsibility for allowing the fraud to take place, as there was a significant deficiency in the system of internal control (i.e. the cashier recorded and made petty cash payments, and appeared to be able to authorise petty cash vouchers).

A more senior employee (e.g. the managing director) should have checked the cashier's work. Also, the managing director would have signed cheques which reimburse the petty cash, and he or she should have been aware that these had increased and investigated the reasons for the increase.

Test your understanding 3

Colwick Enterprises

(a) The sum of $200,000 is immaterial as it represents only 0.22% of profit before tax. Normally, a material item in terms of profit before tax is a misstatement which exceeds 5% of the profit before tax.

However, in terms of the director's remuneration, the $200,000 is 44% of the managing director's annual salary of $450,000.

Directors' remuneration is an important item in the financial statements, both as far as legal requirements are concerned, and to the users of the financial statements, therefore is material by nature.

The company is proposing that the financial statements should show only 69% of the managing director's remuneration, so the understatement is material.

(b) If the managing director refused to change the financial statements, the audit opinion should be qualified and the basis for qualified opinion should state his total emoluments are $650,000.

However, it seems probable that he will try to dismiss the audit firm before they issue their auditor's report on the financial statements. In order to change the auditor, he must:

– Find another auditor who is prepared to accept appointment as auditor, and

– Call a general meeting to vote on the change of auditor.

The auditor has the right to make representations to the shareholders, which can either be sent to the shareholders before the meeting, and/or make the representations at the meeting when the replacement of the auditor is proposed.

Although these representations are likely to have little effect on the change of auditor (as the managing director owns 60% of the shares, and only a majority vote is required to change the auditor), it would alert the other shareholders to the action of the managing director and concealment of information.

As a further point, provided the new auditors are a member of the ACCA, or one of the recognised bodies, the Code of Ethics requires the new auditor to contact the outgoing auditor asking if there are any matters to be brought to their attention to enable them to decide whether or not they are prepared to accept the audit appointment. The outgoing auditor should reply to their letter promptly, saying that the managing director has had $200,000 of benefits-in-kind, which he refuses to allow to be disclosed in the financial statements.

It has been explained to the managing director that the auditor's opinion will be qualified if these emoluments are not disclosed and this is the reason why he is proposing replacement of the auditor. If the proposed new auditors have the expected amount of integrity, they should discuss this point with the managing director, and point out that they will have to qualify the opinion if the benefits of $200,000 are not included in his remuneration in the financial statements.

If the new auditors take over the appointment and give an unmodified opinion, the outgoing auditor should take legal advice. The action taken would include:

–	Disclosing information about the director's remuneration to the new auditor's professional body, and the fact that the auditor's opinion has not been modified.

–	Disclosing the benefit to the tax authorities (as it may not have been subject to income tax).

(c)	If the managing director owned less than 1% of the issued shares, the auditor's position would be much stronger than in part (b) above. If the managing director refuses to increase the remuneration in the draft accounts, the matter should be referred to the audit committee.

If he still refuses to change the remuneration, a meeting with the members should be arranged with the audit committee chair. The auditor would explain that the opinion will be qualified unless the remuneration was increased to $650,000.

However if the audit committee believes the financial statements should not be changed, the audit opinion will need to be modified.

If, at this stage, the directors decide to replace the audit firm, they will have to call a general meeting for this purpose. Representations should be made in writing to the shareholders, and/or circulated at the general meeting.

As Colwick Enterprises is a listed company, this information is likely to be picked up by the press and financial institutions, and result in adverse publicity for the company. It is likely to make shareholders suspicious of the integrity of the managing director and the other directors.

In addition, it is likely that either the company or the managing director is committing an offence by not disclosing this benefit to the tax authorities.

Test your understanding 4

Notes for meeting with finance director

- Engagement letter:
    - Refer to any specific points regarding work in this area.
    - Refer to section on auditor's and directors' responsibilities.
    - Client signed the engagement letter agreeing to the terms.
- Responsibility for detection of fraud is primarily the responsibility of management.
- Implementation of an internal control system is the responsibility of management.
- The auditor's role is to obtain reasonable assurance that financial statements are free from material fraud and error.
- The amounts in question are not material, only 0.3% PBT.
- Ascertain how the finance director discovered the fraud.
- Ascertain how the amounts of diverted funds were quantified.
- Discuss whether there might be further unidentified sums.

Test your understanding 5

The auditor should consider whether there has been a breach of laws or regulations, for example laws and regulations over health and safety, food hygiene, product use by dates etc.

Procedures include:

- Obtain a general understanding of the relevant legal and regulatory framework by:
    - Researching the industry on the internet
    - Considering laws and regulations applicable to other clients in the same industry
    - Enquiring of management.

- Discuss with the directors and other appropriate management whether there have been any instances of non-compliance.

- Inspect correspondence with the local authority and hygiene inspectors regarding instances of non-compliance.

- Evaluate the financial impact of the non-compliance, for example, possible penalties, cost of compensation claims, cost of remedial action, and impact on the value of the brand name.

- Obtain written representation from management that they have provided the auditor with all information in relation to the non-compliance and its impact.

- Consult experts in the area if considered necessary.

Test your understanding 6

Auditors must determine the most effective approach to each area of the financial statements. This may involve a combination of tests of controls and substantive procedures, or substantive procedures only.

Where the auditors choose to test the internal control systems of the company, they must design their work to have a reasonable expectation of detecting any deficiencies which would be likely to result in a material misstatement in the financial statements.

The area of discounts may have been one which did not involve testing of the internal controls as analytical procedures are likely to be effective.

Even if the controls in this area have been tested, the discounts given to customers may have been recorded accurately in the financial statements. In this case, no material misstatement has occurred.

Jubilee Co must be reminded that the control deficiencies included in the report to management is simply a by-product of the audit. It is not intended to be a comprehensive list of all possible deficiencies. Should Jubilee Co require a more comprehensive review, then this could be undertaken as a separate assurance assignment.

Test your understanding 7

For

- Avoids firms exiting from the statutory audit market and thus maintaining choice and competition.

- Clearly quantifies the extent of auditors' liability to the public.

- Reduces the risk of auditors being used as scapegoats.

- Ensures that directors bear their extent of liability.

Against

- Auditors may not be as accountable or be seen to be as accountable.

- May reduce the perceived value of an audit if risk to auditors is reduced.

- Setting a cap may be a difficult and contentious issue to agree with the client.

- Shareholders or other parties to whom the auditors owe a duty of care may find themselves inadequately protected.

Quality control

Chapter learning objectives

This chapter covers syllabus areas:

- C1 – Quality control (firm-wide)

Detailed syllabus objectives are provided in the introduction section of the text book.

PER

One of the PER performance objectives (PO1) is ethics and professionalism. The fundamental principles of ethical behaviour mean you should always act in the wider public interest. You need to take into account all relevant information and use professional judgement, your personal values and scepticism to evaluate data and make decisions. You should identify right from wrong and escalate anything of concern. You also need to make sure that your skills, knowledge and behaviour are up-to-date and allow you to be effective in your role. Working through this chapter should help you understand how to demonstrate that objective.

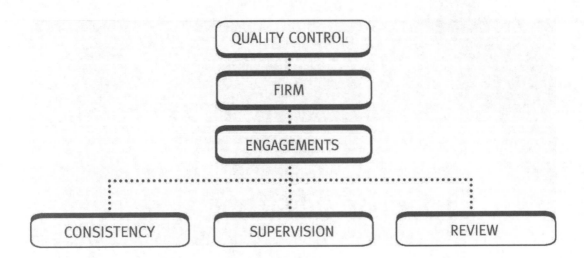

 Quality control relevant to audit engagements was covered in Audit and Assurance at the Applied Skills level. At the Strategic Professional level, you will be expected to evaluate whether quality control procedures have been appropriately applied within the firm.

Exam focus

A common requirement in the exam is to critically evaluate the audit work already performed on an engagement and identify if the audit has been carried out to the required standard of quality. If the firm does not perform work to a high quality it increases the risk of issuing an inappropriate report which could damage the reputation of the firm and the profession.

1 The principles and purpose of quality control

There are two professional standards that set out the responsibilities of auditors regarding quality control:

- ISQC 1 *Quality Control for Firms that Perform Audits and Reviews of Financial Statements, and Other Assurance and Related Services Engagements* which sets out an accountancy firm's responsibilities with regard to their systems of quality control for audits, reviews and other assurance engagements.

- ISA 220 *Quality Control for an Audit of Financial Statements* which applies to audit engagements only. It establishes the responsibilities of the auditor (mainly the engagement partner and engagement quality reviewer) regarding their quality control procedures during audits.

Most of the requirements of ISA 220 are covered by ISQC 1. This chapter therefore focuses on ISQC 1 requirements.

The purpose of assurance services is to enhance the intended user's confidence in the subject matter they are using to make decisions. In order for there to be confidence in the assurance process, engagements must be performed to a satisfactory quality. Failure to do so would not only mean a loss of confidence in the profession as a whole but could lead to professional negligence claims against the assurance provider.

If a professional negligence claim is made, and the firm has followed suitable quality control procedures, they should be able to defend the claim.

Therefore firms must:

- Perform work that complies with professional standards and regulatory and legal requirements.

- Issue reports that are appropriate in the circumstances.

[ISQC 1, 11]

2 ISQC 1

ISQC 1 identifies six key principles:

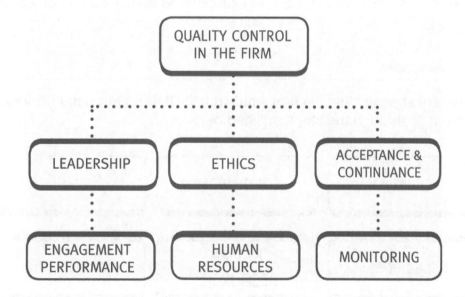

- **Leadership:** Strong and ethical leadership demonstrated by the managing partners.

- **Ethics:** Firms comply with ethical requirements such as the Code of Ethics.

- **Acceptance and continuance:** Only suitable clients and engagements are accepted and retained.

- **Human resources:** A firm and its employees have the necessary knowledge, technical competence, and experience.

- **Engagement performance:** Engagements are performed in an effective manner.

- **Monitoring:** Evaluating the quality control procedures to ensure they are effective.

[ISQC 1, 16]

Ethical considerations and arrangements for the acceptance and continuance of client relationships and specific engagements are covered in chapters 3 and 6 respectively. In this chapter we will focus on the remaining four key principles.

Leadership

Firms must establish policies and procedures to **promote an internal culture that recognises the importance of quality** in performing engagements. This requires the firm's management team (i.e. managing partners) to:

- Establish policies and procedures to address performance evaluation, compensation and promotion to demonstrate commitment to quality.

- Ensure commercial consideration does not override quality.

- Ensure resources are sufficient to support the quality control procedures.

[ISQC 1, A5]

Human resources

The standard stresses that if a firm wants quality flowing through all levels of staff it must go through the steps outlined below.

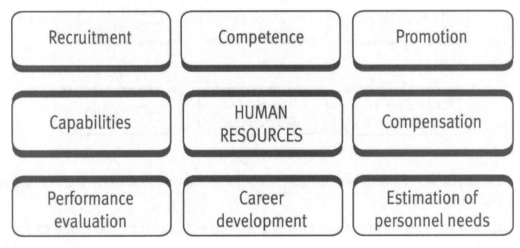

[ISQC 1, A24]

A firm must have policies and procedures in place to ensure an appropriate engagement partner is assigned to an engagement, i.e. one who has the competence, capability and time to perform the role.

The engagement partner should then ensure the right people are allocated to the engagement team, i.e. staff with the relevant knowledge, experience, and training.

Engagement performance

Firms must design policies and procedures to ensure engagements are performed to a satisfactory standard. Policies and procedures should cover:

- Matters relevant to promoting **consistency** in the quality of engagements.

- **Supervision** responsibilities.

- **Review** responsibilities.

[ISQC 1, 32]

Consistency in the quality of engagement performance

Firms promote consistency through their policies and procedures. This is often accomplished through written manuals, software tools and standardised documentation. Particular matters that can be addressed include:

- How engagement teams are briefed to obtain an understanding of the engagement and their objectives.

- Processes for complying with engagement standards.

- Processes of engagement supervision, training and coaching.

- Methods of reviewing work, judgments and reports issued.

- Documentation of work performed and the timing and extent of reviews.

- Processes to keep policies and procedures current.

[ISQC 1, A32]

Supervision responsibilities

Supervision responsibilities include:

- Tracking the progress of the engagement.

- Considering the competence and capabilities of the team members.

- Addressing significant matters that arise during the engagement.

- Identifying difficult or contentious matters for consultation. Areas requiring consultation (both internally and externally) should be organised in advance to facilitate timely, and cost effective, completion of the engagement.

[ISQC 1, A34]

Review responsibilities

Work of less experienced team members should be reviewed by more experienced team members to identify whether:

- The work has been performed in accordance with professional standards.

- Significant matters have been raised for further consideration.

- Appropriate consultations have taken place and resulting conclusions have been documented.

- The work performed supports the conclusions reached and is appropriately documented.

- The evidence obtained is sufficient and appropriate to support the report.

- The objectives of the engagement procedures have been achieved.

[ISQC 1, A35]

Engagement quality control review

An engagement quality control review (EQCR) provides an objective evaluation of the significant judgments made by the engagement team. This may also be referred to as a pre-issuance review or 'Hot' review.

Listed entities and other high risk clients should be subject to an EQCR. [ISQC 1, 35]

High risk clients include those which are in the public interest, those with unusual circumstances and risks, and those where laws or regulations require an EQCR. [ISQC 1, A41]

The EQCR should include:

- Discussion of significant matters with the engagement partner.

- Review of the financial statements and the proposed report.

- Evaluation of conclusions reached in formulating the report and consideration of whether the proposed report is appropriate.

- Review of selected engagement documentation relating to significant judgments the engagement team made and the conclusions reached.

[ISQC 1, 37]

For listed entities, the EQCR should also consider:

- The engagement team's evaluation of the firm's independence.

- Whether appropriate consultation has taken place on matters involving differences of opinion and the conclusions of those consultations.

- Whether documentation selected for review reflects work performed in relation to significant judgments and supports the conclusions reached.

[ISQC 1, 38]

When evaluating significant judgments of the engagement team, the EQCR should consider:

– Significant risks and responses to those risks

– Judgments with respect to materiality and significant risks

– The significance of uncorrected misstatements

– Matters to be communicated to management and those charged with governance, and where applicable, other parties such as regulatory bodies.

[ISQC 1, A45]

Eligibility criteria

The engagement quality control reviewer:

● should have the technical qualifications to perform the role, including the necessary experience and authority, and

● should be objective. To be objective the reviewer should not be selected by the engagement partner and should not participate in the engagement.

[ISQC 1, 39]

Monitoring

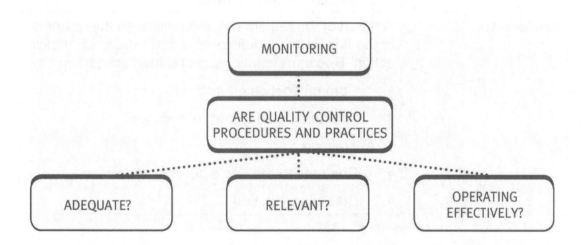

Quality control policies alone do not ensure good quality work. They must be implemented effectively. Therefore the firm must evaluate:

● Adherence to professional standards and regulatory/legal requirements.

● Whether quality controls have been implemented on a day-to-day basis.

● Whether the firm's quality control policies and procedures are effective so that reports issued by the firm are appropriate in the circumstances.

[ISQC 1, A64]

Firms should carry out post-issuance or 'cold' reviews to ensure that quality control procedures are adequate, relevant, and are operating effectively.

	Post-issuance (Cold) review
Purpose...	To assess whether the firm's policies and procedures were implemented during an engagement and to identify any deficiencies therein.
When...	After an engagement has been completed.
Which files...	A selection of completed engagements.
Who by...	A dedicated compliance or quality department/a qualified external consultant/an independent partner.
What considered...	Working papers should demonstrate that: • Sufficient appropriate evidence has been obtained • All matters were resolved before issuing the auditor's report. All working papers should be: • On file • Completed • Signed as completed • Evidenced as reviewed.
Outcomes...	A report of the results will be provided to the partners of the firm flagging deficiencies that require corrective action. Recommendations will be made including: • Communication of findings • Additional quality control reviews • Training • Changes to the firm's policies and procedures • Disciplinary action.

Summary of pre and post-issuance reviews

	Pre-issuance (Hot) review	Post-issuance (Cold) review
Purpose	To enhance the quality of assurance work.	Monitoring – to identify any deficiencies in the firm's processes.
When	Before the auditor's report is issued.	After the auditor's report has been issued.
Which files	<ul><li>Listed clients</li><li>Public interest engagements</li><li>Engagements where there are particular risks</li><li>Each partner should have some of their engagements reviewed.</li></ul>	A selection of completed engagements.
Who by	An independent partner of suitable experience and authority.	A dedicated compliance or quality department/a qualified external consultant/an independent partner.
What considered	Processes underpinning judgments made.	Review of all working papers on an audit file.
Specifically	Processes underpinning judgments about:<ul><li>Significant risks and responses to them</li><li>Matters requiring consultation</li><li>Materiality</li><li>Independence</li><li>Conclusions</li><li>Misstatements</li><li>The audit opinion</li><li>Matters to be communicated to management and those charged with governance.</li></ul>	To ensure that all working papers are:<ul><li>On file</li><li>Complete</li><li>Signed as completed</li><li>Evidenced as reviewed</li><li>The work undertaken is sufficient and has been documented appropriately.</li></ul>

Outcomes...	A reduction in audit risk, i.e. the risk that the auditor expresses an inappropriate audit opinion when the financial statements are materially misstated.	Identify corrective action that should be taken. Recommendations will be made including: • Communication of findings • Additional quality control reviews • Training • Changes to the firm's policies and procedures • Disciplinary action.

3 Documentation

In addition to the main elements of quality control identified in the previous sections, ISA 220 *Quality Control for an Audit of Financial Statements* also requires auditors to document certain matters:

- Issues with respect to ethical requirements and how they were resolved.

- Conclusions on compliance with independence requirements.

- Conclusions reached regarding the acceptance and continuance of engagements.

- The nature, scope and conclusions resulting from consultations undertaken during the course of the audit.

[ISA 220, 24]

During completion of the audit the engagement quality reviewer has to document:

- That the procedures required by the firm's engagement quality review procedures have been performed.

- That the engagement quality review has been completed (on or before the date of the auditor's report).

- That the reviewer is not aware of any unresolved matters that would cause the reviewer to believe that the significant judgments of the team were not appropriate.

[ISA 220, 25]

KAPLAN PUBLISHING

Audit quality monitoring

In the UK, monitoring visits are carried out by the national regulatory body. During 2016/17, 81% of audits were assessed as good or only requiring limited improvements compared with 77% in the prior year.

The five most common areas of concern were:

- Fair value and value in use measurements including impairment testing and property valuations

- Revenue recognition

- Audit committee communication

- Auditor's reports inaccuracies

- Independence and ethics.

Current issue: IAASB Exposure Drafts on Quality Management

Proposed ISA 220 (Revised) Quality Management of an Audit of Financial Statement

ED-220 is one of three proposed quality management exposure drafts issued for consultation by the IAASB. ED-220 covers quality management at the engagement level. The new approach improves the scalability of the standards and is intended to be applied by firms of all sizes and circumstances.

The IAASB aims to address public interest concerns by:

- Encouraging proactive management of quality at the engagement level

- Emphasising the importance of the exercise of professional scepticism

- Enhancing the documentation of the auditor's judgments

- Keeping ISA 220 fit for purpose in a wide range of circumstances and in a complex environment, and

- Reinforcing the need for robust communications during the audit.

In support of these goals, the IAASB agreed to:

- Highlight the importance of the public interest role of audits, and improve the emphasis on the importance of the appropriate application of professional judgment and exercise of professional scepticism.

- Clarify the role and responsibilities of the engagement partner, particularly the required involvement of the engagement partner throughout the audit, and retain the emphasis on the engagement partner's responsibility for managing and achieving quality at the engagement level.

- Modernise ISA 220 for an evolving environment, including changes in audit delivery models and the use of technology.

- Clarify the relationship between ED-220 and the ISQMs, including additional clarification of the engagement partner's and engagement team's interaction with the firm, and the engagement team's, ability to depend on the firm's quality management policies or procedures.

To meet these goals some of the main changes proposed by ED 220 are:

- Highlighting that the public interest is served by consistent performance of quality audit engagements.

- New material on the importance of the use of professional scepticism and professional judgment.

- Changes to the definition of an audit team to recognise that individuals involved in the audit engagement are not necessarily engaged or employed by the audit firm. Nevertheless, their work needs to be appropriately directed, supervised and reviewed.

- Highlighting the growing use of technology in audits. Requirements in the Resources section have been enhanced to cover technology and intellectual resources as well as human resources.

- Clarifying the role and responsibilities of the engagement partner for managing and achieving quality on audits. This includes:

  - taking action to create an environment that emphasises the firm's culture and expected behaviour of engagement team members.

  - a requirement to stand back to determine whether his or her involvement has been sufficient to provide a basis for taking overall responsibility.

  - taking responsibility for the nature, timing and extent of direction, supervision and review of the work performed.

- Moving the requirement to perform an engagement quality review to a new, separate standard, ED-ISQM 2 (covered below).

Proposed International Standard on Quality Management 1, Quality Management for Firms that Perform Audits or Reviews of Financial Statements, or Other Assurance or Related Services Engagements (formerly ISQC 1)

In light of the changing environment and public interest issues, a new approach to quality control at the firm level is needed that emphasises the responsibility of firm leadership for proactively managing quality, while at the same time being scalable to deal with differences in the size of firms and nature of the services they provide. As a result, a new approach for ISQC 1, the quality management approach, has been proposed.

The new approach is to focus firms' attention on risks that may have an impact on engagement quality.

The new approach also requires the firm to:

- Transition from policies and procedures that address standalone elements (currently required by ISQC 1), to an integrated approach that reflects upon the system as a whole.

- Customise the design, implementation and operation of its system of quality management based on the nature and circumstances of the firm and the engagements it performs.

The benefits of a quality management approach are:

- Improved robustness and effectiveness of activities undertaken by the firm to address engagement quality. A tailored system of quality management may also result in improved utilisation of firm resources.

- Facilitating a proactive response by the firm to changing circumstances and proactively managing or mitigating risks, and promoting continual improvement and responsiveness. This new approach will also aid in keeping the standard fit for purpose and adaptable to a changing environment.

- Increased emphasis on monitoring the system as a whole and timely and effective remediation, to promote ongoing improvement of the system.

- Improved integration of the components of the system, thereby promoting an ongoing process of improvement.

ISQC 1 set out six components of a firm's quality control system, ED-ISQM 1 retains or adapts these and includes two more:

- **Governance and leadership** (adapted from 'leadership responsibilities for quality within the firm')

  Establishes the environment in which the system of quality management operates.

  Addresses the firm's culture, decision-making process, actions, organisational structure and leadership.

  Requires that the firm's leadership demonstrate a commitment to quality through their actions and behaviours and establish the expected behaviour of personnel within the firm.

- **The firm's risk assessment process** (new)

  The firm's risk assessment process consists of:

  (a) Establishing quality objectives that, when achieved by the firm, collectively provide the firm with reasonable assurance that the objectives are achieved.

  (b) Identifying and assessing risks to the achievement of the firm's quality objectives (referred to as quality risks).

  (c) Designing and implementing responses to address the assessed quality risks.

- **Relevant ethical requirements**

  The firm must fulfil its responsibilities in accordance with relevant ethical requirements.

- **Acceptance and continuance of client relationships and specific engagements**

  The firm shall establish quality objectives that address the acceptance and continuance of client relationships and specific engagements that are appropriate in the circumstances.

- **Engagement performance**

  The firm shall establish the following quality objectives that address the performance of quality engagements:

  (a) Personnel understand and fulfil their responsibilities in connection with the engagement, including, as applicable:

  (i) The engagement partner's overall responsibility for managing and achieving quality on the engagement and for being sufficiently and appropriately involved throughout the engagement.

  (ii) The appropriate direction and supervision of the engagement team and review of the work performed.

(b) Engagement teams exercise appropriate professional judgment and, when applicable to the type of engagement, professional scepticism, in planning and performing engagements such that conclusions reached are appropriate.

(c) The engagement documentation is appropriately assembled and retained.

- **Resources** (adapted from 'human resources')

    The firm shall establish quality objectives that address appropriately obtaining, developing, using, maintaining, allocating and assigning resources, including human resources, technological resources, and intellectual resources, in a timely manner to enable the design, implementation and operation of the system of quality management.

- **Information and communication** (new)

    The firm shall establish quality objectives that address obtaining, generating or using information regarding the system of quality management, and communicating information within the firm and to external parties on a timely basis.

- **Monitoring and remediation process** (adapted from 'monitoring')

    The monitoring and remediation process involves:

    (a) Designing and performing monitoring activities and evaluating the findings from such activities, the results of external inspections and other relevant information to determine whether deficiencies exist.

    (b) Investigating the root cause(s) of the identified deficiencies and evaluating the severity and pervasiveness of the identified deficiencies.

    (c) Remediating the identified deficiencies.

The eight components in ED-ISQM 1 are intended to be highly integrated. For example, resources and information and communication are essential aspects that enable the operation of each of the other components of the system of quality management. The integration of the components means that the system of quality management does not operate in a linear manner.

Proposed International Standard on Quality Management 2, Engagement Quality Reviews

Currently, the requirements for engagement quality control reviews are contained within ISA 220 and ISQC 1.

ED-ISQM 2 proposes to move these requirements to a separate standard to create the following benefits:

- Emphasises the importance of the engagement quality review.

- Facilitates enhancement of the robustness of the requirements.

- More clearly differentiates the responsibilities of the firm and the EQCR.

- Increases the scalability of ISQM 1 for situations where firms have no engagements for which an EQCR is required.

Requirements and application material have been added to address:

- The eligibility of the individual(s) within the firm responsible for the appointment of engagement quality reviewers with regard to competence, authority and objectivity.

- The eligibility of individuals to assist the engagement quality reviewer in performing the engagement quality review.

- The engagement quality reviewer taking responsibility for the performance of the engagement quality review, including that the work of individuals assisting in the review is appropriate.

- Limitations on the eligibility of an individual to be appointed as engagement quality reviewer for an engagement for which the individual previously served as the engagement partner.

- The need for the engagement quality review to be performed at appropriate points in time during the engagement to facilitate the resolution of issues in a timely manner.

- The need for the documentation of the engagement quality review to be filed with the engagement documentation, and for the documentation to be sufficient to enable an experienced practitioner with no prior connection to the engagement to understand the nature, timing and extent of the engagement quality review procedures performed.

ED-ISQM 2 is designed to operate as part of the firm's system of quality management along with ED-220 and ED-ISQM 1.

FRC Audit Quality Thematic Reviews

Thematic reviews are inspections performed by the FRC which look at specific aspects of the audit process.

Engagement Quality Control Reviews (EQCR)

One tenth of the audits reviewed identified weaknesses in the audit work that the EQCR did not identify which could directly impact audit quality.

Principal findings

- Some EQCRs did not have sufficient specialist experience, limiting their ability to evaluate key judgments specific to the industry.

- The need to be objective is not always adhered to. For example, on one audit the EQCR was to become the audit partner following the audit and had attended audit committee meetings as an observer. In several audits the name of the EQCR was included in the tender document and could therefore have been contacted by the audit committee which would threaten their objectivity.

- In several audits:
    - there was insufficient evidence that the EQCR had been performed.
    - the EQCR had been performed too late to provide meaningful input.
    - the EQCR had not identified deficiencies in the work performed by the audit team that should have been identified and raised by the EQCR.

The FRC has recommended that audit firms evaluate the effectiveness of the EQCR to prevent these weaknesses recurring. When ensuring the EQCR is effective firms must consider:

- The eligibility of the person to perform the EQCR taking into consideration the qualifications and experience of the reviewer.

- Objectivity of the EQCR throughout the whole audit, not just at the start of the audit.

- The EQCR should be performed in a timely and effective manner to ensure there is sufficient time to resolve issues and perform more audit work if necessary.

- There must be evidence of the EQCR.

In order to ensure effectiveness of the EQCR, firms should:

- Complete checklists confirming completion of procedures required by standards.

- Copies of financial statements and reports to the audit committee should be annotated by the EQCR and kept as evidence of review.

- Key audit working papers should be signed off by the EQCR to indicate that they have read them.

- EQCR notes should be kept as evidence.

- Audit file notes of significant matters discussed with the audit team and how they were resolved should be kept as evidence.

- The time spent by the EQCR on the audit should be recorded.

- Firms should ensure the ECQR has sufficient industry experience.

- The EQCR should be required to re-confirm their objectivity at the completion stage to ensure any issues arising during the audit have been appropriately dealt with.

Firms' Audit Quality Control Procedures and Other Audit Quality Initiatives

26 audits from the six largest audit firms were reviewed during 2016/17 with a focus on leadership responsibilities for quality control within the firm, human resources and engagement performance.

Key findings

Leadership

- All firms have audit quality policies and procedures in place.

- All firms have resources at a leadership and management level dedicated to audit quality.

Review of work by more senior members

- All firms have policies where the audit work is reviewed by someone more senior.

- However, 31% of the audits reviewed required more than limited improvement as the quality control procedures were not sufficiently robust.

Inclusion of specialists and experts in the audit team

- Specialists were included in audit teams for all audits reviewed, mainly in the areas of taxation, valuations and IT.

- Where references were made to the specialists' work in the auditor's report some were not described accurately.

Consultation on accounting or audit matters

- Audit teams documented consultations clearly and in line with methodology requirements.

Evaluation of the overall presentation of the financial statements

- All firms have a technical review process to help ensure the quality of the financial statements being audited.

- One firm included a review of the audit file as part of the technical review.

Use of service delivery centres

- Five firms used service delivery centres (SDCs) for the completion of certain elements of audit work.

- Four of these firms stipulated the nature of the audit work that was permitted to be performed by the SDC.

- One firm placed the onus on the audit team to evaluate if the SDC staff had the skills and competence to complete the work assigned.

- Audit firms should consider how audit quality can be maintained or improved as the trend for outsourcing audit work increases.

Real time quality reviews of audit work in progress

- Five firms have implemented a real time independent quality review on a sample of audits.

- One firm performs an independent review of audit work for all audits.

Compliance monitoring

- All firms conducted post-issuance reviews.

- Two firms had post-issuance reviews to provide feedback and coaching to audit teams.

Good practices observed

- Half of the firms have dedicated boards or committees tasked with overseeing, maintaining and continuously improving audit quality.

- One firm has established an audit quality forum where audit staff discuss audit quality improvements.

- Audits with a higher level of partner or director had a greater likelihood of achieving a high quality outcome prior to issuing the auditor's report.

- There is a consultation culture embedded in the firms with a willingness to improve audit quality.

- Having a technical reviewer who considers additional information as well as the financial statements increases the likelihood of potential material undisclosed matters being identified by the technical reviewer.

- Two firms perform periodic pre-issuance reviews of each partner and manager at least once during the year.

All firms are recommended to consider these good practices and implement them where appropriate.

Future activity

The IAASB intends to incorporate a quality management (QMA) approach to strengthen and improve the management of risks to quality. ISQC 1 will be revised to incorporate the principles of the QMA at the firm level. ISA 220 will be revised to incorporate the principles of the QMA at the engagement level. The current standards are no longer deemed sufficient to support audit firms in today's environment.

 Good quality monitoring

Monitoring should be performed on an ongoing, cyclical basis, including an inspection of at least one completed engagement for each engagement partner. The responsibility for this monitoring process should be assigned to a partner and those performing the inspections should not have had any involvement in the engagements under review.

The monitoring process goes beyond the simple enforcement of policies and procedures. It has to consider:

- How the firm responds to new developments in professional standards and regulatory and legal requirements.

- How the firm ensures compliance with independence rules by all its partners and staff. (Usually achieved through the use of independence or 'fit and proper' forms, which should be checked for completeness).

- How the firm ensures all partners and staff comply with continuing professional development requirements. (Often achieved by controlling course bookings centrally, or by maintaining training logs).

- How the firm ensures that appropriate decisions are made about the acceptance of new appointments or the continuance of client relationships. (Should be covered as part of the independent review of assignments).

Arrangements then need to be made for follow up where breaches of policy or ineffective procedures are revealed.

Applying ISQC 1 proportionately with the size and nature of a firm

The IAASB allows proportionate application of the requirements of ISQC 1 for smaller firms.

Firms need only comply with those requirements that are relevant to the services provided.

Firms can exercise appropriate judgment in implementing a system of quality control.

Firms can draw on external resources to meet some of the requirements.

ISQC 1 does not suggest a specific approach to implementation in order to allow smaller firms the flexibility to apply the provisions proportionately.

Smaller firms may have less formal processes, procedures and communication than larger firms.

Smaller firms can use advisory services provided by other firms, professional and regulatory bodies and commercial organisations that provide quality control services.

Monitoring of quality control procedures must still be performed by smaller firms. These may be performed by individuals who are responsible for the design and implementation of the policies and procedures, or who may be involved with the quality control review.

The firm can also choose a qualified external person to carry out inspections.

The existence of an audit regulator inspection program is not a substitute for the firm's own monitoring program.

ISQC 1 requires inspection of at least one completed engagement for each engagement partner on a cyclical basis. This must not be conducted by personnel involved in performing the engagement. Smaller firms may make arrangements with other smaller firms to perform inspections of each other's files.

IAASB: A Framework for Audit Quality

The objectives of the Framework of Audit Quality include:

- Raising awareness of the key elements of audit quality.

- Encouraging key stakeholders to explore ways to improve audit quality.

- Facilitating greater dialogue between key stakeholders on the topic.

The IAASB expects that the Framework will generate discussion, and positive actions to achieve a continuous improvement to audit quality.

The IAASB believes that such a Framework is in the public interest as it will:

- Encourage firms and professional accountancy organisations to reflect on how to improve audit quality and better communicate information about audit quality.

- Raise the level of awareness and understanding among stakeholders of the elements of audit quality.

- Enable stakeholders to recognise factors which require priority to enhance audit quality.

- Assist standard setting, both nationally and internationally.

- Facilitate dialogue between the IAASB and key stakeholders.

- Stimulate academic research.

- Assist auditing students to understand the fundamentals of the profession.

A quality audit is likely to have been achieved by an engagement team that:

- Has exhibited appropriate values, ethics and attitudes.

- Was sufficiently knowledgeable, skilled and experienced and had sufficient time allocated.

- Applied a rigorous audit process and audit quality control procedures compliant with law, regulation and applicable standards.

- Provided useful and timely reports.

- Interacted appropriately with relevant stakeholders.

The Framework contains the following elements:

(1) **Inputs**

The values, ethics and attitudes of auditors.

(2) **Process**

The rigor of the audit process and quality control procedures that impact audit quality. The firm's audit methodology should evolve with changes in professional standards. Whilst methodologies enable an efficient and effective audit to take place, there is a risk that insufficient emphasis will be given to tailoring the audit procedures to the specific circumstances of the client. Therefore a firm's methodologies should be flexible and adapted to each client to ensure a quality audit is performed.

(3) **Outputs**

The reports and information that are formally prepared and presented by one party to another. The outputs from the audit are often determined by the context, including legislative requirements.

(4) **Key interactions within the financial reporting supply chain**

The formal and informal communications between stakeholder groups. Audit quality will be affected by the frequency of communication and the nature of the information communicated. Expectations can be managed through effective communication.

(5) **Contextual factors**

These are environmental factors such as laws and regulations and corporate governance which have the potential to impact the nature and quality of financial reporting and therefore audit quality.

Approach to exam questions: Quality control

A common requirement in the exam is to critically evaluate the audit work already performed on an engagement and identify if the audit has been carried out to the required standard of quality. In order to assess the quality of the audit you should consider factors such as:

- **Have ISAs been followed?**
  If not, sufficient appropriate evidence will not have been obtained and an inappropriate report may be issued.

- **Has the work been allocated to the appropriate level of staff?**
  Areas which are judgmental or subjective, such as goodwill, WIP, impairments, fair values, revenue recognition, material estimates, should be audited by senior members of the team with appropriate experience and professional judgment. Juniors may apply less professional scepticism than someone more senior.

- **Has the audit been time pressured?**
  If the audit has been rushed, insufficient work will have been performed and conclusions may not be appropriate.

- **Has the appropriate type of evidence been obtained?**
  Auditors should try and obtain the most reliable forms of evidence. Too much reliance on enquiry and written representations may mean sufficient appropriate evidence has not been obtained and sufficient scepticism has not been applied.

- **Has the audit been performed in accordance with the audit plan?**
  The audit plan will have been developed in response to the assessed risks of material misstatement. Sample sizes will have been chosen to ensure sufficient appropriate evidence is obtained. If the plan is not followed, inappropriate conclusions may be drawn.

- **Has the audit been properly supervised?**
  Supervision is necessary to ensure issues are identified on a timely basis, the competence of the team is continually assessed and the audit is on track to be completed on schedule. If there is inadequate supervision issues will not be identified. Look for information in the scenario that suggests the supervisor has been too busy with other work, has been absent during the audit, or has not visited the client for a while.

- **Has the audit work been properly reviewed?**
  Reviews should take place on a timely basis to ensure the work has been performed properly. Issues which need to be dealt with by someone more senior can then be resolved. Review of work should take place shortly after the work has been completed, not several weeks later. Reviews should be performed by someone more senior than the person who performed the work to ensure issues are identified. If issues are discovered too late there may not be sufficient time to address them.

Test your understanding 1

You are the manager responsible for the quality of the audits of new clients of Signet & Co, a firm of Chartered Certified Accountants. You are visiting the audit team at the head office of Agnesal Co, a limited liability company, the date is 1 July 20X5. The audit team comprises Artur Bois (audit supervisor), Carla Davini (audit senior) and Errol Flyte and Gavin Holst (trainees). The company provides food hygiene services which include the evaluation of risks of contamination, carrying out bacteriological tests and providing advice on health regulations and waste disposal.

Agnesal Co's principal customers include food processing companies, wholesale fresh food markets (meat, fish and dairy products) and bottling plants. The draft accounts for the year ended 31 March 20X5 show revenue $19.8 million (20X4: $13.8 million) and total assets $6.1 million (20X4: $4.2 million).

You have summarised the findings of your visit and review of the audit working papers relating to the audit of the financial statements for the year to 31 March 20X5 as follows:

(i) Against the analytical procedures section of the audit planning checklist, Carla has written 'not applicable – new client'. The audit planning checklist has not been signed off as having been reviewed by Artur.

(ii) Artur is currently assigned to three other jobs and is working from Signet & Co's office. He last visited Agnesal Co's office when the final audit commenced two weeks ago. In the meantime, Carla has completed the audit of non-current assets (including property and service equipment) which amount to $1.1 million as at 31 March 20X5 (20X4: $1.1 million).

(iii) Errol has just finished sending out requests for confirmation of trade receivable balances as at 31 March 20X5 when trade receivables amounted to $3.5 million (20X4: $1.6 million).

(iv) Agnesal Co's purchase clerk, Jules Java, keeps $2,500 cash to meet sundry expenses. The audit program shows that counting it is 'outstanding'. Carla has explained that when Gavin was sent to count it he reported back, two hours later, that he had not done it because it had not been convenient for Jules. Gavin had, instead, been explaining to Errol how to extract samples using value-weighted selection. Although Jules had later announced that he was ready to have his cash counted, Carla decided to postpone it until later in the audit. This is not documented in the audit working papers.

(v) Errol has been assigned to the audit of inventory (comprising consumable supplies) which amounts to $150,000 (20X4: $90,000). Signet & Co was not appointed as auditor until after the year-end physical count. Errol has therefore carried out tests of controls over purchases and issues to confirm the 'roll-back' of a sample of current quantities to quantities as at the year-end count.

(vi) Agnesal Co has drafted its first 'Report to Society' which contains health, safety and environmental performance data for the year to 31 March 20X5. Carla has filed it with the comment that it is 'to be dealt with when all other information for inclusion in the company's annual report is available'.

Required:

Identify and comment on the implications of these findings for Signet & Co's quality control policies and procedures.　　**(15 marks)**

Test your understanding 2

You are a senior manager with Flute and Co and are a member of the team conducting cold reviews. You are currently reviewing the audit file of Cello Co, a subsidiary of a listed overseas parent, which imports and distributes office furniture, usually manufactured by other group companies.

During your review you notice the following.

- Minutes of the planning meeting are on file but were not signed by the partner.

- The company's year-end is 31 December. Fieldwork was completed by 15 February and the financial statements together with the auditor's report were signed on 15 April. The subsequent events checklist was completed on 15 February.

- The company has very little headroom in its overdraft and apparently no other borrowing facilities.

- There is a letter of support on file from the holding company dated 15 April.

- Materiality is calculated at $60,000, which is in line with the firm's recommended procedures.

- Non-current assets consist of office furniture, office equipment and racking and forklifts for the rented warehouse. The carrying value is $250,000 and additions in the year were $40,000. Copy invoices for all the additions are on file but you find it difficult to see precisely what work was done. The working papers, other than the pre-printed audit programme and lead schedule, have not been initialled or dated.

- The receivables circularisation was successful except for one non-reply for $40,000.

Required:

Comment on the quality of the audit of Cello Co and describe the recommendations would you make to the firm's audit quality committee.

(10 marks)

Test your understanding 3

'The objective of the auditor is to implement quality control procedures at the engagement level that provide the auditor with reasonable assurance that:

–   The audit complies with professional standards and applicable legal and regulatory requirements; and

–   The auditor's report issued is appropriate in the circumstances.'

(ISA 220 *Quality Control for an Audit of Financial Statements*).

Required:

Describe the nature, and explain the purpose of quality control procedures appropriate to the individual audit.   **(5 marks)**

4 Chapter summary

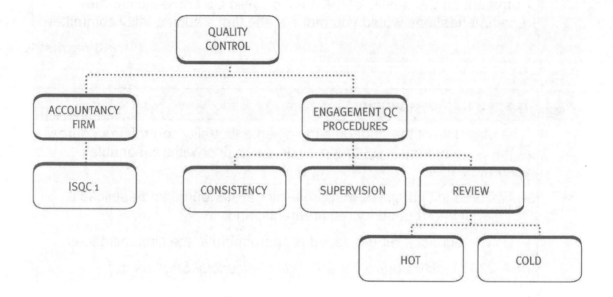

Test your understanding answers

Test your understanding 1

Implications of findings for QC policies and procedures

(i) Analytical procedures

Analytical procedures should have been performed at the planning stage, to assist in understanding the business and in identifying areas of potential risk, in accordance with ISA 315 (Revised) *Identifying and Assessing the Risks of Material Misstatement through Understanding the Entity and Its Environment*. The audit senior should know this.

Audit staff may have insufficient knowledge to assess the risks of the highly specialised service industry in which this new client operates. In particular, Agnesal Co may be exposed to risks resulting in unrecorded liabilities (both actual and contingent) if claims are made against the company in respect of outbreaks of contamination.

The audit has been inadequately planned and audit work has commenced before the audit plan has been reviewed by the audit supervisor. The audit may not be carried out effectively and efficiently.

(ii) Supervisor's assignments

The senior has performed work on non-current assets which is a less material (18% of total assets) audit area than trade receivables (57% of total assets) which has been assigned to an audit trainee. Non-current assets also appears to be a lower risk audit area than trade receivables because the carrying amount of non-current assets is comparable with the prior year ($1.1m at both year-ends), whereas trade receivables have more than doubled (from $1.6m to $3.5m). This corroborates the implications of (i).

The audit is being inadequately supervised as work has been delegated inappropriately. It appears that the firm does not have sufficient audit staff with relevant competencies to meet its supervisory needs.

(iii) Direct confirmation

It is usual for direct confirmation of trade receivables to be obtained where trade receivables are material and it is reasonable to expect customers to respond. However, it is three months after the statement of financial position date and, although trade receivables are clearly material (57% of total assets), an alternative approach may be more efficient (and cost effective).

For example, testing of after-date cash will provide evidence about the collectability of trade receivables as well as corroborate their existence.

Supervision of the audit may be inadequate. For example, if the audit trainee did not understand the alternative approach but mechanically followed circularisation procedures.

Depending on the reporting deadline, there may still be time to perform a circularisation. However, consideration should be given to circularising the most recent month-end balances (i.e. June) rather than the year-end balances which customers may be unable or reluctant to confirm retrospectively.

(iv) **Cash count**

Although $2,500 is very immaterial, the client's management may expect the auditor to count it to confirm that it has not been misappropriated.

The briefing given to the trainee may have been inadequate. For example, Gavin may not have understood the need to count the cash at the time the request was made of the client. However, the behaviour of Gavin also needs to be investigated in that he failed to report back to the audit senior on a timely basis and allowed himself to be unsupervised.

The trainees do not appear to have been given appropriate direction. Gavin may not be sufficiently competent to be explaining sample selection methods to another trainee.

Although it is not practical to document every matter, details should have been recorded to support Carla's decision to change the timing of a planned procedure. Carla's decision appears justified as it is inappropriate to perform a cash count when the client is 'ready' for it. Also, if some irregularity is discovered by the client at a later date (e.g. if Jules is found to be 'borrowing' the cash), documentation must support why this was not detected sooner by the auditor.

(v) **Inventory**

Whilst material, (2.5% of total assets), inventory is relatively low risk given the company has no inventory-in-trade, only consumables used in the supply of service. Therefore it seems appropriate that a trainee should be auditing it. However, the audit approach appears highly inefficient. Such in-depth testing (of controls and details) on a relatively low risk area may be due to a lack of monitoring or a mechanical approach being adopted by a trainee. This provides further evidence that the audit has been inadequately planned, and demonstrates a lack of knowledge and understanding about Agnesal Co's business. This may be a further consequence of the audit having been inadequately planned.

(vi) **'Report to society'**

The audit senior appears to have assumed that this is other information to be included in a document containing audited financial statements (the annual report). To be dealt with presumably means to be read with a view to identifying significant misstatements or inconsistencies. The comment indicates that Carla possibly does not know what needs to be done with the report. By leaving it until the end of the audit, it could cause problems, for instance if the audit firm is actually required to provide assurance on the Report to Society there may not be sufficient time to perform the work required to be able to issue the report by the required deadline.

As the preceding analysis casts doubts on Signet & Co's ability to deliver a quality audit to Agnesal Co, it seems unlikely that Signet & Co has the resources and expertise necessary to provide such assurance services.

Conclusions

The audit is not being conducted in accordance with ISAs e.g. ISA 315 *Identifying and Assessing the Risks of Material Misstatement Through Understanding the Entity and Its Environment* and ISA 520 *Analytical Procedures* which indicates Signet & Co's quality control policies and procedures are not established and/or not being communicated to personnel.

Audit work is being assigned to personnel with insufficient technical training and proficiency which indicates weaknesses in procedures for hiring and/or training of personnel.

Insufficient direction, supervision and review of work at all levels suggests a lack of resources.

In deciding whether or not to accept the audit of Agnesal Co, Signet & Co should have considered whether it had the ability to serve the client properly. The partner responsible for accepting the engagement does not appear to have evaluated the firm's (lack of) knowledge of the industry.

Test your understanding 2

Planning meeting

The planning should be documented fully and approved by the partner before the start of fieldwork. It is possible that evidence of this approval is to be found elsewhere on the file, but it would have been better if the partner had signed off the meeting minutes as soon as they were available.

Going concern and subsequent events

- The subsequent events review should be updated to the date of signing the auditor's report. The review should arguably be more rigorous and comprehensively documented because of the lack of financial facilities and the increased risk of going concern issues.

- The fact that the parent is listed overseas does not mean that the comfort letter is valid evidence that Cello Co is a going concern.

- It may be that the letter of comfort from the holding company is sufficient to eliminate this risk, but this should be made clear on the file, and the checklist still needs updating.

Non-current assets

- Non-current assets might be considered low risk, but the total is material, even if the current year's additions may not be material.

- This section of the file demonstrates a lack of clarity in the approach to the audit and the firm's basic procedures for initialling and dating working papers have not been observed, albeit in what may be a relatively low-risk area.

Receivables

- The uncleared item may not be material but it may be in excess of the tolerable error threshold.

- The item should have been followed up and other evidence obtained and, if this was not possible, the potential misstatement should have been calculated in theoretical terms to see if the misstatement in the financial statements as a whole might have been material.

Conclusions/recommendations

- There is a risk that the auditor's report (on the assumption that an unmodified opinion was given) is wrong because of the going concern and receivables issues.

- Planned audit procedures need to be followed for the planning meeting, subsequent events review, non-current assets working papers and receivables sample.

- Training implications need to be considered.

Test your understanding 3

Quality control procedures

Quality controls are the policies and procedures adopted by a firm to provide reasonable assurance that all audits done by a firm are being carried out in accordance with the objective and general principles governing an audit.

Quality control procedures reduce the risk of litigation claims thereby reducing the risk of reputational damage.

Individual audit level

Work delegated to assistants should be directed, supervised and reviewed to ensure the audit is conducted in compliance with ISAs. This work must be appropriately documented to provide evidence that the work has been performed properly and to provide evidence of the basis for the auditor's report.

Assistants should be professionally competent to perform the work delegated to them with due care.

Direction (i.e. informing assistants about their responsibilities and the nature, timing and extent of audit procedures they are to perform) may be communicated through:

- briefing meetings and on-the-job coaching

- the overall audit plan and audit programs

- audit manuals and checklists

- time budgets.

Supervisory responsibilities include monitoring the progress of the audit to ensure that assistants are competent, understand their tasks and are carrying them out as directed. Supervisors must also address accounting and auditing issues arising during the audit (e.g. by modifying the overall audit plan and audit program).

Review of work should be undertaken by someone more senior to the person who performed the work to ensure:

- it is in accordance with the audit program

- it is adequately documented

- significant matters have been resolved

- objectives have been achieved

- conclusions are appropriate (i.e. consistent with results).

An engagement quality control review (i.e. by personnel not otherwise involved in the audit), to assess the quality of the audit (before issuing the auditor's report) should be undertaken for listed and other public interest or high risk audit clients.

Documentation, which needs to be reviewed on a timely basis includes:

- the overall audit plan and any modifications thereto
- results from tests of control and substantive procedures
- conclusions drawn
- audit adjustments
- financial statements
- the proposed audit opinion.

Practice management

Chapter learning objectives

This chapter covers syllabus areas:

- C2 – Advertising, tendering and obtaining professional work and fees

- C3 – Professional appointments

- G2b – Discuss current developments in business practices, practice management and audit methodology and evaluate the potential impact on the conduct of an audit and audit quality

Detailed syllabus objectives are provided in the introduction section of the text book.

PER

One of the PER performance objectives (PO1) is ethics and professionalism. The fundamental principles of ethical behaviour mean you should always act in the wider public interest. You need to take into account all relevant information and use professional judgement, your personal values and scepticism to evaluate data and make decisions. You should identify right from wrong and escalate anything of concern. You also need to make sure that your skills, knowledge and behaviour are up-to-date and allow you to be effective in your role. Working through this chapter should help you understand how to demonstrate that objective.

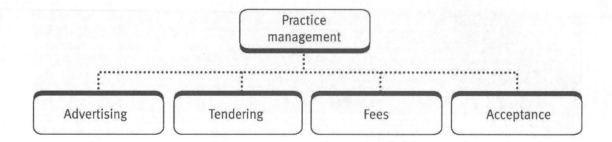

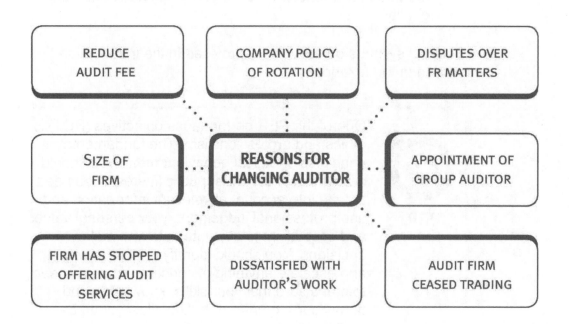

Exam focus

Practice management covers aspects of running an accountancy firm such as winning new business and setting fees. Common requirements cover:

- Matters to be included in a tender proposal.
- Evaluating the suitability of an advertisement.
- Factors to be considered when setting a fee.
- Matters to be considered before accepting an engagement.
- Matters to be included in an engagement letter.

1 Changing auditors/professional accountants

Why change auditors?

Why step down?

Audit firms may not seek re-appointment for many reasons. Examples include:

- Independence issues which cannot be safeguarded
- Doubts regarding the integrity of the company's management
- Strategic decision to concentrate on other services or markets.

2 Tendering

 Tendering is the process of quoting a fee for work before the work is carried out.

Most tenders include a formal written document supported by an oral presentation. All presentations should be dynamic, professional and within the limits of the ethical framework.

Matters to consider before tendering

When invited to tender, a firm must decide whether it wishes to take part in the tendering process.

Specific risks of being involved with the tender include:

- Wasted time if the audit tender is not accepted. The firm will not be paid for the time spent putting the tender proposal together.
- Setting an uncommercial fee in order to win the contract (lowballing covered later in this chapter).
- Making unrealistic claims or promises in order to win the contract.

Information required for the proposal

The preparation of an engagement proposal document is an important step in obtaining new work.

Prior to drafting any proposals an audit firm should consider the following:

- What does the potential client expect from its auditors?
- What timetable does the client expect: an interim audit followed by a final audit or a longer final audit after the year-end?
- By which date are the audited financial statements required?
- What are the company's future plans, e.g. public flotation, expansion, contraction, concentration on certain markets?
- Are there any perceived problems with the potential client's current auditors?
- The format required by the prospective client.

The content of the proposal

The content of the proposal should include:

- The fee and how it has been calculated.

- The nature, purpose and legal requirements of an audit (particularly useful if this is the first time the entity is being audited).

- An assessment of the requirements of the client.

- An outline of how the audit firm proposes to satisfy those requirements and the assumptions made, e.g. on geographical coverage, deadlines, work done by client, availability of information, etc.

- The proposed approach to the audit or audit methodology.

- An outline of the firm and its personnel.

- Quality control procedures of the firm including those relevant to the engagement.

- The ability of the firm to offer other services.

The selection process of the proposal

In 2015 in the UK, a survey of audit committees found that price was not the deciding factor. The selection process for tenders focused on:

- Independence.

- Judgment and scepticism of key audit partners.

- Evidence of internal and external quality reviews.

UK syllabus

The UK Corporate Governance Code states:

- The audit committee should have primary responsibility for making a recommendation on the appointment, reappointment and removal of the external auditors.

- FTSE 350 companies should put the external audit contract out to tender at least every ten years (but can retain the current auditor if they provide the best quality and most effective audit), or explain in the annual report why they have not.

- Public Interest Entities must rotate auditors after at least 20 years.

- If the board does not accept the audit committee's recommendation, it should include in the annual report, and in any papers recommending appointment or reappointment, a statement from the audit committee explaining the recommendation and should set out reasons why the board has taken a different position.

Benefits and drawbacks of tendering process

Benefits

- Firms are forced to look at ways of doing the work more efficiently in order to compete with other firms.

- Companies may look to improve their internal controls and increase the scope of their internal audit departments in order to reduce external audit costs.

- Companies may simplify their group structures to reduce audit costs (among other reasons).

- The threat of familiarity will reduce if tendering results in a change of audit firm as the new firm will bring a fresh insight.

Drawbacks

- Greater market concentration, which has reduced market choice.

- Loss of long-term relationships with auditors.

- Focus on cost of the audit not quality. Lowballing issues.

- The costs involved with the tendering process which affect both the company and the audit firm.

Test your understanding 1

You are an audit manager in Weller & Co, an audit firm which operates as part of an international network of firms. This morning you received a note from a partner regarding a potential new audit client:

'I have been approached by the audit committee of the Plant Group, which operates in the mobile telecommunications sector. Our firm has been invited to tender for the audit of the individual and group financial statements for the year ending 31 October 20X5, and I would like your help in preparing the tender document. This would be a major new client for our firm's telecoms audit department.

The Plant Group comprises a parent company and six subsidiaries, one of which is located overseas. The audit committee is looking for a cost effective audit, and hopes that the strength of the Plant Group's governance and internal control mean that the audit can be conducted quickly, with a proposed deadline of 31 December 20X5. The Plant Group has expanded rapidly in the last few years and significant finance was raised in February 20X5 through a stock exchange listing.'

Required:

Identify and explain the specific matters to be included in the tender document for the audit of the Plant Group. **(8 marks)**

3 Advertising and publicity

The ACCA Rulebook (section B13) states that it is acceptable in principle for ACCA members to advertise their services, but there is a requirement that the advertising must not reflect adversely on:

- the member
- the ACCA, or
- the accountancy profession as a whole.

The aim of adverts should be 'to inform, rather than impress'.

The rules state that advertisements and promotional material should not:

- bring the ACCA into disrepute or bring discredit to the member, firm or the accountancy profession.
- discredit the services offered by others whether by claiming superiority for the member's own services or otherwise.
- be misleading, either directly or by implication.
- fall short of the requirements of any relevant national Advertising Standards Authority's Code of Advertising Practice, notably as to legality, decency, clarity, honesty, and truthfulness.

Firms should be careful that the limited space available in an advertisement does not result in misleading information being communicated.

Promotional material may contain any factual statement which can be justified, but it should not make unflattering references to, or unflattering comparisons with, the services of others.

Restrictions on practice names and descriptions

There are restrictions on practice names and descriptions and the use of the ACCA logo given in the ACCA Rulebook (Section 3 – B4).

Members' descriptions

- Members of the ACCA are entitled to call themselves Chartered Certified Accountants or just Certified Accountants, and may use the letters ACCA (as members) or FCCA (if they are fellows).
- These descriptions may **not** be used in the registered names of companies. For example you may not set up a company called John Smith Certified Accountant Ltd.

Practice descriptions

- An accountancy firm may describe itself as a 'firm of Chartered Certified Accountants', or a 'firm of Certified Accountants', or an 'ACCA practice' provided that:

  - at least half of the partners (or directors) are ACCA members, and

  - these partners (or directors) control at least 51% of the voting rights under the firm's partnership agreement (or constitution).

- A firm in which all partners are ACCA members may use the description 'Members of the Association of Chartered Certified Accountants' on its professional stationery.

- In the case of a mixed firm (e.g. some partners are ACCA members and others are members of other Chartered Accountancy bodies), the firm should not use the description 'Certified Accountants and Chartered Accountants' or similar, since this could be misleading. Instead they may print the following statement on their stationery: 'The partners of this firm are members of either the Association of Chartered Certified Accountants or (e.g.) the Institute of Chartered Accountants in England and Wales'.

Names of practising firms

Generally, members may practice under whatever name they want, but:

- A practice name should be consistent with the dignity of the profession.

- A practice name should not be misleading (e.g. a firm could not trade as 'PQ International Accountants' if all its offices were in one country).

- A practice name should not run the risk of being confused with the name of another firm.

- A sole practitioner should not add 'and partners' to the name under which he practices.

Use of the ACCA logo

- A firm that has at least one ACCA member as a partner (or director) may use the ACCA logo (also called the ACCA 'mark') on its professional stationery and on its website.

- The ACCA logo should be separate from the logo of the firm.

- The positioning, size and colour of the ACCA logo should be chosen so that it is clearly recognisable.

- The logo can be downloaded by members from the ACCA website in electronic format.

4 Fees

The need for guidance

The ACCA Rulebook (Section 3 – 330) contains a number of important provisions in relation to fees in order to:

- Minimise the possibility of a dispute between a member and their clients.

- Ensure that the member behaves at all times in accordance with the fundamental principles.

Determinants for fee-setting

- Members are entitled to charge a fair and reasonable fee for their services. This amount will be:

    - The fee considered appropriate for the work undertaken

    - The fee in accordance with the basis agreed with the client

    - The fee by reference to custom in certain specialised areas.

- Members will usually consider the following matters in setting a fee:

    - Seniority of the persons necessarily engaged on the work

    - Time spent by each person

    - Degree of risk and responsibility that the work entails

    - Urgency of the work to the client

    - Importance of the work to the client

    - Overhead expenses of the firm.

- The fee charged should include the recovery of any expenses properly incurred by the audit staff in the course of the engagement.

- The general basis on which fees are normally computed should be communicated to clients or potential clients in the letter of engagement or proposal document in order to reduce the risk of misunderstandings.

Lowballing

Lowballing is the setting of a low price at the start of an arrangement in order to secure the business, with the intention of later raising it or recovering the losses made on that engagement with other, more lucrative, services.

This could lead to a self-interest threat as the auditor may try and keep their client happy simply in order to win other contracts with them.

Professional competence and due care may be affected if the low fee leads the firm to cut corners on the audit to try and minimise losses.

If a member is investigated following allegations of unsatisfactory work, an inappropriate fee quote may be taken into consideration during the disciplinary process. A reasonable and informed third party may perceive that insufficient time has been taken to do the audit and quality has been affected because of the low fee.

However, it should be noted that there is no evidence that lowballing has actually led to negligent auditing. The regulatory system and the desire of audit firms to maintain their reputation should be sufficient to maintain audit quality regardless of the fee. The cost of litigation and the fear of high profile public scandals is a significant deterrent.

Bases on which fees and commissions may be charged

Contingency fees

A contingency fee is an arrangement made at the outset of an engagement under which a predetermined amount or percentage is payable to the accountant upon the completion of a specified event, or the achievement of a particular outcome.

Contingency fees could lead to practitioners forcing a specific outcome that would not normally have been obtained to try and achieve higher fees. For example, tax fees may be agreed based upon the tax savings the practitioners create or an auditor may be paid for unusually rapid completion of an audit. This could lead to the engagement being conducted without necessary due care and objectivity.

The ACCA's position is that **fees should not be charged on a percentage, contingency or similar basis**, except where that course of action is generally accepted practice e.g. insolvency work.

Fixed fee quotations

Most firms agree a fixed fee as clients prefer the certainty of a known cost. When calculating the fee, the determinants for fee-setting mentioned above will be taken into consideration. This arrangement can raise issues such as setting the fee at a low figure to secure the work or setting the fee at a level that is not profitable for the audit firm because of poor budgeting.

If a fee quoted is so low that it becomes difficult to perform the engagement in accordance with professional standards for that price, then an ethical threat to professional competence and due care may be created.

Safeguards may be applied to eliminate this threat or to reduce it to an acceptable level, for example:

- Make it clear to the client which services are covered by the quoted fees and the basis upon which fees are to be charged.

- Perform a rigorous budgeting process to ensure that costs can be recovered.

- Assign sufficient time and appropriate staff to the assignment to ensure it is performed effectively.

Hourly rates

Alternatively, the accountancy firm can set an hourly rate for each grade of staff and invoice the client for the number of hours involved in the assignment. The final fee will only be known at the end of the engagement which may not be an acceptable arrangement for the client as they will not know how much to budget for the audit fee.

Referral fees

Members may pay a referral fee to a third party, in return for the introduction of a client. The payment of such a fee may create a self-interest threat, therefore safeguards should be established to eliminate the threat or reduce it to an acceptable level. This is usually achieved by disclosing any such arrangements to the client.

References to fees in promotional material

- Where reference is made in promotional material to fees, the basis on which those fees are calculated, hourly or other charging rates, etc. should be clearly stated.

- Members may make comparisons in their promotional material between their fees and the fees of other accounting practices, whether members or not, provided that any such comparison complies with relevant codes of conduct and does not give a misleading impression.

- Promotional material that is based on the offer of percentage discounts on existing fees is permitted but must not detract from the professional image of the firm and the profession as a whole.

- Members may offer a free consultation to potential clients, at which levels of fees will be discussed.

[Section B13]

 Current issue: Downward fee pressure

Ethical considerations relating to audit fee setting in the context of downward fee pressure

Pressure on an audit firm to reduce audit fees arises for several reasons:

- Entities trying to reduce costs

- Increased competition in the audit market

- Mandatory audit firm rotation

- Increased audit threshold.

Reductions in fees can threaten the fundamental ethical principles of professional competence and due care, and objectivity.

A firm may quote whatever fee is deemed appropriate however, the firm must always ensure that the work is performed in accordance with professional standards and that the audit team have the appropriate expertise and experience taking into consideration the nature, size and complexity of the audit engagement. The firm should also recognise that some audits may be more challenging than others which will require an increase in the level of time and expertise needed.

Other stakeholders have an important role to play in ensuring that fee levels do not impair audit quality. In particular, those charged with governance (TCWG) should consider whether adequate time and resources are planned for the audit when negotiating audit fees. Management and TCWG should recognise that high quality audits are part of good corporate governance and therefore audits should not be viewed as a cost to be minimised.

Test your understanding 2

You are a training manager in Hawk Associates, a firm of Chartered Certified Accountants. The firm has suffered a reduction in fee income due to increasing restrictions on the provision of non-audit services to audit clients. The following proposals for obtaining professional work are to be discussed at a forthcoming in-house seminar:

(a) 'Cold calling' (i.e. approaching directly to seek new business) the chief executive officers of local businesses and offering them free second opinions. **(5 marks)**

(b) Placing an advertisement in a national accountancy magazine that includes the following:

'If you have an asset on which a large chargeable gain is expected to arise when you dispose of it, you should be interested in the best tax planning advice. However your gains might arise, there are techniques you can apply. Hawk Associates can ensure that you consider all the alternative fact presentations so that you minimise the amount of tax you might have to pay. No tax saving – no fee!' **(6 marks)**

(c) Displaying business cards alongside those of local tradesmen and service providers in supermarkets and libraries. The cards would read:

Hawk ACCA Associates
For PROFESSIONAL Accountancy, Audit,
Business Consultancy and Taxation Services
Competitive rates. Money back guarantees.

(4 marks)

Required:

Comment on the suitability of each of the above proposals in terms of the ethical and other professional issues that they raise.

(Total: 15 marks)

5 Acceptance considerations

 Acceptance considerations for an audit were covered in Audit and Assurance at the Applied Skills level.

A firm should only take on clients and work of an appropriate level of risk. For this reason, the firm should perform 'client screening'. The firm will consider the following matters before accepting a new engagement or client:

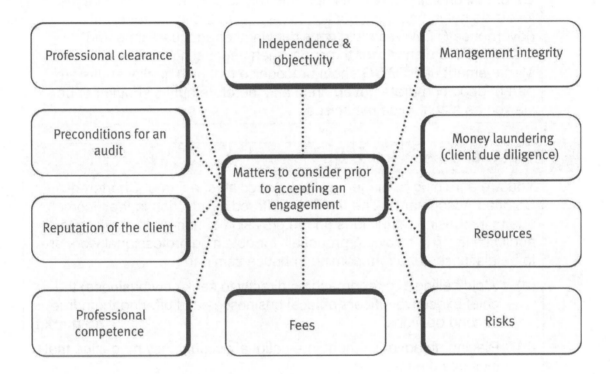

If there are any reasons why the firm believes they may not be able to issue an appropriate report, they should not accept the engagement.

Preconditions for an audit

ISA 210 *Agreeing the Terms of Audit Engagements* and the Code of Ethics and Conduct provides guidance to the professional accountant when accepting new work.

Before accepting (or continuing with) an engagement the auditor must establish whether the preconditions for an audit are present and that there is a common understanding between the auditor and management and, where appropriate, those charged with governance. [ISA 210, 3]

The preconditions for an audit are that management acknowledges and understands its responsibility for:

- Preparation of the financial statements in accordance with the applicable financial reporting framework.

- Internal control necessary for the financial statements to give a true and fair view.

- Providing the auditor with access to all relevant information and explanations.

[ISA 210, 6]

If the client imposes a limitation on the scope of the auditor's work to the extent that the auditor believes it likely that a disclaimer of opinion will ultimately be issued, then the auditor shall not accept the engagement, unless required to do so by law. [ISA 210, 7]

Continuance

Once the engagement is complete, the audit firm must revisit the acceptance considerations again to ensure it is appropriate to continue for the following year. If any significant issues have arisen during the year, such as disagreements with management or doubts over management integrity, the firm may consider resigning.

Acceptance considerations

Professional clearance

The prospective firm must contact the existing accountant to obtain professional clearance and determine whether there are any reasons that would preclude the accountant from taking on this engagement.

The prospective firm should:

- Ask the client for permission to contact the existing auditor (and refuse the engagement if the client refuses).

- Contact the outgoing firm, asking for all information relevant to the decision whether or not to accept appointment (e.g. overdue fees, disagreements with management, breaches of laws & regulations). This is also referred to as a professional etiquette letter.

- If a reply is not received, the prospective firm should try and contact the outgoing firm by other means e.g. by telephone.

- If a reply is still not received the prospective firm may still choose to accept but must proceed with care.

- If a reply is received, consider the outgoing firm's response and assess if there are any ethical or professional reasons why they should not accept appointment.

- The existing firm must ask the client for permission to respond to the prospective firm.

- If the client refuses permission, the existing firm should notify the prospective firm of this fact.

[ACCA Rulebook, section 320]

Independence and objectivity

If the assurance provider is aware, prior to accepting an engagement, that the threats to objectivity cannot be managed to an acceptable level, the engagement should not be accepted.

Management integrity

If the firm has reason to believe the client lacks integrity there is a greater risk of fraud and intimidation.

Money laundering (client due diligence)

The firm must comply with Money Laundering Regulations which require client due diligence to be carried out. If there is any suspicion of money laundering, or actual money laundering committed by the prospective client, the firm cannot accept the engagement.

Resources

The firm should consider whether there are adequate resources available at the time the engagement is likely to take place to perform the work properly. If there is insufficient time to conduct the work with the resources available, the quality of the work could be affected.

Risks

Any risks identified with the prospective client (e.g. poor performance, poor controls, unusual transactions) should be considered. These risks can increase the level of engagement risk, i.e. the risk of issuing an inappropriate report.

Fees

The firm should consider the acceptability of the fee. The fee should be commensurate with the level of risk.

In addition, the creditworthiness of the prospective client should be considered as non-payment of fees can create a self-interest threat.

Professional competence

An engagement should only be accepted if the firm has the necessary skill and experience to perform the work competently.

Reputation of the client

The firm should consider the reputation of the client and whether its own reputation could be damaged by association.

Additional professional work

- Accountants may be asked to undertake work that is complementary or additional to the work of existing accountants, who are not being replaced.

- Before accepting such work, the accountant should communicate with the existing accountants to inform them of the general nature of the work being done.

- If permission is not given to communicate with the existing accountants, the engagement should be declined.

Test your understanding 3

Your firm has been approached by Tomlin Co to provide the annual external audit following the resignation of the previous auditor. The company's year-end is 31 December which is the same as the majority of your firm's other audit clients. Tomlin Co supplies goods to major retailers. Your firm does not audit any other retailers. The company is currently recruiting a new finance director after the previous finance director was found guilty of bribing customers in order to win major contracts.

Required:

Explain the matters to be considered in deciding whether to accept the appointment as auditor of Tomlin Co.   **(6 marks)**

6 Agreeing the terms of engagement

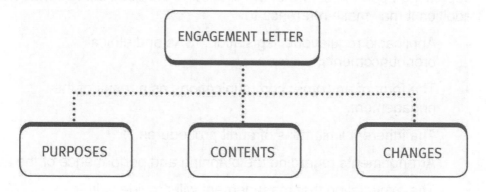

Purpose

The engagement letter specifies the nature of the contract between the firm and client.

Its purpose is to:

- Minimise the risk of any misunderstanding between the practitioner and client

- Confirm acceptance of the engagement

- Set out the terms and conditions of the engagement.

Contents

The auditor will agree the terms of the audit engagement with management or those charged with governance, as appropriate.
[ISA 210, 9]

The terms are recorded in a written audit engagement letter and should include:

- The objective and scope of the audit of the financial statements

- The responsibilities of the auditor

- The responsibilities of management

- Identification of the applicable financial reporting framework for the preparation of the financial statements

- Reference to the expected form and content of any reports to be issued by the auditor.

[ISA 210, 10]

The content of the engagement letter should be agreed with the client before any engagement related work commences.

The client's acknowledgement of the terms of the letter should be formally documented in the form of a director's signature.

 Engagement letter contents in detail

The items noted above should be included in every engagement letter. However the wider form and content of engagement letters may vary depending upon the nature of the client and the audit being conducted. In addition it may make reference to:

- Applicable regulations, legislation, ISAs and ethical pronouncements.

- The form of any other communications as a result of the engagement.

- The inherent limitations of audit procedures.

- Arrangements regarding the planning and performance of the audit.

- The expectation that management will provide written representations.

- The agreement of management to make available to the auditor draft financial statements and any accompanying information in time to allow the auditor to complete the audit in accordance with the timetable.

- The agreement of management to make available to the auditor facts pertinent to the preparation of the financial statements, which management may become aware of during the period from the date of the auditor's report to the date the financial statements are issued.

- The basis upon which fees are computed and billed.

- A request for management to acknowledge receipt of the engagement letter and to agree to the terms of engagement.

- Arrangements concerning the involvement of other auditors and experts (where relevant).

- Arrangements concerning the involvement of internal auditors (where relevant).

- Any restriction on the auditor's liability, when such possibility exists.

- Any obligations to provide audit working papers to other parties.

[ISA 210, A24]

Changes to the engagement letter

The engagement letter should be **reviewed every year** to ensure that it is up to date but does not need to be reissued every year unless there are changes to the terms of the engagement.

ISA 210 requires the auditor to consider whether there is a need to remind the entity of the existing terms of the audit engagement for recurring audits. Some firms choose to send a new letter every year to emphasise its importance to clients.

The auditor should issue a new engagement letter if the scope or context of the assignment changes after initial appointment, or if there is a need to remind the client of the existing terms.

Reasons for changes would include:

- Changes to statutory duties due to new legislation

- Changes to professional duties, for example, due to new or updated ISAs

- Recent changes in senior management

- A significant change in ownership.

[ISA 210, A30]

Audit of components of a group

- Where the auditor of a parent company is also the auditor of a subsidiary, branch or division of the group, the audit firm must decide whether to issue a single engagement letter covering all the components, or a separate letter to each component.

- If the audit firm sends one letter relating to the group as a whole, it is recommended that the firm should identify in the letter, the components of the group for which the firm is being appointed as auditor.

7 After acceptance

New firm

Where an accountant is being appointed they should confirm that:

- the outgoing auditor has vacated office in a correct manner

- they have been properly appointed as the incoming auditor in accordance with relevant local legislation. This is usually achieved through a majority vote at the AGM, which should be documented in a formal minute.

Outgoing firm – transfer of information

On ceasing to hold office, the outgoing firm should return all books and papers belonging to the former client which are in their possession, except where the firm claims to exercise a lien or other security over them in respect of unpaid fees.

In order to ensure continuity of treatment of a client's affairs, the outgoing firm should provide the new accountant with all reasonable transfer information (last set of approved accounts and detailed trial balance) that the new accountant requests, free of charge.

Any information in addition to the reasonable transfer information is provided purely at the discretion of the former accountant, who may render a charge to the person requesting the information.

[ACCA Rulebook, section 320]

 Approach to exam questions: Tendering, acceptance, terms of engagement

In the exam you may be asked for the following:

- Matters to consider before accepting an engagement/deciding whether to take part in the tender process

- Matters to include in the tender proposal.

- Matters to include in the engagement letter.

These requirements may look very similar but the answers to each of them are different. It is important to read the requirement carefully to make sure you understand which of these requirements is being asked so you can provide a relevant answer.

Matters to consider before accepting an engagement/deciding whether to take part in the tender process

Covered in section 5

This requirement could be set in the context of an audit or a non-audit engagement. The principles are the same for most engagements.

The firm should consider reasons why they would not want to accept the work (e.g. lack of integrity of management) and reasons why they cannot accept the work (e.g. not competent to perform the work).

This is a consideration for the accountancy firm. Only the conclusion of the decision is communicated with the prospective client.

Matters to include in the tender proposal

Covered in section 2

The purpose of tendering is to sell the firm's services to the client. Think of the tender proposal as a sales pitch to the prospective client. The tender proposal will be given to the prospective client therefore it should only contain positive points. A prospective client does not want to hear a firm discuss whether it is competent to perform the work. If the firm does not have sufficient competence it should not be taking part in the tender process.

Matters to include in the engagement letter

Covered in section 6

This is the next stage along in the acceptance process. If the firm has decided to accept the engagement they will need to clarify terms and conditions in the engagement letter.

The engagement letter is used to minimise misunderstandings with the client, therefore the matters in this requirement should be points the firm wants to make sure are not misunderstood e.g. who can rely on the report once it is issued, responsibilities of each party, how the fee will be calculated, deadlines, etc.

Test your understanding 4

AB Accountants has been invited to become the auditors of XY Co, a company with a poor reputation since several senior managers were recently convicted of corruption. The company insists that it has now changed its culture, and is hoping that AB Accountants will become its auditors as part of this new ethical outlook.

Required:

Identify possible safeguards AB Accountants might consider using if it accepts appointment as auditor of XY Co. **(4 marks)**

Test your understanding 5

Deidre Jones ACCA

www.djonesacca.co.uk

Advice for small businesses

Friendly and professional service

Business start-up specialist

'The best and friendliest service in this town'

Required:

Comment on whether the proposed advertisement is acceptable.

(5 marks)

8   Chapter summary

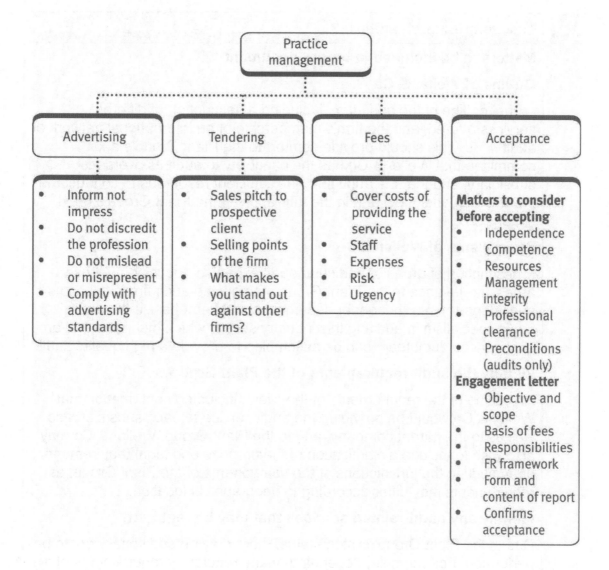

Test your understanding answers

Test your understanding 1

Matters to be included in tender document

Outline of Weller & Co

A brief outline of the audit firm, including a description of different services offered, and the firm's membership of an international network of audit firms. This should provide comfort to the Plant Group's audit committee that Weller & Co has the capability to audit its overseas subsidiary, and that the audit firm has sufficient resources to conduct the Plant Group audit now and in the future, given the Plant Group's rapid expansion.

Specialisms of Weller & Co

A description of areas of particular audit expertise, focusing on those areas of relevance to the Plant Group, namely the audit firm's telecoms audit department. The tender document should emphasise the audit firm's specialism in auditing this industry sector, which highlights that an experienced audit team can be assembled to provide a high quality audit.

Identify the audit requirements of the Plant Group

An outline of the requirements of the client, including confirmation that Weller & Co would be providing the audit service to each subsidiary, as well as to the parent company, and to the Plant Group. Weller & Co may also wish to include a clarification of the purpose and legal requirements of an audit in the jurisdictions of the components of the Plant Group, as requirements may differ according to geographical location.

Identify any audit-related services that may be required

Due to the Plant Group's listed status, there may be additional work to be performed. For example, depending on the regulatory requirements of the stock exchange on which the Plant Group is listed, there may be additional reporting requirements relevant to corporate governance and internal controls. This should be clarified and included in the tender document to ensure that the audit committee understands any such requirements, and that Weller & Co can provide an all-encompassing service.

Audit approach

A description of the proposed audit approach, outlining the stages of the audit process and the audit methodology used by the firm. Weller & Co may wish to emphasise any aspects of the proposed audit methodology which would be likely to meet the audit committee's requirement of a cost effective audit. The proposed audit approach could involve reliance to some extent on the Plant Group's controls, which are suggested to be good, and the tender document should explain that the audit firm will have to gauge the strength of controls before deciding whether to place any reliance on them.

Deadlines

The audit firm should clarify the timescale to be used for the audit. This is very important, given the audit committee's hope for a quick audit. It would be time pressured for the audit of all components of the Plant Group and of the consolidated financial statements to be completed in two months, especially given the geographical spread of the Plant Group, and the public holidays in that time period. The audit firm may wish to propose a later deadline, emphasising that it may be impossible to conduct a quality audit in such a short timeframe.

Quality control and ethics

Weller & Co should clarify its adherence to the Code of Ethics and to International Standards on Quality Control. This should provide assurance that the audit firm will provide an unbiased and credible auditor's report. This may be particularly important, given the recent listing obtained by the Plant Group, and consequential scrutiny of the financial statements and auditor's report by investors and potential investors.

Fees

The proposed audit fee should be stated, with a breakdown of the main components of the fee. The audit firm may wish to explain that the audit fee is likely to be higher in the first year of auditing the Plant Group, as the firm will need to spend time obtaining business understanding and ensuring there is appropriate documentation of systems and controls. The tender document could explain that the audit is likely to become more cost effective in subsequent years, when the audit firm has gone through a learning curve.

Additional non-audit services

The audit firm should describe any non-audit services that it may be able to provide, such as tax services or restructuring services, which may be relevant given the rapid expansion of the Plant Group. The provision of such services would have to be considered carefully by the audit firm due to the threat to objectivity that may be created, so the tender document should outline any safeguards that may be used to reduce risks to an acceptable level. This is particularly important, given the listed status of the Plant Group. This part of the tender document may remind the audit committee members that corporate governance requirements may prohibit the audit firm from offering certain non-audit services.

Test your understanding 2

(a) **Cold calling**

Tutorial note: Recognising that there are three issues to address (i.e. 'cold calling', 'free' and 'second opinions') is likely to earn more marks than focusing on just one.

- Cold calling is prohibited in certain countries, therefore the direct approach may not be suitable. Where cold-calling is allowed, it may still only be permitted for existing business clients (i.e. to offer them additional services). The direct approach to non-business clients may still be prohibited.

- The fundamental ethical principles must be adhered to. Whilst solicitation which is decent, honest and truthful may be acceptable, cold calling which amounts to harassment is not.

- Offering a service for free is not prohibited provided that the client is not misled about future levels of fees.

- There are strict ethical codes regarding second opinions (on accounting treatments). Practitioners are advised NOT to provide second opinions, when requested, without following a procedure of contacting the incumbent auditor/accountant.

Tutorial note: Second opinions should only be given where the auditor has been given permission to speak to the original auditor to ascertain the information available to them at the time of their report. The second auditor should not consider any information that became available subsequently.

(b) **Tax planning**

- Advertising is generally allowed subject to the observance of the fundamental ethical principles.

- Where advertising is permitted, the minimum requirements are that it be decent, honest, truthful and in good taste. These criteria may not be met in this proposal.

- 'The best tax planning advice' is likely to be a self-laudatory statement and not based on verifiable facts. This may be an unjustifiable claim of expertise or specialism in the field of tax. This may also be making an unjustifiable comparison with other professional accountants in public practice.

- 'Can ensure ...' and the assertion of 'all' may not be a supportable claim, therefore the advertisement is not honest in this respect.

- There is a fine line between tax avoidance and tax evasion and 'techniques you can apply' and 'alternative fact presentations' may lean toward the latter and so not be in keeping with the integrity of the profession. This statement may imply an ability to influence taxation authorities.

- The assertion of being able to 'minimise the amount of tax' may expose Hawk Associates to litigation. The engagement risk associated with taking on this work would be high and so should carry commensurately high fees. Expectations of favourable results (lower tax liabilities) may be unjustifiable or created deceptively.

- The 'no tax saving – no fee' offer does not compensate for the risk associated with undertaking the work advertised. Contingency fees, whereby no fee will be charged unless a specific result is obtained, are prohibited except for certain services such as insolvency.

(c) **Business cards**

- Business cards may be considered a form of stationery and should be of an acceptable professional standard and comply with legal and member body requirements concerning names of partners, principals, professional descriptions, etc.

- An advertisement the size of a business card would be sufficient to provide a name and contact details and in this respect is suitable. However, the danger of giving a misleading impression is pronounced when there is such limited space for information.

- The tone of the advertisement may discredit the ACCA name. It is also unsuitable that it seeks to take unfair advantage of the ACCA name. Although the ACCA mark can be used by Hawk Associates on letterheads and stationery (for example) it cannot be used in any way which confuses it with the firm.

- The emphasis on 'professional' may be unsuitable as it could suggest that other firms are not professional.

- It is unlikely that any professional would offer money back. In the event of dispute (e.g. over fees), the matter would be taken to arbitration (with their member body) if a satisfactory arrangement could not be reached with the client. A tradesman may guarantee the quality of his work and that it can be made good in the event that the customer is not satisfied. However, an auditor cannot guarantee a particular outcome for the work undertaken (e.g. reported profit or tax payable). Most certainly an auditor cannot guarantee the truth and fairness of the financial statements in giving an audit opinion.

Test your understanding 3

Reason for the previous auditor resigning

If they have resigned due to difficulties encountered during the audit, the firm may be concerned that the same issues could occur.

Resources

As Tomlin's year-end is the same as most other audit clients, the firm may not have sufficient audit staff available to assign to the audit. This may lead to the work being rushed which could affect the quality of the audit.

Competence

As the firm does not audit any other clients in the retail industry, the audit firm may not be sufficiently experienced to deal with such an audit. The firm may not understand the industry laws and regulations and the risks associated with that industry which increases audit risk.

Absence of a finance director

Without a finance director, the financial reporting processes are not being overseen. The financial statements may not be prepared on time and difficulties could be encountered by the audit team obtaining audit evidence. This could cause work to be rushed to get it finished and material misstatements could go undetected.

Bribery

The previous finance director was found guilty of bribing customers. This indicates high control risk and may cast doubt over the integrity of management if other directors were aware of the bribery. The audit firm may decide the engagement is too risky to accept.

Independence

The firm would need to confirm independence from the client. Ethical threats such as self-interest and familiarity should be considered, and whether effective safeguards could be applied. Where effective safeguards cannot be applied, the engagement should be declined.

Fees

The level of the fee should be considered and whether the fee is acceptable for the amount of work involved and the level of risk associated with the engagement.

Test your understanding 4

AB Accountants must weigh up the possible costs and benefits of accepting appointment. The firm should apply safeguards such as:

- Performing client due diligence in accordance with money laundering regulations.

- Obtaining a detailed knowledge of the client before accepting nomination.

- Securing the client's commitment to implement strong internal controls and the highest standards of corporate governance.

- Allocating the senior partner of the firm to be the engagement partner rather than a more junior partner.

- Performing an engagement quality control review.

If the firm does not believe that any such safeguards could reduce the threats to an acceptable level, then the firm should decline the appointment.

Test your understanding 5

- Deidre Jones is entitled to inform the public of her skills (e.g. advice for small businesses, business start-ups, etc.) but claiming that she offers the best service in the area discredits the services offered by other accountants.

- The smiley symbols are not consistent with an image of professionalism and should be removed.

- She should state a business telephone number or physical address in the advertisement, not just a web address.

- Nowhere in the advertisement does Deidre Jones state that she is an accountant (although the ACCA designation states this for those who know what it means). If this advertisement is to be included in a directory of accountants, there is no need to include this point. However, if the advertisement is to go into a general publication, it is probably best to clearly state the fact that Deidre Jones is a certified accountant or chartered certified accountant (as well as including the ACCA designation after her name).

- Deidre is also not permitted to use the term 'ACCA' in her web address as this indicates that she works for them, when in fact she is simply a professional member of the ACCA.

Planning, materiality and assessing the risk of misstatement

Chapter learning objectives

This chapter covers syllabus areas:

- D1 – Planning, materiality and assessing the risk of misstatement

Detailed syllabus objectives are provided in the introduction section of the text book.

PER

One of the PER performance objectives (PO18) is to is to prepare for and plan the audit process. You plan and control the engagement process, including the initial investigation. You also plan and monitor the audit programme – legally and ethically. Working through this chapter should help you understand how to demonstrate that objective.

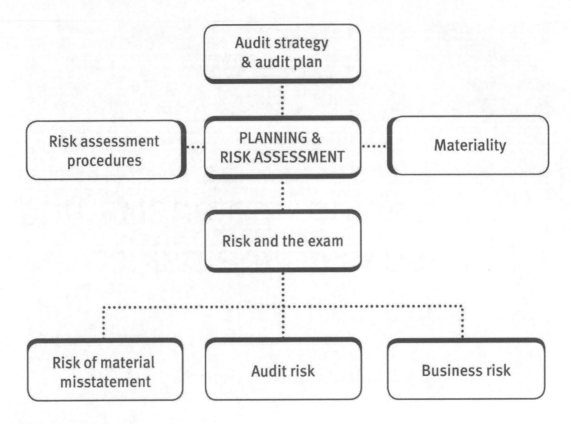

 Planning, materiality and assessing the risk of misstatement were covered in Audit and Assurance at the Applied Skills level. At the Strategic Professional level, you will be expected to evaluate audit risks, risks of material misstatement and business risks. You will also be expected to describe these risks in greater detail than that required for Audit and Assurance.

 Exam focus

Risk assessment and planning normally makes up a significant number of marks of the exam. It is also essential for all areas of the exam that you are able to assess the materiality of a matter.

1 The audit strategy and plan

Planning an audit involves establishing the overall audit strategy for the engagement and developing an audit plan.

[ISA 300 *Planning an Audit of Financial Statements*, 2]

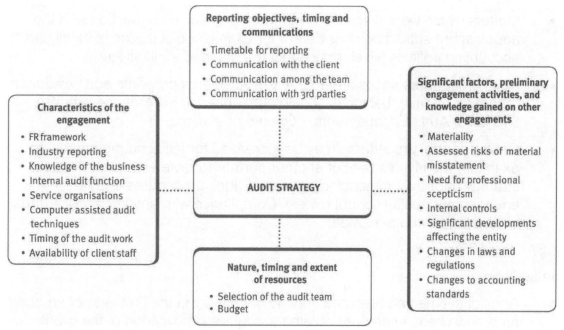

Reporting objectives, timing and communications
- Timetable for reporting
- Communication with the client
- Communication among the team
- Communication with 3rd parties

Characteristics of the engagement
- FR framework
- Industry reporting
- Knowledge of the business
- Internal audit function
- Service organisations
- Computer assisted audit techniques
- Timing of the audit work
- Availability of client staff

AUDIT STRATEGY

Significant factors, preliminary engagement activities, and knowledge gained on other engagements
- Materiality
- Assessed risks of material misstatement
- Need for professional scepticism
- Internal controls
- Significant developments affecting the entity
- Changes in laws and regulations
- Changes to accounting standards

Nature, timing and extent of resources
- Selection of the audit team
- Budget

[ISA 300, Appendix]

Once the strategy has been established, the auditor should develop an audit plan. The audit plan is more detailed than the strategy and should include specific descriptions of:

- The nature, timing and extent of risk assessment procedures.

- The nature, timing and extent of further audit procedures, including:

  - **What** audit procedures are to be carried out

  - **Who** should do them

  - **How much** work should be done (sample sizes, etc.)

  - **When** the work should be done (interim vs. final)

- Any other procedures necessary to conform to ISAs.

[ISA 300, 9]

Both the strategy and the plan must be formally documented in the audit working papers.

Planning procedures for initial engagements

For an initial audit, there are several factors which should be considered, in addition to the planning procedures which are carried out for recurring audits.

- Arrangements should be made with the predecessor auditor to review their working papers.

- Matters which were discussed with management in connection with the appointment should be considered, for example, discussion of significant accounting policies which may affect the planned audit strategy.

- Audit procedures necessary to obtain sufficient appropriate audit evidence regarding opening balances should be planned in accordance with ISA 510 *Initial Audit Engagements – Opening Balances*.

- Quality control procedures may be increased for initial engagements, for example, the involvement of another partner to review the overall audit strategy prior to commencing significant audit procedures and an engagement quality control review. Compliance with any such procedures should be fully documented.

[ISA 300, A22]

In addition:

- Additional time and resource may be necessary in the first year of an audit for a new client, in order to obtain the required knowledge of the client, e.g. documenting the internal control systems of the client for the first time, understanding the business including the legal and regulatory framework applicable to the company.

- It may be difficult to place reliance on analytical procedures as a source of substantive audit evidence as these require knowledge and experience of the client in order to set appropriate expectations, and therefore increased tests of detail may be necessary.

- Given the increased risk associated with initial engagements, consideration should be given to using an experienced audit team in order to reduce detection risk.

The impact of ISAs and IFRS standards

The impact of ISAs

ISA 315 *Identifying and Assessing the Risks of Material Misstatement through Understanding the Entity and Its Environment* requires a risk based approach to the audit.

"The objective of the auditor is to identify and assess the risks of material misstatement, whether due to fraud or error, at the financial statement and assertion levels, through understanding the entity and its environment, including the entity's internal control, thereby providing a basis for designing and implementing responses to the assessed risks of material misstatement." [ISA 315, 3]

ISA 330 *The Auditor's Response to Assessed Risks* further develops the concept by stating that:

"The objective of the auditor is to obtain sufficient appropriate audit evidence regarding the assessed risks of material misstatement, through designing and implementing appropriate responses to those risks."
[ISA 330, 3]

The importance of financial reporting standards

The audit opinion states whether or not the financial statements have been prepared in accordance with the financial reporting framework.

In order to reach this opinion, the auditor must understand the relevant financial reporting standards, and evaluate whether the financial statements comply with these standards. This knowledge and understanding needs to be applied throughout the audit.

At the planning stage, the auditor needs to assess the risk of material misstatement in the financial statements. The auditor must understand the required accounting treatment in order to identify potential omission or incorrect measurement, recognition, presentation or disclosure of an item.

The risk of material misstatement will increase with the complexity of the financial reporting issue, and where the matter requires significant judgment.

2 Risk assessment

ISA 315 requires auditors to perform the following (minimum) risk assessment procedures:

- **Enquiries** of management, appropriate individuals within the internal audit function (if there is one), and others with relevant information within the client entity (e.g. about external and internal changes the company has experienced).

- **Analytical procedures** to identify trends/relationships that are inconsistent with other relevant information or the auditor's understanding of the business.

- **Observation** (e.g. of control procedures).

- **Inspection** (e.g. of key strategic documents and procedural manuals).

[ISA 315, 6]

Analytical procedures at the planning stage

Analytical procedures involve analysis of plausible relationships among financial and non-financial data.

At the planning stage, analytical procedures may be performed using management accounts or the draft financial statements if available.

Analytical procedures will be useful at the planning stage to help identify unusual fluctuations or balances which are not consistent with the auditor's expectation. These areas indicate risks of material misstatement.

In the exam you may be provided with financial information and be expected to perform analytical procedures as part of your risk assessment.

Example risk assessment procedures

It is impossible to prepare a comprehensive list of risk assessment procedures that need to be carried out. The procedures need to be prepared in light of the unique circumstances of the client. However, examples include:

Enquiries of management:

- Have any share issues occurred during the year?

- Has the company invested in any new capital assets during the year?

- Have any new competitors or products entered the market?

- How does the company manage exposure to exchange rate risk?

- Have there been any changes in senior management during the year?

Analytical procedures:

- Compare actual results to forecast to identify any significant differences.

- Compare the client's performance and position to any available industry data to identify significant variations.

- Compare the client's financial statements in comparison to the prior year to identify any unexpected changes in performance or position.

Observe:

- The application of controls over the counting of inventory during the year.

- The performance of year-end reconciliations (bank, supplier statement) to ensure they are performed regularly.

- Month-end adjustments/reconciliations being performed during an interim visit to ensure controls are applied throughout the year.

Inspect:

- Organisation charts to identify changes in key staff.

- Examples of controls operating throughout the year, e.g. evidence of review of month end reconciliations, evidence of review of aged receivables on a monthly basis.

- HR records/payroll records to identify movements in staff.

- News/media reports to identify any significant issues, such as potential legal action.

Understanding the entity and its environment including controls

Auditors should obtain an understanding of:

- Relevant industry, regulatory and other external factors.

- The nature of the entity, including:

  - Its operations
  - Its ownership and governance structures
  - The types of investment the entity makes
  - The way the entity is structured and financed.

- The entity's selection and application of accounting policies.

- The entity's objectives and strategies, and those related business risks that may result in material misstatement.

- The measurement and review of the entity's financial performance.

[ISA 315, 11]

If the entity has an internal audit function, obtaining an understanding of that function also contributes to the auditor's understanding of the entity and its environment, including internal control, in particular the role that the function plays in the entity's monitoring of internal control over financial reporting. [ISA 315, A113]

The auditor may also consider how management has responded to the findings and recommendations of the internal audit function regarding identified deficiencies in internal control relevant to the audit, including whether and how such responses have been implemented, and whether they have been subsequently evaluated by the internal audit function. [ISA 315, A80]

The components of internal control include:

- The control environment

- The entity's risk assessment process

- The information system relevant to financial reporting

- The control activities

- The monitoring system.

[ISA 315, A59]

The auditor must evaluate the design of the controls to determine whether they have been implemented during the financial reporting period and whether they are effective at preventing and detecting potentially material fraud and error. [ISA 315, 13]

 Current developments: Proposed ISA 315 (Revised)

The Exposure Draft 'Proposed ISA 315 (Revised)' sets out the risk assessment procedures that provide a foundation for an audit of financial statements. The revised ISA establishes more robust requirements and detailed guidance to enhance audit quality.

The proposed changes bring the standard up to date with developments in the profession and the business world and are made with the public interest as the main emphasis. The standard has been modernised to:

- Meet evolving business needs, including information technology, and how auditors use automated tools and techniques, including data analytics, to perform audit procedures.

- Enhance the auditor's required understanding of the entity's use of information technology relevant to financial reporting.

- Improve the standard's applicability to entities across a wide spectrum of circumstances and complexities.

- Emphasise the importance of exercising professional scepticism throughout the risk identification and assessment process.

The public interest issues addressed in the ED are:

Scalability

The standard is written to provide guidance that will apply to all entities ranging from small, simple entities to large, complex, multinational entities.

Modernising and updating the ISA for an evolving business environment

The evolution and increasingly complex nature of the economic, technological and regulatory aspects of the markets and environment in which entities and audit firms operate have necessitated revisions to the ISA. The increased use of ISAs by auditors of public sector entities has also prompted the need for specific considerations relevant to public sector audits.

Data analytics

Application material has been developed to provide examples of how automated tools and techniques (including data analytics) are being used when performing risk assessment procedures.

Information technology

The auditor must understand an entity's IT environment, in particular, those aspects relevant to financial reporting. The auditor is required to understand the entity's use of IT in its business and system of internal control. The standard has been revised in a principles-based manner to minimise the risk that rapid changes in IT could date the standard within a short space of time.

Fostering independence of mind and professional scepticism

Several provisions have been included in the revised ISA to enhance the auditor's exercise of professional scepticism, including:

- Emphasising the importance of exercising professional scepticism.

- Clarifying that a thorough understanding of the applicable financial reporting framework is essential to exercise professional scepticism.

- Highlighting the benefits of exercising professional scepticism during the engagement team discussion.

- Highlighting that contradictory evidence may be obtained as part of the auditor's risk assessment procedures.

The auditor's considerations relating to fraud

The standard highlights the need to apply ISA 240 when identifying and assessing the risks of material misstatement due to fraud.

3 Materiality

The objective of an audit is to express an opinion as to whether the financial statements are prepared, in all **material** respects, in accordance with an applicable financial reporting framework. [ISA 200, 11a]

It is therefore of vital importance for auditors to apply the concept of materiality in the planning and performance of the audit.

Misstatements, including omissions, are considered to be material if they, individually or in aggregate, could reasonably be expected to influence the economic decisions of users taken on the basis of the financial statements.

[ISA 320 *Materiality in Planning and Performing an Audit*, 2]

Calculation

ISA 320 *Materiality in Planning and Performing an Audit*, recognises, and permits, the use of benchmark calculations of materiality.

A traditional calculation basis is as follows:

	Value	Comments
Pre-tax profit	5 – 10%	Appropriate where users are primarily interested in the profitability of the company.
Revenue	½ – 1%	Materiality by reference to the size of the business can be measured in terms of revenue.
Total assets	1 – 2%	Size can also be measured in terms of the asset base.

These benchmarks should be used in the initial assessment of materiality.

The auditor must then use judgment to reassess materiality to ensure it is relevant to the unique circumstances of the client.

When deciding on an appropriate benchmark the auditor must consider:

- The elements of the financial statements.

- Whether particular items tend to be the focus of the users.

- The nature of the entity, its life cycle and its environment.

- The ownership and financing structure.

- The relative volatility of the benchmark.

[ISA 320, A4]

Material by nature

Materiality is not just a purely financial concern. Some items may be material by nature because of the impact they have on the financial statements.

Examples of items which are material by nature include:

- Misstatements that affect compliance with regulatory requirements.

- Misstatements that affect compliance with debt covenants.

- Misstatements that, when adjusted, would turn a reported profit into a loss for the year.

- Misstatements that, when adjusted, would turn a reported net-asset position into a net-liability position (or net-current asset to net-current liability).

- Related party transactions including transactions with directors, e.g. salary and benefits, personal use of assets, etc.

- Disclosures in the financial statements relating to possible future legal claims or going concern issues, for example, could influence users' decisions and may be purely narrative. In this case a numerical calculation is not relevant.

Performance materiality

It is unlikely, in practice, that auditors will be able to identify individually material misstatements. It is much more common that misstatements are material in aggregate (i.e. in combination). For this reason auditors must also consider what is known as 'performance materiality.'

 This is an amount, set by the auditor at less than materiality for the financial statements as a whole to reduce to an appropriately low level the probability that the aggregate of uncorrected and undetected misstatements exceeds materiality for the financial statements as a whole. [ISA 320, 9]

 Case Study: Performance materiality

LeJoG Co is a company that organises accommodation, luggage transportation, and support for charitable sporting enthusiasts attempting to travel from one end of the country to the other. All customers pay in full when booking their trip. LeJoG has a complicated cancellation policy, the amount refundable decreases with the length of time before the start of the trip.

The audit team has planned the audit of the financial statements for the year ended 30 June 20X5. The team has determined a materiality level for the financial statements as a whole, of $100,000, which has been calculated using an average of 1% of revenue, 2% total assets and 10% profit before tax.

Performance materiality needs to be applied to revenue and the associated liabilities recognised when taking payment from customers in advance, as revenue recognition is an area of audit risk.

Performance materiality could be determined as a percentage of financial statement materiality, say 75%, i.e. a performance materiality of ($100,000 × 75%) $75,000 could be set for the audit of revenue and the associated liabilities. The audit team could use a higher or lower percentage, or use a different calculation, depending on their professional judgment.

The aim of performance materiality is to reduce the risk that misstatements in aggregate exceed materiality for the financial statements as a whole. For example, if a misstatement was identified of, say $80,000, without performance materiality the auditor would conclude that revenue is not materially misstated. However, the audit may not have detected further misstatements which when added to the $80,000 identified would result in a material misstatement. By using performance materiality, the auditor would conclude that a misstatement of $80,000 could be material, thereby prompting them to do additional work. If no additional misstatements are detected, an unmodified opinion may be issued.

Materiality: Audit Quality Thematic Review

FRC Audit Quality Thematic Review – Materiality

The Financial Reporting Council (FRC) published the results of its audit quality review on materiality in 2017. The determination of materiality affects audit quality.

This review looked at how eight major firms determined materiality in respect of 32 audits of public interest entities (PIEs).

The review also included discussions with audit committee chairs and investors to understand their views on materiality.

Review findings

There are more cases of audit firms basing materiality on adjusted profit figures rather than reported profits. This often included profits adjusted for non-cash items such as amortisation and impairments. The FRC's view is that this is not appropriate as they are part of the business' normal activities.

All firms have detailed guidance on how to determine materiality for the financial statements but do not have a similar level of guidance for determining performance materiality and the methods used do not provide guidance for loss making entities.

All firms considered misstatements of 0 – 5% of overall materiality as clearly trivial.

Overall materiality ranged from 3% to 10% of profit before tax and performance materiality ranged from 40% of overall materiality to 80% of materiality across the eight firms. The FRC considers these differences in approach could lead to significantly different audits and therefore audit outcomes. The FRC has encouraged firms to reassess their guidance.

Some of the firms' own internal quality monitoring found issues in relation to materiality such as:

- Component materiality being incorrectly calculated

- Overall materiality being set too high

- Inappropriate benchmarks being used.

However, the firms did not consider whether these issues were more wide-spread than the individual audit subject to monitoring. The FRC encourages firms to consider whether the issues are firm-wide.

Auditors are required to disclose quantitative materiality to the audit committee. Three of the firms reviewed had not communicated materiality at any point during the audit.

Some audit firms are now basing materiality on a rolling average basis of profit to eliminate volatile situations. Some are using forecast figures based on management information for the same reason. These approaches are not covered by auditing standards and audit firms must be able to justify this approach as being more appropriate.

Recommendations

Audit firms should:

- Consider setting a lower performance materiality level in the first year audit due to the increased level of detection risk.

- Include guidance for audit teams regarding materiality for loss making entities.

- Include guidance on setting component materiality in their methodologies for group audits.

- Ensure the auditor's report includes a clear explanation of the approach taken when an account balance specific materiality is used for certain balances.

Standard setters should:

- Consider the appropriateness of using forecasts to calculate materiality and determine whether this satisfies the requirements of the ISA.

- If deemed necessary, draft additional guidance relating to the use of forecast figures for calculating materiality.

- Consider whether the ISA should include guidance on setting materiality for loss making entities.

- Consider whether the ISA should include guidance on setting component materiality.

Review of audit committees

Audit committee chairs (ACC) were consulted for their views on materiality.

17% of the ACCs said they had not discussed or challenged the appropriateness of the level of materiality set by their audit firm despite corporate governance regulations requiring audit committees to monitor the effectiveness of the audit.

69% regarded the level of materiality was appropriate.

Recommendations

Audit firms should:

- Ensure audit committees are aware of the auditor's responsibility to communicate materiality.

- Disclose quantitative materiality to the audit committee.

Audit committees should:

- During the tender process, consider the appropriateness of the proposed materiality benchmark.

- Discuss with management the level of materiality used when preparing the financial statements.

- Discuss materiality with the audit team and assess its appropriateness.

- Obtain an understanding of those balances considered immaterial by the audit team, and therefore not tested.

Exam focus

The determination of materiality is an important factor in the audit as it influences the extent of testing performed and therefore affects audit quality. You may have to consider some of the matters discussed above in a quality control question.

4 Risk and the exam

In the exam it is likely that you will be asked to perform a risk assessment for an audit client. The three types of risk examinable are:

- Risk of material misstatement
- Audit risk
- Business risk.

It is vital that you understand the difference between these types of risk to ensure you answer the question appropriately.

Risk of material misstatement

Risk of material misstatement is the risk the financial statements are materially misstated (either due to fraud or error), prior to the audit. [ISA 200, 13n]

The financial statements may be materially misstated for three main reasons:

- Numbers are misstated – e.g. overstatement of receivables due to bad debts not being written off.
- Disclosures are missing or inadequate – e.g. going concern disclosures being omitted.
- The basis of preparation is inappropriate – the going concern basis has been used when the break up basis should have been used.

When evaluating the risk of material misstatement it is crucial to discuss the specific impact of the risk on the **financial statements**, i.e.

- The specific account balance, transaction or disclosure affected.
- How it is/may be misstated, i.e. what has the client done wrong/what might the client do wrong when preparing the financial statements.
- Whether the item is/could be overstated, understated, omitted, inappropriately recognised, etc.

Risk of material misstatement comprises **inherent and control risk**.

Inherent risk

Inherent risk is the susceptibility of an assertion about a class of transaction, account balance or disclosure to a misstatement that could be material, before consideration of any related controls. [ISA 200, 13ni]

Requirements of accounting standards can increase inherent risk as the rules laid down may make not be understood or may be misinterpreted by the client resulting in misstatement of the financial statements.

Items presented in the financial statements will be more susceptible to misstatement if they are complicated to account for, particularly balances which involve a significant amount of subjectivity or management judgment.

The financial statements will be materially misstated if they are not prepared in accordance with the applicable financial reporting framework. In order for the auditor to identify material misstatement they need to know what the appropriate accounting treatment is and whether it has been complied with.

In the exam you will have to comment on whether the accounting treatment is appropriate therefore your knowledge from Strategic Business Reporting will be required in this exam. The chapter 'Financial reporting revision' summarises the key points from these standards.

 The auditor is also required to determine whether any of the risks are a significant risk. A significant risk is a risk of material misstatement that requires special audit consideration. [ISA 315, 4e]

Inherent risks

Revenue

IFRS 15 *Revenue from Contracts with Customers* sets out a five step process for revenue recognition. One of these steps is to determine the performance obligations in the contract and consider when they are fulfilled. This may be relatively straightforward for some transactions e.g. when a customer purchases a good from a shop, the performance obligation is fulfilled at the time the customer takes the goods. However, other contracts are not so straightforward. Complications such as contracts which are fulfilled over a period of time or a contract with a variable transaction price dependent on whether certain targets have been met, will make revenue recognition more difficult to account for and as a result, increase the risk of material misstatement.

Impairments

IAS 36 *Impairment of Assets* requires a company to recognise an impairment if the carrying amount of an asset falls below its recoverable amount. Assessing the recoverable amount of an asset requires consideration of how much benefit is expected to be generated by the asset in the future. This is very subjective and open to manipulation which increases the risk of material misstatement.

Provisions

IAS 37 *Provisions, Contingent Liabilities and Contingent Assets* requires a provision liability and expense to be recognised if there is a present obligation which is probable to lead to an outflow of economic benefits. For some provisions, e.g. an assurance type warranty provision, management will need to use its experience and judgment to determine an appropriate provision. This can result in management bias, as management may not want to recognise a liability and cost in order to make the financial performance and position look more positive.

Control risk

Control risk is the risk that a misstatement that could occur will not be prevented, or detected and corrected, on a timely basis by the entity's internal control. [ISA 200, 13nii]

If the client's internal controls are not effective or adequate, transactions processed during the year may contain fraud or error, resulting in misstatement.

Control risks

Control risk is increased if the client's internal controls are not designed appropriately or do not work effectively. This increases the opportunity for fraud and error to occur. Examples include:

- A lack of segregation of duties between recording transactions in the accounting system and responsibility for cash or other assets. If one individual is able to take cash out of the business and record an entry in the accounting system in respect of that money, it will be difficult for the company to detect the fraud.

- If purchase orders are not authorised, a purchase order being placed for a non-business use is unlikely to be identified.

- If customers are not credit checked and credit limits are not set, the company could make sales on credit to uncreditworthy customers which could result in irrecoverable debts.

Audit risk

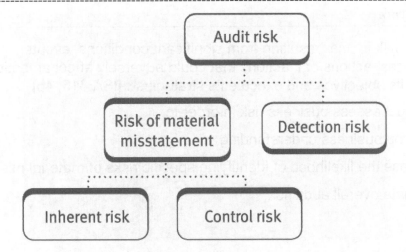

Audit risk is the risk that the auditor expresses an inappropriate opinion when the financial statements are materially misstated. [ISA 200, 13c]

The auditor will express an inappropriate opinion if the financial statements are materially misstated and they fail to detect that misstatement.

Detection risk is the risk that the procedures performed by the auditor to reduce audit risk to an acceptably low level will not detect a misstatement that exists that could be material. [ISA 200, 13e]

Detection risk is the only element of audit risk that that auditor can influence as the risks of material misstatement are created by the client when they prepare the financial statements or process transactions during the year.

 Detection risks

Detection risks include situations such as:

- First year of auditing the client therefore the auditor has a lack of cumulative knowledge and experience.

- The client putting the auditor under undue time pressure to complete the audit resulting in the audit being rushed and misstatements possibly going undetected.

- A client which operates from multiple sites and the auditor may not be able to visit each site during the audit. This will be an issue, for example, if a material amount of inventory is held at sites not visited by the auditor.

 If no detection risks are given in the scenario, an answer to an audit risk question will be identical to an answer to a risk of material misstatement question.

Business risk

A business risk is one "resulting from significant conditions, events, circumstances, actions or inactions that could adversely affect an entity's ability to achieve its objectives and execute its strategies". [ISA 315, 4b]

Auditors must assess business risk in order to:

- Develop business understanding

- Increase the likelihood of identifying specific risks of material misstatement

- Evaluate overall audit risk.

Examples of business risks

Business risks are often categorised as being 'external' or 'internal'

External risks – risks derived from the environment in which the entity operates

- Changing legislation
- Changing interest rates
- Changing exchange rates
- Public opinion, attitudes, fashions
- Price wars initiated by competitors
- Untried technologies and ideas, political factors
- Natural hazards
- Changes in government policy

Internal risks' – risks derived from the entity and its operations

- Employees
- Failure to modernise products, processes, labour relations, marketing
- Overtrading
- Cash flow difficulties
- Rapidly increasing gearing
- Excessive reliance on a dominant CEO
- Fraud
- Computer systems failures
- Reliance on one or few products, customers or suppliers

The relationship between business risk and the risk of material misstatement/audit risk

Most business risks will eventually have financial consequences, and therefore an effect on the financial statements. If the client does not account for these issues in the correct manner, the financial statements could be materially misstated.

Business risk v risk of material misstatement

Operating in a technologically fast paced market could lead to a company's products being outdated by superior products. This is a **business risk** because it may stop a company achieving desired profit margins.

> The **risk of material misstatement** is that inventory may be overstated in the financial statements: the net realisable value of inventory may have fallen below cost, requiring a write-down of the inventory balance.

Additional information to help plan the audit

In the exam you may be asked to suggest additional information to help plan the audit. The scenario will have provided some information on the client, but in order to fully assess the risks, further information will be required.

By obtaining additional information, a greater understanding of the risk areas can be obtained to allow the impact on the financial statements to be considered. This will enable the audit to be planned more effectively.

Additional information

Example 1 – Purchase of shares during the year

The client has purchased 25% of a company's share capital during the year. It is possible that it is being treated as an associate when in fact no significant influence can be exercised. In this case it should be treated as an investment. Additional information is required regarding voting rights attached to the shares to determine whether significant influence has been acquired.

Example 2 – New loan taken out during the year

The client has taken out a ten-year loan during the year. Whilst it would be expected that the loan should be split between current and non-current liabilities, if there are no payments due for the first twelve months, the loan will be a non-current liability for the first year. In this case the loan agreement would provide the additional information required regarding payment terms and details of whether the loan is secured over the company's assets. This will help determine whether the loan should be split between current and non-current liabilities and whether any disclosure needs to be made of any security for the loan.

5 Assessing whether a risk is significant

As part of the risk assessment process the auditor should consider the significance of the identified risks, including:

- Whether the risk is one of fraud.
- Whether it is related to recent economic, accounting or other developments that require specific attention.
- The complexity of the related transactions.
- Whether it involves related parties.
- The degree of subjectivity involved in measuring financial information.
- Whether it involves transactions outside the normal course of business.

[ISA 315, 28]

If the auditor determines that a significant risk exists they must then obtain the necessary understanding of how the entity controls that risk. Only then can the auditor determine an appropriate response in terms of further audit procedures.

6 Response to risk assessment

The main purpose of performing risk assessment is to guide the auditor in the design and performance of further audit procedures to obtain sufficient appropriate audit evidence. The only way the auditor can reduce audit risk is by reducing **detection risk**. Detection risk can be reduced by:

- Emphasising the need for professional scepticism.
- Assigning more experienced staff to complex or risky areas of the engagement.
- Providing more supervision.
- Incorporating additional elements of unpredictability in the selection of further audit procedures.
- Making changes to the nature, timing or extent of audit procedures, e.g.
  - Placing less reliance on the results of systems and controls testing.
  - Performing more substantive procedures.
  - Consulting external experts on technically complex or contentious matters.
  - Changing the timing and frequency of review procedures.

[ISA 330, A1]

7 Professional scepticism

Professional scepticism is defined as: 'An attitude that includes a questioning mind, being alert to conditions which may indicate possible misstatement due to error or fraud, and a critical assessment of audit evidence.'
[ISA 200, 13I]

It is both an ethical and a professional issue. Professional scepticism includes maintaining independence of mind.

Professional scepticism requires the auditor to be alert to:

- Audit evidence that contradicts other audit evidence.

- Information that brings into question the reliability of documents and responses to enquiries to be used as audit evidence.

- Conditions that may indicate possible fraud.

- Circumstances that suggest the need for audit procedures in addition to those required by ISAs.

[ISA 200, A20]

In the exam you may be required to critically evaluate the planning or performance of an audit. This will include assessing whether the auditor has exercised professional scepticism.

Examples of circumstances where professional scepticism has not been applied include:

- Contradictory evidence has not been questioned.

- The reliability of documents and responses to enquiries from the client has not been evaluated.

- The sufficiency and appropriateness of evidence has not been considered.

- The authenticity of a document has not been considered when there are indications of possible fraud.

- Past experience of the dishonesty or lack of integrity of the client has been disregarded.

- The auditor has accepted less persuasive evidence because of their past experience of the honesty and integrity of the client.

If professional scepticism is not exercised, the auditor may:

- Overlook unusual circumstances

- Use unsuitable audit procedures

- Reach inappropriate conclusions.

Exercising professional scepticism

The auditor may make an enquiry of management regarding compliance with laws and regulations. Management may inform the auditor that there have been no instances of non-compliance during the year. Application of professional scepticism would require the auditor to seek alternative, corroborative evidence to support management's claim as they may not wish the auditor to know about any breaches. This may involve speaking with the company's compliance department to confirm management's statement as well as reviewing board minutes for any discussions that indicate non-compliance or reviewing invoices from legal advisers which may indicate advice has been obtained regarding non-compliance.

Current issue: Professional scepticism

IAASB: Toward enhanced Professional Scepticism – observations of the Professional Scepticism Working Group

The importance of professional scepticism to the public interest is increasing due to:

- Increased complexity of business and financial reporting

- Greater use of estimates and management judgment

- Changes in business models due to technological developments

- Reliance by the public on reliable financial reporting.

The main observations of the working group are:

- Strong business acumen and knowledge of the client's business model is essential for robust professional scepticism.

- Professional scepticism can be impeded by tight reporting deadlines and resource constraints.

- Personal traits such as confidence and an inquisitive nature can enhance the exercise of professional scepticism.

- Professional scepticism starts at the beginning of one's career. It needs to be 'part of the auditor's DNA'.

- Standard setters such as the IAASB, IESBA and IAESB can do more to emphasise and provide guidance on how to exercise professional scepticism.

- The concepts of professional scepticism may be relevant to all professional accountants, not just auditors.

- Standard setting alone will not be enough. All stakeholders, such as the audit committee, have a role to play e.g. by challenging the auditor to ask tough questions of management.

This is likely to affect areas such as:

- Quality control – ensuring the auditor is unbiased and that an appropriate audit team is selected.

- Risk assessments – being aware of management incentives and biases, and challenging management.

- Accounting estimates – performing enhanced risk assessment and taking a step back for riskier estimates.

- Group audits – exercising sufficient scepticism when using other auditors.

IAASB: Proposed Application Material Relating to Professional Scepticism and Professional Judgment

Proposed objective

The IAASB has proposed new application material to:

- Describe how compliance with the fundamental principles in the Code of Ethics supports the exercise of professional scepticism in the context of audit and other assurance engagements.

- Emphasise the importance of professional accountants obtaining a sufficient understanding of the facts and circumstances known to them when exercising professional judgment in applying the conceptual framework.

Reasons for the changes

Currently the Code of Ethics only refers to professional scepticism in the context of audit and assurance engagements. The IAASB is looking at whether the Code should refer to the need professional scepticism to be applied by all professional accountants for all services. If a professional accountant accepts information at face value, without regard to whether it could result in being associated with false or misleading information, it would constitute non-compliance with the fundamental ethical principles of integrity and professional competence and due care.

Research suggests that:

- Drivers and impediments to compliance with fundamental principles and the exercise of professional scepticism are the same.

- Auditors who comply with the fundamental principles tend to apply greater scepticism.

- Time pressure which creates a threat to the fundamental principles also impairs the application of professional scepticism.

Details of the proposed changes

1 **Definitions of the fundamental principles to be extended.**

Integrity – being straightforward and honest is consistent with a questioning mind and the critical assessment of audit evidence in exercising professional scepticism.

Objectivity – avoiding bias is consistent with exercising professional scepticism.

Professional competence and due care – exercising professional scepticism enables the auditor to assess whether audit evidence if sufficient and appropriate in the circumstances.

2 **New section on how to exercise professional judgment**

Professional judgment involves the application of training, knowledge and experience. When exercising professional judgment the accountant should identify, evaluate and address threats to the fundamental principles. The accountant should consider whether:

- There is an inconsistency between known facts and circumstances and the accountant's expectations.

- The information provides a reasonable basis on which to draw a conclusion.

- Other reasonable conclusions could be drawn from the information being considered.

- The accountant's own preconception or bias might be affecting the accountant's judgment.

- The accountant's own expertise and experience are sufficient, or whether there is a need to consult with others.

IAASB *Questions and Answers: Professional Scepticism in an Audit of Financial Statements* (February 2012)

Provides additional explanations relating to professional scepticism. Specifically, professional scepticism:

- is fundamentally a mind-set that drives auditor behaviour to adopt a questioning approach.

- is inseparably linked to objectivity and auditor independence.

- forms an integral part of the auditor's skill set and is closely interrelated with professional judgment, both of which are key inputs to audit quality.

- enhances the effectiveness of an audit procedure and reduces the risk of giving an inappropriate opinion.

The Q&A reiterates the importance of the components of quality control in enhancing the awareness of the importance and application of professional scepticism.

In addition, the Q&A emphasises that although professional scepticism is not referred to within each ISA, it is relevant and necessary throughout the audit and is particularly important when considering the risks of material misstatement due to fraud and when addressing areas of the audit that are more complex, significant or highly judgmental (e.g. accounting estimates, going concern, related party transactions, non-compliance with laws and regulations).

Audit documentation is critical in evidencing professional scepticism, particularly documentation demonstrating how significant judgments and key audit issues were addressed, which may provide evidence of the auditor's exercise of professional scepticism.

Effective oversight and inspection of audits by regulators and oversight bodies should incorporate challenging, influencing and stimulating auditors to be sceptical and focusing auditors on the importance of professional scepticism and how it can be appropriately applied through constructive dialogue.

UK syllabus: Professional scepticism

In March 2012, the FRC released a Briefing Paper *Professional Scepticism*.

The briefing paper takes a theoretical approach to discussing the importance of professional scepticism in the audit, specifically:

- Exploring:

    - the roots of scepticism and identifying lessons for its role in the conduct of the audit

    - scientific scepticism

    - the origins of modern audit.

- Concluding about professional scepticism and the audit.

- Discussing the conditions necessary for auditors to demonstrate professional scepticism.

The paper highlights the significance of scepticism to the quality of the audit. It defines scepticism as 'examination, inquiry into, hesitation or doubt' specifically, doubt that stimulates challenge and inquiry.

It explains that scientific scepticism is a 'systematic form of continual informed questioning', or critical appraisal, looking for evidence that contradicts management's assertions and suspending judgment about the validity of those assertions. In the context of an audit, this means actively looking for risks of material misstatement.

Applying ISAs proportionately

Applying ISAs Proportionately with the Size and Complexity of an Entity (IAASB – August 2009)

The auditor's objectives are the same for audits of entities of different sizes and complexities. This, however, does not mean that every audit will be planned and performed in exactly the same way. In particular ISAs explain that the appropriate audit approach for designing and performing audit procedures depends on the auditor's risk assessment and the exercise of appropriate professional judgment.

Often, small and medium-sized entities (SMEs) engage in relatively simple business transactions. This means that their audits will generally be relatively straightforward. For example, consider the requirement in ISA 315 for the auditor to obtain an understanding of the entity and its environment. The typically simpler structure and processes in a SME often mean that the auditor may obtain understanding quite readily and document this in a straightforward manner. Similarly, internal control in the context of a SME may be simpler.

Of particular relevance is the fact that the ISAs include useful guidance that assists the auditor in applying specific requirements in the context of a SME audit. Where appropriate, guidance is included in ISAs under the subheading 'Considerations Specific to Smaller Entities'.

For example:

- Standard audit programs drawn up on the assumption of few relevant control activities may be used for the audit of a SME provided that they are tailored to the circumstances of the engagement.

- In the absence of interim or monthly financial information, the auditor may need to plan analytical procedures when an early draft of the entity's financial statements becomes available.

- Given the potential lack of documentary evidence concerning control activities, the attitudes, awareness, and actions of management are of particular importance to the auditor's understanding of a SME's control environment.

Other guidance indicates that specific aspects of the audit will vary with the size, complexity, and nature of the entity, for example:

- The nature and extent of the auditor's planning activities.

- The auditor's consideration of fraud risk factors.

- The communication process between the auditor and those charged with governance.

- The level of detail at which to communicate significant deficiencies in internal control.

- The judgment as to whether a control is relevant to the audit.

Not all of the ISAs are necessarily relevant in every audit, that is, the circumstances in which an ISA applies may not exist in the engagement. For example, some of the ISAs that may not be relevant in a SME audit include:

- ISA 402 *Audit Considerations Relating to An Entity Using a Service Organisation*, if the client does not use a service organisation.

- ISA 600 *Special Considerations – Audit of Group Financial Statements* (including the work of component auditors), if it is not a group audit.

- ISA 610 *Using the Work of Internal Auditors*, if there is no internal audit function.

Even if an ISA is relevant, not all of its requirements may be relevant in the particular circumstances of an audit. A few examples include:

- Holding an engagement team meeting if it is only a one person team.

- Performing the specified substantive procedures if the auditor has not identified previously unidentified or undisclosed related parties or related party transactions.

- Obtaining sufficient appropriate audit evidence to determine whether a material uncertainty exists if the auditor has not identified any event or condition that casts doubt on the entity's ability to continue as a going concern.

Finally, to further assist the auditor, the ISAs provide examples of how the documentation in a SME audit can be approached in an efficient and effective manner. For example:

- It may be helpful and efficient to record various aspects of the audit together in a single document, with cross-references to supporting working papers as appropriate.

- The documentation of the understanding of the entity may be incorporated in the auditor's documentation of the overall strategy and audit plan.

- The results of the risk assessment may be documented as part of the auditor's documentation of further procedures.

- It is not necessary to document the entirety of the auditor's understanding of the SME and matters related to it.

- A brief memorandum may serve as the documented audit strategy. At the completion of the audit, a brief memorandum could be developed and then updated to serve as the documented audit strategy for the following year's audit.

Auditing significant, unusual or highly complex transactions

In September 2010, the IAASB issued a Questions & Answers publication, **Auditor considerations regarding significant unusual or highly complex transactions** in response to specific requests for information on how the ISAs deal with this particular topic.

The publication highlights that because of their nature, these transactions may give rise to risks of material misstatement of the financial statements and, accordingly, may merit heightened attention by auditors.

The publication does not provide any additional guidance beyond that which is contained within the ISAs themselves. Instead, it highlights the most salient points from the ISAs for auditors to consider when approaching the audit of significant, unusual or highly complex transactions, and in particular highlights:

- What considerations in the ISAs are relevant when forming an opinion on the financial statements.

- What general considerations in the ISAs are relevant in relation to audit documentation, quality control, and interim reviews of financial statements when dealing with such transactions.

- How the ISAs guide the auditor in the auditor's communication with those charged with governance when dealing with such transactions.

The publication highlights many specific requirements of the ISAs, including:

- The requirement to exercise professional judgment and maintain professional scepticism throughout the planning and performance of an audit.

- The need to identify and assess the risks of material misstatement by performing risk assessment procedures designed to obtain the required understanding of the entity and its environment, including the entity's internal control.

- The requirement to design and implement overall responses to address the assessed risks of material misstatement and to design and perform further audit procedures whose nature, timing, and extent are based on and are responsive to the assessed risks of material misstatement at the assertion level.

When approaching the audit of significant, unusual or highly complex transactions, the auditor should consider the need to obtain more persuasive audit evidence in responding to the assessed risks, as the auditor's assessment of risk is likely to be higher, in particular there is the possibility of increased risk of bias in management's judgments due to the complexity involved therein.

Approach to exam questions: Risk assessment

Risk questions in the exam usually contain the largest single allocation of marks, therefore it is important that you can do well on these questions.

Here are some tips to help you score well:

Audit risks and risks of material misstatement

Use analytical procedures to evaluate the risks of material misstatement/audit risks

When asked to perform analytical procedures, do your calculations first and present them neatly in a table. For example:

	20X5	20X4
Gross profit margin	29%	25%
Interest cover	2 times	10 times
Effective tax rate	18%	25%
Receivables collection period	45 days	31 days
Inventory holding period	37 days	67 days

Each calculation is usually worth ½ mark. There will usually be 5 marks available for calculations which are used in the risk evaluation.

Only calculate ratios and trends relevant to evaluating audit risks or risks of material misstatement. Calculation of irrelevant ratios and trends will not score marks.

Refer to your calculations as you perform your risk assessment.

Using the information provided/the results of your analytical procedures, evaluate the risks of material misstatement/audit risks

Each risk will be worth 2 or 3 marks. To earn the full marks for each risk you need to properly explain the risk. If your answers are too brief or do not demonstrate sufficient understanding you will not score the marks.

To ensure your answer is sufficiently detailed, use the following approach:

- Identify the information from the scenario that creates the potential risk.

- If numbers are provided, calculate whether the balance is material. This helps to assess whether the risk is significant.

- State the required accounting treatment from the relevant accounting standard. If the case study provides specific information about the accounting treatment, comment on this in your answer.

- State the risk to the financial statements if the required treatment is not followed, i.e. which balances will be under or overstated.

For example:

Receivables

- A major customer is struggling to pay their debt and as a result the receivables balance is significantly higher than last year.

- The balance outstanding represents 5% of total assets therefore is material and a significant risk.

- In accordance with IFRS 9 *Financial Instruments*, a receivable should be measured at the transaction price less allowance for any expected credit losses.

- There is a risk that receivables and profit are overstated if the debt is not written off or written down.

Foreign currency transactions

- The company purchases all goods from an overseas supplier resulting in foreign currency transactions.

- In accordance with IAS 21 *The Effects of Changes in Foreign Exchange Rates*, foreign currency purchases should be translated using the spot rate or average rate at the date of the transaction. Any payables balance outstanding at the year-end must be revalued using the year-end rate.

- There is a risk that purchases are misstated if the exchange rate used is incorrect or if errors are made when translating the purchase cost. Payables may be misstated if they have not been revalued at the year-end.

Provisions

- The client has this year started offering warranties with products sold but no provision has been recognised for warranty costs.

- In accordance with IAS 37 *Provisions, Contingent Liabilities and Contingent Assets,* a provision is required to be recognised if there is a present obligation as a result of a past event which can be measured reliably and is probable to lead to a transfer of economic benefits.

- The sale of goods with an assurance type warranty creates an obligation for the company to repair or replace goods returned within the warranty period if they do not perform as expected.

- Provision liabilities and expenses are understated if a provision for warranty costs is not recognised.

Note how the explanation of the risks focuses on how the financial statements may be materially misstated.

Evaluate the business risks facing the client

Make sure you explain business risks as risks the directors of the business will care about. The focus here should be on adverse impact to profit, revenue, or cash flow.

- Identify the information from the scenario creating the risk.

- Explain the impact it will have on the business operations.

- Explain the financial impact.

For example:

Major customer

- A major customer is struggling to pay their debt.

- If the customer cannot pay their balance, the company will not receive the cash which will reduce cash inflows.

- The debt will need to be written off which will reduce profit.

- Future revenues will also decrease as the major customer will no longer be trading with the client.

Foreign currency transactions

- The company purchases all goods from an overseas supplier resulting in foreign currency transactions.

- If the company does not use any hedging instruments it will be exposed to exchange rate fluctuations which will affect the price of purchases.

- If exchange rates move in an adverse direction, the cost of purchases will be higher resulting in a reduction in profit.

Professional marks

Professional marks will be awarded in the first question on the exam for clarity of explanation or evaluation, the use of logical structure and an appropriate format. In the exam, you should prioritise risks identified as this adds to the professionalism of the risk assessment performed.

Guidance on exam technique for risk questions is given in the technical article 'Exam technique for Advanced Audit and Assurance: part 2 – risk', available on the ACCA website.

Relevance of the information provided

The scenario for the risk question will be quite detailed and require you to evaluate the information in the context of planning the audit. The information will be presented in the form of a number of exhibits. One or more of the requirements may ask you to use a specific exhibit to answer that requirement. Use these signposts to avoid wasting time in the exam. If told to use exhibit 4, focus attention on exhibit 4 and don't waste time reading the other exhibits again.

Some information may be provided to help set the scene of the scenario and to enable you to understand the client and its operations. If you can't see how the information relates specifically to the requirement, don't try and force it into an answer. This will waste valuable time in the exam that could be better used on a different question.

Test your understanding 1– Yates Co

You are an audit manager in Satey & Co, a firm of chartered certified accountants responsible for the audit of Yates Co, a new audit client. Yates Co is a private national haulage and distribution company with over 2,000 employees. This long-established company provides refrigerated, bulk and heavy haulage transport services to time-sensitive delivery schedules. Planning of the audit for the financial year ended 30 June 20X5 is about to commence.

You are provided with the following exhibits:

1   An email you have received from the audit engagement partner.

2   Draft financial information for the year ended 30 June 20X5.

Required:

Respond to the instructions in the email from the audit engagement partner.   **(21 marks)**

Note: The split of the mark allocation is shown in the partner's email (Exhibit 1)

Professional marks will be awarded for the presentation and logical flow of the briefing notes and the clarity of the explanations provided.

(4 marks)

(Total: 25 marks)

Exhibit 1 – Email from audit engagement partner

Hello

I have provided you with some information in the attached exhibit which you should use to help you with planning the audit of Yates Co for the financial year ended 30 June 20X5.

Using the information provided in Exhibit 2 I would like you to prepare briefing notes for my use in which you:

(a) Evaluate the risks of material misstatement for the audit of Yates Co for the year ended 30 June 20X5. **(12 marks)**

(b) Design the audit procedures to be performed in respect of:

    (i) Leases **(5 marks)**

    (ii) Restructuring provision **(4 marks)**

Thank you

Exhibit 2 – Draft financial information for the year ended 30 June 20X5

Statement of profit or loss

	Notes	30 June 20X5 Draft $m	30 June 20X4 Actual $m
Revenue	1	161.5	144.4
Operating expenses	2	(156.7)	(143.0)
Operating profit		4.8	1.4
Finance costs		(2.9)	(2.2)
Profit/loss before tax		1.9	(0.8)

Statement of financial position

	Notes	30 June 20X5 Draft $m	30 June 20X4 Actual $m
Non-current assets			
Intangible assets	3	7.2	6.2
Tangible assets	4	78.9	83.1
		86.1	89.3
Current assets			
Inventories		0.6	0.5
Trade receivables		13.7	13.4
Cash and cash equivalents		3.4	2.8
		17.7	16.7
Total assets		103.8	106.0
Equity and liabilities			
Equity			
Share capital		25.0	25.0
Retained earnings		38.4	41.5
Total equity		63.4	66.5
Non-current liabilities			
Provisions	5	12.7	14.1
Lease liabilities	6	5.4	4.4
		18.1	18.5
Current liabilities			
Trade and other payables		22.3	21.0
		22.3	21.0
Total liabilities		40.4	39.5
Total equity and liabilities		103.8	106.0

Note 1: Revenue

Revenue is net of rebates to major customers that increase with the volume of consignments transported. Rebates are calculated on cumulative sales for the financial year and awarded quarterly in arrears. Rebates due to be paid are included in liabilities, see note 5.

Note 2: Operating expenses

	20X5 $m	20X4 $m
Materials expense	88.0	74.7
Staff costs	40.6	35.6
Depreciation and amortisation	8.5	9.5
Other expenses	19.6	23.2
	156.7	143.0

Materials expense includes fuel, repair materials, transportation and vehicle maintenance costs.

Note 3: Intangible assets

Purchased intangible assets including software and industrial licences, are accounted for using the cost model.

Internally generated intangible assets, mainly software developed for customers to generate consignment documents, are initially recognised at cost if the asset recognition criteria are satisfied.

Note 4: Tangible assets

	20X5 $m	20X4 $m
Property	55.1	57.8
Vehicles and transport equipment	16.4	16.0
Other equipment	7.4	9.3
	78.9	83.1

The following depreciation rates are applied on a straight line basis:

- Property – 5 years (lease term)
- Vehicles and transport equipment 3 – 8 years
- Other equipment 3 – 15 years

Note 5: Provisions

	20X5	20X4
	$m	$m
Restructuring	9.0	10.8
Rebates	3.7	3.3
	12.7	14.1

The restructuring provision relates to redundancies and other obligations arising on the closure and relocation of distribution depots in December 20X3.

Note 6: Leases

Yates Co leases its head office building and distribution warehouse. Both leases were taken out at the same time and are for an initial period of five years with an option to extend for a further five years. Yates Co intend to exercise the option to extend the leases as they have done since the lease was first taken out ten years.

Test your understanding 2 – Ivor Co

You are an audit manager in Dinwiddy & Co, a firm of chartered certified accountants responsible for the audit of Ivor Co. Planning of the audit for the financial year ending 30 September 20X5 is about to commence.

You are provided with the following exhibits:

1   An email you have received from the audit engagement partner.

2   Draft financial information for the year ending 30 September 20X5.

Required:

Respond to the instructions in the email from the audit engagement partner.   **(16 marks)**

Note: The split of the mark allocation is shown in the partner's email (Exhibit 1)

Professional marks will be awarded for the presentation and logical flow of the briefing notes and the clarity of the explanations provided.

(4 marks)

(Total: 20 marks)

Exhibit 1 – Email from audit engagement partner

Hello

I have provided you with some information in the attached exhibit which you should use to help you with planning the audit of Ivor Co for the financial year ending 30 September 20X5.

Using the information provided in Exhibit 2 I would like you to prepare briefing notes for my use in which you evaluate the audit risks to be considered in planning the audit of Ivor Co. You should use analytical procedures to assist in identifying audit risks. **(16 marks)**

Thank you

Exhibit 2 – Financial information for the year ending 30 September 20X5

Statement of profit or loss

	Notes	30 September 20X5 Forecast $000	30 September 20X4 Actual $000
Revenue	1	12,570	9,960
Cost of sales		(9,556)	(7,603)
Gross profit		3,014	2,357
Operating expenses	2	(1,824)	(1,663)
Operating profit		1,190	694

Statement of financial position

	Notes	30 September 20X5 Forecast $000	30 September 20X4 Actual $000
Non-current assets			
Tangible assets	3	1,073	2,130
Intangible assets	4	54	75
		1,127	2,205
Current assets			
Inventory		1,640	1,200
Trade receivables	5	2,250	1,395
Cash		104	–
		3,994	2,595
Total assets		5,121	4,800

Equity and liabilities

Ordinary share capital	1,700	1,000
Retained earnings	1,894	1,004
	3,594	2,004

Non-current liabilities

Bank loan	500	1,000
	500	1,000

Current liabilities

Bank overdraft	–	129
Trade and other payables	735	1,499
Tax payable	292	168
	1,027	1,796
Total liabilities	1,527	2,796
Total equity and liabilities	5,121	4,800

Note 1 – Revenue

	20X5	20X4
	$000	$000
Revenue	13,095	10,160
Sales discounts	(525)	(200)
	12,570	9,960

Note 2 – Operating expenses

	20X5	20X4
Distribution costs	762	498
Wages and salaries	1,275	960
Directors' salaries	125	115
Rent	35	12
Profit on disposal	(510)	(75)
Other expenses	137	153
	1,824	1,663

Note 3 – Tangible assets

	Land & buildings $000	Plant & machinery $000	Total $000
Cost			
B/f at 1 Oct 20X4	2,000	750	2,750
Disposals	(1,100)	–	(1,100)
C/f at 30 Sept 20X5	900	750	1,650
Depreciation			
B/f at 1 Oct 20X4	200	420	620
Disposals	(110)	–	(110)
Charge	18	49	67
C/f at 30 Sept 20X5	108	469	577
Carrying amount			
At 30 Sept 20X5	792	281	1,073
At 30 Sept 20X4	1,800	330	2,130

Buildings are depreciated over 50 years on a straight line basis.

Plant and machinery is depreciated at 15% using the reducing balance method.

Note 4 – Intangible assets

	Total $000
B/f at 1 Oct 20X4	125
Additions	5
C/f at 30 Sept 20X5	130
Amortisation	
B/f at 1 Oct 20X4	50
Charge	26
C/f at 30 Sept 20X5	76
Carrying amount	
At 30 Sept 20X5	54
At 30 Sept 20X4	75

Development costs are amortised over five years using the straight line method.

Note 5 – Trade and other receivables:

	20X5 $000	20X4 $000
Trade receivables	2,320	1,465
Allowance for credit losses	(70)	(70)
	2,250	1,395

Test your understanding 3

Engine Co

You are an audit manager in Dai & Co, a firm of chartered certified accountants responsible for the audit of Engine Co. Planning of the audit for the financial year ended 30 June 20X5 is about to commence.

You are provided with the following exhibits:

1   An email you have received from the audit engagement partner.

2   Draft financial information for the year ending 30 June 20X5.

Required:

Respond to the instructions in the email from the audit engagement partner.   **(16 marks)**

Note: The split of the mark allocation is shown in the partner's email (Exhibit 1)

Professional marks will be awarded for the presentation and logical flow of the briefing notes and the clarity of the explanations provided.

(4 marks)

(Total: 20 marks)

Exhibit 1 – Email from audit engagement partner

Hello

I have provided you with some information in the attached exhibit which you should use to help you with planning the audit of Engine Co for the financial year ending 30 September 20X5.

Using the information provided in Exhibit 2 I would like you to prepare briefing notes for my use in which you evaluate the audit risks to be considered in planning the audit of Engine Co. You should use analytical procedures to assist in identifying audit risks.   **(16 marks)**

Thank you

Exhibit 2 – Financial information for the year ending 30 September 20X5

Statement of profit or loss

	30.06.20X5 (Draft)		30.06.20X4 (Audited)	
	$m	$m	$m	$m
Revenue		128		107
Cost of sales				
Opening inventory	9		6	
Purchases	87		74	
Closing inventory	(14)		(9)	
	——	(82)	——	(71)
		——		——
Gross profit		46		36
Distribution costs		(11)		(9)
Admin expenses (note 1)		(20)		(18)
		——		——
Operating profit		15		9
		——		——

Statement of financial position

	30.06.20X5 (Draft) $m	30.06.20X4 (Audited) $m
Non-current assets		
Tangible assets (note 2)	77	67
Intangible assets (note 3)	17	13
	94	80
Current assets		
Inventory (note 4)	14	9
Trade receivables	17	13
Cash	3	3
	34	25
Total assets	128	105
Equity and liabilities		
Ordinary share capital	20	20
Revaluation reserve	38	30
Retained earnings	30	25
	88	75
Non-current liabilities		
Bank loan	13	11
	13	11
Current liabilities		
Trade payables	17	13
Other payables	5	3
Tax payable	5	3
	27	19
	40	30
Total equity and liabilities	128	105

Note 1

Included within operating profits are the following items:

	30.06.20X5	30.06.20X4
	$m	$m
Wages and salaries	7	7
Directors' salaries	2	2
Depreciation	3	3
Amortisation	4	3

Note 2

	Land & buildings	Plant & machinery	Total
	$m	$m	$m
Cost			
B/f at 1 July 20X4	70	30	100
Additions	–	5	5
Revaluations	8	–	8
C/f at 30 June 20X5	78	35	113
Depreciation			
B/f at 1 July 20X4	10	23	33
Charge	1	2	3
C/f at 30 June 20X5	11	25	36
Carrying amount			
At 30 June 20X5	67	10	77
At 30 June 20X4	60	7	67

The revaluation relates to land.

Plant and machinery are depreciated at 25% using the reducing balance method.

Note 3

Development costs	Total $
Cost	
B/f at 1 July 20X4	16
Additions	8
C/f at 30 June 20X5	24
Amortisation	
B/f at 1 July 20X4	3
Charge	4
C/f at 30 June 20X5	7
Carrying amount	
At 30 June 20X5	17
At 30 June 20X4	13

During the year significant research and development has taken place with regard to a new product for which commercial production has now commenced.

Note 4

	30.06.20X5 $m	30.06.20X4 $m
Inventory		
Raw materials	3	2
Work in progress	1	1
Finished goods	11	7
Allowance for slow-moving inventory	(1)	(1)
	14	9

Test your understanding 4

(1) Kingston Co operates in the computer games industry, developing new games for sale in retail stores.

(2) Portmore Co is currently waiting for confirmation from their bank that their overdraft facility will be extended. The bank have requested a copy of the audited financial statements as soon as they are available.

(3) Montego Co has recently started selling their products overseas.

(4) Lucea Co, a manufacturer, has negotiated a contract with a new supplier for all its raw materials.

Required:

For each of the scenarios below identify the business risks and state the impact this might have on your assessment of the risk of material misstatement for the planning of the audit. **(8 marks)**

8   Chapter summary

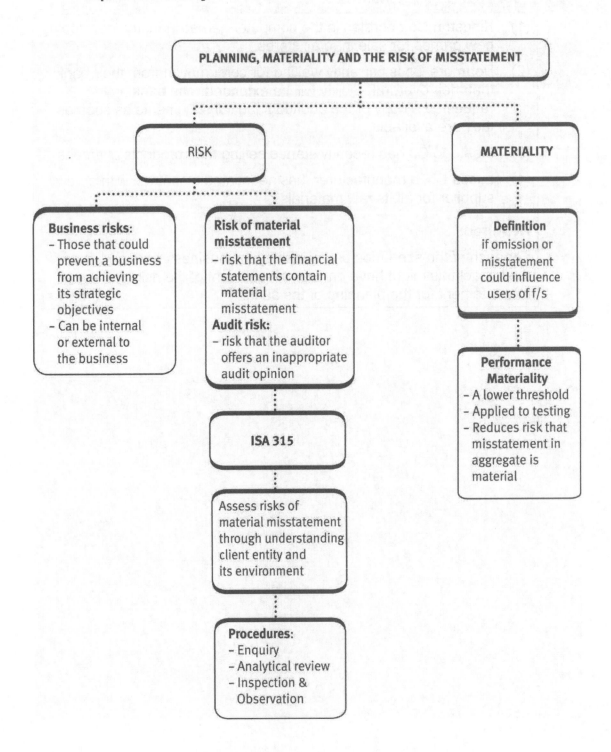

Test your understanding answers

Test your understanding 1 – Yates Co

Briefing notes

To: Audit engagement partner

From: Audit manager

Date: 01 July 20X5

Subject: Planning of the audit of Yates Co for the year ended
             30 June 20X5

Introduction

These briefing notes evaluate the risks of material misstatement and suggest audit procedures to be included in the audit plan in respect of leases and the restructuring provision.

(a) **Risks of material misstatement**

Revenue and rebates

Revenue has increased by 11.8%.

IFRS 15 *Revenue from Contracts with Customers* states that revenue should be recorded at the transaction price which is the amount of consideration expected to be received for delivering the service. If any amount of the transaction price is variable, the company must estimate the amount of consideration expected to be transferred.

The volume related rebates create variability for the transaction price. The company must use experience to estimate the level of rebates that are likely to be paid.

There is a risk of overstatement of revenue if rebates have not been estimated on a reasonable basis or if actual rebates for the last quarter have not been accrued at the year-end.

The rebates have been included as a provision on the statement of financial position within non-current liabilities which is incorrect. The rebates should be shown as a contract liability within current liabilities therefore there is misstatement arising from incorrect classification and presentation.

Operating expenses

The materials expense has increased by 17.8% which is more than the increase in revenue.

This could be legitimate for example if fuel costs have increased significantly. However, the increase could indicate misstatement in relation to capital expenditure treated as revenue (e.g. on overhauls or major refurbishment) or misclassification of expenses.

There is a risk of overstatement of materials expense.

Other expenses have fallen by 15.5% which is unusual given the increase in the level of business. This may indicate understatement of expenses due to misclassification or underestimation of accrued expenses.

Staff costs have increased by 14% and this should also be investigated to ensure this is consistent with movement in employee numbers and pay increases.

Intangible assets

Intangible assets have increased by $1m and represent 6.9% of total assets therefore are material and an area of significant risk.

IAS 38 *Intangible Assets* states that most internally-generated intangibles should not be recognised as they cannot be reliably measured. However, internally generated software is allowed to be capitalised if the company can demonstrate it is technically feasible, will generate future economic benefits through sale or use, and can be measured reliably.

Intangible assets may be overstated if the balance includes internally generated intangibles which do not meet the criteria of IAS 38.

Restructuring provision

The restructuring provision of $9m represents 8.7% of total assets therefore is material and an area of significant risk.

In accordance with IAS 37 *Provisions, Contingent Liabilities and Contingent Assets*, a provision is required to be recognised only if there is a present obligation as a result of a past event that is probable to result in an outflow of benefits and can be measured reliably.

The restructuring occurred 18 months ago and there may no longer be any obligations for the company to fulfil.

There is a risk that the restructuring provision is overstated.

Leases

Lease liabilities represent 5.2% of total assets and are therefore material and an area of significant risk.

In accordance with IFRS 16 *Leases*, leases should be recognised as right-of-use (ROU) assets and a corresponding lease liability recognised at the present value of the lease payments, unless the underlying asset has a low value. Leases of less than twelve months should be expensed.

ROU assets have not been separately classified on the statement of financial position therefore there is a misstatement due to incorrect classification and presentation.

ROU assets should be depreciated over the lease term which should take into consideration any option to extend the lease or terminate the lease early. The lease has an option to extend from five years to ten years and Yates Co intend to exercise this option as they have done in the past. Therefore the ROU assets should be depreciated over ten years. The depreciation policy states that the properties are being depreciated over the initial lease term of five years.

There is a risk that depreciation of ROU assets is overstated and the ROU asset is understated. This could explain why the carrying amount of property is so much lower this year.

Depreciation and amortisation

The depreciation and amortisation expense has fallen by 10.5%. This could be valid if Yates Co has significant assets already fully depreciated or the asset base is lower since last year's restructuring. The restructuring in the prior year may also have resulted in impairment charges increasing last year's depreciation charge.

However, there is a risk of understatement of depreciation and therefore overstatement of assets if not all assets have been depreciated, assets have been depreciated at the wrong rates due to the wide range of rates being used by the company, or if the final month's charge has not been accounted for in the draft figures.

Receivables

Trade receivables have increased by 2.2% although revenue has increased by 11.8%. The receivables collection period has decreased from 34 days to 31 days.

This seems unusual and may indicate understatement of the receivables balance due to a lack of completeness.

Opening balances

Yates Co is a new audit client which means the opening balances were not audited by our firm last year.

There is a risk of misstatement of opening balances if the audit last year failed to detect any material misstatements.

The predecessor auditor should be contacted and their working papers reviewed as part of our firm's testing on opening balances this year.

Tutorial note: the detection risk arising as a result of a lack of cumulative knowledge and experience is an audit risk but is not a risk of material misstatement.

(b) Audit procedures

(i) Leases

- Review the lease agreements to determine the terms and conditions of the lease and confirm details of the option to extend the leases at the end of the term.

- Enquire of management whether the company is likely to exercise the option to extend the lease to determine the appropriate depreciation period for the properties.

- Calculate the expected depreciation charge based on the expected length of the lease term and discuss with management the need for adjustment if depreciation has been calculated on an incorrect lease period.

- Agree lease payments to the bank statements and cash book.

- Calculate the present value of the lease payments and agree to the client's calculations to confirm accuracy.

- Calculate the lease liability at the year end taking into consideration the finance charge element and the lease payments made to date.

- Review the financial statements for appropriate disclosure of the leases in accordance with IFRS 16.

(ii) Restructuring provision

- Review the breakdown of the provision to identify the costs included and assess whether the costs are likely to still be an obligation at the reporting date.

- Enquire of management why the provision is still recognised and whether there are any costs still likely to be paid.

- Trace items from the breakdown of the provision to bank statements and cash book to identify any costs not paid at the year end.

- If the provision is no longer required, discuss the need for adjustment with management.

- Review the financial statements for appropriate disclosure of the provision in accordance with IAS 37.

Conclusion

The above audit risks demonstrate that the audit of Yates Co is a high risk engagement. These risks must be addressed by designing appropriate audit procedures to be included in the audit plan. Appropriately experienced staff must be assigned to the audit team to ensure any material misstatements are detected.

Test your understanding 2 – Ivor Co

Briefing notes

To: Audit engagement partner

From: Audit manager

Date: 1 July 20X5

Subject: Audit risks of Ivor Co to assist the planning of the year-end audit.

Introduction

These briefing notes evaluate the audit risks that should be considered when planning the audit of Ivor Co.

Analytical procedures

Annual movements

Revenue	2,610/9,960 × 100	26.2%
Cost of sales	1,953/7,603 × 100	25.6%
Distribution costs	264/498 × 100	53.0%
Wages/salaries	315/960 × 100	32.8%
Directors' salaries	10/115 × 100	8.7%
Rent	23/12 × 100	191.7%
Other	16/153 × 100	(10.5%)

Ratio analysis

	20X5		20X4	
Gross margin	3,014/12,570 × 100	24%	2,357/9,960 × 100	23.7%
Operating margin	1,190/12,570 × 100	9.5%	694/9,960 × 100	7.0%
ROCE*	1,190/4,094 × 100	29.1%	694/3,004 × 100	23.1%
Asset turnover*	12,570/4,094	3.1	9,960/3,004	3.3
Current ratio	3,994/1,027	3.9:1	2,595/1,796	1.4:1
Acid test/Quick ratio	2,354/1,027	2.3:1	1,395/1,796	0.8:1
Inventory holding period	1,640/9,556 × 365	63 days	1,200/7,603 × 365	58 days
Receivables collection period	2,250/12,570 × 365	65 days	1,395/9,960 × 365	51 days
Payables payment period	735/9,556 × 365	28 days	1,499/7,603 × 365	72 days

* Capital employed is calculated as non-current assets + current assets – current liabilities.

Tutorial note: The table above shows a range of ratios which can be provided. Marks will only be awarded for those ratios correctly calculated and referred to in the risk evaluation.

Revenue

Revenue has increased by 26% during the year. This significant increase suggests a risk that revenue could be overstated.

The increase in revenue may have been generated by offering greater discounts, totalling 4% of revenue as compared with 2% in the prior year.

It is also possible that extended credit terms have been offered due to the lengthening of the receivables collection period from an average 51 days last year to an average of 65 days this year.

As per IFRS 15 Revenue From Contracts With Customers, revenue must be recognised at the amount of consideration that the seller expects to receive for satisfying the performance obligation. In this case, revenue should be recognised net of discounts.

There is a risk that revenue may be overstated.

Disposal of buildings

During the year, buildings with a carrying amount of $990,000 (1,100,000 – 110,000) have been sold for $1,500,000 (990,000 + 510,000). At the same time the company's rental expenses have increased by 192%.

It appears the company has entered into a sale and leaseback arrangement as it is unlikely that the company would be able to increase production so much having sold half of their buildings.

In accordance with IFRS 16 *Leases*, if the sale is not a genuine sale, the building should continue to be recognised by Ivor Co and a financial liability recognised equal to the proceeds received.

Given the profit on disposal included in the statement of profit or loss, it would appear that Ivor Co has treated the sale and leaseback as a full disposal. If this is not the case, the profit on disposal will be overstated.

Irrespective of whether the sale and leaseback is a full disposal, the leased assets should be recognised either as property, plant and equipment if they are still controlled by the entity, or as a right-of-use asset if they are controlled by the lessor. The assets should be depreciated either over the useful life to the entity if controlled by the entity, or over the lease term if controlled by the lessor. A liability should be recognised in respect of the lease payments.

Right-of-use assets and lease liabilities appear to be understated as these do not appear in the statement of financial position.

Development costs

Development costs of $54k represent 1% of total assets and are material.

The costs may not be accounted for in accordance with IAS 38 *Intangible Assets* which requires development costs to only be recognised if the development is technologically feasible, the entity intends to complete the development and has the resources to complete the development. It must also be expected that economic benefits will be generated either through sale or use of the developed assets.

The development assets must be amortised over the period the benefits are expected to be generated. The amortisation policy is five years. This may not be the expected life of the product and therefore may be inappropriate.

There is a risk of overstatement of development costs if the recognition criteria of IAS 38 have not been met or are no longer met, or if the amortisation charge is not appropriate.

Inventory

Inventory represents 32% of total assets therefore is material and an area of significant risk.

Inventory should be valued at the lower of cost and net realisable value in accordance with IAS 2 *Inventories*. The discounts offered must be taken into account when determining the net realisable value. Some products may be used as loss leaders in a drive to tempt new customers.

As the inventory holding period has increased from 58 days to 63 days, this could indicate an increased risk of overvaluation of inventory.

Receivables

The overall increase in credit sales, coupled with the greater credit period increases the risk of irrecoverable receivables. However, the allowance for receivables has not been adjusted from the previous balance of $70,000, which represented 5% of total receivables last year but only 3% of receivables this year. The receivables collection period has increased from 51 days to 65 days.

In accordance with IFRS 9 *Financial Instruments*, receivables must be valued at the transaction price less an allowance for expected credit losses.

There is a risk of overstatement of trade receivables as the allowance for credit losses has not increased despite an increase in revenue.

Going concern

During the year there appears to have been an improvement in the liquidity of the company, with the current and quick ratios improving from 1.4 and 0.8 last year to 3.9 and 2.3 this year, respectively.

Ivor Co has raised a significant amount of cash from the disposal of buildings and the issuing of new shares during the year. In total $2.2m has been raised ($1.5m disposal + $700k share issue) and it appears that this has been used to pay off significant external debts, most notably the bank loan and trade payables.

However, there is very little residual cash left over and the company appears to be having difficulty generating trading cash balances. The inventory holding period and receivables collection period have both increased and this increase in the operating cycle could be caused by offering extended credit in an attempt to win new customers.

The inability to generate cash balances could indicate the company is unable to meet loan or lease repayments. A failure to pay trade payables could lead to a loss of supplier goodwill and have implications for future trade relationships.

If the business is facing uncertainties relating to going concern then the company should disclose these uncertainties in the financial statements.

There is a risk of material misstatement if any going concern issues are not adequately disclosed.

Distribution costs

These have increased by 53% during the financial year which is much higher than the increase in revenue. This could be due to greater geographical spread of customers, rising fuel costs or misallocation of expenses.

Conclusion

The above evaluation demonstrates that the audit of Ivor Co is a high risk engagement. The audit plan will need to include audit procedures to address these risks. The audit team selected will need to have the relevant skills to address the risks.

Test your understanding 3

Briefing Notes

To: Audit engagement partner

From: Audit manager

Date: 1 July 20X5

Subject: Engine Co – audit risk assessment

Introduction

These briefing notes evaluate the audit risks identified during the analytical review of the financial statements of Engine Co and the possible implications for the year-end audit.

Analytical procedures

	20X5		20X4	
Gross margin	46/128 × 100	35.9%	36/107 × 100	33.6%
Operating margin	15/128 × 100	11.7%	9/107 × 100	8.4%
ROCE	15/101 × 100	14.9%	9/86 × 100	10.5%
Asset turnover	128/101	1.3	107/86	1.2
Current ratio	34/27	1.3:1	25/19	1.3:1
Quick/Acid test ratio	20/27	0.7:1	16/19	0.8:1
Inventory holding period	14/82 × 365	62 days	9/71 × 365	46 days
Receivables collection period	17/128 × 365	48 days	13/107 × 365	44 days
Payables payment period	17/87 × 365	71 days	13/74 × 365	64 days
Gearing	13/101 × 100	12.9%	11/86 ×100	12.8%

Profitability

Gross margins have increased during the year from 34% to 36%. Operating margins, however, have increased significantly from 8% to 12%.

The change in gross margin may have been achieved through economies in purchasing, which could be due to bulk purchasing consistent with the increase in revenue.

If this is not the case, there is a risk that cost of sales are understated possibly by overvaluation of closing inventory or incomplete recording of purchases.

A review of operating costs suggests that this has been achieved through labour efficiencies, given the stable salary costs, although this could be caused by misallocation of salary costs (see below).

There is a risk that expenses have not been completely recorded and attention should be paid to cut-off at the year-end.

Salary costs

Salary costs as a percentage of revenue have fallen. During the year Engine Co capitalised $8 million of development costs. It is possible that some salary costs have been capitalised within development costs. Only development costs meeting all the criteria of IAS 38 *Intangible Assets* may be capitalised. Research costs must be expensed.

Salary costs will be understated and development costs overstated if salary costs relating to research have been capitalised incorrectly.

Inventory

Closing inventory levels have increased by over 50% since 20X4, possibly due to increased demand. This has led to an increase in the inventory holding period (from 46 to 62).

Whilst the inventory balance has increased by 50% in the year, the allowance has remained static. Increases in inventory could indicate damage or obsolescence which could reduce the net realisable value to below cost.

There is a risk that the slow-moving inventory allowance is understated and, therefore, inventory is overstated.

Revaluation of land

Land has been revalued by $8 million. The credentials of the valuer should be assessed (competence and independence) to ensure the valuation is reliable.

There is a risk that the revaluation is not appropriate which could lead to overstatement of tangible non-current assets.

In addition, there may be inadequate disclosure of the revaluation and the requirements of IAS 16 *Property, Plant and Equipment* may not have been met.

Depreciation

During the year $5 million was spent on the acquisition of plant and machinery. However it appears as though these items have not been depreciated during the year. Using a rough method of calculation (opening carrying amount + $5m × 25%) the depreciation charge for plant and machinery should be $3 million, not the $2 million presented in the accounts. It therefore appears as though depreciation has not been accounted for as per IAS 16.

There is a risk that the depreciation charge is understated and non-current assets are overstated.

Loan

During the year the company has taken out a loan of $2 million, presumably to help finance the purchase of new plant and machinery.

It will be important to assess the terms of the new loan in case there are any covenants in place. Given the possibility that the directors are excluding salaries, depreciation and inventory allowances from profits, there could be a significant adjustment required to the reported profit, which would adversely affect profitability ratios. The financial statement figures may be being manipulated in order to meet the terms of the covenants. If so, going concern issues may result which would require disclosure in the notes. There is a risk this disclosure is not made.

There is also a risk that the loan has not been correctly split into the current and non-current components as there does not appear to be a loan within current liabilities on the statement of financial position.

Conclusion

The above audit risks demonstrate that the audit of Engine Co is a high risk engagement. These risks must be addressed by designing appropriate audit procedures to be included in the audit plan. Appropriately experienced staff must be assigned to the audit team to ensure any material misstatements are detected.

Test your understanding 4

	Business risk	Audit risk
Kingston Co	Rapidly changing industry with constant product developments. They may not have the resources or expertise to keep up with the pace of change.	Risk of overstatement of inventory (including WIP) where products become obsolete. In the extreme could lead to going concern issues which would require disclosure in the notes to the financial statements.
Portmore Co	Failure of the bank to renew the overdraft facility may increase the risk of insufficient financing or more costly financing.	Directors of Portmore Co will be under pressure to present the financial statements in the best light possible leading to possible manipulation of the financial statements. Lack of confirmation from the bank represents a fundamental uncertainty surrounding going concern which would require disclosure in the notes to the financial statements.
Montego Co	The new venture overseas may not be successful. The market may have been overestimated. Foreign currency fluctuations may affect profits.	Translation errors may occur. Revaluation of foreign currency balances at year-end may not be performed resulting in misstatement of payables.
Lucea Co	Disruption to the manufacturing process if the new supplier does not deliver the right quality of products or at the right time, leading to delays in supplying customers.	Poor quality items may require selling prices to be reduced. This could mean NRV is lower than cost resulting in overstatement of inventory.

Group and transnational audits

Chapter learning objectives

This chapter covers syllabus areas:

- D5 – Group audits
- D1g – Transnational audits.

Detailed syllabus objectives are provided in the introduction section of the text book.

PER

One of the PER performance objectives (PO18) is to is to prepare for and plan the audit process. You plan and control the engagement process, including the initial investigation. You also plan and monitor the audit programme – legally and ethically. Working through this chapter should help you understand how to demonstrate that objective.

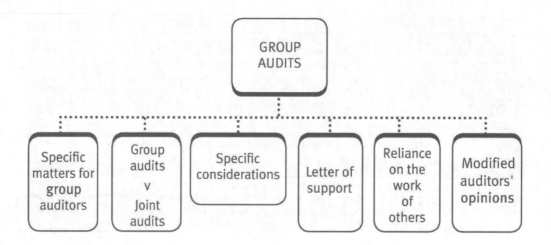

 Exam focus

- A group could appear in any question in the exam, and is relevant to all stages of an engagement.

- Read the scenario to identify whether the question relates to a single entity or a group.

- Take care to identify whether you are the auditor for the entire group (including subsidiaries) or just the parent company. Reliance on the work of other auditors will only be relevant if you are not responsible for the audit of the subsidiaries.

Revision of consolidation

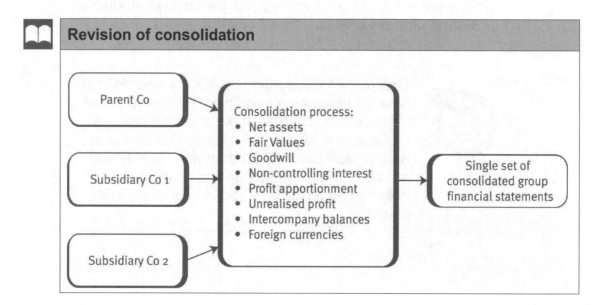

Consolidation involves taking a number of sets of individual company financial statements and adding them all together to form one combined set. Due to various complications, such as companies using different currencies and intergroup trading, a number of adjustments have to be made before the consolidated financial statements can be finalised.

Before the group financial statements can be audited, the individual company's financial statements have to be prepared and audited. In the diagram above this includes Parent Co, Subsidiary Co 1 and Subsidiary Co 2. It is the responsibility of individual company directors/management to prepare their financial statements. These may be audited by the group auditor or another firm of auditors.

Once this process is complete, the financial statements are combined to create a single set of consolidated financial statements. This process is the responsibility of the group's directors.

Once the consolidated financial statements have been prepared, the group auditor performs an audit of the consolidated financial statements.

As the group is a summary of the trading results and positions of the various components of the group (and is itself not a trading entity), the group auditor does not need to audit the group financial statements in the same way. They rely on the audited figures of the individual financial statements to confirm the majority of balances and then audit the consolidation process and adjustments.

1 Group audits – specific considerations

The principles of auditing a group are the same as the audit of a single company and all of the ISAs are still relevant to a group audit. There are, however, some specific considerations relevant to the audit of a group:

- Group financial statements require numerous and potentially complicated consolidation adjustments.

- Specific accounting standards relating to group financial statements must be complied with.

- The components of the group (i.e. the subsidiaries) **may** be audited by firms other than the group auditor.

- The organisation and planning of a group audit may be significantly more complex than for a single company.

The objectives of an auditor with regard to these matters are identified in ISA 600 *Special Considerations – Audits of Group Financial Statements (Including the Work of Component Auditors)*.

The auditor must:

- Determine whether it is appropriate to act as the auditor of the group financial statements.

- If acting as the auditor of the group financial statements:

  - Communicate clearly with the component auditors about the scope and timing of their work on financial information related to components and their findings.

  - Obtain sufficient appropriate evidence regarding the financial information of the components and the consolidation process to express an opinion on whether the group financial statements are prepared, in all material respects, in accordance with the applicable financial reporting framework.

[ISA 600, 8]

Key terms

The auditor with the responsibility for reporting on the consolidated group financial statements (as well as the parent company financial statements) is referred to as the **group auditor**.

The related subsidiaries, associates, joint ventures and branches etc. of the group are referred to as **components**.

The audit firm responsible for the audit of a component is referred to as the **component auditor**.

2 Acceptance

Acceptance as group auditor

In addition to the normal acceptance considerations discussed in Chapter 6, firms should consider whether to accept the role of group auditor. To assist the decision they must consider:

- Whether sufficient appropriate audit evidence can reasonably be expected to be obtained in relation to the consolidation process and the financial information of the components of the group.

- Where component auditors are involved, the engagement partner shall evaluate whether the group engagement team will be able to be involved in the work of the component auditors.

[ISA 600, 12]

If the engagement partner concludes that it will not be possible to obtain sufficient appropriate evidence due to restrictions imposed by group management, and that the possible effect of this will result in a disclaimer of opinion, then they must not accept the engagement. If it is a continuing engagement, the auditor should withdraw from the engagement, where possible under applicable laws and regulations. [ISA 600, 13]

Acceptance as component auditor

The component auditor will consider the following before accepting appointment:

- Whether they are independent of the parent and component companies and can comply with ethical requirements applying to the group audit.

- Whether they possess any special skills necessary to perform the audit of the component and are competent to perform the work.

- Whether they have an understanding of the auditing standards relevant to group audits and can comply with them.

- Whether they have an understanding of the relevant financial reporting framework applicable to the group.

- Whether they can comply with the group audit team instructions including the deadlines.

- Whether they are willing to have the group auditor involved in their work and evaluate it before relying on it for group audit purposes.

3   Planning and performing the group audit

Overall audit strategy and plan

The group auditor is responsible for establishing an overall group audit strategy and plan in accordance with ISA 300 *Planning an Audit of Financial Statements*. [ISA 600, 15]

The group engagement partner is ultimately responsible for reviewing and approving this. [ISA 600, 16]

The audit plan will describe the work to be performed covering areas such as:

- Obtaining an understanding of:

    - the group, its components and their environments [ISA 600, 17]

    - the component auditor [ISA 600, 19]

    - the consolidation process. [ISA 600, 32]

- Setting materiality for the group including the components. [ISA 600, 21]

- Responding to assessed risks, including consideration of whether a component is significant. [ISA 600, 24]

- Reviewing subsequent events in relation to the group. [ISA 600, 38]

Understanding the group, its components and their environments

The group auditor must:

- Enhance its understanding of the group, its components and their environments including group-wide controls, obtained during the acceptance/continuance stage. [ISA 600, 17a]

- Obtain an understanding of the consolidation process, including instructions issued by group management to components. [ISA 600, 17b]

- Confirm or revise its initial identification of components that are likely to be significant. [ISA 600, 18a]

- Assess the risks of material misstatement. [ISA 600, 18b]

Understanding the component auditor

Group auditors cannot simply rely on the work of other auditors. They must evaluate the work of others before relying on it. Therefore the group auditor should obtain an understanding of:

- Whether the component auditor understands and will comply with the code of ethics.

- The professional competence of the component auditor.

- Whether the group auditor will be able to be involved in the work of the component auditor.

- Whether the component auditor operates in a regulatory environment that actively oversees auditors.

[ISA 600, 19]

If the group auditor has serious concerns about any of the above issues then they should obtain evidence relating to the component's financial statements without using the work of the component auditor. [ISA 600, 20]

Understanding the consolidation process

Consolidation adjustments do not pass through the usual transaction processing systems and may not be subject to the same internal controls as other transactions. Therefore the group auditor needs to:

- Evaluate whether the adjustments appropriately reflect the events and transactions underlying them.

- Determine whether adjustments have been correctly calculated, processed and authorised.

- Determine whether adjustments are supported by sufficient appropriate documentation.

- Ensure intra-group balances and transactions reconcile and have been eliminated.

[ISA 600, A56]

Examples of matters to be understood

In order to perform their risk assessment thoroughly, the group auditor must obtain an understanding of a wide range of matters relevant to the unique circumstances of the group and its components. Whilst the list below is not exhaustive, it provides a range of common examples to be considered specific to the circumstances of a group:

- Instructions issued by group management to components:
    - Accounting policies to be applied.
    - Identification of reporting segments.
    - Related party relationships.
    - Intra-group transactions and balances.
    - Reporting timetable.

    [ISA 600, A25]

- Group-wide controls:
    - Regularity of meetings between group and component management.
    - Monitoring process of component's operations and financial results.
    - Group management's risk assessment process.
    - Monitoring, controlling, reconciling and elimination of intra-group transactions.
    - Centralisation of IT systems.
    - Activities of internal audit.
    - Consistency of policies across the group.
    - Group wide codes of conduct and fraud prevention.

- Consolidation process:
    - The extent to which component management understand the consolidation process.
    - The process for identifying and accounting for components.
    - The process for identifying reportable segments.
    - The process for identifying related party transactions.
    - How changes to accounting policies are managed.
    - The procedures for dealing with differing year-ends.
    - The procedures for dealing with differing accounting policies.
    - Group's process for ensuring complete, accurate and timely financial reporting.

> – The process for translating foreign components.
>
> – How IT is used in the consolidation.
>
> – Procedures for reporting subsequent events.
>
> – The preparation and authorisation of consolidation adjustments.
>
> – Frequency, nature and size of transactions between components.
>
> – Steps taken to arrive at fair values.
>
> [ISA 600, Appendix 2]

Materiality

The group auditor is responsible for establishing:

* Materiality and performance materiality for the group financial statements as a whole.

* Materiality for components where they are to be audited by other auditors. In order to reduce the risk of material misstatement in the group financial statements, materiality for the components should be set at an amount below materiality for the group as a whole.

[ISA 600, 21]

Responding to assessed risks

The group audit team has to determine the type of work to be performed on the financial information of the components, irrespective of whether the audit of the component was performed by the group team or another auditor. [ISA 600, 24]

The amount of work required will depend on whether a component is significant to the group.

Significant components

 A significant component is a component identified by the group engagement team that is either:

* of individual significance to the group, or

* likely to include significant risks of material misstatement to the group financial statements.

[ISA 600, 9m]

A significant component is identified by using an appropriate benchmark such as assets, liabilities, cash flows, profit or revenue. The benchmark is a matter of auditor judgment.

ISA 600 gives an example that an auditor may consider a component to be significant if it exceeds 15% of the chosen benchmark, however a different auditor may use a higher or lower amount.
[ISA 600, A5]

 In the exam, use the figure of 15% of profit or revenue as a benchmark to assess whether a component is significant.

Components which are individually significant to the group

For components individually significant to the group a full audit must be performed. [ISA 600, 26]

If the audit of a significant component is to be performed by another auditor, the group auditor should be involved in the component's risk assessment.
[ISA 600, 30]

This includes:

- Discussing with the component auditor the susceptibility of the component to material misstatement. [ISA 600, 30b]

- Reviewing the component auditor's documentation of identified risks of material misstatement. [ISA 600, 30c]

- Performing risk assessment procedures themselves. [ISA 600, 31]

If significant risks of material misstatement are identified in a component that is audited by another auditor, the group auditor should evaluate whether the audit procedures performed were appropriate to address the risks.

Components which include significant risks of material misstatement

Where the component is significant because there is a significant risk of material misstatement to the group financial statements, the auditor can perform:

- An audit of the component's financial statements.

- An audit of one or more account balances which are considered to be a significant risk.

- Specified audit procedures relating to the significant risks.

[ISA 600, 27]

Components which are not significant

Analytical procedures (rather than a full audit) may be performed on components which are not significant. [ISA 600, 28]

Communication with component auditors

The group auditor is responsible for communicating with the auditors of the components on a timely basis. Communication shall include:

- The work to be performed by the component and the use made of this.

- The form and content of the communications made by the component auditor to the group auditor.

- A request that the component auditor cooperates with the group team.

- The ethical requirements relevant to the group audit.

- Component materiality and the threshold for triviality.

- Identified significant risks of material misstatement of the group financial statements.

- A list of identified related parties.

[ISA 600, 40]

As part of the communication process, the group auditor should also request that the component auditor communicates matters that are relevant to the group audit on a timely basis. Such matters include:

- Compliance with ethical standards.

- Compliance with audit instructions.

- Identification of financial information upon which the component auditor is reporting.

- Instances of non-compliance with laws and regulations.

- Uncorrected misstatements.

- Indications of management bias.

- Significant deficiencies in internal control.

- Other significant matters to be communicated to those charged with governance.

- Any other matters relevant to the group audit.

- The component auditor's overall conclusion.

[ISA 600, 41]

Further communications

As well as the matters identified above, the group auditor should also communicate further matters in a letter of instruction. This is likely to include:

- Matters relevant to the planning of the component audit:
    - The timetable for completion.
    - Dates of planned visits by the group auditor.
    - A list of key contacts.
    - Work to be performed on intra-group balances.
    - Guidance on other statutory reporting responsibilities.
    - Instructions for the subsequent events review.
- Matters relevant to the conduct of component auditor's work:
    - The findings of the group auditor's tests of controls on common systems.
    - The findings of internal audit relevant to the component.
    - A request for timely communication of evidence that contradicts evidence used in the group risk assessment.
    - A request for written representations on component management's compliance with the applicable financial reporting framework.
    - Matters to be documented by the component auditor.
- Other information:

    A request that the following be reported in a timely fashion:
    - Significant accounting, financial reporting and auditing matters, including accounting estimates and related judgments.
    - Matters relating to the going concern status of the component.
    - Matters relating to litigation and claims.
    - Significant deficiencies in internal control and information that indicates the existence of fraud.
    - A request that the group auditor be notified of any unusual events as early as possible.

[ISA 600, Appendix 5]

4 Audit risks specific to a group audit

In addition to the risks covered in chapter 7 which could affect any audit, group audits present additional risks. There are specific accounting standards which relate to groups such as:

- IFRS 3 *Business Combinations*
- IFRS 10 *Consolidated Financial Statements*
- IFRS 11 *Joint Arrangements*
- IAS 27 *Separate Financial Statements*
- IAS 28 *Investments in Associates and Joint Ventures*

As always, there is a risk that the client does not comply with the relevant accounting treatment which would mean the financial statements are materially misstated. Some examples include:

- Valuation of goodwill
- Translation of foreign subsidiaries in the consolidation process
- Non-coterminous year-ends
- Inconsistent accounting policies used across the group
- Fair value adjustments
- Calculation of non-controlling interests
- Elimination of intercompany balances and trading
- Profit apportionment where there has been an acquisition or disposal
- Simple transposition or arithmetical errors in the consolidation process.

The auditor must ensure that audit procedures are designed and performed to address these specific risks.

Risk indicators for group audits

The following examples could indicate an increased risk of material misstatement of the group financial statements:

- A complex group structure.
- Frequent acquisitions, disposals and/or reorganisations.
- Poor corporate governance systems.
- Non-existent or ineffective group-wide controls.
- Components operating under foreign jurisdictions that may be subject to unusual government intervention.
- High risk business activities of components.
- Unusual related party transactions.

- Prior occurrences of intra-group balances that did not reconcile.

- The existence of complex transactions that are accounted for in more than one component.

- Differing application of accounting policies.

- Prior occurrences of unauthorised or incomplete consolidation adjustments.

- Aggressive tax planning.

- Frequent changes of auditor.

[ISA 600, Appendix 3]

Dealing with non-coterminous year-ends

IFRS 10 *Consolidated Financial Statements* requires the parent and subsidiaries to have the same year-end or to consolidate based on additional financial information prepared by the subsidiary (or if impracticable, the most recent financial statements adjusted for significant transactions or events). The difference between the parent and subsidiary's year-end must be no more than three months.

Audit risk is increased if there is a difference between the year ends as some of the transactions and adjustments included within the consolidated financial statements will not have been audited.

The group auditor must plan to obtain sufficient appropriate evidence about transactions or events that have not been subject to audit.

5 Auditing the consolidated financial statements

Procedures over the consolidation schedule

- Agree the figures from the component financial statements into the consolidation schedule to ensure accuracy.

- Recalculate the consolidation schedule to ensure arithmetical accuracy.

- Recalculate the translation of any foreign components to ensure accuracy.

- Recalculate any non-controlling interest balances to verify accuracy.

- Agree the date of any acquisitions or disposals and recalculate the time apportionment of the results for these components included in the consolidation.

- Evaluate the classification of the component (i.e. subsidiary, associate, joint venture etc.) to ensure this is still appropriate.

- For investments in associates, ensure that these are accounted for using the equity method of accounting and not consolidated.

- Review the financial statement disclosures for related party transactions.

- Review the policies and year-ends applied by the components to ensure they are consistent across the group.

- Reconcile intercompany balances and ensure they cancel out in the group financial statements.

- Assess the reasonableness of the client's goodwill impairment review to ensure goodwill is not overstated.

- Calculate any goodwill on acquisition arising in the year paying special attention to:

  - Consideration paid – agree to bank statements.

  - Acquisition related costs – ensure they have been expensed and not capitalised.

  - Contingent consideration – whether this has been valued at fair value taking into account the probability and timing of payment.

  - Deferred consideration – should be discounted to present value.

6 Completion and review

Review of the work of the component auditor

The group auditor must review the work of the component auditor to ensure it is sufficient and appropriate to rely on for the purpose of the group auditor's report.

This may be achieved by the component auditor sending the group auditor a questionnaire or checklist which identifies the key aspects of the audit.

The group auditor can then make an assessment as to whether any further work is needed.

- If any significant matters have arisen they should discuss with the component auditor or group management, as appropriate. [ISA 600, 42a]

- If necessary the group auditor should then also review other relevant parts of the component auditor's working papers. [ISA 600, 42b]

- If the group auditor is not satisfied with the component auditor's work they should determine what additional procedures are required. [ISA 600, 43]

- If it is not feasible for the component auditor to perform this then the group auditor must perform the procedures. [ISA 600, A62]

- When all procedures on the components have been completed, the group engagement partner must consider whether the aggregate effect of any uncorrected misstatements will have a material impact on the group financial statements. [ISA 600, A63]

Other completion activities

Subsequent events, going concern and final analytical procedures will need to be considered for the group in the same way as they are considered for a single entity audit.

Letters of support

If a subsidiary has going concern issues, the parent company may offer financial support to enable it to continue trading for the foreseeable future. If this is the case the directors must give the component auditor a letter of support which confirms their intention to support the subsidiary. This is also known as a comfort letter.

The component auditor should not take this at face value. They should consider the position of the parent and the group to help identify whether it has the resources to fulfil its promise of support before accepting the letter as sufficient appropriate evidence of the going concern basis for the subsidiary.

The group auditor must consider the impact of the going concern issues for the group as a whole.

The parent company must disclose this guarantee of assistance in their financial statements.

7 Reporting

Where one or more of the subsidiaries has a modified audit opinion (regardless of who audited the subsidiary) the group auditor must consider the impact of the issue on the group financial statements, according to group materiality levels.

- If the matter is not material in a group context, an unmodified opinion will be issued.

- If the matter is material to both the component and the group the auditor should consider whether the issue causing the modification can be resolved as a consolidation adjustment and aim to resolve the matter with the client. If this is resolved, an unmodified opinion can be issued.

- If the matter is material and cannot be resolved through the consolidation process, the modification should be carried through to the group audit opinion (e.g. if the evidence is not available to support the balance).

- Note that a matter which is pervasive to the component may be material but not pervasive to the group. In which case, a disclaimer of opinion or adverse opinion in a subsidiary will become a qualified opinion in the group auditor's report.

Reporting to management and those charged with governance

Deficiencies in controls identified by either the group audit team or component auditors should be reported to management of the group. [ISA 600, 46]

Any frauds or deficiencies in the group-wide controls identified by either the group auditor or the component auditor should be reported to management of the group. [ISA 600, 47]

The following matters should be reported to those charged with governance of the group:

- Overview of the work performed and involvement in the component auditor's work.

- Areas of concern over the quality of the component auditor's work.

- Difficulties obtaining sufficient appropriate evidence.

- Fraud identified or suspected.

[ISA 600, 49]

8 Joint audit

A joint audit is when two audit firms are appointed to provide an opinion on a set of financial statements. They will work together planning the audit, gathering evidence, reviewing the work and providing the opinion.

Before accepting a joint audit, the firm must consider the level of risk associated with issuing a report alongside the other firm. The auditor's report will be signed by both firms and they will be jointly responsible if the report is wrong.

Each firm should consider the experience and quality of the other firm to ensure they are competent.

If accepted, an engagement letter should be signed and the planning can commence which will involve agreeing an acceptable and fair division of the workload.

Benefits

- Retention of a subsidiary auditor and therefore their cumulative audit knowledge and experience following acquisition.

- Availability of a wider range of experience, technical expertise and resources.

- Possible efficiency improvements as each firm can perform work that plays to their strengths.

- An increase in audit quality as each firm will review the other's work which should reduce the risk of misstatements going undetected. In particular, two audit firms should also be better able to stand up against management who might be trying to introduce management bias into the financial statements through judgemental areas.

- An increase in auditor independence as the threats of intimidation and familiarity should be reduced.

Disadvantages

- Duplication of work will be required in some areas, particularly at the planning and completion stages, which will increase the cost of providing the audit.

- It may be difficult to find an appropriate second firm with relevant experience and expertise with whom to share the audit.

- Clients may need persuading about the benefits of adopting a new approach to the audit.

- A joint audit arrangement will need to be planned in advance of existing audits coming up for tender.

- The two firms may have different cultures leading to cultural clashes when trying to work together.

- There may be difficulty setting a joint approach. One firm may feel the work has not been divided equitably.

Current issue – Joint audits as a solution to audit failures

In many countries, the Big 4 audit firms dominate the audit market for listed companies and public interest entities (PIEs). In light of recent audit failures such as Carillion plc and Patisserie Valerie, regulators and governments are considering mandatory joint audits for PIEs.

The Big 4 are mostly against the introduction of joint audits. This is understandable as they will be the ones who lose out as a result as mandatory joint audits will reduce their power and their fee income. The Big 4 claim that 'challenger' firms do not have the competence or experience to be involved with such large audits and therefore audit quality will reduce.

One of the main drawbacks of a joint audit is the additional cost that is likely to be incurred because of the need for duplication of work as each firm will need to:

- Obtain an understanding of the entity and its internal controls

- Assess risks of material misstatement

- Perform analytical procedures to form an overall conclusion

- Review procedures performed by the other firm of auditors

- Attend meetings with the management and those charged with governance of the client.

However, the additional cost should be compared with the benefits to be obtained by having two firms responsible for the audit which should lead to an increase in professional scepticism and increased audit quality.

There is also an argument that the current lack of competition is driving audit fees higher, so with the introduction of greater competition, audit fees will come down.

The main obstacle that may hinder the introduction of mandatory joint audits is the lack of appropriate challenger firms. There are relatively few firms of sufficient size and experience to be able to perform the audit of PIEs to a satisfactory standard. Even then, firms such as Grant Thornton, Mazars, BDO, RSM, and PKF may consider that the fees earned from providing non-audit services to large companies (who cannot use their audit firms to provide such services for ethical reasons) are worth more than the fees to be earned from a joint audit arrangement with a Big 4 firm, especially for the level of risk involved.

9 Transnational audits

Transnational audit means an audit of financial statements which may be relied upon outside the audited entity's home jurisdiction.

Reliance on these audits might be for purposes of significant lending, investment or regulatory decisions.

The differences between a 'normal' audit, conducted within the boundaries of one set of legal and regulatory requirements, and a transnational audit are largely due to variations in:

- Auditing standards
- Regulation and oversight of auditors
- Financial reporting standards
- Corporate governance requirements.

Auditing standards

Despite the prevalence of International Standards on Auditing, many countries use modified versions and many continue to use local standards. As a result, in a group audit with components from a wide range of geographical backgrounds, it is possible that the audits of the components will be performed according to different standards. This could lead to inconsistency and poor quality for the group audit as a whole.

Regulation and oversight of auditors

As well as differing auditing standards there are many different ways in which the auditing profession is regulated. Some regulatory regimes are more strict than others. This will mean the penalties for not complying with professional regulations are more severe and firms may perform work to a higher standard to avoid such penalties. This can affect the quality of the audit of components from different regimes, which will lead to inconsistency in the quality of a group audit.

Financial reporting standards

Within a multinational group it is likely that adjustments will be required due to the application of different financial reporting standards. These standards will be reflected in the component financial statements but, on consolidation, must be adjusted to reflect the parent's accounting policies. This can lead to some technically complex consolidation adjustments which will increase the risk of material misstatement.

Corporate governance requirements

In some countries there are very strict corporate governance requirements that not only affect the directors of the company, but also the audit firm of the company. Often the auditor is required to perform, and report on, compliance with corporate governance requirements. In other countries the corporate governance requirements, particularly with regard to internal controls, are much more relaxed. This affects the audit as it could indicate that internal controls may be less effective than those of a component that operates in a highly regulated environment.

Auditors must be aware of the different regimes that apply to the audit of a transnational entity because they will be bound by the varying laws and regulations. Given the globalisation of businesses and stock markets this is an increasingly significant concern for many firms of auditors.

The Transnational Audit Committee

The International Federation of Accountants (IFAC) has a committee with specific responsibilities for transnational audits: the Transnational Audit Committee (TAC).

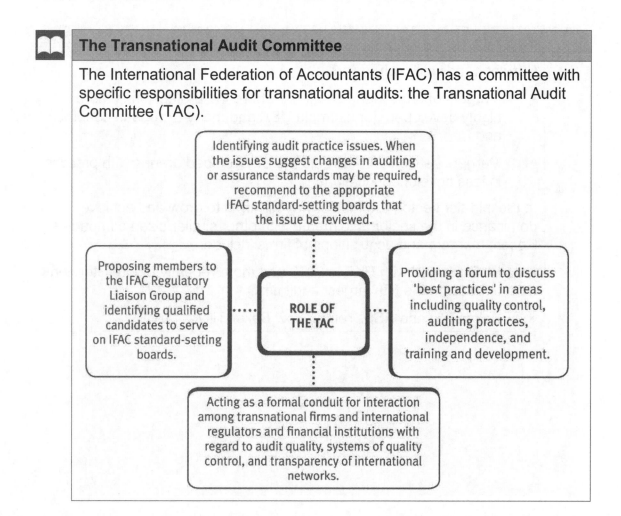

Identifying audit practice issues. When the issues suggest changes in auditing or assurance standards may be required, recommend to the appropriate IFAC standard-setting boards that the issue be reviewed.

Proposing members to the IFAC Regulatory Liaison Group and identifying qualified candidates to serve on IFAC standard-setting boards.

ROLE OF THE TAC

Providing a forum to discuss 'best practices' in areas including quality control, auditing practices, independence, and training and development.

Acting as a formal conduit for interaction among transnational firms and international regulators and financial institutions with regard to audit quality, systems of quality control, and transparency of international networks.

Globalisation

Advantages	Disadvantages
• Wide ranging expertise • Global facilities • Can invest in expensive systems and necessary IT to meet needs of international clients	• Lack of competition and choice, particularly for large companies

The concentration of the audit market into a few very large firms has come about because of globalisation. The larger firms found that amalgamations amongst the audit firms were the way forward leading to a more concentrated audit market:

- **Affiliation** is used by the larger accounting firms to develop an internationally recognised brand name.

- **Co-operation** is used by the mid-tier firms who join international co-operatives of firms who send each other business, but retain their own trading name in their home countries.

Current trends

Current trends still lean towards:

- Mergers of firms in the countries where the profession is more highly developed, for example USA and many European countries, and

- Mergers between firms in the more developed arenas with practices in less developed locations.

In the mid-tier sector, the fastest way for firms to grow and achieve dominance in the sector is to merge with other similar sized companies. Recent mergers and acquisitions of firms include:

- BDO merged with PKF in 2013 and more recently Moore Stephens to become the fifth largest audit firm.

- Baker Tilly and RSM Tenon, now Baker Tilly.

Test your understanding 1

You are an audit manager in Ross & Co, a firm of Chartered Certified Accountants. The principal activity of one of your audit clients, Murray Co, is the manufacture and retail sale of women's fashions and menswear throughout the capital cities of Western Europe.

The following financial information has been extracted from Murray's most recent consolidated financial statements for the year ended 31 March 20X5:

	20X5	20X4
	$000	$000
Revenue	36,367	27,141
Gross profit	22,368	16,624
Profit before tax	5,307	4,405
Intangible assets:		
– Goodwill	85	85
– Trademarks	52	37
Property, plant and equipment	7,577	4,898
Current assets	13,803	9,737
Total assets	21,517	14,757
Equity	13,226	10,285
Non-current liabilities:		
Provisions	201	87
Current liabilities:		
Trade and other payables	8,090	4,385
Total equity and liabilities	21,517	14,757

In May 20X4 Murray purchased 100% of the shareholding of Di Rollo Co. Di Rollo manufactures fashion accessories (for example, jewellery, scarves and bags) in South America that are sold throughout the world by mail order. Murray's management is now planning that clothes manufacture will expand into South America and sold into Di Rollo's mail order market. Additionally, Di Rollo's accessories will be added to the retail stores' product range.

Murray is a member of an ethical trade initiative that aims to improve the employment conditions of all workers involved in the manufacture of its products. Last week Di Rollo's chief executive was dismissed following allegations that he contravened Di Rollo's policy relating to the environmentally-friendly disposal of waste products. The former chief executive is now suing Di Rollo for six months' salary in lieu of notice and a currently undisclosed sum for damages.

Ross & Co has recently been invited to accept nomination as auditor to Di Rollo. Murray's management has indicated that the audit fee for the enlarged Murray group should not exceed 120% of the fee for the year ended 31 March 20X4.

You have been provided with the following information relating to the acquisition of Di Rollo:

	Carrying amount	Fair value adjustment	Fair value to the group
	$000	$000	$000
Di Rollo brand name	–	600	600
Plant and equipment	95	419	514
Current assets	400	–	400
Current liabilities	(648)	–	(648)
Net assets at date of acquisition	(153)	1,019	866
Goodwill arising on acquisition			859
Cash consideration			1,725

Required:

(a) Using the information provided, explain the matters that should be considered before accepting the engagement to audit the financial statements of Di Rollo Co for the year ending 31 March 20X5.

(5 marks)

(b) Explain what effect the acquisition of Di Rollo Co will have on the planning of your audit of the consolidated financial statements of Murray Co for the year ending 31 March 20X5. **(10 marks)**

(Total: 15 marks)

Test your understanding 2

You are the manager responsible for the audit of the Nassau Group, which comprises a parent company and six subsidiaries. The audit of all individual companies' financial statements is almost complete, and you are currently carrying out the audit of the consolidated financial statements. One of the subsidiaries, Exuma Co, is audited by another firm, Jalousie & Co. Your firm is satisfied as to the competence and independence of Jalousie & Co.

You have received from Jalousie & Co the draft auditor's report on Exuma Co's financial statements, an extract from which is shown below:

Qualified Opinion (extract)

In our opinion, except for effects of the matter described in the Basis for Qualified Opinion paragraph, the financial statements give a true and fair view of the financial position of Exuma Co as at 31 March 20X5...'

Basis for Qualified Opinion (extract)

The company is facing financial damages of $2 million in respect of an ongoing court case, more fully explained in note 12 to the financial statements. Management has not recognised a provision but has disclosed the situation as a contingent liability. Under International Financial Reporting Standards, a provision should be made if there is an obligation as a result of a past event, a probable outflow of economic benefit, and a reliable estimate can be made. Audit evidence concludes that these criteria have been met, and it is our opinion that a provision of $2 million should be recognised. Accordingly, net profit and shareholders' equity would have been reduced by $2 million if the provision had been recognised.

An extract of Note 12 to Exuma Co's financial statements is shown below:

Note 12 (extract)

The company is the subject of a court case concerning an alleged breach of planning regulations. The plaintiff is claiming compensation of $2 million. The management of Exuma Co, after seeking legal advice, believe that there is only a 20% chance of a successful claim being made against the company.

Figures extracted from the draft financial statements for the year ending 31 March 20X5 are as follows:

	Nassau Group $ million	Exuma $ million
Profit before tax	20	4
Total assets	85	20

Required:

(a) Identify and explain the matters that should be considered, and actions that should be taken by the group audit engagement team, in forming an opinion on the consolidated financial statements of the Nassau Group. **(10 marks)**

A trainee accountant, Jo Castries, is assigned to your audit team. This is the first group audit that Jo has worked on. Jo made the following comment regarding the group audit:

'I understand that in a group audit engagement, one of the requirements is to design and perform audit procedures on the consolidation process. Please explain to me the principal audit procedures that are performed on the consolidation process.'

Required:

(b) Respond to the trainee accountant's question. **(5 marks)**

(Total: 15 marks)

10 Chapter summary

```
                        ┌─────────────────────┐
                        │    GROUP AUDITS     │
                        └─────────────────────┘
```

Specific matters for principal auditors

- complex FS adjustments
- group accounting standards
- involvement of component auditors
- complexity organising a group audit

Specific considerations

- correct classification of investments
- differing accounting policies and frameworks
- fair values on acquisition
- intangibles
- taxation
- goodwill on consolidation
- intra-group balances, transactions and profits
- related parties
- share options
- subsequent events

Reliance on the component auditors

- compliance with the code of ethics
- competence of component auditors
- involvement of group auditor in audit of component
- regulatory environment of component auditor
- assess materiality and risk at group and component level
- communications with the component auditors

Test your understanding answers

Test your understanding 1

(a) Acceptance matters

Competence

Ross & Co should be sufficiently competent and experienced to undertake the audit of Di Rollo as it has similar competence and experience in auditing the larger Murray Co. However, Ross & Co needs knowledge of conducting businesses in South America including legal and tax regulations.

Independence

Factors that might impair Ross & Co's objectivity in forming an opinion on the financial statements of Di Rollo (and the consolidated financial statements of Murray). For example, if Ross & Co was involved in any due diligence review of Di Rollo, the same senior staff should not be assigned to the audit.

Resources

Adequacy of resources in South America (e.g. in representative/associated offices). Ross & Co must have sufficient time to report on Di Rollo within the timeframe for reporting on the consolidated financial statements of Murray.

Expected limitation of scope

Ross & Co should not accept the nomination if any limitation imposed by management would be likely to result in the need to issue a disclaimer of opinion on Di Rollo's financial statements.

Proposed fee

The proposed restriction in audit fee may compromise the quality of the audit of Di Rollo and/or the Murray group. The 20% increase needs to be sufficient to cover the cost of the audit of Di Rollo and the incremental costs associated with auditing Murray's consolidated financial statements (as well as any general annual price increase that might be applied to audit fees).

Impact on the audit of Murray if the audit of Di Rollo is declined

Di Rollo is material to the Murray group. At acquisition the fair values of Di Rollo's tangible non-current assets, current assets and current liabilities represent 6.8%, 2.9% and 8%, respectively, of those in Murray's consolidated financial statements at 31 March 20X4.

It is usual that a parent company should want its auditors to audit its subsidiaries. If Ross & Co declined the nomination, Murray's management may seek an alternative auditor for the group.

Professional clearance

Murray should give Ross & Co written permission to communicate with Di Rollo's current auditor to enquire if there is any professional reason why they should not accept this assignment.

Murray may provide Ross & Co with additional fee-earning opportunities (e.g. due diligence reviews, tax consultancy, etc.) if it continues to expand in future.

(b) **Effect of acquisition on planning the audit of Murray's consolidated financial statements**

Group structure

The new group structure must be ascertained to identify all entities that should be consolidated into the Murray group's financial statements for the year ended 31 March 20X5.

Materiality assessment

Preliminary materiality for the group will be much higher, in monetary terms, than in the prior year. For example, if a % of total assets is a determinant of the preliminary materiality, it may be increased by 10% (as the fair value of total assets acquired, including goodwill, is $2,373,000 compared with $21,517,000 in Murray's consolidated financial statements for the year ended 31 March 20X4).

The materiality of each subsidiary should be reassessed, in terms of the enlarged group as at the planning stage. For example, any subsidiary that was just material for the year ended 31 March 20X4 may no longer be material to the group.

This assessment will identify, for example:

–   significant components requiring a full audit, and

–   components for which analytical procedures will suffice.

As Di Rollo's assets are material to the group, Ross & Co should plan to inspect the South American operations. The visit may include meeting with Di Rollo's previous auditors to discuss any problems that might affect the balances at acquisition and a review of the prior year audit working papers, with their permission.

Di Rollo was acquired two months into the financial year therefore its post-acquisition results should be expected to be material to the consolidated statement of profit and loss.

Goodwill acquired

The assets and liabilities of Di Rollo at 31 March 20X5 will be combined on a line-by-line basis into the consolidated financial statements of Murray and goodwill arising on acquisition recognised.

Audit work on the fair value of the Di Rollo brand name at acquisition may include a review of a brand valuation specialist's working papers and an assessment of the reasonableness of assumptions made.

Significant items of plant are likely to have been independently valued prior to the acquisition. It may be appropriate to plan to place reliance on the work of expert valuers. The fair value adjustment on plant and equipment is very high (441% of carrying amount at the date of acquisition). This may suggest that Di Rollo's depreciation policies are over-prudent.

As the amount of goodwill is material (approximately 50% of the cash consideration) it may be overstated if Murray has failed to recognise any assets acquired in the purchase of Di Rollo. For example, Murray may have acquired intangible assets such as customer lists or franchises that should be recognised separately from goodwill and amortised (rather than tested for impairment).

Subsequent impairment

The audit plan should draw attention to the need to consider whether the Di Rollo brand name and goodwill arising have suffered impairment as a result of the allegations against Di Rollo's former chief executive.

Liabilities

Proceedings in the legal claim made by Di Rollo's former chief executive will need to be reviewed. If the case is not resolved at 31 March 20X5, a contingent liability may require disclosure in the consolidated financial statements, depending on the materiality of amounts involved. Legal opinion on the likelihood of Di Rollo successfully defending the claim may be sought. Provision should be made for any actual liabilities, such as legal fees.

Group (related party) transactions and balances

A list of all companies in the group (including any associates) should be included in group audit instructions to ensure that intra-group transactions and balances (and any unrealised profits and losses on transactions with associates) are identified for elimination on consolidation. Any transfer pricing policies (e.g. for clothes manufactured by Di Rollo for Murray and sales of Di Rollo's accessories to Murray's retail stores) must be ascertained and any provisions for unrealised profit eliminated on consolidation.

It should be confirmed at the planning stage that intercompany transactions are identified as such in the accounting systems of all companies and that intercompany balances are regularly reconciled.

Other auditors

If Ross & Co plans to use the work of other auditors in South America (rather than send its own staff to undertake the audit of Di Rollo), group instructions will need to be sent containing:

- a request for confirmation of independence
- proforma statements
- a list of group and associated companies
- a list of related parties
- a statement of group accounting policies (see below)
- the timetable for the preparation of the group financial statements (see below)
- a request for copies of written representations from management
- an audit work summary questionnaire or checklist
- contact details (of senior members of Ross & Co's audit team).

Accounting policies

Di Rollo may have material accounting policies which do not comply with the rest of the Murray group. As auditor to Di Rollo, Ross & Co will recalculate the effect of any non-compliance with a group accounting policy that Murray's management would be requested to adjust on consolidation.

Timetable

The timetable for the preparation of Murray's consolidated financial statements should be agreed with management as soon as possible. Key dates should be planned for:

- agreement of intercompany balances and transactions
- submission of proforma statements
- completion of the consolidation package
- tax review of group financial statements
- completion of audit fieldwork by other auditors
- subsequent events review
- final clearance on the financial statements of subsidiaries
- Ross & Co's final clearance of consolidated financial statements.

Test your understanding 2

(a) **Matters that should be considered when forming an opinion on the group financial statements**

Significant component

A significant component is a component identified by the group audit engagement team that is of individual significance to the group. Exuma Co meets the definition of a significant component because it contributes 20% of group profit before tax, and 23.5% of group total assets. Exuma Co is therefore material to the group financial statements.

Materiality of accounting issue

The legal case against Exuma Co involves a claim against the company of $2 million. This is material to the individual financial statements of Exuma Co as it represents 50% of profit before tax, and 10% of total assets. The matter is also material to the group financial statements, representing 10% of group profit before tax and 2.4% of group total assets.

Qualified Opinion – Exuma Co financial statements

Jalousie & Co has expressed a qualified opinion due to a material misstatement regarding the accounting treatment of the court case. Management has treated the matter as a contingent liability as they believe that it is possible, but not probable, that the court case will go against the company. The auditors believe that it should have been recognised as a provision according to IAS 37 *Provisions, Contingent Liabilities and Contingent Assets*. Given the materiality of the matter to the individual financial statements, this opinion seems appropriate (rather than an adverse opinion), as long as the audit evidence concludes that a provision is necessary.

Review and discussion of audit work relating to the court case

Due to the significance of this matter, the audit work performed by Jalousie & Co should be subject to review by the group audit engagement team. Specifically, the evidence leading to the conclusion that a probable outflow of cash will occur should be reviewed, and the matter should be discussed with the audit engagement partner responsible for the opinion on Exuma Co's financial statements.

Evidence should include copies of legal correspondence, a copy of the actual claim showing the $2 million claimed against the company, and a written representation from management detailing management's reason for believing that there is no probable cash outflow.

Further audit procedures

Given the subjective nature of this matter, the group engagement partner may consider engaging an external expert to provide an opinion as to the probability of the court case going against Exuma Co.

Discussion with Nassau Group management

The matter should be discussed with the Group management team as to whether a provision is necessary. Their views should be documented in a written representation. There should also be discussion with management, and communication with those charged with governance regarding the potential impact of the matter on the group audit opinion. The impact depends on whether an adjustment is made in the individual accounts of Exuma Co, on consolidation, or not made at all, as explained below.

Adjustment to Exuma Co financial statements

Exuma Co is a subsidiary of Nassau and by definition is under the control of the parent company. Therefore, management of Exuma Co can be asked to adjust the financial statements to recognise a provision. If this happens, Jalousie & Co's auditor's report can be redrafted with an unmodified opinion, and the group audit opinion will also be unmodified.

Adjustment on consolidation

Even if Exuma Co's financial statements are not amended, an adjustment could be made on consolidation of the group financial statements to include the provision. In this case, the opinion on Exuma Co's financial statements would remain qualified, but the group audit opinion would not be qualified as the matter causing the material misstatement has been rectified.

No adjustment made

If no adjustment is made, either to Exuma Co's individual financial statements, or as a consolidation adjustment in the group financial statements, and if the group engagement partner disagrees with this accounting treatment, then the group audit opinion should be qualified due to a material misstatement. In this case, a paragraph entitled Basis for Qualified Opinion should explain the reason for the qualification, i.e. non-compliance with IAS 37, and should also quantify the financial effect on the consolidated financial statements. Reference to the work performed by a component auditor should not be made.

(b) **Procedures**

- Agree the figures from the component financial statements into the consolidation schedule to ensure accuracy.

- Recalculate the consolidation schedule to ensure arithmetical accuracy.

- Recalculate the translation of any foreign components to ensure accuracy.

- Recalculate any non-controlling interest balances to verify accuracy.

- Agree the date of any acquisitions or disposals and recalculate the time apportionment of the results for these components included in the consolidation.

- Evaluate the classification of the component (i.e. subsidiary, associate, joint venture etc.) to ensure this is still appropriate.

- Review the financial statement disclosures for related party transactions.

- Review the policies and year-ends applied by the components to ensure they are consistent with the group.

- Reconcile intercompany balances and ensure they cancel out in the group financial statements.

- Assess the reasonableness of the client's goodwill impairment review to ensure goodwill is not overstated.

- Review and recalculate the deferred tax consequences of any fair value adjustments.

9

Evidence

Chapter learning objectives

This chapter covers syllabus areas:

- D2 – Evidence and testing considerations

- D3 – Audit procedures and obtaining evidence

- D4 – Using the work of others

- G2c – Discuss current developments in emerging technologies, including big data and the use of data analytics and the potential impact on the conduct of an audit and audit quality.

Detailed syllabus objectives are provided in the introduction section of the text book.

PER

One of the PER performance objectives (PO19) is to collect and evaluate evidence for an audit. Carry out an internal or external audit from collecting evidence, through to forming an opinion. You demonstrate professional scepticism and make sure judgements are based on sufficient valid evidence. Working through this chapter should help you understand how to demonstrate that objective.

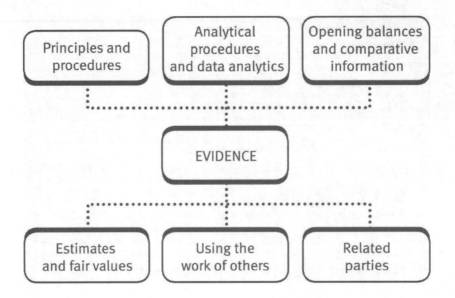

 Audit evidence was covered in Audit and Assurance at the Applied Skills level. The same principles apply here, however, you may be required to obtain evidence over more subjective and judgmental matters.

 Exam focus

More than one question in the exam is likely to feature a requirement to design relevant audit or assurance procedures. It is essential that you understand the principles of obtaining evidence and can apply this knowledge to the scenario and design procedures relevant to the area being tested or the risk to be addressed.

1 The principles of evidence

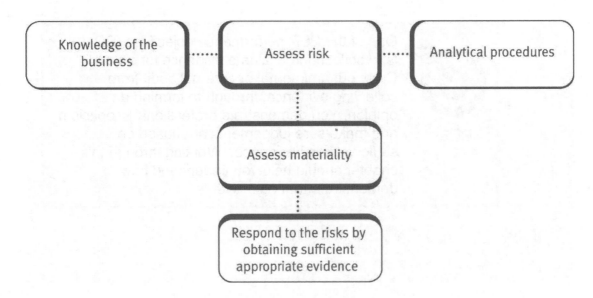

• Audit procedures are designed to obtain evidence in response to the assessment of risk at the planning stage.

- Evidence gathered must be sufficient and appropriate to reduce assessed risk to an acceptable level.

- If, at the review stage, the senior audit staff deem that the risk of misstatement has not been reduced to an acceptable level, more evidence will be required.

2 Obtaining audit evidence

ISA 500 *Audit Evidence* requires the auditor to obtain sufficient appropriate evidence to be able to draw reasonable conclusions. [ISA 500, 4]

Sufficient evidence

- A measure of quantity, i.e. does the auditor have enough evidence to draw a conclusion.

- Affected by risk and materiality of the balances and quality of evidence.

[ISA 500, 5e]

Appropriate evidence

- Measures quality of evidence – **reliability** and **relevance**. [ISA 500, 5b]

- Reliability of evidence depends on several factors [ISA 500, A31]:

  - Independent, externally generated evidence is better than evidence generated internally by the client.

  - Effective controls imposed by the entity improve the reliability of evidence.

  - Evidence obtained directly by the auditor is more reliable than evidence obtained indirectly or by inference.

  - It is better to get written, documentary evidence rather than verbal confirmations.

  - Original documents provide more reliable evidence than copies or documents transformed into electronic form.

- Relevance means the evidence relates to the financial statement assertions being tested. [ISA 500, A27]

Financial statement assertions

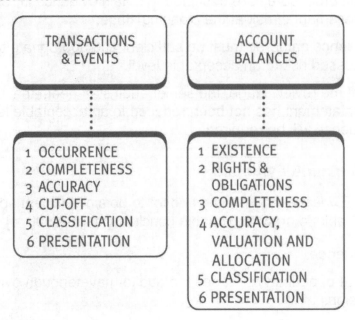

[ISA 315, A129a]

Addressing disclosures in the audit of financial statements

Disclosures are an important part of the financial statements and seen as a way for communicating further information to users. Poor quality disclosures may obscure understanding of important matters.

Concerns have been raised about whether auditors are giving sufficient attention to disclosures during the audit. The IAASB believes that where the term financial statements is used in the ISAs, it should be clarified that this is intended to include all disclosures subject to audit.

Recent changes to ISAs include:

- Emphasis on the importance of giving appropriate attention to addressing disclosures.

- Focus on matters relating to disclosures to be discussed with those charged with governance, particularly at the planning stage.

- Emphasis on the need to agree with management their responsibility to make available the information relevant to disclosures, early in the audit process.

Audit procedures for obtaining evidence

The methods of obtaining evidence are:

- Inspection of records, documents or physical assets.

- Observation of processes and procedures, e.g. inventory counts.

- External confirmation obtained in the form of a direct written response to the auditor from a third party.

- Recalculation to confirm the numerical accuracy of documents or records.

- Re-performance by the auditor of procedures or controls.

- Analytical procedures.

- Enquiry of knowledgeable parties.

[ISA 500, A14 – A22]

The auditor obtains evidence to draw conclusions on which to base the audit opinion. This is achieved by performing procedures to:

- Obtain an understanding of the entity and its environment, including internal control, to assess the risks of material misstatement by performing risk assessment procedures.

- Test the operating effectiveness of controls in preventing, detecting and correcting material misstatements by performing tests of controls.

- Detect material misstatements by performing substantive procedures.

Tests of control and substantive procedures

Tests of controls are designed to check that the audit client's internal control systems operate effectively.

Examples of tests of controls:

- Inspect purchase invoices for evidence of authorisation by a manager before payment is made.

- Observe the process for despatch of goods to ensure the warehouse staff check the goods to the order before despatch.

- Using test data, enter a dummy order over a customer's credit limit to verify that the system will not accept it.

Substantive procedures are designed to find material misstatements (fraud and error) in the financial statements.

Substantive procedures can be tests of detail or analytical procedures.

Substantive tests of detail look at the supporting evidence for individual transactions and traces them through to the financial statements to ensure they are dealt with appropriately.

Examples of tests of detail:

- Inspect a purchase invoice for the amount and trace it into the purchase day book to ensure it has been recorded accurately.

- Recalculate an allowance for doubtful receivables using the client's formula to verify arithmetical accuracy.

Substantive analytical procedures test the balances as a whole to identify any unusual relationships e.g. comparison of a gross profit margin year-on-year might highlight that revenue is overstated if there is no known reason for an increase in the margin. An analytical procedure can be seen as a sense check of a balance or testing the 'reasonableness' of a balance.

Examples of analytical procedures:

- Calculate the receivables collection period and compare with credit terms offered to customers to identify any possible overstatement. If the collection period appears too high, discuss with management the need for an increase in the allowance for doubtful receivables.

- Obtain a breakdown of sales by month and analyse the seasonal trend to ensure it is consistent with the auditor's knowledge of the business. Discuss any unusual fluctuations with management.

- Calculate the expected interest charge for a loan by multiplying the outstanding loan amount with the interest rate and compare with the client's figure. Discuss any significant difference with management.

  Recap: Example audit procedures

Tutorial note

This section is intended to provide examples of audit procedures but is not intended to be a comprehensive list which can be rote-learned to answer any exam question.

Exam questions may focus on specific assertions or issues, and as such, audit procedures will need to be designed to address the specific issues mentioned in the scenario.

Property, plant and equipment

- Select a sample of assets from the asset register and physically inspect them to verify existence.

- Select a sample of assets visible at the client premises and inspect the asset register to ensure they are included for completeness.

- Inspect title deeds or registration documents for the client's name to verify rights and obligations.

- Review purchase invoices to verify cost/valuation.

- Assess the reasonableness of the depreciation rate used by the client by reviewing the company's capital expenditure budget/plan to identify the replacement policy for assets.

- Recalculate the depreciation charge to verify arithmetical accuracy.

- Inspect the physical condition of assets to assess valuation.

- Review any valuation reports to confirm valuation and agree the revaluation surplus to other comprehensive income.

Investment properties

- Inspect title deeds to confirm ownership of the investment property.

- Discuss with management to confirm its intention to hold the property for investment purposes rather than for use by the client.

- Perform a physical inspection of the building to confirm its general condition and that it is not occupied by the client.

- If the property is rented, confirm this by inspecting the rental agreement and bank statements and cash book for rental receipts.

- Obtain an independent expert's market valuation of the property at the reporting date to determine the fair value.

- Calculate the gain or loss arising on valuation and confirm that it has been recognised within the statement of profit or loss.

- Review the disclosures made in the financial statements to ensure they comply with the requirements of IAS 40 *Investment Properties*.

Development costs

- Obtain a breakdown of capitalised costs, cast for mathematical accuracy and agree to the financial statements.

- For a sample of costs included in the breakdown, agree the amount to invoices or timesheets to confirm accuracy.

- Inspect board minutes for any discussions relating to the intended sale or use of the asset.

- Discuss details of the project with the project manager or management to evaluate compliance with IAS 38 criteria.

- Inspect project plans and other documentation to evaluate compliance with IAS 38 criteria.

- Inspect budgets to confirm financial feasibility.

- Review the financial statement disclosures in the draft financial statements to ensure compliance with IAS 38.

- Inspect the budgets/forecasts for the next few years to ascertain the period over which economic benefits are expected to be generated and compare with the amortisation policy, to assess reasonableness of the amortisation period.

Goodwill

- Review the legal documentation pertaining to the acquisition to confirm that the figures included in the goodwill calculation relating to consideration paid and payable are accurate and complete.

- Using the purchase documentation, confirm the level of shareholding acquired and that this conveys control, i.e. the shares carry voting rights and there is no restriction on the Group exercising control.

- Agree the cash consideration paid to the bank statement and cash book of the acquiring company.

- Review the board minutes for discussions relating to the acquisition, and for the relevant minute of board approval.

- For any contingent consideration, obtain management's calculation of the present value, and evaluate assumptions used in the calculation. In particular, consider the probability of payment by obtaining revenue and profit forecasts.

- Discuss with management the reason for using the interest rate used in the calculation, and ensure this is in line with the client's weighted average cost of capital to ensure it is appropriate.

- Confirm that the fair value of the non-controlling interest has been calculated based on an externally available share price at the date of acquisition. Agree the share price used in management's calculation to stock market records showing the share price at the date of acquisition.

- Obtain a copy of the due diligence report (if applicable) and review for confirmation of acquired assets and liabilities and their fair values.

- Evaluate the methods used to determine the fair value of acquired assets, including the property, and liabilities to confirm compliance with IFRS 3 *Business Combinations* and IFRS 13 *Fair Value Measurement*.

- Review the calculation of net assets acquired to confirm that Group accounting policies have been applied.

- Review management's impairment calculations and evaluate the assumptions used to assess reasonableness.

- Review management accounts and cash flow forecasts to assess whether the subsidiary is expected to generate future cash flows in excess of the carrying amount.

- Review the financial statement disclosures in the draft financial statements to ensure compliance with IFRS 3.

Leases

- Obtain a copy of the lease, signed by the buyer-lessor, and review its major clauses such as whether there are any options to terminate the lease early or extend the lease after the initial term.

- Calculate the present value of the lease payments using an appropriate discount rate and compare this to the client's calculations and agree this figure to the initial recognition of the right-of-use asset and lease liability.

- Calculate the expected depreciation charge of the right-of-use assets using the lease term given in the agreement. If there is an option to extend or terminate the contract, discuss the probability of the option being exercised with management, and ensure the depreciation calculation takes this into consideration.

- Inspect bank statement and cash book for lease payments made during the year.

- Perform a physical inspection of the leased assets to confirm that it exists and is being used by the client.

- Recalculate the finance charge in relation to the leased asset.

- For sale and leaseback transactions, assess whether the transaction constitutes the fulfilment of performance obligation as per IFRS 15 to determine the appropriate accounting treatment.

- Review the financial statement disclosures in the draft financial statements to ensure compliance with IFRS 16.

Government grants

- Obtain the documentation relating to the grant and review to obtain understanding of:
  - The terms of the grant, in particular requirements relating to the specific use of the funds
  - The date by which the funds must be used
  - Any clauses relating to repayment of some or all of the grant should certain conditions arise.

- Agree the amount received to the bank statement and cash book.

- Discuss the use of the grant with an appropriate person to confirm that the grant it to be used as intended by the government.

- Obtain a written representation from management that the grant received will be used for the specific purposes required by the government.

Share-based payment plans

- Obtain a copy of the details of the share-based payment plan and review for details of number of share options granted, intended beneficiaries and vesting period.

- Agree the share price at the grant date to stock market records.

- Discuss the assumptions of how many options are expected to be exercised with management and assess the reasonableness of the assumptions.

- Calculate the expected cost of the share-based payment plan and the amount which should be recognised in the current year and agree the amount to the statement of profit or loss.

- Review the financial statement disclosures in the draft financial statements to ensure compliance with IFRS 2.

Revenue recognition

- Review contracts with customers to obtain an understanding of:

  - the performance obligations and whether they are fulfilled over time or at a point in time

  - the transaction price, including whether the price is fixed or variable or a combination of both.

- Inspect supporting documentation to confirm when the performance obligations have been fulfilled e.g. despatch notes, stage payments made, significant milestones reached.

- For any payments made by customers which cannot be recognised as revenue, confirm that they have been recognised as contract liabilities.

- Where the transaction price includes a variable element, e.g. a performance related bonus, assess whether this is highly probable to be received.

- Agree payments received from the customer to the bank statement and cash book.

- Calculate the amount of revenue to be recognised in the current year and agree to the statement of profit or loss.

- Review documentation confirming satisfactory progress towards the fulfilment of performance obligations at the reporting date.

- Review correspondence with customers for any indication that the contract is not progressing satisfactorily and the performance obligations have not been fulfilled and therefore revenue should not be recognised.

Inventory

- Inspect the inventory listing to ensure damaged/obsolete items have been written down to net realisable value (NRV).

- Inspect the inventory listing for the items on the last goods received notes (GRNs) and goods despatched notes (GDNs) obtained to ensure cut-off is correctly applied.

- Trace items on the count sheets obtained during the count into the inventory listing to ensure the quantities have not been changed.

- Calculate the inventory holding period and compare with prior year to identify any slow-moving items requiring write down.

- Inspect the aged inventory listing for old items and discuss the need for write down with management.

- Inspect purchase invoices to verify cost. Inspect post year-end sales invoices to verify NRV and ensure inventory is valued at the lower of the two figures.

- Review calculations of overheads included in work in progress (WIP) and ensure only production related overheads are included.

Receivables

- Request direct confirmation from customers to confirm the balance.

- Inspect GDNs and invoices included in the listing to confirm accuracy of the amount recorded.

- Inspect post year-end cash receipts to confirm valuation.

- Calculate the receivables collection period and compare with credit terms to assess the recoverability of the debts.

- Enquire with management about any long overdue debts and discuss the need for write down with management.

- Inspect correspondence with customers for evidence of disputes which may indicate overvaluation.

- Evaluate the reasonableness of the basis of the loss allowance and recalculate.

Bank

- Obtain a bank confirmation letter for all bank accounts held to verify rights and existence.

- Obtain bank reconciliations for all bank accounts and cast to confirm accuracy.

- Agree the balance per the cash book to the ledger.

- Agree the balance per the bank statement to the bank letter.

- Agree unpresented cheques to the post year-end bank statements to confirm they have cleared in a reasonable time.

- Agree outstanding lodgements to the paying in book and post year-end bank statements.

Payables

- Inspect purchase invoices and GRNs included on the listing to confirm accuracy of recording.

- Obtain/perform supplier statement reconciliations to identify discrepancies which could affect the completeness, existence or valuation assertions.

- Obtain direct confirmation of balances from suppliers where supplier statements are not available.

- Inspect post year-end bank statements for payments made which may indicate unrecorded liabilities.

- Calculate the payables payment period and compare with credit terms given to identify unusual differences and discuss with management.

- Inspect GRNs for before the year-end to ensure completeness.

Provisions

- Enquire with management the basis of the provision to assess reasonableness.

- Recalculate the provision to confirm arithmetical accuracy.

- Obtain written representation from management as to the adequacy and completeness of the provision.

- For a legal provision, obtain confirmation from lawyers regarding the amount and probability.

- Inspect board minutes to confirm an obligation exists at year end.

- Review subsequent events for further evidence.

- Inspect cash flow forecasts to verify the expected timing of the payments and assess whether the provision has been correctly discounted.

ISA 501 Audit Evidence – Specific Considerations for Selected Items

In accordance with ISA 501, auditors are required to obtain sufficient appropriate evidence with regard to three specific matters, as follows:

(1) The existence and condition of inventory

  – Attendance at the inventory count

    – Evaluate management's instructions

    – Observe the count procedures

    – Inspect the inventory

    – Perform test counts

  – Perform procedures over the final inventory records to ensure they reflect actual inventory count results.

  [para 4]

(2) The completeness of litigation and claims involving the entity

  – Enquiry of management and in-house legal counsel.

  – Reviewing minutes of board meetings and meetings with legal counsel.

  – Inspecting legal expense accounts.

  – If there is a significant risk of material misstatement due to unidentified litigation or claims the audit should seek direct communication with the entity's external legal counsel.

  [para 9, 10]

(3) The presentation and disclosure of segmental information

  – Understand, evaluate and test methods used by management to determine segmental information.

  – Perform analytical procedures.

  [para 13]

ISA 505 External confirmations

External confirmations are written responses received from third parties directly by the auditor to help them obtain sufficient appropriate evidence. [para 6a]

Examples include: receivables circularisations and bank letters.

As these provide external, written evidence, they are considered to be reliable. In order to ensure that the evidence sought remains reliable, auditors should maintain control over this process.

To do this they should:

- Determine the information to be confirmed.

- Select the appropriate third party.

- Design the confirmation requests and provide return information for responses to be sent directly to the auditor.

- Send the requests, including a follow up when no response is received.

[para 7]

If management refuses to allow the auditor to send such requests the auditor should consider whether this is reasonable or not in the circumstances. This may affect the auditor's fraud risk assessment and reliance upon written representations from management. The auditor should perform alternative procedures to obtain the evidence. [para 8]

If the auditor concludes that management's request is unreasonable and they cannot obtain sufficient appropriate evidence by any other means, the matter should be communicated to those charged with governance. [para 9]

The auditor must be alert to the risk of interception, alteration or fraud and maintain appropriate professional scepticism when considering the reliability of responses which may have been received indirectly or appear not to come from the intended party. [para A11]

 ISA 530 Audit Sampling

Auditors rarely test every transaction, balance and disclosure relevant to a set of financial statements. ISA 530 states that auditors should select appropriate samples for testing that provide a reasonable basis to draw conclusions about the population from which the sample is selected. [para 4]

When selecting samples the auditor should:

- Consider the purpose of the procedure and the characteristics of the population from which the sample will be drawn. [para 6]

- Ensure the sample size is sufficient to reduce sampling risk to an acceptable level. [para 7]

- Ensure each sampling unit has a chance of selection. [para 8]

If the auditor identifies any misstatements or deviations, the nature and cause should be investigated. [para 12]

If a misstatement is identified when performing tests of details, the misstatement should be projected across the population. [para 14]

When choosing a sampling method there are two broad approaches:

- Statistical sampling, where items in the population are selected randomly so that probability theory may be used to evaluate the results (through extrapolation to the whole population). [para 5g]

- Non-statistical, which is any method that does not meet the characteristics of statistical. [para 5g]

The auditor uses judgment to select sample items (e.g. focusing on high value, or known high risk items). Extrapolation cannot be used when bias has been introduced into the sample because the sample is no longer representative of the whole population.

3 Substantive analytical procedures

ISA 520 *Analytical Procedures* states that the use of analytical procedures as substantive evidence is generally more applicable where:

- There are large volumes of transactions that tend to be predictable over time [ISA 520, A6]

- Controls are working effectively [ISA 520, A9]

In order to design an analytical procedure the auditor should:

- Determine the suitability of analytical procedures for the given assertion.

- Evaluate the reliability of data from which the expectation is developed.

- Develop an expectation and evaluate whether it is sufficiently precise to identify a material misstatement.

- Determine the difference between expected amount and recorded amount.

[ISA 520, 5]

If analytical procedures identify fluctuations or relationships that are inconsistent with the auditor's knowledge of the business then the auditor should investigate those peculiarities through:

- Enquiry of management.

- Other procedures, as deemed necessary, for example, when management's response is considered inadequate.

[ISA 520, 7]

Current issue: The Growing Use of Data Analytics in an Audit

In the past, computer-assisted audit techniques (CAATs) have been used to analyse data. As CAATs were tailored to the specific client they required significant investment and, as a result, were not widely used across all audits.

Technological development means it is now possible to capture and analyse entire datasets allowing for the interrogation of 100% of the transactions in a population – data analytics (DA). Whilst DA can be developed for bespoke issues, a key characteristic is that the development of standard automated tools and techniques allows for more widespread use. Some of the more widely used DA tools started out as bespoke CAATs which have been developed for wider application.

Definitions

Data analytics (DA) is the science and art of discovering and analysing patterns, deviations and inconsistencies, and extracting other useful information in the data of underlying or related subject matter of an audit through analysis, modelling, visualisation for the purpose of planning and performing the audit.

Big data refers to data sets that are large or complex.

Big data technology allows the auditor to perform procedures on very large or complete sets of data rather than samples.

Features of data analytics

- DA allows the auditor to manipulate 100% of the data in a population quickly which reduces audit risk.

- Results can be visualised graphically which can make the reports more user-friendly.

- DA can be used throughout the audit to help identify risks, test the controls and as part of substantive procedures. The results still need to be evaluated using the professional skills and judgment of the auditor in order to analyse the results and draw conclusions.

- As for analytical procedures in general, the quality of DA depends on the reliability of the underlying data used.

- DA can incorporate a wider range of data. For example data can be extracted and analysed from social media, public sector data, industry data and economic data.

Example

The auditor may use DA to analyse journals posted. The analysis identifies:

- The total number of journals posted.
- The number of journals posted manually.
- The number of journals posted automatically by the system.
- The number of people processing journals.
- The time of day the journals are posted.

The auditor may conclude there is a higher risk of fraud this year compared with last if:

- The number of manual versus automatic journals increases significantly.
- The number of people processing journals increases.
- Journals are posted outside of normal working hours.

Benefits of data analytics

- Audit procedures can be performed more quickly and to a higher standard. This provides more time to analyse and interpret the results rather than gathering the information for analysis.
- Audit procedures can be carried out on a continuous basis rather than focused on the year end.
- Reporting to the client and users will be more timely as the work may be completed within weeks rather than months after the year-end.
- The use of DA may result in more frequent interaction between the auditor and client over the course of the year.
- Audit efficiency should increase resulting in a reduction in billable hours. Although this is good news for the client, it will mean lower fees for the auditor.

What it means for the profession

- Larger accountancy firms are developing their own data analytic platforms. This requires significant investment in computer hardware and software, training of staff and quality control.
- Small firms are unlikely to have the resources available to develop their own software as the cost is likely to be too prohibitive. However, external computer software companies have developed audit systems that work with popular accounting systems such as Sage, Xero and Intuit which many clients of small accountancy firms may be using.

- Medium sized firms may also find the level of investment too restrictive and may therefore be unable to compete with the larger audit firms for listed company audits. However, these firms may find that listed companies require systems and controls assurance work which their auditors would not be allowed to perform under ethical standards.

Developments within the profession

Currently, ISAs take a systems-based approach to audit, which seeks to obtain audit evidence by placing reliance on internal controls rather than on carrying out extensive substantive tests of detail. The development of DA represents a significant progression away from traditional auditing methods. Therefore, as they become more widely used, ISAs will need to be updated to reflect this innovation in auditing techniques. ED 315, which is summarised in Chapter 7, contains some guidance on the use of DA when performing risk assessment procedures.

The IAASB has a responsibility to develop standards that reflect the current environment and facilitate a high quality audit. Auditors, audit oversight authorities and standard setters need to work together to explore how developments in technology can support enhanced audit quality.

Auditors and businesses operate in an environment with larger volumes of transactions, greater complexity and greater regulation as a result of corporate failures. Technological change means information systems are capable of capturing, analysing and communicating significantly more data than previously. As a result, stakeholders are expecting the auditor to perform an audit that includes greater use of technology including DA.

The quality of the audit can be enhanced by the use of DA. DA enables the auditor to obtain a greater understanding of the entity and its environment. Professional scepticism and professional judgment are improved when the auditor has a better understanding.

Limitations of Data Analytics

There are still limitations to the audit and therefore auditors need to be careful not to place too much confidence into the use of DA which could have a negative impact on audit quality.

- The data may not be complete, well-controlled or from a reliable source.

- Financial statements still contain a significant amount of estimates.

- DA will not replace the need for auditors to use professional scepticism and professional judgment.

Because of these limitations, the auditor is still only able to give reasonable assurance even though 100% of a population may be tested.

Challenges that impact the use of Data Analytics

Data acquisition and retention – The entity's data will need to be transferred to the auditor raising concerns over data security and privacy as well as creating storage problems for such large data sets.

Conceptual challenges – Auditors will be asking questions they have never asked in the past and the client may be hesitant to provide all of the information requested.

Legal and regulatory challenges – Regulations may prohibit data leaving the jurisdiction the entity is located. This may pose a problem if the IT facilities of the client are located in a different country.

Resource availability – Data scientists may form part of a centralised department which supports all engagement teams within the firm. The resources are likely to be limited which will put a strain on resources.

How regulators and audit oversight authorities maintain oversight – These bodies have little experience themselves of inspecting audits using DA.

Investment in retraining and reskilling auditors – Changing the auditor's mind-set from traditional audit methods will require time and investment.

The use of DA and developments in auditing standards will impact:

Risk assessment – DA may improve the risk assessment process.

Quality control – Audit firms will need to consider how specialist teams are supervised and how they interact with the audit teams they support. Firms will need to consider the integrity of the DA software to ensure it does what it is supposed to.

Group audits – DA may help by enabling better analytical procedures to be performed in respect of components that are not significant components. Also, the audit procedures may be more centralised enabling the group auditor to perform more procedures rather than relying on the work of a component auditor.

Estimates and fair values – Due to large volumes of data that feed into the models used to develop accounting estimates, DA may be valuable in addressing audit risks associated with these data sources.

Smaller audit firms – Smaller firms may not be able to make the required investment to develop DA tools. Audits of public sector entities may prove challenging as home-grown systems are more prevalent and data capture may be more difficult.

Education – Auditors and accountants will need to be re-skilled to realise the potential of DA. Training and qualifications will need to reflect the increased use of DA for new entrants to the profession.

Ethics – Due to auditors having access to large volumes of client data, there may be a need to update the Code of Ethics to enhance the requirements for confidentiality.

Other auditing standards – There is also likely to be a need to revise other auditing standards such as ISA 240 (Fraud), ISA 320 (Materiality), ISA 330 (Responses to risks), ISA 500 (Audit Evidence), ISA 520 (Analytical Procedures) and ISA 530 (Audit Sampling).

FRC Audit Quality Thematic Review – The Use of Data Analytics in the Audit of Financial Statements

With the increasing use of data analytics, the FRC has performed a review to identify what is working well with a view to sharing information to promote continuous improvement in audit quality. The Audit Quality Review team assessed the use of DA in the six largest audit firms.

Current use of data analytics

DA are currently being used by large audit firms to:

- Analyse all transactions in a population, stratify the population and identify outliers for further examination.

- Re-perform calculations.

- Match transactions as they pass through the system.

- Assist in segregation of duties testing.

- Compare client data with externally obtained data.

- Perform sensitivity analysis.

Impact on audit quality

Audit quality is a driver for the implementation of DA. DA can:

- Deepen the auditor's understanding of the entity.

- Facilitate testing of the highest risk areas through stratification.

- Enhance the use of professional scepticism.

- Improve consistency on group audits.

- Enable the auditor to test entire datasets.

- Improve audit efficiency.

- Increase the possibility of identifying fraud.

- Provide a channel for enhanced communication with audit committees.

Good practices observed during the AQR

- Focused roll out of a DA tool.

- Clear positioning within the audit methodology.

- Testing or trial running the DA tool.

- Using specialist staff and clearly defined roles between the specialists and the core engagement team.

- Central running of DA for group audits.

- Clearly documenting the DA tool using flowcharts.

Summary of key findings

- The introduction of mandatory retendering in the UK has provided incentive for firms to develop DA tools as this acts as a key differentiator.

- UK firms are at the forefront of developing DA tools.

- The pace of change is not as fast as expected by audit committees and investors.

- Whilst some firms are investing heavily in DA tools, they are not monitoring their use by audit teams or monitoring their effectiveness at providing appropriate evidence.

- Some audit teams have over-emphasised their use to audit committees. In some cases DA have been used to provide insight to the audit committee rather than to generate audit evidence. In another case a firm described a DA tool as launched in a report but was described to the Audit Quality Review team as being in pilot stage.

- All firms used DA to assist with journal entry testing, however, most firms are not using DA tools routinely in other audit areas.

- For complex entities it can take two years to achieve the full benefits of a DA approach.

- The main barrier to effective use relates to difficulties obtaining entity data and audit teams often lack expertise to extract the data required.

- The use of DA techniques was higher at firms where the audit methodology clearly defines the purpose of the DA.

- In the audits tested, insufficient audit evidence was retained on file.

  - Criteria input into the DA tool was not retained.

  - Screenshots omitted important information.

  - Evidence produced by specialists was omitted.

  - Firm's archiving tools were not able to archive DA evidence.

- It may not be technically, practically or legally possible for the audit firm to retain audit evidence for the file retention period required by auditing standards.

Exploring the Growing Use of Technology in the Audit, with a Focus on Data Analytics

In September 2016, IAASB issued a request for input from accounting firms, regulatory bodies, standard setters, academics and public sector organisations to obtain information about the current use and future direction of the use of data analytics.

The key messages from the Feedback Statement published in January 2018 are:

- ISAs are not 'broken' and should remain principles-based. There should be no rush to change requirements in ISAs at present.

- ISAs should be updated in a way that reflects current technology but remains technologically neutral to provide the ability to accommodate future changes in technology. ISA 500 *Audit Evidence* and ISA 230 *Audit Documentation* were highlighted as priorities for revision.

- Non-authoritative, practical guidance with real-life examples of the use of DA is needed. This process has already commenced.

- The use of DA does not reduce the need to exercise professional scepticism and judgment. Both are integral to understanding the benefits and limitations of using DA in the audit.

Areas of concern

Regulators and oversight authorities are most concerned with data acquisition, auditor skills and compliance with ISAs.

- Audit clients may be reluctant to give access to live systems and this may cast doubt on the reliability of the data being analysed.

- Currently auditors tend to have insufficient understanding of IT to design effective procedures using DA.

- Audit evidence generated from DA must demonstrate that the requirements of the ISAs have been met, particularly the documentation requirements.

Accounting firms are also concerned about retraining and re-skilling, not only auditors, but also regulators and audit committees who will need to understand the DA performed as part of assessing the work of the auditor. There is also concern that these authorities have little experience themselves of inspecting audits involving the use of DA.

Computer-assisted audit techniques (CAATs)

In the past, CAATs such as test data and audit software have been used to analyse data.

Test data is used to test the programmed controls within a computer system allowing the auditor to test aspects that would otherwise not be capable of testing manually.

Audit software is used to:

- Calculate ratios for use in analytical procedures.

- Identify exceptional transactions such as those that exceed predefined limits, e.g. a member of management being paid in excess of $20,000 in any one month. This helps identify balances that require further audit testing.

- Extract samples in a non-biased manner.

- Check the calculations in client prepared reports.

- Prepare lead schedules for the auditor to use in working papers.

Benefits:

- Allows continual auditing of processes and delivery of more frequent reports.

- Facilitates processing of large volumes of data and performing large volumes of calculations, many more than could reasonably be performed manually.

- Test data tests the underlying system data, rather than copies and printouts.

- Once software has been written for a client, it can be applied to their system with few further costs.

- Reduces the need for audit staff to perform procedures, hence further cost savings for clients.

- Reduces the need for paper audit trails (hence reduced environmental impact of the audit process).

Drawbacks:

- There is an initial high cost of designing the software package, although this cost can be recouped over a number of years of use.

- Software may interfere with the client's system and could potentially increase the risk of viruses and data corruption.

- Clients may be concerned for the security of their data.

- They are only usually cost effective if the client's accounting systems are integrated, otherwise auditors would need different software programmes for different systems.

- Lead times tend to be long and the planning has to be carried out well in advance – not just three or four weeks before the start of fieldwork, but perhaps a whole year in advance.

- Audit firms will need to recruit increasingly from an IT, rather than an accounting, background.

- Software has to be tested on a 'live' system before the auditor knows whether it will work or not which creates a risk of the auditor corrupting the system.

- If the client changes its system, the auditor has to incur further costs changing their audit software.

4 Relying on the work of others

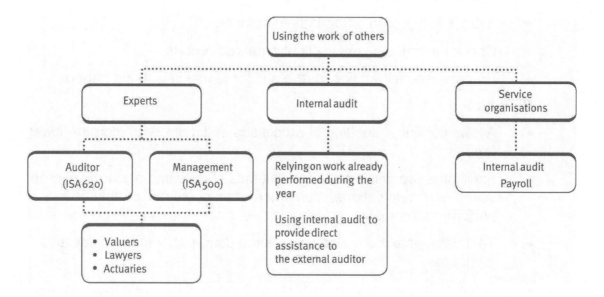

There are two types of expert an auditor may use:

(1) Management's expert – an employee of the client or someone engaged by the audit client who has expertise that is used to assist in the preparation of the financial statements.

(2) Auditor's expert – an employee of the audit firm or someone engaged by the audit firm to provide sufficient appropriate evidence.

Relying on the work of a management's expert

ISA 500 *Audit Evidence* provides guidance on what the auditor should consider before relying on the work of a management's expert. This guidance is very similar to that given for relying on the work of an auditor's expert.

The auditor must:

- Evaluate the competence, capabilities and objectivity of that expert.

- Obtain an understanding of the work of that expert.

- Evaluate the appropriateness of that expert's work as audit evidence for the relevant assertion.

[ISA 500, 8]

The rest of this section focuses on the work of an auditor's expert.

Relying on the work of an auditor's expert

ISA 620 *Using the Work of an Auditor's Expert* provides guidance to auditors.

If the auditor lacks the required technical knowledge to gather sufficient appropriate evidence to form an opinion, they may have to rely on the work of an expert.

Examples of such circumstances include:

- The valuation of complex financial instruments, land and buildings, works of art, jewellery and intangible assets.

- Actuarial calculations associated with insurance contracts or employee benefit plans.

- The estimation of oil and gas reserves.

- The interpretation of contracts, laws and regulations.

- The analysis of complex or unusual tax compliance issues.

[ISA 620, A1]

The auditor must determine if the expert's work is adequate for the auditor's purposes. [ISA 620, 5b]

To fulfil this responsibility the auditor must **evaluate whether the expert has the necessary competence, capability and objectivity for the purpose of the audit**. [ISA 620, 9]

Evaluating competence [ISA 620, A15]

Information regarding the competence, capability and objectivity on an expert may come from a variety of sources, including:

- Personal experience of working with the expert.

- Discussions with the expert.

- Discussions with other auditors.

- Knowledge of the expert's qualifications, memberships of professional bodies and licences.

- Published papers or books written by the expert.

- The audit firm's quality control procedures.

Evaluating objectivity [ISA 620, A20]

Assessing the objectivity of the expert is particularly difficult, as they may not be bound by a similar code of ethics as the auditor and, as such, may be unaware of the ethical requirements and threats with which auditors are familiar. It may therefore be relevant to:

- Make enquiries of the client about known interests or relationships with the chosen expert.

- Discuss applicable safeguards with the expert.

- Discuss financial, business and personal interests in the client with the expert.

- Obtain written representation from the expert.

Agreeing the work [ISA 620, 11]

Once the auditor has considered the above matters they must then obtain written agreement from the expert of the following:

- The nature, scope and objectives of the expert's work.

- The roles and responsibilities of the auditor and the expert.

- The nature, timing and extent of communication between the two parties.

- The need for the expert to observe confidentiality.

Evaluating the work [ISA 620, 12]

Once the expert's work is complete the auditor must scrutinise it and evaluate whether it is appropriate for audit purposes.

In particular, the auditor should consider:

- The reasonableness of the findings and their consistency with other evidence.

- The relevance and reasonableness of significant assumptions.

- The relevance, completeness and accuracy of source data used.

Reference to the work of an expert

Auditors cannot devolve responsibility for forming an audit opinion. The auditor has to use their professional judgment whether the evidence produced by the expert is sufficient and appropriate to support the audit opinion.

The use of an auditor's expert is not mentioned in the auditor's report unless required by law or regulation. Reference to the work of an expert may be included in a report containing a modified opinion if it is relevant to the understanding of the modification. This does not diminish the auditor's responsibility for the opinion. [ISA 620, 14 & 15]

Relying on internal audit

ISA 610 *Using the Work of Internal Auditors* provides guidance.

An internal audit department forms part of the client's system of internal control. If this is an effective element of the control system it may reduce control risk, and therefore reduce the need for the auditor to perform detailed substantive testing.

Additionally, auditors may be able to co-operate with a client's internal audit department and place reliance on their procedures in place of performing their own.

Before relying on the work of internal audit, the external auditor must assess the effectiveness of the internal audit function and assess whether the work produced by the internal auditor is adequate for the purpose of the audit.

Evaluating the internal audit function [ISA 610, 15]

- The extent to which the internal audit function's **organisational status** and relevant policies and procedures support the **objectivity** of the internal auditors.

- The **competence** of the internal audit function.

- Whether the internal audit function applies a systematic and disciplined **approach,** including quality control.

Evaluating objectivity [ISA 610, A7]

- Whether the internal audit function reports to those charged with governance or has direct access to those charged with governance.

- Whether the internal audit function is free from operational responsibility.

- Whether those charged with governance are responsible for employment decisions such as remuneration.

- Whether any constraints are placed on the internal function by management or those charged with governance.

- Whether the internal auditors are members of a professional body which requires compliance with ethical requirements.

Evaluating competence [ISA 610, A8]

- Whether the resources of the internal audit function are appropriate and adequate for the size of the organisation and nature of its operations.

- Whether there are established policies for hiring, training and assigning internal auditors to internal audit engagements.

- Whether internal auditors have adequate technical training and proficiency, including relevant professional qualifications and experience.

- Whether the internal auditors have the required knowledge of the entity's financial reporting and the applicable financial reporting framework and possess the necessary skills to perform work related to the financial statements.

- Whether the internal auditors are members of a professional body which requires continued professional development.

Evaluating the systematic and disciplined approach

- Existence, adequacy and use of internal audit procedures and guidance.

- Application of quality control policies and procedures such as those in ISQC 1.

[ISA 610, A11]

If the auditor considers it appropriate to use the work of the internal auditors they then have to determine the areas and extent to which the work of the internal audit function can be used (by considering the nature and scope of work) and incorporate this into their planning to assess the impact on the nature, timing and extent of further audit procedures. [ISA 610, 17]

Evaluating the internal audit work [ISA 610, 23]

The auditor must evaluate whether:

- The work was properly planned, performed, supervised, reviewed and documented.

- Sufficient appropriate evidence has been obtained.

- The conclusions reached are appropriate in the circumstances.

- The reports prepared are consistent with the work performed.

To evaluate the work adequately, the external auditor must re-perform some of the procedures that the internal auditor has performed to ensure they reach the same conclusion. [ISA 610, 24]

The extent of the work to be performed on the internal auditor's work will depend on the amount of judgment involved and the risk of material misstatement in that area. [ISA 610, 24]

When reviewing and re-performing some of the work of the internal auditor, the external auditor must consider whether their initial expectation of using the work of the internal auditor is still valid. [ISA 610, 25]

Note that the auditor is not required to rely on the work of internal audit. In some jurisdictions, the external auditor may be prohibited or restricted from using the work of the internal auditor by law.

Responsibility for the auditor's opinion cannot be devolved and no reference should be made in the auditor's report regarding the use of others during the audit.

Using internal audit to provide direct assistance

External auditors can consider whether the internal auditor can provide direct assistance with gathering audit evidence under the supervision and review of the external auditor. ISA 610 provides guidance to aim to reduce the risk that the external auditor overuses the internal auditor.

The following considerations will be made:

- Direct assistance cannot be provided where laws and regulations prohibit such assistance. [ISA 610, 26]

  Note that for **UK syllabus**, direct assistance by the internal auditor is not allowed.

- The competence and objectivity of the internal auditor. Where threats to objectivity are present, the significance of them and whether they can be managed to an acceptable level must be considered. [ISA 610, 27]

- The external auditor must not assign work to the internal auditor which involves significant judgment, a high risk of material misstatement or with which the internal auditor has been involved. [ISA 610, 30]

- The planned work must be communicated with those charged with governance so agreement can be made that the use of the internal auditor is not excessive. [ISA 610, 31]

Where it is agreed that the internal auditor can provide direct assistance:

- Management must agree in writing that the internal auditor can provide such assistance and that they will not intervene in that work.
  [ISA 610, 33a]

- The internal auditors must provide written confirmation that they will keep the external auditors information confidential. [ISA 610, 33b]

- The external auditor will provide direction, supervision and review of the internal auditor's work. [ISA 610, 34]

- During the direction, supervision and review of the work, the external auditor should remain alert to the risk that the internal auditor is not objective or competent. [ISA 610, 35]

Documentation

The auditor should document

- The evaluation of the internal auditor's objectivity and competence.

- The basis for the decision regarding the nature and extent of the work performed by the internal auditor.

- The name of the reviewer and the extent of the review of the internal auditor's work.

- The written agreement of management mentioned above.

- The working papers produced by the internal auditor.

[ISA 610, 37]

Use of service organisations

Many companies use service organisations to perform business functions such as:

- Payroll processing

- Receivables collection

- Pension management.

If a company uses a service organisation, audit evidence will need to be obtained from the service organisation instead of, or in addition to, the client. This needs to be considered when planning the audit.

ISA 402 *Audit Considerations Relating to an Entity Using a Service Organisation* provides guidance to auditors.

Planning the audit

The auditor will need to:

- Obtain an understanding of the service organisation sufficient to identify and assess the risks of material misstatement.

- Design and perform audit procedures responsive to those risks.

[ISA 402, 1]

This requires the auditor to obtain an understanding of the service provided:

- Nature of the services and their effect on internal controls.

- Nature and materiality of the transactions to the entity.

- Level of interaction between the activities of the service organisation and the entity.

- Nature of the relationship between the service organisation and the entity including contractual terms.

[ISA 402, 9]

The auditor should determine the effect the use of a service organisation will have on their assessment of risk. The following issues should be considered:

- Reputation of the service organisation

- Existence of external supervision

- Extent of controls operated by service provider

- Experience of errors and omissions

- Degree of monitoring by the user.

Sources of information about the service organisation

- Obtaining a type 1 or type 2 report from the service organisation's auditor.

  A Type 1 report provides a description of the design of the controls at the service organisation prepared by the management of the service organisation. It includes a report by the service auditor providing an opinion on the description of the system and the suitability of the controls. [ISA 402, 8b]

  A Type 2 report is a report on the description, design and operating effectiveness of controls at the service organisation. It contains a report prepared by management of the service organisation. It includes a report by the service auditor providing an opinion on the description of the system, the suitability of the controls, the effectiveness of the controls and a description of the tests of controls performed by the auditor. [para 8c]

  If the auditor intends to use a report from a service auditor they should consider:

  - The competence and independence of the service organisation auditor

  - The standards under which the report was issued.

- Contacting the service organisation through the client.

- Visiting the service organisation.

- Using another auditor to perform tests of controls.

[ISA 402, 12]

Responding to assessed risks

The auditor should determine whether sufficient appropriate evidence is available from the client and if not, perform further procedures or use another auditor to perform procedures on their behalf. [ISA 402, 15]

If controls are expected to operate effectively:

- Obtain a type 2 report if available and consider:

  - Whether the date covered by the report is appropriate for the audit.

  - Whether the client has any complementary controls in place.

> > – The time elapsed since the tests of controls were performed.
> >
> > – Whether the tests of controls performed by the auditor are relevant to the financial statement assertions.
>
> [ISA 402, 17]

- Perform tests of controls at the service organisation.

- Use another auditor to perform tests of controls.

[ISA 402, 16]

The auditor should enquire of the client whether the service organisation has reported any frauds to them or whether they are aware of any frauds, non-compliance or uncorrected misstatements affecting the financial statements of the entity.

[ISA 402, 19]

Impact on the auditor's report

If sufficient appropriate evidence has not been obtained, a qualified or disclaimer of opinion will be issued. [ISA 402, 20]

The use of a service organisation auditor is not mentioned in the auditor's report unless required by law or regulation. Reference to the work of a service organisation auditor may be included in a report containing a modified opinion if it is relevant to the understanding of the modification. This does not diminish the auditor's responsibility for the opinion. [ISA 402, 21]

Benefits to the audit

- Independence: because the service organisation is external to the client, the audit evidence derived from it is regarded as being more reliable than evidence generated internally by the client.

- Competence: because the service organisation is a specialist, it may be more competent in executing its role than the client's internal department resulting in fewer errors.

- Possible reliance on the service organisation's auditors: it may be possible for the client's auditors to confirm information directly with the service organisation's auditors.

Drawbacks

The main disadvantage of outsourced services from the auditor's point of view concerns access to records and information.

Auditors generally have statutory rights of access to the client's records and to receive answers and explanations that they consider necessary to enable them to form their opinion.

They do not have such rights over records and information held by a third party, such as a service organisation.

If access to records and other information is denied by the service organisation, this may impose a limitation on the scope of the auditor's work. If sufficient appropriate evidence is not obtained this will result in a modified audit opinion.

 ISAE 3402: Reporting on Controls at a Service Organisation

ISAE 3402 *Assurance Reports on Controls at a Service Organisation* deals with assurance engagements undertaken to provide a report for use by entities engaging the services of another organisation and the user entities' auditors. It provides guidance to the assurance provider to ensure that where the service is relevant to the user entity's internal controls relating to financial reporting, the reports prepared provide sufficient appropriate audit evidence as required by ISA 402. [para 1]

In order to provide sufficient appropriate evidence, these assurance engagements are required to provide **reasonable assurance**. The engagements are performed as attestation engagements.

The objective of the engagement is to obtain reasonable assurance that:

- The service organisation's description of its system fairly presents the system as designed and implemented

- The controls were suitably designed

- The controls operated effectively throughout the specified period, and

- To report on the above matters.

[para 8]

The evaluation of the suitability of the design and operating effectiveness of the controls needs to be performed to the same standard as an evaluation performed by the external auditor.

The assurance provider can rely on the service entity's internal audit function, in the same way that the external auditor would, where the work of the internal audit function is relevant to the engagement. [para 30]

An assessment of whether the work of the internal auditor is likely to be adequate for the purposes of the engagement should be performed which considers the same matters as those required by ISA 610 e.g. objectivity, competence, etc. [para 32]

5   Related parties

ISA 550 *Related Parties* provides guidance.

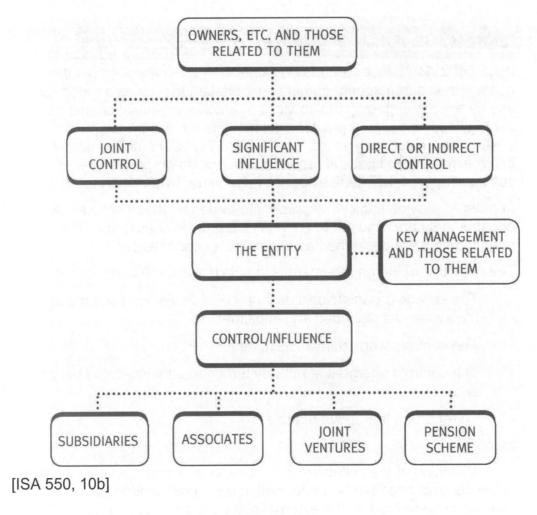

[ISA 550, 10b]

Risks with related party transactions

There is nothing wrong with an entity dealing with a related party.

Related party transactions may increase the potential for the financial results to be manipulated as transactions may be carried out on a basis other than 'arms length'. In these circumstances it is appropriate for such transactions to be brought to the attention of shareholders [IAS 24 *Related Party Disclosures*].

The auditor should obtain sufficient appropriate evidence that the financial statements achieve fair presentation of the related party relationships and transactions and have been accounted for in accordance with the financial reporting framework. [ISA 550, 9]

Disclosure should be made of the following:

- The nature of the related party relationship.

- Information about the transactions including the amount and any balances outstanding at the year-end.

- Any allowance for doubtful receivable or expense recognised in respect of irrecoverable debts.

[IAS 24, para 18–19]

If transactions have not been disclosed in accordance with those requirements, the potentially significant deficiency in the internal control system should be reported to those charged with governance.

Even where related parties have been identified, it can be difficult to spot associated transactions with them for the following reasons:

- Directors may be reluctant to disclose transactions, particularly in the case of family members.

- Transactions may not be easy to identify from the accounting systems because they are not separately identified from 'normal' transactions.

- Transactions may be concealed in whole, or in part, from auditors for fraudulent purposes.

As a result of the risks above, related party transactions are generally deemed material by nature.

Indicators of related party transactions

Related parties are often difficult to identify in practice. It can be hard to establish exactly who, or what, are the related parties of an entity. Indicators of related party transactions include:

- Transactions which are overly complex.

- Transactions with abnormal terms of trade.

- Transactions that appear not to have a logical business reason.

- Transactions that are not processed in the usual or routine way.

- High volumes of transactions, or high value or otherwise significant transactions with individual customers or suppliers.

- Unrecorded transactions such as rent free accommodation, or services provided at no cost.

Risk assessment procedures

The auditor should obtain an understanding of:

- The identity of related parties, nature of related party relationships and the type and purpose of transactions with these related parties. [ISA 550, 13]

- The controls established by the client such as approval and authorisation of the transactions. [ISA 550, 14]

Further audit procedures

- Inspecting prior year working papers.

- Inspecting shareholder records for details of principal shareholders.

- Inspecting minutes of shareholders' meetings and other relevant minutes and records.

- Enquiring of other auditors involved with the audit.

- Inspecting the entity's income tax returns and other information supplied to the regulatory authorities.

Where not prohibited by law or regulation the auditor should:

- Confirm transactions with banks, law firms, or other intermediaries.

- Confirm the terms of related party transactions with the related party.

- Read the financial statements or other relevant financial information of the related party for evidence of the transactions.

[ISA 550, A32]

Members of the audit team need to be aware that they should consider the possibility of undisclosed related party transactions when they carry out audit procedures.

If the auditor identifies related parties that were not previously identified or disclosed they should:

- Communicate that information to the rest of the engagement team.

- Request that management identifies all transactions with the related party and enquire why they failed to identify them.

- Perform appropriate substantive procedures relating to transactions with these entities.

- Reconsider the risk that other, unidentified, related parties may exist.

- Evaluate the implications if the non-disclosure by management appears intentional.

[ISA 550, 22]

If the auditor identifies related party transactions outside the entity's normal course of business they should also:

- Inspect the underlying contracts or agreements to establish:

    - the business rationale

    - the terms of the transaction

    - whether appropriate disclosures have been made.

- Obtain evidence that the transactions were appropriately authorised.

[ISA 550, 23]

6 Accounting estimates

Accounting estimates are inherently risky because management judgment is needed to determine them. As a result, estimates may be used to manipulate the financial statements and show a desired result. It may also be difficult for the auditor to obtain sufficient appropriate evidence regarding the balance.

Professional scepticism is essential for the auditor to ensure the accounting estimates are reasonable and are not being used to introduce bias into the financial statements.

ISA 540 (Revised) *Auditing Accounting Estimates and Related Disclosures* requires the auditor to obtain an understanding necessary to allow the auditor to identify and assess the risks of material misstatement relating to accounting estimates. [13]

This involves obtaining an understanding of:

- The entity's environment including the requirements of the financial reporting framework and regulatory factors relevant to accounting estimates. [13b, c]

- The entity's internal controls related to accounting estimates including the control activities, the need for specialised skills, and the governance in place over the financial reporting process relevant to estimates, and how management reviews the outcome of previous accounting estimates and responds to the results of the review. [13e, f, j]

The auditor must separately assess inherent risk and control risk when assessing the risk of material misstatement relating to accounting estimates. When assessing inherent risk the auditor should consider:

- The degree to which the estimate is subject to estimation uncertainty.

- The degree of complexity and subjectivity involved in the method, assumptions and data used to make the estimate.

- The degree of complexity and subjectivity used in the selection of management's point estimate. [16]

When responding to the risk of material misstatement in the accounting estimates, the auditor must perform the following procedures:

- Obtain evidence from subsequent events.

- Test how management made the estimate.

- Develop an auditor's point estimate or range. [18]

Examples of balances where estimates are relevant include:

- Defined benefit pension schemes

- Share based payment schemes

- Investments in shares

- Investment property

- Property within PPE if the revaluation model is used

- Net assets of a subsidiary at the acquisition date.

 Challenges in Auditing Fair Value Accounting Estimates

IAASB Practice Alert (IAASB – October 2008): Challenges in Auditing Fair Value Accounting Estimates in the Current Market Environment

The practice alert has been prepared in light of difficulties in the credit markets and therefore has a focus on financial instruments. Recent market experience has highlighted the difficulties that arise in valuing financial instruments when market information is either not available or sufficient information is difficult to obtain.

In the current environment, obtaining reliable information relevant to fair values has been one of the greatest challenges faced by preparers, and consequently by auditors.

The nature and reliability of information available to management to support the making of a fair value accounting estimate vary widely, and thereby affect the degree of estimation uncertainty associated with that fair value.

The alert is a comprehensive and lengthy document. A summary of some of the key points is included below:

- Due to the complex nature of certain financial instruments, it is vital that both the entity and the auditor understand the instruments in which the entity has invested or to which it is exposed, and the related risks.

- The auditor's understanding of the instruments may be developed by understanding the entity's processes for investing in particular instruments.

- Factors that may influence the auditor's risk assessment with regard to financial instruments include:

  - Whether the entity has control procedures in place for making investment decisions.

  - The level of due diligence associated with particular investments.

  - The expertise of those responsible for making investment decisions.

  - Whether the entity has the ability to subsequently value the instruments.

  - Management's track record for assessing the risks of particular instruments.

- In the case of fair value accounting estimates, it is necessary that the audit engagement team include one or more members sufficiently skilled and knowledgeable about fair value accounting in order to comply with the required quality control procedures.

- Depending on the nature, materiality and complexity of fair values, management representations about fair value measurements and disclosures contained in the financial statements may also include representations about the following:

  - The appropriateness of the measurement methods and the consistency in application of the methods.

  - The completeness and appropriateness of disclosures related to fair values.

  - Whether subsequent events require adjustment to the fair value measurements.

7 Initial engagements – audit considerations

Where the prior period was audited by another auditor or unaudited, the auditor will need to perform additional work in relation to opening balances.

ISA 510 *Initial Engagements – Opening Balances* requires that when auditors take on a new client, they must ensure that:

- Opening balances do not contain material misstatements

- Appropriate accounting policies have been consistently applied, or changes adequately disclosed.

[ISA 510, 3]

Audit procedures

- Read the most recent financial statements and auditor's report for information relevant to opening balances and disclosures. [ISA 510, 5]

- Determine whether the prior period's closing balances have been correctly brought forward or restated. [ISA 510, 6a]

- Determine whether the opening balances reflect the application of appropriate accounting policies. [ISA 510, 6b]

- Review the previous auditor's working papers. [ISA 510, 6ci]

- Evaluate whether audit procedures performed in the current period provide evidence relevant to opening balances. [ISA 510, 6cii]

- Substantive testing of any opening balances where the above procedures are unsatisfactory. [ISA 510, 6ciii]

[UK syllabus: The predecessor auditor is required to provide access to all relevant information concerning the entity including information concerning the most recent audit in accordance with ISQC 1 (UK).]

Implications for the auditor's report

If there is an inability to obtain sufficient appropriate evidence over the opening balances, a qualified or disclaimer of opinion will be issued. [ISA 510, 10]

If the opening balances contain a misstatement that materially affects the current year's financial statements, or the accounting policies have not been consistently applied, a qualified or adverse opinion should be issued. [ISA 510, 11 & 12]

Initial engagements – further considerations

- Were the previous financial statements audited?

- If the previous financial statements were audited, was the opinion modified?

- If the previous opinion was modified, has the matter been resolved since then?

- Were any adjustments made as a result of the audit? If so, has the client adjusted the accounting ledgers as well as the financial statements?

Difficulties may arise where the prior period audit opinion was modified and the matter remains unresolved. If the matter is material to the current period's financial statements then the current audit opinion will also need to be modified.

For example, if there was a modification on the grounds of a material misstatement of closing inventory in the prior period, this will affect the current period's statement of profit or loss as last year's closing inventory is this year's opening inventory.

8 Corresponding figures and comparative financial statements

ISA 710 *Comparative Information – Corresponding Figures and Comparative Financial Statements* requires the auditor to obtain sufficient appropriate evidence about whether comparative information included in the financial statements has been presented in accordance with the financial reporting framework. [ISA 710, 5a]

 Two categories of comparative information exist:

- *Corresponding figures* – where preceding period figures are included as an integral part of the current period financial statements (i.e. figures shown to the right of the current year figures). [ISA 710, 6b]

- *Comparative financial statements* – where preceding period amounts are included for comparison with the current period (i.e. the prior year's full financial statements are included within the current year annual report). If audited, they should be referred to in the auditor's opinion.
  [ISA 710, 6c]

Audit procedures

Audit procedures in respect of corresponding figures should be significantly less than for the current period and are limited to ensuring that:

- Comparative information agrees to the prior year financial statements, or, when appropriate, has been restated. [ISA 710, 7a]

- Accounting policies reflected in the comparative information are consistently applied or any changes have been properly accounted for and adequately disclosed. [ISA 710, 7b]

- The auditor should request a written representation regarding any restatement made to correct a material misstatement that affects the comparative information. [ISA 710, 9]

Implications for the auditor's report

Corresponding figures

- The auditor's opinion does not refer to the corresponding figures because the opinion is on the current period financial statements as a whole including the corresponding figures. [ISA 710, 10]

- If the prior period's audit opinion was modified and the matter which gave rise to the modification is unresolved, the current audit opinion will also be modified either because of the effects on the current period, or, because of the effects of the unresolved matter on the comparability of the current and corresponding figures. [ISA 710, 11]

- If a material misstatement is identified in the prior period financial statements on which an unmodified opinion was issued, and the corresponding figures have not been restated, a modified opinion should be given in respect of the corresponding figures. [ISA 710, 12]

- If a prior year adjustment has been put through to correct material misstatements arising in the prior year, an unmodified opinion can be issued. An emphasis of matter paragraph will be needed to draw attention to the disclosure note explaining the reason for the restatement of the opening balances. [ISA 710, A6]

Comparative financial statements

- The auditor's opinion will refer to each period. [ISA 710, 15]

- If the prior period financial statements were audited by a different auditor, or were not audited, the auditor may refer to this in an Other Matter paragraph. [ISA 710, 17 & 19]

 Audit documentation

The need for documentation

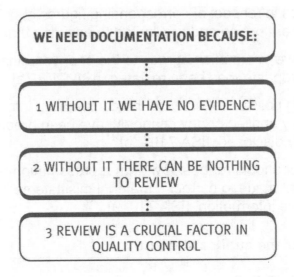

ISA 230 *Audit Documentation* deals specifically with audit documentation and requires:

- Timely preparation of audit documentation necessary to provide a sufficient and appropriate record of the basis for the auditor's report, and evidence that the audit was carried out in accordance with ISAs and applicable legal and regulatory requirements. [ISA 230, 5]

- Audit documentation sufficient to enable an experienced auditor, having no previous connection with the audit, to understand the audit work performed, the results and audit evidence obtained, and the significant matters identified and conclusions reached thereon. [ISA 230, 8]

Special considerations in auditing financial instruments

Financial instruments are susceptible to estimation uncertainty which is the susceptibility of an accounting estimate and related disclosures to an inherent lack of precision in its measurement.

Detection risks when auditing financial instruments

- The auditor may not understand the financial instruments.

- Evidence may be difficult to obtain.

- Undue reliance may be placed on certain individuals who exert significant influence on the financial instrument transactions.

- Transactions may not be significant in value but the risks and exposures associated with them may be significant.

Risk of material misstatement

The risk of material misstatement increases when those responsible for the fair values and estimates:

- Do not fully understand the risks and have insufficient experience to manage those risks.

- Do not have the expertise to value them appropriately in accordance with the financial reporting framework.

- Do not have sufficient controls in place over the financial instruments.

- Inappropriately hedge risks.

Significant transactions may increase the risk of misappropriation of assets.

The risk of fraud may be higher if the employees responsible for accounting for financial instruments are more knowledgeable than management and those charged with governance.

Audit planning considerations

- Understanding the accounting and disclosure requirements.

- Understanding the purpose and risks of the financial instruments.

- Determining whether specialised skills and knowledge are needed in the audit.

- Understanding and evaluating the system of internal control.

- Understanding the internal audit function.

- Understanding management's process for valuing financial instruments.

- Assessing and responding to the risks of material misstatement.

Assessing and responding to the risks of material misstatement

- Testing the controls will be effective in an organisation with well-established controls and systems and where there are significant volumes of transactions which would mean substantive procedures alone would not suffice.

- Organisations with few financial instrument transactions are less likely to have effective controls in place and management may only have a limited understanding which would lead to a substantive audit approach.

- Substantive analytical procedures may not be effective as complex interplay of the drivers of the valuation may mask unusual trends.

- For non-routine transactions, a substantive approach will be the most effective means of obtaining audit evidence.

- As valuations can change significantly in a short period, they should be tested at the year end rather than during the interim audit.

Test your understanding 1

You are an audit manager in King & Co. Your firm has recently been appointed as auditor of Queens Cars Co, a new and second hand motor vehicle dealer with six sites. You are currently planning the audit for the year ended 30 June 20X5. The draft financial statements show revenue of $25 million (20X4: $18.1 million), profit before tax of $2.6 million (20X4: $1.4 million) and total assets of $15.8 million (20X4: $12.6 million).

New cars are purchased on a consignment basis from a single supplier. Queens Cars Co pays the invoice price six months after delivery, or on sale of the vehicle if sooner. Currently, Queens Cars Co records the purchase of the vehicles when they are delivered, along with the associated payable, and the items are included in inventory.

New car sales represent 75% of revenue. All new cars are sold with a warranty of three years or 30,000 miles, whichever is sooner. The warranty provision in respect of new car sales is calculated based on an estimate of 3% of sales which has been estimated using the warranty costs incurred in the last year. Second hand cars are sold with a six month warranty. Customers can purchase an extended warranty for a further three years for an additional fee. The warranty provision in respect of second hand car sales is calculated based on an estimate of 5% of sales as older cars usually experience more issues during the extended warranty period. At 30 June 20X5 the warranty provision was $870,000.

Queens Cars Co also accepts cars in part exchange. One of the company's current promotions is that it will offer a minimum of $500 trade in value for any car used in part exchange for the purchase of a new or second hand car. In addition, many second hand car customers pay cash in order to negotiate a cash discount.

The value of all new cars held across the various sites at the year end, is expected to be $2.4 million. The value of used cars held at the year end is expected to be $600,000.

The finance director has informed you that the inventory count was conducted one week before the year-end. A reconciliation will be performed to calculate the quantity of inventory held at 30 June 20X5.

During the year Queens Cars Co purchased a brand of replacement parts that it will now supply on all servicing and repair jobs. As part of this purchase, $700,000 was paid for the brand name "Quick Fit." This has been capitalised as an intangible asset. No amortisation is being charged as the brand is considered to have an indefinite useful life.

Required:

(a) Evaluate the audit risks that should be considered when planning the audit of Queens Cars Co for the year ended 30 June 20X5.

(10 marks)

(b) Design the principal audit procedures to be used in the audit of the valuation of the Quick Fit brand. **(5 marks)**

(Total: 15 marks)

Test your understanding 2

You are planning the audit of Gig Co for the year ending 31 December 20X5. During the period, Gig Co entered into the following transactions:

On 1 April 20X5 Gig Co purchased 1 million shares in Concert Co for $5 per share. This amounts to a 6% holding of Concert Co's issued share capital, and is not sufficient to give significant influence or control. The shares of Concert Co are not listed.

Gig Co required additional finance and on 1 January 20X5, it issued 1 million $10 bonds at par. Interest is payable at a rate of 5% of the par value annually in arrears. The bonds will be redeemed at a premium on 31 December 20X7. The bonds are held in the financial statements at $10 million and the interest paid during the period has been charged to profit or loss.

Required:

Design the principal audit procedures to be used in the audit of:

(a) The investment in the shares of Concert Co.

(b) The bonds.

(10 marks)

Test your understanding 3

You are a manager in the audit department of Igneous & Co. You are responsible for the audit of Metamorphic Co, which has a financial year ending 31 December 20X5. In April 20X5, Metamorphic Co had all properties revalued by an independent expert. These valuations have been used in the financial statements as at 31 December 20X5.

Required:

(a) Describe the factors Igneous & Co should consider when placing reliance on the work of the expert. **(5 marks)**

(b) Design the principal audit procedures to be used in the audit of the revalued properties. **(5 marks)**

(Total: 10 marks)

9 Chapter summary

Principles and procedures	Analytical procedures	Opening balances and comparatives
• Sufficient appropriate evidence • Substantive procedures • Tests of controls • Inspection, enquiry, observation, etc	• Analysis of plausible relationships • Comparisons • Ratios • Trends • Investigation of unusual fluctuations	• Ensure opening balances and comparative information has been brought forward correctly • Ensure accounting policies are consistently applied

EVIDENCE

Estimates and fair values	Using the work of others	Related parties
• Inherently risky • Subject to management bias • Need for professional scepticism • Test management's process for making the estimate	• Auditor's expert • Internal audit • Service organisations • Must be competent and objective • No reference to use of others in the report	• Material by nature • Increased audit risk • Management may not want to disclose RPTs • Auditor needs to look for undisclosed RPTs

Test your understanding answers

 Test your understanding 1

Study Note: Throughout your answer you must remain specific to the scenario presented in the question. The majority of the marks are for **application** of knowledge. Simply restating the information from the scenario will not score enough for a pass.

(a) **Audit risks**

Consignment purchases

In legal terms, Queens Cars Co does not own the consignment inventory held on site at the year end. The company does not have control over the cars because it does not have the right to direct their use. This is because the supplier can require the return of the car. The fact that it is not obliged to pay for them until the eventual sale is also an indicator that it has not assumed control.

There is a risk that new car inventories, purchases, and payables, are overstated.

Tutorial note: In accordance with IFRS 15 *Revenue from Contracts with Customers*, the ultimate supplier has not made a sale because they still have control over the goods. If the ultimate supplier has control over the goods, Queens Cars Co does not have control, hence Queens Cars Co should not recognise the inventory or purchase until control passes.

Extended warranties

$870,000 is material, being 5.5% of total assets.

A warranty provision has been made in respect of the extended warranties sold with second hand cars.

In accordance with IFRS 15 *Revenue from Contracts With Customers*, this is a service type warranty which gives rise to a separate performance obligation.

The revenue generated by the payment for the extended warranty should be initially recognised as a contract liability and released to the statement of profit or loss over the three year extended warranty period.

No warranty provision should be recognised in respect of estimated costs of extended warranty claims as there is no present obligation in existence.

The warranty provision is currently overstated because the company has provided for future costs of extended warranty claims. Revenue is likely to be overstated and contract liabilities understated as the company may have recognised the extended warranty fees in full.

Warranty provision for new cars

The warranty provision in relation to new cars is $562,500 (75% × 25m × 3%).

This represents 3.6% of total assets and is material.

The new car warranty is an assurance type warranty and must be accounted for in accordance with IAS 37 *Provisions, Contingent Liabilities and Contingent Assets*.

This requires a reliable estimate to be made of the cost of warranty claims during the warranty period. The client has calculated this based on the claims history in the last year which may not provide sufficient evidence over the likely level of claims in future years.

If there is evidence that the level of claims will be significantly different to that in the last year, the warranty provision in respect of new cars may be materially misstated.

Second hand inventories

Second hand inventories of $0.6m represent 3.8% of total assets which is material.

Queens Cars Co offers a minimum trade in value of $500. It is possible that cars may be traded in that do not have a resale value of $500 or more but Queens Cars Co may value them at $500 as this is the cost to the company.

There is a risk that second hand inventories are overstated if they are not valued at the lower of cost and net realisable value as required by IAS 2 *Inventories*.

Cash sales

There is a risk that revenue is misstated due to discounts for cash sales.

There is a risk that the sale may be recorded at the original amount, rather than the renegotiated value.

There is also an increased risk of theft by sales persons, who could record a higher cash discount in the accounts and keep some of the cash for themselves resulting in understatement of revenue.

Inventory count

Inventories are expected to be $3m at the year end which represents 19% of total assets and is material.

There is a risk that quantities have been incorrectly determined at the year end due to the fact that the year-end count was performed before the year-end.

This increases the risk that inventory balances will be misstated.

Brand name

The 'Quick Fit' brand name valued at $0.7m is material, being 4.4% of total assets.

In accordance with IAS 38 *Intangible Assets*, intangible assets should be amortised over their useful life unless the life is indefinite. Indefinite means the company has sufficient resources to maintain the brand strength.

In the absence of amortisation, Queens Cars Co must perform an annual impairment review.

There is a risk that the intangible asset is overstated and impairment charges are understated if there is evidence of impairment.

New audit client

This is the first year our firm has audited this client. Given the firm's lack of cumulative audit knowledge and experience, there is a greater detection risk, and therefore audit risk.

Increased professional scepticism will be required. A more experienced audit team should be selected. Given the multiple sites it will be necessary to visit at least a sample to assess the accounting/control environment. This could increase the time taken to perform the audit and will have consequences for the budget.

(b) **Audit procedures: Valuation of brand name**

–   Inspect the purchase documentation for the brand name to confirm the cost of $0.7m.

–   Enquire of management why they believe the brand has an indefinite life and whether an impairment review has been carried out as required by IAS 38 *Intangible Assets* if this assumption is made. If so, inspect management's assessment and review the assumptions used for reasonableness.

–   Inspect advertising invoices to confirm the amount spent on marketing the Quick Fit brand during the accounting year which may extend the life of the brand and demonstrates that the brand strength is being supported through marketing activity.

–   Inspect marketing expenditure included in forecasts/budgets to ensure marketing is expected to continue at a level considered necessary to maintain the brand name.

–   Review the history of the Quick Fit brand including how long the brand has been trading under that name.

–   Compare the amortisation policies of known competitor brands within the same industry to assess whether non-amortisation is standard within the industry. The accounts should be publicly available and an accounting policy note should be included for amortisation of intangibles.

- Compare the performance of the brand on a month by month basis since acquisition to the present day to identify if performance continues to improve, or at least remain healthy, to confirm management's assumption of brand strength.

- Inspect a breakdown of the repairs and maintenance account after the year end to identify any possible concerns over the quality of the replacement parts which would indicate possible impairment of the brand.

- Review industry journals to identify the risk of new entrants or substitute products to the spare parts industry which may indicate impairment of the brand.

- Obtain written representations from management to corroborate the results of enquiries with management with regard to areas of judgment and estimation.

Test your understanding 2

(a) **Shares**

- Agree the cash paid of $5 million on the purchase of the shares to bank statements and the cash book.

- Inspect the board minutes of Gig Co, or other internal documents, for evidence that the investment has been classified to be measured at fair value through other comprehensive income (FVOCI).

- If classified to be measured at fair value through other comprehensive income, enquire of management to confirm that they do not intend to trade the shares in the short-term.

- Inspect profit and cash flow forecasts to verify that the shares are not expected to be sold within the next year.

- Review past share sales and assess if Gig Co has a history of trading shares in the short-term.

- Enquire of management if legal or broker fees were incurred on the share issue. If so, agree to invoices and ensure that the treatment is appropriate (they should be expensed if the investment is measured at fair value through profit or loss (FVPL), but added onto the carrying amount if measured at FVOCI).

- Enquire of management as to how the fair value of non-listed shares has been determined.

- Review the fair value calculation for accuracy and assess the reasonableness of the assumptions used. Assess the level of input used as per IFRS 13 *Fair Value Measurement*.

> – Inspect the financial statements to see where the revaluation loss has been recorded and assess if this is consistent with the classification of the financial asset (FVPL or FVOCI).
>
> – Inspect the financial statement disclosures, particularly around the level of input used to measure the fair value of the shares.
>
> **(b) Bonds**
>
> – Agree the cash receipt of $10 million to the bank statements and cash book.
>
> – Agree the interest payment to the bank statement and cash book.
>
> – Obtain documentation relating to the bond issue to verify the interest rate and the redemption premium.
>
> – Enquire of management if legal or broker fees were incurred on the bond issue. If so, agree to invoices. An audit adjustment would need to be proposed to deduct these from the initial carrying amount of the liability.
>
> – Recalculate the effective rate of interest on the bonds to confirm arithmetical accuracy.
>
> – Calculate the audit adjustment required so that the finance cost in profit or loss is based on the effective rate of interest.
>
> – Inspect the financial statements to ensure that the liability in respect of the bonds is correctly classified as non-current.

Test your understanding 3

(a) Reliance on the work of an expert

ISA 500 *Audit Evidence* requires auditors to evaluate the competence, capabilities including expertise and objectivity of a management expert.

This would include consideration of the qualifications of the person performing the valuations and assessment of whether they were members of any professional body or industry association.

In addition, the auditor should meet with the expert and discuss with them their relevant expertise such as whether they have valued similar properties to Metamorphic Co in the past. Also consider whether they understand the accounting requirements of IAS 16 *Property, Plant and Equipment* in relation to valuations.

The expert's independence should be ascertained, with potential threats such as undue reliance on Metamorphic Co or a self-interest threat such as share ownership considered.

The valuation should then be evaluated. The assumptions used should be carefully reviewed and compared to previous revaluations at Metamorphic Co.

(b) **Procedures**

- Inspect the valuation report and agree the valuations for each property to the non-current asset register.

- Review property values in the area as at 31 December 20X5 to see if the valuations from April 20X5 are still appropriate.

- Calculate an estimate of depreciation which should have been charged from April to December to assess whether there could be material misstatement of properties.

- Review the financial statement disclosure in respect of the revaluations to ensure compliance with IAS 16 *Property, Plant and Equipment*.

- If necessary, use the work of an auditor's expert to confirm the valuations of the management's expert are appropriate.

Completion and review

Chapter learning objectives

This chapter covers syllabus areas:

- E1 – Subsequent events and going concern

- E2 – Completion and final review

Detailed syllabus objectives are provided in the introduction section of the text book.

PER

One of the PER performance objectives (PO19) is to collect and evaluate evidence for an audit. Carry out an internal or external audit from collecting evidence, through to forming an opinion. You demonstrate professional scepticism and make sure judgements are based on sufficient valid evidence. Working through this chapter should help you understand how to demonstrate that objective.

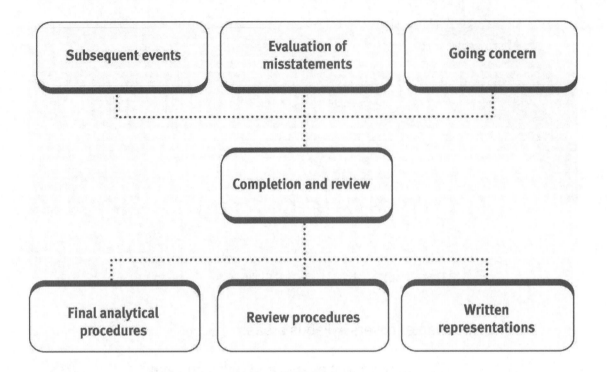

 Completion and review was covered in Audit and Assurance at the Applied Skills level. You are expected to have a greater level of understanding at the Strategic Professional level although the requirements of the ISAs are the same.

 Exam focus

One of the questions in the exam will focus on completion, review and reporting. Recent events may result in adjustments to the financial statements or the need for a disclosure note to be added. The auditor will also evaluate the effect of any uncorrected misstatements as these may lead to a modified audit opinion. In the exam you may have to evaluate misstatements and suggest additional audit procedures to be performed to reach a conclusion on such matters before stating the impact to the report if the issues are not resolved.

1 Subsequent events

A subsequent event is: **An event occurring between the date of the financial statements and the date of the auditor's report, and facts that become known to the auditor after the date of the auditor's report.** [ISA 560 *Subsequent Events*, 5e].

ISA 560 *Subsequent Events,* para 4, requires the auditor to:

*   Obtain sufficient appropriate audit evidence about whether events occurring between the date of the financial statements and the date of the auditor's report, that require adjustment or disclosure are appropriately reflected in accordance with the applicable financial reporting framework.

*   Respond appropriately to facts that become known to the auditor after the date of the auditor's report.

IAS 10 *Events After the Reporting Period* identifies two types of event after the reporting period:

*   Adjusting

*   Non-adjusting.

Illustration 1 – Adjusting and non-adjusting events

Adjusting events

These are events that provide additional evidence relating to conditions existing at the reporting date. Such events provide new information about the items included in the financial statements and hence the financial statements should be adjusted to reflect the new information.

Examples of **adjusting** events include:

*   Allowances for damaged inventory and doubtful receivables.

*   Amounts received or receivable in respect of insurance claims which were being negotiated at the reporting date.

*   The determination of the purchase or sale price of non-current assets purchased or sold before the year-end.

*   Agreement of a tax liability.

*   Discovery of errors/fraud revealing that the financial statements are incorrect.

Non-adjusting events

These are events concerning conditions which arose after the reporting date. In order to prevent the financial statements from presenting a misleading position, disclosure is required in the notes to the financial statements indicating what effect the events may have. Such events, therefore, will not have any effect on items in the statements of financial position or statement of profit or loss for the period.

Examples of **non-adjusting** events include:

- Issue of new share or loan capital.

- Major changes in the composition of the group (for example, mergers, acquisitions or reconstructions).

- Losses of non-current assets or inventory as a result of fires or floods.

- Strikes, government action such as nationalisation.

- Purchases/sales of significant non-current assets.

(IAS 10 *Events After the Reporting Period*)

Auditor responsibilities

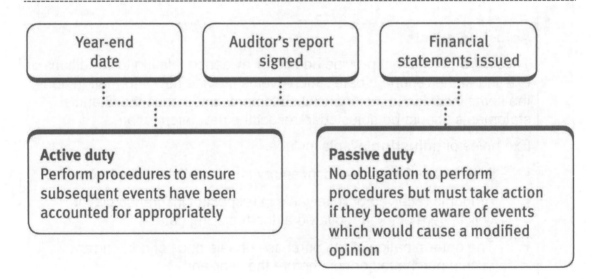

Between the date of the financial statements and the date of the auditor's report

- The auditor should perform procedures to identify events that might require adjustment or disclosure in the financial statements.
  [ISA 560, 6]

- If material adjusting events are not adjusted for, or material non-adjusting events are not disclosed, the auditor will ask management to make the necessary amendments to the financial statements.

- If the identified adjustments or disclosures necessary are not made then the auditor should consider the impact on the auditor's report and whether a modification to the opinion is necessary.

Subsequent events procedures

- Enquiring of management if they are aware of any events, adjusting or non-adjusting, that have not yet been included or disclosed in the financial statements.

- Enquiring into management procedures/systems for the identification of events after the reporting period.

- Reading minutes of members' and directors' meetings.

- Reviewing accounting records including budgets, forecasts, cash flows, management accounts and interim information.

[ISA 560, 7]

- Obtaining a written representation from management confirming that they have informed the auditor of all subsequent events and accounted for them appropriately in the financial statements. [ISA 560, 9]

- Inspection of correspondence with legal advisors. [ISA 560, A8]

- Reviewing the progress of known risk areas and contingencies.
  [ISA 560, A9]

- Considering relevant information which has come to the auditor's attention, from sources outside the entity, including public knowledge, competitors, suppliers and customers.

- Inspecting after date receipts from receivables.

- Inspecting the cash book after the year-end for payments/receipts that were not accrued for at the year-end.

- Inspecting the sales price of inventories after the year-end.

Between the date of the auditor's report and the date the financial statements are issued

- The auditor is under no obligation to perform audit procedures after the auditor's report has been issued, however, if they become aware of a fact which would cause them to amend the auditor's report, they must take action. [ISA 560, 10]

- This will normally be in the form of asking the client to amend the financial statements, auditing the amendments and reissuing the auditor's report.

- If management do not amend the financial statements and the auditor's report has not yet been issued to the client, the auditor can still modify the opinion. [ISA 560, 13a]

- If the auditor's report has been provided to the client, the auditor shall notify management and those charged with governance not to issue the financial statements before the amendments are made.

    If the client issues the financial statements despite being requested not to by the auditor, the auditor shall take action to prevent reliance on the auditor's report. [ISA 560, 13b]

    Legal advice should be sought in this situation as the course of action to prevent reliance on the auditor's report depends on the auditor's legal rights and obligations. [ISA 560, A16]

After the financial statements are issued

- The auditor is under no obligation to perform audit procedures after the financial statements have been issued, however, if they become aware of a fact which would have caused them to amend the auditor's report, they must take action.

- The auditor should discuss the matter with management and consider if the financial statements require amendment.

[ISA 560, 14]

- The auditor should perform audit procedures on the amendments to ensure they have been put through correctly. [ISA 560, 15a]

- The auditor should review the steps taken by management to ensure anyone who is in receipt of the previously issued financial statements is informed. [ISA 560, 15b]

- Issue a new auditor's report including an emphasis of matter or other matter paragraph to draw attention to the fact that the financial statements and auditor's report have been reissued. [ISA 560, 16]

- If management refuses to recall and amend the financial statements, the auditor shall take action to prevent reliance on the auditor's report. [ISA 560, 17]

2 Going concern

Going concern is the assumption that the entity will continue in business for the foreseeable future.

Going concern is a fundamental principle in the preparation of financial statements.

Responsibilities

Management

Management are responsible for preparing the financial statements and must make a specific assessment of the entity's ability to continue as a going concern. [ISA 570 *Going Concern*, 4]

This requires making judgments about the future outcome of events or conditions which are inherently uncertain. [ISA 570, 5]

Management must prepare the financial statements on the most appropriate basis – going concern or break-up basis.

The **'break up' basis** requires that all assets and liabilities are reclassified as 'current' and revalued at net realisable value. Further provisions for liquidation, such as redundancy and legal costs, may also be required.

If management are aware of any material uncertainties which may affect this assessment, IAS 1 *Presentation of Financial Statements* requires them to disclose such uncertainties in the financial statements.

Auditor

ISA 570 *Going Concern,* para 9, states that the auditor must:

- Obtain sufficient appropriate evidence regarding the appropriateness of management's use of the going concern basis of accounting in the preparation of the financial statements.

- Conclude on whether a material uncertainty exists about the entity's ability to continue as a going concern.

- Report in accordance with ISA 570.

Going concern procedures

Audit procedures to assess management's evaluation of going concern

- Evaluate management's assessment of going concern. [ISA 570, 12]

- Assess the same period that management have used in their assessment and if this is less than 12 months, ask management to extend their assessment. [ISA 570, 13]

- Consider whether management's assessment includes all relevant information. [ISA 570, 14]

Audit procedures to perform where there is doubt over going concern

- Analyse and discuss cash flow, profit and other relevant forecasts with management.

- Analyse and discuss the entity's latest available interim financial statements.

- Review the terms of debentures and loan agreements and determining whether any have been breached.

- Read minutes of meetings for reference to financing difficulties.

- Enquire of the entity's lawyer regarding the existence of litigation and claims and the reasonableness of management's assessments of their outcome and the estimate of their financial implications.

- Confirm the existence, legality and enforceability of arrangements to provide or maintain financial support with related and third parties and assessing the financial ability of such parties to provide additional funds.

- Review subsequent events to identify those that either mitigate or otherwise affect the entity's ability to continue as a going concern.

[ISA 570, A16]

- Review correspondence with customers for evidence of any disputes that might impact recoverability of debts and affect future sales.

- Review correspondence with suppliers for evidence of issues regarding payments that might impact the company's ability to obtain supplies or credit.

- Review correspondence with the bank for indication that a bank loan or overdraft may be recalled.

- Obtain written representation from management regarding its plans for the future and how it plans to address the going concern issues.
  [ISA 570, 16e]

Exam tip

Audit procedures should focus on cash flows rather than profits. A company can continue to trade as long as it can pay its debts when they fall due. Therefore identify procedures to obtain evidence about the amount of cash that is likely to be received and the amount of cash that it likely to be paid out and consider whether there is any indication of cash flow difficulties.

Disclosures

Disclosures relating to going concern are required to be made by the directors in the following circumstances:

(1) Where there is any **material uncertainty over the future of a company**, the directors should include disclosure in the financial statements. A material uncertainty exists when the magnitude of its potential impact and likelihood of occurrence is such that disclosure of the nature and implications of the uncertainty is necessary for the fair presentation of the financial statements and for the financial statements not to be misleading. [ISA 570, 18]

The disclosure should explain:

–   the principal events or conditions that cast significant doubt on the entity's ability to continue as a going concern and management's plans to deal with them.

–   the company may be unable to realise its assets and discharge its liabilities in the normal course of business.

[ISA 570, 19]

(2) Where the directors have been **unable to assess going concern in the usual way** (e.g. for less than one year beyond the date on which they sign the financial statements), this fact should be disclosed.

(3) Where the **financial statements are prepared on a basis other than the going concern basis**, the basis used should be disclosed.

Audit conclusions and reporting

Based on the audit evidence obtained, the auditor should determine if, in their judgment:

(a) A material uncertainty exists that may cast significant doubt on the entity's ability to continue as a going concern.

(b) The basis of preparing the financial statements is or is not appropriate in the circumstances.

Situation	Impact on audit opinion	Impact on auditor's report
No material uncertainty exists regarding going concern	Unmodified – Financial statements give a true and fair view	INT syllabus: No impact UK syllabus: The auditor will report by exception in a section headed 'Conclusions Relating to Going Concern' whether they have anything to add or draw attention to in relation to the directors' statement about the appropriateness of the use of the going concern basis.
Material uncertainty exists and is adequately disclosed by management	Unmodified – Financial statements give a true and fair view	Include additional communication: 'Material Uncertainty Related to Going Concern'.
Material uncertainty exists which is not adequately disclosed or is omitted	Modified – Qualified or adverse	Include a 'Basis for qualified/adverse opinion' explaining the going concern issues management have failed to disclose adequately.
Company is not a going concern and has prepared the financial statements on the break up basis appropriately and made adequate disclosure of this fact	Unmodified – Financial statements give a true and fair view	Include additional communication: Emphasis of Matter paragraph.
Company is not a going concern and has prepared the FS on the going concern basis	Modified – adverse opinion	Include a 'Basis for adverse opinion' explaining the going concern issues management have failed to account for appropriately.
The period assessed by management is less than twelve months from the statement of financial position date (INT)/less than twelve months from the date of approval of the financial statements (UK) and management is unwilling to extend the assessment	Modified – qualified or disclaimer due to an inability to obtain sufficient appropriate audit evidence regarding the use of the going concern basis of accounting	Include a 'Basis for qualified/disclaimer opinion' explaining that sufficient appropriate evidence was not obtained to form a conclusion on whether the going concern basis of preparation is appropriate.

Indicators of going concern risk

Auditors should consider the following indicators as possible reasons for doubt over the going concern assumption:

- Rapidly increasing costs
- Shortages of supplies
- Adverse movements in exchange rates
- Business failures amongst customers or suppliers
- Loan repayments falling due in the near future
- High gearing
- Approaching borrowing limits
- Loss of key staff
- Loss of key suppliers or customers
- Technical obsolescence of product range
- Impact of major litigation
- Other fundamental uncertainties
- Significant changes to laws and regulations affecting the entity
- Deteriorating financial ratios

The foreseeable future

The auditor should remain alert to the possibility of events or conditions that will occur beyond management's period of assessment that may bring into question the appropriateness of the going concern assumption. However, due to the uncertainty surrounding such distant events, the indicator needs to be significant to prompt the auditor into further action. If such an event is identified the auditor should request that management consider the significance of the event of condition. [ISA 570, A14]

Other than enquiry of management, the auditor has no other responsibility to perform any other procedures to identify events or conditions beyond the period assessed by management (i.e. at least 12 months from the financial statements date). [ISA 570, A15]

UK syllabus: ISA (UK) 570 Going Concern

ISA (UK) 570 *Going Concern* requires management to assess going concern for a period of at least one year from the (expected) date of approval of the financial statements (rather than 12 months from the reporting date).

The Companies Act 2006 requires company directors to include a business review which describes the principal risks and uncertainties the company faces in the directors' report. The review should be a balanced and comprehensive analysis of the development and performance of the business, and the position of the company at the year-end. This review will include risks and uncertainties surrounding the going concern status of the company.

For companies that report on compliance with the UK Corporate Governance Code, the auditor shall determine whether they have anything material to add, or draw attention to, in the auditor's report in relation to the directors' disclosures on:

- the assessment of the principal risks facing the entity including those that would threaten its business model, future performance, solvency or liquidity.

- how the risks are mitigated.

- the assessment of the going concern basis and identification of material uncertainties related to going concern.

- how they have assessed the prospects of the entity, over what period they have done so and why they consider that period to be appropriate.

The auditor should consider whether they are aware of information that would indicate that the annual report and accounts taken as a whole are not fair, balanced and understandable.

ISA (UK) (Revised) 570 Going Concern

In September 2019, the Financial Reporting Council (FRC) issued a revised going concern standard in response to recent corporate failures where the auditor's report failed to highlight going concern issues of entities which collapsed shortly after. This standard is effective for audits of financial statements with a year end commencing on or after 15 December 2019.

ISA (UK) (Revised) 570 *Going Concern* means UK auditors will follow significantly stronger requirements than those required by current international standards. The FRC hopes that UK experience will lead to further strengthening of requirements at the international level.

The revised standard requires:

- The auditor to more robustly challenge management's assessment of going concern, thoroughly test the adequacy of the supporting evidence, evaluate the risk of management bias, and make greater use of the viability statement.

- Improved transparency, with the auditor of public interest entities, listed and large private companies, to provide a clear, positive conclusion on whether management's assessment is appropriate, and to set out the work they have done in this respect, in a new reporting requirement.

- A stand back requirement to consider all of the evidence obtained, whether corroborative or contradictory, when the auditor draws their conclusions on going concern.

UK syllabus: Going concern guidance in addition to ISA 570

FRC Bulletin 2008/01 – Audit issues when financial market conditions are difficult and credit facilities may be restricted (January 2008)

The bulletin focuses on the risks and uncertainties relating to companies that may not be a going concern due to difficulties obtaining finance as a result of the credit crunch, and the risk associated with the valuation of investments where the company invested in may have significantly curtailed its operations or may have ceased trading.

Difficulties obtaining credit

Whilst the credit crunch mostly affects financial institutions, risks of material misstatement are also higher in other types of company as credit facilities are significantly more difficult to obtain which may cast significant doubt over the going concern assumption.

The audit engagement partner must have particular regard to:

- his own involvement in the direction, supervision and performance of the audit

- the capabilities and competence of the audit team

- consultation with other professionals on difficult and contentious matters

- the nature and timing of communications with those charged with governance.

Where there is an inability to obtain confirmation of borrowing facilities, this must be disclosed in the financial statements in order to give a true and fair view. The auditor's opinion may also need to be modified due to insufficient appropriate evidence.

Valuation of investments

Auditors should evaluate whether the significant assumptions used by management are a reasonable basis for the fair value measurements and disclosures, including whether the assumptions reflect current market conditions and information.

Disclosure requirements include:

- Management judgments in the application of accounting policies.

- Information about key assumptions concerning the future.

- As required by IFRS 7 *Financial Instruments: Disclosures*.

FRC Bulletin 2008/10 – Going Concern Issues During the Current Economic Conditions (December 2008)

This bulletin, along with IAASB practice alert Audit Considerations in Respect of Going Concern in the Current Economic Environment (January 2009), explains the particular challenges the current economic conditions create including the need for increased disclosure about going concern and liquidity risk. It aims to raise auditors' awareness about matters relevant to the consideration of the use of the going concern basis of accounting.

FRC Going Concern and Liquidity Risk: Guidance for Directors of UK Companies 2009

Requires directors to:

- Make a rigorous assessment of whether the company is a going concern by preparing budgets and forecasts and ensure they have adequate borrowing facilities in place.

- Consider all available information for a period of at least 12 months from the date of approval of the financial statements.

- Make balanced, proportionate and clear disclosures about going concern.

3 Final analytical procedures and review

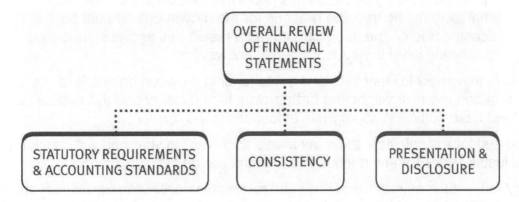

Before forming an opinion on the financial statements and deciding on the wording of the auditor's report, the auditor should conduct **an overall review**.

The auditor should perform the following procedures:

(1) Review the financial statements to ensure:

- Compliance with accounting standards and local legislation disclosure requirements. This is sometimes performed using a disclosure checklist.

- Accounting policies are sufficiently disclosed and to ensure that they are in accordance with the accounting treatment adopted in the financial statements.

- They adequately reflect the information and explanations previously obtained and conclusions reached during the course of the audit.

(2) Perform analytical procedures to corroborate conclusions formed during the audit and assist when forming an overall conclusion as to whether the financial statements are consistent with the auditor's understanding of the entity. [ISA 520, 6]

(3) Review the aggregate of the uncorrected misstatements to assess whether a material misstatement arises. If so, discuss the potential adjustment with management.

Analytical procedures at the completion stage

Final analytical procedures performed at the completion stage involve similar procedures to those performed at the planning stage. Differences to note between the two stages:

- At the completion stage the financial statements are almost finalised and therefore there should be no further changes to the figures. At the planning stage the figures were draft and still subject to change.

- The audit work is almost complete and therefore the auditor should have a full understanding of the client's performance during the year. When analysing the figures, the reasons for the movements should be documented on the audit file, and as a result, this analysis should be confirming what the auditor already knows.

If something new is identified, or if a relationship between balances is not understood, it will highlight that further work is necessary and the auditor does not yet have sufficient appropriate evidence for the opinion.

The auditor will calculate the movements from year to year and will check that the justifications for any unusual fluctuations are on file.

Key ratios such as gross profit margin, receivables collection period, payables payment period and inventory holding period, will be calculated and reasons for movements tied through to the audit file to ensure the outcome is consistent with what is documented.

A review of the financial statements as a whole will be performed to ensure the presentation complies with the applicable financial reporting framework.

The purpose of review procedures

Review forms part of the engagement performance quality control procedures covered in the Quality Control chapter.

As part of the overall review, the auditor should assess whether:

- The audit work was performed in accordance with professional standards.

- Significant matters have been raised for further consideration and appropriate consultations have taken place.

- There is a need to revise the nature, timing and extent of the work performed.

- The audit evidence gathered by the team is sufficient and appropriate to support the audit opinion and report.

[ISA 220, A18]

The auditor should ensure that initial assessments made at the start of the audit are still valid in light of the information gathered during the audit and that the audit plan has been flexed to meet any new circumstances.

4 Evaluation of misstatements

The auditor must consider the effect of misstatements on both the audit procedures performed and ultimately, if uncorrected, on the financial statements as a whole. Guidance on how this is performed is given in ISA 450 *Evaluation of Misstatements Identified During the Audit.*

In order to achieve this the auditor must:

- Accumulate a record of all identified misstatements, unless they are clearly trivial. [ISA 450, 5]

- Consider if the existence of such misstatements indicates that others may exist, which, when aggregated with other misstatements, could be considered material. [ISA 450, 6a]

- If so, consider if the audit strategy and plan need to be revised. [ISA 450, 6]

- Communicate all misstatements identified during the course of the audit to an appropriate level of **management** on a timely basis and request that **all** misstatements are corrected. [ISA 450, 8]

- If management refuses to correct some or all of the misstatements the auditor should consider their reasons for refusal and take these into account when considering if the financial statements are free from material misstatement. [ISA 450, 9]

Evaluation of uncorrected misstatements

If management have failed to correct all of the misstatements reported to them, the auditor should:

- Revisit their assessment of materiality to determine whether it is still appropriate in the circumstances. [ISA 450, 10]

- Determine whether the uncorrected misstatements, either individually or in aggregate, are material to the financial statements as a whole, considering both the size and nature of the misstatements and the effect of misstatements related to prior periods (e.g. on corresponding figures, comparatives and opening balances). If an individual misstatement is considered material it cannot be offset by other misstatements. [ISA 450, 11]

- Communicate the uncorrected misstatements to **those charged with governance** and explain the effect this will have on the audit opinion. [ISA 450, 12]

- Request a written representation from management and those charged with governance that they believe the effects of uncorrected misstatements are immaterial. [ISA 450, 14]

Evaluating misstatements – example

You are at the completion stage of the audit of a client. The PBT for the year is $8 million and total assets are $35 million. The following matters have not been corrected by management and have been left for your attention:

(1)   A major customer has gone into liquidation owing an amount of $200,000 which has not been written off.

(2)   A provision of $300,000 has not been recognised.

The irrecoverable debt of $200,000 represents 2.5% of PBT and 0.57% of total assets therefore is not material.

The provision of $300,000 represents 3.75% of PBT and 0.86% of total assets therefore is not material.

Cumulatively they have a bigger effect on the financial statements:

$500,000 represents 6.25% of PBT and 1.4% of total assets which is material. The two amounts will need to be adjusted to avoid a modified opinion.

The auditor should ask for both issues to be corrected in accordance with ISA 450.

5   Written representations

The value of written representations from management

ISA 580 *Written Representations* requires the auditor to obtain written representations from management:

- That they have fulfilled their responsibility for the preparation of the financial statements. [ISA 580, 6a]

- To support other audit evidence relevant to the financial statements or specific assertions if deemed necessary by the auditor or required by specific ISAs. [ISA 580, 6b]

- That they have provided the auditor with all relevant information. [ISA 580, 11a]

- That all transactions have been recorded and reflected in the financial statements. [ISA 580, 11b]

However, as a form of evidence, representations are low down in the order of reliability because they are internally produced.

On their own, written representations **do not provide sufficient appropriate evidence** about any of the matters with which they deal. [ISA 580, 4]

Audit reporting implications

The auditor should issue a disclaimer of opinion if:

- The auditor concludes there is sufficient doubt about the integrity of management which means the written representations are not reliable, or

- Management does not provide the written representations required in relation to confirming their responsibility to prepare the financial statements and to provide the auditor with information, and confirming completeness of transactions.

[ISA 580, 20]

 The limitations of written representations

When asked for procedures or evidence in the exam be careful not to suggest written representations for all areas of testing. The examiner has stated this is a common issue with weaker students who do not appreciate the nature of 'appropriate' evidence and that it detracts from the quality of an answer. Written representations are only appropriate for matters where better evidence is not available. This is generally areas requiring judgment of management.

 Other written representations

The typical subjects of other representations include:

- Whether the selection and application of accounting policies are appropriate.

- Whether the following matters have been measured, presented and disclosed in accordance with the relevant financial reporting framework:

    - Plans or intentions that may affect the carrying value or classification of assets and liabilities.

    - Liabilities, both contingent and actual.

    - Title to, or control over, assets.

    - Aspects of laws, regulations and contractual agreements that may affect the financial statements, including non-compliance.

    [ISA 580, A10]

- That the directors have communicated all deficiencies in internal control to the auditor. [ISA 580, A11]

- Specific assertions about classes of transactions, accounts balances and disclosures requiring management judgment. [ISA 580, A13]

Written representations required by specific ISAs

Other ISAs that require subject matter specific written representations:

- ISA 240 The Auditor's Responsibilities Relating to Fraud in an Audit of Financial Statements – All known and suspected frauds have been communicated to the auditor.

- ISA 250 Consideration of Laws and Regulations in an Audit of Financial Statements – All instances of non-compliance with laws and regulations have been communicated to the auditor.

- ISA 450 Evaluation of Misstatements Identified During the Audit – Management and those charged with governance consider any uncorrected misstatements to be immaterial.

- ISA 501 Audit Evidence – Specific Considerations for Selected Items – All known actual or possible litigation claims have been disclosed to the auditor and appropriately accounted for.

- ISA 540 Auditing Accounting Estimates, Including Fair Value Accounting Estimates, and Related Disclosures – Significant assumptions used in making the estimates are reasonable.

- ISA 550 Related Parties – All related parties and related party transactions have been disclosed.

- ISA 560 Subsequent Events – All subsequent events have been appropriately accounted for.

- ISA 570 Going Concern – Matters affecting going concern have been disclosed.

[ISA 580, Appendix 1]

Approach to exam questions: Completion

One of the questions in the exam will focus on completion, review and reporting. The scenario will state that the audit is nearly complete and/or the auditor's report is due to be signed soon. This informs you that the majority of the audit work will have been performed and only the last remaining issues need to be resolved. These will be issues that have been left for your attention as the audit manager.

The requirement may ask you to consider several things:

- Matters to consider to enable you to reach a conclusion.

- Matters to be discussed with management to enable you to reach a conclusion.

- Whether sufficient appropriate evidence has been obtained and documented to be able to reach a conclusion.

- What evidence you should expect to find on file when you perform your review of the audit work.

- Further procedures that should be performed to be able to reach a conclusion.

Matters to consider/Matters to discuss with management to enable you to reach a conclusion

This involves:

- **M**ateriality assessment – calculate whether the issue is material.

- **A**ccounting treatment – state what the relevant accounting standard requires and whether the client is complying with that treatment. If they are not compliant, state what they are doing wrong.

- **R**isk of material misstatement – state which balances or disclosures in the financial statements will be materially misstated as a result.

Whether sufficient appropriate evidence has been obtained

This requirement links back to quality control and also requires you to exercise professional scepticism.

- Firstly, consider whether all of the procedures you would expect to be performed have been performed.

- Consider whether the procedures performed are appropriate in the circumstances. In particular, consider whether too much reliance has been placed on enquiries with management or management representations.

- Consider whether sufficient testing was performed. If the sample sizes included in the audit plan have not been tested sufficient evidence is unlikely to have been obtained.

- Consider whether the auditor performing the work has demonstrated sufficient professional scepticism.

Evidence you should expect to find on file

Evidence refers to the audit evidence that should have been obtained and put on file by the auditor performing the work. Evidence is essentially an audit procedure but without the action e.g.

- Copies of board minutes to identify management discussions about the legal provision.

- Copies of bank statements to verify the payment was made by the client during the year.

- Notes of discussions with management regarding their approach for determining the estimate.

Note how the examples above still describe the reason for obtaining the documentation.

Further procedures that should be performed

Further procedures refers to procedures not already carried out. The purpose of these procedures is to provide new information that will enable you to form a conclusion. Make sure you suggest audit procedures that need to be carried out at this stage of the audit and not audit procedures that have already been performed.

Procedures should be an action, applied to a source, to achieve an objective e.g.

- Review the most recent board minutes to identify management discussions about the legal provision.

- Inspect recent bank statements to identify whether a payment has been made by a customer since the last after date cash testing was performed.

- Discuss with management whether any progress has been made in relation to the legal claim e.g. agreement of an out of court settlement.

In most cases the question will go on to ask for the reporting implications if the issue or issues are not resolved. Reporting is covered in the next chapter.

Test your understanding 1

You are the manager responsible for the audit of Phoenix Co, a private limited liability company, which manufactures super alloys from imported zinc and aluminium. The company operates three similar foundries at different sites under the direction of Troy Pitz, the chief executive. The draft accounts for the year ended 31 March 20X5 show profit before taxation of $1.7 million (20X4 – $1.5 million). The audit senior has produced a schedule of 'Points for the Attention of the Audit Manager' as follows:

(a) Included within non-current assets is an investment in ordinary shares of Pegasus Co measured at fair value of $80,000. The most recent published financial statements of Pegasus Co as at 30 September 20X4 show only a small surplus of net assets. A press article published in April 20X5 has reported that Pegasus Co is insolvent and has ceased to trade. In addition to the investment, Phoenix Co's financial statements include a dividend receivable of $15,000 in respect of dividends declared by Pegasus Co in previous years which have not yet been paid. **(5 marks)**

(b) A provision of $500,000 has been recognised within current liabilities. The provision is to cover the cost of overhauling the blast furnaces and other foundry equipment which is expected to take place in August 20X5. **(5 marks)**

(c) All industrial waste from the furnaces is purchased by Cleanaway Co, a government-approved disposal company, under a five-year contract that is due for renewal in October 20X5. A recent newspaper article states that substantial fines have been levied on Cleanaway Co for illegal dumping. Troy Pitz is the majority shareholder of Cleanaway Co. **(5 marks)**

Required:

Evaluate the matters the auditor should consider, and state the sufficient appropriate evidence that should be on file in respect of each of the above issues.

(Total: 15 marks)

Test your understanding 2

You are the manager responsible for the audit of Aspersion Co, a limited liability company, which provides cargo services with a small fleet of aircraft. The draft accounts for the year ended 31 March 20X5 show profit before taxation of $2.7 million (20X4: $2.2 million) and total assets of $10.4 million (20X4: $9.8 million).

The following issues are outstanding and have been left for your attention:

(a) During the year, Aspersion Co sold a cargo carrier to Abra Co, resulting in a loss on disposal of $400,000. The aircraft cost $1.2 million when it was purchased nine years ago and was being depreciated on a straight-line basis over 20 years. The minutes of the board meeting at which the sale was approved record that Aspersion Co's finance director, Iain Joiteon, has a 30% equity interest in Abra Co.

(b) As well as cargo carriers, Aspersion Co owns two light aircraft which were purchased in June 20X2. The two aircraft were purchased to provide business passenger flights to a small island under a three year service contract. It is now known that the contract will not be renewed when it expires at the end of September 20X5 but a decision has not been reached about what to do with the aircraft after this date. The aircraft, which cost $900,000, are included in the financial statements at a carrying amount of $720,000.

(c) Deferred tax amounting to $570,000 as at 31 March 20X5 has been calculated relating to tangible non-current assets at a tax rate of 30% in accordance with IAS 12 *Income Taxes*. On 1 June 20X5, the government announced an increase in the corporate tax rate to 34%. The directors are proposing to adjust the draft accounts for the further liability arising.

Required:

Explain the matters which should be discussed with management in relation to each of the issues. **(10 marks)**

6 Chapter summary

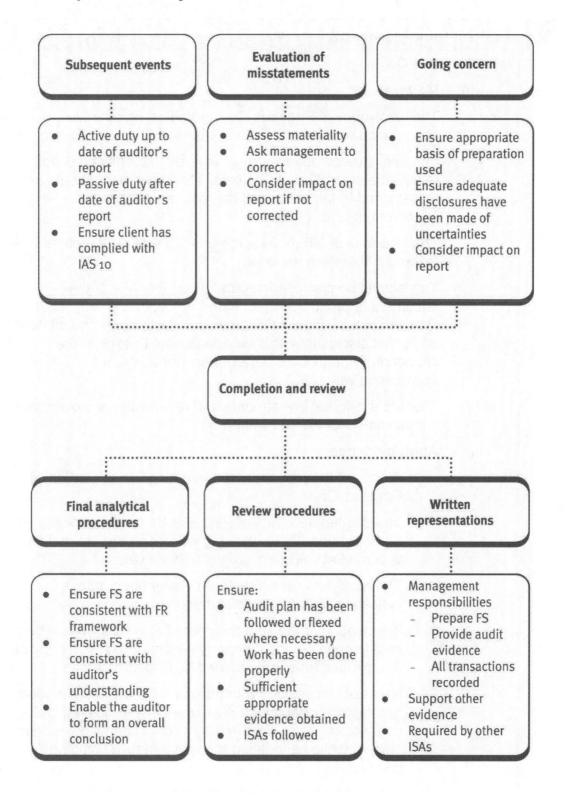

Subsequent events

- Active duty up to date of auditor's report
- Passive duty after date of auditor's report
- Ensure client has complied with IAS 10

Evaluation of misstatements

- Assess materiality
- Ask management to correct
- Consider impact on report if not corrected

Going concern

- Ensure appropriate basis of preparation used
- Ensure adequate disclosures have been made of uncertainties
- Consider impact on report

Completion and review

Final analytical procedures

- Ensure FS are consistent with FR framework
- Ensure FS are consistent with auditor's understanding
- Enable the auditor to form an overall conclusion

Review procedures

Ensure:
- Audit plan has been followed or flexed where necessary
- Work has been done properly
- Sufficient appropriate evidence obtained
- ISAs followed

Written representations

- Management responsibilities
  - Prepare FS
  - Provide audit evidence
  - All transactions recorded
- Support other evidence
- Required by other ISAs

Test your understanding answers

 Test your understanding 1

(a) **Pegasus Co**

(i) **Matters**

The insolvency of Pegasus Co is an adjusting event in accordance with IAS 10 *Events After the Reporting Period*.

The fair value of the investment is likely to be nil and dividends receivable are unlikely to be paid. The investment should be remeasured to fair value and the loss recorded in the statement of profit or loss.

The total loss of $95,000 represents 5.6% of draft profit before tax and is therefore material.

This should be disclosed separately on the face of the statement of profit or loss, or in the notes, in line with IAS 1 *Presentation of Financial Statements*. As this is a one off item, additional disclosures may be appropriate to explain the impact on Phoenix Co's performance for the year in accordance with IAS 1.

There is a risk that investments and receivables are overstated if these amounts are not written off.

(ii) **Audit evidence**

– A copy of the press report confirming the liquidation of Pegasus Co.

– The audited accounts of Pegasus Co for the year ended 30 September 20X4 showing whether there are assets with market values in excess of book values.

– The receiver's (or liquidator's) statement of affairs indicating whether any distribution is possible.

– If a meeting of the shareholders of Pegasus Co has been held to consider the company's state of affairs, a copy of the minutes (may be obtained by Phoenix Co).

– Notes of discussions with the client as to who, if anyone, has replaced Pegasus Co as one of their major shipping contractors. Also, whether any consignments have been held up while negotiating for an alternative shipping contractor.

– A copy of the journal adjustment to write off the investment and dividends receivable.

(b) **Future maintenance**

   (i) **Matters**

      The provision represents 29% of draft profit before tax and is therefore material.

      This provision does not appear to meet the definition of IAS 37 *Provisions, Contingent Liabilities and Contingent Assets* which requires there to be an obligation at the year-end to make a payment which is probable and can be measured reliably.

      There is no obligation for the company to incur the costs of overhauling the furnace. Overhaul expenditure to restore or maintain the future economic benefits expected from the plant and equipment should normally be recognised as an expense when it is incurred.

      No provision should be recorded and if not released, provisions and expenses will be overstated and profit will be understated.

      Draft profit before tax ($1.7m) shows a 13% increase on the previous year. If adjustments are made for points (1) and (2), profit will be increased by $405,000 (i.e. (1) $95k decrease plus (2) $500k increase). Profit before tax of $2.1m would be a 40% increase on the prior year.

      The management of Phoenix Co may have decided that $1.7m is what is to be reported. Management may have made the future maintenance provision as a way of 'setting aside' a reserve to smooth profits in the future. For example, management might be anticipating an increase in costs in respect of waste disposal in (c).

      Tutorial note: It is a higher skill to be able to demonstrate an ability to stand back from the individual items and take an overall view in this part of the question, considering the overall impact on the draft profit.

   (ii) **Audit evidence**

      – A breakdown of the provision, recalculated to verify arithmetical accuracy.

      – Notes of discussions with senior management about their reasons for having made the provision and whether any costs have been contracted for.

      – External tenders or quotes for subcontracted work (and/or internal costings) to verify the amount.

      – Working papers from previous years showing the cost and frequency of overhauls in previous periods.

      – A copy of the journal adjustment to reverse the provision.

(c) **Cleanaway Co**

(i) **Matters**

Troy Pitz has authority and responsibility for Phoenix Co's operational activities as chief executive, and a controlling interest in Cleanaway Co, hence Cleanaway Co is a related party, and the sale of waste is a related party transaction. Related party transactions are material by nature and must be disclosed in the financial statements.

IAS 24 *Related Party Disclosures* requires the following to be disclosed in the notes to the financial statements:

– Nature of the related party relationship

– Amount of the transactions entered into

– Balances outstanding at the year-end.

Non-disclosure of these transactions would result in a material misstatement.

It should be considered whether Phoenix Co has been implicated in Cleanaway Co's illegal dumping, e.g. by Phoenix Co's waste having been dumped, or by Troy Pitz's relationship with the two companies.

The integrity of Troy Pitz may need to be questioned as he may have known about the breach of laws and regulations. If so, this will affect the auditor's assessment of the control environment and control risk.

If the contract is not renewed a legal alternative will need to be found for disposal of waste, for example, another approved provider of waste disposal services or a suitable landfill site (taxes may be substantial), otherwise there may be doubts about going concern.

Possible consequences for Phoenix Co of the contract being renewed:

– A substantial increase in costs of disposal because terms were last agreed five years ago.

– Loss of customer goodwill through associations with Cleanaway Co.

– Risk of investigation by a government agency into the company's environmental practices.

(ii) **Audit evidence**

– A copy of the contract, in particular whether:

– early termination could be an option for Phoenix Co in the light of Cleanaway Co's illegal activities.

– any clauses are relevant to its renewal (e.g. restricting price increases).

– Newspaper articles including any editorial comment or letters from Cleanaway Co or Troy Pitz regarding the issue.

– Notes of discussions with senior management (Troy Pitz and others) whether a suitable alternative service provider exists.

– Prior year working papers and financial statements to identify the disclosure made last year.

– Copies of board minutes to indicate what action, if any, management propose to take to mitigate the adverse publicity surrounding Cleanaway Co.

Test your understanding 2

Matters to be discussed with management

(a) **Related party transaction – sale of cargo carrier**

The $400,000 loss represents 15% of profit before tax and is material. Disclosure as a separate line item may therefore be appropriate.

Abra Co appears to be a related party as Iain:

– is one of the key management personnel of Aspersion Co (being the finance director), and

– has an equity interest in Abra Co which is presumed to constitute significant influence (being greater than 20%).

The sale of the cargo carrier to Abra Co is therefore a related party transaction. The related party relationship and the transaction should be disclosed in a note to the financial statements for the year to 31 March 20X5. The disclosure should include:

– the amount(s) involved (i.e. sale proceeds and loss)

– any outstanding balance of amounts due from Abra Co

– the nature of the relationship.

The transaction must be disclosed even if the transaction took place on an arm's length basis and this fact may only be disclosed if such terms can be substantiated.

If suitable disclosure is not made, there will be a material misstatement with regard to non-compliance with IAS 24 *Related Party Disclosures.*

The reason for the loss on sale should also be considered e.g. whether the:

–   sale was below market value (if the sale to the related party was not at arm's length)

–   aircraft had a bad maintenance history (or was otherwise impaired)

–   useful life of a cargo carrier is less than 20 years.

If the latter, it is likely that non-current assets are materially overstated in respect of cargo carriers still in use. This would lead to overstatement of non-current assets and profits as the depreciation policies may not be appropriate and compliant with IAS 16 *Property, Plant and Equipment.*

(b)   **Impairment – light aircraft**

The carrying amount of the aircraft represents 6.9% of total assets and is material.

The aircraft were purchased for a specific use which will cease six months after the year end. The value of the aircraft may be impaired and Aspersion Co should have performed an impairment review, in accordance with IAS 36 *Impairment of Assets,* to evaluate whether the recoverable amount has fallen below the carrying amount.

The recoverable amount will be affected by management's intentions, for example:

–   to sell the aircraft

–   to find an alternative use for the aircraft (e.g. providing other business or pleasure flights).

If the client can sell the aircraft for more than the current carrying value or if the aircraft can be used in another part of the business, the assets may not be impaired.

There is a risk that non-current assets and profits are overstated if an impairment charge is necessary but hasn't been made.

Additional point: If the passenger business constitutes a business segment, cessation of the contract may result in a discontinued operation (IFRS 5 *Non-current Assets Held for Sale and Discontinued Operations*).

(c) **Deferred tax – change in tax rate**

The total deferred tax provision represents 21% of PBT and is material. (However the deferred tax expense/income for the year may not have been material.)

The increase in liability if calculated at 34% ($570,000 (34/30 – 1) = $76,000) represents 2.8% of PBT. Individually, this amount is not material.

Under IAS 12 *Income Taxes* the tax rate in force at the reporting date should be used for the calculation. The increase in tax rate announced on 1 June is a non-adjusting event in accordance with IAS 10 *Events After the Reporting Period*, and therefore the deferred tax liability does not need to be adjusted. If the impact of the change in tax rate is considered to be material then it should be disclosed in the notes to the financial statements.

If the directors adjust the draft accounts there will be non-compliance with IAS 10 and IAS 12. The tax expense and associated liability will be misstated as a result.

Management should be informed not to make any adjustment for the change in tax rate and should be asked to consider including an appropriate disclosure note.

Reporting

Chapter learning objectives

This chapter covers syllabus areas:

- E3 – Auditor's reports

- E4 – Reports to those charged with governance and management

Detailed syllabus objectives are provided in the introduction section of the text book.

PER

One of the PER performance objectives (PO20) is to review and report on the findings of an audit. You complete an audit, preparing the formal documentation and reporting any control deficiencies to management. You report back to managers in a formal audit report. Working through this chapter should help you understand how to demonstrate that objective.

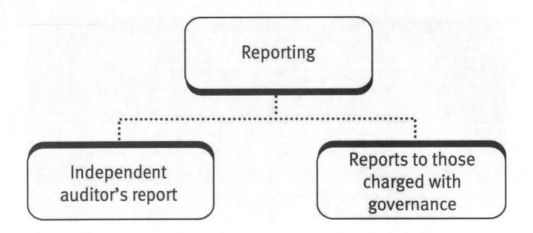

 Auditor's reports and reports to those charged with governance were covered in Audit and Assurance at the Applied Skills level. You are expected to have a greater level of understanding of these reports at the Strategic Professional level although the requirements of the ISAs are the same.

Exam focus

One of the questions in the exam will focus on completion and reporting. Reporting may be examined in several ways. You may be asked to:

- Describe the implications for the auditor's report if issues identified during the audit are not resolved.

- Critically evaluate extracts of a draft report i.e. say what is wrong with it and explain why.

- Explain the matters the auditor should communicate to those charged with governance.

1 The objectives of the auditor

The objectives of the auditor are:

- To form an opinion on the financial statements based on an evaluation of the conclusions drawn from the audit evidence obtained, and

- To express clearly that opinion through a written report.

[ISA 700 *Forming an Opinion and Reporting on Financial Statements*, 6]

2 The independent auditor's report

ISA 700 and ISA (UK) 700 prescribe the following structures for the auditor's report:

INT syllabus **ISA 700** **Para 21 – 49**		**UK syllabus** **ISA (UK) 700** **Para 21 – 49**	
1	Title	1	Title
2	Addressee	2	Addressee
3	Auditor's opinion	3	Auditor's opinion
4	Basis for opinion	4	Basis for opinion
5	[Material uncertainty related to going concern] (if applicable)	5	Conclusions relating to going concern/[Material uncertainty related to going concern]
6	[Emphasis of matter] (if applicable) *1	6	[Emphasis of matter] (if applicable) *1
7	Listed entities: Key audit matters	7	Listed entities: Key audit matters Our application of materiality An overview of the scope of our audit
8	Other information	8	Other information
9	Responsibilities of management	9	Opinions on other matters prescribed by the Companies Act 2006
10	Auditor's responsibilities	10	Matters on which we are required to report by exception
11	Report on other legal and regulatory requirements	11	Responsibilities of directors
12	[Other matter] (if applicable in accordance with ISA 706)	12	Auditor's responsibilities
13	Signature*2	13	[Other matter] (if applicable in accordance with ISA (UK) 706)
14	Auditor's address	14	Signature*2
15	Date	15	Auditor's address
		16	Date

*1 An Emphasis of Matter paragraph may be presented either before or after the Key Audit Matters section depending on auditor judgment.

*2 Reports of listed entities must show the name of the engagement partner as well as the name of the audit firm. Reports of non-listed entities may be signed in the name of the firm only.

The expectation gap

Over time the wording of the auditor's report has grown longer in an attempt to counteract the **expectation gap**, i.e. the difference between what an auditor's responsibility actually is and what the public perceives the auditor's responsibility to be.

The auditor's report is not:

- a certificate of the accuracy of the contents of financial statements

- a guarantee against fraud

- confirmation that an entity is being run in accordance with the principles of good corporate governance.

The wording of the auditor's report is intended to ensure that users of the financial statements understand what level of assurance they are being given and how much reliance they may place on a set of audited financial statements.

INT syllabus: Illustrative auditor's report

INDEPENDENT AUDITOR'S REPORT

To the Shareholders of XYZ Company

Report on the Audit of the Financial Statements [sub-title is not included if there is no separate Report on Other Legal and Regulatory Requirements]

Opinion

We have audited the financial statements of the XYZ Company (the Company), which comprise the statement of financial position as at 31 December, 20X4, and the statement of comprehensive income, statement of changes in equity and statement of cash flows for the year then ended, and notes to the financial statements, including a summary of significant accounting policies.

In our opinion, the accompanying financial statements present fairly, in all material respects, (or give a true and fair view of) the financial position of the Company as at December 31, 20X4, and its performance and its cash flows for the year then ended in accordance with International Financial Reporting Standards.

Basis for Opinion

We conducted our audit in accordance with International Standards on Auditing (ISAs). Our responsibilities under those standards are further described in the Auditor's Responsibilities for the Audit of the Financial Statements section of our report. We are independent of the Company in accordance with the ethical requirements that are relevant to our audit of the financial statements in [jurisdiction], and we have fulfilled our other ethical responsibilities in accordance with these requirements. We believe that the audit evidence we have obtained is sufficient and appropriate to provide a basis for our opinion.

Key Audit Matters [listed companies only]

Key audit matters are those matters that, in our professional judgment, were of most significance in our audit of the financial statements of the current period. These matters were addressed in the context of our audit of the financial statements as a whole, and in forming our opinion thereon, and we do not provide a separate opinion on these matters.

[Description of each key audit matter in accordance with ISA 701]

Other information

Management is responsible for the other information. The other information comprises the [description of other information, for example] Chairman's statement, but does not include the financial statements and the auditor's report thereon.

Our opinion on the financial statements does not cover the other information and we do not express any form of assurance conclusion thereon.

In connection with our audit of the financial statements, our responsibility is to read the other information and, in doing so, consider whether the other information is materially inconsistent with the financial statements or our knowledge obtained in the audit or otherwise appears to be materially misstated. If based on the work we have performed, we conclude that there is a material misstatement of this information, we are required to report that fact. We have nothing to report in this regard.

Responsibilities of Management and Those Charged With Governance for the Financial Statements

Management is responsible for the preparation and fair presentation of these financial statements in accordance with International Financial Reporting Standards, and for such internal control as management determines is necessary to enable the preparation of financial statements that are free from material misstatement, whether due to fraud or error.

In preparing the financial statements, management is responsible for assessing the Company's ability to continue as a going concern, disclosing as applicable, matters related to going concern and using the going concern basis of accounting unless management either intends to liquidate the Company or to cease operations, or has no realistic alternative but to do so.

Those charged with governance are responsible for overseeing the Company's financial reporting process.

Auditor's Responsibilities for the Audit of the Financial Statements

Our objectives are to obtain reasonable assurance about whether the financial statements as a whole are free from material misstatement, whether due to fraud or error, and to issue an auditor's report that includes our opinion. Reasonable assurance is a high level of assurance, but is not a guarantee that an audit conducted in accordance with ISAs will always detect a material misstatement when it exists. Misstatements can arise from fraud or error and are considered material if, individually or in the aggregate, they could reasonably be expected to influence the economic decisions of users taken on the basis of these financial statements.

As part of an audit in accordance with ISAs, we exercise professional judgment and maintain professional scepticism throughout the audit. We also:

- Identify and assess the risks of material misstatement of the financial statements, whether due to fraud or error, design and perform audit procedures responsive to those risks, and obtain audit evidence that is sufficient and appropriate to provide a basis for our opinion. The risk of not detecting a material misstatement resulting from fraud is higher than for one resulting from error, as fraud may involve collusion, forgery, intentional omissions, misrepresentations, or the override of internal control.

- Obtain an understanding of internal control relevant to the audit in order to design audit procedures that are appropriate in the circumstances, but not for the purpose of expressing an opinion on the effectiveness of the Company's internal control.

- Evaluate the appropriateness of accounting policies used and the reasonableness of accounting estimates and related disclosures made by management.

- Conclude on the appropriateness of management's use of the going concern basis of accounting and, based on the audit evidence obtained, whether a material uncertainty exists related to events or conditions that may cast significant doubt on the Company's ability to continue as a going concern. If we conclude that a material uncertainty exists, we are required to draw attention in our auditor's report to the related disclosures in the financial statements or, if such disclosures are inadequate, to modify our opinion. Our conclusions are based on the audit evidence obtained up to the date of our auditor's report. However, future events or conditions may cause the Company to cease to continue as a going concern.

- Evaluate the overall presentation, structure and content of the financial statements, including the disclosures, and whether the financial statements represent the underlying transactions and events in a manner that achieves fair presentation.

We communicate with those charged with governance regarding, among other matters, the planned scope and timing of the audit and significant findings, including any significant deficiencies in internal control that we identify during our audit.

We also provide those charged with governance with a statement that we have complied with relevant ethical requirements regarding independence, and to communicate with them all relationships and other matters that may reasonably be thought to bear on our independence, and where applicable, related safeguards.

From the matters communicated with those charged with governance, we determine those matters that were of most significance in the audit of the financial statements of the current period and are therefore the key audit matters. We describe these matters in our auditor's report unless law or regulation precludes public disclosure about the matter or when, in extremely rare circumstances, we determine that a matter should not be communicated in our report because the adverse consequences of doing so would reasonably be expected to outweigh the public interest benefits of such communication.

Report on Other Legal and Regulatory Requirements

[*As required by local law, regulation or national auditing standards*]

The engagement partner on the audit resulting in this independent auditor's report is [name].

Signature (the name of audit firm, the name of the auditor, or both)

Auditor address

Date

[ISA 700, Appendix]

UK syllabus: Illustrative auditor's report

INDEPENDENT AUDITOR'S REPORT TO THE MEMBERS OF XYZ PLC

Opinion

We have audited the financial statements of (name of company) for the year ended ... which comprise [specify the titles of the primary statements such as the Statement of Financial Position, the Statement of Comprehensive Income, the Statement of Cash Flows, the Statement of Changes in Equity] and notes to the financial statements, including a summary of significant accounting policies. The financial reporting framework that has been applied in their preparation is applicable law and International Financial Reporting Standards as adopted by the European Union.

In our opinion the financial statements:

- give a true and fair view of the state of the company's affairs as at [date] and of its [profit/loss] for the year then ended

- have been properly prepared in accordance with IFRS Standards as adopted by the European Union; and

- have been prepared in accordance with the requirements of the Companies Act 2006.

Basis for opinion

We conducted our audit in accordance with International Standards on Auditing (UK) (ISAs (UK)) and applicable law. Our responsibilities under those standards are further described in the Auditor's responsibilities for the audit of the financial statements section of our report. We are independent of the company in accordance with the ethical requirements that are relevant to our audit of the financial statements in the UK, including the FRC's Ethical Standard as applied to listed entities, and we have fulfilled our other ethical responsibilities in accordance with these requirements. We believe that the audit evidence we have obtained is sufficient and appropriate to provide a basis for our opinion.

Conclusions relating to going concern

We have nothing to report in respect of the following matters in relation to which the ISAs (UK) require us to report to you where:

- the directors' use of the going concern basis of accounting in the preparation of the financial statements is not appropriate; or

- the directors have not disclosed in the financial statements any identified material uncertainties that may cast significant doubt about the company's ability to continue to adopt the going concern basis of accounting for a period of at least twelve months from the date when the financial statements are authorised for issue.

Key audit matters [listed companies only]

Key audit matters are those matters that, in our professional judgment, were of most significance in our audit of the financial statements of the current period and include the most significant assessed risks of material misstatement (whether or not due to fraud) we identified, including those which had the greatest effect on: the overall audit strategy, the allocation of resources in the audit; and directing the efforts of the engagement team. These matters were addressed in the context of our audit of the financial statements as a whole, and in forming our opinion thereon, and we do not provide a separate opinion on these matters.

[Description of each key audit matter in accordance with ISA (UK) 701]

Our application of materiality

[Explanation of how the auditor applied the concept of materiality in planning and performing the audit. This is required to include the threshold used by the auditor as being materiality for the financial statements as a whole but may include other relevant disclosures.]

An overview of the scope of our audit

[Overview of the scope of the audit, including an explanation of how the scope addressed each key audit matter and was influenced by the auditor's application of materiality.]

Other information

The directors are responsible for the other information. The other information comprises the information included in the annual report, other than the financial statements and our auditor's report thereon. Our opinion on the financial statements does not cover the other information and, except to the extent otherwise explicitly stated in our report, we do not express any form of assurance conclusion thereon.

In connection with our audit of the financial statements, our responsibility is to read the other information and, in doing so, consider whether the other information is materially inconsistent with the financial statements or our knowledge obtained in the audit or otherwise appears to be materially misstated. If we identify such material inconsistencies or apparent material misstatements, we are required to determine whether there is a material misstatement in the financial statements or a material misstatement of the other information. If, based on the work we have performed, we conclude that there is a material misstatement of this other information, we are required to report that fact. We have nothing to report in this regard.

Opinions on other matters prescribed by the Companies Act 2006

In our opinion, based on the work undertaken in the course of the audit:

- the information given in the strategic report and directors' report for the financial year for which the financial statements are prepared is consistent with the financial statements; and

- the strategic report and director's report have been prepared in accordance with applicable legal requirements.

Matters on which we are required to report by exception

In the light of the knowledge and understanding of the company and its environment obtained in the course of the audit, we have not identified material misstatements in the strategic report or the directors' report.

We have nothing to report in respect of the following matters in relation to which the Companies Act 2006 requires us to report to you if, in our opinion:

- adequate accounting records have not been kept, or returns adequate for our audit have not been received from branches not visited by us; or

- the financial statements are not in agreement with accounting records and returns: or

- certain disclosures of directors' remuneration specified by law are not made; or

- we have not received all the information and explanations we require for our audit.

Responsibilities of directors

As explained more fully in the directors' responsibilities statement [set out on page ...], the directors are responsible for the preparation of the financial statements and for being satisfied that they give a true and fair view, and for such internal control as the directors determine is necessary to enable the preparation of financial statements that are free from material misstatement, whether due to fraud or error.

In preparing the financial statements, the directors are responsible for assessing the company's ability to continue as a going concern, disclosing, as applicable, matters related to going concern and using the going concern basis of accounting unless the directors either intend to liquidate the company or to cease operations, or have no realistic alternative but to do so.

Auditor's responsibilities for the audit of the financial statements

Our objectives are to obtain reasonable assurance about whether the financial statements as a whole are free from material misstatement, whether due to fraud or error, and to issue an auditor's report that includes our opinion. Reasonable assurance is a high level of assurance, but is not a guarantee that an audit conducted in accordance with ISAs (UK) will always detect a material misstatement when it exists. Misstatements can arise from fraud or error and are considered material if, individually or in the aggregate, they could reasonably be expected to influence the economic decisions of users taken on the basis of these financial statements.

A further description of our responsibilities for the audit of the financial statements is located on the Financial Reporting Council's website at: [website link]. This description forms part of our auditor's report.

[Signature]

John Smith (Senior statutory auditor)

For and on behalf of ABC LLP, Statutory Auditor

Address

Date

[FRC Bulletin: Compendium of illustrative auditor's reports on United Kingdom private sector financial statements]

Explanation of the sections

Section		Purpose
1	Title	To clearly identify the report as an Independent Auditor's Report.
2	Addressee	To identify the intended user of the report.
3	Auditor's Opinion	Provides the auditor's conclusion as to whether or not the financial statements give a true and fair view.
4	Basis for Opinion	Provides a description of the professional standards applied during the audit to provide confidence to users that the report can be relied upon.
5	Key Audit Matters	To draw attention to any other significant matters of which the users should be aware to aid their understanding of the entity. (**Note:** This section is only compulsory for listed entities.)
6	Other Information	To clarify that management are responsible for the other information. The auditor's opinion does not cover the other information and the auditor's responsibility is only to read the other information and report in accordance with ISA 720.
7	Responsibilities of Management and Those Charged with Governance for the Financial Statements	To clarify that management are responsible for preparing the financial statements and for the internal controls. Included to help minimise the expectation gap.

8	Auditor's Responsibilities for the Audit of the Financial Statements	To clarify that the auditor is responsible for expressing reasonable assurance as to whether the financial statements give a true and fair view and express that opinion in the auditor's report. The section also describes the auditor's responsibilities in respect of risk assessment, internal controls, going concern and accounting policies. Included to help minimise the expectation gap.
9	Report on Other Legal and Regulatory Requirements	To highlight any additional reporting responsibilities, if applicable. This may include responsibilities in some jurisdictions to report on the adequacy of accounting records, internal controls over financial reporting, or other information published with the financial statements.
10	Name of the engagement partner	To identify the person responsible for the auditor's report in case of any queries.
11	Signature	Shows the engagement partner or firm accountable for the opinion.
12	Auditor's address	To identify the specific office of the engagement partner in case of any queries.
13	Date	To identify the date up to which the audit work has been performed. Any information that comes to light after this date will not have been considered by the auditor when forming their opinion. The report must be signed and dated after the directors have approved the financial statements. Often the financial statements and the auditor's report are signed on the same day.

UK specific sections

Conclusions relating to going concern

The auditor must state within the auditor's report whether there are any matters to report in relation to the basis of preparation or disclosures of going concern. If there are no matters to report i.e. the auditor is satisfied with the basis of preparation and disclosures relating to going concern, the auditor must make a statement to this effect.

Opinions on other matters prescribed by the Companies Act 2006

In the UK there is a requirement for auditor's to report on whether the strategic report and directors' report are consistent with the financial statements and prepared in accordance with the applicable legal requirements i.e. Companies Act 2006.

All companies must prepare a strategic report unless they are entitled to the small companies exemption.

The purpose of the strategic report is to inform members and help them assess how the directors have performed in their duty to promote the success of the company.

The strategic report must contain:

- A fair review of the company's business including a detailed analysis of the performance of the company and the position of the company at the year-end.

- A description of the principal risks and uncertainties facing the company.

The strategic report must be approved by the board of directors and signed on behalf of the board by a director or secretary.

Matters on which we are required to report by exception

Under the Companies Act 2006, the auditor is required to report by exception on certain matters such as whether they have received all information and explanations for their audit and whether the directors' remuneration has been disclosed as required. In the past these matters were only mentioned in the auditor's report if problems were encountered but are now included in the UK auditor's report specifically and will state whether or not there is anything to report.

3   Forming an opinion

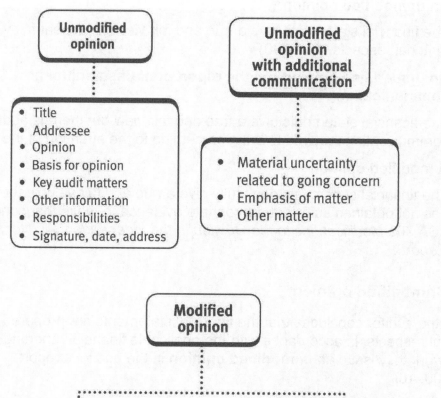

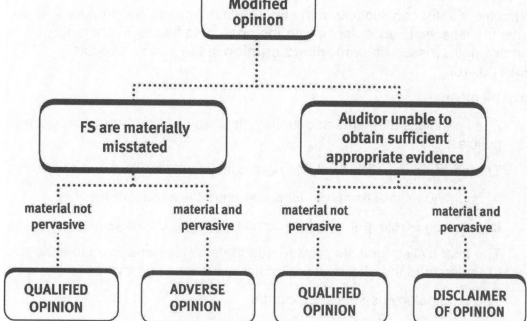

As can be seen from the diagram above, the report can include:

- **An unmodified opinion**

  The financial statements give a true and fair view or present fairly in all material respects. (ISA 700)

- **An unmodified opinion but the report contains additional communication**

  The financial statements give a true and fair view but there is additional communication required to bring something to the attention of the user.

- **A modified opinion**

  The financial statements don't fully give a true and fair view or the auditor has not obtained sufficient appropriate evidence to make that conclusion. (ISA 705 *Modifications to the Opinion in the Independent Auditor's Report*).

4 Unmodified opinion

When the auditor concludes that the financial statements are prepared, in all material respects, in accordance with the applicable financial reporting framework they issue an **unmodified opinion** in the auditor's report.
[ISA 700, 16]

This will mean:

- The financial statements adequately disclose the significant accounting policies.

- The accounting policies selected are consistently applied and appropriate.

- Accounting estimates made by management are reasonable.

- Information is relevant, reliable, comparable and understandable.

- The financial statements provide adequate disclosures to enable the users to understand the effects of material transactions and events.

- The terminology used is appropriate.

[ISA 700, 13]

5 Other Information section

 Other information refers to financial or non-financial information, other than the financial statements and auditor's report thereon, included in the entity's annual report. [ISA 720, 12c]

If the auditor obtains the final version of the other information before the date of the auditor's report, they must read it to identify any material inconsistencies with the financial statements or the auditor's knowledge obtained during the audit. [ISA 720, 3]

Examples of other information include:

- Chair's report

- Operating and financial review

- Social and environmental reports

- Corporate governance statements.

The Other Information section:

- Identifies the other information obtained by the auditor prior to the date of the auditor's report.

- States that the auditor has not audited the other information and accordingly does not express an opinion or conclusion on that information.

- Includes a description of the auditor's responsibilities with respect to the other information.

- States either that the auditor has nothing to report or provides a description of the material misstatement if applicable.

[ISA 720, 22]

Purpose

The auditor must not be knowingly associated with information which is misleading. [ISA 720, 4]

Misstatement of other information exists when the other information is incorrectly stated or otherwise misleading (including because it omits or obscures information necessary for a proper understanding of a matter). [ISA 720, 12b]

Material misstatements or inconsistencies in the other information may undermine the credibility of the financial statements and the auditor's report. [ISA 720, 3]

If the auditor identifies a material inconsistency they should:

- Perform procedures to evaluate the inconsistency. The auditor should consider whether it is the financial statements or the other information that requires amendment. [ISA 720, 16]

- Discuss the matter with management and ask them to make the correction. [ISA 720, 17]

- If management refuse to make the correction, communicate the matter to those charged with governance. [ISA 720, 17b]

- If the matter remains uncorrected the auditor must describe the material misstatement in the auditor's report. [ISA 720, 18a]

- Alternatively, the auditor should withdraw from the engagement if possible under applicable law or regulation as the issue casts doubt over management integrity. [ISA 720, 18b]

Position in the auditor's report

The Other Information section is included in the auditor's report below the Basis for Opinion and Key Audit Matters section (if applicable) and above the Responsibilities of Management.

 Tutorial notes

The auditor must retain a copy of the final version of the other information on the audit file. [ISA 720, 25b]

If the auditor issues a disclaimer of opinion on the financial statements, the Other Information section should not be included in the auditor's report as to do so may overshadow the disclaimer of opinion. [ISA 720, A58]

 UK syllabus: ISA (UK) 720

ISA (UK) 720 The Auditor's Responsibilities Relating to Other Information (Revised June 2016)

In addition to the requirements of ISA 720, ISA 720 (UK) contains additional requirements for UK auditors.

In the UK, an annual report includes at least:

- The statutory other information

- Any other documents that are incorporated by cross-reference in, or distributed to shareholders with, statutory other information either voluntarily or pursuant to law or regulation or the requirements of a stock exchange listing.

A misstatement of the other information exists when the statutory other information has not been prepared in accordance with the legal and regulatory requirements applicable to the statutory other information.

In the UK, the statutory other information includes:

- The directors' report

- The strategic report

- The separate corporate governance statement.

For entities that are required to prepare statutory other information, the auditor shall obtain an understanding of:

- The legal and regulatory requirements applicable to the statutory other information

- How the entity is complying with those legal and regulatory requirements.

The auditor shall perform such procedures as are necessary to identify whether the statutory other information appears to be materially misstated in the context of the auditor's understanding of the legal and regulatory requirements applicable to the statutory other information.

 Other Information: Audit Quality Thematic Review

FRC Audit Quality Thematic Review – Other Information in the Annual Report

This review looked at the auditor's work on the Other Information in the annual report where the auditor has specific reporting responsibilities.

Users are increasingly using the Other Information to aid investment decisions because it is helpful in assessing a company's future prospects.

The nature, extent and quality of the work performed on the Other Information varies considerably from firm to firm and within audit firms. This is likely to be caused by a lack of guidance in auditing standards.

Despite ISA 720 *The Auditor's Responsibilities Relating to Other Information* being revised in 2016, the new standard has not been effective in achieving its objectives. The FRC proposes to look again at these objectives as part of its post implementation review.

Key findings:

- Firms' procedures do not reflect the additional requirements of ISA 720.

- Firms do not require audit teams to obtain supporting documentation supporting the Fair Balanced and Understandable Statement.

- Firms do not generally require audit teams to obtain the company's risk register and consider its completeness as part of their review of the risk disclosures in the Strategic Report.

- Limited work was performed by teams when reviewing the Viability Statement.

- Insufficient procedures were carried out to verify different components of directors remuneration included in the audited parts of the directors remuneration report (DRR). There was no clear evidence that the unaudited parts of the DRR had been assessed.

- Teams did however perform sufficient procedures in respect of KPIs and Alternative Performance Measures.

Improvements required:

- More prescriptive guidance for audit teams to follow.

- Specific consideration of Other Information at the planning stage of the audit.

- Greater emphasis on review of key non-financial information.

- Requirement for Boards to prepare timely information to support the Fair Balanced and Understandable and Viability Assessment/ Statements.

- Assigning audit team members who are competent to review Other Information.

- Audit committees must ensure directors provide auditors with high quality documentation to support their Fair Balanced and Understandable and Viability Assessment/Statements, and must engage with auditors at the planning stage of the audit to fully understand the work to be performed, and completion stage of the audit to understand the work that has been performed on the Other Information.

6 Key Audit Matters section

ISA 701 *Communicating Key Audit Matters in the Independent Auditor's Report* requires auditors of **listed companies** to determine key audit matters and to communicate those matters in the auditor's report. [ISA 701, 5]

Auditors of non-listed entities may voluntarily, or at the request of management or those charged with governance, include key audit matters in the auditor's report.

 Key audit matters are those that in the auditor's professional judgment were of most significance in the audit and are selected from matters communicated to those charged with governance.
[ISA 701, 8]

The purpose of including these matters is to assist users in understanding the entity, and to provide a basis for the users to engage with management and those charged with governance about matters relating to the entity and the financial statements. [ISA 701, 3]

Each key audit matter should describe why the matter was considered to be significant and how it was addressed in the audit.

Key audit matters include:

- Areas of higher assessed risk of material misstatement, or significant risks identified in accordance with ISA 315 *Identifying and Assessing the Risks of Material Misstatement through Understanding the Entity and Its Environment.*

- Significant auditor judgments relating to areas in the financial statements that involved significant management judgment, including accounting estimates that have been identified as having high estimation uncertainty.

- The effect on the audit of significant events or transactions that occurred during the period.

[ISA 701, 9]

Specific examples include:

- Significant fraud risk

- Goodwill

- Valuation of financial instruments

- Fair values

- Effects of new accounting standards

- Revenue recognition

- Material provisions such as a restructuring provision

- Implementation of a new IT system, or significant changes to an existing system.

Note that a matter giving rise to a qualified or adverse opinion, or a material uncertainty related to going concern are by their nature key audit matters. However, they would not be described in this section of the report. Instead, a reference to the Basis for qualified or adverse opinion or the going concern section would be included. [ISA 701, 15]

If there are no key audit matters to communicate, the auditor shall:

- Discuss this with the engagement quality control reviewer, if one has been appointed.

- Communicate this conclusion to those charged with governance. [ISA 701, 17b]

- Explain in the key audit matters section of the auditor's report that there are no matters to report. [ISA 701, 16]

Key Audit Matter	How our audit addressed the Key Audit Matter
Revenue recognition	
Revenue amounted to $X million for the year ended 31st December 20X4. Revenue is recorded when the service is provided, using complex information technology systems to track the point of service delivery and, where necessary, estimates of fair values for the services provided. These fair value estimates involve a significant degree of management judgment.	• Testing controls over the revenue systems • Performing analytical procedures on revenue • Examining manual journals related to revenue to assess the fair values and timings of revenue.
Goodwill	
The Group has goodwill of $X million relating to ABC Co. ABC Co incurred losses in the year ended 31st December 20X5. This has increased the risk that the carrying values of goodwill and other assets may be impaired. Management has concluded that there is no impairment. This conclusion was based on a value in use model that required significant management judgment with respect to the discount rate and the underlying cash flows, in particular future revenue growth.	Our procedures in relation to management's impairment assessment included: • Assessing the valuation methodology • Challenging the reasonableness of key management assumptions based on our knowledge of the business and industry • Reconciling input data to supporting evidence, such as approved budgets and considering the reasonableness of these budgets. We found the assumptions made by management in relation to the value in use calculations to be reasonable based on available evidence.

7 Additional communications

In certain circumstances auditors are required to make additional communications in the auditor's report even though the financial statements show a true and fair view. Issues requiring communication include:

- **Material Uncertainty Related to Going Concern** (ISA 570 *Going Concern*)

- **Emphasis of Matter paragraph** (ISA 706 *Emphasis of Matter Paragraphs and Other Matter Paragraphs in an Auditor's Report*)

- **Other Matter paragraph** (ISA 706)

It is important to note that these **do not impact the wording of the opinion** and do not constitute either a qualified, adverse or disclaimer of opinion.

Material Uncertainty Related to Going Concern

Purpose

This section is included when there is a material uncertainty regarding the going concern status which the directors have adequately disclosed in the financial statements. The auditor uses this section to draw the attention of the user to the client's disclosure note. [ISA 570, 22]

Position in the auditor's report

Below the Basis for Opinion section.

Emphasis of Matter paragraph

Purpose

An Emphasis of Matter paragraph is used to refer to **a matter that has been appropriately presented or disclosed in the financial statements** by the directors. The auditor's judgment is that these matters are **of such fundamental importance to the users' understanding** of the financial statements that the auditor should emphasise the disclosure.
[ISA 706, 7a]

Examples of such fundamental matters include:

- An uncertainty relating to the future outcome of exceptional litigation or regulatory action.

- A significant subsequent event occurs between the date of the financial statements and the date of the auditor's report.

- Early application of a new accounting standard.

- Major catastrophes that have had a significant effect on the entity's financial position.

[ISA 706, A5]

In addition, an Emphasis of Matter paragraph will be used where:

- The financial statements have been prepared on a basis other than the going concern basis.

- The corresponding figures have been restated.

- The financial statements have been recalled and reissued or when the auditor provides an amended auditor's report.

Position in the auditor's report

Below the Basis for Opinion section.

When a Key Audit Matters section is presented in the auditor's report, an Emphasis of Matter paragraph may be presented either directly before or after the Key Audit Matters section, based on the auditor's judgment as to the relative significance of the information included in the Emphasis of Matter paragraph.

The heading of the paragraph can be amended to provide further context, for example, Emphasis of Matter – Subsequent event.
[ISA 706, A16]

 Tutorial notes

An Emphasis of Matter paragraph is not used to draw attention to immaterial misstatements. The fact that they are immaterial means they do not warrant the attention of the shareholders.

An Emphasis of Matter paragraph can only be used when adequate disclosure has been made of the matters mentioned above. The auditor can only emphasise something that is already included.

Where adequate disclosure has not been made the opinion will need to be modified and an Emphasis of Matter paragraph **should NOT be used**.

INT syllabus: An Emphasis of Matter should not be used to highlight an issue already included in the Key Audit Matters section. The auditor must use judgment to determine which section they consider is the most appropriate to highlight the issue.

UK syllabus: Law or regulation may require a matter to be emphasised in the auditor's report in addition to communicating such a matter as a key audit matter in accordance with ISA (UK) 701.

 Example wording of an 'Emphasis of Matter' paragraph

> We draw attention to Note 12 of the financial statements, which describes the effects of a fire at the premises of a third party warehouse provider. Our opinion is not modified in respect of this matter.

BP plc

Between 2010 and 2014, the auditor of BP plc, Ernst & Young LLP, issued auditor's reports containing additional communication in relation to the Deepwater Horizon accident which caused an oil spill off the Gulf of Mexico. The event created significant uncertainty regarding the liabilities that the company might have to pay. BP plc included several disclosures in the notes to the financial statements relating to the uncertainty over the provisions and contingencies. An **Emphasis of Matter** paragraph was included in the auditor's report referring to these disclosure notes. This was removed in 2015 when the auditor concluded that the remaining uncertainties were no longer fundamental to the user's understanding as agreements reached with the government over settlement of the claims significantly reduced the uncertainty of the liabilities.

Other Matter Paragraphs

Purpose

An Other Matter paragraph is included in the auditor's report if the auditor considers it necessary to communicate to the users regarding **matters other than those presented or disclosed in the financial statements** that, in the auditor's judgment, are **relevant to understanding the audit, the auditor's responsibilities, or the auditor's report**.
[ISA 706, 7b]

Examples of its use include:

- To communicate that the auditor's report is intended solely for the intended users, and should not be distributed to or used by other parties. [ISA 706, A14]

- When law, regulation or generally accepted practice requires or permits the auditor to provide further explanation of their responsibilities. [ISA 706, A11]

- To explain why the auditor has not resigned, when a pervasive inability to obtain sufficient appropriate evidence is imposed by management (e.g. denying the auditor access to books and records) but the auditor is unable to withdraw from the engagement due to legal restrictions. [ISA 706, A10]

- To communicate audit planning and scoping matters where laws or regulations require. [ISA 706, A9]

- Where an entity prepares one set of accounts in accordance with a general purpose framework and another set in accordance with a different one (e.g. one according to UK and one according to International standards) and engages the auditor to report on both sets. [ISA 706, A13]

Position in the auditor's report

When an Other Matter paragraph is included to draw the users' attention to a matter relating to other reporting responsibilities addressed in the auditor's report, the paragraph may be included in the Report on Other Legal and Regulatory Requirements section.

When relevant to all auditor's responsibilities or users' understanding of the auditor's report, the Other Matter paragraph may be included as a separate section following the Report on the Other Legal and Regulatory Requirements.

The heading may be amended to provide further context, for example, Other Matter – Scope of the audit.
[ISA 706, A16]

Tutorial notes

An Other Matter paragraph does not include confidential information or information required to be provided by management. [ISA 706, A15]

Example wording of 'Other Matter' paragraph
The financial statements of ABC Company for the year ended December 31, 20X4, were audited by another auditor who expressed an unmodified opinion on those statements on March 31, 20X5. [ISA 706, Appendix 3]

8 Modified opinions

Actions when the opinion is to be modified

Modification of the audit opinion is always the final course of action. As the directors have a legal responsibility to prepare the financial statements to show a true and fair view, the number of modified opinions in real life is very low.

If the auditor is expecting to modify the opinion the following actions will be taken:

(1) Discuss the matter with those charged with governance

   This may lead to the matter being resolved as the client may decide to amend the financial statements or the auditor may be provided with further evidence to conclude that a modification is not necessary.

(2) Consider management integrity

   It is generally expected that the client would want to avoid a modified opinion, therefore if the issue cannot be resolved satisfactorily it casts doubt over management integrity. This will mean that any representations from management may not be reliable. If representations cannot be relied on, this would lead to a disclaimer of opinion in accordance with ISA 580 *Written Representations*.

(3)   Seek external advice

Before resigning, the auditor may decide to seek legal advice or consult with the ACCA about the issues.

(4)   Resign

Where the auditor has reason to doubt management integrity or where the auditor expects in future that there will be a need to issue a disclaimer, resignation must be considered. These are both matters that would have been considered at the acceptance stage and they must be reconsidered at the end of the audit to decide whether to continue with the engagement.

Modifications to the audit opinion

The auditor may decide they need to modify the opinion when they conclude that:

- Based upon the evidence obtained **the financial statements** as a whole **are not free from material misstatement**. This is where the client has not complied with the applicable financial reporting framework.

- They have been **unable to obtain sufficient appropriate evidence** to be able to conclude that the financial statements as a whole are free from material misstatement. This is evidence the auditor would expect to exist to support the figures in the financial statements.

[ISA 705, 6]

The nature of the modification depends upon whether the auditor considers the matter to be material but not pervasive, or material and pervasive, to the financial statements.

Material but not pervasive – Qualified opinion

- If the misstatement or lack of sufficient appropriate evidence is **material but not pervasive**, a **qualified opinion** will be issued. [ISA 705, 7]

- This means the matter is material to the area of the financial statements affected but does not affect the remainder of the financial statements.

- **'Except for'** this matter, the financial statements give a true and fair view.

- Although significant to users' decision making, a material matter can be isolated while the remainder of the financial statements may be relied upon.

Material and pervasive

A matter is considered **'pervasive'** if, in the auditor's judgment:

- The effects are not confined to specific elements, accounts or items of the financial statements

- If so confined, represent or could represent a substantial proportion of the financial statements, or

- In relation to disclosures, are fundamental to users' understanding of the financial statements.

[ISA 705, 5a]

In brief, a pervasive matter must be fundamental to the financial statements, therefore rendering them unreliable as a whole.

Adverse opinion

An **adverse opinion** is issued when a misstatement is considered material and pervasive. [ISA 705, 8]

This will mean the financial statements **do not give a true and fair view**. Examples include:

- Preparation of the financial statements on the wrong basis.

- Non-consolidation of a material subsidiary.

- Material misstatement of a balance which represents a substantial proportion of the assets or profits e.g. would change a profit to a loss.

Disclaimer of opinion

A **disclaimer of opinion** is issued when the auditor has not obtained sufficient appropriate evidence and the effects of any possible misstatements could be pervasive. [ISA 705, 9]

The auditor **does not express an opinion** on the financial statements in this situation.

Examples include:

- Failure by the client to keep adequate accounting records.

- Refusal by the directors to provide written representation.

- Failure by the client to provide evidence over a single balance which represents a substantial proportion of the assets or profits or over multiple balances in the financial statements.

Impact of a disclaimer of opinion

Where a disclaimer of opinion is being issued:

- The statement that sufficient appropriate evidence to provide a basis for the auditor's opinion has been obtained is not included.

- The statement that the financial statements have been audited is changed to 'we were engaged to audit the financial statements'.

[ISA 705, 19]

- The statements regarding the audit being conducted in accordance with ISAs, and independence and other ethical responsibilities, are positioned within the Auditor Responsibilities section rather than the Basis for Disclaimer of Opinion section. [ISA 705, A25]

- The Key Audit Matters section is not included in the report as to do so would suggest the financial statements are more credible in relation to those matters which would be inconsistent with the disclaimer of opinion on the financial statements as a whole. [ISA 705, 29]

9 Basis for Opinion section

When the auditor decides to modify the opinion, they must amend the heading 'Basis for Opinion' to 'Basis for Qualified Opinion', 'Basis for Adverse Opinion' or 'Basis for Disclaimer of Opinion', as appropriate. [ISA 705, 20a]

Where a qualified or adverse opinion is being issued, the auditor must amend the statement '...the audit evidence is sufficient and appropriate to provide a basis for the auditor's qualified/adverse opinion.' [ISA 705, 25]

The section will explain the reason why the opinion is modified e.g. which balances are misstated, which disclosures are missing or inadequate, which balances the auditor was unable to obtain sufficient appropriate evidence over and why. [ISA 705, 20b]

If possible, a quantification of the financial effect of the modification will be included. [ISA 705, 21]

If the material misstatement relates to narrative disclosures, an explanation of how the disclosures are misstated should be included, or in the case of omitted disclosures, the disclosure should be included if the information is readily available. [ISA 705, 22]

The following table illustrates the impact on the audit opinion and auditor's report. [ISA 705, A1]

	Material but Not Pervasive	Material & Pervasive
Financial statements are materially misstated	Qualified Opinion Except for ... Basis for qualified opinion	Adverse Opinion FS do not give a true and fair view Basis for adverse opinion
Inability to obtain sufficient appropriate audit evidence	Qualified Opinion Except for ... Basis for qualified opinion	Disclaimer of Opinion Do not express an opinion Basis for disclaimer of opinion

Management imposed limitation of scope

- If after accepting the engagement, management impose a limitation of scope that will result in a modified opinion, the auditor will request that management remove the limitation. [ISA 705, 11]

- If management refuse, the matter must be communicated with those charged with governance. [ISA 705, 12]

- The auditor should perform alternative audit procedures to obtain sufficient appropriate evidence, if possible. [ISA 705, 12]

- If the auditor is unable to obtain sufficient appropriate evidence and the matter is material but not pervasive, the auditor must issue a qualified audit opinion. [ISA 705, 13a]
  If the matter is considered pervasive, the auditor must withdraw from the audit. [ISA 705, 13bi]

- If withdrawal is not possible before issuing the auditor's report, a disclaimer of opinion should be issued. [ISA 705, 13bii]

- If the auditor decides to withdraw from the audit, the auditor must communicate any material misstatements identified during the audit to those charged with governance before withdrawing.
  [ISA 705, 14]

University of Oxford

The auditors of the University of Oxford, Deloitte and more recently KPMG, have issued a **Qualified Opinion** due to material misstatement for a number of years. The results of Oxford University Press (OUP), a department of the University, are not consolidated in the financial statements of the University because the financial regulations of the Council of the University do not apply to OUP. The financial statements do not comply with UK GAAP in this respect, and are therefore materially misstated.

Example wording of a Qualified Opinion (a)

Example where the auditor concludes that the financial statements are materially (but not pervasively) misstated:

Qualified Opinion

We have audited the financial statements of ABC Company (the Company), which comprise the statement of financial position as at December 31, 20X1, and the statement of comprehensive income, statement of changes in equity and statement of cash flows for the year then ended, and notes to the financial statements, including a summary of significant accounting policies.

In our opinion, except for the effects of the matter described in the Basis for Qualified Opinion section of our report, the accompanying financial statements give a true and fair view................. (remainder of wording as per an unmodified opinion).

Basis for Qualified Opinion

The Company's inventories are carried in the statement of financial position at xxx. Management has not stated the inventories at the lower of cost and net realisable value but has stated them solely at cost, which constitutes a departure from IFRS Standards. The Company's records indicate that, had management stated the inventories at the lower of cost and net realisable value, an amount of xxx would have been required to write the inventories down to their net realisable value. Accordingly, cost of sales would have been increased by xxx, and income tax, net income and shareholders' equity would have been reduced by xxx, xxx and xxx, respectively.

We conducted our audit in accordance with International Standards on Auditing (ISAs). Our responsibilities under those standards are further described in the Auditor's Responsibilities for the Audit of the Financial Statements section of our report. We are independent of the Company in accordance with the ethical requirements that are relevant to our audit of the financial statements in [jurisdiction], and we have fulfilled our other ethical responsibilities in accordance with these requirements. We believe that the audit evidence we have obtained is sufficient and appropriate to provide a basis for our qualified opinion.

Example wording of a Qualified Opinion (b)

Example where the auditor concludes that they have been unable to gather sufficient appropriate evidence and the possible effects are deemed to be material but not pervasive:

Qualified Opinion

We have audited the financial statements of the ABC Company (the Company), which comprise the statement of financial position as at 31 December, 20X1, and the statement of comprehensive income, statement of changes in equity and statement of cash flows for the year then ended, and notes to the financial statements, including a summary of significant accounting policies.

In our opinion, except for the possible effects of the matter described in the Basis for Qualified Opinion section of our report, the accompanying financial statements give a true and fair view.................... (remainder of wording as per an unmodified opinion).

Basis for Qualified Opinion

The Group's investment in XYZ Company, a foreign associate acquired during the year and accounted for by the equity method, is carried at xxx on the consolidated statement of financial position as at December 31, 20X1, and ABC's share of XYZ's net income of xxx is included in ABC's income for the year then ended. We were unable to obtain sufficient appropriate audit evidence about the carrying amount of ABC's investment in XYZ as at December 31, 20X1 and ABC's share of XYZ's net income for the year because we were denied access to the financial information, management, and the auditors of XYZ. Consequently, we were unable to determine whether any adjustments to these amounts were necessary.

We conducted our audit in accordance with International Standards on Auditing (ISAs). Our responsibilities under those standards are further described in the Auditor's Responsibilities for the Audit of the Consolidated Financial Statements section of our report. We are independent of the Group in accordance with the ethical requirements that are relevant to our audit of the consolidated financial statements in [jurisdiction], and we have fulfilled our other ethical responsibilities in accordance with these requirements. We believe that the audit evidence we have obtained is sufficient and appropriate to provide a basis for our qualified opinion.

Example wording of an Adverse Opinion

Example where the auditor has concluded that the financial statements are misstated and deemed pervasive to the financial statements:

Adverse Opinion

In our opinion, because of the significance of the matter discussed in the Basis for Adverse Opinion paragraph, the consolidated financial statements do not give a true and fair view.................. (remainder of wording as per an unmodified opinion).

Basis for Adverse Opinion

As explained in Note X, the Group has not consolidated subsidiary XYZ Company that the Group acquired during 20X1 because it has not yet been able to determine the fair values of certain of the subsidiary's material assets and liabilities at the acquisition date. This investment is therefore accounted for on a cost basis. Under IFRS Standards, the Company should have consolidated this subsidiary and accounted for the acquisition based on provisional amounts. Had XYZ Company been consolidated, many elements in the accompanying consolidated financial statements would have been materially affected. The effects on the consolidated financial statements of the failure to consolidate have not been determined.

We conducted our audit in accordance with International Standards on Auditing (ISAs). Our responsibilities under those standards are further described in the Auditor's Responsibilities for the Audit of the Consolidated Financial Statements section of our report. We are independent of the Group in accordance with the ethical requirements that are relevant to our audit of the consolidated financial statements in [jurisdiction], and we have fulfilled our other ethical responsibilities in accordance with these requirements. We believe that the audit evidence we have obtained is sufficient and appropriate to provide a basis for our adverse opinion.

Example wording of a Disclaimer of Opinion

Example where the auditor was unable to obtain sufficient appropriate evidence and has concluded that the possible effects of this matter are both material and pervasive to the financial statements:

Disclaimer of Opinion

We were engaged to audit the consolidated financial statements of ABC Company and its subsidiaries (the Group), which comprise the consolidated statement of financial position as at December 31, 20X1, and the consolidated statement of comprehensive income, consolidated statement of changes in equity and consolidated statement of cash flows for the year then ended, and notes to the consolidated financial statements, including a summary of significant accounting policies.

We do not express an opinion on the accompanying consolidated financial statements of the Group. Because of the significance of the matter described in the Basis for Disclaimer of Opinion section of our report, we have not been able to obtain sufficient appropriate audit evidence to provide a basis for an audit opinion on these consolidated financial statements.

Basis for Disclaimer of Opinion

The Group's investment in its joint venture XYZ Company is carried at xxx on the Group's consolidated statement of financial position, which represents over 90% of the Group's net assets as at December 31, 20X1. We were not allowed access to the management and the auditors of XYZ Company, including XYZ Company's auditors' audit documentation. As a result, we were unable to determine whether any adjustments were necessary in respect of the Group's proportional share of XYZ Company's assets that it controls jointly, its proportional share of XYZ Company's liabilities for which it is jointly responsible, its proportional share of XYZ's income and expenses for the year, and the elements making up the consolidated statement of changes in equity and the consolidated cash flow statement.

> **Responsibilities of Management and Those Charged with Governance for the Consolidated Financial Statements**
>
> *[Wording as per ISA 700]*
>
> **Auditor's Responsibilities for the Audit of the Consolidated Financial Statements**
>
> Our responsibility is to conduct an audit of the Group's consolidated financial statements in accordance with International Standards on Auditing and to issue an auditor's report. However, because of the matter described in the Basis for Disclaimer of Opinion section of our report, we were not able to obtain sufficient appropriate audit evidence to provide a basis for an audit opinion on these consolidated financial statements.
>
> We are independent of the Group in accordance with the ethical requirements that are relevant to our audit of the financial statements in [jurisdiction], and we have fulfilled our other ethical responsibilities in accordance with these requirements.

[ISA 705, Appendix]

IAASB: Auditor Reporting: FAQ

1   **When a KAM is necessary in respect of the audit of consolidated financial statements, is the auditor also required to communicate a KAM in the auditor's report of the separate financial statements?**

The auditor should determine KAM in respect of each set of financial statements. A matter may give rise to a KAM for both audits. The KAM should be described in the context of each set of financial statements. If the KAM is only relevant to one set of financial statements it should only be included in the relevant auditor's report.

2   **What is the effect on the KAM previously communicated in the auditor's report in circumstances when the auditor reissues the report or amends the report previously issued?**

When the auditor reissues or amends the auditor's report, an emphasis of matter or other matter paragraph will be included which refers to the note to the financial statements that discusses the reason for the amendment. The auditor should consider whether the matter that has resulted in the new or amended report gives rise to an additional KAM. KAMs included in the original report are unlikely to be affected because such matters were previously determined to be matters of most significance. If the matter resulting in the new or amended report affects the KAM, updates to the KAM may be necessary. The KAM should then also cross-reference to the EOM or OM paragraph to clarify that both are in respect of the same matter.

3   **Should KAM be communicated in respect of each period when comparative financial statements are presented?**

KAM should only be communicated in respect of the current period.

4   **Are all significant risks considered to be KAM?**

KAM are matters of most significance. Depending on their nature, significant risks may not necessarily require significant auditor attention and therefore would not be considered KAM.

5   **What are the auditor's responsibilities in relation to other information in circumstances when the auditor reissues or amends the report previously issued?**

The auditor may restrict audit procedures on subsequent events to the subsequent events causing the amendment. The auditor is not required to report on any other information obtained after the date of the original report.

If the auditor does not restrict the audit procedures to the subsequent events causing the amendment, the Other Information section of the reissued report would cover all other information obtained as of the date of the reissued report.

UK syllabus: Recent developments affecting UK Auditor's reports

ISA 700 (UK) (Revised June 2016)

For audits of financial statements of public interest entities, the auditor's report shall:

- State by whom or which body the auditor(s) was appointed.

- Indicate the date of the appointment and the period of total uninterrupted engagement including previous renewals and reappointments of the firm.

- Explain to what extent the audit was considered capable of detecting irregularities, including fraud.

- Confirm that the audit opinion is consistent with the additional report to the audit committee. The auditor's report shall not contain any cross-references to the additional report to the audit committee unless specifically required.

- Declare that the non-audit services prohibited by the FRC's Ethical Standard were not provided and that the firm remained independent of the entity in conducting the audit.

- Indicate any services, in addition to the audit, which were provided by the firm to the entity and its controlled undertaking(s), and which have not been disclosed in the annual report or financial statements.

ISA 701 (UK) Communicating Key Audit Matters in the Independent Auditor's Report

ISA 701 (UK) requires the auditor to communicate other audit planning and scoping matters in the auditor's report.

KAM include the most significant assessed risks of material misstatement (whether or not due to fraud) identified by the auditor, including those which had the greatest effect on the overall audit strategy, the allocation of resources in the audit, and directing the efforts of the engagement team.

In describing each of the key audit matters, the auditor's report shall provide:

- A description of the most significant assessed risks of material misstatement, (whether or not due to fraud)

- A summary of the auditor's response to those risks

- Where relevant, key observations arising with respect to those risks.

Where relevant to the above information provided in the auditor's report concerning each of the most significant assessed risks of material misstatement (whether or not due to fraud), the auditor's report shall include a clear reference to the relevant disclosures in the financial statements.

In describing why the matter was determined to be a key audit matter, the description shall indicate that the matter was one of the most significant assessed risks of material misstatement (whether or not due to fraud) identified by the auditor.

Communicating Other Audit Planning and Scoping Matters

The auditor's report shall provide:

- An explanation of how the auditor applied the concept of materiality in planning and performing the audit, specifying the threshold used by the auditor as being materiality for the financial statements as a whole.

- An overview of the scope of the audit, including an explanation of how such scope:

  - addressed each KAM relating to one of the most significant risks of material misstatement disclosed.

  - was influenced by the auditor's application of materiality disclosed.

Auditing the Directors' Remuneration Report

The Companies Act 2006 requires the directors to prepare a directors' remuneration report. Some of this information is required to be audited. The auditor's report must therefore describe accurately which sections of the remuneration report have been audited. The auditor will ask the directors to make the disclosure of the audited information clearly distinguishable from that which is not audited.

The auditor must form an opinion as to whether the auditable part of the company's directors' remuneration report:

- has been properly prepared in accordance with the Companies Act 2006

- is in agreement with the accounting records and returns.

If this is not the case, the auditor should include in their report the required information.

Companies disclosing compliance with the UK Corporate Governance Code

ISA (UK) 700 requires the auditor to report by exception on the following matters in the auditors' reports of companies disclosing compliance with the UK Corporate Governance Code where the annual report includes:

- A statement given by the directors that they consider the annual report and accounts taken as a whole is fair, balanced and understandable and provides the information necessary for shareholders to assess the entity's performance, business model and strategy, that is inconsistent with the knowledge acquired by the auditor in the course of performing the audit.

- A section describing the work of the audit committee that does not appropriately address matters communicated by the auditor to the audit committee.

- An explanation, as to why the annual report does not include such a statement or section, that is materially inconsistent with the knowledge acquired by the auditor in the course of performing the audit.

- Other information that, in the auditor's judgment, contains a material inconsistency or a material misstatement of fact.

The auditor shall include a suitable conclusion on these matters in the auditor's report.

Bulletin 2009/4 *Developments in Corporate Governance Affecting Responsibilities of Auditors of UK Companies* provides guidance for auditors and require the auditors to review:

- the statement of directors responsibilities in relation to going concern

- the part of the corporate governance statement relating to compliance with the provisions of the UK Corporate Governance Code. The corporate governance statement may be included within the directors' report or may be a separate statement within the annual report or cross referenced to the company's website.

FRC Extended auditor's reports – A review of experience in the second year

A review of experience in the second year found:

Positives

- Investors welcomed extended auditor reporting, particularly where there are fewer sources of other information available about the entity, e.g. smaller companies.

- Reports which were well structured and signposted key information earned the most praise.

- Reports are using better descriptions and less generic language.

Areas for improvement

- More can be done to enhance auditor's reports including providing more complete information about sensitivity ranges used in testing, assessment of the internal controls, and transparency about assumptions made by management and benchmarks used by auditors.

- There is a widespread absence of explanations by auditors of changes in their audit approach and levels of materiality used from one year to the next.

- Only one audit firm provides information on their application of performance materiality. Other firms comment that it is too difficult and technical to explain.

 UK syllabus: Bulletin 2010/1 XBRL tagging of information

In February 2010, the IAASB issued Bulletin 2010/1 XBRL: Tagging of information in audited financial statements – guidance for auditors.

XBRL (eXtensible Business Reporting Language), is a language for the electronic communication of business and financial data. XBRL assigns all individual disclosure items within business reports a unique, electronically readable tags (like a barcode).

HMRC requires companies to file their tax returns online using XBRL for returns submitted after 31 March 2011.

As we have seen, ISA 720 sets out the auditor's responsibilities relating to other information in documents containing audited financial statements. XBRL – tagged data does not represent "other information" as referred to in ISA 720. Auditors are not required to provide assurance on XBRL data in the context of an audit of financial statements.

However, auditors may be able to provide other services in relation to XBRL data, including:

- Performing the tagging exercise.

- Agreed-upon procedures engagements such as the accuracy of the tagging by management.

- Providing advice on the selection of tags.

- Supplying accounts preparation software which automates the tagging process.

- Training management in XBRL tagging.

As a result of these other services, self-review and management threats may arise which will need to be assessed and safeguarded as discussed in the ethics section.

Approach to exam questions: Reporting

There are two common styles of question requirement relating to auditor's reports:

(1) Explain the implications for the auditor's report

(2) Critically appraise the suggested auditor's report.

Below are suggested approaches/considerations you can make when answering these questions.

Explain the implications for the auditor's report

(1) Materiality assessment – if the issue is not material it won't affect the auditor's report. Calculate the percentage of assets and profit the issue represents and state whether this is material or not material.

(2) Identify the type of issue

- Material misstatement – non-compliance with an accounting standard.

- Inability to obtain sufficient appropriate evidence – evidence the auditor would expect to obtain hasn't been obtained.

- Material uncertainty – significant events where the outcome will only be known in the future.

- Inconsistency with the other published information – contradiction between the financial statements and the other information which is not subject to audit e.g. directors' report, chair's statement, CSR report, etc.

- A matter that is of importance to the scope of the audit, the auditor's assessment of materiality, assessment of risk of material misstatement or other key audit matter that the auditor should specifically refer to in their report.

(3) Comment on the issue

- Which accounting standard has not been complied with and why

- Which piece of evidence has not been obtained and why

- What event/outcome is uncertain

- What is the contradiction in the unaudited information

- Explain why the auditor focused specifically on the key audit matters described in greater detail in the auditor's report e.g. involved a high degree of management judgment, required complex accounting treatment creating significant risk of material misstatement.

(4) State whether the issue is material but not pervasive or material and pervasive. If it is isolated or relatively small in impact it will be material but not pervasive. If it makes the financial statements as a whole unreliable it will be material and pervasive.

(5) Conclude on the opinion

- Unmodified if there are no material misstatements and sufficient appropriate evidence has been obtained, or

- Modified if there is material misstatement or the auditor has been unable to obtain sufficient appropriate evidence.

(6) State the name of opinion and the key wording of that opinion

- Unmodified – 'The financial statements give a true and fair view'

- Qualified – 'Except for the matter described in the basis for opinion, the financial statements give a true and fair view'

- Adverse – 'The financial statements do not give a true and fair view'

- Disclaimer – 'The auditor does not express an opinion'

Tutorial Note: Do not list every possible opinion. Select the one which is most appropriate for the situation.

(7) State any other reporting implications

- Basis for modified opinion if the opinion is modified

- Going concern section

- Emphasis of matter paragraph

- Other matter paragraph

- Requires inclusion in the Key Audit Matters section for a listed entity

- UK syllabus: Requires reporting by exception under ISAs or Companies Act.

Critically appraise the suggested auditor's report

In order to say what is wrong with the suggested report you must understand the following:

- The main elements of an auditor's report.

- The order of the paragraphs within the report.

- Appropriate titles for the opinion and basis for opinion paragraphs.

- Professional and appropriate wording and content.

- Which opinion is the appropriate one to use in the circumstances.

- When it is appropriate to use key audit matters, emphasis of matter and other matter paragraphs.

Look out for:

- Paragraphs being included in the wrong order.

- Titles of paragraphs using the wrong wording.

- Incorrect use of KAM, EOM and OM paragraphs.

- An inappropriate opinion being suggested for the issue.

- Inconsistent opinion wording with the name of the opinion e.g. adverse opinion being suggested but the wording within the opinion using 'except for' which is the wording for a qualified opinion.

- Unprofessional wording of the report in general e.g. the auditor 'feels' the financial statements 'may' be materially misstated. The auditor needs to provide greater confidence to the user than just a feeling. If the issue may be material, equally it may not be material and therefore should not be referred to in the report. The auditor needs to use their professional judgment to conclude that the issue is or is not material, they cannot sit on the fence.

- Insufficient explanation of the reason for the modification.

Test your understanding 1

You are a partner of Finbar & Sons, a firm of accountants. You are conducting a review of the draft financial statements of a major client, Holly & Ivy Co, for the year ended 31 March 20X5. According to the draft accounts revenue for the year was $125 million, profit before tax was $9 million and total assets were $100 million. The following issues have been left for your attention:

(1) The accounting policies note state that all development costs are expensed as incurred. The audit work performed shows that these costs totalled $6 million during the year and that of these $1.3 million should have been capitalised as development assets in accordance with relevant financial reporting standards.

(2) The directors of Holly & Ivy Co has, for the first time, stated its intention to publish the annual report on the company's website.

Required:

(a) Explain the implications of the above matters on the auditor's report.

(6 marks)

The audit senior has drafted the following extracts for inclusion in the auditor's report of Holly & Ivy Co:

Explanation of disclaimer of opinion in relation to development assets

The financial statements include development assets which have been expensed rather than capitalised. This deliberate omission contravenes accepted accounting practice and means that the accounts are not properly prepared.

Auditor's opinion

In our opinion, because of the highly material nature of the matter discussed above, the financial statements do not give a true and fair view of the financial position of Holly & Ivy Co as at 31 March 20X5, and of its financial performance and cash flows for the year then ended in accordance with International Financial Reporting Standards.

Emphasis of Matter Paragraph

Because of the significance of the issue, we draw attention to the note to the financial statements which describes the material misstatement in relation to development assets.

(b) Critically appraise the extracts of the draft auditor's report of Holly & Ivy Co for the year ended 31 March 20X5 prepared by the audit senior.

Note: You are NOT required to re-draft the extracts from the auditor's report. **(9 marks)**

(Total: 15 marks)

10 Communicating with those charged with governance

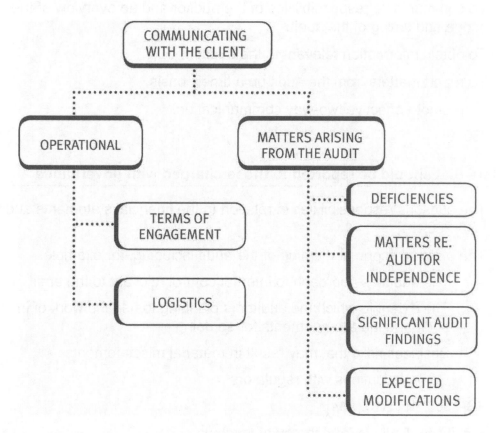

Management and those charged with governance

Those charged with governance and management are defined in ISA 260 *Communication with Those Charged With Governance* as:

 Those charged with governance

The persons with responsibility for overseeing the strategic direction of the entity and obligations related to the accountability of the entity.
[ISA 260, 10a]

This includes the directors (executive and non-executive) and the audit committee.

Management

The persons with executive responsibility for the conduct of the entity's operations. [ISA 260, 10b]

One of the areas of difficulty is that there is assumed to be a distinction between management and those charged with governance. For small and medium-sized entities and particularly for owner-managed businesses, this is often not the case.

There is a possibility, therefore, that the auditor could find themselves reporting to the owners of the business, matters already discussed with them in their capacity as management.

Reasons for communicating to those charged with governance

- To communicate responsibilities of the auditor and an overview of the scope and timing of the audit.

- To obtain information relevant to the audit.

- To report matters from the audit on a timely basis.

- To promote effective two-way communication.

[ISA 260, 9]

Matters that should be reported to those charged with governance

- The auditor's responsibilities in relation to the financial statements audit. [ISA 260, 14]

- The planned scope and timing of the audit including, for example:

  - The auditor's approach to internal control relevant to the audit

  - The extent to which the auditor is planning to use the work of internal audit and the arrangements for so doing

  - Business risks that may result in material misstatements

  - Communications with regulators.

  [ISA 260, 15, A13, A14]

- Significant findings from the audit, such as:

  - The auditor's views about qualitative aspects of the entity's accounting practices/policies

  - Significant difficulties encountered during the audit

  - Significant matters arising during the audit that were discussed with management

  - Written representations the auditor is requesting

  - Circumstances that affect the form and content of the auditor's report, if any. This includes any expected modifications to the opinion and key audit matters to be communicated in accordance with ISA 701 *Communicating Key Audit Matters in the Independent Auditor's Report*

  - Other matters that, in the auditor's opinion, are significant to the oversight of the reporting process.

  [ISA 260, 16 & A24]

- Matters of auditor independence. [ISA 260, 17]

Ultimately what constitutes a matter requiring the attention of those charged with governance is a matter of professional judgment. Typical examples include:

- Delays in obtaining information for the audit.

- An unreasonably brief time within which to complete the audit.

- Expected limitations on the audit, either imposed by management or other circumstances.

- The potential effect on the financial statements of any material risks and exposures, such as pending litigation, that are required to be disclosed in the financial statements.

- A summary of identified misstatements, whether corrected or not by the entity and a request that they are adjusted.

- Material uncertainties related to events and conditions that may cast significant doubt on the entity's ability to continue as a going concern.

- Any other matters agreed upon in the terms of the audit engagement.

Communicating deficiencies in internal control

ISA 265 *Communicating Deficiencies in Internal Control to Those Charged with Governance and Management* requires the auditor to communicate identified deficiencies in internal control that, in the auditor's judgment, are of sufficient importance to merit attention by the entity. [ISA 265, 5]

The first task of the auditor, therefore, is to distinguish between simple deficiencies, which do not require communication, and significant ones that do. Deficiencies have been defined as occurring when:

- A control is designed, implemented or operated in such a way that it is unable to prevent, or detect and correct misstatements in the financial statements on a timely basis. [ISA 265, 6ai]

- A control necessary to prevent, or detect and correct, misstatements in the financial statements on a timely basis is missing. [ISA 265, 6aii]

Significant deficiencies are those which merit the attention of those charged with governance. [ISA 265, 6b]

In their communication the auditor includes:

- A description of the deficiencies and their potential effects.

- An explanation of the purpose of the auditor (i.e. to express an opinion on the financial statements, not to help redesign internal systems).

- An explanation of why consideration of internal control is relevant to the audit.

- An explanation that the matters being reported are only those identified during the audit and considered to be significant enough to report. [ISA 265, 11]

As well as reporting to those charged with governance, the auditor should communicate deficiencies to management on a timely basis (including those significant ones reported to those charged with governance and other, less significant ones, meriting the attention of management). [ISA 265, 10]

UK syllabus

ISA (UK) *260 Communication With Those Charged With Governance:*

- Clarifies that those charged with governance are both executive and non-executive directors (or equivalent), including members of the audit committee, whereas management would not normally include non-executive directors.

- Sets out additional information that the auditors are required to report to those charged with governance:

  - Information relevant to compliance with the UK Corporate Governance Code for relevant entities.

  - Business risks relevant to financial reporting.

  - Significant accounting policies.

  - Management's valuation of material assets and liabilities and related disclosures.

  - Effectiveness of internal controls relevant to financial reporting.

  - Other business risks and effectiveness of other internal controls where the auditor has obtained an understanding of these matters.

- In respect of public interest entities, the following must be communicated:

  - Declaration of independence.

  - The quantitative level of materiality applied to perform the audit.

  - Events or conditions identified during the audit that may cast doubt over the entity's ability to continue as a going concern.

  - Significant deficiencies in the internal financial control systems and whether the deficiency has been resolved by management.

  - Significant matters involving actual or suspected non-compliance with laws and regulations.

  - Any work performed by other auditors that are not part of the same network as the audit firm.

Test your understanding 2

(a) Explain the responsibility of the auditor in respect of corresponding figures and comparatives. **(5 marks)**

(b) Libra & Leo, a small firm of chartered certified accountants, has provided audit services to Delphinus Co for many years. The company, which makes hand-crafted beds, is undergoing expansion and has recently relocated its operations. Having completed the audit of the financial statements for the year ended 31 December 20X4 and issued an unmodified opinion thereon, Libra & Leo have now indicated that they intend to withdraw from the audit.

The chief executive of Delphinus Co, Mr Pleiades, has now approached your firm to audit the financial statements for the year to 31 December 20X5. However, before inviting you to accept the nomination he has asked for your views on the following extracts from an auditors' report:

'However, the evidence available to us was limited because we were not appointed auditors of the company until January 20X5 and in consequence we were not able to attend the inventory count at 31 December 20X4. There were no satisfactory alternative means that we could adopt to confirm the amount of inventory and work- in-progress included in the preceding period's financial statements.

In our opinion, except for any adjustments that might have been found to be necessary had we been able to obtain sufficient evidence concerning inventory and work-in-progress as at 1 January 20X5, the financial statements give a true and fair view of the financial position of the Company as at 31 December 20X5, and its performance and its cash flows for the year then ended, and the notes to the financial statements, including a summary of significant accounting policies.'

Mr Pleiades has been led to understand that such a modified opinion must be given on the financial statements of Delphinus Co for the year ended 31 December 20X5, as a necessary consequence of the change in audit appointment. He is anxious to establish whether you would issue anything other than a modified opinion.

Required:

Comment on the proposed auditor's report. Your answer should consider whether and how the chief executive's concerns can be overcome. **(10 marks)**

(Total: 15 marks)

Test your understanding 3

(a) The purpose of ISA 250 *Consideration of Laws and Regulations in an Audit of Financial Statements* is to establish standards and provide guidance on the auditor's responsibility to consider laws and regulations in an audit of financial statements.

Required:

Explain the auditor's responsibilities for reporting non-compliance that comes to the auditor's attention during the conduct of an audit.

(5 marks)

(b) You are an audit manager in a firm of Chartered Certified Accountants currently assigned to the audit of Cleeves Co for the year ended 31 March 20X5. During the year Cleeves Co acquired a 100% interest in Howard Co. Howard Co is material to Cleeves Co and audited by another firm, Parr & Co. You have just received Parr & Co's draft auditor's report for the year ended 31 March 20X5.

Audit opinion

As more fully explained in notes 11 and 15 impairment losses on non-current assets have not been recognised in profit or loss as the directors are unable to quantify the amounts.

In our opinion, provision should be made for these as required by International Accounting Standard 36 (*Impairment*). If the provision had been so recognised the effect would have been to increase the loss before and after tax for the year and to reduce the value of tangible and intangible non-current assets. However, as the directors are unable to quantify the amounts we are unable to indicate the financial effect of such omissions.

In view of the failure to provide for the impairments referred to above, in our opinion the financial statements do not present fairly in all material respects the financial position of Howard Co as of 31 March 20X5 and of its loss and its cash flows for the year then ended in accordance with International Financial Reporting Standards.

Your review of the prior year auditor's report shows that the 20X4 audit opinion was worded identically.

Required:

(i) Critically appraise the appropriateness of the report extracts given by Parr & Co on the financial statements of Howard Co, for the years ended 31 March 20X5 and 20X4. **(7 marks)**

(ii) Briefly explain the implications of Parr & Co's audit opinion for your audit opinion on the consolidated financial statements of Cleeves Co for the year ended 31 March 20X5. **(3 marks)**

(Total: 15 marks)

Test your understanding 4

Mandolin Co is an unlisted medium-sized company. It has eight directors including two non-executives. The directors together own 60% of Mandolin Co's share capital. The following issues have been highlighted by the audit team during the audit:

(1) The passwords to access the accounting system are written on a sticky label on the inside of the top right-hand drawer of the finance director's desk. The finance director's office is usually locked and access is usually observable by the two personal assistants who assist the directors.

(2) The payroll clerk has access to all aspects of the payroll system and is responsible for processing changes to salary rates, tax deduction codes, and all other payroll items. No one reviews the payroll in detail, although the directors do review the management accounts that are produced promptly each month. The finance director is an experienced, qualified accountant and the CEO and one of the non-executive directors also have financial expertise.

(3) The company has used the same freight company, Trains, Planes and Automobiles Co, for despatching its goods to customers for many years. The audit team has noticed that freight costs have increased considerably as a proportion of sales revenue over the past two years.

(4) The company's inventory includes a material amount of spares inventory against which allowances are made based on a formula calculated on the basis of the period since the last inventory movement. Broadly, the longer the period since the last movement, the higher the allowance. It has emerged that any adjustments to the inventory files, whether or not they represent valid sales, are interpreted by the system as if the inventory is active and therefore current. Such adjustments might include changes of location, the scrapping of small amounts of damaged inventory, or the correction of errors.

(5) The client's system for segregating expenditure on non-current assets from repairs is haphazard. The client's staff are happy to correct mistakes uncovered by the audit team, but seem unconcerned by the distinction between capital and revenue expenditure.

Required:

For each issue, draft a suitable paragraph for inclusion in the report to management or, if appropriate, explain what other action, if any, you would take.

(15 marks)

11 Chapter summary

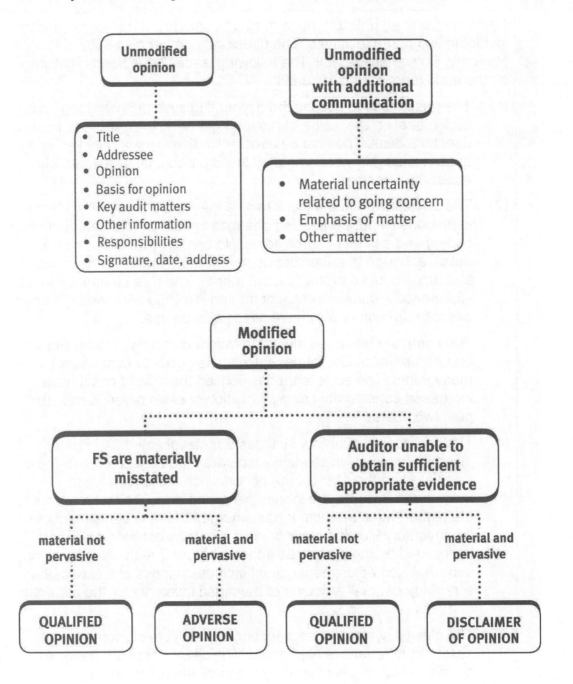

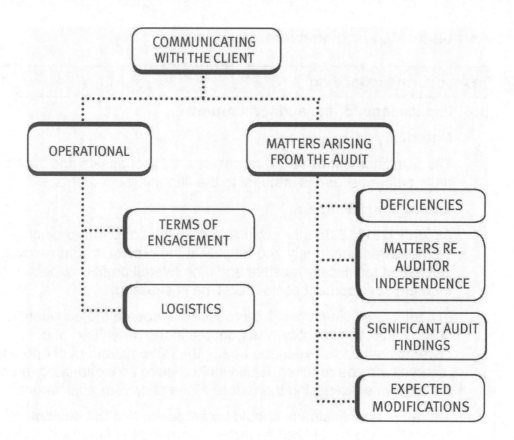

Test your understanding answers

Test your understanding 1

(a) **Implications for the auditor's report**

Materiality

The misstatement of $1.3m represents 1.3% of assets and 14.4% of profit before tax and is material to the financial statements.

Accounting treatment

According to IAS 38 *Intangible Assets*, if the costs of a project can be measured separately and reliably, if the project is commercially viable and technically feasible and if an overall profit is expected then the development costs MUST be capitalised.

In addition the directors will be required to update the accounting policy notes. If this policy was adopted in the prior year, and development costs expensed again, then a restatement of opening reserves may be required. This would require an explanatory note in the accounts discussing the nature of the prior year adjustment.

Therefore an adjustment should be proposed and the directors of Holly & Ivy Co should be requested to amend the financial statements. To achieve this the directors must restate the accounts, removing the $1.3m from the statement of profit or loss and capitalising them as intangible development costs in the statement of financial position, as per IAS 38.

Auditor's report

Failure to make the required adjustments would mean intangible assets and profits are materially understated requiring a modified opinion.

The audit opinion should be qualified 'except for' as a result of the material misstatement.

The issue is material but not pervasive as the matter is isolated to this one area of the financial statements and does not mean the financial statements as a whole are unreliable.

The 'basis for opinion' section will be amended to a 'basis for qualified opinion' and will explain the reason for the qualified opinion and quantify the extent of the misstatement.

Internet report

There is no extension to the auditor's duty of care simply because the report is being published electronically as well as in hard copy. All financial statements are publicly available. The main concern is the extent to which audited information is published on the web.

The directors may choose to exclude some parts of the financial statements. The information will need to be uploaded to the internet and information may be corrupted during this process.

The auditor must check the following:

(a)   The information uploaded is derived from the information contained in the manually signed financial statements (e.g. conversion to PDF or HTML).

(b)   The electronic copy agrees to the hard copy, by proof reading.

(c)   The auditor's signature copied onto the electronic document is protected from modification.

(d)   The conversion has not distorted the information in any way.

Most importantly, the auditor needs to make it clear in the audit opinion which information has and has not been audited (e.g. by use of page numbers).

A point should be included in the written representation that the directors acknowledge their responsibility for implementing a security system that prevents the deliberate corruption or manipulation of the electronic financial statements.

(b)   **Critical appraisal of the draft extracts**

Type of opinion

The title suggests a disclaimer of opinion is required which is not appropriate. A disclaimer of opinion is given when the auditor is unable to obtain sufficient appropriate audit evidence, which is not the case here. In this instance the auditor has identified a material misstatement in the financial statements.

The use of a disclaimer suggests that the matter is being treated as a pervasive issue. This means that the misstatement is so significant that it renders the financial statements unreliable as a whole. If this was the case then an adverse opinion would be given. However, whilst the error represents 14% of profit before tax and 1.3% of total assets and is material, it is unlikely to be pervasive. With full knowledge of the error, the users should still be able to rely on the other information contained in the financial statements as there is no indication of further misstatement.

In this instance, a qualified 'except for' opinion would be expressed on the basis of a failure to comply with the relevant financial reporting standard.

The audit opinion should not refer to the misstatement being 'highly material' as this is subjective. The type of opinion will indicate whether the misstatement is material but not pervasive or material and pervasive. It is unlikely that a misstatement of 14% of profit before tax is considered 'highly material'.

Paragraph titles

The title of the basis for opinion paragraph should not refer to the details that are included within the paragraph itself. In this case, because a qualified opinion is appropriate, the title should be 'Basis for Qualified Opinion'.

The title of the opinion paragraph should state the type of opinion being expressed. This should say 'Qualified Opinion'.

Paragraph order

In an auditor's report, the opinion should be positioned before the basis for opinion paragraph. The opinion will state the auditor's conclusion relating to the fair presentation of the financial statements and if the opinion is modified, the basis for opinion will provide the explanation of why the opinion is modified.

In this extract, the opinion is shown after the basis for opinion and therefore the paragraph order should be changed.

Description of the misstatement

The basis for qualified opinion should provide the user with sufficient information to enable them to understand the issue and the financial impact.

In the extracts there is no reference to the relevant accounting standard that has not been complied with (IAS 38 *Intangible Assets*) and there is no quantification of the misstatement and the impact to the financial statements.

Suggested emphasis of matter

The emphasis of matter paragraph is not required in this situation. An Emphasis of Matter paragraph should be used to draw the user's attention to a matter appropriately disclosed in the financial statements which is fundamental to the user's understanding of those financial statements. An Emphasis of Matter paragraph should not be used to refer to the nature of a modification to the audit opinion as this information is included in the 'Basis for Qualified Opinion' paragraph.

Unprofessional wording

The use of the word 'deliberate' when describing the misstatement is not professional and sounds accusatory. It may also not be correct as an adjustment may have been suggested by the audit firm and may be being considered by management.

Test your understanding 2

It is important that you should not make issues out of information given in a question which is not relevant to answering the question set.

For example, this question refers to a predecessor auditor. Addressing or speculating upon the reasons for the change will not earn marks because (i) it is not relevant; (ii) the tone of the introductory paragraph ('expansion', 'relocation', 'unmodified opinion') does not suggest anything untoward about the change.

(a) Corresponding figures

Amounts and disclosures derived from preceding financial statements are included with, and are intended to be read in relation to, the current period figures. When comparatives are presented as corresponding figures they are not specifically identified in an auditor's report because the audit opinion is on the current period financial statements as a whole, including the corresponding figures.

For initial engagements, the auditor seeks to obtain sufficient, appropriate audit evidence to confirm that:

- Opening balances do not contain misstatements that materially affect the current period's financial statements

- Prior period closing balances have been properly brought forward as the current period's opening balances

- Accounting policies have been consistently applied.

The auditor must be satisfied with the opening position. A new auditor, however, has not previously obtained audit evidence to support transactions and accounting policies of the prior period.

To obtain the necessary assurance on the opening position, additional procedures can be performed, for example:

- Review of working papers and accounting records for the previous year-end kept by the client's management or obtained from the previous auditor.

- Audit work on the current year's transactions and balances will also provide some evidence to support the completeness, valuation, existence and rights or obligations of the opening balances.

In rare circumstances, if these procedures are unsatisfactory, some of the opening balances may need to be substantively tested in order to form an opinion on them.

If the scope of a new auditor's work with respect to the opening position is effectively limited, the lack of audit evidence may result in a modification of the audit opinion.

(b)   Proposed auditors' report

If it is not possible to form an opinion on a material matter, due to lack of evidence, a modified opinion ('except for' qualification or disclaimer) will be required.

The fact that an auditor was not previously appointed to perform procedures on the prior period closing balances is not grounds for modification. For example, a new auditor does not obtain direct confirmations in respect of prior period trade receivable balances, but that does not mean that he cannot form an opinion about the opening trade receivables balance.

Inventory is likely to be a very significant balance in a manufacturing business such as Delphinus Co. It will be more difficult to form an opinion on the opening balance if:

– inventory is not accounted for in the double-entry bookkeeping system

– inventory records are not maintained

– quantities are ascertained by a year-end physical count

– values of work-in-progress, slow-moving and damaged items are a matter of judgment.

Where a modification is warranted (e.g. because sufficient evidence regarding opening inventory quantities cannot be ascertained by alternative means) the 'except for' opinion is a modification of the opinion on the current period's result (i.e. profit or loss) only and not its financial position.

For Delphinus Co, it is likely that sufficient evidence will be available to a new auditor in respect of inventory. In particular:

– Inventory quantities as at 31 December 20X4 and the valuation thereof should be available from Delphinus Co (if Delphinus Co does not have this, Mr Pleaides would be able to request a copy from Libra and Leo).

– Hand-crafted beds are not small or inexpensive items, therefore the auditor will be able to compare quantities as at 31 December 20X5 with those of the prior year.

– Gross profit margins might be expected to be relatively stable, so if opening inventory was materially overstated the current year margin would be deflated and the prior year inflated.

How to overcome chief executive's concerns

Audit procedures such as those outlined above should be undertaken to confirm the opening position. In particular:

– Reviewing prior year-end inventory sheets and comparing quantities of raw materials, WIP and finished beds.

– Comparison of key ratios (e.g. gross profit percentages and inventory turnover) and the relative proportions of raw materials, WIP and finished beds.

Such analytical procedures would take into account known fluctuations which, in the case of Delphinus Co, would arise through recent acquisitions.

To assist the audit, Mr Pleaides should ensure that the following information is readily available:

– Records of physical inventory taking at 31 December 20X4.

– Full details of write-downs and allowances for slow-moving inventory.

– Adjustments, if any, requested to be made by Libra & Leo.

– Analysis of revenue by business segment.

Libra & Leo should make their working papers available to their successor as a matter of professional courtesy.

Whether the chief executive's concerns can be overcome

The change in audit appointment does not necessitate a modified auditor's opinion. For a company such as Delphinus Co, minimal additional procedures should provide sufficient appropriate evidence over the opening position including that of inventory.

However, it is not possible to state, unequivocally, that an unmodified opinion will be issued (since the audit has yet to be performed). If, for example, a material misstatement was to arise in respect of the current year, the auditor would need to report this to the members.

Tutorial note: To agree that the proposed modification is unavoidable or, at the other extreme, promising an unmodified opinion without any reservation would not be a professional stance.

Test your understanding 3

(a) **Reporting non-compliance**

Non-compliance refers to acts of omission or commission by the entity being audited, either intentional or unintentional, that are contrary to the prevailing laws or regulations.

To management

Non-compliance that comes to the auditor's attention should be communicated to management.

If the auditor suspects that members of senior management are involved in non-compliance, the auditor should report the matter to those charged with governance.

Where no higher authority exists, or if the auditor believes that the report may not be acted upon, or is unsure as to the person to whom to report, the auditor should seek legal advice.

To the users of the auditor's report on the financial statements

If the auditor concludes that the non-compliance has a material effect on the financial statements, and has not been properly reflected in the financial statements, the auditor should express a qualified ('except for') or an adverse opinion.

If the auditor is precluded by the entity from obtaining sufficient appropriate audit evidence to evaluate whether or not non-compliance that may be material to the financial statements has (or is likely to have) occurred, the auditor should express an 'except for' qualified opinion or a disclaimer of opinion on the financial statements due to being unable to obtain sufficient appropriate evidence.

To regulatory and enforcement authorities

The auditor's duty of confidentiality ordinarily precludes reporting of confidential information to a third party. However, in circumstances such as these, the duty of confidentiality is likely to be overridden by a professional duty to disclose. In some countries the auditor is required to report non-compliance to a regulatory authority. The auditor should also give due consideration to the auditor's responsibility to report non-compliance in the public interest.

(b) (i) **Appropriateness of audit opinion**

Heading

The opinion paragraph is not properly headed. It does not state the form of the opinion that has been given.

The opinion 'the financial statements do not give a true and fair view' is an 'adverse' opinion.

The opinion paragraph should be headed 'Adverse Opinion'.

Content

It is not appropriate that the opinion paragraph should refer to the note(s) in the financial statements where the matter giving rise to the modification is more fully explained. This should be included in the 'Basis for...' paragraph.

The 'Basis for...' paragraph should include:

–   The reason for impairment.

–   Quantification of the effect. The maximum possible loss would be the carrying amount of the non-current assets identified as impaired.

It is not clear why the directors have been 'unable to quantify the amounts'. Since impairments should be quantifiable, any inability suggests an inability to gather sufficient appropriate evidence, in which case a qualified or disclaimer of opinion should be issued on grounds of lack of evidence rather than material misstatement.

That 'provision should be made', but has not, should be clearly stated as non-compliance with IAS 36. The title of IAS 36 *Impairment of Assets* should be given in full.

The wording is confusing. There must be sufficient evidence to support a claim of material misstatement. Although the directors cannot quantify the amounts it seems the auditor must have been able to (estimate at least) in order to form an opinion that the amounts involved are sufficiently material to warrant a modification.

The first paragraph refers to non-current assets. The second paragraph specifies tangible and intangible assets. There is no explanation why, or how, both tangible and intangible assets are impaired.

The first paragraph refers to profit or loss and the second and third paragraphs to loss. It may be clearer if the first paragraph referred to recognition in the statement of profit or loss.

It is not clear why the failure to recognise impairment warrants an adverse opinion rather than 'except for'. The effects of non-compliance with IAS 36 are to overstate the carrying amount(s) of non-current assets (that can be specified) and to understate the loss. The matter does not appear to be pervasive and so an adverse opinion looks unsuitable as the financial statements as a whole are not incomplete or misleading. A loss is already being reported so it is not that a reported profit would be turned into a loss which is sometimes judged to be pervasive.

Prior year

As the 20X4 auditor's report included an adverse opinion, and the matter that gave rise to the modification is unresolved, the 20X5 opinion should also be modified regarding the corresponding figures (ISA 710 *Comparative Information – Corresponding Figures and Comparative Financial Statements*).

The 20X5 auditor's report does not refer to the prior period modification nor highlight that the matter resulting in the current period modification is not new. For example, the report could say 'As previously reported and as more fully explained in notes ....' and state 'increase the loss by $x (20X4 – $y)'.

(ii) **Implications for audit opinion on consolidated financial statements of Cleeves Co**

As Howard Co is wholly-owned, the management of Cleeves Co must be able to request that Howard Co's financial statements are adjusted to reflect the impairment of the assets which will mean the material misstatements no longer exist and the opinion can be unmodified.

If the potential adjustments to non-current asset carrying amounts and loss are not made to the financial statements of Howard Co, the misstatements may not be material to the consolidated financial statements, in which case there will be no implication for the audit opinion of Cleeves Co.

If the impairment losses are not recognised in Howard Co's financial statements they can nevertheless be adjusted on consolidation (by writing down the assets to their recoverable amounts). The audit opinion on Cleeves Co should then be unmodified in this respect.

> If there is no adjustment of Howard Co's asset values (either in Howard Co's financial statements or on consolidation) it is most likely that the audit opinion on Cleeves Co's consolidated financial statements would be qualified 'except for'.
>
> It is unlikely to require an adverse opinion as it is doubtful whether the opinion on Howard Co's financial statements should be adverse.

Test your understanding 4

(1) This issue should initially be addressed by discussion with the finance director.

If there is a real risk of abuse, this may indicate a lack of controls throughout the company, which should be brought to the attention of those charged with governance.

A possible paragraph for the management letter might be:

'We found a number of instances where the passwords giving access to the company's accounting systems were written down and kept in accessible locations.

We recommend that passwords should always be kept confidential to the intended user. Ideally passwords should be memorised. If this is not feasible, a password management system should be used.'

(2) It is possible that the budgetary controls operated by the board in reviewing the management accounts are sufficient for the detection of possible abuse of the payroll system. If not, the following might be appropriate:

'The payroll clerk has sole control of the payroll system and puts all changes into effect. This provides opportunity to create fictitious employees in the payroll system and commit fraud causing loss to the company.

In our view, the monthly review of the management accounts conducted by the board is insufficiently detailed to detect modest abuses of the system, which, although unlikely to be material on an individual basis, could amount to substantial sums over time.

We recommend that before the instruction to make the monthly transfers is given to the bank, the payroll should be reviewed in detail by either the finance director or the CEO.'

(3) 'We draw your attention to the fact that Trains, Planes and Automobiles Co has been the sole contractor for the company's outward freight business for a number of years.

We have noted that freight charges as a proportion of sales revenue have increased at the rate of x% per annum on average over the past five years and may not be giving best value for money.

We recommend that you consider asking Trains, Planes and Automobiles Co to review their charges, or invite tenders for the business from other companies.'

(4) We have identified a flaw in the operation of the spares inventory system, which has led to an overstatement of spares inventory that we estimate to be $x at the year-end (PY $x). The impact on operating profit for the current year was $x (PY $x).

The errors have arisen because the system recognises any adjustment to spares inventory as a movement on inventory and therefore treats the relevant inventory lines as being current, even though the movements may be minor technical adjustments or even write-downs.

Although the impact on profit is not material year on year, it is possible that the cumulative overstatement of spares inventory values is material.

We recommend that management investigate further the actual level of the overstatement of spares inventory, and take immediate steps to ensure that only valid sales of inventory are recognised as movements for the purpose of deciding whether or not a particular line of inventory is current.

(5) Misallocations between capital and revenue expenditure tend to have tax implications, so the concept of audit materiality may not be relevant.

Possible wording might be:

'We have identified $x of capital expenditure which has been incorrectly treated as repairs. Such errors have an equal impact on the company's profit for the year, which in turn impacts its tax liability.

We recommend that your accounts staff should receive training about the impact of tax sensitive expenditure so that such misallocations do not occur in the future.'

Audit-related services

Chapter learning objectives

This chapter covers syllabus areas:

- F1 – Audit-related and assurance services

- F5a – Analyse the form and content of the professional accountant's report for an assurance engagement as compared with an auditor's report

- F5c – Discuss the effectiveness of the 'negative assurance' form of reporting and evaluate situations in which it may be appropriate to modify a conclusion.

Detailed syllabus objectives are provided in the introduction section of the text book.

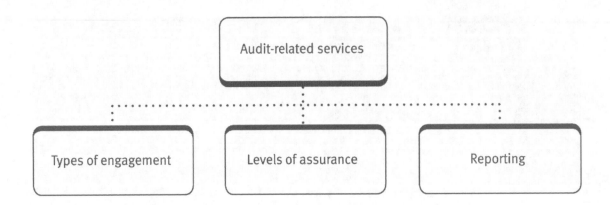

Audit-related services

Types of engagement

Levels of assurance

Reporting

 The key concepts and definitions of assurance engagements were covered in Audit and Assurance at the Applied Skills level and are revised here.

 Exam focus

There will often be one question in the exam that will test your ability to apply your knowledge to a non-audit engagement. The question could cover any area of the engagement process – acceptance, planning, procedures or reporting.

1 Audit-related services

 Audit-related services are those services that professional accountants offer which are not statutory audits, although they are conceptually related and use similar skills.

 An **assurance engagement** is an engagement in which a practitioner obtains sufficient appropriate evidence in order to express a conclusion designed to enhance the degree of confidence of the intended users other than the responsible party about the outcome of the evaluation or measurement of a subject matter against criteria.

[International Framework for Assurance Engagements, 7]

 Agreed upon procedures require the accountant to report on factual findings based upon the procedures agreed with the client and any appropriate third parties, hence no assurance (conclusion) is expressed.

Non-audit engagements include:

Assurance engagements

- Review of interim financial statements

- Due diligence review

- Examination of prospective financial information

- Social and environmental information review.

Agreed upon procedures

- Forensic audit: Fraud investigation

- Forensic audit: Verifying an insurance claim

- Due diligence.

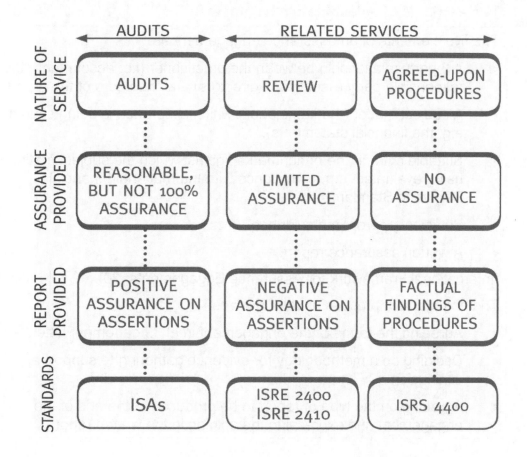

Differences between an audit and audit-related services

	Audit	Audit-related services
Level of assurance	Reasonable assurance	Either limited or no assurance
Scope of work	Established by the auditor in accordance with auditing standards	Established in consultation with client, in accordance with assurance and related services standards
Wording of assurance/other reports	Positive assurance	Negative or no assurance
Required by	Law in many countries	Usually not required by law

The elements of an assurance engagement

The five elements of an assurance engagement are:

- A 3 party relationship between the practitioner (i.e. accountant), the responsible party (usually the directors) and the users of the report.

- A subject matter (the items about which assurance is being sought, e.g. the financial statements).

- Suitable criteria (the benchmarks against which the subject matter is being evaluated, e.g. compliance with International Financial Reporting Standards).

- Sufficient appropriate evidence.

- A written assurance report.

[International Framework for Assurance Engagements, 20]

The engagement process usually involves:

- Agreeing the terms of the engagement in an engagement letter.

- Deciding on a methodology for evidence gathering to support a conclusion.

- Agreeing on the type of report to be produced at the end of the engagement and expressing the opinion in the written report.

Professional standards for audit-related services

IAASB issues specific guidance for other services:

- International Standards on Review Engagements (ISREs)
- International Standards on Related Services (ISRSs)
- International Standards on Assurance Engagements (ISAEs)

Specific examples include:

- ISRE 2400 (Revised) *Engagements to Review Historical Financial Statements*.
- ISRE 2410 *Review of Interim Financial Information Performed by the Independent Auditor of the Entity*.
- ISAE 3000 (Revised) *Assurance Engagements Other than Audits or Reviews of Historical Financial Statements*.
- ISAE 3420 *Assurance Engagements to Report on the Compilation of Pro Forma Financial Information Included in a Prospectus*.
- ISRS 4400 *Engagements to Perform Agreed-Upon Procedures Regarding Financial Information*.
- ISRS 4410 (Revised) Compilation *Engagements.*

2 Levels of assurance

The Framework provides the overall guidance for carrying out assurance engagements such as audits and reviews. It permits only two types of assurance engagement to be performed: either a 'reasonable assurance' or a 'limited assurance' engagement.

Reasonable assurance

The objective of a reasonable assurance engagement is where the practitioner reduces engagement risk to an acceptably low level to conclude that the subject matter conforms in all material respects with identified suitable criteria.

The accountant expresses their conclusion in a **positive form**, giving an opinion on whether the subject matter is free from material misstatement, e.g. statutory audit.

Limited assurance

The objective of a limited assurance engagement is to obtain sufficient appropriate evidence to be able to state whether anything has come to the practitioner's attention that causes them to believe the subject matter is materially misstated.

In other words the subject matter 'appears plausible' in the circumstances.

The accountant expresses their conclusion in a **negative form**, stating that their procedures have not identified any material misstatement of the subject matter, e.g. a review engagement.

The procedures for a limited assurance engagement are therefore less comprehensive than for a reasonable assurance engagement.

No assurance (agreed upon procedures)

The objective of an agreed upon procedures engagement is to perform the procedures requested by the client and report the findings on a factual basis.

The client forms their own conclusion based on the results of the work.

3 Reporting

The assurance report should include the following elements:

- Title – clearly indicating the report is an independent assurance report.

- Addressee – identifies the intended user.

- Identification and description of the subject matter including period of the information, name of the entity to which the subject matter relates.

- Identification of the criteria.

- Description of any significant, inherent limitations.

- Restriction on the use of the report to specific users.

- Statement of responsibilities of the responsible party and practitioner.

- Statement that the engagement was performed in accordance with professional standards.

- Summary of the work performed.

- Practitioner's conclusion.

- Date.

- Name of the firm or practitioner and location.

[ISAE 3000 (Revised), 69]

Assurance conclusion

Unmodified

The conclusion of an assurance report will be unmodified if nothing has come to the practitioner's attention to suggest the subject matter has not been prepared in accordance with the criteria. [ISAE 3000 (Revised), 72b]

If the practitioner wants to highlight a matter to the intended user, this can be done using an Emphasis of Matter paragraph or Other Matter paragraph in the same way as the auditor's report. [ISAE 3000 (Revised), 73]

Modified

A modified conclusion will be expressed if:

- There has been a scope limitation which means the practitioner has not obtained sufficient appropriate evidence to be able to form a conclusion on the subject matter.

- The subject matter is materially misstated.

The modifications are the same as for an auditor's report:

- Qualified – if the effects of the matter are not pervasive.

- Adverse – if the subject matter is not prepared in accordance with the criteria and the effects are pervasive.

- Disclaimer – if the practitioner has not been able to obtain sufficient appropriate evidence to form a conclusion and the effect is pervasive.

[ISAE 3000 (Revised), 74]

Basis for conclusion

If the conclusion is modified, a basis for qualified/adverse/disclaimer of conclusion will be included to explain the circumstances causing the modification.

Illustration 1 – Example of an unmodified review report

A company which does not require a statutory audit may decide to have a review of its financial statements in order to provide some assurance over, and improve the credibility of, those financial statements.

'The objective of a review of financial statements is to obtain limited assurance by performing inquiry and analytical procedures, about whether the financial statements as a whole are free from material misstatement, enabling the practitioner to express a conclusion, on whether anything has come to the practitioner's attention that causes the practitioner to believe that the financial statements are not prepared, in all material respects, in accordance with an applicable financial reporting framework.'
[ISRE 2400 (Revised) *Engagements to Review Historical Financial Statements*, 14a]

The following report illustration is taken from ISRE 2400 Appendix 2, Illustration 1:

INDEPENDENT PRACTITIONER'S REVIEW REPORT TO ... ...

Report on the Financial Statements

We have reviewed the accompanying financial statements of ABC Company, which comprise the statement of financial position as at December 31, 20X1, and the statement of comprehensive income, statement of changes in equity and statement of cash flows for the year then ended, and a summary of significant accounting policies and other explanatory information.

Management's Responsibility for the Financial Statements

Management is responsible for the preparation of these financial statements in accordance with International Financial Reporting Standards, and for such internal control as management determines is necessary to enable the preparation of financial statements that are free from material misstatement, whether due to fraud or error.

Practitioner's Responsibility

Our responsibility is to express a conclusion on the accompanying financial statements. We conducted our review in accordance with the International Standard on Review Engagements 2400 (Revised) *Engagements to Review Historical Financial Statements*. ISRE 2400 (Revised) requires us to conclude whether anything has come to our attention that causes us to believe that the financial statements, taken as a whole, are not prepared in all material respects in accordance with the applicable financial reporting framework. This standard also requires us to comply with relevant ethical requirements.

A review of financial statements in accordance with ISRE 2400 (Revised) is a limited assurance engagement. The practitioner performs procedures primarily consisting of making inquiries of management and others within the entity, as appropriate, and applying analytical procedures, and evaluates the evidence obtained.

The procedures performed in a review are substantially less than those performed in an audit conducted in accordance with International Standards on Auditing. Accordingly, we do not express an audit opinion on these financial statements.

Conclusion

Based on our review, nothing has come to our attention that causes us to believe that these financial statements do not present fairly, in all material respects, (or 'do not give a true and fair view') the financial position of ABC Company as at December 31, 20X1, and of its financial performance and cash flows for the year then ended, in accordance with International Financial Reporting Standards.

Signature

Date

Address

Illustration 2 – Example of a qualified conclusion

Based on our review, except for the effects of the matter described in the Basis for Qualified Conclusion paragraph, nothing has come to our attention that causes us to believe that the financial statements of ABC Company are not prepared, in all material respects, in accordance with the Financial Reporting Framework.

[International Standard on Review Engagements 2400 (Revised) *Engagements to Review Historical Financial Statements*, Appendix 2, Illustration 2]

Provision of other assurance services

The auditor is in a strong position to carry out additional assurance services for their clients as they are already familiar with the company, its operations and systems and controls in operation.

In practice, the skills required to offer a comprehensive range of assurance services means that only the largest firms can offer a complete range of services to clients. Other firms still offer these services and many specialise in certain areas.

The implications of assurance services being provided by auditors are wide-ranging:

- There will be further pressures on the audit firm to maintain independence as the proportion of fees earned from non-audit work continues to grow and the self-review threat increases.

- Practitioners specialising in a range of disciplines (e.g. IT systems, public sector specialists, etc.) will be needed in the firm as well as traditional financial auditors.

- Many assurance services involve reporting on risk (operational, financial, environmental, etc.). Reporting on such matters will increase the auditor's exposure to professional liability claims.

- Clients may be willing to pay for value-adding assurance services but correspondingly less willing to pay for the statutory audit where they perceive less value for their money putting pressure on audit fees.

Attestation and direct engagements

The framework also permits assurance engagements to be performed as either an **attestation** engagement or a **direct** engagement.

In an **attestation engagement**, the accountant's conclusion relates to an assertion made by the party who is responsible for the subject matter. The accountant can either express a conclusion about this assertion, or can provide a conclusion about the subject matter.

In a **direct engagement**, the accountant expresses a conclusion on the subject matter based on identified criteria, regardless of whether the responsible party has made a written assertion on the subject matter. [ISAE 3000 (Revised), 2]

For example: a professional accountant may be engaged to report on a company's internal financial controls.

Attestation engagement	Direct engagement
Management make a written assertion about the effectiveness of the company's control structure. Care must be taken to ensure that management's assertion is clearly understandable and is not subjective. For example, an assertion that the control structure is 'very effective' would be unacceptable since this is a subjective opinion. The accountant gives an opinion on management's assertion.	The accountant simply reports directly on the effectiveness of the control structure in accordance with predetermined performance criteria.

4 Chapter summary

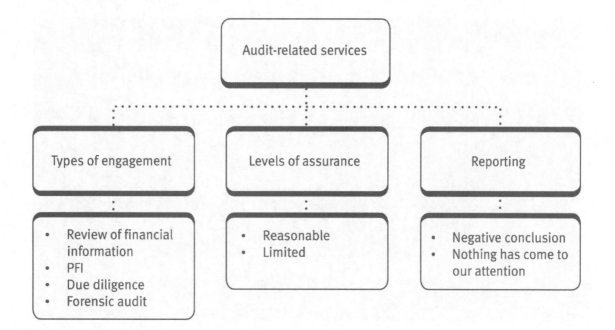

Review of interim financial information

Chapter learning objectives

This chapter covers syllabus areas:

- F2 – Specific assignments: Review of interim financial information

Detailed syllabus objectives are provided in the introduction section of the text book.

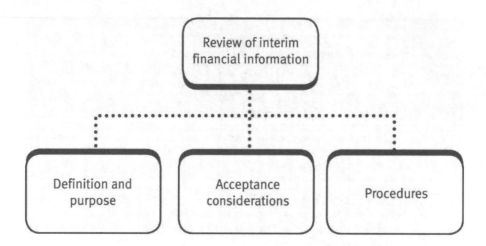

1 Review of interim financial information

In many countries, listed companies are required to publish a half-yearly interim report containing a summarised statement of profit or loss for the first six months of the financial year, as well as certain statement of financial position information and notes.

Companies may choose to, or be required to, have this report reviewed by the company's auditors.

Objective of a review of interim financial information

'The objective of an engagement to review interim financial information is to enable the auditor to express a conclusion whether, on the basis of the review, anything has come to the auditor's attention that causes the auditor to believe that the interim financial information is not prepared, in all material respects, in accordance with an applicable financial reporting framework.'
[ISRE 2410 *Review of Interim Financial Information Performed by the Independent Auditor of the Entity*, 7]

2 Acceptance considerations

In order to express a conclusion on the interim financial information the assurance provider will require a good understanding of the company.

The external auditor is likely to have the greatest understanding of the entity therefore would be best placed to provide this service. Therefore if the company approaches a different firm to provide this service the firm should consider reasons for this.

The engagement is likely to be a recurring engagement. Therefore the engagement fees will need to be considered when assessing fee dependency.

The acceptance matters covered in Chapter 6 should also be considered.

3 Planning and performing the engagement

Main principles of the review engagement

To ensure an appropriate standard of work is performed, practitioners should:

- Comply with ethical requirements.

- Implement appropriate quality control procedures.

- Consider whether the engagement should be accepted, such as whether the practitioner has the necessary competence and available resources.

- Plan and perform the review with an attitude of professional scepticism.

[ISRE 2410, 4 – 6]

Procedures

The accountant must carry out sufficient work to enable them to express limited assurance on the interim financial information.

This involves:

- Identifying the types of potential material misstatements and the likelihood of them occurring.

- Performing procedures such as:

    - Enquiries of relevant parties (usually management)

    - Analytical procedures

    - Other review procedures to obtain sufficient appropriate evidence.

[ISRE 2410, 12]

Analytical procedures should be designed to identify relationships and individual items that appear unusual. Such procedures might include:

- Comparison of the current financial statements vs. prior periods.

- Comparison of the current financial statements vs. forecasts or budgets.

- Review for any relationships within the financial statements that would be expected to conform to a predictable pattern based on previous patterns for the entity or industry norms:

    - Gross profit margin

    - Net profit margin

    - Interest cover

    - Receivables collection period

    - Payables payment period

    - Inventory holding period.

ISRE 2410 Detailed procedures

ISRE 2410 procedures:

- Reading prior year files relating to the audit and interim financial statement review to enable the auditor to identify matters that may affect the current period interim financial information.

- Considering any significant risks, including the risk of management override of controls that were identified in the audit of the prior year's financial statements.

- Reading the most recent annual and comparable prior period interim financial information.

- Considering materiality with reference to the applicable financial reporting framework as it relates to interim financial information, to assist in determining the nature and extent of the procedures to be performed and evaluating the effect of misstatements.

- Considering the nature of any corrected material misstatements and any identified uncorrected immaterial misstatements in the prior year's financial statements.

- Considering significant financial accounting and reporting matters that may be of continuing significance such as significant deficiencies in internal control.

- Considering the results of any audit procedures performed with respect to the current year's financial statements.

- Considering the results of any internal audit performed and the subsequent actions taken by management.

- Enquiring of management about the results of management's assessment of the risk that the interim financial information may be materially misstated as a result of fraud.

- Enquiring of management about the effect of changes in the entity's business activities.

- Enquiring of management about any significant changes in internal control and the potential effect of any such changes on the preparation of interim financial information.

- Enquiring of management of the process by which the interim financial information has been prepared and the reliability of the underlying accounting records to which the interim financial information is agreed or reconciled.

[ISRE 2410, 15]

Written representations

A written representation should be obtained which confirms that management:

- is responsible for internal control to prevent and detect fraud and error.

- has prepared the interim financial information in accordance with the applicable financial reporting framework.

- believe that the uncorrected misstatements are immaterial.

- has disclosed to the auditor:

  - all significant facts relating to fraud or suspected fraud.

  - results of its assessment of risk of material misstatement of the interim financial information.

  - any known or possible non-compliance with laws and regulations.

  - all significant subsequent events that may require adjustment or disclosure.

[ISRE 2410, 34]

Illustration 1 – Example of an unmodified review report

Report on Review of Interim Financial Information

(Appropriate addressee)

Introduction

We have reviewed the accompanying balance sheet of ABC Entity as of March 31, 20X1 and the related statements of income, changes in equity and cash flows for the three-month period then ended, and a summary of significant accounting policies and other explanatory notes.

Management is responsible for the preparation and fair presentation of this interim financial information in accordance with International Financial Reporting Standards. Our responsibility is to express a conclusion on this interim financial information based on our review.

Scope of review

We conducted our review in accordance with the International Standard on Review Engagements 2410 *Review of Interim Financial Information Performed by the Independent Auditor of the Entity*. A review of interim financial information consists of making inquiries, primarily of persons responsible for financial and accounting matters, and applying analytical and other review procedures. A review is substantially less in scope than an audit conducted in accordance with International Standards on Auditing and consequently does not enable us to obtain assurance that we would become aware of all significant matters that might be identified in an audit. Accordingly, we do not express an audit opinion.

Conclusion

Based on our review, nothing has come to our attention that causes us to believe that the accompanying interim financial information does not give a true and fair view (or 'does not present fairly, in all material respects'), the financial position of the entity as at March 31, 20X1, and of its financial performance and its cash flows for the three-month period then ended in accordance with International Financial Reporting Standards.

Signature of auditor

Date

Address

[International Standard on Review Engagements 2410 *Review of Interim Financial Information Performed by the Independent Auditor of the Entity*, Appendix 4]

Test your understanding 1

Describe the procedures that should be performed when reviewing interim financial statements.

(5 marks)

4 Chapter summary

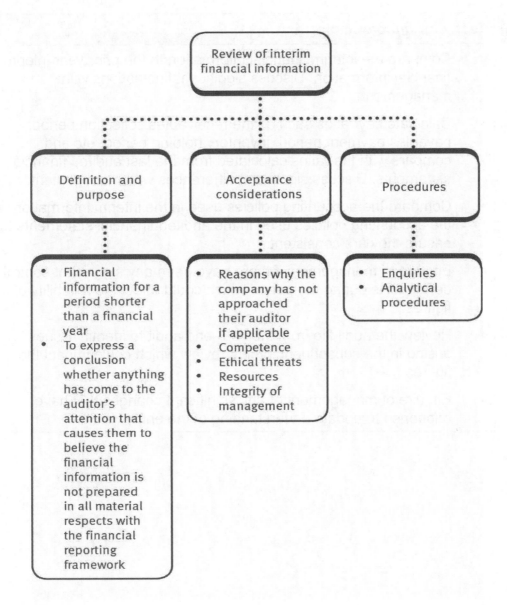

Test your understanding answers

Test your understanding 1

- Compare the interim financial information to the prior year interim financial information. Discuss significant fluctuations with management.

- Calculate key ratios such as the receivables collection period, payables payment period, inventory holding period, etc and compare with the ratios calculated from the last audited financial statements. Discuss significant differences with management.

- Compare the accounting policies used in the interim information with the accounting policies used in the audited financial statements to ensure they are consistent.

- Enquire of management if there have been any significant control deficiencies during the period which could affect the reliability of the figures.

- Review the audit file from the year-end audit to identify issues arising in the subsequent events review which could impact the figures.

- Enquire of management of any significant changes that have happened to update understanding of the entity.

Prospective financial information

Chapter learning objectives

This chapter covers syllabus areas:

- F2 – Specific assignments: Prospective financial information
- F5b – Discuss the content of a report for an examination of prospective financial information.

Detailed syllabus objectives are provided in the introduction section of the text book.

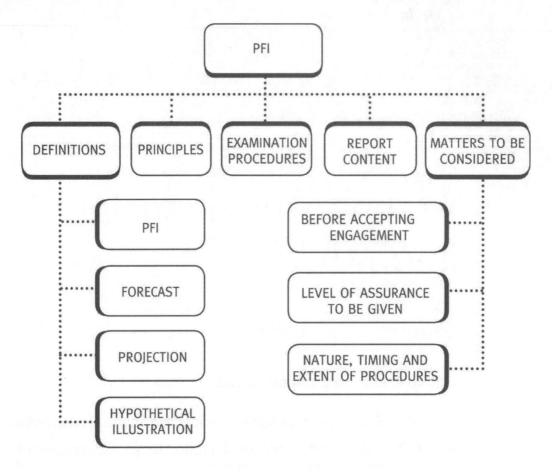

 Exam focus

Examination of projections and forecasts feature regularly in the exam. This is usually in the context of supporting a loan application, or as part of a going concern assessment for an audit. As the transactions haven't happened yet, procedures will focus on testing the reasonableness of the assumptions management has used when preparing the forecast.

1 What is prospective financial information (PFI)?

A reporting accountant may be asked to give an assurance opinion on prospective (i.e. future) financial information. Guidance on examining PFI is given in ISAE 3400 *The Examination of Prospective Financial Information*.

 Definitions

Prospective financial information means financial information based on assumptions about events that may occur in the future and possible actions by an entity. It may be in the form of a forecast or a projection, or a combination of both. [ISAE 3400, 3]

Forecast

PFI prepared on the basis of assumptions as to future events that management expects to take place and the actions management expects to take (best-estimate assumptions). [ISAE 3400, 4]

Projection

PFI prepared on the basis of hypothetical assumptions about future events and management actions that are not necessarily expected to take place, or a mixture of best-estimate and hypothetical assumptions. [ISAE 3400, 5]

A hypothetical illustration is a depiction of anticipated outcomes based on uncertain future events and actions.

Types of forecast

Profit forecast

A profit forecast shows expected revenues and costs prepared on an accruals basis in the same way as a statement of profit or loss.

Forecast revenues will include amounts for sales expected to be made during the forecast period regardless of whether the customer is expected to pay for the goods during the forecast period.

Depreciation will be included based on the expected level of assets held during the forecast period calculated using the company's usual depreciation rate.

Cash flow forecast

A cash flow forecast shows expected cash payments and receipts reflecting the amount and timing of the expected cash flows.

Forecast receipts will take into consideration payment terms given to customers and expected irrecoverable debts (an irrecoverable debt will not result in a cash inflow).

Depreciation is not a cash expense therefore will not appear in a cash flow forecast. Instead a payment to acquire an asset will be included as a cash outflow and proceeds from the disposal of an asset will be included as a cash inflow.

> ## Principles of useful PFI
>
> PFI can be issued:
>
> - as an internal management tool, e.g. to support a possible capital investment, or
>
> - for distribution to third parties in, for example:
>
>   - In a prospectus
>
>   - In an annual report
>
>   - To inform lenders or to support an application for finance.
>
>   [ISAE 3400, 6]
>
> Ultimately the usefulness of PFI depends on the requirements of the end user. Consider, for example, the different decisions and information needs of a prospective lender and shareholder. The unifying qualities of good PFI are that reports must:
>
> - Address the specific needs of the user
>
> - Be prepared on a timely basis to enable decisions to be taken.

2   Acceptance considerations

As with any engagement, the reporting accountant must consider the risk of involvement with the PFI prior to accepting the engagement. The greater the risk of giving an inappropriate report, the greater the risk of legal claims and loss of reputation. Ultimately, if the risk is too high, the engagement should be politely declined.

ISAE 3400, para 10 requires the reporting accountant to consider the following:

Matter under consideration	Reason
The intended use of the information, such as internal management or external users.	Information for external use will be relied upon by third parties, potentially for making investment decisions. This makes it riskier for the accountant because the consequences of issuing an inappropriate report will be more severe.
Whether the information will be for general or limited distribution.	Information for general distribution will result in the engagement being potentially more risky as a larger audience will be relying on it.

The nature of the assumptions (e.g. best-estimate or hypothetical).	Forecasts and projections cannot be verified with any certainty because the outcome is unknown, however: • If information is best-estimate, it should be a reasonable approximation as to what might actually happen. • Where the assumptions are hypothetical, they will be much more difficult to validate as there is likely to be little evidence to support them and therefore the engagement holds higher risk. The engagement should not be accepted if the assumptions are clearly unrealistic or if it is expected that the PFI will be inappropriate for its intended use.
The elements to be included in the information.	The engagement will be higher risk if the PFI includes elements of which the accountant has little knowledge or that are extremely complex or highly subjective.
The period covered by the information.	Short-term forecasts are likely to be more easily verified than projections looking out over a longer period.

The terms of engagement

An engagement to report on PFI does not constitute an audit. However, the prospective client may not appreciate this fact. Agreeing the terms of engagement is therefore critical to avoid misunderstandings with the client. Typically the engagement letter should specify the following terms:

• The nature of procedures performed.

• The type of assurance offered, i.e. limited.

• The form of conclusion given, i.e. negative.

• Management's responsibilities, which are to prepare the PFI and to establish appropriate assumptions.

• Restrictions on the use and distribution of the assurance report.

• The basis of setting the fees.

3   Level of assurance

Due to the uncertainty surrounding forecasts and projections, and due to the limited nature of the procedures performed during the accountant's review, only **limited (moderate) assurance** can be offered for PFI engagements.
[ISAE 3400, 9]

The conclusion will be expressed negatively, i.e. 'Nothing has come to our attention to suggest the assumptions used in the forecast don't provide a reasonable basis for the forecast'.

4   Procedures

The practitioner should obtain a sufficient level of knowledge of the business to be able to evaluate whether all significant assumptions required for the preparation of the PFI have been identified.

This requires knowledge of the processes used to prepare the PFI including:

- Internal controls over the system used to prepare the PFI.

- Nature of documentation to support management's assumptions.

- The extent to which statistical, mathematical and automated tools and techniques are used.

- Methods used to develop and apply assumptions.

- Accuracy of PFI prepared in prior periods and reasons for significant variances.

[ISAE 3400, 13]

The practitioner should also consider the following when determining the nature, timing and extent of procedures:

- The likelihood of material misstatement.

- Knowledge obtained during any previous engagements.

- Management's competence at preparing prospective financial information.

- The extent to which the information is affected by management's judgment.

- The reliability of the underlying data.

[ISAE 3400, 17]

Analytical procedures can be used to identify unusual fluctuations between the forecast and past performance of the company or industry expectations for the forecast period.

Enquiry can be used to follow up on any fluctuations identified as well as being used to establish the assumptions used by management when preparing the forecast.

Inspection may be used where items included in the forecast are already established and in progress, for example:

- Inspection of existing loan or lease agreements to agree the repayments included in the forecast.

- Inspection of quotations or price lists to agree forecast costs for new assets.

- Inspection of recent utility bills to assess the reasonableness of forecast utility costs.

Written representations

The practitioner should obtain written representation from management regarding:

- The intended use of the PFI

- The completeness of significant management assumptions

- Management's acceptance of its responsibility for the PFI.

[ISAE 3400, 25]

It is not appropriate for the practitioner to rely solely on such representations. The practitioner must appropriately plan, perform and review a range of procedures to enable them to obtain sufficient appropriate evidence for the purposes of offering assurance.

PFI procedures: Specific examples

The specific procedures performed on an engagement will depend on the information requirements of the users and the report under scrutiny. However, examples of general procedures include:

- Comparison of forecast amounts to historic performance to ensure consistency. Whilst future results will not always follow previous trends, historical patterns give an indication of the capacity of the business. It is also important to consider that rapid growth is unlikely and potentially damaging to a business (overtrading).

- Comparison of forecast amounts to actual results. It is likely that by the time a PFI review is actually conducted, some of that period may have elapsed. Internally produced management accounts may therefore be available to assess actual performance for the first few months of the forecast period.

- Forecasts for previous periods may also be assessed in comparison to actual results to assess how accurately management have forecast in the past.

- Reasonably certain incomes and costs (such as loan interest) may be verified by inspecting documents such as orders, contracts, loan agreements, lease contracts etc.

- Comparison of accounting policies/estimates used in forecasts in comparison to financial statements, e.g. depreciation rates.

- Inspection of the non-current asset register to identify if assets are approaching the end of their useful lives and require replacement.

- Comparisons of working capital amounts/liquidity to assess whether liabilities can be met and the company can finance its short term resourcing requirements.

- Comparison of the relationships between the reported figures, for example if a significant increase in revenue is supported by increased production costs, advertising costs and distribution costs.

- Calculation of key ratios such as:

  - Gross profit margin

  - Operating margin

  - Receivables collection period

  - Payables payment period

  - Inventory holding period.

- Typical enquiries may include:

  - When do loan agreements expire?

  - Are further forms of finance being sought?

  - Have any new customer/supplier contracts been agreed since the year-end?

  - Have any new capital purchases been agreed?

  - Has the company invested in any product research/ development and if so what are the results?

  - Has the company conducted any market research and again what are the results?

  - Have there been any new competitors/products in the market place.

This list is by no way exhaustive and is very general in nature. The purpose of the examples is that they all consider events or circumstances that will have an impact on the business in the future. Note that none of the enquiries are vague, such as "how do you forecast sales?" They try and identify issues that will directly impact management's forecasts.

In the exam you will be required to suggest procedures that are relevant to the scenario.

5 Reporting

The key elements of the assurance report are summarised below:

- Title and addressee.
- Identification of the subject matter i.e. the forecast information.
- Reference to any applicable laws or standards (e.g. ISAE 3400).
- A statement that it is management's responsibility to prepare the PFI.
- Reporting accountant's responsibilities and basis of opinion.
- A reference to the purpose and restricted distribution of the PFI.
- A statement of negative assurance as to whether the assumptions provide a reasonable basis for the PFI.
- An opinion on whether the PFI is properly prepared on the basis of the assumptions and is presented in accordance with the relevant financial reporting framework.
- Appropriate caveats about the achievability of the results given the nature of assumptions and inherent limitations in the forecasting process.
- Reporting accountant's signature and address.
- Date of the report.

[ISAE 3400, 27]

> **Illustration: PFI report wording**
>
> Based on our examination of the evidence supporting the assumptions, nothing has come to our attention which causes us to believe that these assumptions do not provide a reasonable basis for the forecast. Further, in our opinion, the forecast is properly prepared on the basis of the assumptions and is presented in accordance with...
>
> Actual results are likely to be different from the forecast since anticipated events frequently do not occur as expected and the variation may be material.

Approach to exam questions: PFI

Read the requirement carefully to make sure you are clear on whether you are examining a profit forecast or a cash flow forecast.

- A profit forecast should be based on an accruals assumption i.e. the level of revenue and expenses expected to be earned and incurred during the forecast period.

- A cash flow forecast should be based on a cash basis i.e. the cash inflows and outflows expected during the forecast period.

- In particular, non-cash expenses such as depreciation will not be relevant for a cash flow forecast but will be relevant for a profit forecast.

One way to approach an answer is to assume that the client's starting point for preparing the forecast is the prior year actual results. From here they will:

- Remove items which will not be relevant going forward e.g. if they are discontinuing an activity the costs and revenues/receipts and payments for this activity should not be included in the forecast once it has ceased. Remember to consider one-off costs as a result of the discontinued activity such as profit/loss on disposal of assets or proceeds from the disposal of assets. Redundancy costs should also be included if staff are to be made redundant rather than redeployed within the organisation.

- Add in any new costs or revenues e.g. if they are expanding the business there may be more assets acquired and people employed. Within a profit forecast you would expect to see increased depreciation and payroll costs. Within a cash flow forecast you would expect to see payments to acquire assets and increased payments to employees.

- Adjust revenues and expenses/receipts and payments for inflation or growth in respect of items that are expected to continue.

The assurance provider's procedures will focus on whether the figures included in the forecast look reasonable.

- For new items this might be achieved by inspecting quotations or market research data.

- For items to be excluded, review the forecast to ensure they are no longer included.

- For items of a continuing nature, comparison with prior year management accounts can be performed.

Professional scepticism is important as the company is likely to want the forecasts to be as optimistic as possible in order to secure the finance. Your procedures should challenge the assumptions used by management.

Test your understanding 1– Imperiol Co

Imperiol Co, a limited liability company, manufactures and distributes electrical and telecommunications accessories, household durables (e.g. sink and shower units) and building systems (e.g. air-conditioning, solar heating, security systems). The company has undergone several business restructurings in recent years. Finance is to be sought from both a bank and a venture capitalist in order to implement the board's latest restructuring proposals.

You are a manager at Hal Falcon, a firm of Chartered Certified Accountants. You have been approached by Paulo Gandalf, the chief finance officer of Imperiol Co, to provide a report on the company's business plan for the year to 31 December 20X6.

From a brief telephone conversation with Paulo Gandalf you have ascertained that the proposed restructuring will involve discontinuing all operations except for building systems, where the greatest opportunity for increasing product innovation is believed to lie. Imperiol Co's strategy is to become the market leader in providing 'total building system solutions' using new fibre optic technology to link building systems. A major benefit of the restructuring is expected to be a lower ongoing cost base. As part of the restructuring it is likely that the accounting functions, including internal audit, will be outsourced.

You have obtained a copy of Imperiol Co's Interim Report for the six months to 30 June 20X5 on which the company's auditors, Discorpio, provide a conclusion giving negative assurance. The following information has been extracted from the Interim Financial Report:

(1) **Chair's statement**

The economic climate is less certain than it was a few months ago and performance has been affected by a severe decline in the electrical accessories market. Management's response will be to gain market share and reduce the cost base.

(2) **Statement of financial position**

	30 June 20X5 (unaudited)	31 December 20X4
	$m	$m
Intangible assets	83.5	72.6
Non-current assets	69.6	63.8
Inventory	25.2	20.8
Trade receivables	59.9	50.2
Cash	8.3	23.8
Total assets	246.5	231.2
Non-current liabilities – borrowing	65.4	45.7
Current liabilities	55.6	57.0
Equity and liabilities:		
Share capital	30.4	30.4
Reserves	6.0	9.1
Accumulated profit	89.1	89.0
	246.5	231.2

(3) **Continuing and discontinuing operations**

	Six months to 30 June 20X5 (unaudited)	Year to 31 December 20X4
	$m	$m
Revenue		
Continuing operations		
Electrical and telecommunication accessories	55.3	118.9
Household durables	37.9	77.0
Building systems	53.7	94.9
Total continuing	146.9	290.8
Discontinued	–	65.3
Total revenue	146.9	356.1
Operating profit before interest and taxation – continuing operations	13.4	32.2

Required:

(a) Identify and explain the matters Hal Falcon should consider before accepting the engagement to report on Imperiol Co's prospective financial information. **(5 marks)**

(b) Describe the procedures that a professional accountant should undertake in order to provide an assurance report on the prospective financial information of Imperiol Co for the year to 31 December 20X6. **(10 marks)**

(Total: 15 marks)

6 Chapter summary

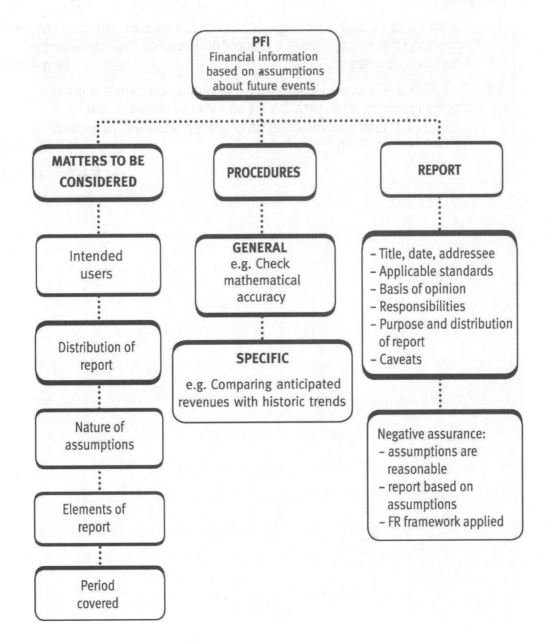

Test your understanding answers

Test your understanding 1 – Imperiol Co

(a) **Matters to be considered before accepting the engagement**

Distribution of the report to third parties

The report is to be used to raise finance. Hal Falcon must agree the distribution of the report prior to accepting. The greater the number of parties that place reliance on the report, the greater the risk involved. Therefore Hal Falcon must seek to reduce this risk by limiting liability to specific parties and by writing appropriate caveats/disclaimers in the final report.

Competence/knowledge of Imperiol Co

Having never audited Imperiol Co, Hal Falcon should consider whether they have the competence and experience to successfully review the PFI. If they have little knowledge of the building system's industry their ability to assess the assumptions about future performance may be questioned. In particular, if the reporting deadlines are tight there will be little room for extensive planning and knowledge gathering. Under those circumstances the existing auditor may be better placed to assign a team.

Period covered by the forecast

Paulo Gandalf has requested a review of the forecasts to 31 December 20X6. This does not appear to be particularly extensive and it is likely that a provider of significant finance would seek a longer forecast period. Before accepting the engagement Hal Falcon should confirm in the engagement letter that the only period being examined (and requested by the financiers) is to 31 December 20X6.

Nature of the assumptions

The nature of assumptions underlying the preparation of the PFI i.e. best-estimate or hypothetical must be considered. Best-estimate assumptions are more likely to have evidence to support them as these relate to actions management are expecting to take. If restructuring plans are already in progress there should be evidence to back this up. Hypothetical assumptions relate to events which are not necessarily expected to occur and as such there will be little evidence for the firm to obtain to assess the reasonableness of these assumptions.

Access to information

Following on from the above point, to enable the engagement to be performed efficiently, Imperiol Co must ensure that access to all relevant information and staff is made available. Any restrictions would lead to a breach of engagement terms and a potential disclaimer of conclusion.

Independence

Hal Falcon is not the auditor of Imperiol Co, therefore independence cannot be assumed. The firm needs to ensure there are no threats to objectivity that would prevent it from accepting the engagement. If the firm is not independent, any user of the report may not trust it to be reliable.

Risk

It appears as though Imperiol Co have undertaken a number of restructuring initiatives. They discontinued some businesses in 20X4 and it appears in the future they will continue to strip away operations until they are left with nothing but building systems. This may suggest that Imperiol Co is unstable and increases the risk that forecasts will be inappropriate.

Form of the PFI

The reporting accountant must consider the form of prospective financial information. This could include any, or all, of the following elements:

– a statement of business objectives and goals

– profit forecasts

– budgeted statements of financial position

– cash budgets

– capital budgets

– a statement of assumptions and variables.

It is vital that Hal Falcon establishes which elements of the report they are being asked to examine. This will significantly affect the risk of the engagement and the procedures they are required to perform, e.g. procedures for a profit forecast will be different from those relevant to a cash flow forecast.

Level of assurance

It must be clarified that only limited assurance can be offered due to the uncertainty of forecasts. The conclusion will be worded negatively.

The conclusion is focused on whether:

– the assumptions are reasonable and consistent with the purpose of the information

– the PFI is properly prepared on the basis of the assumptions

– the PFI is prepared on a consistent basis with historical financial statements, using appropriate accounting principles.

Permission to communicate with auditors

When an accountant is asked to perform work for a client, they should be granted permission to speak to any other accountants or auditors that the company uses in order to obtain relevant information. Hal Falcon should request permission to communicate with Discorpio. If this is not given, the engagement should be declined.

Consider why the auditors, Discorpio, have not been used

To provide a report on the reasonableness of the forecast, a good understanding of the company is required. The auditor is usually the party with the most understanding. The use of a different firm poses a risk as Imperiol Co may be hoping that a different firm will not identify that the assumptions are not reasonable.

Authority of Paulo Gandalf to request the work

Hal Falcon should also establish what authority Paulo Gandalf has to appoint them. He may not be empowered by the board and if he is responsible for the preparation of the PFI it may appear to impair Hal Falcon's objectivity if Paulo makes the appointment.

Other matters

Hal Falcon could also consider the following before deciding whether to proceed:

– Whether there may be an opportunity to offer other services to Imperiol Co, e.g. internal audit.

– Fees and whether the fee will be appropriate for the level of risk of the engagement.

– Integrity of the preparer of the forecast.

(b) **Procedures to be performed**

General procedures

– Compare the forecast for 20X4 to the results achieved in 20X4 to assess management's competence at preparing PFI.

– Compare the forecast to previous performance to identify if they are in keeping with historical trends. Any significant distortions from historical trends would require explanation.

– Compare accounting policies used in the forecast to the historical accounts to ensure consistency.

– Obtain written representation from management that they acknowledge their responsibility for the forecasts, that they believe the assumptions used in the forecast are reasonable and confirmation of the intended use of the forecast.

– Recalculate the forecast to verify the arithmetic accuracy.

Specific procedures

Discontinued operations

–   Enquire of management how soon the remainder of the operations to be discontinued will be wound down or sold and ensure this timescale is reflected in the forecast.

–   Review the forecast costs for impairment charges in respect of the intangible assets. Intangible assets for those activities which are discontinuing may be significantly impaired.

–   Enquire of management whether the non-current assets relating to discontinued activities will be sold, scrapped or used elsewhere in the business.

–   Inspect second hand prices or correspondence from buyers to consider the reasonableness of disposal proceeds in the cash forecast and the consistency of gains/losses on disposals in the profit forecast. There may already be sale agreements in place.

–   Recalculate the forecast profits/losses on disposal using the proceeds verified above to confirm accuracy.

–   Enquire of management whether any of the inventory held relates to discontinued operations. If so, review the valuation to ensure that any write downs have been made if it cannot be sold.

New structure

–   Review the forecast to ensure the new forms of finance have been included e.g. interest charges, and recalculate to confirm accuracy.

–   Enquire whether any amounts or rates have been discussed. If there is documentary evidence (for example, an agreement that is contingent upon the PFI). Review this to ensure it is accurately reflected in the PFI.

–   Review the forecast to ensure the expected increase in fibre optic products has been reflected in the forecast purchases of inventory.

–   Compare the forecasts to actual performance in 20X4 and 20X5. The PFI should reflect a reduction in staff costs and an increase in professional fees due to outsourcing the accounts department.

–   Enquire of the directors what they believe the extent of the benefit will be from outsourcing accounting functions.

–   Compare the forecast outsourcing fees to any quotes/tenders received from professional firms.

–   Obtain details of salaries for the staff to be made redundant and the redundancy terms, and calculate the expected redundancy cost. Compare with the forecast figure to ensure it is reasonable.

Changing performance

- Enquire of management what they consider to be the key variables which underpin building systems revenue growth. Therefore any assumptions of growth for building systems will require close scrutiny as this is to be the only revenue stream.

- Compare forecast sales in the PFI with any internal management accounts or marketing based forecasts to ensure that the amounts are consistent with the key assumptions of future profitability.

- Obtain details of credit terms given to customers and compare with the receivables collection period for June 20X5 of 74 days. This is considerably higher than 20X4 (51 days) and the effect of this should be discussed with management. In particular, the cash flow forecast should be reviewed to ensure that it is consistent with the deterioration in credit control.

- Discuss what might happen if Imperiol Co only manages to raise part of the finance. They may not have sufficient resources to develop the newer fibre optic technology, which could lead to reservations about going concern.

Due diligence

Chapter learning objectives

This chapter covers syllabus areas:

* F2 – Specific assignments: Due diligence

Detailed syllabus objectives are provided in the introduction section of the text book.

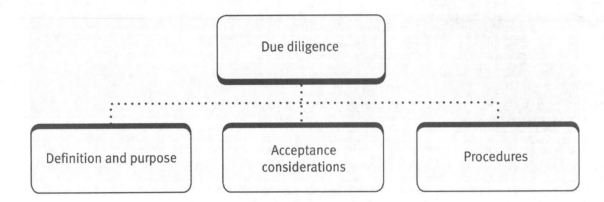

1 Due diligence

 Due diligence is a fact finding exercise, usually conducted to reduce the risk of making poor investment decisions.

Purpose of due diligence

An advisor is engaged by the acquirer of a company to gather information on the target company. This information may:

- Reveal potential problems before an acquisition decision is made and enable the potential acquirer to enter into the transaction with open eyes.

- Provide the client with the information they need to decide

    - whether or not to go ahead with an acquisition

    - when to go ahead with the acquisition

    - how much should be paid for the target company.

- Increase stakeholder confidence in the acquisition decision, for example, if the acquisition is to be financed by a bank loan. The bank will have greater confidence that the investment is sound and the loan is more likely to be repaid.

The due diligence provider will need to look at:

- Current issues affecting the company which could result in additional time and cost to resolve.

- Prospects for the future to ascertain whether the investment is likely to generate the desired rate of return on investment.

- Past performance to establish how successful the company has been and whether it may be able to continue that success into the future.

The main purpose of due diligence is to ensure the acquirer has full knowledge of the target company such as:

- **Financial performance and position**

  Analysing and validating the target's revenue, future cash flows and financial position including identification and valuation of contingent liabilities and key assets.

- **Operational matters**

  Investigating operational risks, capital expenditure requirements, quality of information systems, key customers and suppliers.

- **Market position and commercial matters**

  A comprehensive review of the target's business plan in the context of the industry and market conditions, including the industry life cycle.

- **Legal matters**

  Whether the company has been compliant with the relevant legal and regulatory framework, whether any legal cases are in progress and the likely outcomes of such cases.

- **Tax matters**

  Whether the company is up to date with its tax returns and tax payments. Whether any tax investigations have been performed and whether any issues are still to be resolved.

- **HR matters**

  Whether there are any HR issues affecting the company such as industrial action, staff on long term sick leave, low morale and productivity, contractual disputes, etc.

The acquiring company may decide the issues and risks identified are so significant they do not want to go ahead with the acquisition. They may use the issues to negotiate a reduced price, or require the vendor to resolve the issues before the acquisition completes.

Level of assurance

Depending on the client's requirements, due diligence may either be conducted as:

- an assurance assignment (where a professional conclusion is expressed), or

- an agreed upon procedures assignment (where the accountant presents the client with factual information they have requested about the target company).

Benefits of engaging an advisor to carry out due diligence

- **Decrease management time spent assessing the acquisition decision**

  Due diligence reviews can be performed internally, by the management of an acquiring company. However, this can be time consuming and the directors may lack the knowledge and experience necessary to perform the review adequately. Engaging an external advisor to carry out the review allows management to focus on strategic matters and running the existing group as well as ensuring an impartial review.

- **Identification of operational issues and risk assessment of the target company**

  For example:

  - possible contractual disputes following a takeover

  - potential breaches of covenants attached to any finance

  - the adequacy of the skills and experience of key management within the target company

  - operational issues such as high staff turnover, issues with supplies/suppliers, quality issues with products or the retention of key customers.

- **Liabilities evaluated and identified**

  It is particularly important that the potential acquirer identifies contingent liabilities that may crystallise in the future, and considers the likelihood of them crystallising and the potential financial consequences. These will affect the price the acquirer wishes to pay for the target.

- **Identify assets not capitalised**

  Internally generated intangibles, such as internal brands, will not be included on the statement of financial position but are vital to purchasing decisions as they increase the value of the business.

- **Gathering information**

  The external advisor will gather any other relevant information that could influence the decision of the client.

- **Enhance the credibility of the investment decision**

  Engaging an external advisor to carry out the due diligence will ensure an independent, objective view is obtained on the investment decision, including the price to be paid.

- **Planning the acquisition**

  The due diligence provider can advise on change management following the acquisition, including integrating the new company into the group, which key staff to retain, help with restructuring, as well as the more immediate issues of determining an appropriate price and reviewing the terms of the sale and purchase agreement.

- **Claims made by the vendor can be substantiated**

  For example, future order levels and current finance agreements.

- **Evaluation of possible post-acquisition synergies and economies of scale and potential further costs**

  The advisor will investigate and advise on post-acquisition issues such as consideration of staffing requirements, including identification of management and key personnel who should be retained post-acquisition.

  The advisor should identify potential synergies. The combined entity may be able to utilise distributions systems, staff and non-current assets, allowing for surplus assets to be sold and duplicate roles and processes to be made redundant.

Comparison of due diligence to external audit

	Due diligence	External audit
Objective	To provide the acquirer with sufficient information to make an informed decision about whether the acquisition is a worthwhile investment	To form an opinion as to whether the financial statements are free from material misstatement
Scope of work	• Past performance • Current issues • Future prospects	• Past performance • Cash flow forecasts for going concern review
Focus	• Financial performance and position • Operational matters • Market position and commercial matters • Legal matters • Tax matters • HR matters	Financial performance and position
Level of assurance	• Limited assurance or • No assurance	Reasonable assurance

2 Acceptance considerations

As with any assignment, the practitioner must only take on work of an acceptable level of risk. The acceptance matters given in chapter 6 must be considered.

In addition, the following matters should be considered:

- Why the company is not using their existing firm of accountants if they do not approach their current provider of services.

- Whether the target company's employees know about the acquisition. If not, the firm will need to be careful not to disclose information to the employees when gathering information.

- Whether the acquisition is a hostile takeover. This may affect the ability to obtain sufficient appropriate evidence from the target company.

- Exact scope of the due diligence, e.g. limited assurance or agreed upon procedures, financial due diligence only or consideration of commercial, legal, or operational matters. This will affect the time and resources required.

- The reason for the acquisition. This may affect the type of information that needs to be gathered.

- The deadline for the report. Some due diligence engagements may require the investigations to be performed at short notice.

- Any ethical threats which may be created. If the due diligence involves valuing the target company's assets and liabilities, a self-review threat may be created later on if the audit firm then audits those assets and liabilities which have been purchased by the audit client. If the assets have been overvalued, the audit firm may be reluctant to bring this to the client's attention.

3 Procedures

Due diligence procedures will involve:

- Analytical review of past financial statements to assess the recent financial performance of the target company.

- Review of forecasts including an assessment of the reasonableness of assumptions used in the forecast.

- Review of existing contracts to identify when the contracts expire and whether the contracts will be affected by a change of owner.

- Review of terms and conditions of related party transactions which may have affected the financial performance of the target company.

- Inspection of asset registers and ledgers to identify possible overstatement which would affect the price paid.

- Review of the accounting policies of the target company and how they compare with the acquiring company. The results of the target may be recalculated on the basis of the acquiring company's policies to assess the difference arising from less prudent accounting policies.

- Review of board minutes to identify significant issues affecting the target company which may affect its value.

- Correspondence between the company and its lawyers regarding any outstanding legal issues.

- Correspondence from the tax authority regarding any tax investigations or issues.

- Review of industry data to assess the status of the industry and industry specific risks.

Approach to exam questions: Due diligence

Exam questions will often ask for procedures to be performed for a due diligence engagement. These procedures need to identify the information relevant to the client's investment decision. Based on this information, the client will decide whether to go ahead with the acquisition or it will help them decide the price they are willing to pay.

One way to approach the question is to put yourself in the position of the client.

- What would affect your decision?

- What would make you want to go ahead with the acquisition?

- What would make you think it's not such a good investment?

Examples include:

- Pending legal actions

- Outstanding tax investigations

- Declining market

- Increasing competition

- Damage to reputation

- Old assets in need of replacement

- Declining financial performance

- Quality issues

- Reliability of asset valuations

- Completeness of liabilities

- Human resource issues – e.g. strike action, low morale.

Test your understanding 1

You are a manager in Andando, a firm of Chartered Certified Accountants. You have been approached by Duncan Seymour, the chief finance officer of Plaza, a major food retailer with a chain of national supermarkets, to advise on a bid that Plaza is proposing to make for the purchase of MCM. Plaza has extended its operations throughout Europe and most recently to Asia, where it is expanding rapidly.

You have ascertained the following from a briefing note received from Duncan.

MCM provides training in management, communications and marketing to a wide range of corporate clients, including multi-nationals. The 'MCM' name is well regarded in its areas of expertise. MCM is currently wholly-owned by Frontiers, an international publisher of textbooks, whose shares are quoted on a recognised stock exchange. MCM has a National and an International business.

The National business comprises 11 training centres. The audited financial statements show revenue of $12.5 million and profit before taxation of $1.3 million for this geographic segment for the year to 31 December 20X4. Most of the National business's premises are owned or held on long leases. Trainers in the National business are mainly full-time employees.

The International business has five training centres in Europe and Asia. For these segments, revenue amounted to $6.3 million and profit before tax $2.4 million for the year to 31 December 20X4. Most of the International business premises are leased. International trade receivables at 31 December 20X4 amounted to $3.7 million. Although the International centres employ some full-time trainers, the majority of trainers provide their services as freelance consultants.

Required:

(a) Define 'due diligence' and describe the nature and purpose of a due diligence review. **(3 marks)**

(b) Explain the matters you should consider before accepting an engagement to conduct a due diligence review of MCM. **(5 marks)**

(c) Describe the procedures that should be performed for the due diligence review of MCM. **(7 marks)**

(Total: 15 marks)

4   Chapter summary

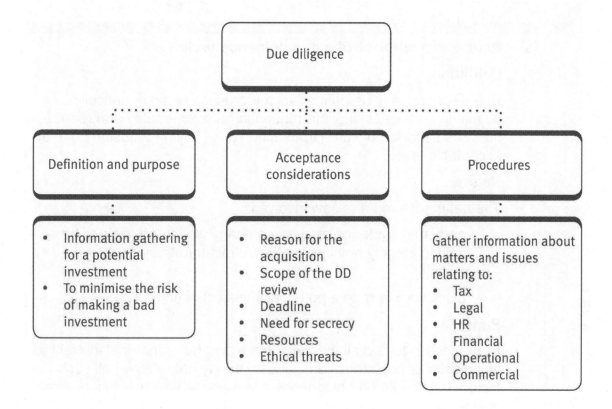

Test your understanding answers

Test your understanding 1

(a) **Nature and purpose of a due diligence review**

Definition

Due diligence may be defined as the process of systematically obtaining and assessing information in order to identify and reduce the risks associated with a transaction (e.g. buying a business) to an acceptable level.

Nature

The nature of such a review involves:

– gathering evidence about a company whose equity is to be sold to identify any information relevant to the investment decision.

– disclosure (e.g. to a potential investor) of findings.

Purpose

Its purpose is to find all the facts that would be of material interest to an investor or acquirer of a business. It may not uncover all such factors but should be designed with a reasonable expectation of so doing.

(b) **Matters to be considered before accepting the engagement**

Tutorial note: Although candidates may approach this part from a rote-learned list of 'matters to consider' it is important to tailor answers to the specifics of Plaza and MCM. It is critical that answer points should not contradict the scenario (e.g. assuming that it is Plaza's auditor who has been asked to undertake the assignment).

Information about Duncan Seymour

Consider the relationship of the chief finance officer to Plaza and whether he has authority to approach Andando to undertake this assignment.

Purpose of the assignment

The purpose must be clarified. Duncan's approach to Andando is 'to advise on a bid'. However, Andando cannot make executive decisions for a client but only provide the facts of material interest. Plaza's management must decide whether or not to bid and, if so, how much to bid.

Scope of the due diligence review

It seems likely that Plaza will be interested in acquiring all of MCM's business as its areas of operation coincide with Plaza's. However it must be confirmed that Plaza is not merely interested in acquiring only the National or International business of MCM.

Andando's competence and experience

Andando should not accept the engagement unless the firm has experience in undertaking due diligence assignments. Even then, the firm must have sufficient knowledge of the territories in which the businesses operate to evaluate whether all facts of material interest to Plaza have been identified.

Resources available

Whether the firm has sufficient resources available (e.g. representative/associated offices) in Europe and Asia to investigate MCM's International business.

Threats to objectivity and independence

For example, if Duncan is closely connected with a partner in Andando or if Andando is the auditor of Frontiers.

Tutorial note: Candidates will not be awarded marks for going into 'autopilot' on independence issues. For example, Andando holding shares in MCM is not possible (since wholly owned).

Rationale for the acquisition

Presumably it is significant that MCM operates in the same territories as Plaza. Plaza may be intending to provide extensive training programs in management, communications and marketing to its workforce.

Relationship between Plaza and MCM

Plaza may be a major client of MCM. That is, Plaza is currently outsourcing training to MCM. Acquiring MCM would bring training in-house.

Tutorial note: Ascertaining what a purchaser hopes to gain from an acquisition before the assignment is accepted as important. The facts to be uncovered for a merger from which synergy is expected will be different from those relevant to acquiring an investment opportunity.

Time available

Andando must have sufficient time to find all facts that would be of material interest to Plaza before disclosing their findings.

Access to information

Whether there will be restrictions on Andando's access to information held by MCM (e.g. if there will not be access to board minutes) and personnel.

Degree of secrecy required

This may go beyond the normal duties of confidentiality not to disclose information to outsiders (e.g. if unannounced staff redundancies could arise).

Plaza's current auditors

Why have they not been asked to conduct the due diligence review, especially as they are responsible for (and therefore capable of undertaking) the group audit covering the relevant countries?

Communication with the current auditor

Andando should be allowed to communicate with Plaza's current auditor:

– to inform them of the nature of the work they have been asked to undertake, and

– to enquire if there is any reason why they should not accept this assignment.

Other services that can be offered

In taking on Plaza as a new client Andando may have a later opportunity to offer external audit and other services to Plaza (e.g. internal audit).

(c) **Procedures**

Tutorial note: These should be focused on uncovering facts that may not be revealed by the audited financial statements (e.g. contingencies, commitments and contracts) especially where knowledge may be confined to management.

– Review management contracts to identify whether any members of MCM's senior/executive management have contractual terms that will result in significant pay-outs to them on change of ownership of the company or being made redundant.

– Enquire of management if there are there any major clients who are likely to be lost, or any contracts with clients that will lapse or be made void in the event that MCM is purchased by Plaza.

– Review lease agreements to identify the principal terms of the leases relating to the International business premises and whether penalties are likely to be incurred if leases are terminated.

– Enquire of management whether MCM has entered into any purchase commitments since the last audited financial statements (e.g. to buy or lease further premises).

– Enquire of management who the best trainers are that Plaza should seek to retain after the purchase of MCM.

- Review board minutes to identify if any events have occurred since the last audited financial statements were published that have made a significant impact on MCM's assets, liabilities, operating capability and/or cash flows.

- Review correspondence with the tax authority to identify any outstanding tax issues, tax investigations or unpaid taxes which could result in additional costs.

- Review legal correspondence to identify any outstanding legal issues which could result in additional costs.

- Review the trend of MCM's profit (gross and net) for the last five years (say). Similarly earnings per share and gearing.

- For both the National and International businesses compare:

  - gross profit, net profit, and return on assets for the last five years

  - actual monthly revenue against budget for the last 2 years

  - actual monthly salary costs against budget for the last 2 years

  - actual monthly freelance consultancy fees against budget for the last 2 years

  - actual monthly premises costs (e.g. depreciation, lease payments, maintenance, etc.) against budget for the last 2 years.

- Review projections of future profitability of MCM against net profit percentage for:

  - the National business (10.4%)

  - the International business (38.1%)

  - overall (19.9%).

- Review disposal values of owned premises against carrying values.

- Compare actual cash balances with budget on a monthly basis and compare borrowings against loan and overdraft facilities.

- Compare the average collection period for International trade receivables month on month since 31 December (when it was nearly seven months, i.e. $3.7/$6.3 × 365 days) and compare with the National business.

– Compare key performance indicators by centre for the last two years, for example:

- number of corporate clients
- number of delegates
- number of training days
- average revenue per delegate per day
- average cost per consultancy day
- gross and net profit margins
- return on centre assets
- average collection period
- average payment period
- liquidity ratio.

Forensic audits

Chapter learning objectives

This chapter covers syllabus areas:

- F2 – Other assignments: Forensic audits.

Detailed syllabus objectives are provided in the introduction section of the text book.

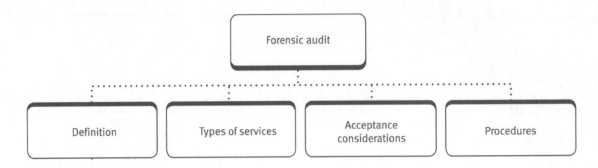

 Exam focus

The field of forensic accounting is a specialist branch of the profession carried out by forensic accountants encompassing forensic auditing and investigation.

Forensic engagements require a much broader range of skills than other typical non-audit engagements. However, they still require the application of traditional auditing skills and techniques.

Two articles have been published on this syllabus area by the examining team: 'Forensic Auditing' (September 2008) and 'Massaging the Figures' (April 2009). These can be downloaded from the ACCA website.

1 What is a forensic audit?

 Definitions

Forensic audit

- This refers to the specific procedures within a forensic investigation in order to obtain evidence.

- This could include the use of traditional financial auditing techniques such as analytical procedures and substantive procedures, for example to quantify a fraud or to determine the amount of an insurance claim.

Some of the major applications of forensic auditing are shown below:

Application	Examples	Type of work performed
Fraud investigations	Theft of company funds, tax evasion, insider dealing.	Funds tracing, asset identification and recovery, forensic intelligence gathering, due diligence reviews, interviews, detailed review of documentary evidence.

Insurance claims	Business interruption, property losses, motor vehicle incidents, personal liability claims, wrongful dismissal.	Detailed review of the policy from either an insured or insurer's perspective to investigate coverage issues, identification of appropriate method of calculating the loss, quantification of losses.
Professional negligence	Loss suffered as a result of placing reliance on a professional adviser.	Advising on the merits of a case in respect of liability and quantifying losses.

As part of the assignment a forensic accountant will:

- Communicate their findings in the form of reports, exhibits and collections of documents.

- Assist in legal proceedings, including testifying in court as an expert witness and preparing visual aids to support trial evidence.

The forensic accountant may be used as an expert witness where:

- They have experience, expertise, and training appropriate to the value, complexity, and importance of the case.

- They have the expertise relevant to the issue on which an opinion is sought.

- It is a reasonable requirement to resolve proceedings.

Accounting fraud examples

Tesco

In 2014, Tesco, Britain's biggest retailer revealed that it had overstated estimated profits by £263 million by overestimating revenues paid to it by suppliers. Tesco was struggling to maintain market share due to pressure from competitors Aldi and Lidl.

Toshiba

In 2015, the electronics company Toshiba admitted that it had overstated its earnings by nearly $2 billion over seven years. An independent investigation found that "Toshiba had a corporate culture in which management decisions could not be challenged" and "Employees were pressured into inappropriate accounting by postponing loss reports or moving certain costs into later years.

Sainsbury's

In June 2012, three men were jailed after defrauding the supermarket Sainsbury's. 2 directors at potato supplier, Greenvale, were found to have overcharged Sainsbury's £8.7 million in agreement with Sainsbury's potato buyer, John Maylam. £4.9 million was paid to Maylam as his share and he also received excessive gifts and hospitality. The Sainsbury's contract was worth £40 million to Greenvale and the directors did not want to risk losing that amount of business and hence bribed Maylam to ensure the contract remained in place.

2 Acceptance considerations

As with any assignment, the practitioner must only take on work of an acceptable level of risk. The acceptance matters given in chapter 6 must be considered.

Most importantly for forensic audits, the practitioner must ensure they can comply with the fundamental ethical principles.

Professional competence and due care

Forensic investigations involve very specialist skills, including:

- Detailed knowledge of the relevant legal framework.

- An understanding of how to gather specialist evidence.

- Skills in the safe custody of evidence, including maintaining a clear chain of evidence.

- Strong personal skills: interview techniques, presentation of material in court.

Confidentiality

During legal proceedings the court will require the practitioner to reveal information discovered during the investigation. There is an overriding requirement to disclose all of the information deemed necessary by the court.

Outside of the court, the practitioner must maintain confidentiality, especially because much of the information they have access to will be highly sensitive.

Objectivity

The practitioner must always be, and be perceived to be, independent.

This is particularly important if the forensic report is going to be submitted to a court of law. Any threat to objectivity could undermine the credibility of the evidence provided. To assess independence, the expert should consider whether the opinion would be the same if they were engaged by the opposing party.

In particular the accountant must safeguard against advocacy and self-review threats.

- An advocacy threat arises because the firm may feel pressured into promoting the interests and point of view of its fee paying client, which breaches the concept of objectivity in court proceedings. In particular, the forensic expert has a duty to provide evidence to the court which overrides any obligation to the client paying them. The practitioner must communicate this duty to the client to prevent any misunderstanding.

- A self-review threat arises when an auditor also becomes involved in forensic work because the investigation is likely to involve fraud or potential misstatement within the financial statements. Separate teams must be used for the different engagements.

Integrity

Given the nature of their work, forensic professionals are likely to deal frequently with individuals who lack integrity or may be involved in criminal behaviour. It is imperative that the practitioner recognises this, and does nothing to damage their own reputation, such as accepting bribes or giving in to other forms of coercion/intimidation.

Professional behaviour

Fraud investigations can become a matter of public interest, and much media attention is often focused on the work of the practitioner. A highly professional attitude must be displayed at all times in order to avoid damage to the reputation of the firm, and of the profession. Any lapse in professional behaviour could undermine the credibility of the practitioner, especially when acting in the capacity of an expert witness.

3 Level of assurance

Forensic engagements are generally conducted as 'agreed upon procedures' assignments. This means:

- No assurance is given.

- The practitioner will report factual findings to the client.

- The procedures are dependent on the requirements of the client.

4 Planning and performing forensic audits

Procedures may include:

- Enquiries/interviews of key staff.
- Detailed inspections and analysis of documentary evidence.
- Tests of control.
- Analytical procedures to compare trends over time or between business segments.
- Automated tools and techniques such as the use of audit software, test date and data analytics.

Planning stage

- Hold a meeting to clarify:
  - The objective of the investigation.
  - The actions taken so far e.g. contact with the police and the result of any investigations carried out by them/contact with the insurance company.
  - The planned deadline for the report.
- Confirm that the investigation team will have full access to the information required, and are able to discuss the matter with the police without fear of breaching confidentiality.
- Confirm the output of the investigation and to whom the report will be addressed. It should be clarified that the report is not to be distributed to any other parties.
- Consider the resources and skills that will be needed to conduct the work. If the firm has a forensic accounting department it is likely they will have staff with relevant skills, but the specific type of investigation must be considered as each will be different.
- Confirm whether the firm will be required to act as an expert witness in the event of a prosecution (if applicable).

Fraud investigation

A company may require a fraud investigation to be performed if it identifies fraud such as fictitious employees being set up on a payroll system or fictitious suppliers being set up on a purchases system.

Objectives and scope

With most fraud investigations, the basic objectives of a forensic engagement include:

- Identification of:
  - the type of fraud that has occurred
  - how long it has been occurring for
  - how the fraud was concealed
  - the main suspects.
- Quantification of the financial losses.
- Gathering of evidence to support legal action/recovery of losses.
- Providing advice to prevent fraud occurring in future.

Specific procedures

- Inspect payments for evidence of authorisation.
- Using audit software, trace all payments made to a particular bank account number.
- Using audit software, identify employees who have not taken any annual leave entitlement or sick leave.
- Inspect reports detailing changes of standing data to identify whether these changes were authorised.
- Use analytical procedures to identify any trends that may indicate when the fraud commenced and the extent of the fraud.
- Interview the suspect to obtain an explanation of what has happened or to obtain a confession.
- Inspect supporting documentation (e.g. contracts of employment, GRNs, invoices) for expenditure to identify whether the expenditure is legitimate or fraudulent.
- Inspect the company's insurance policy to identify whether fraud is covered. If so, the loss to the company will be limited to the extent of any excess on the insurance policy or any limit imposed by the insurance company.

Insurance claim verification

A company may request an insurance claim verification to be performed to ensure the maximum amount possible is claimed from the insurance company in the event of a loss. Examples include insurance claims for theft of assets or claims for business interruption if the business has been affected by a flood or fire.

Specific procedures

- Inspect the insurance policy to clarify the exact terms of the insurance. The period of the insurance cover should be checked to ensure that the client is covered for any claim they intend to make.

- Inspect bank statements to confirm payments to the insurance company are up to date to ensure the cover has not lapsed.

- For assets being claimed, inspect the asset register or invoices to verify the value of the asset.

- Where insurance replaces on a new for old basis, inspect price lists to identify the current price of an asset.

- For business interruption insurance, analyse the level of business generated in previous years' and any growth achieved in the current year to date to quantify the level of business lost during the relevant period.

- Perform a reconciliation of records to physical items to quantify the number of goods lost or destroyed for which insurance can be claimed.

- Discuss with the police whether any items being claimed for have since been recovered.

5 Reporting

Once a forensic investigation is complete, the forensic accountant will submit a report of their findings.

As an agreed upon procedure the most important factor of a forensic report is that the practitioner adequately addresses the requirements of the client, as established in the engagement letter.

A basic report will include:

- a summary of the procedures performed
- a summary of the results of procedures
- any limitations in the scope of the engagement
- a conclusion.

Test your understanding 1

Your firm performs the audit of Jarvis Co, a company which installs windows. Jarvis Co uses sales representatives to make direct sales to customers. The sales representatives earn a small salary, and also earn a sales commission of 20% of the sales they generate.

Jarvis Co's sales manager has discovered that one of the sales representatives has been operating a fraud, in which he was submitting false claims for sales commission based on non-existent sales. The sales representative started to work at Jarvis Co six months ago. The forensic investigation department of your firm has been engaged to quantify the amount of the fraud.

Required:

Recommend the procedures that should be used in the forensic investigation to quantify the amount of the fraud.   **(5 marks)**

Test your understanding 2

You have been asked by the management of The Marvellous Manufacturing Company to carry out a forensic audit into a suspected expenses fraud within the marketing department.

During a routine annual spend review, management noticed that the expenses budget of $300,000 had been exceeded by nearly $30,000 with no known increase in activity.

Required:

(i)   Set out the matters you would consider when planning the forensic audit.   **(5 marks)**

(ii)   Recommend the procedures that should be performed to determine whether or not an expenses fraud has taken place.   **(5 marks)**

(Total: 10 marks)

6   Chapter summary

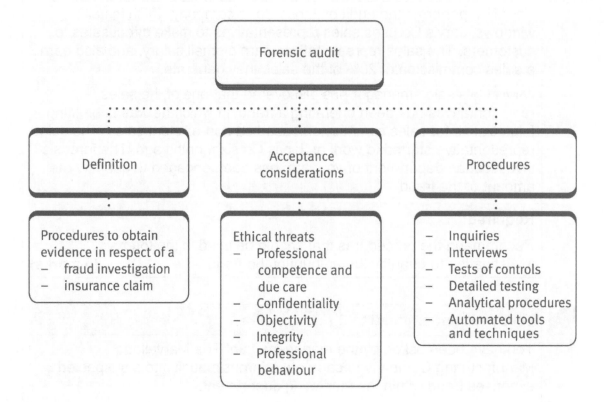

Forensic audit

Definition

Procedures to obtain
evidence in respect of a
-    fraud investigation
-    insurance claim

Acceptance
considerations

Ethical threats
-    Professional
     competence and
     due care
-    Confidentiality
-    Objectivity
-    Integrity
-    Professional
     behaviour

Procedures

-    Inquiries
-    Interviews
-    Tests of controls
-    Detailed testing
-    Analytical procedures
-    Automated tools
     and techniques

Test your understanding answers

Test your understanding 1

- Obtain all of the claims for sales commission submitted by the sales representative for the six months he has worked for the company and total the amount of these claims.

- Reconcile the sales per the sales commission claims to the sales day book.

- Agree all sales per the sales commission claims to customer-signed orders and to other supporting documentation confirming that window installation took place, for example, customer-signed agreement of work carried out.

- Obtain external confirmations from customers of the amount they paid for the work carried out.

- Perform analytical procedures to compare the weekly or monthly sales generated by the sales representative committing the fraud to other sales representatives to identify any significant differences.

Test your understanding 2

(i) **Matters to consider when planning a forensic audit**

- Consider the scope and depth of the investigation and therefore the nature, timing and extent of procedures.

- Determine which staff will perform the assignment ensuring the appropriate skills are included on the team. Consider the availability of the staff and whether any other work needs to be rescheduled and whether this is possible.

- Prepare the budget for the assignment in terms of hours, grades of staff and costs.

- Calculate the fee for the assignment based on the budget.

- Discuss with management why they believe the overspend is through fraudulent behaviour.

- Consider who the intended users of the report will be as this will affect risk and liability levels and therefore the amount of work undertaken.

- Develop an engagement plan that focuses on the areas where fraud could have taken place.

- Ensure the team are fully briefed on the client and the assignment.

- Obtain confirmation from management that the expert will have full access to information needed to perform the investigation.

- Enquire whether the practitioner will be required to be an expert witness if it is found to be fraud and the suspect it taken to court.

(ii) **Procedures**

- Identify risk areas that would provide opportunities for fraud to take place e.g. lack of segregation of duties, poor control environment, etc.

- Obtain management accounts and perform analytical procedures to see if any other significant variances have occurred.

- Speak with the marketing director to identify if there have been more trips required this year that could explain the reason for the increase.

- Enquire if any new customers/contracts have been won in the year that might explain an increase in marketing expenses e.g. entertaining to win new business.

- Enquire with the marketing director whether expenses are authorised and what the authority limits are.

- Enquire if there has been any change in expenses policy that might explain the increase e.g. an increase in the standard of hotels used, meal allowances, etc.

- Enquire when the spending increase was first identified and what measures were taken by the client to find reasons for the increase.

- Analyse expense claims by individual to try to identify a suspect.

- Analyse expenses by type to identify which category of expenses has seen the biggest rise. For example, an increase in fuel costs might be due to fuel prices increasing rather than fraud.

Audit of social, environmental and integrated reporting

Chapter learning objectives

This chapter covers syllabus areas:

- F3 – The audit of social, environmental and integrated reporting.

Detailed syllabus objectives are provided in the introduction section of the text book.

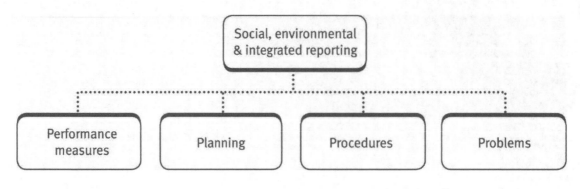

Exam focus

Social and environmental reporting has been examined several times in past exams. Any part of the engagement process could be examined from acceptance through to reporting. You may also be asked to give examples of performance measures and sustainability indicators for a company.

1 The need for social and environmental reporting and assurance

The need for social and environmental reporting

Many companies develop and maintain social, ethical and environmental policies that can range from highly generalised statements of ethical intention to more detailed corporate guidelines.

Today's heightened interest in the role of businesses in society has been promoted by increased sensitivity to, and awareness of, environmental and ethical issues. In addition, businesses are now expected to account for their impact on the social and natural environment.

Integrated reporting is now common where performance measures such as targets in relation to corporate and social responsibility matters are communicated.

Performance in this area is often a factor affecting the decision of employees, customers, and suppliers to engage with an organisation.

Key performance indicators (KPIs)

KPIs, or business performance measures, are financial and non-financial measures that are monitored to determine the strategic performance of an organisation, including those that are critical for the continued success of the organisation.

Monitoring of KPIs enables performance to be evaluated in comparison to benchmark performance criteria or progress to be compared to the results of competitors.

To generate KPIs for the company, management need to:

- Identify the goals of the organisation in relation to social and environmental matters e.g. reduction of electricity and water usage.

- Measure the performance e.g. taking meter readings of electricity and water usage.

- Assess whether the goal has been achieved e.g. compare usage to the prior year to see if it has reduced.

 In the exam you may be asked to suggest KPIs for a company. Make sure your suggestions are measurable, whether this is in:

- $ (e.g. $ spent on charitable activities).

- % (e.g. % of waste that is recycled).

- Number (e.g. number of serious accidents in the workplace).

- Hours/days (e.g. hours/days given to volunteering).

You may also be asked how the assurance provider can verify the validity of the KPI i.e. what evidence would be obtained to provide assurance over the given KPIs.

The need for assurance reports on social and environmental reports

Many companies now publish social and environmental reports within their annual report and auditors may be engaged to report on the fairness and validity of KPIs. This independent review will add credibility to the social and environmental data published and give assurance to external users that the progress claimed by a company's management is in fact real progress. This type of review is an example of an attestation engagement and is often referred to as an environmental audit.

 Attestation engagements are explained in Chapter 12.

The importance of social and environmental policies

- Issues like environmental damage, unethical treatment of workers, and faulty production that inconveniences or endangers customers or staff are highlighted in the media.

- In some countries, government regulation regarding environmental and social issues has increased.

- Some investment fund managers have created ethical funds which take account of a corporation's social and environmental policies for ethically minded investors.

- Some consumers have become increasingly sensitive to the social and environmental performance of the companies from which they buy their goods and services.

- These trends have contributed to the pressure on companies to operate in an economically, socially, and environmentally sustainable way.

The need for social and environmental reporting

Sometimes there is a marked difference between a company's code of ethics and their actual practices, giving rise to the opinion that such policies may be more of a marketing tool than a serious statement of intent.

In addition, environmental and social reporting is normally voluntary, although stakeholder pressure demands it in many industries, and organisations in some industries are required to report on specific targets by law, therefore the extent and selection of reporting measures varies significantly from company to company.

Each company is likely to have differing views on what to measure and how to measure it, making comparisons very difficult. For these reasons environmental and social reporting can be a controversial area.

Generally an organisation will set an overall goal with specific targets to meet in relation to that goal.

There is obviously a great deal of skill and experience required to derive measures for social and environmental responsibility.

Two possible approaches can be used (which are not mutually exclusive):

- Comply with an externally defined set of standards, and/or

- Define one's own set of relevant targets and indicators and monitor progress towards achieving these.

Many companies adopt a benchmarking approach where they work with a market leader in order to derive performance standards that will lead to improvement.

Common accreditations

Fair Trade Foundation

Fairtrade products include coffee, tea, bananas, sugar, cotton, flowers and gold. Consumers of Fairtrade products can be assured that products have been acquired from producers who have been paid a fair price, or where workers have been provided with fair pay and conditions.

Carbon Trust

A company issued with the Carbon Trust Standard must have demonstrated improvements in reducing carbon emissions, water usage or waste. Accreditation can be awarded individually or for all three aspects.

Forest Stewardship Council (FSC)

The FSC promotes responsible management of forests. Consumers purchasing timber or paper products containing the FSC ecolabel can be assured that the trees used have come from sustainable sources, as well as other ethical considerations.

McDonald's Sustainability Report

International fast food chain McDonald's publishes a Sustainability Report which covers:

Food – aiming to improve nutrition of its products and increase the amount of fruit, vegetables and wholegrains served to customers.

Sourcing – working with suppliers who are committed to doing business responsibly. Making sure that they meet McDonald's requirements for ethics, environmental responsibility and economic viability.

Planet – seeking ways to improve restaurant efficiency, energy usage and costs, recycle waste and conserve and reuse water.

People – making a positive impact in employee lives by creating career opportunities and promoting diversity.

Community – giving something back to the community and being a good neighbour.

John Lewis Partnership example

The John Lewis partnership is the largest employee owned organisation in the UK, i.e. not owned by shareholders. The John Lewis partnership includes Waitrose supermarkets as well as John Lewis department stores.

"The Partnership's ultimate purpose is the happiness of all its members, through their worthwhile and satisfying employment in a successful business. Because the Partnership is owned in trust for its members, they share the responsibilities of ownership as well as its rewards – profit, knowledge and power."

The organisation publishes an annual sustainability report. Some of the measures reported include:

- Volunteer hours given
- Number of apprentices
- Net new jobs created
- Value donated to good causes
- % of pre-tax profits given to charitable and community activities
- CO_2 emissions
- Refrigeration and cooling direct emissions
- Food packaging reduction
- Transport emissions
- Waste diverted from landfill
- Distribution mileage
- Sustainable products:
    - Responsible sourcing of fish from wild capture fisheries
    - Soya from certified sustainable sources
    - Wooden products from recycled or certified sustainable sources
    - Own brand paper products from recycled or certified sustainable sources
    - Cotton from sustainable sources.

In addition to measuring these targets internally, the organisation looks to achieve third party accreditation where possible.

Impact of environmental matters on the audit

Certain types of organisation are high risk in terms of social and environmental reporting. Typical examples are companies engaged in oil and gas exploration, shipping and nuclear waste reprocessing.

A company's social and environmental obligations may lead to liabilities that must be recognised in the financial statements.

When an auditor realises that a client may have environmental issues that could impact the financial statements, additional procedures should be designed and carried out to detect any potential misstatements.

Possible areas that might lead to the risk of material misstatements include the following:

- Provisions, e.g. for site restoration costs.

- Contingent liabilities, e.g. arising from pending legal action.

- Impairment of asset values, e.g. non-current assets or inventories that may be subject to environmental concern or contamination.

- Accounting for capital or revenue expenditure on cleaning up the production process or to meet legal or other standards.

- Product redesign costs.

- Product viability/going concern considerations.

The following substantive procedures might be appropriate to detect potential misstatements in respect of social-environmental matters:

- Obtain an appropriate understanding of the company, its operations, and, in particular, its environmental issues.

- Enquire of management as to any systems or controls that are in place to identify risk, evaluate control, and account for environmental matters.

- Seek corroborative evidence of any statements made by management on environmental matters and obtain written representations.

- Obtain evidence from environmental experts where possible.

- Use professional judgment to consider whether the evidence in relation to environmental matters is sufficiently persuasive.

- Review available documentation (board minutes, expert's reports, correspondence with authorities or lawyers etc).

- Review all assets for impairment.

- Review liabilities and provisions to ensure all have been included and contingencies to ensure adequate disclosure.

- Include environmental issues in the review of the appropriateness of going concern.

2 Planning an engagement

There are a number of issues that should be considered when planning an engagement to provide assurance over an entity's business performance measures and sustainability indicators. These include:

- Understanding and agreeing the scope of the engagement, i.e. is assurance to be provided on the outcome and measurement of the KPIs only, or on the fairness and validity of the entire KPI benchmarking exercise (e.g. including the appropriateness and completeness of the measures chosen).

- Obtaining an understanding of the entity.

- Considering the appropriateness of the KPIs chosen in the light of this understanding, ensuring the KPIs chosen represent the priorities of the company.

- Reviewing and agreeing the KPIs over which assurance is to be provided, flagging any KPIs that are not specific enough to measure accurately, and over which assurance can therefore not be provided.

- Identifying the evidence that should be available in relation to each KPI in order to provide an assurance conclusion.

- Considering the potential for manipulation of each KPI, to achieve the desired result, i.e. identifying those KPIs which present the highest engagement risk.

3 Procedures

The same principles for gathering evidence apply for any type of assignment. The assurance provider should obtain sufficient appropriate evidence to be able to form a conclusion on the subject matter. Procedures will include:

- Enquiry of management and experts.

- Recalculation of figures to verify arithmetical accuracy.

- Inspection of supporting documentation.

- External confirmation from third party certification providers.

4 Problems

Measurement problems

- KPIs may not be specific enough to measure accurately

  Take, for example: 'To increase the monetary value of charitable donations by 10% over the next 12 months.'

  Although this appears easy enough to assess in principle, what would happen if the company chose to donate goods or time? How would you value donated goods (cost vs. sales price) and how would you value the time of volunteers (wage cost vs. value of skills contributed)? This becomes much more difficult to measure in practice.

- The concepts involved may lack precise definition

  Consider the concepts of 'sustainability,' 'being green,' 'customer satisfaction,' and 'serious workplace accidents.' All of these are common terms for KPIs but none of them have a standard definition and for that reason may lack credibility.

- Absence of systems and controls

  Companies that have only recently started to report this type of information may not have established a reliable system to record the information. This will affect the completeness and accuracy of the information.

Problems auditing social and environmental reports

Due to the complex and often subjective nature of social and environmental performance, reporting on these matters is a difficult task.

- Accountants lack the specific skills and experience needed to assess many environmental/social matters. For example, it appears unlikely that an auditor would be able to measure carbon emissions or energy consumption.

- There is a significant amount of subjectivity with regard to social and environmental reports, for example, the use of the term 'environmentally friendly.'

- Evidence may not be sufficient or appropriate for the purposes of providing assurance. It is unlikely that companies will establish sophisticated measuring and recording systems to gather the data used for all KPIs. For example: if a company donates goods to charity it is unlikely that there will be invoices, orders, goods despatched notes, remittances, cash transactions etc. In this case how does the auditor determine the quantity and value of goods donated?

- Potential for manipulation

  Due to the problems mentioned above, management has scope to manipulate the figures to make them show what they want to present to stakeholders which increases risk for the auditor.

5 Reporting

Independent verification statements

Where a review is carried out by an independent third party into the environmental matters of an organisation, an **independent verification statement** may be issued. This can take two forms:

* A company can conduct an internal audit on environmental matters and have the internal audit verified by external assessors, or

* A company may engage a third party to perform an independent review of its environmental matters.

Regardless of the type of review undertaken, the report will have some common features:

* Methodology is stated

* Matters reviewed are described

* Reference is made to other documents where applicable

* Conclusion is given.

The integrated report of the company will usually refer to the social and environmental performance indicators the company measures. Where an independent third party verifies this data, a statement will be included in the integrated report to this effect to enhance the credibility of such information.

Illustration of an independent verification statement

Below is an example of a report by an external assessor who might be a Registered Environmental Impact Assessor and/or a member of the Institute of Environmental Assessment or other recognised bodies.

External verification statement

AB & Company has conducted a formal independent verification of the internal audit undertaken by CD Construction plc.

Method and scope of the verification

The verification was conducted by reviewing the internal audit report and by interviewing the senior staff responsible for the audit. The verification examined the audit findings against 50 of the 64 targets in detail. The targets selected were those that had been awarded a maximum score for target achievement (10/10).

Internal audit's role related to auditing progress against targets reported by CD Construction plc's businesses and internal audit's findings are included in the section on Environmental Performance Targets (we have not verified other sections of this report).

Opinion

We are satisfied that the internal audit was conducted against an appropriate methodology. We have reviewed the statements made about progress against targets and confirm that they accurately reflect the audit findings.

Signed

AB & Company

Wolverhampton

March 3 20X4

Current issue: Emerging forms of external reporting

Feedback Statement: Supporting Credibility and Trust in Emerging Forms of External Reporting: Ten Key Challenges

In 2016, the IAASB issued a Discussion Paper on Emerging Forms of External Reporting (EER). The details of the discussion paper are given below this section.

Responses were received from a variety of stakeholder groups including professional bodies, national auditing standard setters and accounting firms.

The key messages from the Feedback Statement published in January 2018 are:

- Demand for assurance is expected to increase as EER evolves, however, demand is limited at present and therefore it is considered too early to develop a subject-matter specific assurance engagement standard. Other reasons given are:

    - Entities do not have sufficiently mature reporting systems, controls and oversight

    - Entities are not following existing EER frameworks consistently

    - A new standard may be too rigid and inflexible

    - ISAE 3000 (Revised) is sufficient for the time being.

- Work performed by auditors under ISA 720 is not considered sufficient when EER information is included and can create an expectation gap, as users expect that the information covered by ISA 720 has been subjected to assurance rather than read for consistency.

There was consensus that the responsibilities of the financial statement auditor should not be extended because:

- EER is not mature enough

- There is no clear demand for doing so

- Financial statement auditors may not possess the specialist knowledge and skills to work with the wide range of topics covered in EER

- Changing auditor responsibilities globally would require involvement of regulators around the world.

- Guidance on EER should be provided by developing existing standards such as ISAE 3000 rather than developing new standards.

- Guidance should be developed in such a way that innovation in EER is not stifled.

- Three of the ten key challenges are considered to be the highest priority:

    - Evaluating the suitability of criteria

    - Addressing materiality

    - Form of the assurance report.

Discussion paper: Supporting Credibility and Trust in Emerging Forms of External Reporting: Ten Key Challenges

Emerging External Reports (EER) background

External reporting by companies is increasingly providing non-financial information to meet the needs of stakeholders. This includes environmental, social and governance matters.

Many types of professional services can be performed in relation to this information, including advisory services, agreed-upon procedures, compilation engagements, assurance engagements and internal reporting to management on the entity's reporting processes and controls.

Whilst some countries have developed their own reporting standards on these matters, there is a need for global guidance to provide consistency and quality around the world.

The auditor will read the additional information in the annual report to identify any inconsistencies between the information and the financial statements and their knowledge obtained during the audit. However, they do not express a conclusion about this this information. A separate assurance engagement covering this information may add credibility to the EER report.

Reason for the discussion paper

The IAASB is looking into whether a specific standard should be developed to address a more specific type of engagement. This will keep international standards fit for purpose, support practitioners and support the quality of assurance engagements.

At present there is a lack of guidance for practitioners performing these assurance engagements. The main form of guidance comes from ISAE 3000 which is a framework neutral standard intended to be applied to a wide range of assurance engagements.

Credibility and trust in relation to EER reports

Credibility and trust are enhanced if there are 4 key factors:

(i) Sound reporting framework – the framework should address the reporting objectives and qualitative characteristics of the information.

(ii) Strong governance – the company should have a strong internal control system to ensure the information in the EER is reliable and available on a timely basis.

(iii) Consistent wider information – the information in the EER report should be consistent with other sources of information likely to be available to users of the report.

(iv) External professional service reports e.g. assurance reports – an accompanying report prepared by an external practitioner can add credibility due to their competence, objectivity, professional scepticism and judgment, and quality control procedures.

Ten key challenges

The IAASB has identified ten key challenges which are barriers to more widespread use of assurance reports in relation to Emerging External Reports (EER):

(1) Determining the scope of the assurance engagement – the scope may be broader and more diverse. It may be difficult to provide a full scope engagement as the costs may outweigh the benefits.

(2) Evaluating the suitability of criteria – EER frameworks are less prescriptive and more ambiguous providing opportunity for management bias.

(3) Addressing materiality – EER has no common unit of measurement making materiality judgments difficult to benchmark. Due to the diversity of users, establishing materiality that applies to all will be difficult.

(4) Establishing appropriate assertions – the diverse nature of EER subject matter makes it more difficult to develop appropriate assertions.

(5) Maturity of governance and internal control processes – entities may not have sufficiently robust EER reporting systems and controls in place. As a result the EER report may not be capable of being assured.

(6) Obtaining assurance over narrative information – narrative information may include management judgments and be more susceptible to management bias.

(7) Obtaining assurance over future-oriented information – future-oriented information is more common in EER reports. There is greater uncertainty over this information. Therefore the assurance may have to be limited to obtaining evidence about the process used in arriving at the future-oriented information.

(8) Professional scepticism and judgment – EER reports are likely to contain information that is more susceptible to management bias resulting in a greater need to apply professional scepticism and judgment.

(9) Competence of practitioners – this type of engagement may call for broad specialised subject matter competence, greater need for experts and the use of multi-disciplinary teams.

(10) Form of the assurance report – to effectively communicate the conclusions to users, the report may need to include the following to ensure they are of use and not seen as ambiguous or difficult to interpret:

– A summary of the work performed which provides the basis for the conclusion

– Additional information such as the terms of engagement, criteria, findings, competencies of the individuals involved, materiality levels and recommendations

– Separate conclusions on one or more aspects of the subject matter.

Test your understanding 1

You are the manager responsible for the audit of The National Literary Museum (NLM), a museum focusing on famous literary works. Entry to the museum is free for all visitors and many visitors make repeat visits to the museum.

NLM receives funding from government departments for culture and education, as well as several large charitable donations. The amount of funding received is dependent on three key performance indicator (KPI) targets being met annually. All three targets must be met in order to secure the government funding.

Extracts from NLM's operating and financial review are as follows:

	KPI target	Draft KPI	Prior year actual
Number of annual visitors:	100,000	102,659	103,752
Proportion of total visitors of school age:	25%	29%	27%
Number of educational programmes run:	4	4	4

Your firm is engaged to provide an assurance report on the KPIs disclosed in NLMs operating and financial review.

Required:

Discuss the difficulties that may be encountered when providing assurance over the stated key performance indicators. **(4 marks)**

Test your understanding 2

You are the manager responsible for the audit of Shire Oil Co, a listed company. Shire Oil Co is primarily an oil producer with interests in the North Sea, West Africa and South Asia. Extracts from the latest interim report shows the following information:

	30 June 20X5	30 June 20X4	31 December 20X4
	Unaudited	Audited	Unaudited
	$000	$000	$000
Revenue	22,000	18,300	37,500
Profit before tax	5,500	4,200	7,500
Total assets	95,900	92,300	88,400
Earnings per share (basic)	$1.82	$2.07	$3.53

In April 20X5, the company was awarded a new five-year licence, by the central government, to explore for oil in a remote region. The licence was granted at no cost to Shire Oil Co but has been recognised at an estimated fair value of $3 million in the financial statements.

The most significant of Shire Oil Co's tangible non-current assets are its 17 oil rigs (20X4: 15). Each rig comprises numerous items including a platform, buildings thereon and drilling equipment. The useful life of each platform is assessed annually on factors such as weather conditions and the period over which it is estimated that oil will be extracted. Platforms are depreciated on a straight line basis over 15 to 40 years.

A provision for the present value of the expected cost of decommissioning an oil rig is recognised in full at the commencement of oil production. One of the rigs in South Asia sustained severe cyclone damage in October 20X5. Shire Oil Co's management believes the rig is beyond economic recovery and that there will be no alternative but to abandon it where it is. This suggestion has brought angry protests from conservationists.

In July 20X5, the company entered into an agreement to share in the future economic benefits of an extensive oil pipeline.

Last year your firm issued a modified audit opinion due to a lack of evidence to support management's schedule of proven and probable oil reserves to be recoverable from known reserves.

Required:

(a) Using the information provided, evaluate the audit risks to be considered when planning the final audit of Shire Oil Co for the year ending 31 December 20X5. **(12 marks)**

(b) Describe the principal procedures to be performed in respect of the useful lives of Shire Oil Co's rig platforms. **(5 marks)**

You have just been advised of management's intention to publish its yearly marketing report in the annual report that will contain the financial statements for the year ending 31 December 20X5. Extracts from the marketing report include the following:

'Shire Oil Co sponsors national school sports championships and the 'Shire Ward' at the national teaching hospital. The company's vision is to continue its investment in health and safety and the environment.

Our health and safety, security and environmental policies are of the highest standard in the energy sector. We aim to operate under principles of no-harm to people and the environment.

Shire Oil Co's main contribution to sustainable development comes from providing extra energy in a cleaner and more socially responsible way. This means improving the environmental and social performance of our operations. Regrettably, five employees lost their lives at work during the year.'

Required:

(c) Suggest performance indicators that could reflect the extent to which Shire Oil Co's social and environmental responsibilities are being met, and the evidence that should be available to provide assurance on their accuracy. **(8 marks)**

(Total: 25 marks)

6 Chapter summary

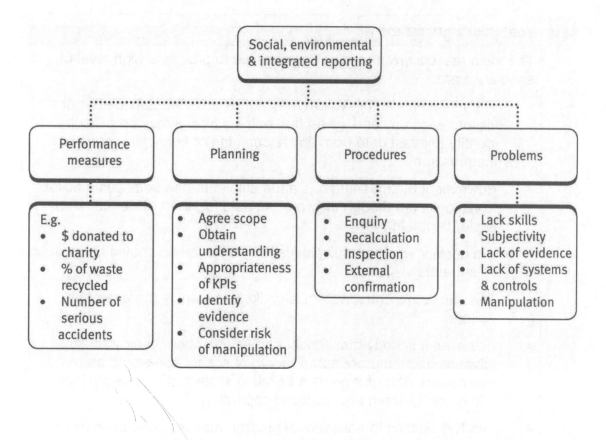

Social, environmental & integrated reporting

Performance measures

E.g.
- $ donated to charity
- % of waste recycled
- Number of serious accidents

Planning
- Agree scope
- Obtain understanding
- Appropriateness of KPIs
- Identify evidence
- Consider risk of manipulation

Procedures
- Enquiry
- Recalculation
- Inspection
- External confirmation

Problems
- Lack skills
- Subjectivity
- Lack of evidence
- Lack of systems & controls
- Manipulation

Test your understanding answers

Test your understanding 1

The main reason why it may not be possible to provide a high level of assurance are:

- The museum's entry system may not record the total number of visitors each day and, given that entry is free, it may be difficult to identify relevant data from any accounting or financial systems of the museum.

- However, if the museum has a turnstile entrance or issues a ticket to visitors even though they are not paid for, then evidence will be easier to obtain.

- It is unclear whether multiple visits by one person should be counted as separate visitors.

- The museum's entry system is unlikely to identify the age of all visitors.

- However, it is likely that school parties must book their visits in advance and therefore some record of school age would be maintained. Also, if there is a ticketing system, it is possible that adults and children are recorded separately.

- The KPI relating to educational programmes is poorly defined – what constitutes an educational programme? How long does it have to run? How many users have to benefit from it running?

- If however, an educational programme means an exhibition or event that covers a national curriculum area, it may be easier to verify this KPI.

Tutorial note: When given a requirement of 'discuss', it is advisable to gives reasons both for and against the argument being stated.

Test your understanding 2

(a) **Audit risks**

Licence – initial recognition

A five-year licence has been granted to Shire Oil Co at no cost. This is recognised at an estimated fair value of $3m.

A licence may be valued at either cost or fair value. However, valuation other than at cost ($nil) is inherently risky as fair value has been estimated by management.

The licence may be unique (being for five years in a remote region) and in the absence of an active market, or recent transactions for which prices can be observed, it seems unlikely that any estimate of fair value made by management can be substantiated.

There is a risk of overvaluation of the licence.

Licence – amortisation

Assuming the recognition of the licence at fair value is deemed appropriate, it should be accounted for under IAS 38 *Intangible Assets* which requires the asset to be amortised over its useful life.

There is a risk that the licence is overstated if it has not been amortised over the five year period of the licence.

Research and development

Research and development costs (may also be described as exploration and evaluation costs or discovery and assessment) must be expensed unless/until Shire Oil Co has a legal right to explore the area in which they are incurred.

In respect of the remote region, Shire Oil Co can only capitalise costs incurred from April.

There is a risk of overstatement of intangible assets if research costs are capitalised incorrectly.

Property, plant and equipment

Item replacements (e.g. of drilling equipment) should be recognised as items of property, plant and equipment (and the replaced items as disposals) in accordance with IAS 16 *Property, Plant and Equipment.*

Constituent items of each rig should be depreciated over their useful lives. Management should reassess the useful life of each rig annually to ensure they are being depreciated appropriately.

Assets will be misstated if not depreciated over an appropriate period.

Decommissioning provision

One of the company's oil rigs sustained severe damage in October and management have decided to abandon it. A decommissioning provision is recognised in full in respect of the oil rig.

A provision should only be recognised if there is a present obligation as a result of a past event that is probable to lead to an outflow of economic benefits and can be measured reliably (IAS 37 *Provisions, Contingent Liabilities and Contingent Assets*).

As management intend to abandon the rig, this would imply that there will be no dismantling of the rig and therefore no costs incurred.

There is a risk that the decommissioning provision is overstated if the company intends to abandon the rig and there is no obligation to take it down.

Abandoned rig – value

The cost of the rig includes the cost of decommissioning the rig at the end of its life. The rig is likely to have a value of $nil as there is no value in use and the rig is to be abandoned rather than decommissioned.

As the rig is no longer in use, depreciation should cease and an impairment review performed.

There is a risk the abandoned rig is overvalued in the financial statements as it is now impaired.

Abandonment of rig – liabilities

Further liabilities may result from the abandonment of the rig. This could include provision for redundancy of rig workers, fines/penalties as a result of abandoning the rig (IAS 37).

There is a risk that adequate disclosure is not made of the contingent liabilities and a risk that provisions are understated if not recognised in accordance with IAS 37.

Pipeline agreement

The oil pipeline is a jointly controlled asset that should be accounted for to reflect its economic substance in accordance with IAS 28 *Investments in Associates and Joint Ventures*.

Shire Oil Co must recognise its share of the asset, liabilities and expenditure incurred and any income from the sale of its share of the oil output (as well as its own liabilities and expenses separately incurred).

There is a risk that appropriate disclosure of the joint venture is not made.

Previous year's auditor's report

The prior year auditor's report was modified due to a lack of sufficient appropriate evidence over the oil reserves.

If there is a similar lack of evidence in the current year the opinion should be similarly qualified.

Even if the correct position at 31 December 20X5 is determinable, the auditor's opinion at that date should be modified in respect of the impact, if any, on the opening position and comparative information (unless the opening oil reserves position has since been ascertained and can be corrected with a prior period adjustment).

Manipulation

As Shire Oil Co is a listed company there will be pressure on management to meet the expectations of users, in particular shareholders and analysts.

The fall in basic EPS (as compared with the first six months of the previous half year) may increase management bias to overstate performance in the second half year (to 31 December 20X5).

There is a risk of manipulation of the financial statements in order to impress the shareholders.

Operating segments

As a listed company, Shire Oil Co is required to comply with the extensive disclosure requirements of IFRS 8 *Operating Segments*.

There is a risk that this disclosure has not been made or has not been made adequately.

Going concern

The oil industry is exposed to a volatile market. Shire Oil Co operates in different regions with exposure to economic instability, currency devaluation and high inflation.

In addition, the company can only operate if it has a licence. Licences may be withdrawn if, for example, the company does not comply with environmental legislation.

There is a risk of inadequate disclosure of going concern issues.

(b) **Principal audit work – useful life of rig platforms**

- Review management's annual assessment of the useful life of each rig at 31 December 20X5 and corroborate any information that has led to a change in previous estimates. For example, for the abandoned rig where useful life has been assessed to be at an end, obtain:

    - weather reports

    - incident report supported by photographs

    - insurance claim, etc.

- Consider management's past experience and expertise in estimating useful lives. For example, if all lives that are initially assessed as short (c. 15 years) are subsequently lengthened (or long lives consistently shortened) this would suggest that management is being over (or under) prudent in its initial estimates.

- Review the useful lives used by other oil companies as published in their annual reports to assess reasonableness of Shire Oil Co's depreciation rates.

- Compare actual maintenance costs against budget to confirm that the investment needed to achieve the expected life expectancy is being made.

- Compare actual output (oil extracted) to budget. If actual output is less than budgeted the economic life of the platform may be:

    - shorter (e.g. because there is less oil to be extracted than originally surveyed)

    - longer (e.g. because the rate of extraction is less than budgeted).

- Review the results of management's impairment testing of each rig to assess reasonableness.

- Recalculate the cash flow projections (based on reasonable and supportable assumptions) discounted at a suitable pre-tax rate.

- Review of working papers of geologist/quantity surveyor(s) employed by Shire Oil Co supporting estimations of reserves used in the determination of useful lives of rigs.

(c) **Performance indicators**

Performance indicator	Evidence
Absolute ($) level of investment in sports sponsorship, and funding to the Shire Ward	• Cash book to verify actual level of investment ($)
Average bed occupancy	• Reports from the hospital regarding the Shire Ward occupancy
Number of patients treated successfully during the year	• Reports from the hospital regarding the Shire Ward occupancy
Number of sporting events/ medals/trophies sponsored	• Correspondence with event organisers to confirm sponsorship of events/ medals/trophies • Press articles covering sponsored events • Copies of advertisements showing sponsorship by Shire Oil Co
Number of oil spills	• Correspondence with industry regulator regarding non-compliance • Press articles covering publicised breaches • Board minutes
Number of breaches of health and safety regulations and environmental regulations	• Correspondence with industry regulator regarding breaches • Press articles covering publicised breaches • Board minutes

Number of accidents and employee fatalities	• Accident book • Correspondence with insurance company relating to claims made • Board minutes • Press articles
Number of insurance claims	• Cash book to verify amounts settled on insurance claims • Correspondence with the insurance company relating to claims made
Staff turnover	• HR records
Average number of days absent per person per annum	• HR records

INT syllabus only: Audit of performance information in the public sector

Chapter learning objectives

This chapter covers syllabus areas:

- F4 – The audit of performance information (pre-determined objectives) in the public sector.

Detailed syllabus objectives are provided in the introduction section of the text book.

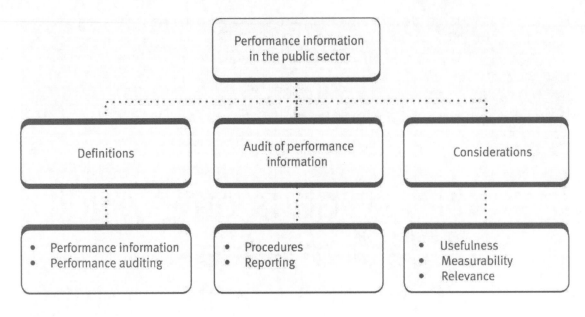

 Exam focus

This syllabus area is only relevant to students sitting the International variant of the syllabus. The concepts covered in this chapter are very similar to the concepts covered in the chapter on social and environmental reporting.

1 Public sector audit requirements

Public sector audit requirements

Public sector organisations are subject to greater regulation and reporting requirements than profit making organisations due to the fact that they are funded by taxpayer money.

There are 2 types of audit that must be performed for public sector organisations:

(1) Financial statement audit

(2) Performance audit.

2 Performance audit

Performance audits aim to provide management with assurance and advice regarding the effective functioning of its operational activities.

A performance audit uses auditing skills (planning & risk assessment, gathering sufficient appropriate evidence, reporting) and applying them to activities of the organisation that an external auditor of the financial statements wouldn't normally consider.

Performance audits may include

(1)   Performance information

(2)   Value for money – economy, efficiency and effectiveness of operations

(3)   Operational audits.

 3   Performance information

Performance information is information published by public sector bodies regarding their objectives and the achievement of those objectives.

This information should have the same qualitative characteristics of general purpose financial reports such as relevance, completeness, reliability, neutrality, understandability, timeliness, validity and accuracy.

The external auditor may have a responsibility to report on this information to the users of such information.

Performance measures for public sector bodies

Hospital Performance Measures

- Reduce number of medical errors

- Reduce number of cases of MRSA (a bacterium responsible for causing infections particularly prevalent in hospitals)

- Reduce waiting times for operations

- Improve satisfaction with hospital food

- Decrease mortality rates.

Local Council Performance Indicators

- % of streets that have unacceptable levels of litter on them to be 7% or less

- % residents satisfied with the local environment to be 79% or above

- At least 200 dwellings improved by the actions of the council

- To have no more than 45 households living in temporary accommodation

- At least 57% of bids for external finance/grant applications to be approved.

Police Performance Measures

- Reduce number of priority crimes e.g. burglary, theft of cars by 18%

- Increase serious violence detection rates by 68%

- Reduce number of anti-social behaviour incidents by 40%

- Reduce reoffending rates by 50%

- Increase public satisfaction to 80%.

Performance measures such as these are important to various stakeholder groups for example:

- The government who want to see that the money they provide to the relevant departments is being used effectively.

- The users of the services to assess how well their police force/hospital/council is performing in comparison with others.

- Potential users of the services e.g. where there is a choice of hospital to use, the patient may look at this information to decide which hospital at which to have their treatment.

---

4 Planning an audit of performance information

At the planning stage the auditor will:

- Obtain an understanding of the information to be reported on including how it is collected, aggregated, reporting processes, systems and controls.

- Make enquiries with management and staff to obtain an understanding of the data and how it is processed and reported.

- Establish materiality (see below).

- Examine the processes, systems and controls in place to collect, aggregate and report the performance information.

Materiality for non-financial information

Materiality for non-financial information is just as important as for financial information. For example if the entity is reporting that a target has been met when it hasn't this will affect the penalties faced.

For performance information such as mortality rates for a hospital, the indicator is highly sensitive and therefore material.

Setting materiality for non-financial information is more difficult to apply as compared with financial information and there is a risk that different assurance providers would reach different conclusions. As a result, this will undermine the credibility of the report.

One way of overcoming this issue is to disclose the materiality level used in the assurance report. Where performance measures apply across a variety of public bodies, a consistent approach should be adopted.

5 Procedures

Procedures to gather evidence will be the same as for a normal audit:

- Inspection of the supporting documentation for the information.

- Enquiry of management and other personnel within the organisation.

- Perform analytical procedures on the information such as comparison with prior year or other organisations of a similar size.

- Obtain written representation from management regarding the accuracy and completeness of the information.

- Recalculation of amounts included in the performance information.

Audit procedures

Following on from the illustration above, below are some procedures that could be performed to obtain evidence over the hospital performance measures.

Hospital performance measure	Procedures
Reduce number of medical errors	Enquire of hospital management what the definition of a medical error is.
	Inspect Department of Health publication to confirm management's understanding of the definition.
	Inspect hospital records and board minutes to confirm the number of medical errors.
Reduce number of cases of MRSA and C-Diff	Inspect hospital records of the number of cases of MRSA/C-Diff.
	Compare with prior years and re-calculate the % change.
Improve satisfaction with hospital food	Review patient feedback questionnaires regarding hospital food.
	Recalculate the average score generated from the feedback and compare with prior years.
Decrease mortality rates	Inspect hospital records of the number of deaths.
	Review board minutes for evidence of any unrecorded deaths.
	Compare with prior year and re-calculate the % change.

6   Reporting

Reports on performance information may be in the form of reasonable assurance or limited assurance.

A reasonable assurance report would express the conclusion positively e.g. 'In our opinion the number of deaths reported by the hospital is fairly stated'.

A limited assurance report would express the conclusion negatively e.g. 'Nothing has come to our attention that causes us to believe that the number of deaths reported by the hospital is not fairly stated.

The assurance report will contain the usual elements of an assurance report:

- Title

- Addressee

- Introductory paragraph identifying the subject matter – the performance information being reported on

- Scope including the applicable standards and guidance followed e.g. ISAE 3000 *Assurance Engagements other than Audits or Reviews of Historical Financial Statements*

- Respective responsibilities of management and the assurance provider

- Inherent limitations of the report

- Summary of the work performed

- Conclusion based on the work performed

- Signature of the assurance provider

- Date.

7   Usefulness, measurability and reliability

Usefulness

Performance information is now more commonplace with the introduction of government targets, league tables and measures for public sector organisations to demonstrate accountability to the taxpayer.

This information is reported to the relevant regulatory authority but may also be published on the organisation's website and included in their annual report.

Users of the information are able to assess the performance of government departments or to help make choices such as which hospital to choose for treatment.

Measurability

Some measures may be subjective in terms of definition and as a result may be easily manipulated by management in order to ensure they are being seen to achieve the target.

This may lead the way for some organisations to include measures which are not relevant to their main strategic aims but which have been included to make it appear as though the organisation has achieved something.

There is a risk that organisations are deliberately vague when composing performance measures so that they can claim to have met their target.

For these reasons, measurement of the target may be difficult and therefore difficult for the auditor to prove or disprove.

Whilst there are national performance measures in place which all organisations of a particular type will need to report, each organisation can also determine their own performance objectives they wish to measure. This inconsistency means comparisons cannot be drawn between different entities and may cause confusion for users of the performance information who see that different criteria are being used to assess the same information.

Reliability

It is important that detailed criteria are developed to avoid different entities and assurance providers interpreting them differently. These criteria should be referred to in the assurance report, either via a link to the website detailing the criteria or as an appendix to the report.

Quality assurance processes within the public sector compare the assurance provider's work and results to ensure that a level of consistency exists between the different firms and give comfort to users that the conclusions drawn would be the same irrespective of which assurance firm performed the work.

These pre-determined standards and quality assurance processes should improve reliability of the performance information.

Test your understanding 1

Suggest 3 performance measures for a government treasury department and list the audit procedures that an auditor of the performance information could perform to obtain evidence to support the figures reported.   **(6 marks)**

Test your understanding 2

Explain the difference between a performance audit and an audit of performance information.   **(2 marks)**

8 Chapter summary

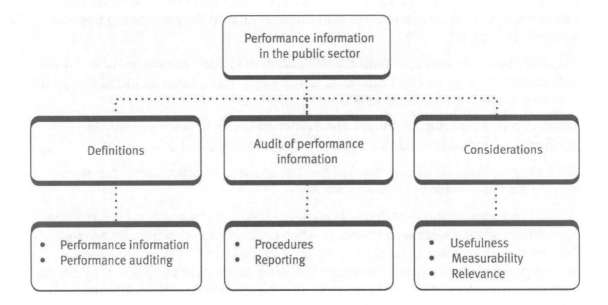

Test your understanding answers

Test your understanding 1

Performance measures	Audit procedures
Gross domestic product (GDP) per head of population	Review department reports for GDP and population.
	Recalculate the GDP per head of population to verify the figure reported.
Employment rate	Review department reports for the number of people in employment and calculate this as a % of the working population.
Public sector net debt as a % of GDP	Review the department report for the level of debt and calculate this as a % of GDP.

These are procedures assuming a limited assurance engagement. If a reasonable assurance engagement was being performed, tests of controls could be performed to evaluate the systems and processes used to collect the information.

Test your understanding 2

Performance audit

A performance audit is an audit of the operational activities of an organisation, typically with a view of assessing value for money.

Value for money is concerned with the 3 Es – economy, efficiency and effectiveness.

- Economy – obtaining the lowest cost for the required level of quality.

- Efficiency – achieving the maximum output for the minimum input.

- Effectiveness – achieving the objectives set.

In the context of a public sector organisation, value for money is concerned with stewardship of the public pound i.e. not wasting taxpayer money.

Performance information audit

Public sector organisations have targets set by the government which must be reported to assess the organisation's performance. This is referred to as 'performance information'.

An audit of the performance information will be concerned with obtaining evidence that the results reported by the organisation against such targets are:

- Accurate – data is recorded correctly.

- Valid – data has been produced in compliance with relevant requirements.

- Reliable – data has been collected using a stable process in a consistent manner over a period of time.

- Complete – all relevant information has been included.

UK syllabus only: Auditing aspects of insolvency

Chapter learning objectives

This chapter covers syllabus areas:

- F4 – Auditing aspects of insolvency (and similar procedures).

Detailed syllabus objectives are provided in the introduction section of the text book.

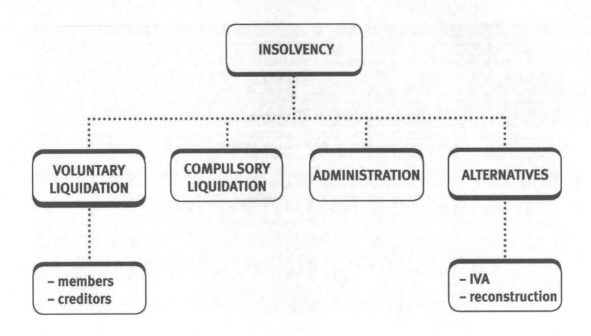

 Exam focus

This chapter is relevant to students taking the UK variant of the exam only.

Insolvency will not appear in every exam, however, it is advisable to be familiar with the different mechanisms for winding up a company, the alternatives to winding up and the advantages of these and the difference between fraudulent and wrongful trading.

 Insolvency

There are two tests for insolvency:

(1)   If assets are exceeded by liabilities, or

(2)   If a company is failing to discharge its debts as and when they fall due.

If a company meets either criteria then it is technically insolvent.

 Liquidation is the process of terminating a company, thus ending its life. The assets of the company are physically liquidated, i.e. they are sold, so that cash can be used to pay off company creditors and equity holders.

1   Voluntary liquidation

Introduction

There are two forms of voluntary liquidation:

*   Members' voluntary liquidation

*   Creditors' voluntary liquidation.

Members' voluntary liquidation

This form of liquidation is used when a company is solvent (i.e. has assets greater than its liabilities). In order to facilitate this, the members must pass one of two resolutions:

- An ordinary resolution, where the articles provide for liquidation on the expiry of a fixed date or a specific event, or

- A special resolution, for any other reason.

Once the resolution has been passed the directors must make a **declaration of solvency** stating that they are of the opinion that the company will be able to pay its debts within 12 months. A false declaration would constitute a criminal offence.

The members will then appoint a named insolvency practitioner to act as the liquidator by passing an ordinary resolution. The insolvency practitioner will realise the company's assets and distribute the proceeds accordingly.

Once the liquidation process is complete the liquidator must send a copy of the final account to the members. The company will be dissolved three months later.

Creditor's voluntary liquidation

This form of liquidation is used if a company intends to liquidate voluntarily but is insolvent. A resolution of members must be passed (as with a members' voluntary liquidation). However, no declaration of solvency can be made.

Both the members and the creditors are entitled to appoint a liquidator. However, in the case of a disagreement, the creditors' choice must prevail over the members' choice. In addition, the creditors may appoint up to five people to sit on a liquidation committee.

The directors must send to the creditors a **statement of affairs** within 7 working days. The statement of affairs contains full details of all creditors, including names and addresses, and the amounts of their claims.

The liquidator will realise the company's assets and distribute the proceeds accordingly.

Once the liquidation process is complete the liquidator submits his final report to the members and creditors and a copy of this report is sent to the registrar of companies.

The company will be dissolved three months later.

Decisions made by the creditors during the insolvency proceedings will be made using the 'deemed consent' process.

Deemed consent is a process by which an insolvency practitioner can seek a decision by the creditors which does not require the creditors to vote on the proposed decision. Provided that the insolvency practitioner does not receive objections from 10% or more of the creditors by value, the proposed decision will be deemed to have been taken.

In the event that 10% or more of the creditors object to the proposal, the insolvency practitioner will use an alternative decision-making procedure such as a virtual meeting, correspondence or electronic voting.

2 Compulsory liquidation

Introduction

Companies may be obliged to liquidate if a winding up order is presented to a court, usually by a creditor or member. Such a petition may be made for a number of reasons, which include:

- A public company has not been issued with a trading certificate within a year of incorporation.

- The company is unable to pay its debts.

  A company is deemed to be unable to pay its debts if:

  - a creditor who is owed more than £750 has served a formal demand for an undisputed sum and the company has failed to pay the sum due within 21 days.

  - a creditor has attempted to enforce a judgment against a company in respect of a debt without success.

  - it is proven to the satisfaction of the court that this is the case (the 'cash flow test') or if assets are less than liabilities (the 'balance sheet test').

- It is **just and equitable** to wind up the company. However, the court will only make an order under this ground if no other remedy is available.

  If a member petitions on this basis, this will only be considered if the company is solvent and the member has been a registered shareholder for at least six of the prior eighteen months.

Consequences

If successful, the court will appoint an Official Receiver (an officer of the courts) as liquidator. They may be replaced by a practitioner at a later date. The receiver investigates the company's affairs and the cause of its failure. The petition also has the following effects:

- All actions for the recovery of debt against the company are stopped.

- Any floating charges crystallise.

- All legal proceedings against the company are halted and none may start unless the courts grant permission.

- The company must cease trading activity, unless it is necessary to complete the liquidation, e.g. completing work-in-progress.

- The directors relinquish power and authority to the liquidator, although they may remain in office.

- Employees are automatically made redundant. The liquidator may choose to re-employ them to help complete the liquidation process.

Procedures

Within 12 weeks of appointment, the Official Receiver will propose the appointment of a licensed insolvency practitioner. Creditor approval of the insolvency practitioner is sought via the 'deemed consent' process.

The liquidator will realise the company's assets and distribute the proceeds.

The liquidator returns to the court and the court passes an order dissolving the company.

Once the liquidation process is complete the liquidator files the order and their final report with the Registrar.

The company will then be dissolved.

3 Allocation of company assets

Liquidators in a compulsory liquidation must pay debts in the following order of priority:

- Fixed charge holders

- Expenses of liquidation, including liquidator's remuneration

- Preferential creditors, including employee's wages and accrued holiday pay

- Prescribed part set aside for unsecured creditors*

- Floating charge holders

- Unsecured creditors (ranked equally)

- Preference shareholders

- Members.

It is likely that liquidators will also adhere to these principles in a voluntary liquidation as well.

*Prescribed part

The prescribed part is an amount set aside to give unsecured creditors some protection. In many liquidations, if the prescribed part was not in place, the unsecured creditors would be unlikely to receive anything as it is likely that fixed charge holders, liquidation fees, preferential creditors and floating charge holders would receive any monies crystallised.

The calculation is based on the 'net property' of the company. This is the amount of assets remaining after paying fixed charge holders, liquidator's fees and preferential creditors.

If the net property is less than £10,000, the prescribed part will not apply and any remaining monies will be paid to the floating charge holders.

The prescribed part is calculated as:

(1) 50% of the first £10,000 of the net property figure

(2) 20% of £2,985,000 less £10,000

(3) Subject to a maximum of £600,000.

If net property is less than £2,985,000 the calculation at step 2 should use the figure of net property remaining.

Example – prescribed part

Assets	£6,000,000
Fixed charge creditors	£2,500,000
Floating charge creditors	£750,000
Preferential creditors	£650,000
Unsecured creditors	£8,000,000
Ordinary share capital	£20,000,000
Liquidators costs	£200,000
Net property calculation:	
Assets	6,000,000
Less fixed charge creditors	(2,500,000)
Less liquidator's costs	(200,000)
Less preferential creditors	(650,000)
Net property	2,650,000
Prescribed part calculation (applicable as net property > £10,000)	
50% × £10,000	5,000
20% × (2,650,000 – 10,000)	528,000
Prescribed part	533,000

4 Administration

Introduction

Administration is the process whereby an insolvency practitioner is appointed to manage the affairs of a business (Enterprise Act 2002). It is often used as an alternative to liquidation with a view to:

- Rescuing a company in financial difficulty with the aim of allowing it to continue as a going concern
- Achieving better results for creditors than could be achieved through liquidation
- Realising property to pay off secured creditors.

Appointment

An administrator can be appointed by any one of the following:

- The courts, in response to a petition
- The holder of a qualifying floating charge over company assets
- Members or directors, providing that liquidation has not already begun.

A court will only appoint an administrator if the company is, or is likely to become, unable to pay its debts and if it feels that administration will help meet the objectives listed above.

The administrator must act in the best interests of all of the company's creditors.

Consequences

The administrator takes over control of the management of the company. They must follow any proposals approved at any meeting of creditors or dictated by the courts. However, particular powers include:

- Removal or appointment of directors
- Calling meetings of creditors and/or members
- Making payments to secured or preferential creditors
- Making payments to unsecured creditors, if it is felt that this will assist the objectives of the administration
- Presenting or defending a petition for liquidating the company.

Upon appointing an administrator, certain protections are afforded to the company, namely:

- The rights of creditors to enforce security over the company's assets are suspended
- Petitions for liquidation are dismissed
- No resolutions to wind up the company may be passed
- The directors continue in office, although their powers are suspended.

The proposals of the administrator must be approved by the creditors of the company. This approval can be given by:

- Deemed consent process
- Virtual meeting
- Electronic voting
- Correspondence

If the creditors do not approve the proposals, the court may dismiss the administrator or make such provisions as it sees fit.

The administration will end when it is completed or when the administrator is discharged by the court:

The administration must normally be completed within 12 months of the date on which it commenced. However, this term can be extended with the consent of the court or by a majority of the creditors.

Advantages of administration over liquidation

- Administration provides time to develop an alternative plan for survival. Liquidation results in the cessation of the company and therefore any future benefits that might have been generated will be lost.

- Members are less likely to lose their investment.

- Creditors are more likely to be paid. In a liquidation, unsecured creditors are likely to receive nothing.

- Creditors will still be able to trade with the company if the administration is successful. If the company is liquidated, the creditor loses a customer.

5 Alternatives to winding up

Introduction

Often businesses have no alternative but to face up to administration or, in the worst-case scenario, liquidation. However, there are alternatives that exist to help both unincorporated businesses and companies survive, namely:

- Voluntary arrangements
- Reconstructions.

Individual Voluntary Arrangements (IVAs)

- An IVA is an arrangement available to individuals, sole traders and partnerships to help them reach a compromise with creditors with the aim of avoiding the closure of their business and, perhaps, bankruptcy.

- Such an arrangement usually facilitates lower payments of debt over an extended period, usually five years.

- Once an individual (or their insolvency practitioner) submits a proposal to the courts for an interim order, creditors may no longer take action against the individual (a 'moratorium on actions'). A creditors meeting must be held within 14 days of the order to include the proposals made by the individual with regard to their debt. The creditors may accept the proposals with a 75% majority (by value of creditors present) vote.

- The main benefit is obviously that the individual may continue in business and work towards the payment of their debt in a more flexible manner.

- They are also not penalised by bankruptcy laws, such as restrictions on becoming a director.

- Creditors also benefit as it is likely that they will receive more under the terms of an IVA than if the business is wound up.

Company Voluntary Arrangements (CVAs)

- A company or limited liability partnership can apply for a CVA if all the directors or partners agree.

- Similar to an IVA, it allows an insolvent company to pay creditors over a fixed period and so continue trading.

- A proposed CVA cannot be approved by deemed consent. At least 75% (by value) of the creditors who vote on it must approve it.

Reconstructions

It may be possible for companies facing problems to survive by taking up new contracts or exploiting market opportunities. However, such ventures usually require cash injections and when faced with liquidity problems this can pose a problem, not least because such businesses may not appear attractive to external investment.

Typical traits of such companies include:

- Accumulated losses

- Debenture interest arrears

- Cumulative preference shares dividend arrears

- No payment of ordinary dividends

- Share price below nominal value

- Share price decline.

To become more attractive to investment the company could reorganise or reconstruct.

Permitted reconstructions

Capital structures protect stakeholders' interests. Therefore changes to these structures are restricted by company law. However, under various mechanisms of the Companies Act 2006 companies are able to:

- Write off unpaid share capital
- Write off share capital which is not represented by available assets
- Write off paid up share capital which is in excess of requirements
- Write off debenture interest arrears
- Replace existing debentures with a lower interest debenture
- Write off preference dividend arrears
- Write off amounts owing to trade creditors.

By altering the capital structure of the business and by removing some of the debt of the business, companies may be able to reduce their accumulated losses to the point that they have profits available to begin paying debts and dividends in the future. The reduction in the debt burden also frees up resources for investment in future opportunities and new growth.

To do this the company must ask its stakeholders to surrender some or all of their existing rights and amounts due. They do this in exchange for new rights under a new or reformed company and a share of the benefits that could arise due to future investment. This may be more appealing than the alternatives, which include:

- To remain as they are, with the prospect of no return from their investment and no growth in their investment, or
- To accept whatever return they could be given in a liquidation.

Modernisation of insolvency rules

One of the purposes of the Insolvency Rules 2016 is to modernise the requirements and remove unnecessary regulatory burdens.

Meetings of creditors

Prior to the Insolvency Rules 2016, physical meetings were the default mechanism for seeking decisions from creditors in insolvency proceedings. Physical meetings are no longer required and the deemed consent process is the default mechanism for decision making. There are two exceptions to this:

1   The liquidator may call a physical meeting of creditors at the request of 10% or more by value or number of the creditors, or by 10 individual creditors. The creditors may request this at any time they are asked to make a decision.

2   The appointment of a liquidator in a creditors' voluntary liquidation may only be approved using either a virtual meeting or deemed consent. If creditors object to the use of deemed consent, the company must immediately call a physical meeting.

Final meetings of creditors and members

Final meetings were held to allow the liquidator to give a concluding report and be released from office. Stakeholders have said that these meetings were rarely attended and therefore the requirement to hold these meetings has been removed.

Electronic communication

Prior to the Insolvency Rules 2016, if debtors and creditors used electronic communication before insolvency proceedings commenced, they had to obtain written consent from the creditors to continue doing so. The 2016 Rules allows electronic communication to continue if this was used pre-insolvency.

Use of website

Prior to the Insolvency Rules 2016, a liquidator had to obtain a court order to put future documents relating to a case on a website after notifying the creditors. The 2016 Rules allow a liquidator to send a notice to creditors stating that all future documents will be made available on a website without the need for a court order.

6   Wrongful and fraudulent trading

Fraudulent trading

 Fraudulent trading is where a company carries on a business with the **intention of defrauding creditors** or for any other fraudulent purposes. This would include a situation where the director(s) of a company continue to trade whilst insolvent, and enter into debts knowing that the company will not be in a position to repay those debts.

Fraudulent trading is also a criminal offence under the Companies Act 2006.

Wrongful trading

 Wrongful trading is when the director(s) of a company have **continued to trade** when they: "knew, or ought to have concluded that there was **no reasonable prospect of avoiding insolvent liquidation**".

A director can defend an action of wrongful trading if they can prove that they have taken sufficient steps to minimise the potential loss to creditors.

Wrongful trading is an action that can be taken only by a company's liquidator, once it has gone into insolvent liquidation (either voluntary or compulsory liquidation).

Wrongful trading needs no finding of 'intent to defraud', unlike fraudulent trading.

Wrongful trading is a civil offence (fraudulent trading is a criminal offence), it only needs to be proven "on the balance of probabilities" (i.e. it is more likely than not that the director(s) are guilty of wrongful trading).

Fraudulent trading needs to be proven "beyond reasonable doubt" (i.e. it is almost certain that the director(s) are guilty of fraudulent trading).

For these reasons, wrongful trading is more common than fraudulent trading.

Penalties

Fraudulent trading

- Directors can be made **personally liable** for the debts of the company (a civil liability under the Insolvency Act)
- **Disqualified** as a director for between two and 15 years
- **Imprisoned** for up to 10 years.

Wrongful trading

- Directors can be made **personally liable** for the debts of the company
- **Disqualified** as a director for between two and 15 years.

Test your understanding 1

(a) Explain the procedures involved in placing a company into compulsory liquidation. **(10 marks)**

(b) Explain the consequences of compulsory liquidation for a company's creditors, employees and shareholders. **(5 marks)**

(Total: 15 marks)

Test your understanding 2

Tommy Co is in compulsory liquidation. The insolvency practitioner has liquidated the company's assets and has £1.125 million available for distribution. The following points are relevant:

- The company has an issued share capital of 2.5 million £1 shares.
- The directors declared, but have not paid, a dividend of 10 pence per share six months ago.
- The insolvency practitioner's costs total £50,000.
- Tommy Co's bank has a floating charge over the company's stock, which has now crystallised. The value is £400,000.

- The company's employees have been paid, with the exception of £275,000 of accrued holiday pay.

- Unsecured creditors total £500,000.

Required:

Identify and explain how the available funds will be distributed to the stakeholders of Tommy Co by the insolvency practitioner. **(5 marks)**

Test your understanding 3

Compare and contrast the characteristics of a members' voluntary winding up and a creditors' voluntary winding up. **(5 marks)**

Test your understanding 4

Poppy and Rosie registered their pet food business as a private limited company, Wag Ltd, in January 20W9. They injected £1,000 of share capital of £1,000 into Wag Ltd, and appointed themselves as directors of Wag Ltd.

Wag Ltd made a small profit in its first few years of trading, after the salaries paid to Poppy and Rosie. However, following difficult economic conditions, Wag Ltd made a loss of £15,000 in the year ended 31 December 20X2.

In early 20X3, Poppy said she thought the company should cease trading and be wound up. Rosie, however, insisted that the company would be profitable in the long-term so they agreed to carry on the business. Poppy was no longer involved in the day-to-day running of the business and stopped drawing a salary (although she retained her position as company director).

During 20X3 and 20X4, Rosie falsified Wag Ltd's accounts to disguise the fact that the company had continued to suffer losses, until it became obvious that they could no longer hide the company's debts and that it would have to go into insolvent liquidation, with debts of £75,000.

Required:

Advise Poppy and Rosie as to any potential liability they might face in respect of:

- Fraudulent trading, and

- Wrongful trading.

(8 marks)

7 Chapter summary

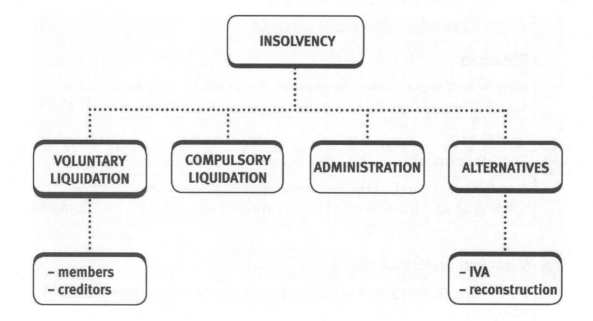

Test your understanding answers

Test your understanding 1

(a) A company is usually placed into compulsory liquidation by a creditor, who uses compulsory liquidation as a means to recover monies owed by the company. The creditor must petition the court and the petition is advertised in the London Gazette. There are various grounds for a petition to be made for compulsory liquidation.

The most common ground is that the company is unable to pay its debts. In this case the creditor must show that he or she is owed more than £5,000 by the company and has served on the company at its registered office, a written demand for payment. This is called a statutory demand. If the company fails to pay the statutory demand within 21 days and does not dispute the debt, then the creditor may present a winding up petition at court.

The application for a winding up order will be granted at a court hearing where it can be proven to the court's satisfaction that the debt is undisputed, attempts to recover have been undertaken and the company has neglected to pay the amount owed.

On a compulsory winding up the court will appoint an Official Receiver, who is an officer of the court. Within a few days of the winding up order being granted by the court, the Official Receiver must inform the company directors of the situation. The court order is also advertised in the London Gazette.

The Official Receiver takes over the control of the company and usually begins to close it down. The company's directors are asked to prepare a statement of affairs. The Official Receiver must also investigate the causes of the failure of the company.

The liquidation is deemed to have started at the date of the presentation of the winding up petition.

At the end of the winding up of the company, a final return is filed with the court and the Registrar. At this point the company is dissolved.

Tutorial note: Credit will be awarded to candidates who explain other, less common, means by which a company may face a compulsory liquidation:

A shareholder may serve a petition for compulsory liquidation. The grounds for doing so would normally be based on the fact that that the shareholder is dissatisfied with the management of the company, and that it is therefore just and equitable to wind up the company. This action by the shareholder is only allowed if the company is solvent and if the shareholder has been a shareholder for at least six months prior to the petition.

Very occasionally, if the Crown believes that a company is contravening legislation such as the Trading Standards legislation or is acting against the public or government interest, it is possible for the company to be liquidated compulsorily. This is very serious action to take and is not used very regularly.

(b) **Creditors** – The role of the Official Receiver (or Insolvency Practitioner, if appointed), is to realise the company's assets, and to distribute the proceeds in a prescribed order. Depending on the amount of cash available for distribution, and whether the debt is secured or unsecured, creditors may receive some, all, or none of the amount owed to them.

Employees – All employees of the company are automatically dismissed. A prescribed amount of unpaid employee's wages, accrued holiday pay, and contributions to an occupational pension fund rank as preferential debts, and will be paid before creditors of the company.

Shareholders – Any surplus that remains after the payment of all other amounts owed by the company is distributed to the shareholders. In most liquidations the shareholders receive nothing.

Test your understanding 2

The stakeholders of Tommy Co will be paid in the following order:

(1) Liquidator's costs of £50,000.

(2) Preferential creditors: i.e. the employee's accrued holiday pay of £275,000.

(3) Floating charge holders i.e. the bank's debt of £400,000.

(4) Unsecured creditors of £400,000.

At this point, £1.125 million is fully allocated. The unsecured creditors must forfeit the other £100,000 owed to them.

The members' declared but not paid dividends rank below the above stakeholders and will therefore not be paid. Likewise there will be no residual assets left to distribute to the members, who will receive nothing at all upon the liquidation of Tommy Co.

Test your understanding 3

A voluntary winding up takes place when the company resolves by special resolution to be wound up for any cause whatsoever, or by ordinary resolution where the articles provide for liquidation on the expiry of a fixed date or a specific event.

In the case of a members' voluntary winding up, the directors make a declaration of solvency stating that after full inquiry into the company's affairs they are of the opinion that the company will be able to pay its debts within 12 months of the commencement of the winding up.

In a creditors' voluntary winding up, such a declaration is not possible owing to the circumstances leading to the winding up.

In a members' voluntary winding up, the liquidator is appointed by the members and is accountable to them.

In a creditors' voluntary winding up, both members and creditors have the right to nominate a liquidator and, in the event of dispute, subject to the right of appeal to the courts, the creditors' nominee prevails. Here the liquidator is primarily accountable to the creditors.

In a creditors' voluntary winding up it is possible for a liquidation committee to be appointed.

Test your understanding 4

Fraudulent trading occurs where, in the course of a winding up, it appears that the business of a company has been carried on with intent to defraud creditors, or for any fraudulent purpose.

In such cases, the court, may declare that any persons who were knowingly parties to such carrying on of the business are liable to make such contributions (if any) to the company's assets as the court thinks proper. There is a high burden of proof involved in proving dishonesty on the part of the person against whom it is alleged.

It should be noted that there is a criminal offence of fraudulent trading under the Companies Act 2006, which applies to anyone who has been party to the carrying on of the business of a company with intent to defraud creditors or any other person, or for any other fraudulent purpose.

Given that it is stated that Rosie hid the fact that Wag Ltd was insolvent it is possible that she might be liable under the fraudulent trading provisions both civil and criminal. As a consequence she may well be liable for a maximum prison sentence of 10 years and may have to contribute to the assets of the company to cover any loss sustained by creditors as a result of her actions.

There is no evidence to support either action against Poppy.

Wrongful trading does not involve dishonesty but it still makes particular individuals potentially liable for the debts of their companies. Where a company is being wound up and it appears that, at some time before the start of the winding up, a director knew, or ought to have known, that there was no reasonable chance of the company avoiding insolvent liquidation, they would be guilty of wrongful trading.

In such circumstances, unless the directors took every reasonable step to minimise the potential loss to the company's creditors, they may be liable to contribute such money to the assets of the company as the court thinks proper.

It is clearly apparent that Rosie will be personally liable for the increase in Wag Ltd's debts from £15,000 to £75,000. However, as a director of the company Poppy will also be liable to contribute to the assets of the company.

Financial reporting revision

Chapter learning objectives

This chapter is designed to assist you with revision of key financial reporting topics. Given the relationship between financial reporting and auditing it is inevitable that the auditing exam will encompass many aspects of financial reporting that you have encountered in previous studies.

For further clarification with regard to the importance of financial reporting standards please refer to the technical article entitled "The Importance of Financial Reporting Standards to Auditors" (Nov 2008).

This can be found in the AAA section of the ACCA website.

IAS 1 Presentation of Financial Statements

This standard provides formats for the statement of profit or loss and other comprehensive income, statement of financial position, and statement of changes in equity.

Accounting policies should be selected so that the financial statements comply with all international standards and interpretations.

IAS 1 requires that other comprehensive income is presented in two categories, namely items that:

- will not be reclassified to profit or loss, and

- may be reclassified to profit or loss in future reporting periods.

IAS 2 Inventories

Inventories should be valued **'at the lower of cost and net realisable value'** (IAS 2, para 9). Net realisable value is selling price less any necessary costs which must be incurred to make the sale.

IAS 2 says that the cost of inventory includes:

- Purchase price including import duties, transport and handling costs

- Direct production costs e.g. direct labour

- Direct expenses and subcontracted work

- Production overheads (based on the normal levels of activity)

- Other overheads, if attributable to bringing the product or service to its present location and condition.

IAS 2 specifies that cost excludes:

- Abnormal waste

- Storage costs

- Indirect administrative overheads

- Selling costs.

Some entities can identify individual units of inventory (e.g. vehicles can be identified by a chassis number). Those that cannot should keep track of costs using either the first in, first out (FIFO) or the weighted average cost (AVCO) assumption.

Some entities may use standard costing for valuing inventory. Standard costs may be used for convenience if it is a close approximation to actual cost, and is regularly reviewed and revised.

Example: Inventory with a cost of $200 can only be sold to a customer for $220 if rectification work is undertaken which will cost of $30. The inventory should be valued at net realisable value of $190 ($220 – $30).

IAS 7 Statement of Cash Flows

IAS 7 requires a statement of cash flow that shows cash flows generated from:

- Operating activities

- Investing activities

- Financing activities.

IAS 8 Accounting Policies, Changes in accounting estimates and errors

IAS 8 covers the following issues:

- Selection of accounting policies

- Changes in accounting policies

- Changes in accounting estimates

- Correction of prior period errors.

Accounting policies

Accounting policies are the **'principles, bases, conventions, rules and practices applied by an entity in preparing and presenting financial statements'** (IAS 8, para 5).

Changes in accounting policies

Accounting policies should remain the same from period to period in order to allow for consistency of treatment.

A change in accounting policy must be dealt with retrospectively. The opening balance on retained earnings is recalculated on the basis that the new policy had always been in force. The resulting change in the retained earnings brought forward will be shown as a prior period adjustment in the statement of changes in equity and comparatives will be restated as if the new policy had been in force during the previous period.

The change and its effects must be described in the notes to the accounts.

Accounting estimates

Changes in accounting estimates, such as depreciation rates, are recognised in the statement of profit or loss in the same period as the change. If the change is material then it should be disclosed in the notes to the financial statements.

Prior period errors

Prior period errors are **'omissions from, and misstatements in, the financial statements for one or more prior periods arising from a failure to use, or misuse of, reliable information'** (IAS 8, para 5).

IAS 8 requires that prior period errors are dealt with by:

- Restating the opening balance of assets, liabilities and equity as if the error had never occurred, and presenting the necessary adjustment to the opening balance of retained earnings in the statement of changes in equity

- Restating the comparative figures presented, as if the error had never occurred.

These adjustments should also be disclosed in the notes.

 ## IAS 10 Events After the Reporting Period

Definitions

Events after the reporting period are **'those events, favourable and unfavourable, that occur between the statement of financial position date and the date when the financial statements are authorised for issue'** (IAS 10, para 3).

Adjusting events after the reporting period are those that **'provide evidence of conditions that existed at the reporting date'** (IAS10, para 3a).

Non-adjusting events after the reporting period are **'those that are indicative of conditions that arose after the reporting period'** (IAS 10, para 3b).

Accounting treatment

Adjusting events affect the amounts stated in the financial statements so they must be adjusted.

Non-adjusting events do not concern the position as at the reporting date so the financial statements are not adjusted. If the event is material then the nature and its financial effect must be disclosed.

Example 1: A legal provision of $5,000 is included in the financial statements as at 31 December 20X4. In January 20X5 the legal case is settled resulting in an actual cost of $7,500. This is an adjusting event and the financial statements should be adjusted to reflect a provision of $7,500.

Example 2: In January 20X5 the company purchases 100% of the shares of another company. This is a material non-adjusting event which must be disclosed in the notes to the financial statements.

IAS 12 Income Taxes

Scope of standard

IAS 12 covers both current and deferred tax, but deferred tax is the most examinable and will be reviewed here.

Deferred tax

Deferred tax is recognised on temporary differences between the carrying amount of an asset or liability and its tax base.

Tax base is the **'amount attributed to an asset or liability for tax purposes'** (IAS 12, para 5).

Temporary differences can be either:

(i)   Taxable temporary differences. This is when the carrying amount of an asset exceeds its tax base, giving rise to a deferred tax liability.

(ii) Deductible temporary differences. This is when the tax base of an asset exceeds the carrying amount of that asset, giving rise to a deferred tax asset.

Deferred tax should be measured by applying the applicable tax rate to the temporary difference. The applicable tax rate is the rates expected to be in force when the temporary differences reverse. This is usually the current tax rate.

Sources of taxable temporary differences

- Depreciation of an asset is accelerated for tax purposes.

- Development costs that were capitalised and amortised in the accounts, but deducted as incurred for tax purposes.

- A revaluation surplus on non-current assets as the carrying amount of the asset increases but the tax base of the asset does not change. Deferred tax is provided on the revaluation.

- Interest revenue received in arrears, which is accounted for on an accruals basis in the statement of profit or loss but taxable on a cash basis.

- Temporary differences can arise on a business combination if assets or liabilities are increased to fair value but the tax base remains at cost. Deferred tax is recognised on these differences and is included as part of net assets acquired.

Sources of deductible temporary differences

- Losses in the statement of profit or loss where tax relief is only available against future profits.

- Intra-group profits in inventory that are unrealised for consolidation purposes but taxable in the individual company that made the unrealised profit.

- Accumulated depreciation of an asset in the statement of financial position is greater than the cumulative depreciation for tax purposes.

- Pension liabilities that are recognised in the financial statements but only allowable for tax when the contributions are made to the scheme in the future.

- Research expenses are recognised as an expense in determining accounting profit but not deductible for tax until a later period.

- Income is deferred in the statement of financial position but has already been included in taxable profit.

Accounting treatment

- Deferred tax assets can be recognised for all deductible temporary differences to the extent it is probable that taxable profits will be available for these differences to be utilised.

- IAS 12 does not permit the discounting of deferred tax liabilities.

- The charge for deferred tax is recognised in the statement of profit or loss unless it relates to a gain or loss that has been recognised in other comprehensive income e.g. revaluations, in which case the related deferred tax is also recognised in other comprehensive income.

Example 1: During the year a company performs a revaluation of its property portfolio resulting in a revaluation surplus of $100,000. The current tax rate is 20%. A deferred tax liability of $20,000 must be recognised in respect of the revaluation. DR tax expense, CR deferred tax liability.

Example 2: During the year a company makes a loss of $50,000. This loss can be offset against future profits to reduce the tax bill. The current tax rate is 20%. A deferred tax asset of $10,000 can be recognised provided it is probable the company will make a taxable profit in future to utilise the deferred tax asset.

IAS 16 Property Plant and Equipment

Cost and depreciation of an asset

IAS 16 states that property, plant and equipment is initially recognised at cost.

An asset's cost is its purchase price, less any trade discounts or rebates, plus any further costs directly attributable to bringing it into working condition for its intended use.

Subsequent expenditure on non-current assets is capitalised if it:

- Enhances the economic benefits of the asset e.g. adding a new wing to a building.

- Replaces part of an asset that has been separately depreciated and has been fully depreciated; e.g. a furnace that requires new linings periodically.

- Replaces economic benefits previously consumed, e.g. a major inspection of aircraft.

The aim of depreciation is to spread the cost of the asset over its life in the business.

- IAS 16 requires that the depreciation method and useful life of an asset should be reviewed at the end of each year and revised where necessary. This is not a change in accounting policy, but a change of accounting estimate.

- If an asset has parts with different lives, (e.g. a building with a flat roof), the component parts should be capitalised and depreciated separately.

Example 1: A hotel company undertakes building work to extend its hotel from 20 rooms to 25 rooms. This increases the earning capacity of the hotel and represents an enhancement of economic benefits. The cost of the extension should be capitalised.

Example 2: A hotel company undertakes a refurbishment of its hotel involving repainting of all guest rooms. Repainting the rooms does not enhance the economic benefits generated by the hotel. The cost of the repainting should be expensed.

Revaluation of property, plant and equipment

Revaluation of PPE is optional. If one asset is revalued, all assets in that class must be revalued.

Valuations should be kept up to date to ensure that the carrying amount does not differ materially from the fair value at each statement of financial position date.

Revaluation gains are credited to **other comprehensive income** unless the gain reverses a previous revaluation loss of the same asset previously recognised in the statement of profit or loss.

Revaluation losses are debited to the statement of profit or loss unless the loss relates to a previous revaluation surplus, in which case the decrease should be debited to other comprehensive income to the extent of any credit balance existing in the revaluation surplus relating to that asset.

Depreciation is charged on the revalued amount less residual value (if any) over the **remaining useful life** of the asset.

An entity may choose to make an annual transfer of excess depreciation from revaluation reserve to retained earnings. If this is done, it should be applied consistently each year.

Example 3: A hotel chain undertakes a revaluation of its properties for the first time in 20X4 resulting in a revaluation gain of $250,000. The revaluation gain should be taken to other comprehensive income.

In 20X5, the properties are revalued again resulting in a loss of $50,000. The loss should be taken to other comprehensive income as a gain had previously been recognised in respect of the same assets. The balance on the revaluation reserve will be reduced to $200,000.

Had a gain not previously been recognised in respect of the same assets, the loss would have been recognised in the statement of profit or loss.

IAS 19 Employee Benefits

IAS 19 deals with accounting for pensions and other employee benefits in the employer's accounts.

Defined contribution pension schemes

A defined contribution pension scheme is where the employer pays a fixed amount to a separate entity in respect of pension contributions. The employer has no obligation to make any further payments if the fund does not have sufficient assets to pay all employee benefits.

Example 1: An entity pays fixed contributions of 5% of employee's salaries into a pension plan each month. The entity has no obligation to make further payments outside of the fixed contributions. The monthly salaries total $100,000. The entity will recognise an expense of $5,000 in the statement of profit or loss.

Defined benefit pension schemes

The most complex accounting issue is defined benefit pension schemes. These are where the employer has an obligation to provide an employee with a specific level of pension on retirement, usually based on a percentage of final salary.

To estimate the fund required, an actuary will have to calculate the contributions required to ensure the scheme has enough funds to pay out its liabilities.

This involves estimating what may happen in the future, such as the age profile of employees, retirement age, etc.

A pension scheme consists of a pool of assets (cash, investments, shares etc.) and a liability for pensions owed to employees when they are at retirement age. The assets are used to pay out the pensions.

Measurement and recognition of defined benefit schemes

Statement of profit or loss

- Service cost components: current and past service costs, including any gains or losses arising on curtailments and settlements.

- Net interest component.

Statement of financial position

- Net scheme asset or liability, where assets are measured at fair value and liabilities measured at present value.

Other comprehensive income

- Remeasurement of the net defined benefit liability or asset such as actuarial gains or losses, and return on plan assets.

Definitions

- **Current service cost** is the increase in the actuarial liability (present value of the defined benefit obligation) resulting from employee service in the current period. This is part of the service cost component.

- **Past service cost** is the increase in the actuarial liability relating to employee service in previous periods but only arising in the current period. Past service costs usually arise because there has been an improvement in the benefits to be provided under the plan. They are part of the service cost component and are recognised when the plan amendments occur.

- A **curtailment** occurs when an entity is demonstrably committed to making a material reduction in the number of employees covered by a plan, or amends the terms of a plan such that a material element of future service by current employees will qualify for no or reduced benefits. This may occur, for example if an entity closes a plant and makes those employees redundant. Any gain or loss on curtailment is part of the service cost component.

- A **settlement** occurs when an entity enters into a transaction to eliminate the obligation for part or all of the benefits under a plan. Any gain or loss on settlement is part of the service cost component.

- The **Net interest** component is computed by applying the discount rate to the net liability (or asset) at the start of the reporting period.

- The **Remeasurement component** results from increases and decreases in the pension asset or liability due to changes in actuarial estimates and assumptions. This component is recognised in other comprehensive income and is not recycled to profit or loss.

Example 2:

The following information relates to a defined benefit pension plan:

Present value of obligation at 1 January 20X4	$140,000
Fair value of plan assets at 1 January 20X4	$80,000
Discount rate at 1 January 20X4	4%
Current and past service cost for 20X4	$30,000
Benefits paid during 20X4	$20,000
Contributions into plan during 20X4	$25,000
Present value of obligation at 31 December 20X4	$200,000
Fair value of plan assets at 31 December 20X4	$120,000

The financial statements will show the following for the year ended 31 December 20X4

Statement of financial position

Closing net liability (200,000 – 120,000)	$80,000

Statement of profit or loss

Service cost component	$30,000
Net interest component (4% × (140,000 – 80,000))	$2,400

Other comprehensive income

Remeasurement component (calculated below)		$12,600
Net obligation brought forward	$60,000	
Service cost component	$30,000	
Net interest component	$2,400	
Contributions into plan	($25,000)	
Remeasurement component (β)	$12,600	
	———	
Net obligation carried forward	$80,000	
	———	

IAS 20 Accounting for Government Grants and Disclosure of Government Assistance

Government grants are **'assistance by government in the form of transfers of resources to an entity in return for past or future compliance with certain conditions'** (IAS 20, para 3).

Government assistance is **'action by government designed to provide economic benefit to a specific entity'** (IAS 20, para 3).

Accounting treatment

- IAS 20 says that grants are not to be recognised until there is reasonable assurance that:
    - The conditions attached to the grant will be complied with, and
    - The grant will be received.

- Grants shall be recognised in the statement of profit or loss so as to match them with the expenditure towards which they are intended to contribute.
    - Income grants given to subsidise expenditure should be matched to the related costs.
    - Income grants given to help achieve a non-financial goal (such as job creation) should be matched to the costs incurred to meet that goal.
    - Grants for purchases of non-current assets should be recognised over the expected useful lives of the related assets.

There are two acceptable accounting treatments for grants related to non-current assets:

- Deduct the grant from the cost of the asset and depreciate the net cost, or

- Treat the grant as deferred income and release it to the statement of profit or loss over the life of the asset.

Grants that become repayable

A government grant that becomes repayable shall be accounted for as a change in accounting estimate.

Example 1: An entity receives a government grant of $1,500,000 to subsidise the cost of employing people in areas of low employment over the next three years.

The grant should be matched to the related costs in each year. Therefore the grant should be initially recognised as deferred income and each year $500,000 should be credited to the statement of profit or loss to offset the related payroll costs.

Example 2: An entity receives a government grant of $0.5 million towards the purchase price of a building. The purchase price of the building is $3 million. The useful life of the building is 50 years and depreciation is charged on a straight line basis.

The grant can be accounted for in two possible ways:

(a) Reduce the cost of the building by $0.5 million.

The building will be included within property, plant and equipment at $2.5 million. Depreciation of $50,000 ($2.5 million/50 years) will be charged each year.

(b) Recognise the grant as deferred income and amortise to the statement of profit or loss over the useful life of the building.

The building will be recognised at cost of $3 million. Depreciation of $60,000 ($3 million/50 years) will be charged each year. Income of $10,000 ($0.5 million/50 years) will be credited to the statement of profit or loss each year and the deferred income liability in the statement of financial position will reduce by $10,000 each year.

IAS 21 The Effects of Changes in Foreign Exchange Rates

IAS 21 provides guidance on accounting for foreign currency transactions.

Functional and presentation currencies

A company must determine both its functional and presentation currency.

Functional currency is **'the currency of the primary economic environment in which the entity operates'** (IAS 21, para 8).

IAS 21 says that presentation currency is the currency in which the entity presents its financial statements.

In determining **functional currency**, IAS 21 specifies that an entity should consider the following:

- The currency that influences its sales prices for its goods and services.

- The currency that influences the costs associated with providing its goods and services.

If the company is a foreign-owned subsidiary then it will have the same functional currency as its parent if it operates with little autonomy.

Once determined, functional currency should not be changed.

Presentation currency can be any currency and can be different from functional currency. This is particularly the case if the company is foreign-controlled as the presentation currency may be that of the parent. If the presentation currency is different from the functional currency, then the financial statements must be translated into the presentation currency.

Individual transactions in foreign currency

If a company enters into **foreign currency transactions** the results of these transactions should be translated and recorded in the accounting records in the functional currency:

- at the rate on the date the transaction occurred, or

- using an average rate over a period of time providing the exchange rate has not fluctuated significantly.

At subsequent statement of financial position dates, the following process must be applied.

- Foreign currency monetary items (receivables, payables, cash, loans) must be translated using the closing rate. The closing rate is the exchange rate at the statement of financial position date.

- Foreign currency non-monetary items (non-current assets, investments, inventory) are not retranslated. They are left at the exchange rate used at the transaction date (called the historic rate).

- Exchange differences relating to monetary items are recognised in the statement of profit or loss.

Foreign subsidiaries

If a company has foreign subsidiaries whose functional currency is their local currency, their financial statements must be translated into the parent's presentation currency.

- All assets and liabilities are translated into the parent's presentation currency at the closing rate at the statement of financial position date.

- Goodwill is calculated in the functional currency of the subsidiary, and translated at each reporting date at the closing rate into the presentation currency of the parent.

- Income and expenses in the statement of profit or loss must be translated at the average rate for the period.

- Exchange differences arising on consolidation are recognised in other comprehensive income until disposal of the subsidiary when they are part of the gain or loss on disposal reported in profit or loss for the year.

- Exchange differences arise from:
  - Retranslation of the opening net assets using the closing rate.
  - Retranslation of the profit for the year from the average rate (used in the statement of profit or loss) to the closing rate (for inclusion in the statement of financial position).

IAS 23 Borrowing Costs

IAS 23 requires finance costs to be capitalised providing they are directly attributable to the construction or acquisition of a qualifying asset. A qualifying asset is one which takes a substantial period of time to get ready for its intended use or sale.

Capitalisation commences when construction expenditure is being incurred and ceases when the asset is ready for use. Borrowing costs incurred after the asset has been completed or while work is suspended must be expensed in the statement of profit or loss.

Capitalised borrowing costs are those actually incurred, although this may be estimated if the entity is financing the cost out of general borrowings.

Example: On 1 August 20X4 a company borrowed $400,000 from the bank to help fund the construction of a new office building with an expected cost of $500,000. The interest rate on the loan is 6%. Expenditure relating to the construction of the building commenced 1 October 20X4 and was completed 30 June 20X5. Borrowing costs of $18,000 ($400,000 × 6% × 9/12) should be capitalised as part of the cost of the asset. Depreciation should commence once the asset is ready for use.

IAS 24 Related Party Disclosures

A related party is a person or entity that is related to the entity that is preparing its financial statements. IAS 24 gives the following rules which should be used to determine the existence of related party relationships:

(a) **'A person or a close member of that person's family is related to a reporting entity if that person:**

   (i) **has control or joint control of the reporting entity**

   (ii) **has significant influence over the reporting entity**

   (iii) **is a member of the key management personnel of the reporting entity or of a parent of the reporting entity.**

(b) **An entity is related to a reporting entity if any of the following conditions apply:**

(i) **The entity and the reporting entity are members of the same group (which means that each parent, subsidiary and fellow subsidiary is related to the others).**

(ii) **One entity is an associate or joint venture of the other entity (or an associate or joint venture of a member of a group of which the other entity is a member).**

(iii) **Both entities are joint ventures of the same third party.**

(iv) **One entity is a joint venture of a third entity and the other entity is an associate of the third entity.**

(v) **The entity is a post-employment benefit plan for the benefit of employees of either the reporting entity or an entity related to the reporting entity. If the reporting entity is itself such a plan, the sponsoring employers are also related to the reporting entity.**

(vi) **The entity is controlled or jointly controlled by a person identified in (a).**

(vii) **A person identified in (a)(i) has significant influence over the entity or is a member of the key management personnel of the entity (or of a parent of the entity).**

(viii) **The entity, or any member of a group of which it is a part, provides key management personnel services to the reporting entity or to the parent of the reporting entity'** (IAS 24, para 9).

A related party transaction is **'the transfer of resources, services or obligations between related parties regardless of whether a price is charged'** (IAS 24, para 9).

Disclosures

- Relationships between parents and subsidiaries irrespective of whether there have been transactions between the parties.

- The name of the parent and the ultimate controlling party (if different).

- Key management personnel compensation in total and for each short term employee benefits, post-employment benefits, other long term benefits, termination benefits and share based payment.

- For related party transactions that have occurred, the nature of the relationship and detail of the transactions and outstanding balances.

- The disclosure should be made for each category of related parties stated above and include:

  (a) The amount of the transactions

  (b) The amount of outstanding balances and their terms

  (c) Allowances for doubtful debts relating to the outstanding balances

  (d) The expense recognised in the period in respect of irrecoverable or doubtful debts due from related parties.

Example: A vehicle has a carrying amount of $10,000 and a market value of $12,000. At a board meeting, the directors of the company authorised the purchase of the vehicle by the finance director for $8,000. At the year end, the invoice relating to this transaction was unpaid.

This is a related party transaction as the finance director is a member of key management personnel. The related party disclosure notes must disclose the transaction amount of $8,000 and the balance outstanding of $8,000. If the debt is considered to be doubtful, any allowance made in respect of the invoice must also be disclosed.

IAS 27 Separate Financial Statements

This standard applies when an entity has interests in subsidiaries, joint ventures or associates and either elects to, or is required to, prepare separate **non-consolidated financial statements**.

If separate financial statements are produced, investments in subsidiaries, associates or joint ventures can be measured:

- at cost

- using the equity method

- in accordance with IFRS 9 *Financial Instruments*.

IAS 28 Investments in Associates and Joint Ventures

Joint ventures

A joint venture is a **'joint arrangement whereby the parties that have joint control of the arrangement have rights to the net assets of the arrangement'** (IAS 28, para 3). This will normally be established in the form of a separate entity to conduct the joint venture activities.

Associates

An associate is defined as an entity **'over which the investor has significant influence'** (IAS 28, para 3).

Significant influence is the **'power to participate in the financial and operating policy decisions of the investee but is not control or joint control over those policies'** (IAS 28, para 3).

It is normally assumed that significant influence exists if the holding company has a shareholding of 20% to 50%.

Equity accounting

In the consolidated financial statements of a group, an investment in an associate or joint venture is accounted for using the equity method.

The **consolidated statement of profit or loss** will show a single figure in respect of the associate or joint venture. This is calculated as the investor's share of the associate or joint venture's profit for the period.

On the **consolidated statement of financial position**, the 'investment in the associate/joint venture' is presented in non-current assets. It is calculated as the initial cost of the investment plus/(minus) the investor's share of the post-acquisition reserve increase/(decrease).

Associates and joint ventures are not part of the group. Therefore transactions and balances between group companies and the associate or joint venture are not eliminated from the consolidated financial statements.

Example: P Co prepares group accounts. On 1 January 20X5, P Co purchased a 30% shareholding in A Co for $30,000. At that date A Co had retained earnings of $25,000. At the year end of 30 June 20X5, the retained earnings of A Co are $40,000. A Co's profit after tax for the year was $5,000.

The consolidated statement of financial position will include an investment in associate within non-current assets of $34,500 (30,000 + 30% × (40,000 – 25,000)) which represents the cost of the investment plus P Co's share of the post-acquisition increase in reserves.

The consolidated statement of profit or loss will include a share of A Co's profit after tax, time apportioned for the ownership period. Therefore $750 (5,000 × 30% × 6/12) will be included as the share of profit of the associate for the year. If the investment in A Co was impaired for any reason, an impairment charge would be deducted from the share of profit of the associate.

IAS 32 Financial instruments: Presentation

IAS 32 *Financial Instruments*: Presentation classifies financial instruments as a financial liability (debt) or equity according to the substance of the contractual arrangement.

IAS 32 says that a financial instrument is classified as **debt** if the issuer has a contractual obligation either to deliver cash or another financial asset to the holder or to exchange another financial asset/liability with the holder under conditions that are potentially unfavourable to the issuer.

A financial instrument is classified as **equity** if it does not give rise to such a contractual obligation.

For example, preference shares are classified as:

- Equity if they are irredeemable
- Debt if they are redeemable.

Compound instruments

A compound instrument is one which has both a liability and an equity component. An example would be a convertible bond that can be redeemed in cash or a fixed number of the entity's own ordinary shares.

Compound instruments must be 'split' into a liability element and an equity element. The liability is initially measured as the present value of the repayments. The difference between the proceeds and the liability element is the equity element.

Example: On 1 January 20X4 a company issued $10 million 3% bonds at par. Interest is paid in arrears. The loan notes will be redeemed in cash at par on 31 December 20X6, or in the form of a fixed number of ordinary shares. The interest rate on similar bonds without a conversion option is 6%.

The bond has characteristics of debt and equity so must be split into a liability and equity component. The liability component is calculated as the present value of the cash repayments, discounted using the rate on a similar non-convertible bond.

The present value of the cash repayments is $9.2m:

31/12/X4	$10m × 3% × 1/1.06	$0.28m
31/12/X5	$10m × 3% × 1/1.06^2	$0.27m
31/12/X5	$10m × 3% × 1/1.06^3 + $10m	$8.65m

The initial double entry required is:

DR Cash	$10 million
CR Liability	$9.2 million
CR Equity (β)	$0.8 million

At 31/12/X4, $0.55m ($9.2m × 6%) will be charged to the statement of profit or loss and the liability will be $9.45m (9.2 + 0.55 – (10 × 3%)). The equity is not remeasured.

IAS 33 Earnings Per Share

IAS 33 applies to all listed companies. Private companies must follow the standard if they disclose an EPS figure.

Basic earnings per share is:

$$\frac{\text{Profit or loss for the period attributable to the equity shareholders}}{\text{Weighted average number of equity shares outstanding in the period}}$$

The weighted average number of equity shares takes into account when the shares were issued in the year.

Diluted earnings per share

IAS 33 requires diluted earnings per share to be disclosed as well as basic EPS.

Diluted EPS shows the effect on the current EPS if all the potential equity shares had been issued under the greatest possible dilution.

Potential equity shares consist of:

- Convertible loan stock

- Share options

- Rights granted under employee share schemes

- Rights to equity shares that are contingent upon future events.

Example: An entity issued 200,000 shares at full market price on 1 January 20X5. The number of ordinary shares in issue at 30 June 20X5 is 1,000,000 (20X4 – 800,000). Profit attributable to the ordinary shareholders for the year ended 30 June 20X5 is $550,000.

To calculate the basic EPS for the year ended 30 June 20X5, the weighted average number of equity shares must be calculated:

(800,000 × 6/12) + (1,000,000 × 6/12) = 900,000

EPS = $0.61 (550,000/900,000)

IAS 36 Impairment of Assets

Impairment is measured by comparing the carrying amount of an asset or cash generating unit with its recoverable amount.

If the carrying amount exceeds the recoverable amount, the asset is impaired and must be written down.

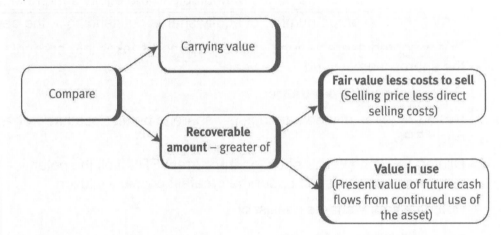

Indicators of impairment

Unless an impairment review is required by another standard (e.g. IAS 38 *Intangible Assets* or IFRS 3 *Business Combinations*), then impairment reviews are required where there is an indicator of impairment.

Examples of impairment indicators

Internal indicators include:

- Physical damage to the asset

- Management committed to reorganisation of the business

- Obsolete assets

- Idle assets

- Major loss of key employees

- Operating losses in the business where the assets are used.

External indicators include:

- Competitor actions

- Increasing interest rates (affect value in use)

- Market values of assets falling

- Change in the business or market where assets are used (e.g. government action).

Cash-generating units (CGU)

A **cash-generating unit**, per IAS 36, is the smallest identifiable group of assets that generates external cash inflows.

- It will not always be possible to base the impairment review on individual assets as an individual asset may not generate a distinguishable cash flow. In this case the impairment calculations should be based on a CGU.

- The impairment calculation is performed by comparing the carrying value of the CGU to the recoverable amount of the CGU. This is achieved by allocating an entity's assets including goodwill, to CGUs.

- Impairment losses are allocated to assets with specific impairments first, then allocated in the following order:

  (1) Goodwill

  (2) Remaining assets on a pro rata basis. Assets cannot be written down below the higher of fair value less costs to sell, value in use and zero.

Recognition of impairment losses

Assets held at cost: The amount of the impairment is charged to the statement of profit or loss for the period in which the impairment occurs.

Revalued assets: The impairment is charged first to OCI to reverse any previous surplus on that asset in the same way as a downward revaluation. Any further impairment is charged to the statement of profit or loss.

Example: A CGU has a carrying amount of $150 million and a recoverable amount of $132 million resulting in an impairment loss.

The nets assets of the CGU comprise:

Goodwill	$10 million
Property *	$20 million
Plant and equipment	$45 million
Net monetary assets **	$15 million

* The property has a market value of $25 million.

** The net monetary assets will be realised in full.

The impairment loss of $18 million cannot be set against the property or the net monetary assets as these assets are not impaired.

The impairment loss must first allocated to the goodwill, reducing its carrying amount to nil.

The balance of the impairment loss of $8 million will be set against the plant and equipment in proportion to their carrying amounts.

IAS 37 Provisions, Contingent Liabilities and Contingent Assets

A **provision** is **'a liability of uncertain timing or amount'** (IAS 37, para 10).

A provision must be recognised when:

– the entity has a present obligation as a result of a past event

– it is probable that an outflow of economic benefits will be required to settle the obligation, and

– a reliable estimate of the obligation can be made. The amount recognised as a provision should be the best estimate of the expenditure required to settle the obligation at the reporting date. Where time value of money is material, the provision should be discounted to present value.

IAS 37 provides specific guidance in several areas:

- A provision for future operating losses cannot be recognised.

- A restructuring provision can only be recognised where an entity has a constructive obligation to carry out the restructuring. A constructive obligation arises when there is a detailed formal plan setting out the business affected, the principal location, function and approximate number of employees being made redundant, when the plan will be implemented, the expenditure that will be incurred and there is a valid expectation that the plan will be carried out by either implementing the plan or announcing it to those affected.

- A decommissioning provision must be recognised in relation to assets where there is an obligation to remove the assets after the end of their useful lives and restore the site to its original state. Examples include an oil rig or a nuclear power plant.

A **contingent liability** is a possible obligation arising from past events whose existence will only be confirmed by an uncertain future event outside of the entity's control. Contingent liabilities should not be recognised. They should be disclosed unless the possibility of a transfer of economic benefits is remote.

A **contingent asset** is a possible asset that arises from past events and whose existence will only be confirmed by an uncertain future event outside of the entity's control. Contingent assets should not be recognised. If the possibility of an inflow of economic benefits is probable they should be disclosed.

Example: A company makes an announcement to employees that it intends to restructure, which will involve redundancies to be made in one department and other restructuring costs to be incurred. The announcement is made on 28 March 20X5 and the company has a year end of 31 March 20X5. A restructuring provision must be recognised for the cost of the restructure, including the redundancies, as the announcement before the year end has created a constructive obligation.

Example: A company publishes in its annual report its impact on the environment and the actions it takes to minimise the damage caused by its operations. The company has a well-documented record of taking full responsibility and corrective action for the environmental damage it causes. On 1 October 20X4 the company brought a self-constructed machine into use at a cost of $10 million. The machine caused damage to local land as soon as it was used and the cost of repairing this damage is estimated at $2 million. The machine will be disassembled and decommissioned on 30 September 20X7. The interest rate representing risks specific to the company is 8%.

Bringing the machinery into use and causing damage to the local land as a result of the machine being operational are past events. The company's well-documented policy of taking full responsibility and action for correcting environmental damage creates a constructive obligation to repair the damage. Therefore a provision must be recognised for the initial damage caused when the machine was first brought into use. The provision will be $1.59 million ($2m × $1/1.08^3$). The cost of the provision will be debited to property, plant and equipment as part of the cost of the asset. Each year, the provision will be unwound to increase the carrying amount of the liability and a finance cost will be recognised in the statement of profit or loss.

Any further damage caused in subsequent periods can only be recognised once the damage has been caused as future damage can be avoided if the machine is decommissioned earlier than 20X7. As such there is no present obligation.

Example: The warehouse of a company is damaged in a fire. The company makes a claim on its insurance to cover the cost of repairing the warehouse and replacing the assets damaged in the fire. At the year end the company has not received confirmation from the insurance company as to whether the insurance claim is successful, although from review of the insurance policy, there is no reason to assume the claim will not be paid. Until the insurance claim is virtually certain to be paid, a contingent asset cannot be recognised in the financial statements. If it is considered probable that the claim will be settled, a disclosure should be included in the notes to the financial statements detailing the amount expected to be received from the insurance company in respect of the claim.

IAS 38 Intangible Assets

IAS 38 says that an intangible asset is **'an identifiable non-monetary asset without physical substance'** (IAS 38, para 8).

Initial recognition

IAS 38 states that an intangible asset is initially recognised at cost if all of the following criteria are met.

(1) It is identifiable – it could be disposed of without disposing of the business at the same time.

(2) It is controlled by the entity – the entity has the power to obtain economic benefits from it, for example patents and copyrights give legal rights to future economic benefits.

(3) It will generate probable future economic benefits for the entity – this could be by a reduction in costs or increasing revenues.

(4) The cost can be measured reliably.

If an intangible does not meet the recognition criteria, then it should be charged to the statement of profit or loss as expenditure is incurred. Items that do not meet the criteria are internally generated goodwill, brands, mastheads, publishing titles, customer lists, research, advertising, start-up costs and training.

Subsequent treatment

Intangible assets should be amortised over their useful lives.

If it can be demonstrated that the useful life is indefinite no amortisation should be charged, but an annual impairment review must be carried out.

Intangible assets can be revalued but fair values must be determined with reference to an active market. Active markets have homogenous products, willing buyers and sellers at all times and published prices. In practical terms, most intangible assets are likely to be valued using the cost model.

Research and development

The recognition of internally generated intangible assets is split into a research phase and a development phase.

Costs incurred in the research phase must be charged to the statement of profit or loss as they are incurred.

IAS 38 says that costs incurred in the development phase should be recognised as an intangible asset if they meet the following criteria:

(a) The project is technically feasible

(b) The asset will be completed then used or sold

(c) The entity is able to use or sell the asset

(d) The asset will generate future economic benefits (either because of internal use or because there is a market for it)

(e) The entity has adequate technical, financial and other resources to complete the project

(f) The expenditure on the project can be reliably measured.

Amortisation of development costs will occur over the period that benefits are expected.

Example: A company has incurred $100,000 on initial design work for a new product. It is anticipated that the design will be taken forward over the next two years to be developed with a view to production in three years' time. $500,000 has been spent on testing another product. The testing has been successful and the development team are confident the product will be able to go into commercial production in three months' time.

The design work of $100,000 must be expensed as a research cost as the criteria of IAS 38 have not been met. At this stage there is not enough evidence that the design will be technically feasible or that the asset will be able to be sold or generate future economic benefits.

The costs of $500,000 appear to be development costs as the testing has been successful, which indicates the product is technically feasible. The company is expecting to move the product into commercial production in the near future which they would be unlikely to do if it was unlikely to generate future economic benefits.

 IAS 40 Investment Property

IAS 40 defines **investment property** as property or land held to earn rentals or for capital appreciation or both.

Investment property is not:

- Owner occupied property (dealt with under IAS 16 *Property, Plant and Equipment*)

- Property held for sale in the normal course of business (dealt with under IAS 2 *Inventories*)

- Property being constructed for third parties (dealt with under IFRS 15 *Revenue from Contracts with Customers*)

- Property leased to another entity (dealt with under IFRS 16 *Leases*).

Accounting treatment

- An entity can choose either the cost model or the fair value model.

- The cost model in IAS 40 is the same as the cost model in IAS 16 *Property, Plant and Equipment*.

- The fair value model requires that investment properties are recognised in the statement of financial position at fair value. Gains and losses on revaluation when using the fair value model are recognised in the statement of profit or loss.

Example: A company purchases a property for $1 million on 1 January 20X4. The land component is $400,000 and the buildings are expected to have a useful life of 50 years. At 31 December 20X4 the property has a market value of $1.1 million. The property is not occupied by the company and has been purchased for its investment potential.

Using the cost model, the property should be initially recognised at a cost of $1 million and depreciation of $12,000 ($600,000 / 50) should be charged each year. At 31 December 20X4 the property should be included in the financial statements with a carrying amount of $988,000 (1,000,000 – 12,000).

Using the fair value model, the property should initially be recognised at cost of $1 million. At 31 December 20X4, the property should be recognised at fair value of $1.1 million and the $0.1 million gain should be included in the statement of profit or loss. No depreciation will be charged.

If the company purchases any further investment properties they must all be accounted for using the same basis.

IAS 41 Agriculture

A biological asset is **'a living plant or animal'** (IAS 41, para 5).

Agricultural produce is **'the harvested product of the entity's biological assets'** (IAS 41, para 5).

Biological assets should be valued at fair value less estimated costs to sell and revalued each year-end. Any changes in fair value should be recognised in the statement of profit or loss.

At the date of harvest, agricultural produce should be recognised and measured at fair value less estimated costs to sell. It is then accounted for under IAS 2 *Inventories*.

Example: A herd of goats was held at 1 January 20X4 with a fair value less estimated costs to sell of $1,000. On 1 July 20X4, a goat was purchased for $250. The fair value of the goats at 31 December 20X4 was $1,450. The gain of $200 (1450 – (1000 + 250)) will be recognised in the statement of profit or loss.

IFRS 1 First-time Adoption of International Reporting Standards

IFRS 1 sets out the procedures to follow when an entity adopts IFRS Standards in its published financial statements for the first time.

The **date of transition** is **'the beginning of the earliest period for which an entity presents full comparative information under IFRS Standards in its first IFRS financial statements'** (IFRS 1, App A).

IFRS 1 requires entities to prepare an opening IFRS statement of financial position at the date of transition. This statement must:

- Recognise all assets and liabilities required by IFRS Standards.

- Not recognise assets and liabilities not permitted by IFRS Standards.

- Reclassify all assets, liabilities and equity components in accordance with IFRS Standards.

- Measure all assets and liabilities in accordance with IFRS Standards.

Any gains or losses arising on the adoption of IFRS Standards are recognised in retained earnings.

IFRS 2 Share Based Payments

A **share based payment** transaction is one where an entity obtains goods or services from other parties with payment taking the form of shares or share options issued by the entity.

There are two types of share based payment transactions:

(1) Equity-settled share based payment transactions where an entity receives goods or services in exchange for equity instruments (e.g. shares or share options).

(2) Cash-settled share based payment transactions, where an entity receives goods and services in exchange for a cash amount paid based on its share price.

Accounting

- If an entity issues share options (e.g. to employees), the fair value of the option at the grant date should be used as the cost of the services received.

- For cash settled share based payments, the fair value of goods and services is measured and a liability recognised. The liability is re-measured at each statement of financial position date until it is settled with changes in value being taken to the statement of profit or loss.

- The expense in relation to the share based transaction must be recognised over the period in which the services are rendered or goods are received (vesting period).

Grant date: the date a share based-payment transaction is entered into.

Vesting date: the date on which the cash or equity instruments can be received by the other party to the agreement.

Example: A company grants share options of 5,000 shares due to vest in 5 years' time. The fair value of the option at the grant date is $3.

Assuming that 5,000 shares are expected to vest, the cost to the company will be 5,000 × $3 = $15,000 which is spread over the vesting period. Therefore $3,000 is charged to the statement of profit and loss.

Each year the cost should be remeasured and any adjustment taken through the statement of profit or loss with a corresponding credit to equity.

At the end of year two it is expected that only 4,000 options will vest. The total cost of the scheme will be 4000 × $3 = $12,000. A cost of $4,800 needs to be recognised ($12,000 × 2/5). As $3,000 was charged in year one, the charge for year two needs to be $1,800.

Assuming no further changes in the number of shares expected to vest, $2,400 will be charged to the statement of profit or loss in year's three to five.

IFRS 3 Business Combinations

On acquisition of a subsidiary, the purchase consideration transferred and the identifiable net assets acquired are recorded at fair value.

Fair value is 'the price that would be received to sell an asset or paid to transfer a liability in an orderly transaction between market participants at the measurement date' (IFRS 13, para 9).

Purchase consideration

Purchase consideration is measured at fair value. Note that:

- Deferred cash consideration should be discounted to present value using a rate at which the acquirer could obtain similar borrowing.

- The fair value of the acquirer's own shares is the market price at the acquisition date.

- Contingent consideration is included as part of the consideration at its fair value, even if payment is not probable.

Non-controlling interest

The non-controlling interest (NCI) at acquisition is measured at either:

- Fair value = number of shares owned by NCI × subsidiary share price, or

- The NCI's proportionate share of the fair value of the subsidiary's identifiable net assets = NCI % × fair value of net assets at acquisition.

Goodwill

Goodwill is the excess of the consideration transferred and amount of any non-controlling interest over the net assets of the subsidiary at the acquisition date. Positive goodwill is capitalised as an intangible non-current asset and tested annually for impairment. Any impairment charge will be charged as an expense in the consolidated statement of profit or loss.

Gain on bargain purchase

If the net assets acquired exceed the fair value of consideration, then a gain on bargain purchase (negative goodwill) arises.

After checking that the calculations have been done correctly, the gain on bargain purchase is credited to profit or loss.

Other adjustments

Other consolidation adjustments need to be made in order to present the parent and its subsidiaries as a single economic entity. Transactions that require adjustment include:

- Interest on intragroup loans.

- Intragroup management charges.

- Intragroup sales, purchases and unrealised profit in inventory.

- Intragroup transfer of non-current assets and unrealised profit on transfer.

- Intragroup receivables, payables and loans.

Example: On 1 July 20X5, P Co purchased 100% of the ordinary share capital of S Co for $1.8 million. The carrying amount of S Co's net assets at that date was $1.35 million. The fair value of S Co's net assets was $150,000 greater than its carrying amount.

The goodwill on acquisition will be calculated as the difference between the consideration paid and the fair value of the net assets at the date of acquisition. The fair value of the net assets is $1.5 million, therefore the goodwill on acquisition is $0.3 million (1.8 – 1.5).

IFRS 5 Non-current Assets Held for Sale & Discontinued

A **discontinued operation** is a **'component of an entity that either has been disposed of, or is classified as held for sale; and**

- **Represents a separate major line of business or geographical area of operations**
- **Is part of a single coordinated plan to dispose of a separate major line of business or geographical area of operations**
- **Is a subsidiary acquired exclusively with a view to resale'** (IFRS 5, App A).

IFRS 5 says that a non-current asset or a disposal group is classified as held for sale if its carrying amount will be recovered primarily through a sale rather than continued use in the business.

A **disposal group** is a group of assets, and associated liabilities, which will be sold together in a single transaction.

Assets can only be classified as held for sale (and therefore a discontinued operation) if they meet all of the criteria below:

- Management commits itself to a plan to sell.
- The asset (or disposal group) is available for immediate sale in its present condition.
- A sale is highly probable and is expected to be completed within a year from date of classification.
- The asset (or disposal group) is being actively marketed for sale at a reasonable price compared to its fair value.
- It is unlikely that significant changes will be made to the plan or it will be withdrawn.

If the criteria are met after the statement of financial position date but before the accounts are authorised for issue, the assets should **not** be classed as held for sale but the information should be disclosed.

Measurement

- A non-current asset (or disposal group) classified as held for sale should be measured at the lower of its carrying amount and fair value less costs to sell.
- Assets classified as held for sale should not be depreciated, regardless of whether they are still in use by the reporting entity.

Presentation

IFRS 5 says that information about discontinued operations should be presented on the face of the statement of profit or loss as a single amount. This comprises:

- Profit or loss from the discontinued operations.
- Gain or loss on the measurement to fair value less costs to sell or on the disposal of the discontinued operation.

IFRS 7 Financial Instruments: Disclosures

IFRS 7 requires two main categories of disclosures in relation to financial instruments:

(1) Information about the significance of financial instruments

(2) Information about the nature and extent of risks arising from financial instruments.

Qualitative disclosures must describe:

*   Risk exposures for each type of financial instrument

*   Management's objectives, policies, and processes for managing those risks

*   Changes from the prior period.

Quantitative disclosures include:

*   Summary quantitative data about exposure to each risk at the reporting date

*   Disclosures about credit risk, liquidity risk, and market risk

*   Concentrations of risk.

IFRS 8 Operating Segments

IFRS 8 requires an entity to disclose information about each of its operating segments.

An **operating segment** is defined as a component of an entity:

*   that engages in business activities from which it may earn revenues and incur expenses

*   whose results are reviewed by the entity's chief operating decision maker(s)

*   for which financial information is available.

Reporting thresholds

IFRS 8 requires that an entity separately reports information about any operating segment that meets one of the following quantitative thresholds:

*   Sales are 10 per cent or more of the combined revenues of all operating segments, both international and external sales revenues.

*   Its reported profit or loss is 10 per cent or more of the greater, in absolute amount, of:

    –   The combined reported profit of all operating segments that did not report a loss, and

    –   The combined reported loss of all operating segments that reported a loss.

- Its assets are 10 per cent or more of the combined assets of all operating segments.

At least 75% of the entity's **external revenue** should be included in reportable segments. If the quantitative test results in segmental disclosure of less than this, other reportable segments should be identified until this 75% is reached.

Disclosures

For each reportable segment IFRS 8 requires an entity to disclose:

- A measure of profit or loss

- A measure of total assets

- A measure of total liabilities (if such an amount is regularly used in decision making).

IFRS 9 Financial Instruments

Financial assets

Investments in equity

Investments in equity instruments (such as an investment in the ordinary shares of another entity) are normally measured at fair value through profit or loss. It is possible to designate an equity instrument as fair value through other comprehensive income, provided that the following conditions are complied with:

- The equity instrument must not be held for trading, and

- There must have been an irrevocable choice for this designation upon initial recognition of the asset.

Investments in debt

IFRS 9 requires that financial assets that are debt instruments are measured in one of three ways:

(1) **Amortised cost**

An investment in a debt instrument is measured at amortised cost if:

- The financial asset is held within a business model whose aim is to collect the contractual cash flows.

- The contractual terms of the financial asset give rise on specified dates to cash flows that are solely payments of principal and interest on the principal amount outstanding.

(2) Fair value through other comprehensive income

An investment in a debt instrument is measured at fair value through other comprehensive income if:

- The financial asset is held within a business model whose objective is achieved by both collecting contractual cash flows and selling financial assets.

- The contractual terms of the financial asset give rise on specified dates to cash flows that are solely payments of principal and interest on the principal amount outstanding.

(3) Fair value through profit or loss

An investment in a debt instrument that is not measured at amortised cost or fair value through other comprehensive income will be measured at fair value through profit or loss.

Financial liabilities

Financial liabilities held for trading are measured at fair value through profit or loss.

Most financial liabilities are measured at amortised cost.

IFRS 9 allows measurement of a financial liability at fair value, rather than amortised cost, if doing so will eliminate or reduce an accounting mismatch. Where this is the case, the change in the fair value of the financial liability due to a change in credit risk is recorded in other comprehensive income, and the balance of any change in fair value is recorded in profit or loss.

Impairments of financial assets

Definitions

Credit loss: The difference between the contractual cash flows and the cash flows that the entity expects to receive (i.e. all cash shortfalls), discounted at the original effective interest rate.

Lifetime expected credit losses: The expected credit losses that result from all possible default events over the expected life of a financial instrument.

12 month expected credit losses: The expected credit losses that result from default events possible within 12 months of the reporting date.

Loss allowances

Loss allowances must be recognised for financial assets that are debt instruments and which are measured at amortised cost or at fair value through other comprehensive income:

- If the credit risk on the financial asset has not increased significantly since initial recognition, the loss allowance should be equal to 12-month expected credit losses.

- If the credit risk on the financial asset has increased significantly since initial recognition then the loss allowance should be equal to the lifetime expected credit losses.

Adjustments to the loss allowance are charged (or credited) to the statement of profit or loss.

Measuring expected losses

An entity's estimate of expected credit losses must be:

- Unbiased and probability-weighted

- Discounted to present value

- Based on information about past events, current conditions and forecasts of future economic conditions.

Receivables

The loss allowance should always be measured at an amount equal to lifetime credit losses for trade receivables that do not have a significant financing component.

Derivatives

IFRS 9 defines a derivative as a financial instrument with all three of the following characteristics:

(1) Its value changes in response to the change in a specified interest rate, security price, commodity price, foreign exchange rate or similar variable.

(2) It requires little or no initial investment.

(3) It is settled at a future date.

Derivatives which are not part of a hedging arrangement are classified to be measured as fair value through profit or loss.

Hedge accounting

Hedge accounting is an optional accounting treatment where the gains or losses on the **hedging instruments** are recognised in the same performance statement and in the same period as the offsetting gains or losses on the **hedged items**.

In order to follow the hedge accounting rules in IFRS 9 the following criteria need to be met:

- The hedging relationship consists only of eligible hedging instruments and hedged items.

- At the inception of the hedge there must be formal documentation identifying the hedged item and the hedging instrument.

- The hedging relationship is effective.

- If the hedged item is a forecast transaction, then the transaction must be highly probable.

Accounting treatment of a fair value hedge

At the reporting date:

- The hedging instrument will be remeasured to fair value.

- The carrying amount of the hedged item will be adjusted for the change in fair value since the inception of the hedge.

The gain (or loss) on the hedging instrument and the loss (or gain) on the hedged item will be recorded:

- in profit or loss in most cases, but

- in other comprehensive income if the hedged item is an investment in equity that is measured at fair value through other comprehensive income.

Accounting treatment of a cash flow hedge

For cash flow hedges, the hedging instrument will be remeasured to fair value at the reporting date. The gain or loss is recognised in other comprehensive income.

However, if the gain or loss on the hedging instrument since the inception of the hedge is greater than the loss or gain on the hedged item, then the excess gain or loss on the instrument must be recognised in profit or loss.

IFRS 10 Consolidated Financial Statements

IFRS 10 states that consolidated financial statements must be prepared if one company controls another company.

Control, according to IFRS 10, consists of three components:

(1) **Power** over the investee: this is normally exercised through the **majority of voting rights,** but could also arise through other contractual arrangements.

(2) **Exposure** or rights to variable returns (positive and/or negative), and

(3) The **ability to use power** to affect the investor's returns.

It is normally assumed that control exists when one company owns more than half of the ordinary shares in another company.

IFRS 11 Joint Arrangements

A joint arrangement is a contractual arrangement whereby two or more parties undertake an economic activity that is subject to joint control.

IFRS 11 says that joint arrangements may take one of two forms:

- **Joint operations:** the parties that have joint control have rights to the assets and obligations for the liabilities. Normally, there will not be a separate entity established to conduct joint operations.

- **Joint ventures:** the parties that have joint control of the arrangement have rights to the net assets of the arrangement. This will normally be established in the form of a separate entity to conduct the joint venture activities.

IFRS 11 requires that:

- **Joint operators** recognise their share of assets, liabilities, revenues and expenses of the joint operation.

- **Joint ventures** are accounted for using the equity method.

 IFRS 12 Disclosure of Interests in Other Entities

IFRS 12 details **disclosure** requirements for entities that have an interest in subsidiaries, joint arrangements and associates, i.e. where there is control, joint control or significant influence.

IFRS 12 is designed to provide relevant information to users of financial statements. It requires disclosure of:

- Details relating to the composition of the group

- Details of non-controlling interests within the group

- Identification and evaluation of risks associated with any interests held in other entities which give rise to control, joint control or significant influence.

IFRS 13 Fair Value Measurement

The objective of IFRS 13 is to provide a single source of guidance for fair value measurement.

Note that IFRS 13 does not apply to IFRS 2 *Share-based Payment* and IFRS 16 *Leases*.

Fair value is defined as **'the price that would be received to sell an asset or paid to transfer a liability in an orderly transaction between market participants at the measurement date'** (IFRS 13, para 9).

In order to increase comparability between entities, IFRS 13 establishes a hierarchy that categorises the inputs used when measuring fair value:

* **Level 1** inputs comprise quoted prices ('observable') in active markets for identical assets and liabilities at the measurement date.

* **Level 2** inputs are observable inputs, other than those included within Level 1. Level 2 inputs include quoted prices for similar (but not identical) asset or liabilities in active markets, or prices for identical assets and liabilities in inactive markets.

* **Level 3** inputs are unobservable inputs for an asset or liability.

IFRS 13 gives priority to level 1 inputs.

IFRS 15 Revenue from Contracts with Customers

IFRS 15 outlines a five step process for revenue recognition.

(1) **Identify the contract**

A contract is an agreement between two or more parties that creates rights and obligations.

(2) **Identify the separate performance obligations within a contract**

Performance obligations are, essentially, promises made to a customer.

(3) **Determine the transaction price**

The transaction price is the amount the entity expects to be entitled in exchange for satisfying all performance obligations. Amounts collected on behalf of third parties (such as sales tax) are excluded.

(4) **Allocate the transaction price to the performance obligations in the contract**

The total transaction price should be allocated to each performance obligation in proportion to stand-alone selling prices.

(5) Recognise revenue when (or as) a performance obligation is satisfied

For each performance obligation an entity must determine whether it satisfies the performance obligation over time or at a point in time.

An entity satisfies a performance obligation over time if one of the following criteria is met:

(a) **'The customer simultaneously receives and consumes the benefits provided by the entity's performance as the entity performs.**

(b) **The entity's performance creates or enhances an asset (for example, work in progress) that the customer controls as the asset is created or enhanced, or**

(c) **The entity's performance does not create an asset with an alternative use to the entity and the entity has an enforceable right to payment for performance completed to date'** (IFRS 15, para 35).

For a performance obligation satisfied over time, an entity recognises revenue based on progress towards satisfaction of that performance obligation.

If a performance obligation is not satisfied over time then it is satisfied at a point in time. The entity must determine the point in time at which a customer obtains control of the promised asset.

Example: Construction contract

A Co enters into a contract with B Co to construct a building. Construction started on 1 October 20X1. The contract price was agreed at $4 million, plus a bonus of $1 million that would be payable if construction is completed by 30 September 20X2. The building has been designed especially for B Co and could not be sold to another entity without significant modifications. Although A Co believes that it is more likely than not that it will meet the bonus criteria, it has some doubt due to the unique nature of this particular project. The terms of the contract specify that B Co must pay A Co within 30 days of the end of each quarter based on the progress of construction as at the end of each quarter. A Co measures progress to completion in terms of the contract costs incurred as a proportion of total estimated contract costs. Total contract costs are estimated at $2.5 million. If B Co cancels the contract, it is liable to pay A Co for the work completed.

By 31 December 20X1, A Co has incurred costs of $0.5 million on the contract. The estimate of total contract costs remains unchanged. Although progress on the contract has been satisfactory, there are still doubts about whether the $1 million bonus will be received.

Accounting treatment

A Co has entered into a contract with a customer that contains a single performance obligation: to construct a building.

The contract includes $4 million of fixed consideration and $1 million of variable consideration. The variable consideration should only be included in the transaction price if it is highly probable that it would not need to be reversed once the uncertainty is known. Due to the bespoke nature of this building, and the doubts expressed by A Co, the variable consideration should be excluded from the transaction price. The transaction price is therefore $4 million, all of which relates to the construction of the building.

Revenue from the construction should be recognised as or when the performance obligation is satisfied. A Co must therefore consider whether it satisfies the performance obligation over time or at a point in time. A Co is creating an asset with no alternative use and has a right to payment for performance completed to date. Therefore, per IFRS 15, this should be accounted for as a performance obligation satisfied over time.

For performance obligations satisfied over time, revenue should be recognised based on progress towards the completion of the performance obligation. Based on costs incurred, the performance obligation is 20% ($0.5m/$2.5m) complete. Revenue of $0.8 million ($4m × 20%) should be recognised.

A Co should show a corresponding receivable for $0.8 million because it has an unconditional right to receive the money.

Example: Non-refundable deposit

Flight Co is an airline which sells flights directly to customers via a website. Flights must be paid for in full at the time of booking and all flights are non-refundable. Flight Co enters into a contract with a customer that contains a single performance obligation (to provide a flight) which is satisfied at a point in time (when the flight has been taken). Flight Co should recognise revenue once the flight has been taken by the customer.

IFRS 16 Leases

Identifying a lease

Lessees are required to recognise an asset and a liability for all leases, unless they are short-term or of a minimal value. As such, it is vital to assess whether a contract contains a lease, or whether it is simply a contract for a service.

A contract contains a lease if it **'conveys the right to control the use of an identified asset for a period of time in exchange for consideration'** (IFRS 16, para 9).

Lessee accounting

If the lease is short-term (less than 12 months at the inception date), or of a low value, the lessee can choose to recognise the lease payments in profit or loss on a straight line basis.

In all other cases, IFRS 16 requires that the lessee recognises a lease liability and a right-of-use asset at the commencement of the lease:

- The right-of-use asset is initially recognised at cost. This will be the initial value of the lease liability, plus any lease payments made at or before the commencement of the lease, as well as any direct costs.

- The right-of-use asset is subsequently measured at cost less accumulated depreciation and impairment losses (unless another measurement model is chosen).

- The lease liability is initially measured at the present value of the lease payments that have not yet been paid.

- The carrying amount of the lease liability is increased by the interest charge, which is also recorded in the statement of profit or loss. Cash repayments reduce the carrying amount of the lease liability.

Lessor accounting

The lessor must assess whether the lease is a finance lease or an operating lease. A finance lease is a lease where the risks and rewards of ownership substantially transfer to the lessee. Key indicators of a finance lease, according to IFRS 16, are:

- Ownership of the asset transfers to the lessee at the end of the lease term.

- The lessee has the option to purchase the asset at the end of the lease term, or to continue to lease it, for less than fair value.

- The lease term is for the major part of the asset's economic life.

- The present value of the lease payments amounts to substantially all of the asset's fair value.

If the lease is a finance lease then the lessor will:

- Derecognise the asset.

- Recognise a lease receivable equal to the net investment in the lease (the present value of the payments).

- Interest income arising on the lease receivable is recorded in profit or loss.

If the lease is an operating lease then the lessor recognises the lease income in profit or loss on a straight line basis over the lease term.

Sale and leaseback

The treatment of a sale and leaseback depends on whether the 'sale' represents the satisfaction of a performance obligation as per IFRS 15 *Revenue from Contracts with Customers*.

	Transfer is not a sale	Transfer is a sale
Seller – lessee	Continue to recognise the asset. Recognise a financial liability equal to the proceeds received.	Derecognise the asset. Recognise a right-of-use asset as the proportion of the asset's previous carrying amount that relates to the rights retained. Recognise a lease liability. A profit or loss on disposal will arise.
Buyer – lessor	Do not recognise the asset. Recognise a financial asset equal to transfer proceeds.	Account for the asset purchase. Account for the lease by applying lessor accounting requirements.

Example: N Co sells a property to F Co for $20 million. The property has a carrying amount at the date of disposal of $7 million. N Co enters into a contract to lease the property back from F Co for five years. The present value of the annual lease payments is $5.7 million.

If the sale and leaseback transaction represents the satisfaction of a performance obligation in accordance with IFRS 15, N Co must recognise a right-of-use (ROU) asset at the proportion of the asset's previous carrying amount that relates to the rights retained.

The ROU asset will be recognised at $2 million ((5.7/20) × 7). A lease liability will be recognised for the present value of the lease payments of $5.7 million.

The double entry to record the transaction will be:

DR Cash	$20 million
DR ROU asset	$2 million
CR Lease liability	$5.7 million
CR Property, plant and equipment	$7 million
CR Profit on disposal (β)	$9.3 million

If the sale and leaseback transaction does not represent the satisfaction of a performance obligation in accordance with IFRS 15, N Co must continue to recognise the asset within PPE and recognise a financial liability for the proceeds received of $20 million.

Questions and Answers

Test your understanding 1

You are an audit manager in Compton & Co, responsible for the audit of the Stow Group (the Group). You are planning the audit of the Group financial statements for the year ending 31 July 20X5.

You are provided with the following exhibits:

1   An email which you have received from Chad Woodstock, the audit engagement partner

2   Company information

3   Changes in group structure during the year

4   Information about Zennor Co's internal audit team

5   Request from the audit committee

Required:

Respond to the instructions in the email from the audit engagement partner.   **(46 marks)**

Note: The split of the mark allocation is shown in the partner's email (Exhibit 1)

Professional marks will be awarded for the presentation and logical flow of the briefing notes and the clarity of the explanations provided.

(4 marks)

(Total: 50 marks)

Exhibit 1 – Email from audit engagement partner

To: Audit manager

From: Chad Woodstock, Audit engagement partner

Subject: The Stow Group – audit planning

Hello

I have provided you with some information in the form of a number of exhibits which you should use in planning the audit of the Stow Group (the Group). I held a meeting yesterday with the Group finance director, Marta Bidford, and we discussed a number of issues which will impact on the audit planning.

Using the information provided, I require you to prepare briefing notes for my use in which you:

(a)   (i)   Evaluate the risks of material misstatement to be considered in planning the Group audit, commenting on their materiality to the Group financial statements.   **(18 marks)**

      (ii)   Identify any further information that may be needed. **(5 marks)**

(b)   Design the principal audit procedures to be used in the audit of the disposal of Broadway Co.   **(10 marks)**

(c) Using the information provided in Exhibit 4, discuss how Marta's suggestion impacts on the planning of the audit of Zennor Co's and of the Group's financial statements, and comment on any ethical issue raised. **(7 marks)**

(d) Taking into consideration the information provided in Exhibit 5, discuss the issues that should be considered by Compton & Co in determining the audit fee for the Group audit. **(6 marks)**

Thank you.

Exhibit 2 – Company information

The Group is a car manufacturer. Its operations are divided between a number of subsidiaries, some of which focus on manufacturing and distributing the cars, while others deal mainly with marketing and retail. All components of the Group have the same year end. The Group's projected profit before tax for the year is $200 million and projected total assets at 31 July 20X5 are $2,500 million.

Exhibit 3 – Changes in group structure during the year

The Group has been restructured during the year. A new wholly-owned subsidiary has been acquired, Zennor Co, which is located overseas in Farland. Another subsidiary, Broadway Co, was disposed of.

Acquisition of Zennor Co

In order to expand overseas, the Group acquired 100% of the share capital of Zennor Co on 1 September 20X4. Zennor Co is located in Farland, where it owns a chain of car dealerships. Zennor Co's financial statements are prepared using International Financial Reporting Standards and are measured and presented using the local currency of Farland, the Dingu.

At the present time, the exchange rate is 4 Dingu = $1. Zennor Co has the same year end as the Group, and its projected profit for the year ending 31 July 20X5 is 90 million Dingu, with projected assets at the same date of 800 million Dingu.

Zennor Co is supplied with cars from the Group's manufacturing plant. The cars are sent on cargo ships and take approximately six weeks to reach the main port in Farland, where they are stored until delivered to the dealerships. At today's date there are cars in transit to Zennor Co with a selling price of $58 million.

A local firm of auditors was engaged by the Group to perform a due diligence review on Zennor Co prior to its acquisition. The Group's statement of financial position recognises goodwill at acquisition of $60 million.

Compton & Co was appointed as auditor of Zennor Co on 1 October 20X4.

Disposal of Broadway Co

On 1 April 20X5, the Group disposed of its wholly-owned subsidiary, Broadway Co, for proceeds of $180 million. Broadway Co operated a distribution centre in this country. The Group's statement of profit or loss includes a profit of $25 million in respect of the disposal.

Broadway Co was acquired by a retail organisation, the Cornwall Group, which wished to bring its distribution operations in house in order to save costs. Compton & Co resigned as auditor to Broadway Co on 15 April 20X5 to be replaced by the group auditor of the Cornwall Group.

Exhibit 4 – Information about Zennor Co's internal audit team

Zennor Co has a well established internal audit team which was established several years ago. The team is headed up by a qualified accountant, Jo Evesham, who has a lot of experience in designing systems and controls. Jo and her team monitor the effectiveness of operating and financial reporting controls, and report to the board of directors. Zennor Co does not have an audit committee as corporate governance rules in Farland do not require an internal audit function or an audit committee to be established.

During the year, the internal audit team performed several value for money exercises such as reviewing the terms negotiated with suppliers.

Marta has suggested that we use the internal audit team as much as possible when performing our audit of Zennor Co as this will reduce the audit fee.

Exhibit 5 – Request from the audit committee

The Group audit committee appreciates that with the audit of the new subsidiary there will be some increase in our costs, but has requested that the audit fee for the Group as a whole is not increased from last year's fee.

Test your understanding 2

You are an audit manager in Attica & Co, a firm of chartered certified accountants responsible for the audit of Hydrasports Co.

Hydrasports Co is a national leisure group with sixteen centres around the country. Planning of the audit for the financial year ending 31 July 20X5 is about to commence.

You are provided with the following exhibits:

1   An email you have received from the audit engagement partner.

2   Background information about Hydrasports Co.

3   An email from the finance director regarding assistance with suggesting performance measures which could be used to increase the centre managers' awareness of social and environmental responsibilities.

Required:

Respond to the instructions in the email from the audit engagement partner. **(36 marks)**

Note: The split of the mark allocation is shown in the partner's email (Exhibit 1)

Professional marks will be awarded for the presentation and logical flow of the briefing notes and the clarity of the explanations provided.

(4 marks)

(Total: 40 marks)

Exhibit 1 – Email from audit engagement partner

Hello

You need to start planning the audit of Hydrasports Co for the financial year ending 31 July 20X5, and to help with this I have provided you with some relevant information. I met with the finance director yesterday to discuss a number of matters including some recent business developments.

Using the information provided in Exhibit 2 I would like you to prepare briefing notes for my use in which you:

(a) Evaluate the business risks faced by Hydrasports Co. **(10 marks)**

(b) Evaluate the risks of material misstatement to be considered when planning the audit of Hydrasports Co. **(12 marks)**

(c) Design the audit procedures to be performed in respect of:

    (i)   deferred income, and

    (ii) the hydrotherapy pool.

(8 marks)

d) Using the information in Exhibit 3, recommend performance measures that could be set to increase the centre managers' awareness of Hydrasports Co' social and environmental responsibilities and the evidence which should be available to provide assurance on their accuracy. **(6 marks)**

Thank you

Exhibit 2 – Background information

Facilities at each centre are of a standard design which incorporates a heated swimming pool, sauna, air-conditioned gym and fitness studio with supervised childcare. Each centre is managed on a day-to-day basis, by a centre manager, in accordance with company policies. The centre manager is also responsible for preparing and submitting monthly accounting returns to head office.

Each centre is required to have a licence from the local authority to operate. Licences are granted for periods between two and five years and are renewable subject to satisfactory reports from local authority inspectors. The average annual cost of a licence is $900.

Members pay a $100 joining fee, plus either $50 per month for 'peak' membership or $30 per month for 'off-peak', payable quarterly in advance. All fees are stated to be non-refundable.

The centre at Verne was closed from February to April after a chemical spill in the sauna caused a serious accident. Although the centre was reopened, Hydrasports Co has recommended to all centre managers that sauna facilities be suspended until further notice.

In response to complaints to the local authorities about its childcare facilities, Hydrasports Co has issued centre managers with revised guidelines for minimum levels of supervision. Centre managers are finding it difficult to meet the new guidelines and have suggested that childcare facilities should be withdrawn.

Staff lateness is a recurring problem and a major cause of 'early bird' customer dissatisfaction with sessions which are scheduled to start at 07.00. New employees are generally attracted to the industry in the short-term for its non-cash benefits, including free use of the facilities, but leave when they require increased financial rewards. Training staff to become qualified lifeguards is costly and time-consuming and retention rates are poor. Turnover of centre managers is also high, due to the constraints imposed on them by company policy.

Three of the centres are expected to be loss-making for the year to 31 July 20X5 due to falling membership. Hydrasports Co has invested heavily in a hydrotherapy pool at one of these centres, with the aim of attracting retired members with more leisure time. The building contractor has already billed twice as much and taken three times as long as budgeted for the work. The pool is now expected to open two months after the year-end.

Cash flow difficulties in the current year have put back the planned replacement of gym equipment for most of the centres.

Insurance premiums for liability to employees and the public have increased by nearly 45%. Hydrasports Co has met the additional expense by reducing its insurance cover on its plant and equipment from a replacement cost basis to a net realisable value basis.

Exhibit 3 – Email from the finance director

Hello

I am looking at ways in which we can increase the centre managers' awareness of Hydrasports Co' social and environmental responsibilities. I would like your firm to suggest a variety of social and environmental performance measures that we can assess our centre managers against to ensure consistency throughout the organisation.

Thank you

Test your understanding 3

You are an audit manager in Scarlet & Co, a firm of chartered certified accountants responsible for the audit of Cerise Co.

Cerise Co manufactures computer controlled equipment for production-line industries such as cars, washing machines, cookers, etc. Planning of the audit for the financial year ending 31 July 20X5 is about to commence.

You are provided with the following exhibits:

1   An email you have received from the audit engagement partner.

2.   Background information about Cerise Co and information about events occurring during the year to date.

Required:

Respond to the instructions in the email from the audit engagement partner.   **(26 marks)**

Note: The split of the mark allocation is shown in the partner's email (Exhibit 1)

Professional marks will be awarded for the presentation and logical flow of the briefing notes and the clarity of the explanations provided.

(4 marks)

(Total: 30 marks)

Exhibit 1 – Email from audit engagement partner

Hello

You need to start planning the audit of Cerise Co for the financial year ending 31 July 20X5, and to help with this I have provided you with some relevant information. I met with the finance director yesterday to discuss a number of matters including some recent business developments.

Using the information provided in Exhibit 2 I would like you to prepare briefing notes for my use in which you:

(a)   Evaluate the audit risks to be considered when planning the audit of Cerise Co.   **(15 marks)**

(b)   Explain how the extent of the reliance to be placed on analytical procedures and written representations should compare with that for the prior year audit.   **(6 marks)**

(c)   Design the audit procedures to be performed in respect of the amounts due from distributors.   **(5 marks)**

Thank you

Exhibit 2 – Background information

On 1 April 20X5 the shareholder-managers decided, unanimously, to accept a lucrative offer from a multinational corporation to buy the company's patented technology and manufacturing equipment.

By 10 April 20X5 management had notified all the employees, suppliers and customers that Cerise Co would cease all manufacturing activities on 31 May 20X5. The 200-strong factory workforce and the majority of the accounts department and support staff were made redundant with effect from that date, when the sale was duly completed.

The marketing, human resources and production managers will cease to be employed by the company at 31 July 20X5. However, the chief executive, sales manager, finance manager, accountant and a small number of accounting and other support staff expect to be employed until the company is wound down completely.

Cerise Co's operations comprise fourteen premises, nine of which were put on the market on 1 June 20X5. Cerise Co accounts for all tangible, non-current assets under the cost model (i.e. at depreciated cost). Four premises are held on leases that expire in the next two to seven years and cannot be sold or sub-let under the lease terms. The small head office premises will continue to be occupied until the lease expires in 20X8.

All Cerise Co's computer controlled products carry a one-year warranty. Extended warranties of three and five years, previously available at the time of purchase, have not been offered on sales of remaining inventory from 1 June 20X5 onwards.

Cerise Co has three-year agreements with its national and international distributors for the sale of equipment. It also has annual contracts with its major suppliers for the purchase of components. So far, none of these parties have lodged any legal claim against Cerise Co. However, the distributors are withholding payment of their account balances pending settlement of the significant penalties which are now due to them.

Test your understanding 4

Bellatrix Co is a carpet manufacturer and an audit client of your firm. Bellatrix Co has identified a company in the same business, Scorpio Co, as a target for acquisition in the current year.

As audit manager to Bellatrix Co and its subsidiaries for the year ending 31 December 20X5, you have been asked to examine Scorpio Co's management accounts and budget forecasts. The chief executive of Bellatrix Co, Sirius Deneb, believes that despite its current cash flow difficulties, Scorpio Co's current trading performance is satisfactory and future prospects are good. The chief executive of Scorpio Co is Ursula Minor.

The findings of your examination are as follows:

Budget forecasts for Scorpio Co, for the current accounting year to 31 December 20X5 and for the following year, reflect a rising profit trend.

Scorpio Co's results for the first half year to 30 June 20X5 reflect $800,000 profit from the sale of a warehouse that had been carried in the books at historical cost. There are plans to sell two similar properties later in the year and outsource warehousing.

About 10% of Scorpio Co's sales are to Andromeda Co, a limited liability company. Two members of the management board of Scorpio Co hold minority interests in Andromeda Co. Selling prices negotiated between Scorpio Co and Andromeda Co appear to be on an arm's length basis.

Scorpio Co's management accounts for the six months to 30 June 20X5 have been used to support an application to the bank for an additional loan facility to refurbish the executive and administration offices. These management accounts show inventory and trade receivables balances that exceed the figures in the accounting records by $150,000. This excess has also been reflected in the first half year's profit. Upon enquiry, you have established that allowances, to reduce inventory and trade receivables' to estimated realisable values, have been reduced to assist with the loan application.

Although there has been a recent downturn in trading, Ursula Minor has stated that she is very confident that the negotiations with the bank will be successful as Scorpio Co has met its budgeted profit for the first six months. Ursula believes that increased demand for carpets and rugs in the winter months will enable results to exceed budget.

Required:

(a)   Identify and comment on the implications of your findings for Bellatrix Co's plan to proceed with the acquisition of Scorpio Co.

(10 marks)

(b)   Explain what impact the acquisition will have on the conduct of your audit of Bellatrix Co and its subsidiaries for the year to 31 December 20X5. **(15 marks)**

(Total: 25 marks)

Test your understanding 5

You are the manager responsible for the audit of Volcan Co, a long-established limited liability company. Volcan Co is a national supermarket chain with 23 stores, five of which are in the capital city, Urvina. All the stores are managed in the same way with purchases being made through Volcan Co's central buying department and product pricing, marketing, advertising and human resources policies being decided centrally. The draft financial statements for the year ended 31 March 20X5 show revenue of $303 million (20X4: $282 million), profit before taxation of $9.5 million (20X4: $7.3 million) and total assets of $178 million (20X4: $173 million).

The following issues arising during the final audit have been noted on a schedule of points for your attention:

(a) On 1 May 20X5, Volcan Co announced its intention to downsize one of the stores in Urvina from a supermarket to a 'City Metro' in response to a significant decline in the demand for supermarket-style shopping in the capital. The store will be closed throughout June, re-opening on 1 July 20X5. Goodwill of $5.5 million was recognised three years ago when this store, together with two others, was bought from a national competitor. 60% of the goodwill has been written off due to impairment. **(7 marks)**

(b) On 1 April 20X4 Volcan Co introduced a reward scheme for its customers. The main elements of the reward scheme include the awarding of points to customers' loyalty cards for every $1 spent, with extra points being given for the purchase of each week's special offers. Customers who hold a loyalty card can convert their points into cash discounts against future purchases on the basis of $1 per 100 points. **(6 marks)**

(c) In October 20X4, Volcan Co commenced the development of a site in a valley of outstanding natural beauty on which to build a retail megastore and warehouse at the end of 20X5. Local government planning permission for the development, which was received in April 20X5, requires that three 100-year-old trees within the valley be preserved and the surrounding valley be restored in 20X6. Additions to property, plant and equipment during the year include $4.4 million for the estimated cost of site restoration. This estimate includes a provision of $0.4 million for the relocation of the 100 year-old trees.

In March 20X5 the trees were chopped down to make way for a car park. A fine of $20,000 per tree was paid to the local government in May 20X5. **(7 marks)**

Required:

Comment on the matters to be considered and explain the audit evidence you would expect to find during your review of the audit working papers in respect of the issues described above. **(Total: 20 marks)**

Test your understanding 6

You are the manager responsible for the audit of Albreda Co and its subsidiaries. The group mainly operates a chain of national restaurants and provides vending and other catering services to corporate clients. All restaurants offer eat-in, take-away and home delivery services. The draft consolidated financial statements for the year ended 31 March 20X5 show revenue of $42.2 million (20X4: $41.8 million), profit before taxation of $1.8 million (20X4: $2.2 million) and total assets of $30.7 million (20X4: $23.4 million).

The following issues arising during the final audit have been noted on a schedule of points for your attention:

(a)   In March 20X5, the management board announced plans to cease offering home delivery services from the end of the month. These sales amounted to $0.6 million for the year to 31 March 20X5 (20X4: $0.8 million). A provision of $0.2 million has been made as at 31 March 20X5 for the compensation of redundant employees (mainly drivers). Delivery vehicles have been classified as non-current assets held for sale as at 31 March 20X5 and measured at fair value less costs to sell, $0.8 million (carrying amount, $0.5 million).

(8 marks)

(b)   Historically, all owned premises have been measured at cost and depreciated over 10 to 50 years. The management board has decided to revalue these premises for the year ended 31 March 20X5. At the statement of financial position date two properties had been revalued by a total of $1.7 million. Another 15 properties have since been revalued by $5.4 million and there remain a further three properties which are expected to be revalued later in 20X5. A revaluation surplus of $7.1 million has recognised in other comprehensive income.

(7 marks)

(c)   During the year Albreda Co paid $0.1 million (20X4: $0.3 million) in fines and penalties relating to breaches of health and safety regulations. These amounts have not been separately disclosed but included in cost of sales.   **(5 marks)**

Required:

Comment on the matters to be considered and explain the audit evidence you would expect to find during your review of the audit working papers in respect of the issues described above.

Note: The split of the mark allocation is shown against each of the issues above.

(Total: 20 marks)

Test your understanding 7

You are the manager responsible for the audit of Visean Co, a company, which manufactures health and beauty products and distributes them through a chain of 72 retail pharmacies. The draft accounts for the year ended 31 March 20X5 show profit before taxation of $1.83 million (20X4: $1.24 million) and total assets $18.4 million (20X4: $12.7 million).

The following issues are outstanding and have been left for your attention:

(a) Visean Co owns nine brand names of fragrances used for ranges of products (e.g. perfumes, bath oils, soaps, etc), four of which were purchased and five internally generated. Purchased brands are recognised as intangible assets with a total cost of $589,000 and amortised on a straight-line basis over 10 years. The costs of generating self-created brands and maintaining existing ones are recognised as an expense when incurred. Demand for products of one of the purchased fragrances, 'Ulexite', fell significantly in April 20X5 after a marketing campaign in the previous month caused offence to customers. **(8 marks)**

(b) In March 20X5 the directors announced plans to discontinue the range of medical consumables supplied to hospital pharmacies. The factory which manufactured these products closed in April 20X5. A provision of $800,000 has been made as at 31 March 20X5 for the compensation of redundant employees and a further $450,000 for penalties relating to early cancellation of contracts with customers and suppliers. **(7 marks)**

(c) Historically the company's statement of cash flows has reported net cash flows from operating activities under the 'indirect method'. However, the statement of cash flows for the year ended 31 March 20X5 reports net cash flows under the 'direct method' and the corresponding figures have been restated. **(5 marks)**

Required:

Comment on the matters to be considered and explain the audit evidence you would expect to find during your review of the audit working papers in respect of the issues described above.

Note: The split of the mark allocation is shown against each of the issues above.

(Total: 20 marks)

Test your understanding 8

(a)   Explain the importance of the role of objectivity to the auditor-client relationship. **(5 marks)**

(b)   You are the audit engagement partner in a firm which provides a variety of accountancy-related services to a large portfolio of clients. The firm's gross practice income is $1 million. The firm has a particularly successful tax department, which carries out a great deal of recurring and special tax work for both audit and non-audit clients. The tax manager has recently involved you in discussions with a major tax client, Rainbow Co, who is considering changing its auditors. Rainbow Co would expect audit fees of around $100,000. Your adult daughter has been working as an administrative assistant in the sales department of Rainbow Co for a year, after being introduced by the tax manager. She has just joined an employee share benefit scheme.

The client is keen to use the firm to provide audit services as they are pleased with the taxation services provided. The managing director and major shareholder, Kar Parkes, has therefore offered an incentive to the audit fee of an additional 1% of profits in excess of $20 million, annually where relevant. The current recurring taxation fees from Rainbow Co are $35,000, and last year special tax work amounted to $25,000. Last year's fees remain outstanding.

The managing director has suggested that you give consideration to the matter while staying for the weekend at his villa in Tenerife. He has arranged flights for both you and your spouse.

Required:

Comment on the matters that you should consider in deciding whether or not your audit firm can accept appointment as auditor of Rainbow Co. **(10 marks)**

(Total: 15 marks)

Test your understanding 9

You are an audit manager in Sepia & Co, a firm of Chartered Certified Accountants. Your specific responsibilities include advising the senior audit partners on the acceptance of new assignments. The following matters have arisen in connection with three prospective clients:

(a)   Your firm has been nominated to act as auditor to Squid Co, a private limited company. You have been waiting for a response to your letter of professional enquiry to Squid Co's auditor, Krill & Co, for several weeks. Your recent attempts to call the current engagement partner, Anton Fargues, in Krill & Co have been met with the response from Anton's personal assistant that 'Mr Fargues is not available'. **(5 marks)**

(b) Sepia & Co has been approached by the management of Hatchet Co, a company listed on a recognised stock exchange, to advise on a takeover bid which they propose to make. The target company, Vitronella Co, is an audit client of your firm. However, Hatchet Co is not. **(5 marks)**

(c) A former colleague in Sepia & Co, Edwin Stenuit, is now employed by another audit firm, Keratin & Co. Sepia & Co and Keratin & Co and three other firms have recently tendered for the audit of Benthos Co. Benthos Co is expected to announce the successful firm next week. Yesterday, at a social gathering, Edwin confided to you that Keratin & Co lowballed on their tender for the audit as they expect to be able to provide Benthos Co with lucrative other services. **(5 marks)**

Required:

Comment on the ethical and professional issues raised by each of the above matters and the steps, if any, that Sepia & Co should now take.

Note: The mark allocation is shown against each of the three issues.

(Total: 15 marks)

Test your understanding 10

(a) Explain why quality control may be difficult to implement in a smaller audit firm and illustrate how such difficulties may be overcome.

(5 marks)

(b) Kite Associates is an association of small accounting practices. One of the benefits of membership is improved quality control through a peer review system. You are reviewing a sample of auditor's reports issued by Rook & Co, a firm only recently admitted to Kite Associates, and you have identified the following modified opinion on the financial statements of Lammergeier Group:

Qualified opinion arising from material misstatement accounting treatment relating to the non-adoption of IAS 7

The management has not prepared a Group statement of cash flows and its associated notes. In the opinion of the management it is not practical to prepare a Group statement of cash flows due to the complexity involved. In our opinion, the reasons for the departure from IAS 7 are sound and acceptable and adequate disclosure has been made concerning the departure from IAS 7. The departure, in our opinion, does not impact on the truth and fairness of the financial statements.

'In our opinion, except for the non-preparation of the Group statement of cash flows and associated notes, the financial statements give a true and fair view of the financial position of the Company as at 31 March 20X5 and of the profit of the Group for the year then ended, and have been properly prepared in accordance with ...'

Your review of the prior year auditor's report has revealed that the 20X4 audit opinion was identical.

Required:

Critically appraise the appropriateness of the audit opinion given by Rook & Co on the financial statements of Lammergeier Group for the years ended 31 March 20X5 and 20X4.　　　　**(10 marks)**

(c)　You are also the audit manager responsible for the audit of Hegas Co. The audit is nearly complete and you are reviewing the other information contained in the annual report before your firm's auditor's report is signed. The financial statements of Hegas Co, a privately owned civil engineering company, show total assets of $120 million, revenue of $261 million, and profit before tax of $9.2 million for the year ended 31 March 20X5.

The chair's statement contains the following information:

'Hegas Co has now achieved a position as one of the world's largest generators of hydroelectricity, with a dedicated commitment to accountable ethical professionalism'.

Audit working papers show that 14% of revenue was derived from hydro-electricity (20X4: 12%). Publicly available information shows that there are seven international suppliers of hydro-electricity in Africa alone, which are all at least three times the size of Hegas Co in terms of both annual revenue and population supplied.

Required:

Explain the auditor's responsibilities for other information in documents containing audited financial statements and identify and comment on the implications of the above matter for the auditor's report on the financial statements of Hegas Co for the year ended 31 March 20X5.　　　　**(10 marks)**

(Total: 25 marks)

Test your understanding answers

Test your understanding 1

Briefing notes

To:	Chad Woodstock, audit engagement partner
From:	Audit manager
Date:	01 July 20X5
Subject:	Audit planning – Stow Group

Introduction

These briefing notes contain an evaluation of the risks of material misstatement to be considered in planning the audit of the Stow Group. The risks which have been explained focus on a restructuring of the Group which has taken place during the year. Materiality has been considered where information permits, and further information which would be useful in planning the audit has also been identified. The briefing notes also contain recommended audit procedures to be performed in respect of the disposal of Broadway Co. The Group finance director's suggestion that our firm makes use of the new subsidiary's internal audit team when performing our audit has been discussed, along with the ethical implication of the suggestion. Finally, the matters that should be considered when determining the audit fee have been discussed.

(a)   (i)

and (ii)   Zennor Co

Materiality of Zennor Co

To evaluate the materiality of Zennor Co to the Group, its profit and assets need to be retranslated into $. At the stated exchange rate of 4 Dingu = $1, its projected profit for the year is $22.5 million (90 million Dingu/4) and its projected total assets are $200 million (800 million Dingu/4).

Zennor Co's profit represents 11.3% of Group projected profit for the year (22.5/200), and its assets represent 8% of Group total assets (200/2,500). Zennor Co is therefore material to the Group and may be considered to be a significant component of it. A significant component is one which is identified by the auditor as being of individual financial significance to the group.

Zenner Co is likely to be considered a significant component due to its risk profile and the change in group structure which has occurred in the year.

The goodwill arising on the acquisition of Zennor Co amounts to 2.4% (60/2,500) of Group assets and is material.

Because the balances above, including goodwill, are based on a foreign currency, they will need to be retranslated at the year-end using the closing exchange rate to determine and conclude on materiality as at the year-end.

Materiality needs to be assessed based on the new, enlarged group structure. Materiality for the group financial statements as a whole will be determined when establishing the overall group audit strategy. The addition of Zennor Co to the group during the year is likely to cause materiality to be different from previous years, possibly affecting audit strategy and the extent of testing in some areas.

Risks of material misstatement

Retranslation of Zennor Co's financial statements

According to IAS 21 *The Effects of Changes in Foreign Exchange Rates*, the assets and liabilities of Zennor Co should be retranslated using the closing exchange rate. Its income and expenses should be retranslated at the exchange rates at the dates of the transactions.

The risk is that incorrect exchange rates are used for the retranslations. This could result in over/understatement of the assets, liabilities, income and expenses that are consolidated, including goodwill.

It would also mean that the exchange gains and losses arising on retranslation and to be included in Group other comprehensive income are incorrectly determined.

Measurement and recognition of exchange gains and losses

The calculation of exchange gains and losses can be complex, and there is a risk that it is not calculated correctly, or that some elements are omitted, for example, the exchange gain or loss on goodwill may be missed out of the calculation.

IAS 21 states that exchange gains and losses arising as a result of the retranslation of the subsidiary's balances are recognised in other comprehensive income. The risk is incorrect classification, for example, the gain or loss could be recognised incorrectly as part of profit for the year.

Initial measurement of goodwill

In order for goodwill to be calculated, the assets and liabilities of Zennor Co must have been identified and measured at fair value at the date of acquisition. Risks of material misstatement arise because the various components of goodwill each have specific risks attached, for example:

- Not all assets and liabilities may have been identified, for example, contingent liabilities may be omitted.

- Fair value is subjective and based on assumptions which may not be valid.

There is also a risk that the cost of investment is not measured correctly. For example:

– there may be contingent consideration that has not been included in the calculation, or

– there may be consideration that is not measured at fair value, for example, deferred consideration should be measured at the present value of the future payment.

Subsequent measurement of goodwill

According to IFRS 3 *Business Combinations*, goodwill should be subject to an impairment review on an annual basis. The risk is that a review has not taken place, and so goodwill is overstated and Group operating expenses understated if impairment losses have not been recognised.

Consolidation of income and expenses

Zennor Co was acquired on 1 September 20X4 and its income and expenses should have been consolidated from that date. There is a risk that the full year's income and expenses have been consolidated, leading to a risk of overstated Group profit.

Disclosure

Extensive disclosures are required by IFRS 3 to be included in the notes to the Group financial statements, for example, to include the acquisition date, reason for the acquisition and a description of the factors which make up the goodwill acquired. The risk is that disclosures are incomplete or not understandable.

Intra-group transactions

There will be a significant volume of intra-group transactions as the Group is supplying Zennor Co with inventory. There is a risk that intra-group sales, purchases, payables and receivables are not eliminated, leading to overstated revenue, cost of sales, payables and receivables in the Group financial statements.

There is also a risk that intercompany transactions are not identified in either/both companies' accounting systems.

The intra-group transactions are by definition related party transactions according to IAS 24 *Related Party Disclosures*, because Zennor Co is under the control of the Group. No disclosure of the transactions is required in the Group financial statements in respect of intra-group transactions because they are eliminated on consolidation.

However, both the individual financial statements of the Group company supplying Zennor Co and the financial statements of Zennor Co must contain notes disclosing details of the intra-group transactions. There is a risk that this disclosure is not provided.

In addition, the cars may be supplied including a profit margin or mark up, in which case a provision for unrealised profit should be recognised in the Group financial statements for inventory that remains unsold at the year end. If this is not accounted for, Group inventory will be overstated, and operating profit will be overstated.

Completeness of inventory

There is a risk that cars which are in transit to Zennor Co at the year-end may be omitted from inventory. The cars spend a significant amount of time in transit and awaiting delivery to Zennor Co, and without a good system of controls in place, it is likely that items of inventory will be missing from the Group's current assets as they may have been recorded as despatched from the seller but not yet as received by Zennor Co.

The inventory in transit to Zennor Co represents 2.3% of Group total assets (58/2,500) and is therefore material to the consolidated financial statements.

Further information in relation to Zennor Co:

- Prior years' financial statements and auditor's reports.
- Minutes of meetings where the acquisition was discussed.
- Business background, e.g. from the company's website or trade journals.
- Copies of systems documentation from the internal audit team.
- Confirmation from Zennor Co's previous auditors of any matters which they wish to bring to our attention.
- Projected financial statements for the year to 31 July 20X5.
- A copy of the due diligence report.
- Copies of prior year tax computations.

Broadway Co

Materiality

The profit made on the disposal of Broadway Co represents 12.5% of Group profit for the year (25/200) and the transaction is therefore material to the Group financial statements.

Given that the subsidiary was sold for $180 million and that a profit on disposal of $25 million was recognised, the Group's financial statements must have derecognised net assets of $155 million on the disposal. This amounts to 6.2% of the Group's assets and is material. This is assuming that the profit on disposal has been correctly calculated, which is a risk factor discussed below.

Risk of material misstatement

Derecognition of assets and liabilities

On the disposal of Broadway Co, all of its assets and liabilities which had been recognised in the Group financial statements should have been derecognised at their carrying value, including any goodwill in respect of the company.

There is therefore a risk that not all assets, liabilities and goodwill have been derecognised leading to overstatement of those balances and an incorrect profit on disposal being calculated and included in Group profit for the year.

Profit consolidated prior to disposal

There is a risk that Broadway Co's income for the year has been incorrectly consolidated. It should have been included in Group profit up to the date that control passed and any profit included after that point would mean overstatement of Group profit for the year.

Calculation of profit on disposal

There is a risk that the profit on disposal has not been accurately calculated, e.g. that the proceeds received have not been measured at fair value as required by IFRS 10 *Consolidated Financial Statements*, or that elements of the calculation are missing.

Classification and disclosure of profit on disposal

IAS 1 *Presentation of Financial Statements* requires separate disclosure on the face of the financial statements of material items to enhance the understanding of performance during the year. The profit of $25 million is material, so separate disclosure is necessary. The risk is that the profit is not separately disclosed, e.g. is netted from operating expenses, leading to material misstatement.

Extensive disclosure requirements exist in relation to subsidiaries disposed of, e.g. IAS 7 *Statement of Cash Flows* requires a note which analyses the assets and liabilities of the subsidiary at the date of disposal. There is a risk that not all necessary notes to the financial statements are provided.

Treatment of the disposal in parent company individual financial statements

The parent company's financial statements should derecognise the original cost of investment and recognise a profit on disposal based on the difference between the proceeds of $180 million and the cost of investment. Risk arises if the investment has not been derecognised or the profit has been incorrectly calculated.

Tax on disposal

There should be an accrual in both the parent company and the Group financial statements for the tax due on the disposal. This should be calculated based on the profit recognised in the parent company. There is a risk that the tax is not accrued for, leading to overstated profit and understated liabilities. There is also a risk that the tax calculation is not accurate.

(b) **Procedures to be performed on the disposal of Broadway Co**

- Obtain the statement of financial position of Broadway Co as at 1 April 20X4 to confirm the value of assets and liabilities which have been derecognised from the Group.

- Review prior year Group financial statements and audit working papers to confirm the amount of goodwill that exists in respect of Broadway Co and trace to confirm it is derecognised from the Group on disposal.

- Confirm that the Stow Group is no longer listed as a shareholder of the company.

- Obtain legal documentation in relation to the disposal to confirm the date of the disposal and confirm that Broadway Co's profit has been consolidated up to this date only.

- Agree or reconcile the profit recognised in the Group financial statements to Broadway Co's individual accounts as at 1 April 20X4.

- Perform substantive analytical procedures to gain assurance that the amount of profit consolidated appears reasonable and in line with expectations based on prior year profit.

- Recalculate the profit on disposal in the Group financial statements to confirm arithmetical accuracy.

- Agree the proceeds received of $180 million to legal documentation, and to cash book/bank statements.

- Confirm that $180 million is the fair value of proceeds on disposal and that no deferred or contingent consideration is receivable in the future.

- Review the Group statement of profit or loss and other comprehensive income to confirm that the profit on disposal is correctly disclosed as part of profit for the year (not in other comprehensive income) on a separate line.

- Using a disclosure checklist, confirm that all necessary information has been provided in the notes to the Group financial statements.

- Obtain the parent company's statement of financial position to confirm that the cost of investment is derecognised.

- Using prior year financial statements and audit working papers, agree the cost of investment derecognised to prior year's figure.

- Recalculate the profit on disposal in the parent company's financial statements.

- Reconcile the profit on disposal recognised in the parent company's financial statements to the profit recognised in the Group financial statements.

- Obtain management's estimate of the tax due on disposal, recalculate the figure and confirm the amount is properly accrued at parent company and at Group level.

- Review any correspondence with tax authorities regarding the tax due.

- Possibly the tax will be paid in the subsequent events period, in which case the payment can be agreed to cash book and bank statement.

(c) **Internal audit team and ethical issue**

It is not improper for Marta to suggest that Compton & Co use the work of Zennor Co's internal audit team. ISA 610 *Using the Work of Internal Auditors* contains requirements relating to the evaluation of the internal audit function to determine in what areas, and to what extent, the work of internal audit can be used by the external audit firm.

It would be beneficial for Compton & Co to use the internal audit team as it may result in a more efficient audit strategy, for example, the internal audit team's monitoring of controls should have resulted in a strong control environment, so a less substantive approach can be used on the audit.

In addition, the internal audit team should be able to provide Compton & Co with systems documentation and information on control activities which have been implemented. This will help the audit firm to build its knowledge and understanding of the new audit client. The internal audit team will also be able to assist Compton & Co in gaining more general business understanding with respect to the new subsidiary.

Compton & Co may also decide to rely on audit work performed by the internal audit team, for example, they may be asked to attend inventory counts of cars held at the port and awaiting delivery to Zennor Co.

All of the benefits described above are particularly significant given Zennor Co's overseas location, as reliance on the internal audit team would reduce travel time and costs which would be incurred if the external auditor had to perform the work themselves.

However, there will be a limit to the amount of work that can be delegated to the internal audit team. Before deciding to what extent the work of internal audit can be used, ISA 610 requires the external auditor to evaluate various matters, including the extent to which the internal audit function's organisation status and policies and procedures support the objectivity of the function; the level of competence of the internal audit team; and whether the internal audit function applies a systematic and disciplined approach, including quality control.

To perform these evaluations the external auditor may wish, for example, to discuss the work of the team with Jo Evesham including a consideration of the level of supervision, review and documentation of work performed, and also review the qualifications held by members of the team.

The fact that the internal audit team does not report to an independent audit committee may reduce the reliance that can be placed on their work as it affects the objectivity of work performed.

If Compton & Co chooses to use the work of the internal audit team, this will be relevant to the audit of both Zennor Co's individual financial statements, and the Group financial statements and will affect the audit strategy of both.

Marta states that reliance on the internal audit team will reduce the external audit fee, and the Group audit committee has requested that the Group audit fee remains the same as last year. An audit firm being pressured to reduce the extent of work performed in order to reduce fees is an example of an intimidation threat.

It should be brought to Marta's attention that the audit fee will not necessarily be reduced by reliance on internal audit, especially as this is the first year that Compton & Co have audited Zennor Co, so there will be a lot of work to be performed in developing knowledge and understanding of the client whether or not the firm chooses to rely on the work of the internal audit team.

(d) **Matters to be considered in determining the audit fee**

The commercial need for the firm to make a profit from providing the audit service needs to be considered alongside the client's expectations about the fee level and how it has been arrived at.

The audit firm should consider the costs of providing the audit service. This will include primarily the costs of the audit team, so the firm will need to assess the number and seniority of audit team members who will be involved, and the amount of time that they will spend on the audit. There may be the need for auditor's experts to be engaged, and the costs of this should be included if necessary.

Compton & Co will have standard charge out rates which are used when determining an audit fee and these should be used to estimate the total fee.

Travel and accommodation costs may also need to be included as Compton & Co was appointed as auditor of Zennor Co which is located in Farland. These costs may be reduced if Compton & Co has an office in Farland and can utilise local staff to perform the audit of Zennor Co.

As Zennor Co is a new subsidiary, additional work will be required this year, in particular:

- obtaining an understanding of the company and its interaction with the rest of the Group

- documenting the control systems

- testing opening balances.

Marta has suggested that we use the internal audit team as much as possible when performing our audit of Zennor Co as this will reduce the audit fee. However, as discussed above, Compton & Co will need to consider whether the work performed by the internal audit department is adequate for audit purposes. If reliance can be placed on their work, the time needed for the audit will decrease and this will result in a reduction to the fee.

The Group finance director has asked that the audit fee for the Group as a whole is not increased from last year's fee. This is unlikely to be possible given the changes to the group structure during the year. One of the problems of a low audit fee is that it can affect audit quality, as the audit firm could be tempted to cut corners and save time in order to minimise the costs of the audit.

Offering an unrealistically low audit fee which is below market rate in order to retain an audit client is known as lowballing, and while this practice is not prohibited, the client must not be misled about the amount of work which will be performed and the outputs of the audit. The issue for the client is that an unrealistically low audit fee is unlikely to be sustainable in the long run, leading to unwelcome fee increases in subsequent years. Compton & Co should explain to the finance director that the audit fee will be determined by the level of audit work which needs to be performed. The fee will be determined by the grade of staff that make up the audit team and the time spent by each of them on the audit.

UK syllabus: FRC Ethical Standard section 4 states that the audit engagement partner must be satisfied and able to demonstrate that the audit engagement has assigned to it sufficient partners and staff with appropriate time and skill to perform the audit in accordance with all applicable auditing and ethical standards, irrespective of the audit fee to be charged. This means that the audit fee should be high enough to allow the use of appropriate resources and that a low fee cannot be tolerated if it would impact on audit quality.

Conclusion

The Stow Group's financial statements contain a high risk of material misstatement this year end, due to the restructuring which has taken place. The audit plan will contain numerous audit procedures to reduce the identified risks to an acceptable level. Compton & Co may choose to place reliance on Zennor Co's internal audit team, but only after careful consideration of their competence and objectivity, and communication between the external and internal audit teams must be carefully planned for. The firm should be careful not to give in to pressure to reduce the audit fee if it is not appropriate to do so as this may affect the quality of the audit. The basis of the fee should be discussed with the audit committee to minimise the risk of disputes.

Test your understanding 2

Briefing notes

To:	Audit engagement partner
From:	Audit manager
Date:	01 July 20X5
Subject:	Planning of the audit of Hydrasports Co for the year ending 31 July 20X5

Introduction

These briefing notes evaluate the business risks and risks of material misstatement in respect of Hydrasports Co. Audit procedures in respect of the deferred income and hydrotherapy pool have been included. Performance indicators in relation to social and environmental responsibilities along with the evidence that should be obtained to provide assurance over the indicators have been suggested.

(a) **Business risks**

Customer dissatisfaction

Sauna facilities are currently not available for members to use. Childcare facilities are considering being withdrawn due to complaints about levels of supervision. Hydrasports Co's inability to retain lifeguards increases the risk that pools cannot open due to health and safety regulations. In addition, gym equipment is obsolete and therefore will not reflect the most up to date technology.

These issues are likely to lead to customer dissatisfaction. Additional expenditure will need to be incurred to resolve any problems. Members may ask for a partial refund on their membership fees as they do not have use of all of the facilities for which they are paying which will reduce future revenue.

Health and safety

Hydrasports Co could be sued if a member suffers injury as a result of unsafe equipment or due to a lack of qualified lifeguards. This will result in legal costs and may result in compensation payments.

Serious accidents may prompt investigation by local authority resulting in penalties, fines and/or withdrawal of licence to operate.

Licence

Hydrasports Co cannot operate a centre if a licence is suspended, withdrawn or not renewed (e.g. through failing a local authority inspection or failing to apply for renewal). Revenue will fall as a result.

Advance payments

Membership fees are received in advance. If cash flow is not managed properly, Hydrasports Co may not have the money in the bank to be able to meet pay future liabilities when they fall due.

Monthly accounting returns

Centre managers prepare monthly accounting returns. The managers may not have sufficient knowledge to do this accurately or efficiently. This could result in submission of inaccurate returns and incorrect management information being used for decision making. Centre managers may not have enough time to fulfil their day-to-day responsibilities (e.g. relating to customer satisfaction, human resources, health and safety) if the management information to be reported takes up too much of their time.

Centralised control

Centralised control through company policy is resulting in inefficient and ineffective operations as managers cannot respond on a timely basis to local needs. This may lead to poor decision making which will reduce profitability and customer dissatisfaction which may affect reputation and the ability to generate revenues.

Insurance cover

The reduction in insurance cover reduces the recoverable amount of assets in the event of loss. Due to Hydrasports Co's cash flow issues, they may not have adequate resources to replace any assets not covered by insurance. This will impact the facilities that can be offered to members limiting the amount of revenue that can be earned.

High staff turnover

High staff turnover will lead to higher recruitment and training costs. Employees will not be fully productive until they are familiar with Hydrasports Co's working practices. This will reduce profitability.

(b) **Risks of material misstatement**

Non-compliance with health and safety regulations

There are several potential health and safety issues present in Hydrasports Co:

- Childcare facilities are not adequately supervised.

- Obsolete equipment may be unsafe to use.

- Accidents may occur due to pools being operated without a qualified lifeguard on duty.

Breaches of regulations could lead to fines and penalties.

Liabilities may be understated if adequate provision for fines/penalties imposed by the local authority has not been made.

Overstatement of assets

There are several indicators of impairment:

- The saunas are no longer in use.

- Childcare facilities may be withdrawn.

- Pools may need to close if there are no qualified lifeguards to supervise.

- The continued construction of the hydrotherapy pool may be threatened by cash flow problems. This may mean it does not get completed.

- Gym equipment needs to be replaced. Assets which are obsolete but not fully depreciated will be overstated if an impairment review is not performed.

The carrying amount of non-current assets may be overstated if an impairment review is not performed.

Provision for refunds

Although fees are non-refundable, suspension of a facility (e.g. sauna) may result in customers asking for partial refund. In particular Hydrasports Co may have an obligation to refund fees paid in advance when centres are closed (e.g. the Verne centre).

Liabilities may be understated if provisions for refunds are not adequately made.

Revenue

Revenue should only be recognised when the performance obligations of the membership contract are fulfilled in accordance with IFRS 15 *Revenue From Contracts with Customers*. The performance obligations in this situation are fulfilled over time when the customer has had the opportunity to use the facility. As fees are paid in advance, revenue will need to be deferred and recognised at the end of each month of service the customer has received.

If Hydrasports Co's revenue recognition policy does not comply with IFRS 15, revenue is likely to be overstated and contract liabilities are likely to be understated.

Licences

Hydrasports Co requires a licence to operate from the local authority. The licence should be capitalised as an intangible asset and amortised over the licence period in accordance with IAS 38 *Intangible Assets*.

Intangible assets may be overstated if the licences have not been amortised appropriately or if there is any indication of impairment affecting the ability of a leisure centre to generate future economic benefits.

Going concern disclosure

Due to the problems mentioned above which are likely to lead to a loss of future revenue, in addition to the cash flow problems already being experienced, Hydrasports Co may have difficulty continuing as a going concern.

Going concern uncertainties may not be adequately disclosed in the financial statements.

Control risks

Accounting information flowing into the financial statements may not be properly captured, input, processed or output by the centre managers resulting in misstatements in the financial statements.

Management circumvention or override of control procedures laid down by head office may result in system deficiencies and increased control risk.

If errors arising are not detected and corrected the risk of misstatement in the financial statements is increased.

(c) Audit procedures

(i) Contract liabilities

- Trace a sample of peak/off-peak membership fees and joining fees to member contracts to verify the income that should be deferred.

- Reconcile membership income to fees paid. If customers can renew their membership without payment there should be no deferral of income (unless the debt for unpaid fees is also recognised).

- Inspect correspondence from members to identify any disputes which may mean membership fees should be refunded.

- Recalculate the contract liability element of fees received in the three months before the statement of financial position date to verify arithmetical accuracy.

- Compare the year-end contract liability balance with prior year and investigate any significant variance.

(ii) **Hydrotherapy pool**

- Inspect the contract with the builder, contractor billings and stage payments to confirm the cost of the asset.

- Review the expert's assessment of stage of completion as at the statement of financial position date, estimated costs to completion, etc. Hydrasports Co is likely to be advised by its own expert (a quantity surveyor) on how the contract is progressing.

- Physically inspect the construction at the year-end to confirm work to date and assess the reasonableness of stage of completion.

- Agree borrowing costs associated with the construction to the loan agreement to confirm finance terms and payments.

- Recalculate the borrowing costs capitalised to confirm arithmetical accuracy.

- Confirm that the basis of capitalisation complies with IAS 23 *Borrowing Costs* (e.g. interest accruing during any suspension of building work should not be capitalised).

- Critically evaluate management's assessment of possible impairment (of the hydrotherapy pool and the centre). As the construction has already cost twice as much as budgeted, its value in use (when brought into use) may be less than cost.

(d) **Performance measures**

Member satisfaction

- Number of people on membership waiting lists (if any).

- Number of referrals/recommendations to club membership by existing members.

- Proportion of renewed memberships.

- Actual members: 100% capacity membership (sub-analysed between 'peak' and 'off-peak').

Membership dissatisfaction

- Proportion of members requesting refunds per month/quarter.

- Proportion of memberships lapsing (i.e. not renewed).

Staff

- Average number of staff employed per month.

- Number of starters/leavers per month.

- Staff turnover/average duration of employment.

- Number of training courses for lifeguards per annum.

Predictability

- Number of late openings (say more than 5, 15 and 30 minutes after advertised opening times).

- Number of days closure per month/year of each facility (i.e. pool, crèche, sauna, gym) and centre.

Environment

- Number of instances of non-compliance with legislation/regulations (e.g. on chemical spills).

- Energy efficiency (e.g. in maintaining pool at a given temperature throughout the year).

- Incentives for environmental friendliness such as discouraging use of cars/promoting use of bicycles (e.g. by providing secure lock-ups for cycles and restricted car parking facilities).

Other society

- Local community involvement (e.g. facilities offered to schools and clubs at discount rates during 'off-peak' times).

- Range of facilities offered specifically to pensioners, mothers and babies, disabled patrons, etc.

- Participation in the wider community (e.g. providing facilities to support sponsored charity events).

Safety

- Incident reports documenting the date, time and nature of each incident, the extent of damage and/or personal injury, and action taken.

- Number of accident free days.

Evidence

- Membership registers clearly distinguishing between new and renewed members, also showing lapsed memberships.

- Pool/gym timetables – showing sessions set aside for 'over 60s', schools, clubs, special events, etc.

- Staff training courses and costs.

- Staff timesheets – showing arrival/departure times and adherence to staff rotas.

- Documents supporting additions to/deletions from payroll standing data (e.g. new joiner/leaver notifications).

- Engineer's inspection reports – confirming gym equipment, etc is in satisfactory working order.

- Engineer and safety check manuals and the maintenance program.

- Levels of expenditure on repairs and maintenance.

- Energy saving equipment/measures (e.g. insulated pool covering).

- Safety drill reports (e.g. alarm tests, pool evacuations).

- Accident report register – showing date, nature of incident, personal injury sustained (if any), action taken (e.g. emergency services called in).

- Any penalties/fines imposed by the local authorities and the reasons for them.

- Copies of reports of local authority investigations.

- The frequency and nature of insurance claims (e.g. to settle claims of injury to members and/or staff).

Conclusion

The risks detailed above demonstrate that the audit of Hydrasports Co is a high risk engagement. These risks must be addressed by designing appropriate audit procedures to be included in the audit plan. Appropriately experienced staff must be assigned to the audit team to ensure any material misstatements are detected.

Test your understanding 3

Briefing notes

To:	Audit engagement partner
From:	Audit manager
Date:	1 July 20X5
Subject:	Planning of the audit of Cerise Co for the year ending 31 July 20X5

Introduction

These briefing notes evaluate the audit risks to be considered when planning the audit of Cerise Co. Audit procedures in respect of the amounts due from distributors have been included. The briefing notes also cover the extent to which reliance on analytical procedures and written representations will differ from the prior year audit.

(a) **Audit risks**

Cessation of trade

Cerise Co ceased to trade during the year. The financial statements therefore should not be prepared on a going concern basis, but on a break-up or other realisable basis.

This has implications for:

- the reclassification of assets and liabilities (from non-current to current)
- the carrying amount of assets (at recoverable amount)
- the completeness of recorded liabilities.

There is a risk that the basis of preparation used is inappropriate.

Inventory

Cerise Co has ceased manufacturing two months prior to the year-end. Any items remaining in inventory at the year-end will need to be written down to the lower of cost and net realisable value (NRV) in accordance with IAS 2 *Inventories*.

NRV is likely to be nil and therefore the inventory must be written-off in full.

There is a risk that inventory is overstated if sufficient allowance is not made for items that will not be sold.

Sale of technology and manufacturing equipment

All assets sold should be derecognised and the profit on disposal arising from the discontinuance of operations separately disclosed in the statement of profit or loss.

There is a risk of incorrect disclosure if the profit or loss on disposal is not separately made or if the profit or loss on disposal is not calculated correctly.

Plant and equipment will be overstated if:

- manufacturing equipment that has been sold is still included in the financial statements
- assets that were not part of the sale are not written down to the lower of carrying amount and recoverable amount, in accordance with IAS 36 *Impairment of Assets*.

Premises held for sale

If the unsold properties meet all the criteria of IFRS 5 *Non-current Assets Held for Sale and Discontinued Operations* at the statement of financial position date they should be:

- separately classified as held for sale
- carried at the lower of carrying amount (i.e. depreciated cost) and fair value less estimated costs to sell.

Any after-date losses on disposal would provide evidence of impairment.

The financial statements will be materially misstated if non-current assets held for sale are not separately disclosed in accordance with IFRS 5.

Redundant workforce

Although statutory redundancy pay, holiday pay, accrued overtime etc. may have been settled before the year-end, there may be additional liabilities in respect of former employees e.g. pension obligations.

Liabilities may be understated if there are claims arising from the redundant workers if their statutory or contractual rights have been breached.

Accounts department

Fewer staff will be employed in the accounts department until the company is wound down completely. This may increase the risk of errors arising as staff will need to assume wider areas of responsibility. Staff may also not take as much care with their work as they know they will not be working for the company in the near future.

The risk of errors arising not being detected by the control system is also likely to increase as levels of supervision and segregation of duties may be reduced.

There is a greater risk of misstatement in the financial statements as a result.

Leased premises

Four of Cerise Co's premises are leased and cannot be sold or sub-let under the lease terms.

The right of use asset will be impaired if the recoverable amount (value in use) is less than the carrying amount in accordance with IAS 36 *Impairment of Assets*.

There is a risk that tangible assets are overstated if the impairment is not recognised.

A liability will need to be recognised in respect of the onerous lease payments. Liabilities will be understated if the future lease payments do not continue to be recognised as a liability.

Product warranties

Cerise Co's products have been sold with a one-year assurance type warranty which require a provision to be recognised for the estimated cost of warranty claims as per IAS 37 *Provisions, Contingent Liabilities and Contingent Assets*.

As Cerise Co can no longer undertake the warranty work itself, arrangements will have to be made to honour the warranty obligations, e.g. by transferring the warranty obligations to another company which may be more expensive than performing the work in-house.

There is a risk of understatement of the warranty provision if the estimate has not been appropriately revised.

Three and five-year extended warranties are service type warranties which should be accounted for under IFRS 15 *Revenue From Contracts With Customers*. The payments for these warranties should have been recognised as a contract liability and the revenue recognised over the period of the service provided.

If the company is no longer planning to provide that service, either a refund must be given or the contracts must be sold to another provider.

If a refund is to be given, a liability will need to be recognised in respect of the refund payments required.

If the contracts are sold to another provider, the revenue should be recognised.

Breach of agreements/contracts

Since Cerise Co no longer has the means of fulfilling contracts with distributors, provision should be made for any compensation or penalties arising. Where the penalties due to distributors for breach of supply agreements exceed the amounts due from them, the receivables should be written down.

Adequate provision should be made for breaches of contracts with suppliers. If suppliers do not exercise their rights to invoke penalty clauses, disclosure of the contingent liability may be more appropriate than a provision.

There is a risk that provisions are understated or contingent liabilities are not adequately disclosed.

(b) **Reliance on audit work**

(i) **Analytical procedures**

Overall, the extent of reliance on analytical procedures is likely to be less than that for the prior year audit as the scale and nature of Cerise Co's activities will differ from the prior year.

There are a number of individually material transactions in the current year which will require detailed substantive testing (e.g. sale of patented technology and manufacturing equipment and sale of premises).

Budgetary information used for analytical procedures in prior periods (e.g. budgeted production/sales) will have less relevance in the current year as the cessation of trade is unlikely to have been forecast.

Information will only be comparable with the prior year for 10 months. Costs incurred in June and July will relate to winding down operations rather than operational activities therefore cannot be compared with the prior year.

The impact of the one-off circumstances on carrying amounts is more likely to be assessed through detailed substantive testing (e.g. after-date realisation) than reliance on ratios and past history.

For example, analytical procedures on an aged trade receivables analysis and calculation of average collection period used in prior years will not be relevant to assessing the adequacy of the write-down now needed. Similarly, inventory turnover ratios will no longer be comparable when inventory is no longer being replenished.

Some reliance will still be placed on certain analytical procedures, for example, in substantiating charges to the statement of profit or loss for the 10 months of operations.

(ii) **Written representations**

Overall, the extent of reliance on written representations is likely to be increased as compared with the prior year audit.

The magnitude of matters of judgment and opinion is greater than in prior years. For example, inventory and trade receivable write-downs, impairment losses and numerous provisions.

The auditor will seek to obtain as much corroborative evidence as is available. However, where amounts of assets have still to be recovered and liabilities settled, management will be asked to make representations on the adequacy of write-downs, provisions, and the completeness of disclosures for claims and other contingent liabilities. Where negotiations are under discussion but not yet formalised (e.g. with a prospective buyer for premises), management may be the only source of evidence (e.g. for the best estimate of sale proceeds).

The extent to which reliance can be placed on representations depends on the extent to which those making the representation can be expected to be well-informed on the particular matters. As the human resources and production directors will not be available after the statement of financial position date, particular thought should be given to obtaining representations on matters pertaining to areas of judgment, before they leave.

(c) **Audit procedures**

Amounts due from distributors

– Review after-date cash to assess whether payments have been received post year-end.

– Review agreements with distributors to confirm the unexpired period (up to three years) and the penalties stipulated.

– Recalculate amounts due to distributors for the early termination of the agreements with them.

– Review correspondence with distributors relating to financial settlement, and any responses received.

– Discuss with management whether they can provide any further evidence regarding amounts due to be received from distributors or penalties imposed.

– Review board minutes for discussions of management relating to disputes with distributors.

Conclusion

The risks detailed above demonstrate that the audit of Cerise Co is a high risk engagement. These risks must be addressed by designing appropriate audit procedures to be included in the audit plan. Appropriately experienced staff must be assigned to the audit team to ensure any material misstatements are detected.

Test your understanding 4

Tutorial note:

The first part of this question is essentially a due diligence question. You have been asked to examine the management accounts and forecasts of a target company that your client is interested in acquiring.

(a) **Implications of findings**

$800,000 profit on sale of property

Although the profit on sale of the property arises from ordinary activities, it needs to be separately identified (IAS 1) so that Scorpio Co's current trading performance can be assessed (by Bellatrix Co and the bank). It should be excluded from any trading results that are being extrapolated to provide figures for profit forecasts. To include it would result in a distortion of sustainable profits.

Scorpio Co's properties are being valued at historical cost in its financial statements. Bellatrix Co should obtain an independent valuation of the properties before finalising a purchase price for the acquisition of Scorpio Co.

The property sale could have been made to realise cash and so mitigate current cash flow difficulties. The proposed sale of two more properties and outsourcing of warehousing may further improve the cash flow situation in the short-term. However, outsourcing warehousing could place a further burden on cash flow if an agreement is entered into and no buyer can subsequently be found for the properties.

Scorpio's management is seeking (or negotiating with) a suitable organisation to provide warehousing. However, one of the synergies to be obtained from acquiring Scorpio Co may be utilising Bellatrix Co's spare warehousing capacity. Bellatrix Co should therefore obtain warranties and indemnities in the purchase contract in respect of any contingent liabilities that could arise. For example, penalties may be incurred if an agreement to outsource warehousing is entered into and subsequently cancelled.

Sales to Andromeda Co

The two members of the management board of Scorpio Co will be related parties, as per IAS 24, if they are key management personnel (i.e. having authority and responsibility for planning, directing and controlling the activities of Scorpio Co).

Andromeda Co will be a related party if the management board members have the ability to exercise influence over Andromeda Co's financial and operating policy decisions. This seems likely, as 10% of Scorpio Co's sales constitutes material inter-company transactions. (Control of Andromeda Co is not an issue as the two members have only a minority interest.)

Sales to Andromeda Co appear to be related party transactions which should be disclosed in Scorpio Co's financial statements for the year to 31 December 20X5.

Although prices appear to be on an arm's length basis, the transactions may not be at arm's length if other trading terms (e.g. delivery or payment terms) are more or less favourable than transactions with unrelated parties. If credit terms are not normal commercial terms these sales could be contributing to Scorpio Co's current cash flow difficulties.

The sales to Andromeda Co are material to Scorpio Co and may be lost after the acquisition (e.g. if the two minority shareholders do not continue to hold positions on the management board of Scorpio Co). A proportional (i.e. 10%) reduction in gross profit would also be expected (assuming margins on sales to Andromeda Co are not dissimilar to those on other sales).

Bank loan application

The $150,000 discrepancy between the current asset values per the management accounts and the balances per the accounting records appears to be an irregularity that could constitute a fraud against the bank. It casts serious doubts over the integrity of Scorpio Co's management. Revising the accounting estimates for allowances against asset values downwards is clearly inappropriate as it is most likely that they should be increased (as inventory levels increase with falling demand and receivables are more likely to be bad or doubtful debts).

Refurbishing the offices is unlikely to constitute essential expenditure when the company is experiencing cash flow difficulties. Also it is possible that refurbishment may not be required when Bellatrix Co acquires Scorpio Co because the functions of the executive and administration offices may be relocated elsewhere within the Bellatrix group of companies.

Although current trading performance is clearly below budget (after deducting the profit on disposal and reinstating the allowances for inventory and receivables), the loan finance is not being sought for a purpose that would increase the company's revenue-earning opportunities. This may cast doubt on the business acumen of Scorpio Co's management. It is possible that the loan finance would not be forthcoming if the bank were aware of Scorpio Co's true position.

Bellatrix Co should seek to have the negotiations with the bank suspended until after the acquisition, when the need for loan finance can be reassessed. Bellatrix Co should obtain guarantees from Scorpio Co's executives in the event that they pursue the loan application (which may possibly create charges over Scorpio Co's assets).

Budget forecast

The profit estimates made by the management of Scorpio Co appear to be unduly optimistic because the first six month's budget has only been met by the inclusion, in the reported results of:

- a non-sustainable profit on disposal of a warehouse

- unwarranted reversals of allowances against asset values.

Perhaps it is more likely that the forecast 'rising profit trend' will be achieved (and the annual budget exceeded) through profits arising on the disposals of two more properties rather than increased demand.

Budgeted profits should therefore be disregarded in the determination of the purchase price.

(b) **Impact of acquisition on audit**

Tutorial notes:

(1) The acquisition will be completed before 31 December 20X5 (see 1st para 'acquisition in current year').

(2) Accounting year-ends will be coterminous ('first half year to 30 June 20X5').

(3) You will be appointed as auditor to Scorpio Co ('as audit manager to Bellatrix Co and its subsidiaries').

(4) 'Conduct of your audit' requires consideration of the whole audit process, not just audit testing.

Practice management

It is possible that audit objectivity may appear to be impaired (e.g. due to a closer relationship between Bellatrix Co's management and the audit team having developed during the acquisition assignment). An engagement quality control review may therefore be required as an appropriate safeguard.

Bellatrix Co's individual company accounts

The acquisition will constitute an addition to investments in subsidiaries in Bellatrix Co's own financial statements. The purchase consideration paid (or contingently payable) should also be disclosed.

The cost of acquisition should be verified to the sale agreement. Cash consideration must be agreed to entries in the cash book and bank statements. Company minutes and entries in the share register will evidence consideration in shares.

Bellatrix Co's consolidated accounts

Statement of financial position

Scorpio Co's assets and liabilities, at fair value to the group, will be combined on a line-by-line basis and any goodwill arising recognised.

The fair value of such assets may be material to the consolidated statement of financial position. Assuming that the properties were independently valued prior to the acquisition, it will be appropriate to seek to place reliance on the work of the expert valuer.

The calculation of the goodwill arising on acquisition must be recalculated and the component figures agreed. Goodwill must be reviewed for impairment by Bellatrix Co's management. The auditor will need to assess this impairment review for appropriateness to ensure the asset is not overstated.

Statement of profit or loss

As Scorpio Co will be acquired quite late on in the year (certainly the second half of the year) it is possible that its post-acquisition results are not material to the consolidated statement of profit or loss.

Unless accounting adjustments are required (e.g. to bring any accounting policies of Scorpio Co into line with Bellatrix Co) the addition of one more subsidiary into the consolidation working papers is unlikely to have a significant impact.

Other subsidiaries

The materiality of other subsidiaries, in the group context, should be reassessed in terms of the enlarged group. The existence of another company (Scorpio Co) in the same business within the group may extend the scope of analytical procedures available. This could have the effect of increasing audit efficiency.

Scorpio Co's financial statements

Planning

Much of the collection of background information associated with planning the conduct of a new audit assignment will have already been obtained as a result of the pre-acquisition work.

Materiality assessment

Material matters requiring attention will include:

– sales to Andromeda Co

– property valuations

– inventory valuations (raw materials, WIP and finished goods)

– trade receivables balances

– liabilities (including bank loans).

The management accounts for the six months to 30 June should provide information sufficient to make an initial evaluation of materiality. However, as the reliability of certain management information is in doubt, this should be reassessed before detailed work commences.

The materiality of these items should also be assessed in the context of monetary amounts in the consolidated financial statements.

Risk assessment

Specific areas of audit risk have already been identified, thereby reducing the time required to assess the risk of misstatement at the planning stage.

In particular:

- Inherent risk is high due to Scorpio Co's management overstating profit (even if the management board has since been replaced)

- Inventory may be overstated/allowances understated due to inventory having increased (due to a fall in demand)

- Trade receivables may be overstated/allowances for irrecoverable and doubtful debts understated due to Scorpio's management having manipulated these figures to achieve their profit estimates.

Ascertaining the systems and internal controls

Some systems review work may have already been undertaken (e.g. when considering the source of information used in the preparation of Scorpio Co budgetary information).

The relevance of Scorpio Co's current accounting systems and internal controls will depend on Bellatrix Co's plans for change. For example, a Bellatrix Co office may account for Scorpio Co's transactions. If significant changes are proposed it may be more appropriate to adopt a substantive approach to the first audit of Scorpio Co.

Audit evidence

Some audit evidence should have been obtained for the due diligence file e.g. concerning the sales to Andromeda Co and the sale of property. This should be copied and referenced to the audit working papers to ensure that work is not unnecessarily re-performed.

As Scorpio Co is in the same business as Bellatrix Co, ratio analysis and other substantive analytical procedures should provide a more cost-effective approach to obtaining audit evidence than tests of detail.

Review

The relationship between the two members of Scorpio Co's management board and Andromeda Co after the date of acquisition must be established and the extent of transactions between them, if any. For example, these non-controlling interests of Andromeda Co may no longer hold board positions, and/or sales to Andromeda Co may have ceased.

The proportion of sales should be disclosed (e.g. 10%) along with factual information concerning the pricing policy. Audit tests must verify, for example, that price is determined based on a published price list.

Test your understanding 5

(a) **Store impairment**

(i) **Matters**

The carrying amount of goodwill of $2.2m ($5.5m × 40%) represents 1.2% of total assets and 23% of PBT, and is also material.

If more than $475,000 of goodwill is attributable to the supermarket, then its write-off would be material to PBT ($9.5m × 5% = $475,000).

The event provides evidence of a possible impairment of the supermarket which is a cash-generating unit. The goodwill assigned to it is also likely to be impaired.

Management should have considered whether the other four stores in Urvina (and elsewhere) are similarly impaired.

There is a risk that assets including goodwill are overstated in the financial statements if an appropriate impairment review has not been undertaken.

The announcement is after the statement of financial position date and is therefore a non-adjusting event insofar as no provision for restructuring (for example) can be made.

(ii) **Audit evidence**

– Board minutes approving the store's refurbishment and documenting the need to address the fall in demand for it as a supermarket.

– Recalculation of the carrying amount of goodwill (40% × $5.5m = $2.2m).

– A schedule identifying all assets that relate to the store under review and the carrying amounts agreed to the underlying accounting records (e.g. non-current asset register).

– Recalculation of value in use and/or net selling price of the cash-generating unit that is to become the City Metro as at 31 March 20X5.

– Agreement of cash flow projections to approved budgets/forecast revenues and costs for a maximum of five years, unless a longer period can be justified.

– Written representation from management relating to the assumptions used in the preparation of financial budgets.

- Agreement that the pre-tax discount rate used reflects current market assessments of the time value of money (and the risks specific to the store) and is reasonable. For example, by comparison with Volcan Co's weighted average cost of capital.

- Inspection of the store (if this is the month it is closed for refurbishment).

- Actual after-date sales by store compared with budget.

- Revenue budgets and cash flow projections for:

    - the two stores purchased at the same time

    - other stores in Urvina

    - the stores elsewhere.

(b) Reward scheme

(i) Matters

If the entire year's revenue ($303m) attracted loyalty points then the cost of the reward scheme in the year is at most $3.03m. This represents 1% of revenue and 31.9% of profit before tax which is material.

To the extent that points have been awarded but not redeemed at 31 March 20X5, Volcan Co will have a liability at the statement of financial position date.

In accordance with IFRS 15 *Revenue from Contracts with Customers*, some of the proceeds from the initial sale should be allocated to the liability and only recognised in revenue as the points are redeemed.

The calculation of the liability will need to take into consideration

- Any restrictions on the terms for converting points (e.g. whether they expire if not used within a specified time).

- The proportion of reward points awarded which are not expected to be claimed (e.g. the 'take up' of points awarded may be only 80%, say).

- The proportion of customers who register for loyalty cards and the percentage of revenue (and profit) which they represent (which may vary from store to store depending on customer profile).

There is a risk that liabilities in relation to the reward scheme are understated and revenue is overstated.

(ii) **Audit evidence**

- New/updated systems documentation explaining how:

    - loyalty cards (and numbers) are issued to customers

    - points earned are recorded at the point of sale

    - points are later redeemed on subsequent purchases.

- Reconciliation of the total balance due to customers at the year-end under the reward scheme to the sum of the points on individual customer reward cards.

- Documentation of walk-through tests (e.g. on registering customer applications and issuing loyalty cards, awarding of points on special offer items).

- Results of tests of controls supporting the extent to which audit reliance is placed on the accounting and internal control system. In particular, how points are extracted from the electronic tills (cash registers) and summarised into the weekly/monthly financial data for each store which underlies the financial statements.

- Analytical procedures on the value of points awarded by store per month with explanations of variations. For example, points might be expected to increase following any promotion of the loyalty scheme by a store.

- Results of tests of detail on a sample of transactions with customers undertaken at store visits. For example, for a sample of copy till receipts:

    - check the arithmetic accuracy of points awarded (1 per $1 spent + special offers)

    - agree points awarded for special offers to that week's special offers

    - for cash discounts taken confirm the conversion of points is against the opening balance of points awarded (not against purchases just made).

(c) **Site restoration**

(i) **Matters**

The provision for site restoration of $4.4 million represents nearly 2.5% of total assets and is therefore material.

As per IAS 16 *Property, Plant and Equipment,* the estimated cost of restoring the site is a cost directly attributable to the initial measurement of the tangible non-current asset to the extent that it is recognised as a provision under IAS 37 *Provisions, Contingent Liabilities and Contingent Assets.*

As per IAS 37, a provision should only be recognised for site restoration if there is a present obligation as a result of a past event that can be measured reliably and an outflow of economic benefits is probable.

The provision is overstated by nearly $0.34m since Volcan Co is not obliged to relocate the trees and only has an obligation of $60,000 as at 31 March 20X5 (being the penalty for having felled them). When considered in isolation, this overstatement is immaterial (representing only 0.2% of total assets and 3.6% of PBT).

It seems that even if there are local government regulations calling for site restoration there is no obligation unless the penalties for non-compliance have been imposed (unlike the fines for the trees).

It is unlikely that commencement of site development has given rise to a constructive obligation, since past actions (disregarding the preservation of the trees) must dispel any expectation that Volcan Co will honour any pledge to restore the valley.

Consideration should also be given to whether commencing development of the site and destroying the trees conflicts with any statement of environmental responsibility in the annual report.

There is a risk that provisions are overstated and profit understated if this provision does not meet the criteria of IAS 37.

(ii) **Audit evidence**

- Payment of $60,000 to local government in May 20X5 agreed to the bank statement.

- The present value calculation of the future cash expenditure making up the provision.

- Agreement that the pre-tax discount rate used reflects current market assessments of the time value of money (as for (a)).

- Asset inspection at the site as at 31 March 20X5.

- A copy of the planning application and permission granted setting out the penalties for non-compliance.

Test your understanding 6

(a) **Cessation of home delivery service**

(i) **Matters**

$0.6m represents 1.4% of reported revenue (prior year 1.9%) and is therefore material.

The home delivery service is not a component of Albreda Co and its cessation does not classify as a discontinued operation in accordance with IFRS 5 *Non-current Assets Held for Sale and Discontinued Operations* because:

– It is not a cash-generating unit because home delivery revenues are not independent of other revenues generated by the restaurant kitchens.

– 1.4% of revenue is not a major line of business.

– Home delivery does not cover a separate geographical area (but many areas around the numerous restaurants).

The redundancy provision of $0.2m represents 11.1% of profit before tax (10% before allowing for the provision) and is therefore material. However, it represents only 0.6% of total assets and is therefore immaterial to the statement of financial position.

As the announcement was made before the year-end, there is a present obligation and a probable outflow of economic benefits in respect of the redundancies, therefore the provision is appropriate.

The delivery vehicles should be classified as held for sale if their carrying amount will be recovered principally through a sale transaction rather than through continuing use. For this to be the case the following IFRS 5 criteria must be met:

– the vehicles must be available for immediate sale in their present condition, and

– their sale must be highly probable.

However, even if the classification as held for sale is appropriate, the measurement basis is incorrect. Non-current assets classified as held for sale should be carried at the lower of carrying amount and fair value less costs to sell.

It is incorrect that the vehicles are being measured at fair value less costs to sell which is $0.3m in excess of the carrying amount. This amounts to a revaluation and should be reversed. $0.3m represents just less than 1% of assets and 16.7% of profit which is material.

Comparison of fair value less costs to sell against carrying amount should have been made on an item by item basis and not on their totals.

There is a risk that the delivery vehicles held for sale are overstated.

(ii) **Audit evidence**

- Copy of board minute documenting management's decision to cease home deliveries (and any press releases/internal memoranda to staff).

- An analysis of revenue (e.g. extracted from management accounts) showing the amount attributed to home delivery sales.

- Redundancy terms for drivers as set out in their contracts of employment to assess adequacy of the redundancy provision.

- A proof in total for the reasonableness/completeness of the redundancy provision (e.g. number of drivers × number of years employed × payment per year of service).

- A schedule of depreciated cost of delivery vehicles extracted from the non-current asset register to confirm carrying amount of assets held for sale.

- Second hand market prices as published/advertised in used vehicle guides to verify fair value.

- After-date net sale proceeds from sale of vehicles and comparison of proceeds against estimated fair values to confirm fair value.

- Physical inspection of the condition of unsold vehicles to assess whether they are likely to be sold for the estimated fair value in their current condition.

- Draft financial statements to assess the appropriateness of the disclosure of assets held for sale on the face of the statement of financial position or in the notes, and shown in the reconciliation of carrying amount at the beginning and end of the period.

(b) **Revaluation of owned premises**

(i) **Matters**

The revaluations are material as $1.7m, $5.4m and $7.1m represent 5.5%, 17.6% and 23.1% of total assets, respectively.

The change in accounting policy, from a cost model to a revaluation model, should be accounted for in accordance with IAS 16 *Property, Plant and Equipment* (i.e. as a revaluation).

Independence, qualifications and expertise of valuer(s) should be considered to determine the reliability of the valuations.

IAS 16 does not permit the selective revaluation of assets therefore the whole class of premises should have been revalued.

The valuations of properties after the year-end are adjusting events (i.e. providing additional evidence of conditions existing at the year-end) per IAS 10 *Events After the Reporting Date*.

The revaluation exercise is incomplete. If the revaluations on the remaining three properties are expected to be material and cannot be reasonably estimated for inclusion in the financial statements the change in policy should be deferred until next year.

There is a risk that property is overstated as the revaluations do not comply with the requirements of IAS 16.

(ii) **Audit evidence**

- A schedule of depreciated cost of owned premises extracted from the non-current asset register.

- Calculation of the difference between valuation and depreciated cost by property to assess materiality.

- Copy of valuation certificate for each property to confirm the valuation amount.

- Physical inspection of properties with the largest surpluses (including the two valued before the year-end) to confirm condition.

- Extracts from local property guides/magazines indicating a range of values of similarly styled/sized properties.

- Financial statements to confirm adequacy of the IAS 16 disclosures in the notes including:

  - the effective date of revaluation

  - whether an independent valuer was involved

  - the methods and significant assumptions applied in estimating fair values

  - the carrying amount that would have been recognised under the cost model

  - reconciliation of carrying amount at the beginning and end of the period

  - revaluation surpluses in the statement of changes in equity.

(c) **Fines and penalties**

(i) **Matters**

$0.1m represents 5.6% of profit before tax and is therefore material.

The payments may be regarded as material by nature as they are payments related to non-compliance with regulations. However, separate disclosure may not be necessary if, for example, there are no external shareholders.

The accounting treatment (inclusion in cost of sales) should be consistent with prior year.

The reason for the fall in expense should be investigated. This may due to an improvement in meeting health and safety regulations or due to incomplete recording of liabilities (understatement).

There is a risk of inadequate disclosure of the fines and penalties and a risk of understatement of fines and penalties if they have not been completely recorded.

(ii) **Audit evidence**

- Cash book and bank statements confirming payment of fines.

- Review/comparison of current year schedule against prior year for any apparent omissions.

- After-date cash book and bank statements for payments made in respect of liabilities incurred before 31 March 20X5.

- Correspondence with relevant health and safety regulators (e.g. local authorities) for notification of liabilities incurred before 31 March 20X5.

- Notes in the prior year financial statements confirming consistency, or otherwise, of the lack of separate disclosure.

- Written representation from management that there are no fines/penalties other than those which have been reflected in the financial statements.

Test your understanding 7

(a) **Brand names**

(i) **Matters**

The cost of the purchased brands represents 3.2% of total assets and 32% of profit before tax (carrying amount will be less). Annual amortisation amounts to 3.2% of profit before tax. Brands as a whole are therefore material.

Ulexite is a purchased brand and is therefore included in intangible assets on the statement of financial position. If the carrying amount of Ulexite at the year-end is greater than $91,500 (i.e. 5% PBT) its total write-off due to impairment is likely to be regarded as material.

The fall in demand as a result of the marketing campaign in March 20X5 is an adjusting event (IAS 10 *Events After the Reporting Period)* providing evidence about the valuation of assets as at 31 March 20X5.

There is a risk that the value of intangible assets (brands) and profits are overstated if an impairment charge has not been recognised.

There is also a risk the net realisable value of inventory of Ulexite products may be less than cost and inventory is overstated.

There could be a loss of customer goodwill to Visean Co as a whole if customers boycott Visean Co's other products by the association of Ulexite with Visean Co. This could result in overstatement of the other purchased brands.

(ii) **Audit evidence**

– Cost/carrying amount of Ulexite agreed to prior year working papers, less current year's amortisation charge.

– Comparison of actual after-date sales (and/or inventory turnover) against budget, month on month, and by fragrance to identify:

– the significance of the fall in demand of Ulexite

– whether other fragrances have been similarly affected

– if demand has picked up in recent months.

– Monthly sales analysis returns received from retail pharmacies.

– The advert, promotional literature or slogan relating to Ulexite which caused the offence.

– Media reports, if any, arising from bad publicity.

– Board minutes reflecting any decisions taken by management e.g. to discontinue the fragrance.

      –   Schedule of expenses incurred since April (reflected in the cash book and/or after-date invoices) to rectify the damage done (e.g. a new marketing campaign).

      –   Copy of correspondence and notes concerning any pending legal action and possible quantified outcomes.

(b) Discontinued operation

(i) Matters

The provisions have reduced profit before tax by 40% (i.e. 1.25 ÷ [1.83 + 1.25]) and now represent 68% of profit before tax and are therefore considered to be material.

The plan to close the factory is likely to result in a discontinued operation if hospital medical consumables are a separate line of business which can be distinguished operationally and for financial reporting purposes (IFRS 5 *Non-Current Assets Held for Sale and Discontinued Operations*).

The initial disclosure event will be the earlier of:

–   the directors' announcement in March 20X5 (that the factory closed in April strongly suggests that a formal detailed plan existed and was approved before it was announced)

–   a binding sale agreement for substantially all the related assets (i.e. equipment and inventory).

Tutorial note: The announcement is the more likely in the context of the given scenario.

Assuming that the announcement in March 20X5 raised valid expectations that a detailed formal restructuring plan would be carried out, a constructive obligation to restructure arises (IAS 37 *Provisions, Contingent Liabilities and Contingent Assets*). The provision made should include:

–   Redundancy costs (but not any costs of retraining or relocating continuing staff).

–   Penalty clauses relating to contracts with customers and suppliers. For example, hospitals (as public sector bodies) are likely to have contracts with Visean Co containing penalty clauses for non-performance, breach of contract, etc.

The disposal of any assets in April 20X5 is a non-adjusting event (IAS 10) which will require disclosure in the financial statements if material. No provision should be made for the loss on sale of related assets after the year-end unless a binding sale agreement was entered into before the year-end.

However:

- Plant and equipment should be reviewed for impairment (IAS 36 *Impairment of Assets*), and

- Inventory of hospital consumables should be valued at the lower of cost and net realisable value (IAS 2 *Inventories*).

(ii) **Audit evidence**

- Segmental information in the prior year financial statements showing hospital medical consumables to be a business segment (e.g. if this activity accounted for 10% or more of Visean Co's revenue, profit or assets).

- Initial disclosure of:

  - carrying amounts of assets being disposed of (if any), and

  - revenue, expenses, pre-tax profit or loss and income tax expense attributable to the discontinuing of medical consumable supplies.

- Agreement of initial disclosure to underlying financial ledger accounts, management reports, etc.

- Comparison of separate disclosure with budgeted amounts and prior year.

- Board minutes approving the formal plan to discontinue the product range, close the factory and make staff redundant.

- Copies of announcements e.g. press releases and letters to customers and employees.

- The binding sale agreement (if any) for plant, equipment and inventory.

- Contracts with hospitals and suppliers to identify penalty clauses, if any.

- Calculations of the provisions and evaluation of the assumptions made.

- Redundancy terms for employees (both contractual and statutory) to enable verification of any redundancy provision calculation.

- Past redundancy settlements (as compared with statutory and contractual obligations).

- After-date sales of hospital medical consumables.

(c) **Statement of cash flows**

(i) **Matters**

The statement of cash flows should be prepared in accordance with IAS 7 *Statement of Cash Flows* i.e. reporting cash flows classified under the standard headings (including operating activities, returns on investments, taxation, capital expenditure, etc).

IAS 1 *Presentation of Financial Statements* requires comparative figures for all items in the primary statements (and therefore for the statement of cash flows).

Cash flows from operating activities may be reported using either:

– the 'direct' method (i.e. showing relevant constituent cash flows) or

– the 'indirect' method (i.e. calculating operating cash flows by adjustment to the operating profit reported in the profit and loss account).

IAS 7 the permits a change from the indirect to the direct method. It is appropriate, in the interest of comparability that the corresponding figures have been restated. The reason for reclassification should be disclosed.

Given the nature of the disclosure, this is likely to be material by nature.

In accordance with ISA 710 *Comparative Information – Corresponding Figures and Comparative Financial Statements*, the auditor has a responsibility to obtain sufficient appropriate audit evidence that corresponding figures have been correctly reported and appropriately classified.

There is a risk of material misstatement if the corresponding figures have not been restated appropriately or if disclosure of the restatement has not been made adequately.

(ii) **Audit evidence**

– Agreement of corresponding amounts for 'Net cash from operating activities' downwards to the prior year statement of cash flows.

– For the prior year, agreement (or reconciliation) of profit before tax adjusted for non-cash items (e.g. depreciation) and working capital changes to cash receipts from customers less cash paid to suppliers and employees.

– Schedules of cash receipts (per analysis of cash book receipts) agreed to the receivables ledger control account.

> – Schedules of cash payments to suppliers and employees (per analysis of cash book payments) agreed to the payables ledger and payroll control accounts respectively.
>
> – Analytical procedures such as the comparison of the trade receivables collection period with average credit periods given to customers, and the trade payables payment period with average credit periods received from suppliers.

Test your understanding 8

(a) Objectivity is defined in the ACCA's Code of Ethics and Conduct as being free from bias, conflicts of interest or undue influence of others which may override professional or business judgments.

Objectivity is one of the fundamental principles for a member of ACCA. Objectivity is particularly important to an auditor, whose role it is to provide an independent opinion on financial statements. Objectivity can only be assured if the member is independent.

The ACCA provides detailed guidance on how auditors should maintain their objectivity and independence. The guidance covers issues such as dependence on an audit client (fee-related issues), close relationships with the client, provision of other accountancy or other services to the client, and accepting goods and services.

The auditor must always strive to maintain objectivity in all dealings with the client.

(b) **Matters to be considered**

Undue dependence

Accepting the work of Rainbow Co may lead to the firm having an undue dependence on the client creating a self-interest threat. The firm may be reluctant to raise issues with the client for fear of losing the work.

The audit fee discussed is substantial and, in connection with the tax work, may affect the objectivity of the firm. Ethical guidance states that an audit firm should not be dependent on a client for fees. However, as Rainbow Co is not a listed client, the restrictions are less stringent than for a listed company.

INT: There is no specific limit set but the firm must ensure objectivity is not impaired by the level of fees earned from a client.

UK: For non-listed clients, fees must not exceed 15% of the firm's fee income on a regular basis.

An engagement quality review should be carried out to ensure objectivity has not been impaired and the outcome of the audit has not been influenced.

Contingency fee

Linking the audit fee to the success of the client's business creates a self-interest threat. The firm may not request audit adjustments that should be made but would lead to a reduction in profit as this would reduce the audit fee.

This type of fee arrangement is not acceptable and the firm should not accept these terms.

Unpaid fees

Overdue fees can be construed as a loan to the client, which would create a self-interest threat. The firm may be reluctant to raise issues with the client in case the fees remain unpaid.

The auditor should consider whether the unpaid fees are overdue, or whether it is normal practice for the firm to have such outstanding fees. The amount outstanding should be considered to see if the threat is significant. The length of time that the fees have been overdue would also affect the significance of the threat.

The firm should discuss the outstanding fees with the client and make arrangements for payment. If the fees are significant, an engagement quality control reviewer should be assigned to the audit.

Relationships

The audit engagement partner is related to a member of the client's staff which creates a familiarity threat. The partner may be too trusting of the client and not apply sufficient scepticism when conducting the audit.

The significance of the threat is reduced as the staff member appears to be junior in the organisation and does not work in the finance department therefore does not have a direct influence over the financial statements. The daughter is no longer a dependent of the audit engagement partner which may further reduce the significance of the threat.

The daughter has just joined the employee share benefit scheme which means a close family member is a shareholder in the audited entity. This increases the significance of the threat.

The partner should be changed to remove any threat.

Other services

Provision of other services to an audit client can create a self-review threat. If an auditor is responsible for auditing work they were responsible for preparing, they are unlikely to be critical of it and errors may remain uncorrected.

It appears that different staff would be involved in tax and audit work so (other than the fee issue above) this should not pose any issues in relation to objectivity.

The firm must also be careful not to assume management responsibilities in respect of any other services.

Hospitality

Auditors should not accept excessive gifts as this can create self-interest and familiarity threats. The offer of hospitality may be seen as a bribe for an unmodified opinion.

The weekend in Tenerife appears to be excessive and should not be accepted.

The auditor should consider whether the offer of the free holiday casts significant doubt over the integrity of the director, and whether this would affect his decision to accept the audit work.

Test your understanding 9

(a) **Professional enquiry**

Krill & Co has a professional duty of confidentiality to its client, Squid Co. If Krill & Co's lack of response is due to Squid Co not having given them permission to respond, Sepia & Co should not accept the appointment. However, in this case, Anton Fargues should have:

–   notified Squid Co's management of the communication received from Sepia & Co

–   written to Sepia & Co to decline to give information and state his reasons.

Krill & Co should not have simply failed to respond.

Krill & Co may have suspicions of some unlawful act (e.g. defrauding the taxation authority), but no proof, which they do not wish to convey to Sepia & Co in a written communication. However, Krill & Co has had the opportunity of oral discussion with Sepia & Co to convey a matter which may provide grounds for the nomination being declined by Sepia & Co.

Steps by Sepia & Co

Obtain written representation from Squid Co's management that Krill & Co has been given Squid Co's written permission to respond to Sepia & Co's communication.

Send a further letter to Krill & Co by a recorded delivery service (i.e. requiring a signature) which states that if a reply is not received in the next seven days, Sepia & Co will assume that there are no matters of which they should be aware and so proceed to accept the appointment. Advise also that unless a response is received, a written complaint will be made to the relevant professional body.

Make a written complaint to the disciplinary committee of the professional body of which Anton Fargues is a member so that his unprofessional conduct can be investigated.

(b) **Takeover bid**

A conflict of interest will be created if Sepia & Co accepts the engagement to advise on a takeover bid between Hatchet Co and Vitronella Co.

Sepia & Co has a professional duty of confidentiality to its audit client, Vitronella Co. This may be difficult to achieve given the existing relationship with Vitronella Co.

If the engagement with Hatchet Co was accepted, Sepia & Co would need to ensure no member of the audit team of Vitronella Co was assigned to provide the advice to Hatchet Co.

Vitronella Co may ask Sepia & Co to give corporate finance advice on Hatchet Co's takeover bid which would be incidental to the audit relationship. This would create a further conflict in terms of objectivity. It would be difficult to act as adviser to both parties involved in the takeover and remain unbiased to both.

Steps by Sepia & Co

As it is clear that a material conflict of interest exists, Sepia & Co should decline to act as adviser to Hatchet Co.

Advise Vitronella Co's management that Hatchet Co's approach has been declined.

(c) **Lowballing**

Lowballing is a practice in which auditors compete for clients by reducing their fees for the external audit. Lower audit fees are compensated by the auditor carrying out more lucrative non-audit work (e.g. consultancy and tax advice).

The fact that Keratin & Co has quoted a lower fee than the other tendering firms (if that is the case) is not improper provided that Benthos Co is not misled about:

– the precise range of services that the quoted fee is intended to cover, and

– the likely level of fees for any other work undertaken.

Although an admission to lowballing may sound improper, it does not breach current ethical guidance provided Benthos Co understands the situation. For example, Keratin & Co could offer Benthos Co a free first-year audit with an understanding that future audits will be chargeable and how the cost will be calculated.

The risk is that if the non-audit work does not materialise, Keratin & Co may be under pressure to cut corners or resort to irregular practices (e.g. the falsification of audit working papers) in order to keep within budget. If a situation of negligence was then to arise, Keratin & Co could be found guilty of failing to exercise professional competence and due care.

Provided the auditor performs the audit to the required level of quality, and issues an appropriate opinion in the circumstances, the level of fee is not an issue.

Keratin & Co may not just be lowballing on the first year audit fee, but in the longer term, perhaps indicating that future increases might only be in line with inflation. If Keratin & Co was to later increase Benthos Co's audit fees substantially, a fee dispute could arise. In this event Benthos Co could refuse to pay the higher fee. It might be difficult then for Keratin & Co to take the matter to arbitration if Benthos Co was misled.

Steps by Sepia & Co

There are no steps which Sepia & Co can take to prevent Benthos Co from awarding the tender to whichever firm it chooses.

If Keratin & Co is successful in being awarded the tender, Sepia & Co should consider its own policy on pricing in future competitive tendering situations.

Test your understanding 10

(a) **Quality control in a smaller audit firm**

Why difficult to implement

Audit quality depends on the quality of the people performing the service. Smaller firms may lack resources and specialist expertise. In particular, small firms may not be able to offer the same reward structures to attract and retain staff as larger firms.

Larger firms can afford to recruit staff in sufficient numbers to allow for subsequent leavers and provide for their training needs. Smaller firms may not be able to offer the same training opportunities. Prospective trainees may perceive a smaller firm's client base to be less attractive than that of a larger firm.

Smaller practices may have less scope to provide staff with internal and on-the-job training due to their smaller client base.

The cost of external training may be prohibitive for smaller firms and also fail to provide the hands-on experience necessary for professional development.

Audit committees play an oversight role which contributes to quality control in larger firms (e.g. on matters of client acceptance/retention, independence issues, etc). When the client base is largely of owner-managed businesses, as for many smaller audit firms, there are no non-executive directors to support the auditor when difficult issues arise.

Quality control requires leadership within the firm. In a larger firm, one senior partner may have responsibility for establishing quality control policies and procedures and a different partner may have responsibility for monitoring work performed. Splitting these roles may not be practical for a smaller firm and is impossible for sole practitioners.

Small firms operate in a highly competitive environment for audit work, are often busy with non-audit work, and may be under-resourced. Technical updating on audit matters may not be as regular as desirable and audit practice may become inefficient.

How overcome

Quality control procedures in a smaller firm can be distributed between the reporting partners.

Smaller firms may draw on the expertise of suitably qualified external consultants (e.g. on technical matters). Small firms and sole practitioners have the same access to a wide range of technical and ethical advisory services provided by ACCA (and other professional bodies) and should take advantage of these.

Small firms may work together as a network to share training opportunities and sometimes staff. For example, an association of small firms may adopt the same methodology and meet periodically for technical updates.

(b) **Lammergeier Group – auditor's report**

The opinion paragraph should be positioned above the basis for opinion paragraph and should have a title referring to the type of opinion being issued i.e. Qualified Opinion.

The explanation of the material misstatement should be given in a separate section called the Basis for Qualified Opinion.

The report is clearly headed 'Qualified opinion arising from material misstatement ...' yet the reasons for departure from IAS 7 are 'sound and acceptable'. This is confusing.

The heading is a statement of disagreement with the application of a standard, the latter a statement of concurrence. If the auditor concurs with a departure, the opinion should not be modified.

The title of IAS 7 should be stated in full, i.e. 'International Accounting Standard 7 *Statement of Cash Flows*. The full title of the accounting standard not being complied with should be stated in the basis for qualified opinion paragraph.

The auditor should not be expressing an opinion of Lammergeier's management in their report. This is not professional.

Management's justification should be set out in a note to the financial statements (e.g. in the accounting policies section). The auditor's report should clearly state that there is non-compliance with IAS 7.

It cannot be true that the departure 'does not impact on the truth and fairness ...'. The requirement to prepare a statement of cash flows (and its associated notes) stems from the need to provide users of financial statements with information about changes in financial resources. If this information is omitted the financial statements cannot show a true and fair view.

'Except for [the non-preparation of the group statements of cash flows and associated notes] ....' is a qualified auditor's opinion. This contradicts Rook & Co's assertion that the matter 'does not impact on the truth and fairness ...'.

The grounds for non-compliance is 'the complexity involved', which does not seem likely. IAS 7 offers no exemption on these, or any other grounds.

A statement of cash flows is required by IAS 7 and as a result the failure to include one will mean the financial statements do not give a true and fair view. This will require an adverse opinion.

A basis for adverse opinion will explain the reason for the adverse opinion. This section should be distinguishable from the opinion section by including a title 'Basis for Adverse Opinion'.

The fact that the audit opinion was similarly modified in the prior year shows that the matter has not been resolved. It is possible that the auditor thought it was an easy option to do the same again rather than draft a more appropriate opinion for the current year.

The 20X4 opinion makes no reference to the fact that the matter is not new and that the opinion was similarly modified in the prior year.

(c) **Auditor's responsibilities in relation to Other Information**

The auditor has a professional responsibility to read other information to identify material inconsistencies with the audited financial statements (ISA 720 *The Auditor's Responsibilities Relating to Other Information in Documents Containing Audited Financial Statements*).

A material inconsistency arises when other information contradicts that which is contained in the audited financial statements or which contradicts information obtained by the auditor about the entity. It may give rise to doubts about:

– the auditor's conclusions drawn from the audit evidence

– the basis for the auditor's opinion on the financial statements.

As a result, the credibility of the financial statements and the auditor's report thereon may be undermined by any inconsistency.

Any inconsistencies should be discussed with management, who should be asked to remove the misleading information in the chair's statement.

If management refuse to remove the inconsistency, the auditor should communicate this to those charged with governance.

If the inconsistency remains, the auditor should provide a description of it in the 'Other Information' section of the auditor's report.

Alternatively the auditor may withhold the auditor's report or withdraw from the engagement. In such cases legal advice should be sought, to protect the interests of the audit firm.

Implications for the auditor's report

The assertion in the chair's statement claims two things:

– the company is 'one of the world's largest generators of hydro-electricity', and

– the company has 'a dedicated commitment to accountable ethical professionalism'.

The first statement presents a misleading impression of the company's size. In misleading a user of the financial statements with this statement, the second statement is not true as it is not ethical or professional to mislead the reader and potentially undermine the credibility of the financial statements.

The first statement is materially inconsistent with the auditor's understanding of the entity because:

–   the company is privately-owned, and publicly-owned international/multi-nationals are larger

–   the company's main activity is civil engineering not electricity generation (only 14% of revenue is derived from HEP)

–   as the company ranks at best eighth against African companies alone it ranks much lower globally.

Hegas Co should be asked to remove these assertions from the chair's statement.

If the statement is not changed there will be no grounds for modification of the opinion on the audited financial statements as the chair's statement does not form part of the financial statements.

The 'Other Information' section should include a description of the inconsistency between the chair's statement and the auditor's understanding of the company.

References

Chapter learning objectives

The Board (2019) IAS 1 *Presentation of Financial Statements. London*: IFRS Foundation.

The Board (2019) IAS 2 *Inventories*. London: IFRS Foundation.

The Board (2019) IAS 7 *Statement of Cash Flows*. London: IFRS Foundation.

The Board (2019) IAS 8 *Accounting Policies, Changes in Accounting Estimates and Errors.* London: IFRS Foundation.

The Board (2019) IAS 10 *Events after the Reporting Period*. London: IFRS Foundation.

The Board (2019) IAS 12 *Income Taxes*. London: IFRS Foundation.

The Board (2019) IAS 16 *Property, Plant and Equipment*. London: IFRS Foundation.

The Board (2019) IAS 19 *Employee Benefits*. London: IFRS Foundation.

The Board (2019) IAS 20 *Accounting for Government Grants and Disclosure of Government Assistance*. London: IFRS Foundation.

The Board (2019) IAS 21 *The Effects of Changes in Foreign Exchange Rates*. London: IFRS Foundation.

The Board (2019) IAS 23 *Borrowing Costs*. London: IFRS Foundation.

The Board (2019) IAS 24 *Related Party Disclosures*. London: IFRS Foundation.

The Board (2019) IAS 27 *Separate Financial Statements*. London: IFRS Foundation.

The Board (2019) IAS 28 *Investments in Associates and Joint Ventures*. London: IFRS Foundation.

The Board (2019) IAS 32 *Financial Instruments: Presentation*. London: IFRS Foundation.

The Board (2019) IAS 33 *Earnings per Share*. London: IFRS Foundation.

The Board (2019) IAS 36 *Impairment of Assets*. London: IFRS Foundation.

The Board (2019) IAS 37 *Provisions, Contingent Liabilities and Contingent Assets*. London: IFRS Foundation.

The Board (2019) IAS 38 *Intangible Assets*. London: IFRS Foundation.

The Board (2019) IAS 40 *Investment Property*. London: IFRS Foundation.

The Board (2019) IAS 41 *Agriculture*. London: IFRS Foundation.

The Board (2019) IFRS 1 *First-time Adoption of International Financial Reporting Standards.* London: IFRS Foundation.

The Board (2019) IFRS 2 *Share-based Payment*. London: IFRS Foundation.

The Board (2019) IFRS 3 *Business Combinations*. London: IFRS Foundation.

The Board (2019) IFRS 5 *Non-current Assets Held for Sale and Discontinued Operations*. London: IFRS Foundation.

KAPLAN PUBLISHING

The Board (2019) IFRS 7 *Financial Instruments: Disclosure*. London: IFRS Foundation.

The Board (2019) IFRS 8 *Operating Segments*. London: IFRS Foundation.

The Board (2019) IFRS 9 *Financial Instruments*. London: IFRS Foundation.

The Board (2019) IFRS 10 *Consolidated Financial Statements*. London: IFRS Foundation.

The Board (2019) IFRS 11 *Joint Arrangements*. London: IFRS Foundation.

The Board (2019) IFRS 12 *Disclosure of Interests in Other Entities*. London: IFRS Foundation.

The Board (2019) IFRS 13 *Fair Value Measurement*. London: IFRS Foundation.

The Board (2019) IFRS 15 *Revenue from Contracts with Customers*. London: IFRS Foundation.

The Board (2019) IFRS 16 *Leases*. London: IFRS Foundation.

Index

KAPLAN PUBLISHING